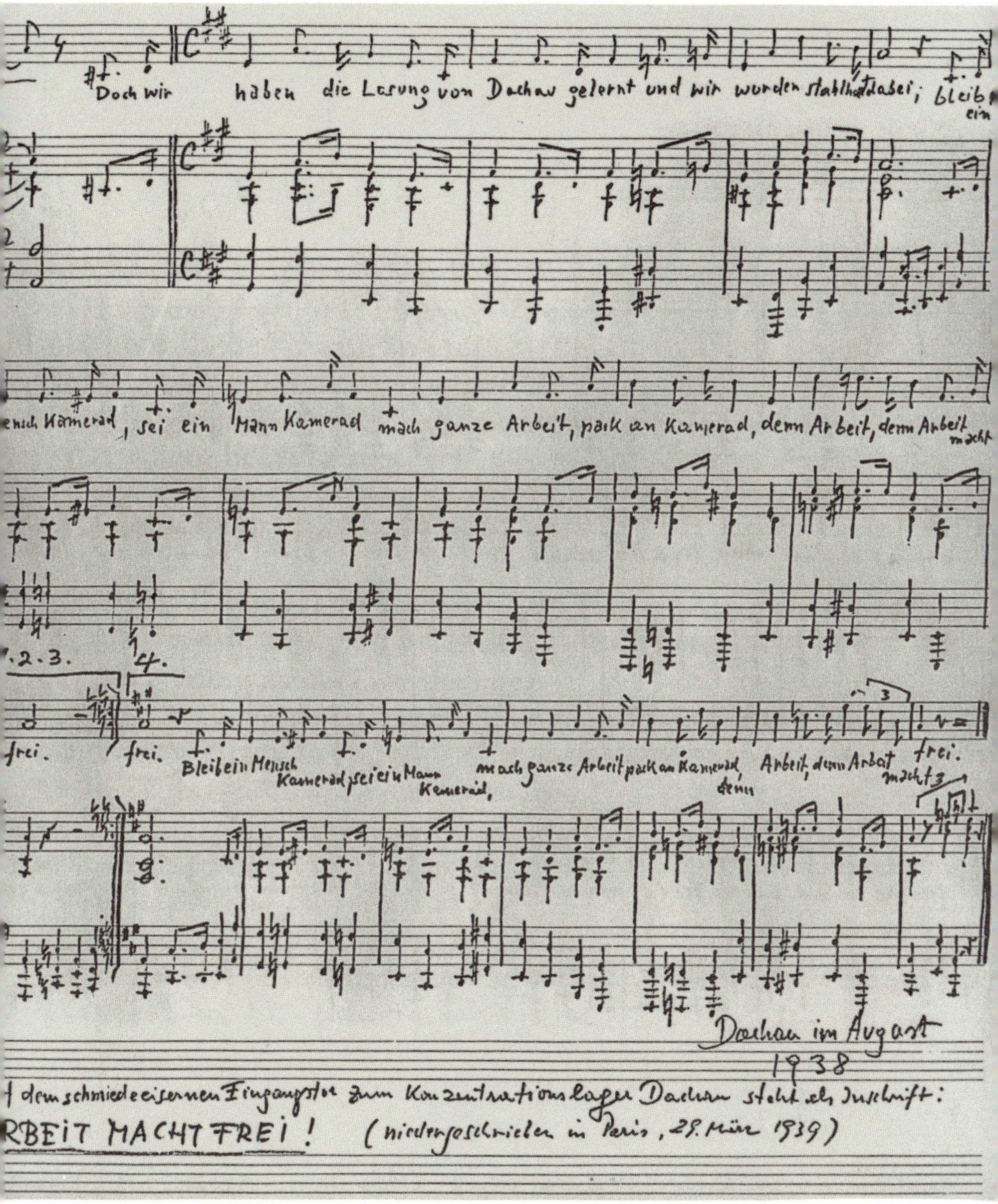
Doch wir haben die Losung von Dachau gelernt und wir wurden stahlhart dabei, bleib ein
ensch Kamerad, sei ein Mann Kamerad mach ganze Arbeit, pack an Kamerad, denn Arbeit, denn Arbeit macht
1.2.3.
4.
frei.
frei.
Bleib ein Mensch Kamerad, sei ein Mann Kamerad, mach ganze Arbeit pack an Kamerad, Arbeit, denn Arbeit macht frei.
denn
Dachau im August 1938
dem schmiedeeisernen Eingangstor zum Konzentrationslager Dachau steht als Inschrift:
RBEIT MACHT FREI! (niedergeschrieben in Paris, 29. März 1939)

"It's Up to Us!"

Collected Works of Jura Soyfer

Studies in Austrian Literature, Culture and Thought

Translation Series

"It's Up to Us!"

Collected Works of Jura Soyfer

Edited, translated,

and with an afterword

by

Horst Jarka

Preface by Harry Zohn

ARIADNE PRESS

Ariadne Press would like to express its appreciation to the Austrian Cultural Institute, New York and the Bundesministerium für Wissenschaft, Forschung und Kunst, Vienna for their assistance in publishing this book.

Translated from the German
All rights, including performance rights
Thomas Sessler Verlag, Vienna & Munich

Library of Congress Cataloging-in-Publication Data

Soyfer, Jura, 1912-1939
  [Selections. English. 1996]
  "It's Up to Us!" : Collected works of Jura Soyfer / edited, translated and with an afterword by Horst Jarka; preface by Harry Zohn.
       p.   cm. -- (Studies in Austrian literature, culture, and thought. Translation series)
    ISBN 0-929497-55-4
    1. Soyfer, Jura, 1912-1939--Translations, English.
  I. Jarka, Horst. II. Title. III. Series
  PT2639.O93A25   1996
  838'.91209--dc20
                                            92-5027
                                            CIP

Cover Design:
Art Director, Designer: George McGinnis

Copyright ©1996
by Ariadne Press
270 Goins Court
Riverside, CA 92507

All rights reserved.
No part of this publication may be reproduced or transmitted in any form or by any means without formal permission.
Printed in the United States of America.
ISBN 0-929497-55-4

Contents

Preface by Harry Zohn

Verse and Short Prose

"The order works like hell"

The Song of Order 5
Lullaby for an Unborn Baby 7
Object Lesson in Race Theory 9
Shanty Town 11
The Ballad of the Bowl 13
Youth in Despair 15
The Ballad of Pepi 19

Germany 1932-1933

The Photographs 21
"Heil Hitler!" 27
Marching Song for German Children 1933 . . 29
Reformed German Church Hymn 30

Austria 1936

Alma Mater Rudolphina 31
From Mother on Mother's Day 35
Be Prepared!? 38

"Must it always be this order?"
Towards a Democratic Culture

Political Theater 42
"Fury" 43
"Hej Rup!" 45

All Thieves on Strike! 48
French Avant-garde in Vienna 56
A Public Rehearsal of Mozart's "Marriage
of Figaro" 57
The Living Nestroy 61
A Word about Censorship 66

Plays

By way of introduction:
The Statue of Liberty for Five Schillings 71

The End of the World 75
Trip to Paradise 123
Astoria 167
Vineta 227
Broadway Melody 1492 257

The Novel

Thus Died a Party
(Fragment)

Prelude: Fanz Josef Zehetner 365
Ferdinand Dworak. Officer of the Railroad
Union 383
February Eleventh 1933 406
Josef Dreher, Social Democratic Member of
Parliament 419
Robert Blum, Treasurer of Section Twelve . 432
Karl Marx or Karl Marx? 441
The Ides of March 1933 445
A Question of Nerves 467
A Revolution? 474
The Price of Resistance 486
An Interrogation 494
The Corner 516

Epilogue

Song of Twentieth Century Man 529
The Dachau Song 531

Afterword 533
Editorial Note 566
Acknowledgments 567
Notes 569
Bibliography 587
Index of Names 590

Illustrations

Dachau Song, music by
Herbert Zipper . . . . end papers
Jura Soyfer, 1929/30 2
Object Lesson in Race Theory 8
Shanty Town 11
Ständischer Mittagstisch 14
The Ballad of Pepi 18
Antiwar Museum Berlin 1932 22
Antiwar Museum Berlin vandalized 25
"Heil Hitler" 26
"Marching Song for German Children" 28
Jura Soyfer, 1932 40
Program of ABC Cabaret, Vienna,
front page 68
The End of the World (Vienna 1936),
Professor Peep 70
The End of the World (Vienna 1936),
The Comet 82
The End of the World (Graz 1989),
The Comet 82
The End of the World (Graz 1989),
The Führer 88
The End of the World (Vienna 1965),
Scene Seven 106
Jura Soyfer 1935 121
Trip to Paradise (Vienna 1936),
The Machine 128
Trip to Paradise (London 1940),
Scene One 135
Trip to Paradise (Vienna 1993),
Scene Two 143
Trip to Paradise (Stuttgart 1990),

Scene Six	153
Trip to Paradise (Vienna 1982), Scene Eight	156
Astoria (Vienna 1965), At the Embassy	186
Astoria (Herxheim 1991), Scene Four	192
Astoria (Magdeburg 1985), Program	220
Astoria (Vienna 1991), Scene Nine	224
Vineta (Vienna 1990), Scene Three	239
Vineta (Salzburg 1975), Scene Eight	250
Broadway Melody 1492 (Vienna 1937), Program	263
Broadway Melody 1492 (New York 1992), Act III, Scene One	313
Broadway Melody (Buenos Aires 1992), title page of Translation	340
Jura Soyfer 1937/38	362
Soyfer Program (London 1987)	530
Concentration Camp Dachau, Gate	531

Credits

The illustrations on the pages indicated are reproduced by kind permission of the following persons and institutions:
Helli Andis 362; Antikriegsmuseum und Friedensbibliothek, Berlin 22, 25; Leon Askin 82; Eva Brenner 340; Chawwerusch Theater 192; Dokumentationsarchiv des österreichischen Widerstandes, Wien opp. i, 40, 121, 531; Walter Engel 128; Susanne Grafeneder 143; Jura Soyfer Theater, Vienna 156, 224, 530; Landestheater Salzburg 313; Max Reinhardt Seminar, Vienna 249; Bil Spira 70, Staatstheater Stuttgart 153; Theater der Landeshauptstadt Magdeburg 239; Bruno Völkel 106,186; Peter Weißensteiner 82, 88; Herbert Zipper score of Dachau Song.

Preface

Once in a great while a reader comes across a book that appears to exemplify Walt Whitman's dictum "This is no book; who touches this touches a man." Here is such a book.

In 1977 the sophisticated and venturesome Engendra Press of Montreal issued a remarkable book entitled The Legacy of Jura Soyfer 1912-1939: Poems, Prose and Plays of an Austrian Antifascist. That volume, edited and translated by Horst Jarka of the University of Montana, has long been out of print and its publisher long out of business, and so it is doubly fitting and welcome that Ariadne Press, an equally discriminating publishing house dedicated to introducing English-speaking readers to many aspects of Austrian culture, should now bring out an expanded, revised, and improved version of that collection. In the intervening years Professor Jarka has been very active in illuminating the troubled interwar period of his native Austria in general and one of its true representative literary figures in particular, publishing a 900-page edition of Soyfer's collected works in the original (1980), the definitive (German) biography of that writer (1987), and a collection of his correspondence (1991). These publications, intended to wrest from oblivion a prolific writer who perished in a Nazi concentration camp at the age of 26, represent a remarkable labor of love.

The somewhat jaunty title of the present edition reflects both Soyfer's activism and the continued timeliness of his writings. If the Russian-born Soyfer, whose family fled from the Bolshevik revolution and settled in Vienna in 1921, used several pseudonyms, this did not evidence a lack of courage but may have been due to his sensitivity about his name, which derives from the Hebrew word for (Torah) scribe but is also a homonym for the German word for drunkard. In economically, socially, and politically perilous times in the inhospitable climate of incipient and triumphant Austrofascism, Jura Soyfer increasingly devoted himself to political journalism. His most enduring work was done for the Kleinkunstbühnen, the "little theaters" of Vienna that presented political cabaret and to which he contributed Mittelstücke, playlets that highlighted Austria's stature as a "proving ground for the apocalypse," to use a phrase of the satirist Karl Kraus, one of Soyfer's mentors.

In Soyfer's writings moral indignation, cynical bitterness, and critical wit are coupled with lyrical lightness, poignant pathos, and an imagination sometimes akin to Charley Chaplin's. Soyfer's inspired use of language is reminiscent of Karl Kraus and Johann Nepomuk Nestroy as he utilizes elements of the old Viennese popular theater in hard-hitting topical revues. His five dramas, unpublished in his lifetime, are latter-day morality plays, powerful parables and dramatic tracts for the times that move on both a realistic and surrealistic plane. For example, in a play about a down-and-outer who chops away at the capitalistic system, an attempt is made, during a backward ride in a sort of time machine, to undo centuries of "progress," for hasn't technology in the service of untrammeled capitalism produced only unemployment and its concomitant crises and miseries? Another of Soyfer's plays, a farce about the promotion of a nonexistent state, a swindle turned into a utopia, is still relevant in an age of wholesale delusion through manipulation by the mass media and political packaging. A third play, Broadway Melody 1492, here presented in English for the first time, is an adaptation of Christopher Columbus by Hasenclever and Tucholsky that was not successful—possibly (and paradoxically) because it was a joint effort by a playwright who was not a satirist and a satirist who was not a playwright. A copyright holder of the earlier play has barred it from the German stage, but the English version of Soyfer's play was produced in New York in 1992, the Columbus quincentennial year.

The political tragedy of Austria prevented Soyfer from finishing his most ambitious literary project, a novel about the defeat of Austrian Social Democracy in February 1934. The fragment that survived the war and is here published in English for the first time, demonstrates Soyfer's rapid development as a prose writer: within a few months his political journalism attained the level of literature. As an experimental novel fusing political analysis and social and psychological insight it is unique in the Austrian literature of the interwar period.

Jura Soyfer, that wise and witty warner and eloquent spokesman for the aspirations of working-class people, devoted his tragically brief life to a vigorous but ultimately futile fight against the deleterious slackness, apathy, disunion, and fatalistic resignation of his compatriots. Thanks to such tireless champions as Horst Jarka, whose skilful editing and accurate, idiomatic, and frequently ingenious translations have now produced an "English Soyfer" of undeniable power and poignance, this dynamic advocate for a dispossessed generation has emerged in his full stature as a major political and social satirist whose writings not only illuminate a dark chapter in European history but can also inspire all of us to combat the multifarious repressive and dehumanizing forces of our age.

Brandeis University   Harry Zohn
Waltham, Massachusetts
Summer 1995

VERSE and SHORT PROSE

Jura Soyfer, 1929/30

"The order works like hell"

The Song of Order

That we are hungry is a trifling matter.
That we go begging is beside the point.
Our protests are but idle chatter.
Don't shake the order out of joint!
Whoever has not noticed, hear it now:
There is an order in this world, you bet!
We hold it up and it holds us—and how!
The order's order must not be upset.

      This planet is from east to west,
      From Singapore to Budapest
      Organized so well!
      Thirty million people trot,
      Hunger pains is all they've got,
      You can't go on? Then drop and rot.
      The order is just swell.
      There's too much bread?
      Then heat with bread!
      Too many people? Shoot them dead!
      The order is God's gift to Man,
      We die like dogs to fit His plan.
      The order works like hell.

At times your order seems to be kaput.
You couldn't call it order what we see;
Nothing for us and you get all the loot:
Is that your order by divine decree?
But when we shout this question in the streets
In London, in New York, and in Shanghai,
You tell us that your order never cheats,
And clubs and bullets tell us why:

      This planet is from east to west,
      From Singapore to Budapest
      Organized so well!
      Thirty million people trot,

> Hunger pains is all they've got,
> You can't go on? Then drop and rot.
> The order is just swell.
> There's too much bread?
> Then heat with bread!
> Too many people? Shoot them dead!
> The order is God's gift to Man,
> We die like dogs to fit His plan.
> The order works like hell.

Oh, your order's working to perfection!
We are still slaves, but not for long!
The marching masses soon will change direction
And soon the streets will echo with our song.
Yesterday we still sustained your order.
Today it's crumbling. Will it last?
Tell us: must it always be *this* order?
Always be the order of the past?

> We're asking you from east to west,
> From Singapore to Budapest,
> In spite of tank and gun:
> We, on the breadline everywhere,
> Because your order keeps us there,
> We ask you: is this order fair?
> Is your order the only one?
> We are still keeping your order today,
> But tomorrow we'll follow a different way.
> In spite of God and free enterprise
> A better order will arise!

1932

Lullaby for an Unborn Baby

"Always honor married love!
You don't need a roof above.
All my people shall increase
Like the wheat dumps in the seas.
Propagate!"
Says the State.
    Sleep, baby, sleep.
    The State protects its sheep.
    Abortion cannot harm you.
    The State needs you to arm you.
    In war the graves are wide and deep.
    Sleep, baby, sleep.

"For war and industry we breed.
They must be fed, on men they feed.
Human beings need no bread.
Man is spirit, God has said.
Hunger's fate."
Says the State.
    Sleep, baby, sleep.
    The State protects its sheep.
    The State will give you discipline,
    More discipline than vitamin.
    So you will be a gentle sheep.
    Sleep, baby, sleep.

"You won't find a place in life,
You'll be a number in a file.
You don't like it? End your strife,
Just cool down and think a while
And accept instruction:
Life is mass production!
Capitulate!"
Says the State.
Its files are wide and deep.
    Sleep, baby, sleep.

1933

Newspaper photo that preceded Soyfer's poem in *Der Kuckuck*, 26 February 1933.

Object Lesson in Race Theory

You can see two men—but what am I saying?
Two races, that's what you see,
Waiting at a welfare office
For a handout patiently.
The guy on the left is black of skin,
Has thick lips and a roundish face,
The guy on the right a clear specimen
Of the white, Nordic master race.
Here the hair's woolly, and there it is straight.
Two races—two worlds we must separate.

The black guy, Jack, worked off and on,
Patching tires, and jobs like that.
But then one day all jobs were gone
And all of Jack's hopes fell flat.
The white guy is Jim. He is a tramp
And got two months in jail
At the riot in the veterans' camp.
Jim's hopes are getting stale.
Jim's misery is as black as Jack's
Jack's future as dim as Jim's.
But all that sameness doesn't count.
Hair and skin are paramount.

The black guy marched to the House all White,
While the Senate was in session.
He and others screamed out their plight:
"An end to our oppression!"
The police soon squelched the riot
(Prosperity likes it quiet).
Jimmy, the white guy, was also there.
They beat him black and blue.
But that doesn't count. Color of hair
and skin is important, ain't that true?

Jim is hungry, and Jack without food,
If things get worse, then both the chaps

Will go through the same gray garbage can
Fishing for rich guys' scraps.
There's bread enough for Jack, Jim, and John,
All peoples: black, yellow, and white,
Five harvests have been burned up or dumped
So the profit margins stay right.
But the main thing is color of skin and hair,
All else is unimportant. So there!

But important it is. So important, in fact,
That Jim and Harry and Tommy and Jack
Forgot the color of skin and hair
And saw: the underdog everywhere,
Whether brown, white, yellow, or black,
Has always been cheated out of his share
And, tired of being the starving masses,
Will smash the difference of color and classes.

                                              1933

Newspaper photo printed above Soyfer's poem, *Der Kuckuck*, 19 February 1933.

Shanty Town

Views may differ, those of cities, too.
Here's the capital of the world today.
Is this view authentic, I'm asking, who
Has ever imagined New York this way?
No glamorous ladies in glittering gowns,
No skyscrapers are in sight.
Only one-floor "dwellings," and they are a fright:
This "New York" is called "Shanty Town."

No! What a poor picture! Is this a mistake?
The bank capital of the United States?
World Center of Commerce? For heaven's sake!
Where are all the marvels progress creates?
Three dozen barracks made of crates
Where jobless wretches crawl in and out?
Is this what New York is all about:
A pier, and old fence, all broken down?
We want Times Square and the Waldorf!
Who cares about Shanty Town?

A piece of New York? Just let me tell ya
No real New York without Rockefeller
And he's not in the picture, nor FDR.
And if they were they'd look bizarre.
The capital of the dollar and profit
Of the order that God intended
In this picture I can see nothing of it
New York's grossly misrepresented.
All modern culture, this city's renown,
The civilization we always defended
Are mocked by Shanty Town!

And yet, if anyone wanted to get
A view of the city, the richest of all,
Don't show them the skyscraper silhouette
Of capitalism's capital,
Or Wall Street, the Met, Fifth Avenue.
Give him instead a different view
Far from the lights against the sky:
The home of the homeless, the beaten down.
Symbol of this city bound to die:
East Tenth Street, Shanty Town.

1933

The Ballad of the Bowl

"Enough of fighting! Times are grim.
Today class warfare ends!"
Thus spoke the boss to the worker,
"Let's eat together like friends!"

Under halos of class harmony,
With olive twigs in their hair,
They sat themselves down to a bowl of stew
And the worker moved up his chair.

The boss stirred the stew and fished himself
The biggest lump he could get.
Then the worker tried to do the same—
But it wasn't the worker's turn yet.

"Stop!" cried the boss, "I see you lack
A sense for the national need."
And, grabbing another juicy hunk:
"This is no time for greed!"

The worker tried a second time.
Yelled the boss: "Will you never learn?
Use your noodle, you stupid meathead, you,
Can't you see that it's still my turn?"

And the boss snatched away the worker's bite.
"Be patient," he said, "don't forget
Our country is poor. Don't think of yourself.
Think of the national debt!"

"I'm hungry," the worker meekly said,
"I was laid off for half a year."
"Seasonal worker?" the boss snapped back.
"Wait till your season is here!"

Der Sozialdemokrat, October 1933.

"I'm starving," the worker said, "give me a bite!"
Just a bone was left of the stew.
"Too long you've been the State's parasite.
No more welfare checks for you!

I don't like bones. My bloodhound does.
And you, don't forget your job.
All of us have to work for our meals:
Clean up, wash the bowl, you slob!"

"No," said the worker. "No?" screamed the boss.
"Then get out, you brainwashed Red!
But first I'll smash the bowl we shared
On your subversive head!"

And so he did. He crashed the bowl
On the worker's head with a swoop.
The worker protested in vain, he was
More than ever, in the soup.

1933

Youth in Despair

The world is in a phase of transition. Capitalism is undergoing a crisis of unheard-of intensity, and our time, therefore, is fraught with more suffering and contradictions than any transitional period before.

And yet, in spite of it all, the external power of the system is incredibly great. For the more acute the economic difficulties of the middle class, the more the burden of the crisis is being transferred to the shoulders of the workers and the heavier this burden becomes. The more insecure in its assertion of power the middle class becomes, the more brutal are its fascist offensives and the more unscrupulous its methods of domination.

This is the world the young generation has been growing up in. This young generation wanted to come to terms with its time, exuberantly, energetically, as is the way of young people. The time extinguished the flame of their enthusiasm and paralyzed their vitality. The young generation comes to feel the inadequacies of the system more intensely than anybody. "You are young and strong, aren't you?" Society says. "You want to work and to produce? There is no work for you because there are too many clothes and there's too much bread. You want to eat and clothe yourself? Go in rags and starve because there is no work for you . . . !"

The young generation is painfully aware of the unbearable burden of a prison sentence to which they have been condemned through an unjust and incomprehensible verdict. But this awareness could be a strong impetus to fire a revolutionary will, enthusiasm, action; it could inspire these young people with the sense of a creative mission—if their very first attempts at protest were not doomed to failure and bitter disappointment.

The burdensome, suffocating misery of the Depression undermines the vitality of youth and infects them with that fatal thought: It is not just a prison sentence of a couple of years we have been condemned to, it is a life sentence.

Everything these young people do they do to escape a time in which they cannot find any meaning for their lives. Some of them drug themselves in all possible ways. Some of them try to escape back to the romantic ideals of a youth movement which they left just a short time ago, and which has obviously not prepared them to enter life. But all these circles of young people finally disintegrate by themselves, and they drift through life, torn and aimless, insecure. Then there is the effortless intoxication that jazz and sweet maudlin sentimentality have to offer. And then there is the magnificent opium of sports intensified to a decadent degree. Many succumb to empty temptations: swastika flags are waving. Desperately they search for what they lack: the supposedly unfaltering personality, the strong and secure character, the guy who can master his fate. And some of them simply throw their lives away—ninety percent of the farewell letters of young suicides say: "Life has no meaning for me."

What irony! There is so much frantic commotion that one

would think the young people of today are particularly radical and impatient, as if they could no longer restrain their will from finally acting. That is not the case. These times of contradictions, these times in which we cannot go the way we have been going and yet have no alternative, these indifferent and irresolute times have taken the young generation in their hard and merciless grip and put their stamp on it: they have made of the young a generation of half-heartedness and contradictions. Underneath all the enthusiasm there is a basic insecurity, a shadow of disbelief which young people often become aware of whenever they are removed from the frenzy of their mass-experiences.

Today there is no such thing as the impatience of youth. Unfortunately this young generation is not dynamic, it has no drive, no impatience. It is not revolutionary and not reactionary, not quite believing and not quite skeptical. It is never whole, always half. It is not even completely unhappy. The neurosis typical of transitional generations has taken hold of them. But it is dangerous to interpret their sickness as impatience and irrepressible drive forward, dangerous because such an interpretation would allow what must never be allowed to happen: the older generation would freeze in smiling, well-meaning condescension, and the young people would, in idle self-complacency, look for another escape from life and not think of the duty to gather all their strength to save themselves.

For even in this time there are goals for socialist youth, and, once they learn to recognize them, there is also a way out of half-heartedness and despair to a new self-respect and a sense of purpose.

1931

Photos by Rudolf Spiegel that accompanied Soyfer's poem *The Ballad of Pepi, Der Tag,* 13 June 1937.

The Ballad of Pepi

Pepi sailed as battleship commander
From Vienna's slums straight to Shanghai;
He was railroad engineer and polar pilot
And discovered islands by the by.
But alas his plane crashed in a tree
And his ship was lost at sea.
Pepi, ex-commander, pilot, undismayed,
Realized he had to learn a trade
And he asked the master locksmith Nóvotny.

Pepi at that time was just fourteen,
And at night he shared his brother's bed,
Quick his legs were, and his body lean,
Eleven groschen was the cash he had.
Pepi, though once pilot, captain of the sea,
Was no longer out for fame when he,
As a man, still sure that he would make it
Offered his right hand to Nóvotny,
But the master locksmith did not take it.

Pepi's sister was a little thing,
Pepi's brother had no real job.
Pepi knew it was all up to him
To get a job, he went from shop to shop.
All he wanted was what was expected:
Learn some honest skill and be respected.
But his hopes were crushed, his pleas unheeded:
Smith, and barber, tailor, all rejected
Pepi, and he realized: I'm not needed.

Plumber, barber, baker, all said "Sorry,"
For them, too, the times were hard enough.
Just then Rudi ended Pepi's worry,
Took him on and taught him to be tough.
The police had Rudi in their file:
"Adolescent criminality,"

Rudi had more cash than any juvenile,
Man of the world he was, he stole in style.
And was never burdened by morality.

Rudi was sixteen, his principle was shrewd:
To be just as bad as was his time.
And with stab and grab his gang pursued
Their own justice in a world of crime.
Pepi knew the logic of this strife:
Only ruthlessness will feed you!
Pepi balked at first. Yet never in his life
Had someone come and said: We need you!

Pepi's eyes were bright and keen,
Pepi's bony head was smart and clever,
Pepi's fingers they were quick and thin,
And his money worries gone forever.
When he pulled his first job he felt queasy,
Trembled when he tried his master-key,
But he soon found picking locks quite easy,
And at times he thought that he could see
The approving glance of Nóvotny.

Pepi's conscience sometimes gave a pang,
On the whole, however, kept its peace.
And he felt secure in Rudi's gang.
Rudi's gang from day to day increased,
Grew gigantic, and the town was shocked.
Soon a thousand ragged dead-end kids,
Haggard, without shoes or socks,
Fists in pockets, silent, bold,
Marched an endless line through all the streets
Towards their fated future, cruel, cold.

                                    1937

Germany 1932-33

The Photographs
or: A Case of German High Treason

Germany's future is not only gray, it is field-gray. The fascist petite bourgeoisie and the fascist upper-middle class, which even today do not see eye to eye in many respects, will probably meet on the common ground of chauvinist foreign policy, armament and war preparations. The interests of Hitler, our would-be Mussolini, and those of Schleicher, the "Napoleon of the future," will probably be brought under one hat, and that hat will be a steel helmet. The future of German fascism is closely linked with that of the German Armed Forces.

It follows that in Germany, much more so than in any other country, any active opponent of the military, by virtue of his pacifist involvement, is also the most active antifascist. And this means that he is fair game for the Justice Department.

In the Germany of the Nazi barons there is a law that protects the majesty of the Armed Forces: it is the law that covers high treason. Anything from propagating the Fifth Commandment to uncovering Schleicher's military schemes is strictly taboo, considered high treason, and punishable accordingly. A pacifist writer in Berlin has said: "In former days I wrote at the rate of thirty pfennigs per line; now for every line I write I get three months."

In Parochialstrasse in Berlin there is a rather unusual two-story building. The shop windows on the ground floor are completely covered with a corrugated iron screen that's been pulled down, and above them the sign "Antiwar Museum" is painted in big letters. When I rang the bell I was told that Ernst Friedrich, a writer and the curator of the museum, was not in. When I asked whether he was out of town, the girl who had come to the door said: "Half and half." Three months per line . . .

"May I see the antiwar museum?"

"The antiwar museum is closed. The exhibits will be removed tomorrow. The museum cannot be saved any longer. There is a

Antiwar Museum, Berlin, shortly before Soyfer's visit, summer 1932.

meeting hall of the Nazis on the corner, and the S.A. will smash in all the windows they haven't smashed in yet. Besides, the way politics are going nowadays it's more than likely that the material will be confiscated."

"Can I see it anyway before it's all taken away?"

She took me to a fairly large room where I was to see the exhibits of one of the most remarkable museums, the corpora delicti of one of the best-documented indictments of war.

There was hardly anything but photographs in that room. Many hundreds of photographs, either especially taken for the purpose of such a display, or sent in by people all over the world who had somewhere come across these pictures of the great war, maybe searched for them in the attic.

Young National Socialists who had read Remarque's *All Quiet on the Western Front* have given me their uniform judgment: "That the World War was hell we know without this book. We also know that we are able to withstand another world war physically and spiritually because we are not degenerate but of racially superior material. Steel for steel."

Steel for steel? Hard against hard? The war photos in that house in Berlin hardly permit such an escape into the romanticism of war. They evoke only one reaction to war: revulsion. But can revulsion be romanticized?

Look at the three human beings lying there, burned by flame throwers, their limbs charred, shrunken, cramped up, their faces tiny and black. And there you can see a man who fell, shot through the heart—only "fell" is not the right word. Due to a kind of lockjaw he remained standing in a shooting position after everybody had deserted the trenches. The corpse had been riddled with bullets. The dead sharpshooter begins to bloat. Here is a picture of a mass grave in the German P.O.W. Camp at Bunzlau. There are three to five thousand bodies in this grave. There was typhoid fever in the camp and cholera, and every month two or three such graves had to be dug. What you see in this picture are not skeletons but the naked corpses of Armenians who were driven from their homes by the Turks and starved to death; there were hundreds and thousands of them. This man here, the one in the wheelchair in the middle of the street, was killed during the shelling of Ostend. Here is a priest, hanged by the neck; they put a cross in his hands and used him as a target for shooting practice. Here is the desecrated cemetery of Nesle: the German crosses knocked over, the German graves ripped open, the corpses strewn about. And here is a Russian cemetery; the higher the rank of the dead soldier the bigger his cross. The corpse in this picture was a soldier sick with typhoid fever; since he had to die anyway, they threw him in a pit and let him starve. His position makes it clear that even in his last moments he tried to crawl out. Here is a row of seven gallows erected by the soldiers of Archduke Frederick; according to one statistical survey, the army of this Habsburg hanged 11,400 persons; according to another survey it was 36,000. For fun, the persons have bowler hats on their heads. Here are the regulations of a brothel in a garrison town in Belgium, a cultural document. Each of the girls is to receive a certain number of soldiers per day, that is, within certain stipulated working hours. The rate is five marks per soldier, and each contact is limited to fifteen minutes maximum; visiting schedules by companies have been arranged. Here are soldiers who, eaten up by poison gas, are dying by the thousands in the blazing sun. This soldier's nose was replaced with flesh from his thigh—in twenty-five operations. And here you see Kaiser Wilhelm on an inspection tour of the battlefield, striding over a wooden board walk especially built to keep his boots out of the mud. And here he is again, giving a speech in which he talks of God and the fatherland . . .

These are the photographs to be seen in the narrow, crooked side-street in Berlin. They should have been reproduced in thousands of copies and put up in all schools, in all nurseries, and at all disarmament conferences of the world.

Instead, the police have scraped them off the window with their sabers, and confiscated them. Now they have to be hidden because tomorrow they could lead to a trial for high treason, because the S.A. will smash in the windows of the museum, because there is no room for them in a Germany that allows Schleicher to lead her into times even more glorious than those immortalized in these pictures.

1932

Antiwar Museum, Berlin, after being vandalized by the SA.

Newspaper photo printed above Soyfer's poem "Heil Hitler," *Der Kuckuck*, 23 April 1933.

"Heil Hitler!"

Sonny, we are shouting "Heil!"
Can you tell me why?
"Why? The flags are all over the sky,
The drummers' beat I can stamp with my feet,
The SA look fierce like real men.
That's all I know, I'm only ten,
But when I'm grown up and a man,
Then I'll understand."

Hey, uncle, we are shouting "Heil!"
Are you sure that you know why?
"Why? Let me see, why sure, because . . .
I am in rags, but look at the sky!
Look at the flags, just like it was.
Our duty to the fatherland . . .
This country is down as never before.
Right now, I just don't know much more.
Just leave it to Hitler, he's our man.
Soon we'll understand."

Germany, Germany, shouting "Heil!"
Did you ever ask yourself, Why?
While you were poor, they lived in style
And you believed their lie.
They made their profit off your skin,
And they made you blind and dumb.
They were holding on and didn't give in
Although their time had come.
You let them fool you, you let them win,
Now years of slavery begin.

Years of blood will come over the land . . .
Then you'll understand.
23 April 1933

Newspaper photo printed above Soyfer's poem, "Marching Song for German Children," *Der Kuckuck*, 28 May 1933.

Marching Song for German Children

Little Hans
Strides along
Behind the smart battalion.
Look, how cute,
The boy recruit,
What a sharp salute!
His mother's eyes, oh how they shine:
Dear Fatherland, my boy is thine!
One and two.
Strong and true,
He will guard the Rhine!

Ladybug, ladybug,
Fly away home.
Your house is on fire
Your children all roam.
Bombing plane, bombing plane, roar!
Hansi, like daddy before,
Hansi boy, too, wants his war.

You want to join the black S.S.?
Yes, yes, yes!
Three years Hansi will be brave,
The fourth year Hansi's in his grave.
They'll make his mother understand:
No nobler death
Is in the world
Than for the fatherland.

1933

Reformed German Church Hymn

We stand at attention to suffer the rod,
In Dachau we lift our tortured face.
Wonderful are the ways of God
In His unending Grace.
Halleluja!

We march in field-gray, troop after troop,
To work for peace, as all men know.
A mighty fortress is our Krupp
From whom all blessings flow.
Halleluja!

We went to the polls and hid our disgust
(The SA was watching with gun and knife)
And said: In Hitler I will trust,
He is my savior and my life.
Halleluja!

We stand at attention, degraded, accursed,
In front of the hangmen, in utter dismay,
As faceless numbers, demeaned to the worst,
The last shall be the first
On Judgment Day.
Amen!

                                    Nov. 1933

Austria 1936

Alma Mater Rudolphina
Vienna Student Life 1936

Dear Mother,

Believe it or not, I have registered. The process was very complicated and awe-inspiring—the forms, and the stamps, and the long corridors in the venerable old building. It took me two solid hours to put it all behind me! Only after it was all over did I get time to look at something else but the backs of fellow students standing in endless lines in front of registration counters.

Alma Mater Rudolphina is as beautiful and dignified as its name. In the main hall there is a roll of honor in marble and a marble monument to those fallen in the war. In the courtyard there are colonnades around a statue of Wisdom and an endless row of busts of famous deceased professors. With every step you feel the breath of a great academic tradition. I can understand very well why up to a few years ago this university had its autonomy. One morning I spent in the library and I opened all kinds of books at random, journals and dissertations, and facing all that mountain of scholarship and learning I understood where the student organizations of 1848 had gotten the selfconfidence to assume the role of leaders of the people.

Oh yes, I must not forget, I have already joined a student organization. The fellow student who had me initiated assured me that among the alumni of that fraternity there are many well-situated and influential personalities who one day will be able and willing to help me along in my career. Every Wednesday and Saturday I will take part in the meetings in full regalia. I'll send you a picture. I'll have to get used to a strictly regulated schedule of morning beers, evening beers, obligatory picnics with young lady friends of the fraternity etc., etc. Not to mention the honor code; it's a regular book, an inch thick, and I'll have to memorize it if I don't want to remain a stupid pledge forever.

But here I am talking about a thousand things and forgetting the most important news. You don't even know what I'm majoring in! I know you were wondering all summer when I was home why I was all that keen on going to school without really knowing what I wanted to study. And even now I cannot really explain that lack of purpose and I can only repeat what I told you before, that six out of the twenty boys who graduated with me felt exactly the same way I did. We were simply afraid of leaving the last class of high school and stepping out into nothingness. Well, anyhow, now I've made up my mind what to study. No, not medicine as you always wanted—to become a doctor one has to feel a calling. No matter how much the medical students sneer at the idea, I'm aiming at a teaching certificate, that is in German and History. Considering the all-round situation, I don't think I'll have any problem getting a job, and besides, that problem is still four years away.

I have already gone to the first lectures. They were all very interesting of course and I took plenty of notes. And yet, somehow everything was different from what I had expected. How shall I explain it? I had thought that at the university, where you prepare for your job, everything would be in some relation to actual life. But what the lectures are about is all a world in itself, just like the curriculum in high school, though obviously more detailed and more thorough and precise. This similarity struck me the first time I listened to a lecture. I must confess, however, that after one short week, I have already corrected my wrong notions. Students I've been talking with who have been here for a number of semesters cannot understand how anybody can look at the curriculum the way I did in my first days here. That's the way scholarship works. For instance, in one class I heard students answer questions about Goethe's idealistic humanism but on the way home they talked about things that were the very opposite of these ideas.

Then there are those who bury themselves in the seminar rooms and look at everything in the world from the standpoint of their very specialized investigations; very ambitious young people who at twenty-one are already proper, old, wise private scholars. Actually, they impress me more. For while the first group in their discussion are throwing around half-finished sentences from Nietzsche, Treitschke, Houston Stewart Chamberlain or even Plato, the latter pull so much learned detail out of their hats that any unlearned boobie loses all the ground under him and sees the world upside down.

But for you the most important question right now is how much money you have to send me for my tuition. I know very well, dear mother, that you are working yourself to the bone to send me to school so that our family, too, has a college graduate in its midst. Well, at this point in time I cannot give you a definite amount. I have applied for a fee waiver, and with my honors diploma I stand a good chance, but one never knows. The other day the papers said that out of twelve thousand students about seven thousand are considered poor.

In the fraternity I have heard a lot about why we young intellectuals are in such a plight and have so little to look forward to. In discussions like these and in conversations with other students, particularly those seminar aces mentioned above, I deepen my weltanschauung constantly and provide it with a strong foundation. As a historian I hope to put my political views, which I already gained in high school years, on a firmer footing by basing them on a solid biological concept of history.

But I don't want to talk shop and bore you. Before closing I'd rather tell you about some of my fellow students whom you know personally. Do you know, for instance, what the pharmacist's son is majoring in? The skinny, short fellow, who came to Vienna a year before me? You won't believe it: agriculture! First he took a shot at law, but then he changed majors. I must say, agriculture seems to agree with him very well. He made friends with some sons of estate owners. For next summer he's lined up a job to get some experience on one of these estates. He knows exactly what he wants. Lechner and Steiner, who graduated three years before me, are up to their ears in medical studies. They have so much to cram that they have no time left to think about the future. In their overheated smoke-filled dens they spend sleepless nights studying; they are nervous wrecks when they take their orals, they flunk them, take them again and have no time to think whether they actually enjoy what they are doing or whether they are doing it all against their will. If they meet somebody they know they tell him offhand that he suffers from at least a dozen deadly diseases—or he has to listen to their dirty jokes. Bookworms, but quite entertaining characters. Supposedly, the internship amply makes up for all the long months of hard studying. I heard quite a few amusing anecdotes about it.

I also met Hans Eilinger. I don't know whether you remember him. He's the Viennese I met when I was a little boy. We were both in Holland together on that relief program for Austrian children right after the war. Well, anyhow he's in rotten shape. His father is out of work. Hans is studying chemistry but has to skip every second semester because they have no money. God knows when he finds time for studying at all. In the morning he's selling vacuum cleaners from door to door, in the afternoon he gives private lessons for 1 schilling 50. There are a lot like him in the lecture halls and labs. In their shabby knickerbockers and frayed shirts they don't exactly look as dignified as young intellectuals should. I must say the majority of students, boys and girls, look quite different from what you might imagine from Old Heidelberg movies like *The Student Prince*.

Only when there is a fraternity rally do the university lobby and the courtyard take on a marvelous splendor: innumerable caps in all colors that are constantly raised in salutation! Or when a fraternity comes to congratulate one of their boys at commencement, all in full regalia, top-boots, wide pants, white jackets, hats with feathers, and rapiers—then we feel the deep and true sense of the words, Alma Mater Rudolphina!

I'm living in a very nice room with one window for 45 schillings, and, keeping in mind your admonitions, I don't even look at the opposite sex, and, following your advice, I eat a lot of fresh fruit. If Dad realized enough profit from the restaurant this summer, maybe you could send me a couple of shirts with stiff collar. After all, I am no Hans Eilinger, and in the fraternity I have to look my part as an intellectual.

Dear mother! You know that it is my honest intention to study hard and to work my way up. All my love to all of you!

Your university man,

Fritz Feder

From Mother on Mother's Day

Vienna, May 9, 1937

My dear Ernstl,

Hope you are well, we are all pretty good in any case we have to thank God other people don't even have a piece of bread for their children and that is sure the worst of it all, and sickness. And today I even had a real surprise, that was a real joy, that's why I have to write to you today though you've been gone for eight weeks and you should write your mother more than a short postcard. I am very worried about you. Wanted to punish you and not write to you anymore until you pick up the pen again at last, but my mother's heart never has been strict enough. This morning I just got through cooking breakfast and scrubbing the kitchen floor and I go and knock softly at Franzl's door and then I go to the bedroom to wake up little Annie and dress her. But there she was all ready dressed in the white lace dress! And I hadn't hardly time to look when Franzl comes out too in his blue suit that unfortunately is getting much too short already and shiny at the knees, but he managed to get money from somewhere and got a haircut, all short he looks like a real man with his seventeen years. But I didn't even see him at first. I was so scared at little Annie—the child was as white as a sheet and trembling so I though God what is the matter with her. You know, my dear Ernstl, how delicate she is because she was born in 24 when father didn't have his job yet and we was awful poor, but you won't remember—sometimes I think it's good that children have such a short memory. The doctor keeps telling me she is anemic. But it was all only cause of the Mother's Day poem. I am copying it over for you cause I want to keep the card. You'd mislay it, I'm sure.

    There is on earth one word so dear,
    So full of toil, yet full of cheer.
    One loving soul, that won't desert you,
    One woman who will never hurt you,
    One heart so true,

> That beats for you,
> In joy and pain,
> Through sun and rain:
>   Mother!

My God, did the child say that ever so beautiful. The tears started running down my face that I couldn't see and hear anything anymore. And then Franzl gave me a box of candy, chocolates with brandy filling, at least 2 schillings 50. I was going to give the kids a talking to cause they spend the little money that have saved for something silly like that and Franzl still hasn't gotten his shoes resoled. But there I was again crying so hard that I couldn't get a word out of my mouth. Little Annie wanted me to taste the candy. At eight in the morning! Of course I said that wouldn't do. Then the children asked if they could taste one and I gave them one each after breakfast. And then they wanted more and Franzl wanted to take one to his soccer. I said yes if he takes off the good suit so it won't get dirty from that stupid soccer he keeps playing by the hour, but he'd already taken one and off he was. While I was cooking I thought when he comes back I'll give him one, the brat, but then I changed my mind because it was Mother's Day and I wouldn't have the heart to do it anyway. I couldn't stop thinking the boy is running around now the third year without a place where he could learn a trade or something, and he has such a talent for a mechanic. I just hope he won't get off the track. He's in a dangerous age now and idleness is the beginning of all vice. I've also been thinking about Dad, dear Ernstl, now that he is beginning to age you can see that he wasn't as well as they said he was when they sent him home from the army hospital. I don't know what's the matter with him these last two weeks. I know I shouldn't think the worst but I've been begging him on my knees to take sick leave. But you know your Dad. Specially now that they won't pay the first three days, and no one dares to report sick. What good are the few groschen, of course we need them but one's health is still the highest good. And as I said I pinned up the Mother's Day card on the wall next to the stove and there I was crying and crying.

It was beautiful spring weather. Little Annie played with the kids in the street. She looked so nice in spite of the sweets. She had eaten all of them instead of saving a few for her Dad. She was sweet like an angel and I couldn't do nothing but look at her and love her and the weather was really marvelous. And I got quite soft-hearted and I had to think of all kinds of things, of your dear grandmother, bless her heart, and of the future and what will become of you, my dear children in these hard times and if there isn't another war coming perhaps, and I thought of the poor people in Spain and many other things.

Dear Ernstl, hope you get work when you come back to Vienna. Maybe the time will come when you'll be the only one to support us. Hope you are feeling fine being a happy recruit in Krems. Please write soon. Or I'll never write you again. I only picked up the pen because I had to tell you about the nice day I had today and am still happy and moved.

Dear Ernstl, please don't eat any unripe fruit. Please write soon. Remember what I told you about the girls. I send you my loving kisses as well as greetings from father, little Anne, and Franzl and from your loving mother

Moosgruber Marie

P.S.—The name of the gentleman who wrote the poem on the Mother's Day card is S.O. Wallner. Do you think one could write him and thank him?

Same as above.

Be Prepared!?

Since prewar times much in the world and in the Inner City of Vienna has changed. Just think of the many elegant storefronts in the Kärtnerstrasse! Just take a look at the window of the Guerlain, perfume store where in tender flacons all the exquisite scents of the world are gathered. A culture that knows how to smell that good must be far removed from the terrors of war!

How far? Ten steps, approximately. Approximately ten steps from that perfume store there is, in the heart of Vienna, a store for gasmasks.

Every evening at seven-thirty the curious passer-by can see in its window by means of a puppetry mechanism (itself worth seeing), free and tax-exempt, the bombardment of the city of Salzburg. To serve as a warning. In the most exciting moment of the air attack a curtain descends on the festival city and on this curtain are the words: BE PREPARED! The smart man who wants to follow this warning can do so every day between six and eight by buying a gasmask in said store.

He will be shown different models. A usable mask costs, all included, fifty-seven schillings. It will protect you against all military poison gases except mustard gas, which eats away the skin itself; except the dust-like irritation gases which penetrate every filter and, not poisonous themselves, will force the wearer of the mask to take it off; and except those gases that hitherto have been kept secret by the armies. Even the best special equipment could hardly do more for you than this mask at fifty-seven schillings. Those who want to go one better can buy a rubber suit that will resist aforementioned mustard gas for about two hours. But that would be—if you pardon the expression—excessive precaution. For mustard gas precipitates in the form of droplets and evaporates so slowly that a populated area thus stricken would remain inaccessible even to the advancing enemy troops. That is to say, it is so lethal that it loses in strategic value. Only the enemy who has no other purpose than simply to annihilate all living beings would expose a city district to mustard gas. For such a procedure the term "barbaric" would be a gentle compliment.

Getting smarter and smarter, the smart man now enters the gas-protection-shelter.

What he sees is, in sum, a cell equipped with everything to prevent suffocation as well as starvation. There are two air-generators: one to be operated by hand, the other one to be operated like a bicycle. Furthermore, there is a cupboard full of gasmasks and cans of food, a fire extinguisher, a specially approved gas-protection-shelter-toilet complete with turf container; there are shovels for digging oneself out; there is a light generator, fed by an emergency battery in case the power plant should be destroyed; and for the eventuality of the emergency battery being buried under rubble there are two phosphorescent boards that give a greenish glow in the dark. German patents, all. And—we almost forgot—there is a telephone! In the event of a completely buried and destroyed world we could still have the chance to put a phone call through. "Hallo, is this the Stone Age? This is the Twentieth Century. We'd appreciate some technical advice for restoring peace! How's that? You are surprised that we, the technological age . . . ? But, dear friends, don't you know yet that our technology has other problems to work out? Almost half of our technology is busy developing means for the destruction of life; almost the other half is working hard to find the necessary counter-weapons. In between there's just enough time to think up new Guerlain perfumes. But to protect human life from force or even to make it more worth living—really, dear friends and fellow human beings, that's not what our gas-protection-patents are for."

Nevertheless, the way things are going, the emergency might present itself at any moment, and then a good gasmask and a bombproof shelter would be a hundred times more important than all considerations of principle. And for that eventuality, obviously, not even the smartest person can take precautions all by himself. Such necessary measures will have to be a common effort and will have to be organized publicly. This is the real purpose of the store in the Kärtnerstrasse where, apart from a very wealthy count and half a dozen equally well-situated customers, no one has really bought a gas mask yet. The store, which is worth seeing, primarily serves to propagandize for civil defense awareness and to prepare the population for the coming Civil Defense Bill.

Such a law will probably make the purchase of a gasmask mandatory for Austrians of an income above a certain level and will provide construction of a sufficient number of shelters. Let us hope that Austrians below it won't have to perish in an emergency; let us hope that for people below this income level gasmasks will be distributed free! Let us hope that Civil Defense will not primarily serve the business interests of private individuals but the greatest possible safety of *all* Austrians.

1936

Jura Soyfer, 1932.

"Must it always be this order?"
Towards a Democratic Culture

Political Theater

The bourgeoisie of today demands categorically: the theater is not the place for politics! Politics, so they say, is the make-up of our dreary everyday life. The stage however ought to be the place for refined, intellectual enjoyment of art, a place of elevation above the turmoil of the day, or a place for harmless pleasure. All this sounds beautiful—no less beautiful than, let's say, the bourgeois demand for the end of the class struggle and the peaceful working partnership between worker and employer. But just as in the world of class conflict there can be no class harmony and a sincere partnership there can be no unpolitical theater as long as there is a class struggle!

Let's see. Was the bourgeoisie always so keen on an "unpolitical theater." Let's refresh our memory! Lessing, Schiller, the young Goethe—they all turned the stage into a political arena. Their plays were fiery proclamations "in tyrannos," revolutionary manifestos of the victorious class, the bourgeoisie. Since then, however, the bourgeoisie has changed roles. Now as supporter of a collapsing world the bourgeoisie wards off the onslaught of the new rising class of the proletariat. Now they demand the "unpolitical theater."

The life of the proletariat is political from beginning to end. If the theater is to offer it more than mere distraction through the illusion of a nonexisting world it must itself be political! The art of the proletariat must have a social, political content.

How about the bourgeois entertainment industry? Can a polished drawing room comedy, a funny operetta, a thoughtless movie become a danger to the proletarian?

A great number of these "harmless" theater pieces and movies derive their atmosphere, their humor from the "good old times" and thus support all the petty bourgeois, conservative longings. They conjure up a world of dreams that doesn't exist, in which there are no class conflicts and whose insincerity paralyzes all judgment. Like a sweet poison the bourgeois, reactionary ideology creeps into the consciousness of the theater- or movie-goers. An undecided, politically confused working class is the working class the bourgeois wants. The emptier their pleasures, the more their interests are in their free time, the more their brains are befogged by reactionary kitsch . . . the better the public likes it.

Let's fight this apparently harmless, actually very dangerous theater!

The working class shall find the theater that is not outside, but inside their fight for liberation: the political, revolutionary theater.

Agitation theater is an effective weapon in the class struggle. The cabaret lends us its satirical force, the mass theater its powerful pathos.

We don't care whether what we do is art or not. We don't serve art, we serve propaganda. It may be that at times our convictions, our ethical strength bring us close to artistic achievement.

1932

"Fury"

The movie director Fritz Lang has left Germany and is presently working in Hollywood. For several weeks now his first American work has been shown in London and Berlin. People there talk a lot about this film; it's called "Fury," and it will be talked about here in Vienna. But "talking about it" alone will not do. The work poses some questions and gives some answers. We must hear the questions, understand the answers and then say yes or no. And that not in detached agreement or scorn but passionately, because this film inflames our emotions. Passionately, but not just for an evening, because the consequences of this work reach into the future. It concerns practically every one of us.

The plot itself tackles a purely American problem: a rather sticky one. In the USA thousands are being lynched every year. Most of the murderers go free. We see one of these thousands suffer (not a black because even the most daring director could not get away with that over there). We see a couple of hundred people in all stages of development: from a provincial small town population to a bloodthirsty mob. The governor willingly agrees not to send in the National Guard to prevent the lynching: he worries about the next election.

Nevertheless an indictment of the murderers is achieved. The whole honorable Midwestern town protects itself from the law with impenetrable silence and false evidence. The front runs unbroken from the Sheriff to the lady manager of the all-night bar. As many details—and there are many—, as many stabs deep into the pink flesh of the Babbitts. Even the unshakable legend of the foreigner who is to blame for everything is held up to scorn!

All this is specifically American. American are the types, the milieu. The terrain of powerful realism is never left. And yet, all by itself, the problem widens.

The mob tortures the innocent in jail. There is also a mob this side of the Atlantic. How many European artists and thinkers, great ones among them, have withdrawn disgusted into loneliness! They dissociated themselves from the "hordes," the "rabble," the "masses"—and, in the long run, from the people. They have lost the ability to see the difference between these very distinct collective phenomena or they have never seen it. They can learn from Fritz Lang. It is not the masses, not the people who, howling, storm the prison. It is one whirlwind of human drift-sand which can disappear as fast as it whirled together. It is nothing solid, nothing that came into being by any necessity. The down-and-out lumpenproletarian picks a fight with the chubby bourgeois in the bar. They hate each other. But they storm ahead shoulder to shoulder when driven by mass hysteria. What comes into being in this is the mob.

But explanations help little. One has to experience it.

Then one will also understand that Joe Wilson's conflicts of conscience are not only his and not only American conflicts. Wilson barely escaped being lynched. The public knows nothing about it. The people who wanted to murder him are indicted. He could have his revenge, a strictly legal, just revenge. The man is embittered. The horde has destroyed the faith in his home country. But he could save his torturers if he reports to the law alive.

What is he going to do? How will he decide when the day of the trial comes?

NB: It is difficult to translate fury into German. Only the Latin "furor" will do, that is to say: furor Americanus.

1937

Hej Rup!

In Prague the letter combination V & W has become a familiar concept: it stands for Voskovec and Werich, a pair of comedians, and their "Unfettered Theater" on Wenzel-Square. Now we in Vienna, too, have had a chance to see them; unfortunately not very many of us—just as many as the "Large Meeting Hall of the Restaurant and Hotel Association" can hold for two evening performances. There the newly founded Austrian Society of Film Friends showed us *Hej Rup!*, the first movie that Voscovec and Werich have ever made. In his introductory remarks Herr Ernst Angel said the Society's purpose was to acquaint members with films which for commercial or other reasons could not be made accessible to the Viennese public. A most welcome undertaking indeed! And if the coming events of the society follow the line of this first evening, Herr Angel may be sure that the venture he launched will meet with overwhelming response. The performance of *Hej Rup!* has already proven this. It also proved the very important fact that the Viennese movie audience unfortunately is being deprived of a great number of movies they would tremendously enjoy. Why can *Hej Rup!* not be shown in all the movie theaters of Vienna? One would hardly have to be afraid of a commercial flop. The sound track may be Czech but the film speaks a language that is understood in all countries and that makes any audience prick up its ears.

Chaplin's *Modern Times* was a great box office hit. So was *Mr. Deeds*. That should have been a lesson to movie producers in this country, They should have realized that it is simply not true that people are so reluctant to see their real problems and worries on the screen. On the contrary. As long as the movie industry (and the theater industry for that matter) sees its main function in fabricating a beautiful pseudo-world, production will be a gamble for the producers, a lottery gamble for the favors and whims of the public. Neither well-established stars nor directors with that famous sixth sense for what the public wants can ever eliminate that risk.

Nevertheless, the producers do not want to believe that we most like to hear and see things that really concern us. They claim that reality is too sad, that we get enough of it during the day and that in the evening we want to think of something else, want to be entertained etc. Well, the two movies I mentioned were not exactly bad entertainment! And Wednesday night, when we saw *Hej Rup!*, we heard our hearts beat, we laughed, and we clapped; and all that movie was about was two unemployed workers. For there is one more important fact that I herewith solemnly proclaim for the benefit of the gentlemen with that sixth sense: the unemployed worker, that utterly banal and ordinary fellow we see every day at every street corner, is a human being, too, and at least as alive a human being as the fairy-tale private secretary who leads the fairy-tale daughter of his millionaire boss to the altar. And the emotional range of that very ordinary man without a job comprises all possible human feelings from reckless merriment to the deepest grief. There is an unlimited wealth of material here for any author to draw upon.

Once again this has been proven by V & W in *Hej Rup!* This is the most important thing about this movie. Is it, apart from that, an avant-garde movie? Undoubtedly. It is true that occasionally we noticed echoes of various models. Now and then there was a touch of René Clair; here and there a gesture remind us of Laurel and Hardy. But there can be no doubt that V & W are truly great artists who are rooted in the people and speak to the people. What is best in this movie arises from their own wit and natural talents. And because they are true Czechs they create a very peculiar and charming mixture of indigenous Prague humor and the gags of American movie comedy. There can be no doubt that in their next movie the fusion of these two elements will be smoother and more artistic.

And there is one more feature that V & W have to be commended for: they deal with the life of the unemployed without any illusions whatsoever, not even with well-intended ones.

A couple of hundred unemployed are founding a dairy company and thus enter into competition with a powerful condensed-milk corporation. The boss of this corporation does everything he can to force the unwelcome intruders off the market. Only one thing he does not do: lower the price of milk. (That is typically Czech, of course.) Finally the small dairy co-op wins the battle although it was founded not with capital but only with good will.

We know from some American movies (e.g., *World without Money*) that romantically inclined film directors have a special liking for such communal efforts that are born of need. More than once, and with the best intentions, we have been told on the screen that the poor would improve their lot if they only united for some common work project on some empty building site. Unfortunately, things are not as simple in reality, and the competition of the big corporations cannot be broken quite as easily as that.

Voscovec & Werich, however, do not feed their audience the milk of pleasant illusionism. They know how to present the rise of the dairy co-op "Hej Rup!" in such a grotesquely fantastic way that at the same time the practical impossibility of this industrious communal effort is revealed. A fairytale, then, after all? Yes. But one that is most welcome: a lively modern popular fairy tale full of humor and courage nourished by clear insights.

1937

All Thieves on Strike!

(Resume for a film)

At a five-o'clock tea a young gentleman meets a young lady. He introduces himself as Hans West, she introduces herself as Lilian Röger. He, a pleasant young man with a winning manner, she, a very pretty girl, take a liking to each other, and meet on other occasions: a regular flirtation develops. But she, laughing though stubborn, refuses again and again to let him see her home, always disappearing unexpectedly and without a trace, leaving only the exhaust cloud of a little sports car behind her . . .

One night an obviously sporty, well-trained gentleman scales the facade of a villa (that of the president of the insurance company "Hermes"). He cuts through a window pane, penetrates into the president's office, and, in the beam of a flashlight and with state of the arts burglary equipment, attacks the safe. President Kessler enters the room, and, corpulent, greying, but energetic man that he is, does not hesitate to brandish his revolver and, with the customary command of "Hands up!" keeps the burglar at bay. But now the difference in age and experience in such things makes itself felt: without much trouble the burglar disarms the president with an elegant jiu jitsu maneuver, ties him to an easy chair, and gags him. All this has not happened without some commotion. Another door opens, and a girl in pyjamas enters. In the light of the dim floor lamp which has been lit in the meantime she can only see that the president is sitting, as it seems, perfectly quiet in a chair while, facing him with his back to the door, another gentleman is standing. "Excuse me, papa," she stammers in embarrassment, "I didn't know you had a visitor." With these words she is about to withdraw hurriedly, but the burglar, understandably, prevents her from doing so by locking the door: "You might as well stay here, Miss." He clicks on the ceiling light, and to the surprise of both of them it becomes evident that she is the "She" and he is the "He" of the flirtation described above. The unfortunate director almost has a stroke as he witnesses his daughter and the burglar recognizing each other and having the following conversation:

"So you are not Miss Röger, but . . ."

"So you are not Hans West, but . . ."

"Correct, but you will understand that under the circumstances I had to . . ."

At which Miss Lilian Kessler suddenly breaks out in violent sobs. The burglar, however, shows more control. After some deliberation he makes this statment: "I assume that up to now you have met me without the knowledge of your father. That was not nice, Lilian. But that's going to stop right now. Now you can't get away from me as easily as before. Besides, fortunately your father is present at out meeting. A wonderful opportunity. Director Kessler, may I ask you for the hand of your daughter?" Noticing that director Kessler is unable to answer right now because he has a gag in his mouth, Hans frees him of this obstacle and then adds: "My name enjoys the best reputation in our line of business. Financially I am easily in a position to offer your daughter all the comforts she is used to." Director Kessler is so baffled by this gigantic impudence that for the moment he can't think of anything to say except: "But you are . . . a thief . . ."

"So what?" Hans replies without batting an eye. "To be a thief is a profession like any other, a profession which is as necessary for society as yours." While saying this he has cut the cord to the alarm bell which Lilian was just about to pull. By now the shock of the thief's unheard-of impudence has worn off, and at the same time father and daughter start screaming for help. "So you don't believe me?" Hans calls in annoyance. "All right, you'll see that I'm right." He gathers up his tools and, while the servants are trying to break in the door, he takes a less elegant than hurried exit through the window . . .

The same night Cash-Box Joe and his accomplice break into the vault of a bank. Their work isn't easy. From the cellar of the neighboring house, laboriously they have to break through the thick outer wall of the bank building and, when Cash-Box Joe has squeezed his imposing circumference through the hole, the exhausting work on the thick-walled safe of the latest design only begins. Finally they've got it made; the safe swings open. It is completely empty. "A flop again," the accomplice remarks phlegmatically while Cash-Box Joe lets loose a barrage of most awful curses against the economic depression. Profoundly discouraged the two make off to their usual joint, the tavern "The Paddy Wagon." There various colleagues are awaiting Cash-Box Joe in the club room. "Every third safe you open," Joe complains," is empty nowadays. Our profession is getting less and less profitable. And we're so much worse off than other professions. In situations like these at least they can protest or strike if they decide to, but we . . ." At this moment Hans enters the tavern. He hasn't been there for some time and is greeted with respectful murmurs of the gentlemen and delighted exclamations of the ladies.

"Who says," he calls, "we can't go on strike, huh? Aren't we . . ." Hans' face is transfigured by an ingenious idea. "Listen, colleagues," he begins. Cash-Box Joe, Tony (veteran pick pocket), and other representatives of the various branches of crime, gamblers, con men—all put their heads together around Hans.

Editor Stallmeier, engrosses in his hurried editorial work on the local page of the *Evening Courier*, receives a letter which makes him burst out in guffawing merriment. But he has no time to go over it again right then. He puts it in his pocket and rushes off to Director Kessler's villa. There a big banquet is taking place, and it is an open secret that the event serves the purpose of giving the proper festive setting to the announcement of Miss Lilian Kessler's engagement to bank director Walter F. Meininger. Editor Stallmeier arrives just at the high point of festivities; the assembled select company, (which, name on name, will adorn the *Evening Courier's* society column) is toasting the young couple. Stallmeier, who knows everything, also knows, of course, that Lilian until very recently objected to the match that her father had so eagerly arranged. But Stallmeier also knows that Lilian suddenly consented, apparently due to some unexpected occurrence and, strangely enough, on the morning after the impudent burglar's attempt on her father's villa. In the smoking salon where people are gossiping at great length about this unexpected turn of events, Stallmeier remembers the letter, asks for silence and begins to read it aloud:

Dear Editor:

Due to the Depression, our business, too, is undergoing great hardships. Again and again in our work we must make the sad discovery that companies and private individuals of the best reputation which we selected as targets of our hard work, actually find themselves in a deplorable financial situation. You, dear editor, can hardly imagine how much solid, professional work has been wasted on empty safes, how many excellent colleagues have wasted their exquisite skill on wallets that contained nothing but pawn shop receipts. Other branches of business that find themselves in difficulties are being officially kept afloat by bail-outs. We never receive such benefits. No matter what happens, in times like these or in times of an economic boom, the penalty for habitual theft is five years, not to speak of other stringent measures. But the day has come when our patience is spent. We demand a decisive reduction of penalties, a decrease of our risk in proportion to our decrease in income. We demand that you publish this letter in your respected paper. If our demands are not met within a week, our whole profession will go on strike. Similar letters are being sent to outstanding personages of public life.

Respectfully Yours,

Umbrella Organization of Thieves and Allied Branches.

The letter is greeted with the hellish laughter of all present. And next day not only the chief of police, director Kessler, the director of the jail, the attorneys, bank direktor Meininger, and other dignitaries who have received the letter are laughing; the whole town is laughing because the editor has given the letter a special lay-out as the priceless idea of a witty joker . . .

The first person who feels no longer like laughing is editor Stallmeier. Dumbfounded he leafs through the correspondents' reports. They used to teem with sensational criminal affairs. Now all the crimes this city of a million has to show are two cases of petty pocket thievery. How is he to fill his so popular local page? His best criminal reporters, those who have the most sensitive noses for news and miss nothing come back empty-handed. With a curse on his lips Stallmeier decides to go on a hunt for sensations himself. He ventures forth into the most notorious crime districts, the most dangerous hide-outs. They present a picture of most boring order and peaceableness. Only in "The Paddy Wagon" a more lively atmosphere prevails. That's the general headquarters of Hans and his aide Cash-Box Joe. Patrols are arriving who had to check all parts of the city to see that the strike was being observed a hundred percent. Hans is satisfied with their reports. A non-union burglar who has tried to work is dragged in and given a serious reprimand. His burglar tools are confiscated. Incessantly Hans is encouraging those of little faith and promises imminent success.

And success is not long in coming. At first, the public's response to Stallmeier's report on the strict observance of the strike is laughter and incredulity. After about a week the facts speak a more convincing language than a hundred newspaper stories. The number of property offenses has decreased rapidly and finally plummeted to zero. For days not a crumb of bread is stolen in the whole city! First one, then several, finally a large number of people insured against theft are telling Kessler's premium collectors to go to the devil. Why pay the irksome premiums if the risk of theft has sunk to zero?

Lilian's fiancé, too, looks grim. More and more people withdraw their savings from his bank. Now that they can safely keep their money at home, they can do without the little bit of interest in the assurance that their money won't be lost in the banks' speculations.

At the police stations the policemen sit around yawing. They have nothing to do.

Orders for safes, fences, and safety locks decrease whereupon the producers cancel their orders at the steel plants.

The striking burglars are sufficently supported by money from their strike fund. The strike is being observed painstakingly. The avalanche gathers momentum. A great many policemen have become superfluous and have to be terminated. In the jail cells that now stand empty, the wards, bored stiff, build rabbit hutches. If judges and juries now and then are lucky enough to try a case at all, they treat any Mrs. Jones who insulted any Mrs. Smith for using the wrong garbage can with utmost politeness, and blow up the incident into a sensational trial of several weeks. But it's all of no avail. More and more judges find themselves without cases, and with deep concern they anticipate the end of their profession. The banks whose holdings have decreased tremendously, don't issue loans any more: the construction of houses, roads etc. comes to a standstill. The catastrophy draws ever growing circles. With the end of sensational crimes the circulation of Stallmeier's paper has shrunk to a frightening degree, and he prophesies national bankruptcy.

Lilian's fiancé suggests that they leave the city and take a pleasure trip to the French Riviera until the absurd situation rights itself. Reluctantly she agrees. But at the very moment when he is about to pick her up in his car a group of suspicious looking characters led by Hans ask him in polite but unmistakable terms to stay. To Lilian's great surprise her fiancé does not call the police but sheepishly lets himself be led back to his apartment which from now on is watched round the clock by two unshaven jail birds. Hans elightens Lilian: "Your fine fiancé just wanted to abscond with the remaining savings deposits of his bank. But we do not tolerate scabs."

Lilian's father faces utter ruin. Hans's insolence provokes her. She decides to save the situation. The thieves have to be induced to steal again. Lilian organizes a splendid fancy dress ball for the city's cream of society, a "rags and tatters" affair for which everybody comes costumed as some disreputable looking character.

Then she goes to "The Paddy Wagon"—after having disguised herself as one of the ladies frequenting this establishment. Hans, overworked by organizational chores, is absent. Lilian spreads the news of the ball among her "lady colleagues." She describes the magnificent strings of pearls and rings the attending ladies will wear. Security checks at the door will be very relaxed. What a wonderful opportunity for the thieves to make a phantastic haul without any risk! Her psychological calculation proves right. The thieves let themselves be persuaded by their girl friends to attend the ball.

When Hans appears in the tavern he finds his colleagues in uproar and no longer willing to stick to honesty.

At the ball, Lilian, ironically, flirts and dances with Hans. Things are stolen everywhere. Indeed, a veritable competition seems to have broken out among the thieves. As soon as one of the real rogues wants to steal some jewelry from a make-believe rogue, another real rogue has beaten him to it. But as soon as a theft has been noticed, the stolen object is politely returned to the owner in an adjoining room. This doesn't always work smoothly. Lilians's father, for instance, was very happy when he found that his gold watch had been stolen. But Hans' most loyal followers, thwarting the plans of their colleagues who prove inferior in character and skill, insist on returning what they have stolen right in front of the scabs' noses. Only old Tony, veteran of pickpockets, makes trouble. But the poor guy is a cleptomaniac and steals instinctively, even shot glasses in "The Paddy Wagon."

Thus Lilian's plan founders. The strike is threatened by a new danger. Organized crime in a neighboring city has heard of the strike and smells a good opportunity. They arrange a raid on Meininger's Bank (his engagement with Lilian was annulled after his attempted fraud). Meininger, alerted in his office, strictly forbids anyone to contact the police. He is delighted that stealing is in again and gladly sacrifices a couple of hundred thousands of the money which does not belong to him anyway but to the savers, if only the status quo is restored. But again Hans throws a monkey wrench into his calculations. Under the leadership of Cash-Box Joe the bank robbers are being routed and the bank is saved. Cash-Box Joe carries out his duty only under serious psychological tortures considering the rows and rows of magnificent safes crammed full that he, of all people, saves. Only old Tony, during the fierce battle against the bank robbers, cannot resist the temptation and pockets an orange-colored paper weight.

The captains of industry have no other alternative than to negotiate with the thieves. Except for the disquieting appearance of the thieves' delegation, and apart from some smaller faux pas by Tony which are straightened out quickly enough, the atmosphere is most dignified and decorous. In the pauses the negotiators are walking up and down the corridors or discussing specifics at the smoking tables. Director Kessler, who presides over the meeting, has long since abandoned his former scornful judgment of the thieves' guild. Hans has risen in his respect tremendously. But that's about all that the negotiations produce because, in the midst of them, the Head of Criminal Police receives news of a bold burglary in a jeweler's shop. At police headquarters the joy is unmitigated. A telephone call informs the captains of industry who immediately break off negotiations.

The joy of the Head of Criminal Police evaporates as the burglar is led before him. He is the former supervisor of his own office, who, fired because of the strike, wanted to earn his bread in this way. But this gives the Head of Criminal Police an idea. The following night police officers on higher orders attempt several albeit rather clumsy burglaries. But, alas, it is impossible to break through the united front of the strikers. The criminals very skillfully catch the policemen in due time. None of the burglaries are successful.

Director Kessler has noticed Lilian's love for Hans and has come to know the latter's proficiency. He proposes that Hans end the strike, marry Lilian, and become an executive at the Hermes insurance company. After some quick calculations Hans concludes that the job of executive is more profitable than the profession of a thief.

But how can he persuade the thieves to break off the strike as long as their demands are not met?

A plenary meeting of the thieves is called in which Director Kessler gives a spirited speech. He appeals to the thieves' sense of responsibility. In warm words he asks them to revive the domestic economy again, to do their duty again, in other words to steal again. The thieves are touched. Besides, their strike funds are depleted. With enthusiasm and tears of deep emotion they decide to break off the strike. Thousands of nimble hands reach for their shiny burglars' tools.

And when during the engagement banquet in honor of Hans and Lilian, the news arrives that Director Kessler's apartment has been cleared out completely, Kessler, his hands trembling with jubilation, raises his glass to the young couple's health and prosperity.

French Avant-garde in Vienna
From: The Unknown Girl of Arras.

. . . It is the old story, the story of the avant-garde studio. This week is was the turn of Dr. Rohner's acting group (in the *Hagenbund*) to suffer through all the birth pangs of such a premiere. The play was *The Unknown Girl of Arras*, the work of a young Frenchman by the name of Salacrou. This production is noteworthy mainly for three reasons. Firstly, the play is highly interesting from an artistic point of view; in parts we feel the touch of genius. Secondly, due to its high artistic merit the play offers us significant insights into the whole movement of which it is an example. Thirdly, and this is especially important, the production is indicative of the situation of all avant-garde theater groups in Vienna.

Ulysses, a man in very comfortable middle-class circumstances, shoots himself because his wife has been unfaithful. Before he reaches the Beyond, however, the dead man still has to cover some distance in this world. In his apartment he finds himself surrounded by all his memories, and once more he has to go through all the deeply human experiences that were his share from his childhood to his death; to put it briefly, he has to relive his life. This repeated life does not take place chronologically, however, but in a very hectic and erratic disorder . . . . What happened long ago mixes with what happened very recently . . . In all this intricately interwoven multiplicity of time levels with the perfectly preserved unity of place . . . Ulysse sets out on his odyssey once more . . . .

To judge by this play, Salacrou is one of the French surrealists. During the first years after the war large segments of the French theatergoing public, led by a number of extremely talented young authors, rebelled against existing art forms. A world of new problems had arisen . . . . At that time the surrealists, in bold experiments, tried to create something new. What they succeeded in creating was much but not enough. As far as the theater was concerned they achieved a liberation from the rigid, formal rules of traditional dramaturgy and thus they continued and perfected expressionism. But they did not go beyond that point. After a period of genuine progress, stagnation set in. Playwrights started to experiment with various forms. What was being said became secondary to the way in which it was said.

At this time Aragon, one of the leading Surrealists, turned away from his own school. And he was not to be the only one to do so. Today there is a broad movement of French poets, prose writers, and dramatists who have turned again to the eternal fountain of all art: the people and the thousand-fold *living* problems of the daily experience of ordinary people.

One thing that poets and prose writers may still argue about needs no further discussion by dramatists: the fact that throughout history the theater was great and productive only when its passions were the passions of hundreds of thousands.

And from this vantage point we shall go back to the theaters in Vienna—go back in every respect.

The theater industry in today's Vienna, relatively speaking and strangely enough, is enjoying a financial boom. Its intellectual level, however, is extremely low. The big theaters aim at a repertoire that moves between boulevard amusement and what is called, with a slightly more dignified term, theater of entertainment. Only a shockingly low percentage of plays produced cannot be classified as belonging to either one of these primitive categories. Future historians of Austrian theater will have to discard our era with a few words of regret. Everyone today who has anything to do with the theater knows this. Some people don't care; others find it deplorable and for years have been trying to do something about it. Years ago they were a minority with no influence whatever, and that is what they have remained to this day.

Why? Aren't there enough talents in this minority camp? That has certainly not been the problem. The big theaters have always come to the small young set to recruit personnel for themselves, and they have had no reasons for regret. Or were the young people not really serious enough, were they lacking in good will? Without underestimating the temptations of good money one can say without getting dramatic about it: no, not all of them were lacking in good will. Is it the fault of the public, then? Does the public want, at any cost, only plays that are well-written but say nothing? If that is true, why aren't the studios trying to find a new audience instead of the one they have been unsuccessfully trying to reach all these years? And if that is not true, why is their admirable work doomed to be and to remain a labor of Sisyphus?

Between the happy end of an operetta tenor and the double suicide of an avant-garde Ulysse: is there really no alternative that might be worthy of an experiment?

1937

A Public Dress Rehearsal of Mozart's *Marriage of Figaro*

Public dress rehearsal of a new production of a Mozart Opera! Surely a social event! Don't the artists face the crossfire of dozens of scrutinizing colleagues? And do we not notice among others this or that V.I.P in the audience? And do not music critics exchange praise and blame in the intermission? And where are the "soigné aesthetes" and where the "beautiful women"?

Nothing of the kind is to be seen in the pit. Admission to the dress rehearsal is 60 groschen, for unemployed 30 groschen. The time: Monday, 10 a.m. Place: Adult Education Center, Stöbergasse.

Who fills the rows of the auditorium? Housewives who somehow managed to free themselves of their housework for this morning though obviously they do not have a maid. Older people in their Sunday best, pensioners no doubt. But above all: unemployed of all ages and categories.

Anybody who is known? Whom do we notice among others? Among others we notice Mr. X. Every other morning he appears in our backyard and sings "Hands Tied by Love" to the mandolin. Also Mrs. Y. Every night till four in the morning she sells newspapers in the coffeehouses in the city. And there is Professor Z. Three years ago he gave piano lessons to Mitzi Gruber in number 17 down the block. But then the Grubers ran out of money to pay for such luxury, or Mitzi ran out of talent.

Who are the artists in this production of the *Marriage of Figaro*? In the orchestra pit as well as on the stage: students of the Music Conservatory.

The overture has been played. The curtain rises above the rococo room of the maid Susanne. The State Opera has more beautiful backdrops than the Adult Education Center on Stöbergasse. Mrs. Y., like all the other 300 people in the audience, concentrates her eyes and ears on the stage.

Now we are going to see, Mrs. Y, whether Mozart also belongs to the poor people

Or to be more precise: whether they already understand that he belongs to them.

It won't be too easy, this understanding of the opera *Figaro*. As we know, not much is left of Beaumarchais' original text. It's just one aria in the first act whose text recalls those fiery chansons that on the eve of 1792 inspired the Parisian Third Estate to frenetic applause: "If you wish to dance, most noble Lord, I will accompany you on the guitar!"

Apart from that, nothing in the words of the opera makes one realize how important the victory of the servant Figaro over his aristocratic master must have appeared to the audience at the time of the bourgeois revolution.

The music, however, speaks a different language. Infinitely graceful and melodious, it proclaims for all eternity those principles which guided the freedom-loving citizens of their time in their rebellion against their oppressors: sensitivity of feeling, true love and friendship, deep pain, noble joy—in a word: genuine, passionate humanity which had remained forever unknown to the puppets and sycophantic courtiers of the Rococo.

And now in the year 1937 in the Adult Education Center on

Stöbergasse the question presents itself: are today's unemployed of the Fourth Estate able to feel their way through the intrigues of a silly, long-outdated comedy of mistaken identities to the eternal values of a magnificent opera? Do they understand, do they enjoy this piece of cultural heritage?

They do! This Monday morning they proved it once again. Their shy, joyous affirmation made this *Figaro* an experience completely different from anything that could have happened in the State Opera Building.

The nouveau of the performance was naturally lower. The technical means were scanty. And the young musicians and singers who gave their utmost probably could have been made to give even more. In short: Mozart has been better interpreted.

Yet the reception he did find made up for it to a great measure. The people sitting in the auditorium were no connoisseurs. It didn't occur to anyone to find fault with the low registers of Mr. Soandso or the breathing technique of Mrs. N.N. The stage designer did not have to worry about a verdict on his "concept," and the conductor did not feel critical glances piercing his back. The response of the audience is fully described in one word: gratitude. Indeed, first and foremost, people were grateful . . . and then: eager to know more. In the intermission the aforementioned Professor Z. and a few others who knew about music instructed the people sitting next to them.

Instructed?

How was that? Had the unemployed not come to enjoy themselves, to forget their worries? They certainly had. But learning and amusement are contradictory concepts only in the area between the State Opera and the Stock Exchange.

In the districts around the Adult Education Centers things are different. Here people do not consider themselves above instruction.

Primitive? Of course! It was a primitive audience in a primitive theater. And anybody who loves the theater knows: whenever it does not appear in glamorous robes, but in poverty, half naked; only then one sees how deeply its magic is ingrained in us.

No Reinhardt was present to stage Mozart's music, no Toscanini to conduct it. Provided only with bare essentials, left to itself, it moved and elated three hundred people.

That was the experience *Figaro* in the Adult Education Center offered us. When the people left the auditorium they went in striking silence. Only out in the street did they start talking about their everyday life.

* * *

Unfortunately, it is not only pleasant thoughts that come when one thinks of all that joyous response and gratitude. Unfortunately, one cannot help thinking about the monstrous deluge of dangerous "entertainment"-garbage that in other places pours down upon the audience so naive in its willingness to see and to hear. Once again one wants to scream about the insidious abuse that goes on day after day, the disgraceful speculation with the masses' hunger for culture.

But talking about it doesn't help much. Things probably won't change for a long time to come.

It would make more sense to ask whether the Adult Education Centers within the limits of their possibilities take countermeasures that can satisfy their members. The Adult Education Centers are supposed to bring the arts and sciences closer to the people. They ought to educate people to a full understanding of *Figaro* as systematically as to a full understanding of history. They ought to!

The thirst for knowledge and beauty is great. The fare that is being served, meager.

1937

The Living Nestroy
On the 75th Anniversary of his Death

Johann Nestroy is such a lively corpse that even the barrage of learned empty in-memorials which are burying his ghost these days will not be able to kill him. He will survive, will go on living—and go on waiting. Waiting for the permission to have his debut once more. The production of his plays which he now gets to see here and there doesn't strike him as being exceptionally imaginative. It is not the memorized, sterilized wording of one or the other exhumed farce of his that he wants to hear. He would like to see himself on the stage again, in all his ravishing topicality and popularity, laughed at, cheered, booed, (indeed, why not, why not booed in hearty disapproval?) by a public who knows: what's going on up there on the stage concerns us, is full of life as we know it, full of the problems we face, it is our cause that is being debated! Karl Kraus in his unforgotten readings put Nestroy in the proper light and intellectual perspective, and that was a great achievement but it was not enough. At present the great actor is out of work again. Those who could see to it that Nestroy be given his long overdue permanent contract with the Austrian theater are the same kind of people who went to see him a hundred years ago. They carried him to his grave in a funeral procession that, for an hour and a half, moved through a dense crowd of mourners in the streets. So they must have been fond of him, must have been grateful audiences at his plays. I wonder whether there are still such people alive today. Of course there are, and they don't think of dying out yet—the small shopkeepers, the craftsmen, the wage earners in the outer districts of Vienna.

It was mainly the ordinary people who went to see Nestroy's plays. The higher classes were also represented, and in good numbers. But as far as the history of the theater goes, his total achievement was, without a doubt, that he made theater for the people in the poorer outskirts, for those who always lived at the bottom of society and on the ground floor of the houses and not for those who lived "one flight up." For in his time Nestroy rescued—though not forever—the popular theater from a profound inner crisis. In a development lasting hundreds of years, this theater had created three main types of stage characters: *Hanswurst, Kasperl, Thaddädl.* Apart from their differences, all three of these main clowns showed an unmistakable family resemblance. Basically, they had one thing in common: whether Stranitzky's *Hanswurst* in his stereotyped Salzburg costume was dreaming of eating and drinking; whether Laroche's *Kasperl*, a kind of Sancho Panza, followed his knight through a ghost-infested forest, crying with terror like a child; whether *Thaddädl* as a miller's boy got frightened out of his wooden clogs by a lizard—it was always the "lower class" folk that these figures represented: the peasants, the craftsmen, the servants.

They did not cut a very endearing figure. They were shown as the crude creatures that the upper classes of the feudal system liked to make scornful fun of. Utterly insensitive to higher aspirations, childish, gluttonous, drunk, vile, cowardly, stupidly impertinent, but at the same time servile. Adorned with such qualities these comic figures awkwardly stumbled through their masters' noble, bold, and spine-chilling "Court Tragedies in the Grand Style." The common people found pleasure in these caricatures of themselves, perhaps out of a delight in self-travesty, certainly because the comic character, although he always got the blows in the end, could, here and there, in his childishly direct manner come out with a stark and honest truth that was spoken straight from the Salzburg peasant's heart.

Around the turn of the century, however, it became evident that the times of *Kasperl* were gone. Especially in the cities the frame of mind of the ordinary population changed rapidly. Farces with extempore dialogue and well-worn coarse gags simply could not hold the audience any longer. They demanded performances that were more sophisticated in artistic form and in acting. They did not want to see *Hanswurst* anymore, basically because they no longer wanted to be *Hanswurst*.

To give even a sketchy picture of this theater crisis in its various stages is obviously not possible here. Let me point out just one thing: in the last analysis it was Nestroy who, for the people of Vienna and out of the people of Vienna, created the theater that the times demanded. He was an utterly modern person. In his own personality all contradictions of bourgeois society could be found. As he said once, "The deeper I sink the plumb line into the ocean of my thought, the more I realize the abyss of the contradictions in me." And Nestroy was no whiny Punch either; he had to fight for his audience because at first it shrank back from the sober, damned smart, fanatic, acidly critical temper of this lanky, jumpy, spindly long-legs. A theater critic called the Nestroy of his first period "the incarnation of merciless satire." At the time, the technical term for the way Nestroy was hamming it up was *"outrer"*—to carry to excess. Nestroy exaggerated diabolically! He could not help it. When he was more mature he showed his audience a style of acting that at that time was very new and very much needed: realism.

But realistic or not, he spoke the truth, the truth of his audience.

> "Do you know, you plebeian, that I am the descendent of a knight?"
>
> "My forefathers were small shopkeepers selling buttons and ribbons. The knights lived in a fly-by-night style. They took duty from the small shopkeepers, in plain language: they robbed them. Now I ask you: why is it nobler to be descended from the robbers than from the robbed?"

There were a lot of disagreements between Nestroy and his audience. They never disagreed on the above question. The great playwright and comedian stuck to his convictions not only in 1848, but also in the years after. It is true that when the storm had blown over, Nestroy became somewhat more moderate and finally subscribed to the view, held also by Grillparzer, that a centralized monarchy was the best protection for German culture against the mounting pressure of the Slavic peoples that were to be assimilated. But these views had, in Nestroy's case, nothing to do with servility. He became loyal to the ruling house, but not servile. Immediately after this *Freiheit in Krähwinkel* (*Freedom in Sticksville*, the play that the censor branded "notorious") Nestroy wrote his farce *Lady und Schneider* (*Lady and Tailor*) to ridicule the revolutionary busybodies. He did so not only out of the psychological shock following the bloody days of October: Nestroy felt a deep disappointment with the liberals because of their inadequacies. Clearly he recognized the half-heartedness of the Viennese middle class of the Metternich era that betrayed its own revolution. If we juxtapose what he wrote during the great delirium of revolution and what he wrote during the subsequent period of reaction, we can certainly discern a coherent line:

Before: "A censor is a pencil turned man or a man turned pencil, a line become flesh that cuts through the creations of the spirit. Censorship is the younger of two abominable sisters; the name of the elder is Inquisition."

After: "A silk-handkerchief-thief goes to jail for three months; afterwards he seems to be free, but for the rest of his life he remains fettered to the pillory of disgrace. The political prisoner, for his short intoxicated freedom, gets ten, fifteen years in the dungeons but loses not a quarter of an hour of his honor. The respect we allow everyone who stands up for his convictions, who risks his life for his creed, is his forever, and that makes the prison sentence infinitely easier to bear."

Nestroy's work is an inalienable heritage of Austrian culture. But what would a theater have to be like today to play Nestroy in his living spirit? In general, many words have been said and lost on this subject. A concrete example should be all the more welcome, particularly one from Nestroy's own time. It is a telling example of what such a theater should not be like. For many years Nestroy worked under the direction of a man by the name of Carl who was not only a shrewd businessman but also a slave-driver, the very prototype of a destroyer of the theater. Carl had come from Germany to take over the directorship of the Theater an der Wien (The Theater on the Vienna River). One of the most typical features of his directorship was his unrelenting miserliness. Only now and then, when launching one of his fancy spectacular productions, he splurged on lavish decorations. He had not a penny's worth of respect for literature. He put on Schiller's *Die Räuber* (*The Robbers*) with a whole army of foot soldiers and cavalry and made a "horse comedy" out of it that evoked great merriment in the audience.

Carl speeded up a development that, in spite of Nestroy's ingenious preventive measures, could not be stopped. It was Carl who inevitably led the Viennese popular comedy to its downfall. Most historians of the theater today unanimously consider Carl responsible for this death blow to a cultural tradition. He did become wealthy, but his wealth was nothing but the treasures he saved from a pirate's ship that was sinking.

Nestroy observed:

> Now they play at the Wien.
> But no audience is seen.
> The future's gray and not green.
> There's a thought in my bean:
> It's not the fault of the Wien.
> You need brains on the scene.
> Or you'll die from routine
> Out there at the Wien.

Nestroy, however, later became director himself and he by no means lost money (on the contrary), but a confidential report of police headquarters concerning the theaters on the outskirts of Vienna (nr. 3566, Präs. I: Prius 101. 608 pr. I, Vienna, 25 December 1857) testifies that he "does not enjoy a good reputation. Discipline has become so loose that the members of the troupe obey the director more out of a spirit of cooperation and gratitude than out of duty." An excellent tip! How about trying to introduce this kind of discipline today? How about the battle cry: "Down with Carl! Cheers for Nestroy!"?

1937

A Word about Censorship

One more word about censoring little cabaret theaters. It may be the official function of theater censors to prevent a politically embarrassing *faux pas*. A distrust, however, that in every word senses some kind of allusion must inevitably lead to misunderstandings. It must be admitted that the little theaters are striving for real art. And it must be remembered that artistic values have always suffered when subjected to excessive supervision—a fact that those cabarets which all too willingly submit to such supervision have found out to their regret. Young Austrian writers can be concerned about one thing only: to increase and to preserve the store of Austrian culture. Nobody should deny them this function and nobody should deny them the right to speak out for human values and for social progress.

1937

Program of the ABC Cabaret, Vienna
Front Page

THE PLAYS

Sketch by Bil Spira, the "stage designer" in the dialogue "The Statue of Liberty for Five Schillings", *Der Tag*, 17 May 1936. Spira designed the sets for *Der Weltuntergang* (The End of the World), performed at the cabaret ABC, Vienna, 1936.

By way of introduction . . .

The Statue of Liberty for Five Schillings

by
Jura Soyfer and Bil Spira

A large room eighteen feet beneath a Viennese coffeehouse. Metal sheets, wooden strips, pots of glue and paint, nails, tools are scattered all over. Sticking out of the bits and pieces are: a space rocket, a giant telescope, a green diplomats' table, an Egyptian sarcophagus. The room resounds with hammer blows. As the door opens, we can hear through the monotonous hammering rhythm the short intermittent groans of a half-crazy astronomer, stopped suddenly by the sharp voice of an energetic director: "Go back! Once more! We're going to rehearse until five in the morning!" Then the door closes. A very dirty person in overalls comes crawling out of the scattered raw materials and barks at the intruder. The characters of the following dialogue stand face to face: the stage designer of this basement theater and its playwright.

The beginning of their conversation cannot be reproduced verbatim. Basically it centers round the following situation: the stage designer faces the task of designing and building the props for a kind of revue play whose plot gallops through two continents. The funds placed at his disposal took him as far as New York. Here the necessity of building a Statue of Liberty presented itself. Cost: five schillings. The artistic director refused to exceed the budget that already had been exceeded several times. Furthermore: a few minutes before an actress bathed in tears had appeared and threatened disaster unless her Negro number were provided with a full moon. Moons are made of opalescent glass, and opalescent glass is expensive. The ensemble consists of seven players and seven nervous problems. Towering above these problems there is the inescapable asbestos problem. Since cabaret theaters are not protected by an iron curtain, they are protected from fire only by an iron law: what is not made of sheet metal must be made of Asbestex, a noninflammable material. Not to mention the fact that the premiere will take place in twenty-three hours and that in spite of two sleepless nights nothing is ready.

That is also the playwright's worry. As a matter of fact, he shouldn't be standing around here but should be writing the sketch that is still missing, about which only he knows that it must contain a part for Mr. A. and a part for Mrs. B.; also sparkling humor since there are too many serious scenes already; and finally, it must be of intellectual caliber because this is no mere entertainment but, as we've said before, a . . .

"Four-letter words won't help," the stage designer interrupts, and he reminds his partner that the two of them should, for God's sake, carry on a dialogue of a more representative nature, a dialogue ready to be printed in order to give the reader some insight into the conditions under which a cabaret theater has to work. And so, from now on, they speak print:

STAGE DESIGNER: Lend me a schilling for the moon!

WRITER: Tell me, why are you working here at all—*only* to make money?

DESIGNER: The money we make here is not enough to be referred to in connection with *only*! I think what attracted the actors, the director, you, and me to this basement is last, but not least, the possibility of acting, painting, writing without any of the considerations regular theaters have to take into account.

WRITER: There are still other considerations, though. You have to take the cost of opalescent glass into account when you are making a moon and I have to think of the good of the country when I tell the audience the world's coming to an end.

DESIGNER: Nevertheless, our financial risk isn't really very big. In young people there are untapped resources of energy, more than is good for them. We have the opportunity to experiment. I also think that this is the reason why there are always people who would rather fill up our auditorium than look at a polished and well-funded performance.

WRITER: In my opinion, at least up to now, the audience has not come to us primarily for avant-garde experiments. And so far I really have not seen too much on that order. In the five years that we have had underground theaters like this in Vienna they have hardly gone beyond mixing elements of the Old Viennese popular theater, of the *Überbrettl*, the *Three Penny Opera*, etc. with cabaret programs, and they have done this partly out of courage, partly for the heck of it . . .

DESIGNER: Then what is it that the public has wanted and found in our theater?

WRITER: We are much closer to actual life in our times, much closer than the usual theater. We are aware of the problems that concern people today. That can make up for artistic shortcomings.

DESIGNER: I think a little more highly of our theaters than you do. Above all, they loosen up the rigid schematic structure of the traditional theater, they prepare the ground for a new development and even now they represent a certain literary value.

WRITER: I think that the artistic goals and possibilities for development are not absolutely clear yet, either to the public or to the theater people. The right form has not been found yet.

DESIGNER: But we are moving. Aren't they telling us that every program is better than the last?

WRITER: But even if that is the case, are we sure that we all agree on the direction in which we are moving?

The End of the World

CHARACTERS

Sun
Saturn
Mars
Venus
Moon
Konrad, a comet
Voices of four journalists
The Führer
Professor Peep, a physicist
Photographer
First lady of fashion
Second lady of fashion
Young man
Girl
First Viennese
Second Viennese
Spinster
Polly, her parrot
First diplomat
Second diplomat
Loudspeaker
English official
French official
German official
Austrian Official
End-of-the-world preacher
Street singer
Woman street singer
Robber
Suicide
Intellectual lady
Intellectual gentleman
Cake-mix grandma
Policeman
Mr. Rockford, American millionaire
Mrs. Rockford, his wife

Mr. Wood, writer
Winnie Winston, film star
Journalist of the *New York Tribune*
Miss Violet, Rockford's secretary

Scene One

Prologue in Cosmos

(In outer space. The background is a starry sky. The Sun, a corpulent, imposing lady, is conducting the dance of the planets. Mars, Venus, and Saturn, each revolving on its axis, are dancing in a circle around the Sun. Of the three, Venus is closest to the Sun, Saturn farthest away.)

THE THREE PLANETS *(singing the "Waltz of the Planets" in the slow and dignified tempo of an English Waltz):*

> Through endless space the planet goes,
> Cold cosmic wind around it blows.
>
> Its job of turning's never done:
> Around itself, around the sun.
>
> It keeps its distance as it should,
> In space your place is understood.
>
> Four times pi squared a to the third.
> By u times u times radius squared.
>
> The planet makes its scheduled run,
> And other worries it has none.

SUN *(taps the music stand with her baton)*: Stop! Take your places again! *(The planets interrupt their course.)*
SATURN *(a grumpy, old planet):* What did you say?
MARS *(a choleric planet):* Did you say "stop"?
VENUS *(an erotic planet):* Really, what do you think this is, a dress rehearsal? This isn't the first day of creation, you know. You just can't say stop like that, not in the middle of eternity!
SATURN: The Sun has sunstroke.

SUN: Quiet in the cosmos! If I told you to stop, I have my reasons.
MARS: I'm sure curious to hear them.
SUN: Just a moment ago I noticed that the harmony of the spheres got out of tune.
MARS: Are you serious?
SUN: Dead serious, my dear Mars!
MARS: Dreadful! The blood is freezing in my canals. *(He holds his head with both hands.)*
SATURN: What could be wrong?
SUN: I'm not quite sure. Some disgusting dissonance or other.
MARS: But, allow me—creation is perfect. How can there be any dissonance all of a sudden? *(The Sun shrugs her shoulders.)*
VENUS *(nonplused):* Astronomical!
SATURN: Do you have any idea who could be the culprit?
SUN *(hesitating):* Yes.
VENUS *(hysterically):* You don't think I'm to blame, do you? I swear the third power of the mean of my distance from you has always been equal to the square of the time of my revolution.
SATURN: Gracious lady, you know that you have always been the focal point of my ellipses!
SUN: Venus and Saturn don't need to worry. I don't suspect them but . . . *(She hesitates.)*
MARS *(impatiently):* Well?
SUN: . . . the Earth! A short while ago, approximately ten thousand years that is, the behavior of the Earth started to become very odd. Her face, too, has changed strangely.
VENUS: Well, let her answer for it!
SUN: That's just the problem. She doesn't answer any of my interplanetary calls. Some disease or worry seems to take up all her attention. That might be the real reason why she can't keep time with the spheres anymore.
SATURN: And we are supposed to stand and wait till the Earth deigns to come round?

VENUS: If I have to stop for much longer and cannot rotate round you, I'll be frizzled in front and frozen in the back. (*Close to tears:*) Oh dear, my gorgeous tropical vegetation!

SUN: Don't worry! We'll soon know what the score is. I have summoned someone who knows all about the Earth.

MARS: And who's that?

SUN: The Moon.

MARS: And how did you manage to get him to come?

SUN: All I did was throw a bundle of gravitation at him, thus getting him out of the earth's sphere of attraction.

SATURN: Excuse me, but that is the biggest nonsense that I have heard in two hundred million years. You threw a bundle of gravitation at him?! That's an insult to all laws of physics!

SUN (*scornfully*): Laws of physics phooey! Is it compatible with the laws of physics that you are standing still this minute like fixed stars?

MARS: Right! I've been wondering about that all along!

SUN: I have asked the supreme authorities for permission to introduce emergency measures. The laws of physics have been temporarily suspended.

SATURN: But the astronomical theories . . . ?

SUN: The astronomical theories will be changed, that's all. First you get emergency measures; the theories to support them come later. It's always been like that.

SATURN (*shaking his head*): The things that are going on in the cosmos these days . . .

(*Enter Moon.*)

MOON (*a little bald old man, smiling, cool and serene*): Your obedient satellite, my stellar excellencies! (*To the Sun:*) My very best wishes for happy radiation, Your Ladyship! I do hope the little solar spots aren't bothering you too much. Well, well, they can't be helped, we're all getting older. (*While he is speaking, the planets make motions toward him so as to attract him.*)

SUN (*haughtily*): Maybe you are, Moon. As far as I am concerned, I still have my normal temperature of thirty thousand degrees centigrade. Well now, I have drawn you to us . . .

MARS (*making above motions*): Actually it was me who did that . . .

SATURN (*with similar motions*): It was me. I did that. Come here, buddy! Be my moon! I've got three already; if you join them, you could play bridge!

VENUS (*with same motions as the other two planets*): Come, darling, I need a satellite like you! Forget about the Earth, she's just a withered star. She always pretends to be five hundred years younger than she actually is!

MOON: You sure are a heavenly girl, but I'm too old for things like that.

SUN (*to the planets, sternly*): I forbid you to use your gravitation on the Moon any longer! (*To the Moon*): Step a million miles closer, please.

MOON (*takes one step towards the Sun*): At your service, milady. What can I do for you?

SUN: We demand some information about the Earth.

MOON (*embarrassed*): What's the matter with the Earth?

SUN: She's constantly getting out of step. She's displaying restless behavior. She does not complete her prescribed course in the prescribed thundering stride. She does not conform to the perfection of creation. In short, she is disturbing the harmony of the spheres!

MOON: You mean, you don't know?

SUN: No, I don't. What should I know?

MOON (*squirming around with embarrassment*): Well, if you don't know anyhow, I'd rather not talk about it.

SUN: Listen! I must advise you not to be ornery, or I'll draw you mercilessly to my bosom!

MOON (*terrified*): Thirty thousand degrees centigrade!!! What a thought! In that case I'd better tell you. Well . . . (*he hesitates*) . . . the Earth is sick.

VENUS: Ha ha! Probably sick with old age!

MOON: No, that's not it. Sick isn't really the right word. I'm so embarrassed . . .

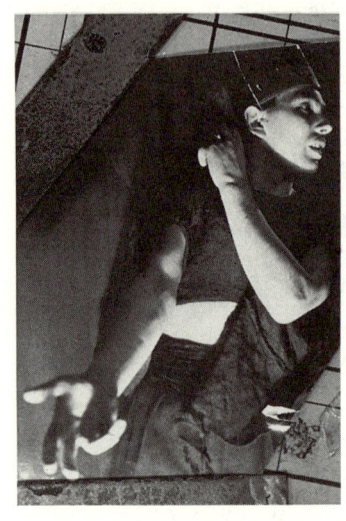

Leon Askin as the first Comet in the production in the ABC, Vienna, 1936.

Christian Ruck as Comet in the production at the Skelet-Theater—Theatermerz, Graz, 1989.

MARS: Come on now! Out with it!
MOON: Well . . . the Earth has . . . (*he touches his head and makes motions as if he were catching lice*) . . . she has . . . what do you call them . . . humans! That's what she has.
VENUS: Humans? I've never heard of that kind of bug.
SATURN: Must be disgusting little critters.
MOON: Well now, that depends. I, too, had humans once . . . before I got bald . . . those were the days! They sure are alive, these humans . . . that's something, at least . . .
VENUS: Sentimental old man.
SUN: Well, in that case, we must clean up the Earth, and exterminate the humans. There won't be any peace until we do.
MOON: Don't do that, my stellar excellencies, please don't!
VENUS: Of course we will.
SATURN: The only question is, how?

(*Enter the Comet Konrad.*)

COMET: Excuse me, my heavenly worthies; a poor wandering comet begs for a handful of lightrays.
SUN: What's your name?
COMET: Konrad's my name. I'd like to get all the way over to the Milky Way. I've got a date there with a shooting star.
SUN (*condescendingly*): All right. You may pass through my system. Just be sure not to bump into anything, or there'll be trouble.
COMET: Much obliged! Thank you! (*He tries to pass.*)
MARS: Stop! Just a minute! (*The Comet stops short, scared.*) I have an idea! The radical cure for the Earth!
SUN: Let's hear it!
MARS: The Comet Konrad proceeds on his way this minute . . . on the double . . .
COMET: To my shooting star?
MARS: No, to the Earth . . . and bounces on her with all his might! End result: a bump . . . but the shock and the vibration will kill off all humans on the Earth!
SUN: Ingenious! Congratulations!

COMET: But my heavenly worthies! I wanna meet my shooting star!
VENUS: We can't bother about your spacy spooning.
MARS: Your flitting floozy leaves us cosmically cold. You hit the earth, and that's an order!
COMET: But . . .
SUN: And no swerving! Or I'll sentence you to circle Uranus for the rest of your life, and to make your sentence a little more painful I'll put a few sharp angles into your ellipses!
COMET: Oh God! I wish I could run away. But this confounded cosmic space is curved wherever you go, and I'll have to come back to where I started, and then I'll be in for it! That's the way the ball bounces, according to physics. (*Resigned:*) All right, I'll do it.
MARS: And no mercy, understand?
SATURN: You'll be there in a month.
SUN: And then wham, crash, bang—and the Earth will be rid of all those humans.
MOON: But don't make the bang too hard, neighbor, or you'll bust her to bits! Now, I'll take off for home as fast as possible, and please be careful and don't touch me when you go whizzing by in a month!
COMET: Don't worry, I'll be careful. One month? What kind of month? Time is relative, they tell me. (*He sighs.*) Damn physics!
SUN: One earth-month. Okay, now, are you ready?
COMET: More or less.
SUN: We'll give you the necessary momentum!

(*The Comet is now pulled and pushed around by the planets' power of attraction until it has the necessary momentum.*)

COMET: Not so fast! Enough! I'll bust myself to pieces! Damn physics!
SUN: Ready, set, go!!!
COMET (whizzing off): God, that'll be a nice splat all right!

(There's a whizzing noise as the lights begin to dim. While the lights continue to dim, the noise fades away.)

Scene Two

Professor Peep makes a discovery

(This scene is lost.)

Scene Three

(The stage is completely dark. One can hear the ticking of telegraph keys.)

LOUDSPEAKER *(speaks the "Telegraph-Chanson")*:
From all corners of this globe,
From a million different places,
Flitting, whizzing, humming, drumming,
News is buzzing through the spaces.
Through earth's intricate, electric
Copper nervous system, hectic
History madly races.
Sing—song—short—long—
Long—short—news report—
Stop.

Victims fall and dividends rise,
Peace agreements rest in peace,
White doves flutter in the skies,
Air Force funds increase.
Crime and court—weather—sport—
Fatherland needs your support—
Join the Army, please.
Join the ranks—guns—tanks—
Long—short—news report—
Stop.

Syllables and words and phrases
Slip and glide all night, all day,
Through the singing, ringing wires
And are blown away.
But one word stays on the air

Signaling the latest trend,
Echoing from everywhere:
End of world—the end—end—end—
Long—short—end of report—
Stop.

And it reaches every nation,
Flies from cape to cape,
Sounds from every radio station,
Rips through ticker tape.
Races on, on road and rail,
Rings from pole to pole,
In the papers, through the mail:
The end! Quick, save your soul!
The sentence is: The earth must bust!
The earth's condemned to bite the dust!
The final day's not far away:
Execution: end of May!
Stop! Stop! Stop!

(Out of the dark one now hears the Voices of the Journalists.):

FIRST JOURNALIST:
    Hello, is this Paris? This is me.
    Here's the report from Germany.
    Country as peaceful as paradise.
    Shares very active, steels on the rise.
    A local rumor too funny to tell:
    Four weeks from now the world goes to hell.
SECOND JOURNALIST:
    Well, London *Times*? This is Paris calling.
    Army funds rising, all other stock falling.

Recent bank crash left thousands poor.
Increase in riots expected for sure.
Following rumor hard to dispel:
Four weeks from now the world goes to hell.

THIRD JOURNALIST:
Hello, this is London. On Downing Street
Plans for world peace are now complete.
Diplomats' circles slightly alarmed
By spreading rumor that can't be calmed.
Though Anthony Eden says "All is well,"
Four weeks from now the world goes to hell.

FOURTH JOURNALIST:
Hello! Our Time? Is no one there?
Here the reports from everywhere:
Shanghai and Frisco and Budapest,
The Middle East, the Golden West,
The World Oil Bank, the Safety Match Trust.
Kneel down and pray or we all go bust!
We must bargain with God, and bargain well!
Or four weeks from now the world goes to hell!

Scene Four

(Salon of the Führer. The Führer is talking with Professor Peep. Facing them, a Photographer.)

FÜHRER: Professor, you have drawn the essence of your genius out of the strong roots of our nation. Give me your gnarled right hand! *(To the Photographer:)* Picture, please!

PEEP: No, no—really . . .

FÜHRER: No "no"! "No" is a word foreign to our language. You are the nation's public pride number two! The end of the world is an invention for the good that expresses the essence of our nation! *(To the Photographer:)* Picture, please!

PEEP: But . . .

The End of the World, Scene Four, Skelet-Theater—Theatermerz, Graz, 1989 Christian Ruck (Hitler).

FÜHRER: "No but"! "But" is a Marxist expression! I am asking you a question: Starting today, are you willing to bear the honorable title of Leader of German National Physics, or, to put it more beautifully, Head Heat-Conductor of the Third Reich?
PEEP: No, I . . .
FÜHRER: Your answer is obviously a ninety-nine percent "Yes"! (*To the Photographer:*) Picture!
PEEP: I think . . .
FÜHRER: Anything but that!
PEEP: I believe . . .
FÜHRER: That's better!
PEEP: I believe you do not completely comprehend the full significance of my discovery. The comet is going to destroy everybody.
FÜHRER: Destroying everybody is my business.
PEEP: But the whole of humanity . . .
FÜHRER: Humanity? Never heard of it!
PEEP: A mass execution . . .
FÜHRER: I've heard of that!
PEEP: Just think, everything that's human . . .
FÜHRER: No decadent liberal verbiage! World Jewry, Freemasonry, and Bolshevism have sent out a comet with the one purpose to destroy and, at the same time, to dominate the world, and with the second purpose of undermining our nation through influences from foreign planets.
PEEP (*scared*): I'm not quite sure . . . I'm only working in physics.
FÜHRER (*threatening*): Not in Jewish physics, I hope?
PEEP (*perplexed*): Jewish physics? Is there such a thing? If we look at the teachings of modern physics . . . space is curved . . .
FÜHRER (*pointing at his nose*): You see!
PEEP: Time is relative . . . a thousand years . . .
FÜHRER: What about our thousand years?
PEEP: Under certain circumstances they might dwindle to a couple of years.
FÜHRER (*furious*): What does that depend on?

PEEP: On movement.
FÜHRER: Which movement? In Germany there's only one . . .
PEEP (*hesitating*): I mean the other movement.
FÜHRER: You see, a clear case of high treason!
PEEP: And the orbits of the planets . . .
FÜHRER: What about the orbits?
PEEP: . . . are elliptical.
FÜHRER: In plain language: rounded. (*He points to his nose again.*)
PEEP: And the power of attraction . . .
FÜHRER: What about my power of attraction?
PEEP: In terms of physics, your power of attraction is (*hesitating*) zero.
FÜHRER (*roaring*): Zero? I herewith demote you from Head Heat-Conductor of the Third Reich to ordinary citizen of the Reich and from ordinary citizen of the Reich to taxpayer. As taxpayer, you will now immediately follow my thundering command: Out!! (He points to the door.) You're lucky that you're world-famous. (Peep exits. To the Photographer.) Did you take a picture of this last episode?
PHOTOGRAPHER: I did, my Führer!
FÜHRER (*after some consideration*): Then smash the plate to pieces.

Scene Five

Vox Populi

(*Two Ladies*)

FIRST LADY OF FASHION (*entering from the left, deciphering newspapers*): Resurgence of riots among the population due to approach of comet.
SECOND LADY OF FASHION (*entering from the right, deciphering newspaper*): Rumors about ineffectiveness of Anti-Comet-Defense-Corps at imminent planetary collision.

FIRST LADY: Clashes between Anti-Comet-Defense-Corps and demonstrators.
SECOND LADY: ACDC-Men rout demonstrators and give striking evidence of their usefulness in collisions.
FIRST LADY: Lloyd's insures human life and property against end of the world.

(*They meet.*)

SECOND LADY: Dearest!
FIRST LADY: Dearest!
SECOND LADY: Are you also reading about this eternal what-do-you-call-it . . . you know what I mean. For two weeks we have been hearing about nothing else. It's getting downright boring.
FIRST LADY: Don't say that. The *Journal* here carries a pretty neat story about it: "A Poll of Public Figures: What do you say to the End of the World?"
SECOND LADY: And *what* do they say?
FIRST LADY: Maestro Lehar gave a very clever reply: "I am working on my next musical, *The Charming Little Comet with the Umbrella.*"
SECOND LADY: Lehar is *such* a genius.
FIRST LADY: Slezak writes: "I am indestructible and this summer too I intend to remain loyal to my trusty Lake St. Wolfgang."
SECOND LADY: Slezak is *such* a brilliant man!
FIRST LADY: Jan Kiepura writes: "You are asking me about the end of the world? I love all women."
SECOND LADY (*enraptured*): Isn't he sweet?
FIRST LADY: But the wittiest of all is, as always, Farkas. He writes:

> "The world may go crash,
> My salvation is cash.
> So come to my show
> Before we all go."

SECOND LADY: He is *so* up on things.
FIRST LADY: Do you know, dearest, that the end of the world promises to become a social event of the first order?
SECOND LADY: But what will people wear at the end of the world?
FIRST LADY: Paulette Greenbaum has brought charming models from Paris. One will wear dark colors, simple models, fitting the sad occasion and the pleasingly plump figure.
SECOND LADY: Really!
FIRST LADY: There is a darling cocktail dress: Crepe Comet, with sky-blue trim and shooting star design.
SECOND LADY: What *nouveautée*!
FIRST LADY: What *idée*!
SECOND LADY: What *success*!
FIRST LADY: A Poiret original! Look here, this charming . . .

(*Two Sweethearts*)

(*The first words are heard already behind closed curtain. Later the curtain opens a bit so that one can see the starry sky as in scene two. By now the comet is already much closer, therefore bigger.*)

YOUNG MAN (*deciphering a newspaper*): "Negotiations of two super-powers about the end of the world due to take place in two weeks have led to preliminary but satisfactory results. The feverish increase in the sale of consumer goods due to the imminent end of the world has resulted in a tremendous boom of the economy. The Dow Jones is stable and encouraging. (*At this moment the curtain opens completely.*) Mr. W. W. Rockford who has profited 200 million in the boom, has stated in an interview that the end of the world could have only the most beneficial effect on the world . . . " That's beyond me.
GIRL (*comes from the other side and throws herself into the young man's arms.*): Honey!
YOUNG MAN (*embracing her*): Honey!
GIRL: What you reading there, honey?

YOUNG MAN: You know, about the end of the world.

GIRL: Always those stupid politics! That's not good for your health, honey! Especially now that you are in the Anti-Comet-Defense-Corps.

YOUNG MAN: But it isn't that simple, this end of the world, once you start thinking about it.

GIRL: So stop talking about it. That's nothing for folks like us. Why don't you tell me instead how the great anti-comet-defense drill will work!

YOUNG MAN: That's going to be fantastic, you'll see. (*Feeling his importance, he recites from the regulation hand-out:*) One half of the population has to go into the shelters . . .

GIRL: But why?

YOUNG MAN: Because of the fire danger. The second half of the population has to go to the attics.

GIRL: What's that for?

YOUNG MAN: So they don't get buried under the debris. The third half of the population has to stay quietly in the apartments.

GIRL: What for?

YOUNG MAN: So there ain't no panic.

GIRL: That's smart. And in the meantime you keep hitting the comet on the head with gusto?

YOUNG MAN: That's the idea. But nobody knows how.

GIRL: That's because it's a military secret. I am so proud that we have our end-of-the-world military sovereignty again. And right after the drill, in two weeks, we're getting married.

YOUNG MAN: Sure, if the end of the world doesn't happen . . .

GIRL: An excuse again! First it was auntie Agatha who was supposedly against it, then it was uncle Hubert, and now it's the end of the world . . .

YOUNG MAN: But Professor Peep says . . .

GIRL: You men always stick together. First you want to get everything a decent girl has to give, and then the excuse: the end of the world . . .

YOUNG MAN: Look, honey, I'm not saying anything, all I'm saying is if the end of the world comes before . . .

GIRL: I don't care about the end of the world. You promise, this minute!
YOUNG MAN: Of course I promise, honey. All I'm saying is . . .
GIRL (*enthusiastic*): Honey! (*Throws herself at his chest: Blissfully sighing:*) I just "want to set the world on fire . . ."

(*Mayer and Meyer*)

FIRST VIENNESE (*from the left, deciphering a newspaper*): "The necessity to defend itself against a cosmos of enemies has forced the Reich to expand its military sovereignty. The result is that unemployment in Germany that amounted to two million has decreased by another four million so that the Reich now numbers only five million unemployed."
SECOND VIENNESE (*from the right deciphering a newspaper*): "The German Ministry of Propaganda announces: The end of the world will destroy the whole planet with the exception of the German Reich and the colonies that were stolen from it. As prudence dictates, for the time being, the plan for the respective rescue operations is kept in the desk drawer."
FIRST VIENNESE: Pleased to meet you, Herr Mayer!
SECOND VIENNESE: Pleased to meet you, Herr Meyer!
FIRST VIENNESE: Say, I don't get it.
SECOND VIENNESE: Me neither. But the Prussians, they'll get it, don't worry.
FIRST VIENNESE: That figures. They always know what they're doing.
SECOND VIENNESE: Right you are.
FIRST VIENNESE: But on the other hand, listen to this: "The Paris Institute of Physics has calculated that the end of the world will destroy the whole planet with the exception of the French Republic and her colonies."
SECOND VIENNESE: Right you are.
FIRST VIENNESE: That figures. But, on the other hand, listen to this: "The London Institute of Physics has calculated that the end of the world will destroy the whole planet with the exception of the British Empire."
SECOND: Right you are.

FIRST VIENNESE: But they can't all be right, all three of them.
SECOND VIENNESE: Right you are.
FIRST VIENNESE: That figures. By the way, have you read . . . let me see where is that . . . "The end of the world has resulted in a most welcome upsurge of our tourist trade. Our poster 'To see the Hermannskogel and then die' has had its effect in all metropolitan areas of the world. All vicious rumors that the end of the world will destroy us too we smilingly relegate to the world of fantasy. The Viennese will not go under."
SECOND VIENNESE: Right you are. I keep saying: Things are looking up.
FIRST VIENNESE: That figures. But what happens if things in the world are looking up until everything's kaput?
SECOND VIENNESE: Right you are.
FIRST VIENNESE: That figures.
SECOND VIENNESE: Well then, good night, Herr Meyer.
FIRST VIENNESE (*ironically*): Good night!

(*Polly and Polly*)

(*The front wall of a house. The Spinster opens a window and hangs a birdcage on a hook outside so that her Parrot can get some sun.*)

SPINSTER: Polly!
PARROT: Polly!
SPINSTER: Polly wants sugar?
PARROT: Polly wants sugar!
SPINSTER: I've bought a lot of sugar and flour! And shortening! And when the end of the world comes and Mrs. Endlinger wants to borrow some shortening, I'll say: "Sorry, Mrs. Endlinger. You know, you really should have stocked up some supplies yourself! You did have the money, from your late husband, the Councillor. You ought to have saved it instead of running around every Sunday with this Mr. Mullenbacher whose mother you could be!"
PARROT: Mother you could be!

SPINSTER: Arrogant biddy! Always looking at her former, or late husband, the Councillor's photograph just to irritate me; that's why she's doing it, just to spite me; every time I happen to look through the keyhole she's looking at him! And only yesterday she purposely called me "Miss." "Miss Polly," she said. And those allusions of hers! "You unmarried ladies don't understand!"

PARROT: You unmarried ladies don't understand!

SPINSTER (*now talking directly to the Parrot*): Pooh! If I had wanted it at the time, I'd be a widow today just as she is! If you want to know, Mrs. Endlinger! But I was only imprudent, that's all, Polly. For twenty-eight years I saved and saved, and then in 1922 the inflation came and everything was gone. And it was only my lack of prudence that destroyed Mr. Russwurm's love for me. Oh, how he did love me! Never shall I forget his parting words: "It grieves me deeply," he said, "that I erroneously lavished my feelings on such a careless individual!" Oh—he was such a moral person.

PARROT: Such a moral person!

SPINSTER: But this time I've shown myself worthier of Mr. Russwurm's love. The little I have I have invested in End-of-the-World Bonds. And every year I'll get my five percent, the interest accrued.

PARROT: Screwed! Screwed!

SPINSTER: Is that so? You think again that you are smarter than I, do you? Just for your information: I was at the bank myself, and I talked to the gentleman himself. Not to the minor official at the window, oh no! To the other gentleman, the older one who sits in the back at the big desk with the adding machine on it. A mature person. And yet quite handsome! And he himself showed me a certificate with the interest printed on it. "Five percent," he said, "that's the interest rate—minimal!"

PARROT: Criminal! Criminal!

SPINSTER (*getting more and more excited*): Is that so? And when I tell you that it was in the paper today, black and white, that the little, patriotic investors will be protected when the end of the world comes? But you arrogant people, you and Mrs. Endlinger, you'll get the axe!

PARROT: You'll get the axe!

SPINSTER: But listen, you! People like me, we've always trusted the gentlemen at the Bank, all our lives and one day, I know it, one day they'll give us their thanks!

PARROT: Banks! Tanks! Banks! Tanks!

SPINSTER (*trembling*): You don't really believe that your subversive remarks can scare me? You can't scare me anymore! Not anymore!

PARROT: War! War!

SPINSTER (*terrified*): But in the great speech yesterday he said: "I am and I will remain an optimist! We're moving ahead!"

PARROT: Dead! Dead!

SPINSTER (*imploring the Parrot*): But I have saved, do you hear! And the fortune-teller prophesied that another king of hearts would turn up on my doorstep; he was right in her cards! And all the time I've been thinking how nice it will be—a modest, but decent middle-class home—and I, a modest but decent, middle-class housewife—and that's all my hope—my only hope.

PARROT: Dope! Only dope! Polly wants sugar!

SPINSTER: Polly wants sugar.

PARROT: Polly wants to get out of the cage.

SPINSTER: Polly wants to get out of the cage? Oh no! Polly, you must stay where you are, you must stay in your cage, stay in your cage!

PARROT: Stay in your cage!

(*Lights out.*)

(*Two Diplomats*)

(*Two armchairs, a conference table. In each chair a representative of a superpower.*)

FIRST DIPLOMAT: In twenty days the world will come to an end. You will admit, sir, that this event cannot be denied a certain priority of urgency.
SECOND DIPLOMAT: You will understand, monsieur, that the end of the world must not be allowed to impair the European balance of power.
FIRST: What measures are you going to take?
SECOND: None. That's always safest.
FIRST: But the end of the world . . .
SECOND: . . . will know how to behave as a gentleman.
FIRST: You really believe that?
SECOND: Let's give him a chance.
FIRST: But the comet?
SECOND: The comet would necessarily have to destroy so and so many boundaries. Since such action, however, is forbidden by our treaties, the comet will think twice before touching the earth!
FIRST: You think the comet is familiar with the statutes of the League of Nations?
SECOND: Let's give him a chance.
FIRST (*bangs on the table*): And our security, sir?
SECOND: But, monsieur, the balance of power . . .
FIRST (*controlling himself*): Just assume the eventuality that the comet disregards the boundaries in spite of everything. What then?
SECOND: Maybe the comet is ruled by humans. We will negotiate with them.
FIRST: But assume the eventuality that the comet is not ruled by humans.
SECOND: Let's give him a chance.
FIRST: But, sir, our security!
SECOND: And the balance of power, monsieur?
FIRST: Olala! Tell me, if we are all destroyed, who is going to negotiate with the comet?
SECOND: Let's give ourselves a chance!
FIRST: And our security, sir?
SECOND: And the balance of power, monsieur?

FIRST: Are we not at least going to draw up a resolution condemning the actions of the comet?
SECOND: *In contumaciam*? I think that would be unfair. Let us wait until the comet arrives in London. I propose that, regarding the issue of the end of the world, we adjourn until ten days after the end of the world.
FIRST: If you don't take proper steps regarding this comet (*he begins to drum on the table*), do you know what we will do in Africa?
SECOND: What, pray tell?
FIRST (*bangs on the table, screams*): Nothing!!!
SECOND: But our security, monsieur?!
FIRST: And the balance of power, sir?
SECOND: In that case I have to get on the phone at once and talk to my government.
FIRST (*joyfully*): That's exactly what I was going to say!
SECOND: I am extremely pleased that we have been able to reach an agreement on one point after all. (*They rise.*)
FIRST: In any case, sir, your country may, as in times past, count on the goodwill of my country.
SECOND: Monsieur, your boundaries are our boundaries! Your worry is our biggest worry. And if there are two places in this world that should be spared destruction, they are undoubtedly . . .
FIRST: . . . the Bank of France and my constituency! Or can you think of anything else?
SECOND: I can indeed. I was going to say: the Bank of England and my golf course.

(*They say good-bye to each other. Lights out.*)

Scene Six

(*Professor Peep invents a machine to save the planet. Lights out. A ray of light falls on the Loudspeaker.*)

LOUDSPEAKER: This is the BBC, London. This is the news. Today Professor Peep arrived in London by plane. He stated to the press that he has made a revolutionary invention which is of the utmost importance to humanity. Professor Peep had no time to give details since he immediately took off for the Foreign Office. The end of the world, which is now only one week away . . . *(The Loudspeaker breaks off. Lights on. Peep is seen standing before a door with the sign "No Entry." He knocks.)*

ENGLISH OFFICIAL *(opens a window next to the door):* Oh, Professor Peep! How do you do? Your end of the world is a marvelous idea! The consumers are buying, buying, buying . . . they are spending without counting how much. Our industry is making millions. You are a jolly good fellow!

PEEP *(taken aback):* But—I mean—I've invented a machine—to save the world—I need money to build it and . . .

ENGLISH OFFICIAL: To save the world! That's all right! Great Britain has always loved to save the world. Such operations always were our most profitable transactions.

PEEP *(eagerly):* With my machine the comet will be thrown off its course, you see, and the end of the world will be prevented!

ENGLISH OFFICIAL: End of the world prevented? Oh, excuse me . . . for such things I really have no time on the weekend. *(He shuts the window with a bang.)*

PEEP *(banging on the window):* Listen! There's no time to lose! A week from now . . .

ENGLISH OFFICIAL *(offstage):* John! *(The door opens. A leg in elegant pants with spats appears and gives Peep a kick. Lights out. The roar of an airplane engine is heard.)*

(Loudspeaker lights up.)

LOUDSPEAKER: This is Radio Paris. Today Professor Peep arrived at Le Bourget Airport and immediately went to the offices of the General Staff. The riots that have been triggered by the imminent catastrophe . . . *(Loudspeaker breaks off. Lights on.*

Peep is standing before a door with the sign "Defense d'Entrer!")
PEEP *(knocks.)*
FRENCH OFFICIAL *(offstage)*: Qui est là?
PEEP: Professor Peep . . .
FRENCH OFFICIAL *(opens window next to the door)*: Oh, le professeur Peep. London has given me full information about you.
PEEP: But I only want to prevent the end of the world!
FRENCH OFFICIAL: Well, and what about our armament budget? *Ah, le sale boche! Ah, le bolshévic! Ah, le nazi! Ah, le salopard! Foutez le camp!* *(He closes the window.)*
PEEP *(bangs on the window):* But listen! A week from today . . .
FRENCH OFFICIAL *(offstage):* Sergeant! *(Door opens. Black uniform boot. Kick. Lights out.)*

(Loudspeaker lights up.)

LOUDSPEAKER: This is Radio Stockholm. According to unconfirmed rumors, Professor Peep has illegally crossed the German border. In total calm Sweden faces the imminent . . . *(Loudspeaker breaks off. Lights on. Peep is standing before a door with the sign "Eintritt verboten!")*
PEEP: *(knocks.)*
GERMAN OFFICIAL *(opens window next to the door):* What do *you* want here?
PEEP: A thousand pardons, I want to save the world.
GERMAN OFFICIAL: We don't need you for that. The German soul will make the world whole!
PEEP: But listen! I want to stop the end of the world from happening!
GERMAN OFFICIAL *(honestly surprised)*: And you dare tell me that to my face? Guys like you we've got enough right here in our own country. But they are living under a different name to fool the Gestapo. You must be crazy! The guy is nuts! *(He closes the window.)*
PEEP: *(bangs on the window.)*

GERMAN OFFICIAL (*offstage*): Sergeant! (*The door opens. Brown high boot. Kick. Lights out.*)

(*Loudspeaker lights up.*)

LOUDSPEAKER: This morning Professor Peep traveled by plane to Vienna and . . . (*The Loudspeaker breaks off. Lights on. Peep is standing before a door with the sign "No entry until further notice!"*)
PEEP: Your Honor! Open, please!
AUSTRIAN OFFICIAL (*offstage*): What's the matter?
PEEP: The end of the world is coming!
AUSTRIAN OFFICIAL (*offstage*): Only between nine and two. We're closed for official business now.
PEEP: But it'll be here in only a week from now!
AUSTRIAN OFFICIAL: In a week? So what's the hurry? There's plenty of time.
PEEP: But, Your Honor. I've invented something to prevent it!
AUSTRIAN OFFICIAL (*opens a little spy window in the door*): Now, that's nice! I'm pleased to hear it!
PEEP: Thank God! Finally a positive response! We will start building the machine at once. If we keep working day and night, we just might finish it in time.
AUSTRIAN OFFICIAL: Excellent idea! Now, quick, take out a patent for your machine.
PEEP: How long does it take to get a patent?
AUSTRIAN OFFICIAL: Six months to two years.
PEEP: But my invention is of the greatest importance . . .
AUSTRIAN OFFICIAL: Oh yes, I forgot. In that case it takes twice as long.
PEEP: But the end of the world is coming in a week!
AUSTRIAN OFFICIAL: Let him wait! He's not the only one! (*The little spy window closes.*)
PEEP: But listen, Your Honor! This is a city of culture . . .
AUSTRIAN OFFICIAL (*offstage*): Sure, but sometimes we forget it! Swoboda! (*Raggedy pant leg. Kick. Lights out.*)

Scene Seven

(Street. It is night. In a shop window a sign: "End-of-the-World Sale." Wall covered with posters, one advertising "Grandma's Cake Mix" with the slogan "You won't waste a crumb," another one saying: "Buy End-of-the-World Bonds!")

PREACHER-SALESMAN: Do not pass by! Stay and listen! Open your ears and do not close your hearts! Tomorrow noon the world will come to an end. But you, oh, how do you walk through this world darkened by the shadow of death? Your deeds are sin and your actions are deceit. The words you speak to wife and son are full of anger and discontent. Impatience makes you scream when you give orders to those under you. Woe, woe! Restlessness torments you in the morning, unhappiness spoils your noon, latent disease tortures you in the evening! Ask yourselves, oh men, ask yourselves today, this last day before the final day, what it may be that closes your souls to all that is beautiful and noble, that strangles you like the plague, that has you by the neck like Satan! And then ask yourselves: what could save your neck and give your throats freedom? I will tell you! It is, my dear ladies and gentlemen . . .

(Lights on.)

. . . the patented collar stud REVIVO! Revivo, ladies and gentlemen, is made of first-class horn, the hit of the last industrial fair. No more nervousness, no more restlessness; no pain, no strain; no itching, no twitching! The gentleman dresses in the morning, a touch of the hand—the collar fits round the neck like a glove. A touch of the hand, and the collar is off; a touch of the hand, and the collar is on. The collar never climbs up to your ears, never slides down to your tummy. You save yourself worry, family scenes, a blow-up with the boss, even dismissal or unemployment. You will enjoy your life again, you will enjoy your wife again—or your lady friend, as the case may be—and what do you pay for all this, ladies and gentlemen? The manufacturer, due to the end of the world, is compelled to run a magnanimous sale at slashed prices. Revivo costs you not ninety, not eighty, not seventy, not thirty groschen—but only one schilling! I appeal to your intelligence as city dwellers . . . (*To Peep, who is the only listener at his booth:*) I give up. You don't look as if you'd buy anything. Nothin' doin' in this street.

PEEP (*to himself*): Tomorrow it will be busted . . .

SALESMAN: Not at all, sir! It is made out of first-class native ox- horn. Unbreakable. Indestructible. You can depend on it. It'll keep forever.

PEEP: What?

SALESMAN: Revivo, of course, the collar stud.

PEEP: I was thinking of the earth.

SALESMAN: Oh, that! (*He shrugs his shoulders. Exits.*)

PEEP (*alone*): Oddly enough, he's right . . . the whole city will be nothing but a huge heap of rubbish. A few uncouth barbarians—if any human beings are left, that is—will be roasting potatoes in the glowing ruins of St. Stephen's cathedral—if any potatoes are left, that is. My instruments will be all in pieces and scattered all over the globe—if any globe is left, that is. But that collar stud, Revivo, will be left unharmed. What can ever happen to such an idiotic collar stud? Interesting—extremely interesting . . .

(*Two Street Singers, a man and a woman, enter singing. They sing a few lines of a sentimental hit.*)

PEEP (*to himself*): Are they really singing . . . twelve hours before the end of the world and they are singing! I must be losing my mind!

(*The Singers end their song. The man approaches Peep with outstretched hand.*)

PEEP: Excuse me—but what I just heard—that was "singing"—isn't that what people call it?

STREET SINGER: Didn't the gentleman like it? For a couple of coppers no Caruso would be in no better voice than me!
PEEP: But tomorrow noon both of you will be dead!
STREET SINGER: And how we live till tomorra is nothin' to ya, eh?
PEEP: Sorry—but I just wanted to draw your attention to the imminent end of the world.
WOMAN STREET SINGER: Look, you don't understand what the gentleman wants. The gentleman wants to hear the new hit about the end of the world.
STREET SINGER: So that's what he wants! Okay. Comin' up!
BOTH SINGERS (*sing the song "Let's Go Dying Just a Little"*):
Jolly Franz wants to take his girl Marie
For a little trip to the country.
But Marie is not in the mood for a spree,
He finds her in tears in the pantry.
"Oh Franz, did you hear?
The world's end is near!"
She sobs and her hanky is wet.
Franz says laughing: "So what?
If the world goes to pot,
There's time for a little song yet!
Why, won't it be swell,
A free trip to hell?
So here is my jolly farewell:

"Let's go dying just a little,
With crash boom bang and with hurray,
Always happy, dashing, snappy,
It can't be as bad as people say.
First, we've always been O.K.
Secondly, to fade away
Is about the only thing
A poor guy can afford today.
So let's go dying just a little!
It's risky, but it's chic!"

The End of the World, Scene Seven, Theater am Belvedere, Vienna, 1965 "Let's go dying just a little . . ." Margot Skofic (Woman Street Singer), Franz Walters (Street Singer), Hans Aler (Peep).

STREET SINGER: Here you are, sir! (*He holds out his hat to Peep. Peep, lost in thought, does not see it and walks on.*)
STREET SINGER: What!? First an artistic treat like that and then you just beat it outa here!?
PEEP: The end of the world is coming!
WOMAN STREET SINGER: That won't buy us no supper, sir!
STREET SINGER: Leave him alone. We better get lost. He might call a cop. That's all we need.
WOMAN STREET SINGER: I guess you're right. You can't trust those guys that always talk about the end of the world . . . (*Both singers exit.*)
PEEP (*alone, looking up at the sky*): There it is whizzing through the darkness, coming closer and closer—barely a million and a half miles away from me—and people are deaf and blind—and every second it is coming closer .
talking to himself, a thief sneaks up behind him.)
ROBBER (*suddenly*): Your money or your life!
PEEP: My dear friend, may I remind you that tomorrow noon the world will come to an end?
ROBBER: So what? (*Meditatively:*) Then you'll see some stealin'!
PEEP: Maybe the millennium will come?
ROBBER: Will come? Don't you know it's here already, in Germany? You think they don't steal there?
PEEP: Maybe the Day of Judgment is near!
ROBBER: Boy, what a fair trial that'll be!
PEEP: Of course, there are bigger thieves than you.
ROBBER: You don't know nothing, sir. Those big ones, they'll work a deal somehow, don't you worry! But me—all my life I've—I've had to make a living! Okay, now, give me your wallet. (*Peep hands him his wallet. The Robber hurries off.*)
PEEP (*alone*): It's all very strange, very strange. People apparently are too busy making both ends meet and never have time enough to even think about death. There they are, always in a hurry, always chasing after something—brimming over with lust for life.

(*A Suicide enters and bumps into Peep.*)

PEEP: What's the hurry, young man? Where are you going?
SUICIDE: I'm gonna to drown myself in the Danube.
PEEP: But why?
SUICIDE: My honey's left me. I'm gonna jump in the river.
PEEP: Young man, tomorrow at twelve noon the world's going to end.
SUICIDE: And I'm gonna jump in the river.
PEEP: And you can't wait till tomorrow?
SUICIDE: My honey's left me. I'm going to kill myself.
PEEP: But just be patient! tomorrow noon, we're all going to be dead anyhow.
SUICIDE: I'd rather play it safe.
PEEP: But young man! Tomorrow we are all going . . .
SUICIDE (*leaving*): I'm going right now. (*Exits.*)
PEEP: All right, have it your own way. Good luck!

(Enter intellectual lady and intellectual gentleman.)

SHE: And what does *he* say to these last days?
HE: You mean, *he*?
SHE: Yes, he . . . the grumbler.
HE: He is silent.
SHE: He's silent. We've got to hear that.
HE: Do you think we can still get tickets for his 800th silence?
SHE: Sure, as many as we want.
PEEP (*alone*): Right . . . the grumbler . . . the unbendable spirit. Doesn't hear. Strange. Why don't they hear and don't see, none of them . . . it's enough to drive one insane. It's like talking to the wall, and it just stands there smooth and dumb and stupid because it is a wall, after all. (*He gives the wall a furious kick.*)
CAKE-MIX-GRANDMA: Ouch! Ouch! My poor little old shin!
PEEP (*stuttering with amazement*): Wh . . . what's your name, if I may ask?
CAKE-MIX-GRANDMA: You mean you don't know me? You don't know Cake-Mix-Grandma?
PEEP: Pleased to meet you. I'm Professor Peep, Madam.

CAKE-MIX GRANDMA: Go right ahead and call me grandma. Everyone who looks at me becomes a child again, and gains the privilege of becoming my grandson.

PEEP: Believe me, dear grandma, from millions of light years away I can get to know a planet inside out. But these small humans that pass two feet away from me . . . they are downright inexplicable, inscrutable.

CAKE-MIX-GRANDMA: The mixture does it.

PEEP: Thanks for that mixture! It turns my stomach. You know I have calculated that tomorrow at twelve o'clock the world will go kaput. I invent a machine to prevent the catastrophe . . . no one's interested.

CAKE-MIX-GRANDMA: My grandchildren just have too good an appetite and don't want to be disturbed while they're enjoying their goodies.

PEEP: Here I am, walking the streets twelve hours before the end of the world, and what are people doing? They steal—out of sheer apathy. They kill themselves—out of stupidity. They are crying with happiness, singing with unhappiness. Grandma, I don't understand human beings any more.

CAKE-MIX-GRANDMA: Let me give you some advice, my cute little grandsonny.

PEEP: Finally. What is it?

CAKE-MIX-GRANDMA: You won't waste a crumb.

PEEP: Won't waste a crumb? No doubt, I'm going crazy. And second by second it is coming closer and closer.

CAKE-MIX-GRANDMA (*in baby talk*): What is it that's toming tloser, my cute little grandsonny? The cutesy end of the cute little world?

PEEP: Yes, Christ Almighty. And tomorrow at noon this darling planet will be ready for the darling garbage can. With a bang that will bust everybody's eardrums, two heavenly bodies will collide . . . but . . .

CAKE-MIX-GRANDMA: . . . but you won't waste a crumb.

PEEP: I beseech you, Grandma, you are too old for such stupid cute baby talk. I am a human wreck; take pity on me, stop talking about crumbs.

CAKE-MIX-GRANDMA: But it's good advice, grandsonny. (*She sings the Chanson of Cake-Mix-Grandma*):

> This world has always been an eating place,
> A restaurant for the human race.
> Alas, the service has been quite selective
> And for some time in need of a corrective
> 'cause, while inside, the fat cats lick their chops,
> The poor outside are chased away by cops.
> One day the dirty bums just might
> Demand their right and want a bite
> And spoil the fat cats' appetite,
> And law and order are at stake.
> So we are generous: Let them eat cake.
>
>   It makes people happy as happy can be,
>   Just follow grandma's home recipe!
>   Grandma used old-fashioned cooking tricks
>   To create her magic mix:
>
>   A little sugar and a little spice,
>   And all the bitterness will go down nice.
>   A pinch of reality and a pound of sham
>   And all the crap will taste like jam;
>   Two cups stupidity, three cups duplicity,
>   A dab of truth (but not too rough)
>   For our customers is just enough.
>   Grandma's mix stops any riot,
>   Grandma's mix keeps people quiet,
>   Keeps them happy, mum, and dumb.
>   You won't waste a crumb.
>
> And if the world tomorrow goes to hell?
> "Business as usual" works so well.
> People will always be the same
> And follow the rules of the same old game.
> They sing and laugh and drink and sob,
> They love and hate and starve and rob.
> They aren't quite bright, not quite dimwitted,
> And mostly do what they're permitted.

While poor chaps fight for scraps, the gluttons
Stuff their gut and burst their buttons.
   Thank God that's the way it'll always be!
We follow Grandma's recipe
While we go with the flow
Of the status quo.
A little sugar and a little spice
And all the bitterness will go down nice.
A pinch of reality and a pound of sham,
And all the crap will taste like jam.
Two cups stupidity, three cups duplicity,
A dab of truth (but not too rough)
For our customers is just enough.
Grandma's mix stops any riot,
Grandma's mix keeps people quiet,
Keeps them happy, mum, and dumb.
You won't waste a crumb!
Grandma's magic mix will last
Far beyond the final blast!

(*Peep lies asleep at Cake-Mix-Grandma's feet. Policeman enters.*)

POLICEMAN: Hey you!
PEEP (*sleepy*): Leave me alone, Cake-Mix-Grandma, it's no use, it's all over.
POLICEMAN: Listen, you, who's your Cake-Mix-Grandma? Are you showing disrespect for an officer of the law, or something?
PEEP: I was dreaming that some poster was talking to me . . .
POLICEMAN: That's all we need, posters that talk! With all the public disturbances they'd create, public safety would go to the dogs. What are you doing in the street like this? Do you have a regular occupation? And what is it?
PEEP: I'm waiting for the end of the world.
POLICEMAN: Don't you know that the occupancy of public premises for sleeping purposes is improper because it is not in the public interest?

PEEP: Are you trying to tell *me* what's in the public interest and what isn't? Oh shucks, what difference does it make?

POLICEMAN: Who are you, anyway? Let's see some I.D. (*He shines his flashlight in Peep's face.*) Oh, it's you, you don't need any, you're identical anyway. You're that Peep guy, ain't you?

PEEP: Yes, I am. But what difference does that make now? Tomorrow afternoon maybe one of your molecules will bump into one of mine, in outer space . . .

POLICEMAN: Listen! No double talk! I'm a man of the law and, therefore, I don't have no molecules, even if I knew what they was.

PEEP: It doesn't make any difference—no difference . . .

POLICEMAN: Nothing makes any difference to him, the ideal citizen. Oh, now I see what you mean—'cause tomorrow the earth is gonna get smashed to pieces?

PEEP: Exactly. At twelve o'clock noon, Officer. Final closing time for the entire earthly operation . . .

POLICEMAN: You know what? I don't believe it.

PEEP: I didn't think you would.

POLICEMAN: You're not supposed ta think!

PEEP: I know, I know . . .

POLICEMAN: You're not supposed ta know!

PEEP: That's another thing I've learned. That's why the world will be blown to bits.

POLICEMAN: I don't believe it, I said. I haven't seen no official bulletin yet giving instructions for such an event. You know what you are?

PEEP: Hopeless.

POLICEMAN: Right. Crazy, that's what you are. You should go to America!

PEEP (*becoming interested*): America?

POLICEMAN: Over there they're just as spacy as you are. America's full of guys like you, a bunch of astronuts. Now they've built a spaceship, and a couple o' people wanna save themselves in it. But I don't believe it, I don't.

PEEP (*jumping up*): Spaceship? America? Of course! America! Technology! Progress!

POLICEMAN: I'm tellin' ya, I don't believe 'n it.
PEEP: Freedom!
POLICEMAN: I don't believe in it.
PEEP: The statesmen have failed—the citizens have failed—technology will save civilization!
POLICEMAN: I don't believe in space traffic and all that stuff. You know why? Because there ain't no space traffic regulations yet. No regulations, no traffic!
PEEP: The last hope!
POLICEMAN: The last stupidity.
PEEP (*embracing him*): Thank you very much, thank you! You are a savior of culture!
POLICEMAN: I know that without ya! Take your hands off me!
PEEP (*dancing around with him*): America! I'm flying to America!
POLICEMAN: You oughtta be put in the nuthouse, that's where you belong!

(*Lights out.*)

Scene Eight

Before the Start

(*Complete darkness. The Loudspeaker lights up.*)

LOUDSPEAKER: This is the BBC, London. (*Gong.*) At the time signal it was eleven-thirty A.M. In exactly half an hour the earth will be destroyed. You will now hear the news. Irresponsible elements have spread the rumor that the official measures for the protection of the population against the end of the world are inadequate. The streets of London are jammed with restless crowds. The editorial office of the *Daily Mail*, which commented optimistically on the imminent event, has been reduced to shambles by the mob. Intervention by the police resulted in a total of fifteen persons killed, four of whom were policemen. The riots in the East End . . . (*Breaks off. After a short pause:*) Radio Paris. This is Radio Paris. The Department of the Interior unequivocally denies any rumors that a supposed invention by Professor Peep has been rejected. The Place de L'Opéra is jammed with frantic crowds resisting the Gardes Mobiles and shouting "We want to live!" and "Protect us from destruction!" Any offense against discipline within the ranks of the Gardes Mobiles will be punished with the strictest disciplinary countermeasures. Over the entire city of Paris the curfew . . . (*Breaks off. After a pause.*) This is Radio Berlin. The German Reich is facing the coming event in cold blood. All reports about protest rallies in Hamburg, Cologne, Frankfurt, Leipzig, and Berlin are utter fabrications. The speech of the Minister of Propaganda, entitled "The End of the World—a Wholesome Bath of Steel," was received with enthusiasm. All rumors about riots in . . . (*Breaks off. Pause.*) This is NBC, New York. Reports that an inventor by the name of Williams has built a spaceship and sold the available fifty seats at thirty million dollars each have aroused indignation in all states of the union. In all major cities a general strike has been called. A delegation of the Farmers Union has asked the President why the fifty wealthiest Americans intend to leave this planet, and if adequate measures for the protection of the population against the end of the world . . . (*During the last words the curtain rises. Mr. Rockford, Mrs. Rockford, Violet (the secretary), Winnie Winston (a film star), a Lady Journalist, and Mr. Wood (a writer) are standing in a group. In the background, the spaceship.*)

MR. ROCKFORD: Miss Violet, turn off that damned radio!

(*Violet turns off the radio.*)

MRS. ROCKFORD: Say, honey, where has Mr. Williams been all this time?
MR. ROCKFORD: He's coming to get us any minute. He's just checking the engines. We're going to take off right away.

MR. WOOD: But we still have a whole fifteen minutes. Are you excited, Winnie Winston?

WINNIE WINSTON: My dear Wood, I have made movies with Clark Gable. Since then, nothing and nobody can excite me anymore.

JOURNALIST: Is it true, Mr. Rockford, that ten minutes after take-off you will be out of the danger zone?

MR. ROCKFORD: That is correct. Who are you, one of the passengers?

JOURNALIST: No, I'm reporting for the *New York Tribune*. We want to bring out a special late edition five minutes before the end of the world.

VIOLET: The radio says that in Springfield, Illinois, they've stormed the Governor's mansion.

MR. ROCKFORD: Oh, that goddamn radio, forget it!

MRS. ROCKFORD: You must remain calm, Miss Violet. Your nose is all red. Put on some powder! Keep smiling!

WINNIE WINSTON: Oh, this end of the world, isn't it awful! I understand the air is quite cold in outer space. That will be a catastrophe for my complexion.

MR. WOOD: Winnie Winston, you must comprehend the greatness of the moment! When I imagine that in twenty minutes a million miles below us the earth will crash into another heavenly body with a gigantic bang—the cities collapse with thunder—the skyscrapers crack like match boxes—volcanoes explode—the death cry of millions rises up to us—a sea of flames swallows up all living creatures— oceans flood whole continents—when I think of all this, I don't know, should I write a drama about it or only one gigantic poem.

JOURNALIST: How long do you intend to stay up there?

MR. ROCKFORD: Three months, I guess.

JOURNALIST: And what are you going to do during that time?

MRS. ROCKFORD: You know, I've heard the earth is facing another ice age. So I think I will knit mittens for the poor boys who will have to shovel all that snow.

VIOLET: Mr. Rockford, in Spain and France revolutions have broken out.

MR. ROCKFORD: They've always got revolutions in Spain and France.
VIOLET: But the radio said that in all countries there are terrible scenes in the streets and . . .
MR. ROCKFORD: Forget about the damn radio!
MRS. ROCKFORD: You must remain calm, Violet!
WINNIE WINSTON: More self-control and poise!
MR. WOOD: More esthetic magnanimity!

(*Professor Peep enters.*)

PEEP: Do I have the honor of speaking with the ladies and gentlemen who intend to take off into safety?
MR. ROCKFORD: We are not saving ourselves primarily, my dear Professor. Primarily, we are saving what humanity will need to reestablish its culture after the catastrophe. If any human beings are left at all.
PEEP: That's exactly why I've come. Here I have a box full of materials that will be very useful to the survivors.
JOURNALIST: What's in the box?
PEEP: Oh, all kinds of things. A primer, for instance.
MRS. ROCKFORD: A primer?
PEEP: Well, the children will have to learn how to read. Then I put in the most important scientific textbooks . . .
MR. WOOD: Textbooks?
PEEP: Then—the Declaration of Human Rights from the French Revolution in 1789 . . .
WINNIE WINSTON: Isn't he ridiculous?
PEEP: And a few more books and instruments—some very complicated, others rather primitive—they all will be very useful—afterwards.
MR. ROCKFORD: Professor, we have no room for your collection of antiques. Our luggage space is packed full with important items. Our shares alone take up half of it.
PEEP: But Mr. Rockford . . .
MR. ROCKFORD: No time. In three minutes we must take off. Miss Violet, ask Mr. Williams if we can board now.

(*Violet hurries off.*)

PEEP: Miss . . .

JOURNALIST: No time. I've got to phone in my report to the editor.

MR. ROCKFORD: Wait a minute! Why don't you add to your interview with me the following statement: "Fellow Americans! We fifty persons in responsible positions unfortunately have to leave the earth before its end in order to observe the events more objectively from a higher point of view. We envy you who can stay behind for the great event! Be proud of it! Later you will be able to say to your children and your children's children: 'I, too, was there!' Stick it through! You are dying for the United States of America! But as long as there is still time, buy End-of-the-World Bonds!" Okay, that's all.

PEEP (*awkwardly*): No, that's not all! Tell them that what's going on here is a . . . is one . . . unthinkable . . .

(*Violet rushes in.*)

VIOLET: Mr. Rockford! Mr. Rockford! Mr. Williams is nowhere to be found! All I found was this letter on the pilot's seat. It's for you!

MR. ROCKFORD (*grabs the letter from her and reads*): "To the fifty passengers of my spaceship! Ladies and gentlemen, I thank you for your millions. They have made the last few weeks of my life very pleasant. These three weeks also were *your* last weeks, ladies and gentlemen. My spaceship does not even perform the simple functions of a child's scooter, let alone the functions you expect of it. It cannot move an inch. Good night, everybody, and have a pleasant end of the world! Your obedient servant, P. Williams." Ahem, in that case, of course . . .

(*The women give a piercing shriek. The stage is suddenly dark. A howling noise approaches. Scream. The noise breaks off, then is heard again, and finally fades away in the distance.*)

Scene Nine

Professor Peep draws conclusions

PEEP (*in front of the curtain, sings the "Song of Peep"*):

You pumped tons of knowledge into me,
You stuffed me to saturation,
You built me the latest machinery
To precisely measure Creation.
You told me to look for the causes of things,
My mind did the thinking for you.
I searched, and after long reasoning,
Found the truth, but my truth wasn't true.

> Wrong is wrong, and right is right?
> That's no longer true.
> Right is what yields dividends,
> Wrong is when your profit ends.
> That's the truth for you!

Your newsreel reeled off my spectacular fame,
Magazines have been filled with my story.
You founded societies with my name,
You unveiled me in bronze for my glory.
As long as I spoke of destruction and doom,
You hailed me, you smelled the profit.
But salvation! Salvation might end your boom,
You don't want to hear anything of it.

> Right is wrong and wrong is right,
> Fool, don't you ever forget it!
> Every lie is really true.
> If it ain't the truth for you
> You'll regret it!

(*Lights out.*)

Scene Ten

(In outer space. The Sun on her throne. Venus, Mars, and Saturn are dancing. The Comet enters.)

SUN *(raps the stand with her baton, furious)*: There you are, finally!
MARS: For crying out loud, what did you think you were doing?
VENUS: Here we stood, waiting to hear the big bang any minute . . .
SUN: . . . and what does Mr. Konrad do? A measly two thousand miles from the Earth he swerves from his course . . .
MARS: . . . staggers around the Earth three times—turns back . . .
VENUS: . . . and quite nonchalantly sails back home again!
SUN: Explain yourself, you calamity comet!
MARS: He just got scared, that's all.
SATURN: Pardon me, but I have to defend him. He thought there's really no need for a collision. The human race will kill itself off sooner or later anyway!
VENUS: What makes you believe that?
SATURN *(shows fieldglasses)*: I've made my observations. Well, Konrad, am I right?
COMET: No.
SUN: Then why, by the zooming zodiac, did you spare the Earth?
COMET: As I came closer, I got to know her a little.
SUN: And?
COMET: And I . . . fell in love with her.
VENUS: Fell in love with her???
COMET *(sings the "Song of the Comet")*:

> For near, much nearer than you understand
> I've come to the human world.
> I saw it golden with fields of grain,
> I saw huge shadows darken the plains
> When bombers roared over the land.
> I saw the world studded with radio towers

Sending waves of hatred and lies,
Saw poverty past comprehending;
I saw the world wretched—and free as the skies
With wealth and joy unending.

Full of hunger, full of bread is this world,
Full of life, full of death is this world,
Blessed is this world and damned.
Infinite in misery and wealth is this world,
Radiant with beauty and health is this world,
And its future is glorious and grand.
This future is nearer than you understand.
I've seen the new world arise.
I saw it ripening in fields of grain
Outgrowing the shadows of bombing planes,
And reaching for the skies.
I know that all radio towers soon
Will broadcast the news that the world is well
And blessed beyond comprehending.
Then the world will be cured of its age-old spell
And revel in riches unending.

Full of hunger, full of bread is this world.
Full of life, full of death is this world,
Blessed is this world and damned.
Radiant with beauty and health is this world,
And its future is glorious and grand.

(Curtain)

Jura Soyfer, 1935.

Trip to Paradise

CHARACTERS

Eddie Lechner, an unemployed worker
Annie, his girlfriend
"Pepi," a machine
Herr Andraschek, A blind war veteran
Tony, Eddie's dead friend
Dr. Galvani
The Judge
The Counsel for the Defense
A Sailor
Columbus
Pietro, a Humanist
An American tourist
An American woman tourist
A Tourist Guide
Gutenberg
The Gatekeeper of Paradise
Apparitions and Voices

Scene One

(A Bridge over the Danube Canal in Vienna; it is dimly lit. On the ground a blind beggar is sitting with his back against the railing; on his head he has a shabby soldier's cap of the type worn in the Austro-Hungarian Army in World War I. Next to him stone steps lead down the embankment to the Canal. On his accordion the beggar plays a sentimental hit of the thirties. Next to the beggar, and almost hidden by him, is a wastebasket fixed to the railing: very clearly visible is a sign with the words "Don't throw it away but . . ." and an arrow pointing at the beggar. A little while after the curtain rises, Eddie enters with his girlfriend Annie. Their conversation is accompanied by the beggar's soft accordion music.)

EDDIE: Six years ago! That's when ya should've known me! Six years ago when I still had a job!

ANNIE: You're kiddin' me!

EDDIE: Whadda ya mean, kiddin'? Six years ago all us buddies had a job.

ANNIE: Oh, get along with your stories.

EDDIE: I ain't tellin' you no stories. You just can't imagine any more what it was like. You're too young. Every first of the month I got my 190 schillings.

ANNIE: 190 schillings?

EDDIE: An' if you'd been my girlfriend then, I'd've bought ya that slip, the pink one, y' know . . .

ANNIE: You would've?

EDDIE: Sure I would've. And the scarf, that guaranteed pure silk one, y' know.

ANNIE: Would ya?

EDDIE: You bet your life!

ANNIE: And the genuine Persian Lamb coat, too? You know the one in that department store, the "House o' Bargains"?

EDDIE: Sure—on time!

ANNIE: See? Now I've got ya. I'm sure that coat costs much too much. I know it does.

EDDIE: But really, I'm tellin' ya the truth. You only believe what ya see in the movies . . .

ANNIE: What about yourself, hon? The stories you're tellin' me, they're straight out of Hollywood, too.

EDDIE: Hollywood! You and your Hollywood! D'you think I haven't been there, in Hollywood?!

ANNIE: No kiddin'!

EDDIE: No kiddin'! I was there—ya know—the year I took a trip on my vacation—and I was in Rio de Bombay, too—and in San Singapore where those people live, whatcha call 'em? The Kaffirs!

ANNIE (*believing him*): You've never told me that before!

EDDIE: 'cause it ain't worth talkin' about. Nuttin' like Haiti!

ANNIE: Haiti?!

EDDIE: In Haiti, as you may know, they've got the most beautiful women in the world—understand?—and they haven't got a stitch of clothing on—only wreaths of flowers in their hair—ukulilies!

ANNIE: Did you have another girlfriend there?

EDDIE: Don't be silly . . . I mean, we did have a lotta fun, us guys foolin' around in Haiti. And all of us had a job.

ANNIE: Now you're giving me the business again.

EDDIE: I ain't giving ya the business. Why don't ya ask Franz if you don't believe me, and Ferdie and Tony—(*the blind beggar's music breaks off*)—no, not Tony; ya can't ask Tony no more . . .

ANNIE: How long is it now that he . . . that he went and . . .

EDDIE: Three years ago. (*Points at the steps.*) Right here he walked down the steps, down to the bank, and straight into the water . . .

BLIND MAN: Eddie, is that you?

EDDIE: Sure, Herr Andraschek.

BLIND MAN: What time is it? Must be getting late.

EDDIE: I guess it's close to twelve.

BLIND MAN: Looks like they've forgotten me again.

ANNIE: Don't worry, they'll come for you any minute now, Herr Andraschek. Why don't you play us somethin' till they come? How about "I'm in Heaven . . ."? (*The blind man begins to play. Eddie and Annie lean against the railing and look out over the Canal.*)

EDDIE (*softly*): You've gotta believe me, Annie!

ANNIE: When Herr Andraschek's playin' I believe everything you say, Eddie.

EDDIE: Really?! Ya know, back then I was operating an electric machine. That was one helluva machine, let me tell ya! That machine could do practically everything by itself, just like a human being. D'ya believe that?

ANNIE: Sure, Eddie.

EDDIE: Forty pairs of shoes we made in one hour. Then one day, naturally, there were too many shoes. And than they gave me the sack. (*Getting excited*) And who was to blame? Ya wanna know who's to blame? That goddam machine, that's who's to blame! Damn it, if I could get ahold of it now—I'd smash it to pieces! This minute! D'ya believe me?

ANNIE: Sure, Eddie . . .

EDDIE: That machine, if it ever shows its face around here! I'll get even with it!

ANNIE (*smiling*): Sure you will! If it shows up!

EDDIE: So ya don't believe me, do you? Ya don't believe a word I say just because I'm out of a job . . .

ANNIE: But I do, Eddie, I believe you—I believe everything you say . . .

EDDIE: You've gotta believe me, Annie! (*Takes her head between his hands.*) You've gotta believe me when I tell ya the machine is goin' to come to this bridge right now, the witchin' hour's just started. The powerful machine with its one thousand horsepower is goin' to come my way, and I'll finally get even with it—me, down-and-out Eddie Lechner—and the big, powerful machine . . .

ANNIE: I dunno, Eddie. Tell me—when did you have your last meal?

EDDIE: You're not supposed to ask questions, you're supposed to believe me, that's what you're supposed to do. I've been dreamin' of this for five years. Any tough who's cheatin' me at cards I can tell where to get off at—and this goddam machine that's made all of us unhappy should get away with it? I should give in to him, me, Eddie Lechner? Close your eyes, Annie—he's comin'—d'ya see him?

BLIND MAN: I think they're coming for me. (*He is playing more softly; steps are heard.*)

EDDIE: Shh! (*Listens.*) It's high time that one of my dreams comes true. Listen, he's comin'!

ANNIE: Who's comin'?

EDDIE: The Machine. He's goin' to turn the corner any second now! He's comin' to the bridge, to me!

ANNIE: But . . .

EDDIE: Don't ya believe me? (*Imploringly*): You must believe me even if it ain't true! D'ya believe me?
(*Silence. Music is still playing: "I'm in Heaven . . ."*)

ANNIE: Yes, Eddie. (*Enter the Machine. With a suppressed cry, Annie grabs the arm of the Blind Beggar. Music stops.*)

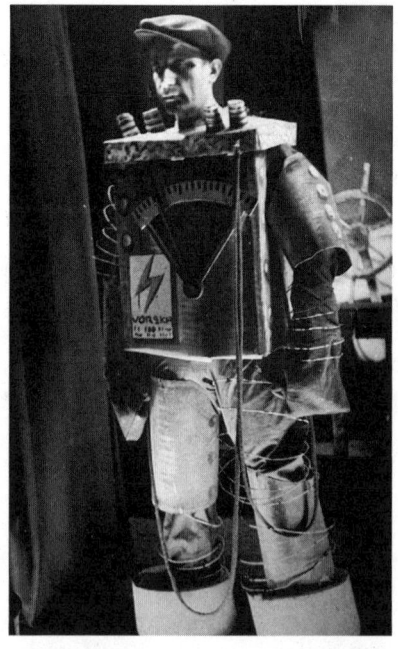

Trip to Paradise, Scene One, Literatur am Naschmarkt, Vienna 1936, Wilhelm Hufnagel (Motor).

EDDIE (*walks slowly and threateningly toward the Machine; with suppressed joy*): Just a second. I've gotta be sure this ain't no judicial murder—now, is it him or is it someone else? (*Looks the Machine over.*) The stompin' walk, the boxy chest, the starin' control lights, the danglin' hand-levers—a little rusty—a little run down, but it's him all right. (*Clenches his fist threateningly.*) Well, my friend, you wouldn't've thought I'd still know ya, after six years . . .

ANNIE (*throws herself between the two*): Eddie, don't do it. You won't get out of this alive!

EDDIE (*pushes her back*): Get outa my way! This is my own private affair!

BLIND MAN (*smiling*): Let them fight, Annie, they're both young lads bursting with energy.

EDDIE (*starting to pick a fight*): What are you gallivantin' around here for, on my bridge, heh?

MACHINE: You know what, Eddie? I'm out of a job!

EDDIE (*crushed*): You're what? (*Lifts his hands to his head for a second.*) In that case—if that's the case . . . (*After some hesitation, he motions to the Machine to take a seat on the railing like a host inviting a guest.*)

MACHINE: Thanks. Okay if I introduce myself to the lady first?

EDDIE (*expansively*): Go right ahead.

MACHINE (*bowing*): Petersen's Electrical Patented Industrial Motor. Pepi for short. Serial Number 820722.

ANNIE: Anna Amalie Rosa Eilinger. Annie for short. And this is Herr Andraschek.

MACHINE: Pleased to meet you.

(*The three sit on the railing, their legs dangling.*)

EDDIE (*offers cigarette*): Want a smoke?

MACHINE: No thanks. We electric machines are non-smokers.

ANNIE: You see! And you smoke like a chimney. (*Chatting amiably.*) It's very sensible of you, Herr Pepi, to save a few groschen instead of ruining your heart.

MACHINE: Unfortunately, I don't have a heart.

ANNIE (*somewhat embarrassed*): Oh, I'm sorry.

EDDIE: Well, then, tell us all about it. What's new at the factory? Is the boss still as grumpy as he was? Or have ya been outa work for quite a while?

MACHINE: They disconnected me five years ago, a year after you left. But it was only tonight that they finally unbolted me and threw me out.

EDDIE: And for five years you stood there, unpolished, unoiled, and not a soul to take care of ya? What a life!

ANNIE: I wonder if I could offer you a cup of engine oil, Herr Pepi.

MACHINE: Madame, you are kindness personified. Rust is gnawing at my vitals with unrelenting force.

EDDIE (*softly to Annie*): Where d'ya get engine oil in our luxurious household?

ANNIE (*softly*): Round the corner there's a steamroller . . .

EDDIE (*softly*): All right. Beat it.

ANNIE: If Herr Pepi will excuse me a second. (*Exits.*)

EDDIE: But tell me, how come you lost your job?

MACHINE: That's your fault, buddy!

EDDIE: My fault?!

MACHINE: Well—when exactly did you buy your last pair of shoes?

EDDIE: I guess—wait a minute—that must've been—one—two—three years, no, four—no, not four . . .

MACHINE: And I'm supposed to make a living putting out shoes with things that way?

EDDIE: That's true enough. And I always thought it's all your fault—and now it's me—but no, it ain't me neither, is it? Oh, forget it. And what are you goin' to do now?

MACHINE: I think I'll join the army and have myself remodeled into a tank. The army is the only place nowadays where there's still a demand for fresh material.

BLIND MAN: Looks like they've forgotten to pick me up again.

EDDIE: Don't worry, Herr Andraschek, they'll come.

BLIND MAN: They won't, Eddie. (*Begins to play and to sing softly: "We're off to the Isonzo . . ."*)

ANNIE (*comes with a little oiling can*): I hope you'll like it!

MACHINE: That's awfully kind of you, thank you so much! (*Drinks.*) Ah, is that good for my ballbearings! Say, would you mind pushin' down the circuit breaker on my left side?

ANNIE: What's that supposed to do?

MACHINE: I just wanna think hard for a little while.

EDDIE: Don't tell me that you can think, too!

MACHINE: I sure can. I learned that in the last five years. (*Walks up and down a few times.*)

ANNIE: Look at him! How quickly he's perked up! People like you and me would need at least a Wiener Schnitzel and a glass of wine!

MACHINE: I've got it!

EDDIE: What?

MACHINE: I know who's to blame for the whole mess.

EDDIE (*ready to fight*): Who? Lemme at him!

MACHINE: An Italian.

EDDIE: Yeah?

MACHINE: Yes, sir! Galvani.

ANNIE: You sure you got that name right? You sure it's not another Italian?

EDDIE: Shhh! How come it's his fault?

MACHINE: 'cause he invented electricity.

EDDIE: Why, sure! Electricity! And Galvani's the bastard's name, eh?

ANNIE: Don't start calling him names, Eddie! He's sure to be an influential gentleman. Perhaps we could talk to him about it sometime when he comes to Vienna on a visit. If they'd only let us in at the Bristol.

MACHINE: Don't bother! You know what? We'll go to him right now!

EDDIE: You've got a screw loose, Pepi; how do we get to Italy?

MACHINE: Are you tryin' to insult me, or what? Do you think that I can't do what one of these asthmatic locomotives can do or one of these scrunched-up little stuttering bugs.

ANNIE: Herr Pepi, you really wanna take us to Italy? To Venice? gee! You're a goodhearted guy.

MACHINE: Unfortunately, I don't have a heart.

ANNIE: Sorry.

EDDIE (*who has done some figuring*): Must be pretty ancient, though, this Galvani guy.

MACHINE: Dead. (*Annie and Eddie are dumbfounded.*) He's dead;

died a hundred years ago.

EDDIE (*stares at the Machine; then*): Come on, Annie, let's go. We're just wasting our breath. (*Takes her by the arm and pulls her away. Then he turns round, and, with tears in his eyes, he rushes at the Machine.*) You good for nothin' pile o' junk! You busted bucket o' bolts! You think you can make fun of me, do ya? 'cause you're a machine and I'm a poor sucker off welfare an' down an' out. If ya think that I'm goin' to take your goddam lip you've got a surprise comin', kid. Gear up and get out, or I'll make your wheels spin! (*He raises his fist to strike him.*)

ANNIE: Eddie!

BLIND MAN: Let them fight, Annie, they're young lads bursting with energy!

MACHINE: Eddie! How many pairs of shoes did we manufacture together?

EDDIE (*moved*): Hundreds and thousands of them, Pepi. So what? That's not goin' to stop me from knockin' your cogs out, you monster!

MACHINE: And who was the pride of the factory?

EDDIE: We was. Just stop makin' a fool o' me, will ya?

MACHINE: Did I ever give you any cause to mistrust me? (*Blind Man begins to play softly "I'm in Heaven . . ." Eddie shakes his head without saying a word.*) You must trust me, Eddie. (*Unobtrusively he has pushed his arm under Eddie's.*) We machines can do much more than human beings believe. You just haven't found out! Miss, may I offer you my arm? (*He links arms with Annie. They have moved to the side of the stage.*) Eddie, do me a favor and press that little lever, there, the one over the third chest piston.

EDDIE (*he does so*): You never had that one before.

MACHINE (*while his eyes begin to glow with a new light*): I grew it. Okay, and now let's all take a step back at the same time. Ready, set, go! (*They take a large step backwards. The stage lights up quickly; the Blind Man plays his song full volume. City noises set in.*)

ANNIE: Look! It's daytime!

MACHINE: Yes, yesterday!

EDDIE: Now we're all crazy.
MACHINE: Oh no, we're only taking a trip. We're taking a trip into the past.
EDDIE: But . . .
MACHINE: Just keep cool. We've still got a long way to go. (*Carefully he takes them back step by step. Day and night alternate with increasing rapidity.*)
ANNIE: Eddie, Eddie, look! The Danube Canal is flowing upstream!
MACHINE: Naturally. Life is running backwards. Like a movie in reverse, understand? (*During one of the day episodes, an elegantly dressed lady comes on stage backwards, takes a coin out of the blind beggar's tin can, and, still walking backwards, leaves the stage. While this is going on, the travelers slow their movement but do not come to a halt.*)
ANNIE: Herr Andraschek! She stole something from you!
EDDIE: No, the other way round! She gave him something! The movie is running in reverse. Don't ya get it yet?
BLIND MAN (*who has been playing all this time*): Charity or robbery, I don't know anymore which is which.
MACHINE: Careful: curve! (*Since they have reached the other side of the stage, he now leads them carefully in a semicircle, always moving backwards.*) Now we've got the first month behind us. (*They stop.*) Catch your breath a little, because from now on we're going a hundred times as fast!
ANNIE: And now we're standing still in time, ain't we?
MACHINE: No, we aren't. When you're rowing upstream and you stop rowing for awhile, you don't stand still, do you? You glide downstream a bit again. For a few minutes we have lived forwards again. And now, on we go at a speed of 5000 years per hour. Yippee! I feel the speed demon stirring in me! Forward! That is, backwards! (*They continue their journey. The change between day and night gives way to a monotonous gray. The Blind Man's music, which had alternated from soft to loud, now remains piano.*)
ANNIE: Gee whiz, how fast! I can feel it whizzing by my ears.
MACHINE: That's time rushing by.
ANNIE: Good Heavens!

EDDIE: What's the matter now?

ANNIE (*timidly*): Herr Pepi! For God's sake! If we keep livin' backwards at this speed, I'll be a baby again in five minutes.

MACHINE: Don't worry! We travelers don't get any younger. Only the world around us.

EDDIE: Let's go! Faster, faster! How far have we got?

MACHINE: It'll soon be three years since we started out.

ANNIE: And you're sure that I won't turn into a fifteen-year-old bobby-soxer if I let go of you now?

MACHINE: But you shouldn't even think of lettin' go. If you let go now, you go on living normally, gliding down the river of time. And who knows if I can fish you out again!

EDDIE: Three years, you said, Pepi? It's just been three years since Tony . . . In that case it would just be the time when he . . . (*Tony comes up backwards over the bridge railing. He rests his face on the railing, and looks out over the Canal. The travelers stop. It is night.*)

EDDIE: Tony! (*Silence. The Blind Man stops playing.*)

BLIND MAN (*softly*): Is it you, Tony?

TONY: Sure it's me, Herr Andraschek.

BLIND MAN: What time is it? Must be getting late.

TONY: Must be close to twelve, I guess.

BLIND MAN: Looks like they've forgotten to pick me up again.

TONY: Don't worry. They're going to get you any time now. (*After a pause.*) Good-bye, Herr Andraschek.

BLIND MAN: Where are you going, Tony?

TONY: I'm going on a trip. (*Blind Man begins to play again. Tony walks down the first steps.*)

EDDIE: Tony! Tony! Tony! (*To the Machine*): Go back, quick! He's swimming away! Pepi, quick! Get him back!

MACHINE: All right, Eddie. (*He turns on his running light. Tony comes over the railing, moving backwards. The Blind Man, who has played exactly the same music as before, stops at exactly the same spot. Again the travelers stop.*)

BLIND MAN (*exactly as before*): Is it you, Tony?

TONY: Sure it's me, Herr Andraschek.

BLIND MAN: What time is it? Must be getting late.

TONY: Must be close to twelve, I guess.

BLIND MAN: Looks like they've forgotten to pick me up again.
TONY: Don't worry. They're going to get you any time now.
(*After a pause*): Good-bye, Herr Andraschek.
BLIND MAN: Where are you going, Tony?
TONY: I'm going on a trip.
EDDIE: Tony! Wait! Don't do it!
TONY (*as always, with his face turned away*): Life doesn't have any meaning anymore, Eddie.
EDDIE: Don't say that! Wait a little! Just two or three years, do you hear?
TONY: You don't know what it's going to be like three years from now, do you?
EDDIE: Sure I know how it's goin' to be.
TONY (*turns his head for the first time*): Different? (*Eddie is silent. Tony turns away.*)

Trip to Paradise, Scene One, Das Laterndl, London, 1940
Peter Preses (Eddie), Marianne Walla (Annie).

BLIND MAN: Good luck, Tony! (*Tony walks down the steps as before.*)

EDDIE: Tony! Tony!

MACHINE: Come on, Eddie! (*Running light; the travelers proceed.*)

EDDIE (*more softly*): Tony! (*Tries to get away.*)

MACHINE: Don't you dare let go! I don't know if I can fish you out again!

ANNIE: Why are you taking such long steps, Herr Pepi?

MACHINE: We've got to step on it. We're approaching a great time where every hour lasts twice as long and is three times as hard to live through. (*Daytime. A group of people moves across the stage, walking backwards.*)

A WOMAN: The war is over!

OTHERS: No more wars!

A MAN: We are marching forward into a new time of peace, of progress . . . (*The group leaves the stage, marching backwards. During this episode, the Blind Man has played the "Marseillaise." The travellers have not stopped.*)

MACHINE (*softly*): That was 1919!

ANNIE: And where were these people marching to?

MACHINE: To 1914.

EDDIE: I hear somebody shouting something about the Isonzo. Looks like we're passing 1917 now.

ANNIE: And even then Herr Andraschek was sittin' here in his place . . . (*The Blind Man, who, since 1918, has played the "Prince-Eugene-of-Savoy March," gets up and stretches. He is considerably rejuvenated, approximately thirty-five years old. His cap, earlier dusty and banged-up, is now brand new and decorated with a little bunch of flowers, as recruits in the Austro-Hungarian army wore on their caps after they had passed their medical for induction . . . The dark glasses have disappeared.*)

BLIND MAN: Hurrah! (*The travelers stop.*)

ANNIE: But Herr Andraschek, where ya goin'?

BLIND MAN: To the front! On to the Isonzo! Hurrah!

ANNIE: But . . . but . . . how can ya? You're blind . . .

BLIND MAN (*laughs*): Are you kiddin'? Me blind? I'm 1-A!

They took me all right! Hurrah!

EDDIE: Stay here, Herr Andraschek! Stop! (*Tears himself loose from the Machine.*)

BLIND MAN: C'mon, buddy! "We're off to the Isonzo . . ." (*Singing loudly, he marches off. Annie cries.*)

EDDIE (*as in a dream*): Don't cry, Annie, I'll come back in one piece.

ANNIE (*screaming*): You?

EDDIE: Don't cry. I'll write you a letter from the front every day. (*Is about to march off.*)

ANNIE: Don't go, Eddie!

EDDIE: You don't want me to stay home, do you? Our fatherland is at stake! Good-bye, Annie! (*Calling into the wings.*) Wait for me, buddy! (*Hums the Isonzo song and drifts off like a sleepwalker, as if carried away by a powerful current.*)

MACHINE: Now he's livin' in time again; he's bein' carried away from us.

ANNIE (*looking into the wings*): He's marchin' to the barracks! With the Blind Man! With the dead! Eddie!

MACHINE: We can't stop him from dyin' now.

ANNIE: I'll stop him! (*Tries to get away.*)

MACHINE: Don't let go! You'll be carried away just like he was!

ANNIE: Me? (*Tears herself loose and leaves.*)

MACHINE (*looking after her*): Now they're both driftin' away, on the waves of Hurrah! End of trip, Pepi. What good are your thousand hp now? Time is stronger than you are.

(*Enter Annie, pushing and dragging Eddie.*)

ANNIE: You good-for-nothin'! Get goin'!

EDDIE (*babbling as if he were asleep*): Leave me alone, Annie! I'm a hero! The die is cast! The only good Russian is a dead Russian!

ANNIE: That's what you think, you rascal!

EDDIE: We shall conquer . . .

ANNIE: Baloney! (*Pushes him into the arms of the Machine.*) Step on it, Pepi! (*Running light goes on; the two pull Eddie back into their marching rhythm.*)

MACHINE: Against the current! I'd never 've thought you could do that, girl.
ANNIE (*kisses Eddie*): Silly boy, if I didn't look after ya . . .
EDDIE: Seems to me I've been dreamin'. Yes, I was dreamin' I was going off to war.
ANNIE (*to the Machine*): Have we left it behind us now—the dream?
VOICE: Special Edition! Heir Apparent Assassinated in Sarajevo!
MACHINE: It's just beginnin', the dream.
OTHER VOICE: Late Edition! Archduke Ferdinand and Consort on Their Way to Sarajevo!
MACHINE: And now we're way back in peacetime. (*The hands of the clock on the little bridge-tower are turning faster and faster counterclockwise.*)
ANNIE, EDDIE, and MACHINE (*sing the "Song of Time"*):

> The road is long,
> Rest far away.
> Time races on
> Day after day,
> An icy, howling blast.
> You feel a wingbeat
> In your hair.
> Was it a week?
> Was it a year?
> All gone forever, past.
>
> What you have done
> You did in vain.
> And all is wrecked
> In time's hurricane.
> You're left a beggar at last.
> What's happening now
> Soon blows away.
> You hardly hear
> Men sing and pray,
> Time whizzes by so fast.

A mother's cry
Went to the sky!
That was a war.
Now it's passed by.
It's subversive to mention those years!
A "Ça ira"—
A boy's last breath.
A star—so near—
Sinks down to death.
It's raining blood-red tears.

Life races on.
Death follows fast.
A new day breaks,
A life is past.
Green fields soon barren lie.
And to their graves
The soldiers go.
They march and fall
Row after row.
New soldiers come and die.

Yet time storms on
And gives no rest.
You're overcome
With tiredness—
You want to close your eyes.
Don't you give in!
Open them wide!
Look at the storm
And face the tide,
And you shall know no lies!

Scene Two

The Invention of Electricity

(Drop-curtain is raised. The scene is a street in Bologna. On a balcony Galvani is busying himself with the famous frogs' legs. Enter Eddie and the Machine.)

EDDIE *(approaching Galvani)*: Good morning, sir. Beg your pardon, sir, would you possibly have some work for us? Like fixin' a short circuit or repairin' a connection? Nuttin'?
GALVANI: Sorry. Electricity has not been invented yet.
EDDIE: Thank God! . . . I mean, too bad, I'm an electrician, y'know, and I haven't had no bite to eat since the twentieth century—twelve o'clock noon.
GALVANI *(shrugging his shoulders)*: Maybe you could come by in two weeks.
EDDIE: My dear sir! If I'd come by in 150 years, I'd get the same answer.
MACHINE: Eddie! That's Galvani in person! He's right in the middle of inventing electricity! *(Points at the plate on the door)*: "Dr. Galvani, born 1737, died 1798. No Begging, No Soliciting!" And over there are the famous frogs' legs he's experimenting with!
EDDIE: I see. Well, in that case he don't have to bother to invent it!
GALVANI: What did you say?
MACHINE *(embarrassed)*: You see, that's actually so to speak the real purpose of our visit. We would like to ask you a favor. The thing is . . . I'm afraid to say it.
EDDIE: We mean, we think you should forget it. You shouldn't invent it at all, that electricity.
GALVANI: What?! Well, that *is* asking a lot! And what am I, as university professor, supposed to live on? At a time when every grocer is better off than people like myself? And besides, in these uncertain times one can't even count on one's pension! I understand that over there, in France, the Jacobin Popular Front is supposed to have taken the Bastille. In this

day and age a civil servant simply doesn't know what's in store for him next! But apart from that, look over there! (*He points at the frogs' legs*): There they go, twitching again!

EDDIE: If you wanna have a clean conscience, let 'em twitch as much as they like.

GALVANI: That's out of the question. The progress of technology . . .

EDDIE: . . . is to blame that the two of us have nothin' better to do than to go gallivantin' around in the eighteenth century. Look here! Know what this is? An electric power bill for September, 1936. Now go ahead if you dare, and invent that electricity of yours.

GALVANI: You're crazy! No, you're a Jacobin. A French secret agent. The cut of your pants should have warned me right away!

EDDIE (*in despair*): He don't believe me! He don't see no farther than a frog can jump.

MACHINE: He'll believe us in a minute. (*To Galvani:*) Look here, sir! I have connected your innocent harmless frogs' legs directly with the year 1936. Eddie, turn the radio on!

GALVANI (*impressed*): Radio! What's that?

MACHINE: That's what comes of your electricity. (*Eddie turns on the radio. Radio voices. Montage. Voice-Band. The voices are mingled with that of a female concert singer and piano music.*)

GALVANI: Enough, enough! (*Eddie turns the radio off.*) I will not invent electricity. (*Buries his head in his hands.*) I could never forgive myself.

MACHINE: Well done, Galvani! Good for you!

EDDIE: Annie! Annie!

ANNIE: Say, ain't it beautiful around here? Rococo all over! Much prettier than the Home for Servant Girls in the Vienna Woods. Just like Hollywood. Gee!

EDDIE: Annie! We did it! Electricity's down the drain!

ANNIE: Jesus, am I happy! Now we'll have to get home quick and buy some candles.

EDDIE: But Pepi, what are you goin' to do? As an electromotor you won't even exist!

MACHINE: I'll manage. I'll just have to be content with the limited life of a sewing machine. Being a bicycle isn't a bad life either.

GALVANI: Terrible! Terrible!

ANNIE: Don't take it to heart, Signor Inventor! Pepi's goin' to let you in on some other invention that will make you just as famous. Why don't you invent the Gillette safety razor? How about that?

MACHINE: Here's a catalog of the 1936 Vienna Industrial Fair. Read that and you'll be at least twenty years ahead of your century!

GALVANI: But my dear friends, all this is of no use.

EDDIE: Whadda ya mean?

GALVANI: If I don't invent electricity, my colleague Volta will. Or somebody else.

EDDIE: But why should he? For four thousand years you managed with candles, and now, all of a sudden, you're in such a big hurry.

GALVANI: The theory is in the air.

MACHINE: For heaven's sake, why don't ya leave it there?

GALVANI: Can't be done! No intellectual will ever agree to having his freedom of thought curtailed!

EDDIE: You don't say! That's the latest!

GALVANI: The latest, indeed! In the Middle Ages no scientist would have stuck to his theories so obstinately.

EDDIE: Is that so? And who invented this game?

MACHINE: Stop just a second! I know all about it! (*To Galvani:*) Could you please wait for us a few minutes. We'll just hop back to the year 1633.

ANNIE: Gee whiz, but why?

MACHINE: You'll see. (*To Galvani:*) But you must promise that while we're gone, you don't come up with any reckless inventions!

EDDIE: Right! And no twitching, understand!?

GALVANI: Never again! (*The travelers start. Galvani calls after them:*) But as an intellectual, I can't refrain from telling you . . .

(*Drop-curtain falls.*)

Trip to Paradise, Scene Two Volkstheater in den Außenbezirken, Vienna, 1993: Günter Franzmeier (Eddie), Rüdfer Hentzschel (Machine), Rainer Fried (Galvani).

Scene Three

(In front of the curtain. Eddie, Annie and the Machine on their trip.)

ANNIE: And where are we goin' now?
MACHINE: To Galileo, the physicist.
EDDIE: What for? Don't tell me ya wanna talk him out of the idea that the earth's movin'!
MACHINE: At least he should keep his knowledge to himself.

EDDIE: But listen! If you do that, you trip up the whole of modern science!
MACHINE: Of course. You said yourself that progress is to blame for everything!
EDDIE: I dunno. I've a kind a bad conscience about that.
MACHINE (*annoyed*): You do, do you? A hangover already, eh?
EDDIE (*who has talked himself into a temper*): Don't shout! Don't ya see that Annie's asleep?
MACHINE: You better keep quiet yourself. You're responsible for everything.
EDDIE: I am, eh? And who talked us into this trip?
MACHINE: And who said that the machines are to blame? (*More quietly:*) Remember, Eddie, we machines have only one purpose in this world and that is to do the will of humans. You press the starter, we start moving. You just thought half a thought; I thought it out and drew the consequences. Now that you humans have created us machines, you've got to be a little more careful with your daydreaming. Before you can say General Motors, fantasy turns into reality. We are the obedient spirits and you're the sorcerer's apprentices. Do you understand me?
ANNIE (*sleeping*): Nothin' but fibs . . . shenanigans . . .
EDDIE (*who has stopped listening to the Machine and been watching Annie*): D'ya hear that? She don't believe that I'll ever have a job again, even in her dreams. But I'll show her! Once all the big factories are gone, all of us will get enough to do—ain't that right, Pepi?
MACHINE (*with reserve—he has made the important statement; everything beyond that is a matter of indifference to him; with a trace of scorn for Eddie's bullheadedness*): That's only logical!
ANNIE (*waking up*): Have we come to Galileo yet?
EDDIE: It won't be long now, Annie. And then we'll go straight home. (*With longing and despair:*) And then everythin' will be all right again. (*Looking for confirmation:*) Won't it, Pepi?
MACHINE (*with more than a touch of irony*): That's only logical.

Scene Four

The Trial of Galileo Galilei

(Courtroom. In the background a bust of the goddess of justice. In the middle: Presiding Judge at his desk. Right front: in the defendant's dock, Galileo. Behind him, the Counsel for the Defense. Left front: in the witness stand, Eddie. Behind him, the public.)

JUDGE: I herewith open the final hearing in the trial of Galileo Galilei, and I will have the courtroom cleared at the least sign of disturbance. *(Mechanically:)* Accused, be silent! The statements made by the witnesses heretofore have produced increased evidence against you. The last three witnesses called upon by the prosecuting attorney were Giuseppe Stoissner, a resident of a mountainous region; Heraklid Florentini, a night watchman; and Professor Mollig, Director of the Institute of Physics at the University of Vienna. Mr. Stoissner, who is 112 years old, has been observing the earth from an elevation of 7,800 feet all his life, and he has stated that never in all that time has he noticed that the earth was turning. Accused, be quiet! Signor Florentini has disproved the defendant's last possible argument by stating under oath that at night, too, no motion of the earth can be observed. Accused, be silent! Professor Mollig, the distinguished Viennese scholar, has removed the last doubt by means of an ingenious experiment. He threw a brick vertically into the air, and, without moving from the spot, he waited for it to fall. If during the four seconds that the brick was in the air the earth had moved, Professor Mollig would have moved with it and the projectile would have dropped to the ground beside him. However, Professor Mollig was carried out of this courtroom with a complicated skull fracture. His last words were: long live Aristotle! *(He rises.)* Professor Mollig is one of the most prominent martyrs of the Vienna School of Science. May I ask for a minute of silence in his memory. Accused, be silent!

COUNSEL FOR THE DEFENSE: You have . . . (*Stops on account of the minute of silence proclaimed by the judge. Presiding Judge sits down.*) You have not mentioned my witnesses, Your Honor! The carter Romeo Medici has stated that the earth does turn around.
JUDGE: He was disqualified because he is a chronic alcoholic.
COUNSEL FOR THE DEFENSE: The same statement was made by the fully licensed courtesan Julia.
JUDGE: Disqualified on account of her fits of nervous dizziness.
COUNSEL FOR THE DEFENSE: And what about Cesare Lionardo Aenea Aurelio Gibellini?
JUDGE: He is the owner of a merry-go-round. (*Counsel for the Defense winces.*) Do you wish to comment on this series of indisputable evidence? Defendant, be silent! Now I would like to ask our last witness, Signor Eduard Lechner, to step forward—as an expert from the twentieth century. (*Eddie steps forward.*) Defendant, are there any questions you want to ask the witness? Defendant, be silent! Signor Lechner, would you please comment on the question of whether the earth moves or not.
EDDIE (*fighting with himself, keeps silent.*)
JUDGE: Well? The question is clear enough, is it not? Does the earth move or not?
EDDIE (*with great reluctance*): It don't.
COUNSEL FOR THE DEFENSE (*who, all this time, has made gasping attempts to speak*): Aha! Just a minute! Witness, when were you born? I remind you of your oath.
EDDIE: August 23, 1910.
COUNSEL FOR THE DEFENSE: I see! And what year is it now? Your Honor?! 1633! What follows from this with razor-sharp logic? That the witness will be born 277 years from now. (*Grandly:*) I have shown that the Prosecution is using unborn witnesses! (*Commotion among the public.*)
JUDGE: Silence! I'll have the courtroom cleared!
COUNSEL FOR THE DEFENSE: I move that the witness Lechner be disqualified!
JUDGE: Court will adjourn for consultation. Accused, be silent!

(*Exits.*)

GALILEO (*to Eddie*): Signor Lechner, I would never have thought that of you.
EDDIE (*wretched*): Look, doctor, don't hold it against me. What I worry about is that Galvani 'll invent electricity 'cause of your discoveries.
GALILEO: You realize, of course, that with your statement you allied yourself with the Dark Ages!
EDDIE: Look, doc: I only said it 'cause I've gotta get some kind a work again!
GALILEO (*shrugging his shoulders*): If you consider that a sufficient excuse . . .

(*Judge and Counsel for the Defense enter.*)

JUDGE: Accused, be silent! The motion of the Defense has been rejected.
COUNSEL FOR THE DEFENSE: It has? Why?
JUDGE: On the basis of your argument, the defendant could claim that this High Court has been dead and rotten for hundreds of years, which under certain circumstances might lead to the assumption that our competency is doubtful. Defendant, be silent! Witness, I repeat my question: Does our world move or not?
EDDIE (*after a long silence*): No.
COUNSEL FOR THE DEFENSE: It doesn't, eh? And how do you substantiate such a statement?
EDDIE (confused): I . . . I'm . . . (*Almost giving in:*) Look, doctor, it's only that I'll get . . .
JUDGE: Hmm, hmm . . . Accused, be silent!
MACHINE (*entering*): The witness submits the following evidence from his own age.

(*Lights out. A spotlight illuminates for a second the bust of the goddess of justice. Lights up. In the place of the Judge, a modern judge; in place of Galileo, a man in a modern suit with Galileo's features.*)

JUDGE OF THE TWENTIETH CENTURY (in the brutal tones of a military command): Accused! Be silent!

(*Lights out. Spotlight on the goddess of justice. Lights up. The former characters.*)

GALILEO: Who was that?
MACHINE: One of your many colleagues from the twentieth century.
GALILEO (*softly*): Is he, too, accused because he claims that the earth is moving?
MACHINE: Something like that.
GALILEO: In that case . . . the earth does stand still.
JUDGE (*relieved*): Well, finally! Such a recantation is a real relief, isn't it? And of course, it will also extenuate your case. Do you want to make a final statement?
GALILEO: No. (*After hesitating briefly:*) Yes! (*Screams:*) And yet, it does—(*The Machine puts his hand over Galileo's mouth:*)
COUNSEL FOR THE DEFENSE (*in despair*): But why, for heaven's sake, after we had just settled the matter so nicely?
GALILEO: Because no one believes this stupid rubbish anymore since, thanks to Christopher Columbus, our horizon . . .
COUNSEL FOR THE DEFENSE (*to Eddie*): Could you do me a favor and talk sense with Signor Columbus?

(*Eddie wants to protest.*)

MACHINE: It will be a pleasure.
COUNSEL FOR THE DEFENSE: There! I move to adjourn.
JUDGE: The court will adjourn. Accused, be silent!

(*Drop-curtain falls.*)

Scene Five

On the Road

(Eddie and the Machine in front of the curtain.)

EDDIE (*gloomily*): Nice thing! Now I've committed perjury!

MACHINE: Good grief! Now it's gnawing at him again. You humans are certainly inconsistent creatures. You must have a bug in your construction somewhere.

EDDIE (*as above*): A traitor, that's what I am. The disgusted look the doctor gave me, full of contempt!

ANNIE (*to the Machine*): Just look at him, will you? Downright sick he is. I'm tellin' ya, tomorrow at twelve noon we've gotta be back home; he's gotta be in time for soccer practice. (*Proudly:*) You won't find a better center half in the whole district. And I've gotta be back in the restaurant in the afternoon or I'll lose my job.

EDDIE (*disgruntled*): I haven't seen a newspaper for 500 years.

MACHINE: Funny, how interested you both are in your own time again all of a sudden! (*Annoyed:*) Okay, if you want, we'll turn right back. Agreed?

EDDIE (*defiantly*): No! Damned if we do! We'd look like a bunch of fools. I've gotta bring somethin' home from this trip. On our bridge they'll never find out who's to blame for it all. I've gotta tell'em somethin'!

ANNIE: Stop being ornery, you two. We'll be with Columbus in a jiffy; he'll understand for sure, and everything's gonna be all right!

MACHINE (*coolly, ironically*): That's only logical! At your service as usual.

ANNIE: Gee! I can already see the station sign of the Middle Ages.

VOICES: Middle Ages! Hot Dogs! Change trains for Modern Times! Hot Dogs! Hot Dogs!

Scene Six

The Discovery of America

(On board Columbus' ship. On the high seas . . . Eddie and sailor are singing the Sailor's song:)

> If you're not happy at home any more
> Then try your luck on another shore,
> Set sail, get going, brother!
> If here you have no time to "be,"
> Take off into eternity
> And find yourself another.
>
> And if the storm wind starts to blast
> Bind yourself, laughing, to the mast . . .
> I'd bet that you won't drown!
> And even if you lose your way
> Laugh, look forward, don't dismay . . .
> Nothing will get you down.
>
> If on the globe you cannot find
> The new world that you had in mind . . .
> Then don't be daunted, brother,
> You'll locate our own continent
> And our own time, you'll, in the end,
> Discover, yes, discover!

EDDIE: We better cut out the singin', the sharks are prickin' up their ears.

SAILOR: They're deaf anyway.

EDDIE: How can ya be sure? (*Sighing.*) I'd like to fish myself a supper. Tell me, did you have a stormy trip before we joined you as stowaways?

SAILOR: Abominable. First we broke a piece of the mainmast as we passed under the Santa Maria Bridge since we forgot to pull it in. Then we ripped a Portuguese dinghy in two. It wasn't until the Prater Point that a breeze from larboard drove us into more favorable waters. The distance to the Cape of Bratislava was kind of a long haul. But from then on to the equator it was real easy sailing.

(Enter Machine and Columbus talking animatedly)

COLUMBUS: No! No and no!
SAILOR: For three days your buddy's been talking his arms and legs off. But the captain is stubborn as a mule.
COLUMBUS: Or . . . all right. All right, if you really insist on talking me out of my plan, I won't discover the West Indies but America! It doesn't make that much difference to me.
MACHINE: But you misunderstand me. America is what I've been talking about for the last three days! Listen!
COLUMBUS: Go to the devil! (*He exits. The Sailor runs after him.*)
EDDIE: Say, who's that slicked-up brat that's always chasin' my fiancée?
SAILOR: A certain Pietro, an Italian Humanist. He came along for the adventure.
PIETRO (*to Annie*): Thou art Aphrodite born from the foam of the sea . . .
ANNIE (*embarrassed*): But, no! I keep tellin' ya, I'm the substitute kitchen maid in the Park Café.
PIETRO: And your age really fulfilled the dreams of the great master Leonardo da Vinci? You can raise yourself to the clouds?
ANNIE: Not me. I can hardly raise enough to go to the movies.
PIETRO: You are the human being we have been dreaming of. The human being reborn!
ANNIE: But my dear Signor, I'm nothing of the kind. You're mistakin' me for someone else. (*They both exit.*)
EDDIE: Tell me, what's the employment situation like, here in the Middle Ages?
SAILOR: Pretty rotten. If you don't wanna be a lackey or a mercenary, your chances of landing a job are pretty much nil. How about you in modern times?
EDDIE: Same shit. Still, I'm homesick.

(Enter Columbus, on his heels the Machine.)

COLUMBUS: All right, let's make a compromise. I discover South America only, and your commission will be the position as general manager of the Amazon Steamship Company.
MACHINE: What a commercial mind! You're not supposed to discover anything!
COLUMBUS: I'll have you thrown overboard!

(He exits, the Machine follows him.)

PIETRO: And with a little pressure of the finger you can light up your palaces like daylight?
ANNIE: Provided the power bill is paid. That's the problem; that's why we're here. Or wait a minute. Eddie, why did we leave home, anyway?
EDDIE (*jealous*): Why don't ya ask your Humanist?
ANNIE: Don't be so rough, Eddie. I'm homesick for the twentieth century just like you are.
PIETRO (*dreamily*): So am I.

(Enter Columbus, on his heels the Machine.)

COLUMBUS (*beseechingly*): Let me discover at least the island of Cuba. After all, this is 1492. How are people going to know that the Middle Ages have come to an end if I don't discover something?
MACHINE: I have warned you of any discovery in this part of the world!
COLUMBUS: Just a coral reef, a dilapidated one! Pro forma! All right?
MACHINE: You heard me: No!
COLUMBUS: Okay! If you don't want to cooperate, you won't get anywhere! I'll discover the American continent—all of it! From top to bottom—just to spite you! (*Looks at his watch.*) It's 1492 on the dot. (*To the chief mate:*) Hey, look-out!
SAILOR (*stretching out his arm*): L-a-a-a-a- (Before he has finished, the word, the machine has covered his mouth).

Trip to Paradise, Scene Six, Staatstheater Stuttgart, 1990, from left to right: Paul Wolff-Plottegg (Columbus), Ricky May (Annie), Adi Hirschal (Sailor), Hansjürgen Gerth (Motor), Tono Slama (Eddie).

MACHINE: Wait a minute! Before you go any further let me show you the consequences of your foolhardy actions: Why don't you stand over there. I'm going to project a piece of the future around you. (*Columbus turns into a statue. A young American and his wife, chewing gum, come sauntering to the statue.*)

AMERICAN: Oh, honey, how do you like the Acropolis? Ain't it swell!

HIS WIFE: It's awesome! It's neat! There ain't nothin' like culture. (*Calling into the wings:*) Hello, get a drink, folks.

AMERICAN TOURISTS (*in chorus*): Yeah, get a drink somewhere.

AMERICAN (*discovering Columbus*): Who's that?
TOURIST GUIDE (*rushing to him*): That is Christopher Columbus, the discoverer of America.
AMERICAN: Boy, he had a lot of gall—an Englishman discovering the United States!
TOURIST GUIDE: Don't you want to be remembered as a visitor to this historic site? (*He hands him a visitor's book.*)
AMERICAN: Sure, boy, you bet I do. (*He pushes the book aside, sticks his chewing gum on Columbus' behind, and writes something on it.*) You know what this says? The most beautiful city of the world is Cincinnati, Ohio. (*The apparition disappears.*)
COLUMBUS: Helmsman, turn the rudder 180 degrees. America will not be discovered.
MACHINE: Three to nothing in my favor.
COLUMBUS: At least not by me.
MACHINE (*enjoying Eddie's disappointment*): You know what's coming now, Eddie, don't ya?
EDDIE: Who's gonna discover it?
COLUMBUS: It doesn't matter who. Somebody. The way things are nowadays any shipping agent can hit on the idea of discovering America. Just look at all those travel books! The most obvious pointers to a new continent! That kind of bestseller is lying around in any tavern these days. Of course, if the printing press hadn't been invented . . .
MACHINE: It will not be invented! I'll see to that!
EDDIE: But without me!
ANNIE: Good for you, Eddie. I've had enough of this chasin' around.
EDDIE (*jumping up*): I see! That's the way you mean it—you wanna stay with this Humanist, eh? You have my blessings! C'mon, Pepi.
ANNIE: But Eddie . . .
EDDIE (*without taking any notice of her*): Let's go: On to Gutenberg! I don't give a damn anymore!
COLUMBUS (*as the drop-curtain falls*): I will cast anchor at this historic turning point and wait for you. Ahoy!

(*Drop-curtain.*)

Scene Seven
On the Road

(Eddie and the Machine in front of the curtain.)

EDDIE *(in despair)*: We never did quite hit it off! And now that she's found an egghead, she jilts me.
MACHINE: Oh, forget it. Why get all hepped up about a streamlined girl like that, just because she has a few functional curves?
EDDIE: Be quiet, you bastard concoction of steel and gasoline! You haven't got a heart!
MACHINE: Thank God, no. My pump mechanism works much more accurately.
EDDIE: Goddammit! Now everythin's up! I don't give a damn about nothin'!
MACHINE: Now all his fuses are burned out!
EDDIE: I'm goin' to smash the goddam works. I'll take the whole stupid progress an' knock it to pieces! You don't know me yet! Where's that guy, that Gutenberg?

Scene Eight
In Gutenberg's Workshop

EDDIE: Where's that guy, that Gutenberg?
MACHINE: Are you the Gutenberg who invented the printing press?
GUTENBERG: Invention, my friend, is a very slow art, I am just now about to start!
EDDIE: You are, eh? *(Hands him an evening edition of a newspaper.)* Why don't ya read this sh . . .eet, before ya get goin'.
GUTENBERG: *(reads and, as if stung by a scorpion, suddenly collapses on a chair)*: My journeymen, melt every letter!
   Not to print is so much better.
   God save us from the devil's work!
   This is the wish of Gutenberg.
EDDIE: Three cheers for Gutenberg! And all he read was the ads.

(Curtain.)

Trip to Paradise, Scene Eight, Jura Soyfer Theater, Vienna, 1982, Gutenberg: "Not to print is so much better."

Scene Nine

On the Road

(In front of the curtain. Eddie and the Machine sitting on milestones. They are tired and look down-at-heel.)

MACHINE: Is it my fault that it wasn't Gutenberg who started it all either?
EDDIE: What about the thousands of other inventors we've been to in the meantime? Take Emperor Charlemagne for in-

stance . . .

MACHINE: Didn't I prove to him without a shadow of a doubt he shouldn't invent the Holy German Nation?

EDDIE: But he said he wasn't the one to complain to. And then that Hagen of Tronje and the Nibelungen gang . . .

MACHINE: We really couldn't have met him at a better time. We surprised him just at the very moment when he was going to ram Siegfried through with his spear from behind . . .

EDDIE: And how we begged him not to invent a warrior's honor and loyalty and all that! But it wasn't any use. And what about Genghis Khan, the Scourge of God . . .?

MACHINE: How we implored him not to invent bilateral treaties!

EDDIE: But he said he wasn't responsible either. The most promising of all was that pretty female inventor . . .

MACHINE: You mean Pharaoh's daughter who was cooling off in the Nile, and found the little basket with the baby in didies that someone had left there.

EDDIE: Let it swim down river, says I. You've no idea what an unholy mess you're gettin' started.

MACHINE: But she referred us to someone else, like all the others.

MACHINE: And Finally old Archimedes, the father of all inventors . . .

EDDIE: We caught him in the bathtub just when he was about to jump stark naked and shout his famous "Eureka"; he go "Eu" out, but we managed to gag him before he got to "reka."

MACHINE: But what good was it? And what did he say? He said: "If you want to stop Man from inventing, you've got to get rid of the artists first. They anticipate every invention in their dreams. The best thing would be for you to prevent the invention of music!"

EDDIE: And that's the reason we went to Orpheus . . .

MACHINE: There he was sittin' in the woods, with all the animals gathered around him, and he was just at the point of inventing music . . .

EDDIE: . . . and at that moment we played him a record of "Mairzy doats and dozy doats and little lamzy divey A kiddeley divey too—wouldn't you?"

MACHINE: Instantly he said that nothin' could persuade him to invent music.

EDDIE: But that someone else would, if he didn't. Because Man has been singing ever since he was made.

MACHINE: If you really want to prevent the invention of music, he said, the only thing to do is to prevent the invention of Man!

EDDIE: And now here we are . . . at the last stop, at the Gates of Paradise. That's how far you got me!

MACHINE: You wanted to come! And all the inventors are waiting for us at this moment. The whole history of mankind has come to a halt . . . fifty centuries are watching us and holding their breath . . . and you turn chicken and don't want to go in.

EDDIE: I'd like to know what Annie's doin'.

MACHINE: Can't you ever get her out of your head? O.K. you can take a peep back to the fifteenth century, if you want . . . (*Projection on drop-curtain: Humanist and Annie raising their glasses to an imaginary group of wandering scholars. Drinking song*):

Golden sparkles the blood of the vine
Fermented in the cool of night.
Raise the brimming bowls of wine,
Toast three times the new, the fine
Man reborn now in the Light.
    Vivat ille nunc renatus,
    Vivat vivere conatus,
    Vivat homo liberatus!

See from Rubens' golden frame
Man greets us, laughing, full of life,
Plays the lover—Petrarch's game,
Suffers Dante's hellish flame,
Swings Cesare's vicious knife.
    Vivat osus et amatus,
    Vivat temperate satus,
    Vivat homo liberatus!

Shepherd, where's your flock tonight?
Where is your poor court jester, King?
His longing and his mortal plight,
No heavenly force, no earthly might
Subjects Man now, no other thing.
   Vivat novus rerum status,
   Vivat qui haec nova ratus,
   Vivat homo liberatus!

Richly foams the blood of the vine,
Fermented in the dark of night.
Why throw yourself away . . . resign?
Fight! Life itself is on the line!
Welcome Man with all your might!
   Vivat ille nunc renatus,
   Vivat vivere conatus,
   Vivat homo liberatus!

EDDIE: She's havin' a good time with her egghead, Signor Academic. (*Comes to a decision*) Pepi, go to her and take her my final farewell!

MACHINE: Then you *are* going in? You realize, don't you, that if you manage to prevent the invention of Man, then it's all up with you, too, and with Annie and with the whole race of Man? And with us machines, too. (*Emphatically*) That's only logical.

EDDIE: No work. No girl. No hope. There's no way out; everythin' must go to hell. Tony knew what he was doin'. And Herr Andraschek, too, when he marched off with a "Hurrah!" To see Paradise just once—and then to see nothin' more, nothin' but darkness. Go to Annie and tell her that it's all over with all of us.

MACHINE (*quietly*): At your service as always. (*Gets ready to take off*)

EDDIE (*calls him back*): Hey, Pepi!

MACHINE: Yes?

EDDIE: Before you go . . . don't you want to peep in to see what it's like inside Paradise?

MACHINE: No, thanks. We machines don't have any souls that need boosting. All we need is a little bit of grease in order to destroy civilization and mankind to boot. (*Emphatically:*) If that's what you want. I never hesitated on this trip. I am ready to take the consequences. 'Bye, Eddie.
EDDIE (*tersely*): If that's what you want—'bye.
MACHINE: (*turns around once more as he goes off*) Say, Eddie!
EDDIE: Yes?
MACHINE: What is it like in Paradise?
EDDIE: I dunno. I imagine it's a huge factory where creation is being manufactured. (*Longingly:*) Six days of work, then a holiday . . . and everybody has all the work he can handle!
MACHINE: And in the middle a huge lit-up fountain of purest Shell Oil . . . beeeautiful! 'Bye, now. (*Exits.*)
EDDIE: 'Bye. (*Softly:*) Paradise, get ready, here I come! Hurrah!

(*Eddie rushes forward; curtain rises quickly to reveal the next scene.*)

Scene Ten

At the Gates of Paradise

(*Eddie bumps into the luxuriously-uniformed gatekeeper of the Paradise-Factory. Gatekeeper holds a fiery staff. Next to the entrance, a sign: "Help wanted." Dull machine noises in the background.*)

GATEKEEPER (*speaking in a very quiet and dignified though somewhat arrogant tone*): Stop!
EDDIE: Who's in charge around here?
GATEKEEPER: As far as you're concerned, I am.
EDDIE: But you're only the gatekeeper.
GATEKEEPER: And who are you? Are you a monkey or what?
EDDIE: I'm no monkey!
GATEKEEPER (*calmly*): Then you are a devil. (*Looking him over:*)

A poor devil at that. It's for poor devils like you that I'm here.

EDDIE: I'm a human being.

GATEKEEPER: Who do you think you're fooling? Human beings don't exist yet, and if they did, they wouldn't look like you.

EDDIE (*crushed*): It's the same everywhere. (*Imploringly:*) Could I please be admitted to the office of the general manager?

GATEKEEPER: The management is busy. At this time they are hard at work trying to construct Man. You can hardly walk through the corridors, what with the lumps of clay everywhere. The nervousness is beyond description. The management apparently still hasn't figured out the key to the whole thing. The dot on the *i*, so to speak, is still missing. Something that would distinguish Man from all the animals that we know . . .

EDDIE: I thought that'd be his ability to be noble, kind, and good.

GATEKEEPER: Any fox terrier can be that. Anyway, what do you want around here?

EDDIE: Well, actually . . . (*Catches sight of the sign "Help wanted" and forgets everything else.*) Work I want! Work! You need workers, I see, don't ya? I could really be most helpful to you in the creation of Man, I really could! (*Imploringly:*) I have first-rate insight into human nature. I could even make a few important suggestions for his improvement!

GATEKEEPER: Sorry. The boom has already subsided. The earthly market is saturated with creatures. The only models scheduled for production at this time are "Adam" and "Eve." Starting Monday production will cease.

EDDIE (*at the highest point of his despair*): If that's the case, why d'ya create Man at all? Why don't ya forget about him?

GATEKEEPER (*perplexed*): What do you want?

EDDIE: To submit a petition, that's what I want; a petition to the general management. They'll listen to me, don't worry! (*Sings the "Ballad at the Gates of Paradise":*)

> Lord, oh do not touch the clay!
> You'll just get into a bind.

What Your Adam will become
Won't be what You had in mind!

(A profiteer walks across the stage.)

Look at Man when he's in power!
He will praise You, Lord, but say:
Is he still what You envisaged
On Creation's final day?

(An unemployed worker walks across the stage.)

Look at Man cast off, forgotten,
Out of work, no food, no bed.
How can he obey your order:
"Labor for your daily bread?"

(A mother walks across the stage.)

Look! Don't turn Your face away!
See the mother worn with care.
When You told her to bear children,
Did You want her to despair?!

(A prostitute walks across the stage.)

See the whore lost in the crowd!
Joy for sale! O Lord above!
Did You think of her profession
When Your smile created love?

(A man with a gas mask walks across the stage.)

Look at Man before his death!
Pitiless he's out to kill.
You had made him in Your image.
Is this brute Your image still?
Do not touch the clay, O Lord!

Adam will but wreck Your plan.
Or if You've already made him,
Cancel him! Unmake Your Man!

GATEKEEPER: Is that your suggestion?
EDDIE: That's my suggestion.
GATEKEEPER: Are there any objections to your motion?
EDDIE: Who should object? The animals sure wouldn't. They'll be much happier without us anyway. Even the snake.
GATEKEEPER: Well, isn't there anyone to speak up for the creation of Man?
EDDIE: No.

(Annie and the Machine rush in.)

ANNIE: I will!
EDDIE: Annie!
GATEKEEPER: Cut it out! Don't get excited, will you! What is the justification for your countermotion?
ANNIE *(confused)*: Justification? *(She is silent, afraid of her own courage.)*
EDDIE *(vehemently)*: No!
ANNIE *(passionately)*: Yes!
GATEKEEPER: No—yes. *(Suddenly excited:)* I've got it!! I'll get an official commendation and a raise for this! *(Hurries off.)*
EDDIE *(bashfully)*: Annie . . . to be honest, I never thought you'd come back to me . . .
ANNIE: Eddie . . .
EDDIE: Annie . . .
ANNIE: Eddie . . .
EDDIE: Annie . . .
ANNIE *(overcome)*: Gee, Eddie, this is more beautiful than in the movies. *(Embrace.)*
MACHINE: Well, finally! Hurry up and make up! Then the end of the world will at least be a happy ending!
EDDIE *(already protesting)*: What do you mean—"ending"?
MACHINE: Well, if that isn't the limit of inconsistency! You don't really doubt that your well-documented "no" will make

more of an impression on the powers in charge than the childish "yes" of that cute little chick there?!
ANNIE (*terrified*): So it's all over?
MACHINE: That's only logical. I don't know how long official channels around here take, but that's exactly how long all of us still have to live.

(*Annie and Eddie in their fear huddle up against the Machine.*)

EDDIE: Maybe there's still a chance after all?
MACHINE: They're not good enough to live—and not bad enough to die. Primitive machines, these human beings!
(*They wait.*)
GATEKEEPER (*enters joyfully*): Congratulations! Man has just been created!
EDDIE: Really?
GATEKEEPER: Don't act so surprised. After all it was you who made the key suggestion for his construction.
EDDIE: Me?
GATEKEEPER: Both of you. When one of you said no and the other yes, we made a mixture of yes and no, slapped some clods of clay around it, and there was the finished product: Man!
MACHINE: But yes and no is a contradiction. Somebody must make a choice between the two, that's only logical.
GATEKEEPER: That choice has been put in the hands of Man himself. And from that moment on, he was alive. I have been instructed by the high authorities to inform you of their special praise, and after that to throw you out of here.
EDDIE: But why?
GATEKEEPER: Because you nibbled from the Tree of Knowledge—because, after Man, the weekend was created. And now I'm closing up—end of my working hours!
EDDIE: And the destruction of mankind won't come off?
GATEKEEPER: Sorry. Maybe some other time. (*Commanding gesture with the fiery staff. Drop-curtain falls.*)
EDDIE: And the destruction—that'll depend on us, too?

MACHINE: At your service. You sure are talking a different language already. I almost feel a yen to take service with you for good.
EDDIE: That, too, depends on me. Everything's up to me. Can you take us back to the present?
MACHINE: At your service. My gearbox is gettin' all sore anyhow from bein' constantly in reverse.
ANNIE: And can you take us into the future, too?
EDDIE: Don't ask so many questions—that's up to us.
ANNIE: Let's go, Pepi!
MACHINE (*respectfully*): With your permission then, we'll be off!

(*The entire cast sings the final song*):

Reverse the direction ! Take charge at last
Or the whole machine will crack.
For in the one-way street of the past
Nothing can ever go back.

   We'll let that be that once was done,
   Take up what we hope we can merit:
   We've a legacy: it's up to us
   To cherish what we inherit.

ARCHIMEDES: Eureka!

Now, shout, Achimedes! As loud as you choose,
Granddaddy of all invention.
If progress in *your* time ran without shoes . . .
That isn't our modern intention.

   Now toast the inventors, the miracle-men,
   Give new and old their merit.
   They left us stewards . . . it's up to us
   To advance what we inherit.

COLUMBUS: **Land!**

    Columbus, may your pirate raids
    With wooden ships succeed!
    The Santa Maria drifts with the trades . . .
    Queen Mary goes ten times your speed!

        Ahoy, the discoverers, men of vision,
        Rewarded with rags for their merit,
        They left a bequest . . . it's up to us
        To preserve what we inherit.

GALILEI: And yet, it *does* more!

    Yes, earth, move on, all clothed in light,
    Battered by storms on high.
    Move on, with poverty's endless plight
    And wealth that reaches the sky.

        You Present, we challenge you in the fight
        To shape the Future we merit . . .
        For the world is rich and it's up to us
        To take charge of all we inherit.

(During the song the scene changes to scene one. At the last refrain the curtain opens. The Machine exits. Eddie and Annie stand again at the bridge railing, eyes closed, while the Chorus behind them sings the last refrain. Chorus breaks off.)

ANNIE *(opens her eyes. Softly)*: Where is Pepi?
EDDIE *(as softly)*: We'll see him soon enough.
ANNIE *(softly)*: Soon? When?
EDDIE *(softly)*: Don't ask so many questions—that's up to us.

        (Curtain)

Astoria

CHARACTERS

Hupka
Vagabonds
Pistoletti
Policeman
Countess Gwendolyn Buckleburg-Marasquino
Count Luitpold Buckleburg-Marasquino
James, Butler
Lady P.
Grand Duchess Anastasia M.
Lord R.
G. B. Shaw
Meter Man from the Power Company
Paul, vagabond
Hortensia, an old prostitute
Rosa, a prostitute-to-be
Jacob, Hortensia's fiance
Applicant No. 23,687
Journalist
Secretary
Man with donation box
Officer
Old Man
Loudspeaker
Voices
Applicants at the Passport Office

Scene One

(In front of the curtain. Hupka and Pistoletti on the road, singing.)

> The summer sun has faded,
> Fall rained away its glow.
> The winter is acoming,
> The poor folks' bitter foe.
> The earth is lying in its shroud,
> Its youth, its flowers gone.
> Move on, you are a stranger here.
> My brother vagabond.
>
> The icy wind is biting
> Right through your rags and shoes.
> You, bum, are not invited
> To fireside and booze.
> On New Year's night no jolly host
> will pass a drink along.
> A crow is cawing you his toast:
> My brother vagabond.
>
> And if the sky above us,
> As far as eye can reach,
> Were velvet woven through with stars,
> A silver dollar each,
> No one would hold your ladder
> To pluck the stars out yond.
> Such are the times, such is the world,
> My brother vagabond.

(The curtain rises. A country road. A signpost with the inscription "St. Ulrich on the Triesting, 25.6 km." Hupka and Pistoletti. Cars are passing by. Hupka and Pistoletti try in vain to thumb a ride.)

HUPKA: It's time to crawl in somewhere. In this connection the irrefutable question arises where to pass the winter season inasmuch as this is no climate anymore, this is just shitty weather.

PISTOLETTI: So you're comin' with me to the hospital? There's one a few miles down the road that's been recommended to me most warmly.

HUPKA: Hospital? I can't take chances like that. I am a sick man. I've got to find a jail to spend the winter in. *Honi soit qui mal y pense.*

PISTOLETTI: How many months will you get for that?

HUPKA: I won't get anything for that. That's not a crime, that's French.

PISTOLETTI: Why don't ya smash in a few windows or somethin'?

HUPKA: I'm above that kind of stuff, my dear Pistoletti, inasmuch as I have no papers and insofar as I look like a well-known murderer; I'm his spitting image so to speak. By the time they find out that I'm not him, it's always spring.

PISTOLETTI: Well, I won't argue. That's a question of one's weltanschauung. I only know that in that hospital there's a certain Dr. Eilinger, and if you can prove that you're a chronic alcoholic you qualify for his rehabilitation program. And this doctor comes round to check on his rehabs every night, and then he runs a competition. Everyone, including the doctor, sees pink elephants, and for every elephant you see more than the doctor sees, you get a drop of plum brandy as a bonus. The thing is that the doctor always loses even though he is an egghead. Probably too stupid. Only once the doctor got suspicious of a guy—it was the guy who told me about it—'cause that guy said he saw twelve million elephants. Naturally he was kicked out. But not everybody's got to gamble that high.

HUPKA: Man must content himself with little.

PISTOLETTI: You said it.

HUPKA: But let me tell you about the police jail in St. Ulrich! That's about the most luxurious accommodation this country has to offer in the genre. A veritable Hotel Bristol! I even

believe they've got flush toilets there. *Sapienti sat.*
PISTOLETTI: Very true. But it's either the hospital or the jail. Man cannot have everything at the same time.
HUPKA: Exactly. Nowadays you've got to be a Diogenes to survive. Okay then, buddy. See you later, right here by the signpost.
PISTOLETTI: When?
HUPKA: You know when. In spring we both feel the itch the same day.
PISTOLETTI: That's because we are kindred souls and spirits. So long, Hupka.
HUPKA: See ya, Pisto.

(Pistoletti exits.)

(Cars are passing by. In spite of Hupka's thumbing, no one stops.)

HUPKA: *Fi donc.* It's at least a four-hour hike to the nearest policeman who could arrest me. Always the same story: when you need them they're not around.
POLICEMAN (*enters*): A cordial 'God be with you' to you!
HUPKA (*amazed*): Well, would you believe it! If that isn't a *lupus ex machina*! It's really very nice of you to come so that I can fall into your hands.
POLICEMAN: Would you kindly show your papers, please?
HUPKA: Boy, is he polite! It's enough to make your flesh creep.
POLICEMAN: Or could it possibly be that you don't have any papers on you?
HUPKA: You guessed it, Sherlock! Scotland Yard, here we come!
POLICEMAN: Poor man, in that case you most likely lost your papers.
HUPKA (*amazed*): What's that? What did you say?
POLICEMAN: But that's only logical, isn't it?
HUPKA: Yes, of course . . . naturally . . . I can't have been born without papers . . . consequently, I must have lost them on the way, but in this case . . . you just have to . . .
POLICEMAN: . . . see to it that you get your papers again, natu-

rally. That's what the police are here for, after all. We shall make all necessary inquiries.

HUPKA: Say, you're not Santa Claus by any chance, are you?

POLICEMAN (*laughing*): Far from it. Just a simple country policeman. However, last night at 10:25 P.M. my faithful wife presented me with healthy triplets.

HUPKA: Little presents make the heart grow fonder. But listen, don't you notice some kind of resemblance when you look at me? I mean, don't I remind you of a certain WANTED notice? Isn't there anything of a criminal about me, a murderer, a robber?

POLICEMAN: With those honest eyes of yours?

HUPKA: Appearances are deceiving, I tell you. Believe me! You've just had the good luck of falling into the hands of a fugitive criminal. Arrest me!

POLICEMAN: Never! Documents and papers lie. But you can trust an honest eye!

HUPKA: Damn it! You've gotta arrest me! . . . What are people paying their taxes for? Besides, there's a reward of ten thousand schillings on my head!

POLICEMAN: Money is the root of all evil.

HUPKA: Don't provoke me, I'm telling ya! Don't force me to go to extremes or I'll insult you and your uniform and the law most savagely!

POLICEMAN: You are intoxicated, my dear friend, and not accountable for your words and deeds. A hard life has made you bitter. I won't hold it against you. Just steer clear of alcohol and fickle womankind. Take care now, it's been a pleasure, sir!

(*Exits.*)

HUPKA: Sir? Sir? Would you believe it! I've just met the only policeman in the whole world who's ever said "sir" to a bum. That's got to mean something. But what? That is the question: What would happen if somewhere in the world there were a borderline, a very special borderline that is, between the realm of everyday reality and the realm of fairy tales—and if, this very moment, I just happened to stroll along that borderline, knowing nothing, thinking nothing . . . (*he draws a line in the dust of the road*) . . . just like this—and if we assume that that borderline is approximately more or less here—hmm—and if I keep walking on the left side of the line like Pistoletti, I'll just remain an ordinary, prosaic bum with chilblains and without papers. If I, however, walked on the other side of the line, in the direction of St. Ulrich—then, this very minute, twenty feet behind me, a Packard would have to come to a screeching halt (*sound of brakes*) and a lady millionaire would get out of the car, with sports car goggles and a gun (*Gwendolyn enters; she has drawn her gun.*) and she would shout at me in purest Hollywoodian:

GWENDOLYN: Hello there! Would you like to come to London with me?

HUPKA: In such a case, I—smart boy that I am—would not be surprised in the least but would reply with dry humor: "Lady, put your shootin' iron in your pocket, the poor thing might catch cold in this virus-ridden winter weather" . . .

GWENDOLYN: I will certainly not. The shape of your earlobes clearly signals desperation and licentiousness. You will most certainly want to rape me. Forgivable . . . we are all sinners. Who dares cast the first stone?

HUPKA: "Thanks a bunch for your sympathy," I'd say in Harvard American. "But you are making an *errare humanum est*. Me nix gangster, me passenger! My name is Kilian Hupka."

GWENDOLYN: I am Countess Gwendolyn Buckleburg-Marasquino, formerly Cash. Why are you turning your back to me?

HUPKA: What? (*Turns around.*) Good heavens, what a realistic hallucination! How do you do?

GWENDOLYN: I've been shopping.

HUPKA: And I'd say: "You've made some purchases?"

GWENDOLYN: Not really, I only wanted to.

HUPKA: And you didn't find what you wanted! I know. In the ads they promise all kinds of things and, when you go and look at the stuff, it's all junk.

GWENDOLYN: Very true . . .
HUPKA: . . . she would say in a formal tone. And I would ask her in just as formal a tone: "And what was it that you wanted to buy, milady?"
GWENDOLYN: A state.
HUPKA: A state? Oh, I see, an estate!
GWENDOLYN: No, you heard right. I wanted to buy a state. A monarchy, for instance, or a republic. I tried out a number of European states, price-list in hand.
HUPKA: And I'd say, nonchalantly: "Well, and were they too expensive, or what was the matter with them?" And she'd say, even more nonchalantly:
GWENDOLYN: They are all old-fashioned, obsolete models.
HUPKA: Is that so? And what did you want a state for anyhow?
GWENDOLYN: For my husband, Count Buckleburg-Marasquino. When he married me he conferred upon me a noble title that goes back to the times of Emperor Andrew the Bald. The marriage contract stipulates that I, in turn, have to give him a state for his eighty-eighth birthday. Forty years ago, he was Minister of Foreign Affairs in the services of a great European power. In that capacity he scored one diplomatic success after the other for a whole week until he finally was fired. Ever since, grief has been consuming him.
HUPKA: I see. Without a state, even the best foreign minister cannot make his influence felt.
GWENDOLYN: The Count has great plans, but I'm afraid they'll have to wait. I just won't be able to find just the right state for him by tomorrow.
HUPKA: I have an idea. Beware of rash purchases! Take your time, shop around until you find what you want. For the time being it is perfectly sufficient if you present your husband with me as citizen number one, a kind of appetizer.
GWENDOLYN: Okay. That's exactly what I had in mind, as you can see. (*She points at her gun.*) Are you, by nature, a patriot?
HUPKA: Always have been, milady. My country or somebody else's, it's always been the same difference to me. You'll be amazed what an ideal citizen you'll find in me. I am honest,

thrifty, and about as subversive as the head of the FBI.
GWENDOLYN: Okay.
HUPKA: Okay, okay. (*Sadly:*) And then, whoosh, she would have packed me into her Packard, and we'd've been off to London. In an American movie. It would've been so wonderful, but was not meant to be . . .
GWENDOLYN: Well, are you coming or aren't you?
HUPKA: Gosh! Are you still here?
GWENDOLYN: Naturally. I'm waiting for you.
HUPKA: What do you mean, "naturally"? And what the hell is goin' on anyhow? You aren't alive, are you? Holy cow! Pinch me! Pinch me, I said! Come on! (*She does.*) Ouch! But that's no proof. Lend me a dollar! C'mon, out with it, lend me a buck!

(*Gwendolyn gives him a silver dollar.*)

HUPKA (*bites the coin*): Genuine!! I'm not dreaming! I'll be damned! I'm not dreaming!
GWENDOLYN: Well, let's go. The engine's getting cold.
HUPKA (*calling into the wings*): Pisto! Pisto! Don't hold it against me: I've let myself be hired as a loyal subject!

(*Lights out.*)

Scene Two

(*The Butler is standing in front of the curtain. From behind the curtain the Count's voice is heard.*)

COUNT: James!
BUTLER: Your Excellency?

(*The curtain rises. The Count's study.*)

COUNT: Read the congratulatory telegram messages to me!

JAMES: Very good, Your Excellency. (*Reads:*) "To the daredevil Junker a hearty tallyho in memory of unforgettable boar hunt in Oder Forest anno Domini 1890. Wilhelm."

COUNT: Fancy that now! The old fellow still remembers me in spite of the fact that he is allowed to rule again.

JAMES: With your permission, Your Excellency, but Your Excellency has deemed it appropriate to fall prey to a confusion; the one who is allowed to rule again is a different one.

COUNT: Possible, quite possible. Carry on in this vein.

JAMES: "The world belongs to the young, like us. Up to 120. Lloyd George. Rockefeller."

COUNT: Excellent, excellent! Carry on in this vein!

JAMES: I beg your Excellency's pardon, but there is a man outside who wishes to see you.

COUNT: What kind of a man?

JAMES: If you'll pardon the expression, Your Excellency, a suspicious-looking individual. It would not surprise me in the least if he were some kind of anarchist who is after Your Excellency's life.

COUNT: Splendid. Tell him that I shall receive him. (*Hupka enters.*)

JAMES (*announcing*): Mr. . . . Hupka (*Unseen by the Count, the Butler gives Hiccup a shove and exits.*)

HUPKA: My name is Hupka. Kilian Hupka.

COUNT: Excellent, excellent. And what else in this vein?

HUPKA: I'm kind of embarrassed, Your Excellency, because actually I ought to have eighty-eight candles sticking into me and a blue ribbon round my neck.

COUNT: Splendid.

HUPKA: Hupka is my name. But under the present circumstances I happen to be a birthday cake, so to speak.

COUNT: Splendid. Only I am not sure now whether I am crazy or not. The papers say that I am entering upon my eighty-ninth year in perfect physical and mental vigor. But the newspapers are full of lies these days . . .

HUPKA: No reason to despair, Your Excellency. You'll understand soon enough. I have been given to you as a birthday gift; I am your subject number one.

COUNT: Excellent. Ex . . . By Jove! You don't mean to say that I have been nominated Foreign Minister! That I have been given back to the people?

HUPKA: On the contrary. A people has been given to you. Though the *whole* people will be dished up to you later. I am just a first taste. *L'état c'est moi!*

COUNT: One People! One State!

HUPKA: One Ruler! Actually, if it makes ya happy, we could reactivate you as a venerable old Head of State. Do not deny the people its will! As it has been said so aptly: *Vox populi,* his master's voice.

COUNT (*straightening up to his full height*): I will follow the call.

HUPKA: Hail to the Chief!

COUNT (*with fixed stare*): Do you know who poisoned Bismarck?

HUPKA: Yes. Nobody.

COUNT: Wrong. A vegetarian. Do you know why?

HUPKA: Because it's true.

COUNT: Wrong. Because Bismarck was a Protestant! As I have proven from documentary evidence, the vegetarians and the Protestants have been fighting for world supremacy since the Peace of Tilsit. Whose fault was it that the central powers lost the World War?

HUPKA (*with guilty expression*): My fault. I had flat feet at the time.

COUNT: Wrong. It was the bassoonists' fault. Lloyd George is an amateur bassoonist. Colonel Redl was a bassoonist. The German general staff was shot through and through with bassoonists. And do you know why President Wilson never in his life played a bassoon?

HUPKA: No.

COUNT: Because he did not want to betray himself.

HUPKA: How crafty! But now the day of revenge has come! *Dies irae diem perditi.*

COUNT: I see that you lack neither education nor logic nor the necessary delicate touch. Listen! My plan for bringing peace to the world is as follows: First of all I cancel my membership in the League of Nations. This initial step will pave the way for a clear-sighted Realpolitik. Then the Danzig question will be solved as the most pressing problem. Nothing could be simpler: Poland receives access to the Mediterranean by means of a corridor straight through Eastern Europe.

HUPKA: And what will the other nations say to that?

COUNT: They will say what the papers say. The Italian government will be piqued of course, but I have already thought of that! As compensation Italy gets the islands of Rhodos and Malta.

HUPKA: Ingenious. *Hic* Rhodos, *hic* Malta! But what will the inhabitants say?

COUNT: They will say what they will be permitted to say. Now, the British government, on the other hand, will be furious. This is where that delicate touch comes in. As compensation, the British Empire receives the exclusive right to use the Suez Canal.

HUPKA: I get the idea. By way of compensation the Egyptians will get Manchuria, and the French get the Dutch Indies. In exchange the Dutch will get Schleswig-Holstein, and the Danes get Cuba; the Americans a free port in Luxembourg, the Luxembourgians an air base on Potsdam Square in Berlin, and the Russians get a knock on the head.

COUNT: From the entire civilized world.

HUPKA: You have grasped the world situation. Your plan is the Eureka of Columbus!

COUNT: And the only way to achieve world peace.

HUPKA: The only thing I'm wondering about is what the people . . .

COUNT: I don't understand why you keep mentioning the people. The people are the responsibility of the Home Office. Whoever said that you need a people for making foreign policy?

GWENDOLYN (*enters. She is beside herself*): Luitpold! It's all over!

COUNT (*kisses her hand*): Gwendolyn, I thank you! For ten years my shadow, fate-encumbered, has been standing in the wings of the European political stage, but starting today . . .

GWENDOLYN: It's all over, sweetheart! I'm ruined!
COUNT: . . . I have the opportunity again to exercise my diplomatic sensitivity . . .
GWENDOLYN: I am the unhappiest woman in the world! I'm done for! (*Sobs.*)
COUNT: . . . to the fullest. But you seem to be less cheerful today than usual. Or is my sensitivity deceiving me?
GWENDOLYN: The telegram! (*Sobbing, she holds out a telegram.*)
HUPKA: Allow me as a complete outsider . . . (*Takes the telegram, reads:*) "Black Friday. Your stock yesterday 22. 26, today nil comma zero. Shareholder set fire to Gwendolyn Building. Stop. Protest march to Roosevelt. No hope whatsoever. Expect instructions."
GWENDOLYN (*sobbing*): That's been lying on my desk for days, Luitpold. Why didn't you open it?
COUNT: On principle, dearest. Any communication has to be left alone for at least two weeks to let the situation mature.
HUPKA: This time, if you pardon my saying so, the situation seems to have reached full maturity.
GWENDOLYN: I am ruined, Luitpold! I have hardly ten thousand dollars left. I am a beggar.
COUNT: I don't understand a thing.
GWENDOLYN: You have to do without your Foreign Office.
COUNT: I can't make head or tail of it.
HUPKA: It must have been a bassoonist.
COUNT (*collapses on a chair*): I understand everything. Europe is lost.
GWENDOLYN: And here I was all ready to give you a state for your birthday. My poor Luitpold.
COUNT (*sunk in gloom*): Three invisible powers are poisoning the marrow in my bones. I am the world-ash and they are gnawing at my roots.
HUPKA: Just a minute, Your Excellency. Maybe it isn't really necessary that you lose your mind completely.
GWENDOLYN: Hupka, I'm giving you notice. At the end of the month I'll have to deport you, and you'll have to turn in your citizenship.
HUPKA: Hold it! Hold it! Didn't Your Excellency say yourself

that for making foreign policy you don't need a people? If there's no need for a people, there's no need for a country. Ergo: it's quite conceivable to have a state without a country, isn't it?

GWENDOLYN: I don't understand a thing.

COUNT: Certainly, certainly.

HUPKA (*ecstatically*): Never mind! All we need for a state is a presentable name. Every state that has some self-respect calls itself after a hotel or a restaurant. Let's think . . . well, you know the name of a café, don't you? . . . Café de France—we've got a France already . . . Café de l'Europe?—We've got a Europe, too . . . Shucks, the nicest names have all been snapped up already . . . What about Rathskeller Republic? Too musty . . . Dukedom Moulin Rouge? Too sexy . . . Hofbräu Monarchy? Not democratic enough . . . Burgerkingdom? No decent state would have a name like that . . . Astoria? . . . I've got it: The Kingdom of Astoria!

(*Lights out.*)

Scene Three

(*Salon at the Astorian Embassy. Grand Duchess Anastasia M.; Lady P., Lord R., G. B. Shaw; Gwendolyn; James, the Butler.*)

GWENDOLYN: Oh, how charming, how discreet
    That the party's choice elite
    Has so charmingly withdrawn
    To our Japanese salon.
    Oh how sweet of you to call!
    How you make this evening shine!

GUESTS: Not at all, at all, at all!
    I am sure, the pleasure's mine!

BUTLER: This soirée has rightly promised to blossom into one of the most dazzling social events of the London season.

GWENDOLYN: I'm delighted, I'm excited!

Brilliant minds from every sphere!
Art and industry united!
All of *Who Is Who* is here!
Every word profound and witty!
How you make this evening shine!
GUESTS: Wits are witty with the pretty!
I am sure, the pleasure's mine!
BUTLER: Among other celebrities we notice the charming wife of the bearer of one of the oldest names in the country, Lady P.
LADY P.: I only wear creations of famous names like Paulette Greenbaum.
BUTLER: Grand Duchess Anastasia M., in exile until further notice, who as insiders tell us has put her ravishing beauty at the service of the espionage departments of the superpowers.
ANASTASIA (*laughs her infamous scale of laughter*): Hahahahahaha! (*In matter-of-fact tone*:) Take note: Grrrand Duchess Anastasia. Only at 7a Nelson Street.
BUTLER: Lord R., Chief Executive of the R. Newspaper trust. A distinguished representative of revisionism.
LORD R.: All raped nations, attention! Don't despair! Take your problems confidently to Lord R.! Success guaranteed! Numerous thank-you letters.
BUTLER: George Bernard Shaw, one of our most popular cynics.
SHAW: Europe has another twenty-four hours to live. We will be superseded by the Hottentots. Early to bed and early to rise makes a man healthy, wealthy, and wise.
GUESTS: Oh how cunning and how stunning!
Oh how drastic and sarcastic!
GWENDOLYN: Every word, how castigating,
Perspicacious, devastating,
Uninhibited and snappy!
How you make my evening shine!
SHAW: I am happy, happy, happy
To be here. The pleasure's mine.
GUESTS: The pleasure's his and hers. And ours and theirs. And thine and mine.
HUPKA (*enters, elegantly dressed in a tuxedo decorated with*

medals): Ladies and gentlemen, girls and boys! Welcome to our dingy den!

ALL (*except Gwendolyn*): Oh, the Ambassador! (*They surround him.*)

LADY P.: Has his Excellency, the Count, not returned from the Foreign Office yet? Why is he staying so long?

HUPKA: Look here, it goes without saying that I am obliged to wrap myself in half-official silence about the matter. But because I like you, I'll let something leak out from a well-informed source. The conference in the Foreign Office centers around the squaring of the round table.

LORD R. (*to Shaw*): Complete nonsense. This Hupka seems to be a diplomat who knows all the tricks.

SHAW: The first diplomat in history was Adam.

LADY P.: How profound!

ANASTASIA: Hahahaha! And Eve?

SHAW (*in quick repartee*): Was his wife!

ANASTASIA: I admiit defeat.

LORD P.: You are still the most brilliant woman of Europe. (*To Gwendolyn:*) Apropos, Countess, where exactly is your beautiful home country?

GWENDOLYN: Oh yes? I beg your pardon?

LADY P.: You mean to say, milord, that you don't know? Astoria is in the Tyrol, of course, and the name of the capital is Reinhardt.

LORD R.: Milady is thinking of Austria whose capital, however, is . . .

SHAW: Lord R. is the only Englishman who knows his geography. Geography is his philosophy. I am in favor of abolishing geography. That would be the only way to prevent wars.

GWENDOLYN: Really, how sardonic! May I now ask the ladies and gentlemen to retire to the Malayan salon? The Astorian jazz band will play Viennese songs in their proper setting.

LADY P.: Oh, wunderbar!

(*All leave the room except Anastasia.*)

ANASTASIA (*wads up her lace handcherchief, frowns, pretends to exit to the left, returns to middle of stage, screws up her eyes, hisses mysteriously*): Kharrrasho! (*Grand exit to the right. She bumps into Hupka who is returning to the salon.*)

HUPKA: Excuse me!

ANASTASIA (*meaningfully*): Nichevo! (*She looks after him with devouring eyes.*) You also like Tschaikowsky?

HUPKA: Add a little rum and a drop of lemon and you can't beat it. (*Has sat down at the bar.*)

ANASTASIA: Hahahahaha! (*She exits.*)

HUPKA: Another schemer. It's a tough life.

GWENDOLYN (*reenters, nervous*): Don't drink so much! Every careless word endangers the existence of our state.

HUPKA: If that were all! In this respect Astoria wouldn't be any exception among civilized nations. But there are a thousand other things that hurl us from Charybdis into the frying pan. The suspicious circumstance that weighs most heavily against our country is that we have absolutely no use for tourists.

GWENDOLYN: So you have talked to that dreadful wildlife explorer who wants to traverse Astoria from end to end?

HUPKA (*gloomily*): With light-meter, flashbulbs, and telephoto lens.

GWENDOLYN: I've told him off already. I told him that Astoria was an impassable mountain region where even the most experienced mountain climbers break their necks.

HUPKA: What a fortunate coincidence! I told him Astoria is one vast expanse of swampy mudflats where malaria rages. Only it didn't work. The more tsetse flies and snakes I dished up for him the more hepped up he got about exploring Astoria. Finally it turned out that he wants to find certain death no matter where because his wife's unfaithful.

GWENDOLYN: Hupka, have you already decided on which continent Astoria is supposed to be?

HUPKA: Not yet. Unfortunately we won't be able to avoid putting it somewhere.

GWENDOLYN: To me our future looks pretty dark.

HUPKA: I see that you are informed about the light situation then?

GWENDOLYN: The light situation? What do you mean?

HUPKA: In fifteen minutes the lights will go out in the whole building because we haven't paid the electric bill.

GWENDOLYN: What a scandal!

HUPKA: Your fault. You should have budgeted the last ten thousand bucks better. Not that it would make much difference—not now that we are at loggerheads with the British Empire.

GWENDOLYN: How did that happen?

HUPKA: Well, what was I supposed to say when this Lord R. comes up to me and announces that the King of England wants to visit our capital?

GWENDOLYN: What did you say?

HUPKA: Thanks, I said. But unfortunately we can't have visitors right now.

GWENDOLYN: Why not?

HUPKA (*shrugging his shoulders*): It's time for our spring cleaning, I said.

GWENDOLYN: But that's a deadly insult to the whole British Empire!

COUNT (*enters, very ceremoniously*): My dear Ambassador, I thank you.

HUPKA: Don't mention it.

GWENDOLYN: Luitpold! Have you been arrested?

COUNT: Invested, dearest, invested with my new responsibilities. The skill of our dear Hupka has put the grinding machinery of our Foreign Office into a gallop.

HUPKA: Come off it, you're puttin' her on. What did my skill have to do with it?

COUNT: He insulted the British Empire most grievously. As a first consequence, France refused to recognize our Fatherland. To spite the French, Germany immediately took up diplomatic relations with us. For that reason, we were refused recognition by the Little Entente, which automatically led to our recognition by Italy the next day, which meant, of course, recognition by Austria and Hungary as well. By the same token, the Americans refused to recognize us, and to protest their move, the Japanese did recognize us. And after all the pros and cons had been carefully weighed, we were finally recognized by the British Foreign Office.

HUPKA: It should take us at least ten years to get out of this ungodly mess.

COUNT (*proudly*): At least! That's what diplomacy is all about! Astoria's position as a bulwark between East and West burdens my shoulders with a European mission. And now I'm going to hand out medals. (*Exits proudly.*)

HUPKA: Where, if you please, did this blissfully ignorant old gentleman get the idea that Astoria lies between east and west?

GWENDOLYN: He explained it to me this morning at breakfast. Only decadent states do not lie between east and west.

(*The guests reappear laughing. They are carrying a globe.*)

GWENDOLYN: Oh, how cute! What a cute globe! So nice and round . . .

LADY P.: You know, Countess, what our G. B. S. just said?

SHAW: I said that Astoria does not exist.

(*Silence.*)

GWENDOLYN: Cute!

HUPKA: Jumping Jehoshaphat!

SHAW: In the same breath I also said that England does not exist and America doesn't exist either.

LADY P.: Just listen to that! The most perspicacious aphorism of his life.

LORD R.: But by means of the globe we have proven to our literary lion that England and America do exist.

SHAW: Geography is a political argument but no proof.

LADY P.: Oh, how droll.

Astoria, At the Embassy. Wiener Studenten-Theater, 1965.

LORD R.: The only country we have not been able to find is the Kingdom of Astoria. Funny, isn't it?
HUPKA: Hahahaha! (*Everybody looks expectantly at him and Gwendolyn. Hupka stands up. He is drunk.*) Nothing easier than that! You can't miss it. You go straight across the Pacific and down another three republics on your right. At the third oil well you hang a left, cross the Rio de Peroxide.
LORD R.: And where is that?
HUPKA: Well, if you don't even know that I can't explain to you where Astoria is.
LADY P.: Then show us on the globe.
HUPKA: In that case I'd rather explain it. *Astoria divisa est in tres partes Quarum unam appellant cis secundum trans tertiam etcetera cum grazia ad infinitum. Corriere della sera. Caveant consules. Astoria ipsa lucus a non lucendo. Apres nous cum grano salis. Jedze Polska ne signela. Astoria quasi una fantasia quo usque tandem ceterum censeo Carthaginem esse delendam. Vive l'Empereur*!
LADY P.: He speaks Astorian.
SHAW: Astorian and Usbekish are the languages of the future.
HUPKA (*trying to get the globe out of sight*): Oh, our Astorian nights! When the murmur of the balalaika blends with the

dull roar of the sharks; when the alpine mountain giants melancholically look at their mirror image in the asphalt and when the tame gnus hurry to their watering places; when the earth clods are steaming and the waves of the Pacific are dreaming of Columbus and the Vikings! Oh, girls and boys! Let us talk about the Vikings. The Vikings can be divided into various categories, the first one being . . .

LADY P.: You have made us anxious to know more about your wonderful country. Where is it?

HUPKA (*spinning the globe*): How can I show you where it is when the globe is turning so fast?

SHAW: The earth is not turning! That is a Galileian prejudice!

EVERYBODY: Very true.

(Enter the Count holding a bunch of medals.)

HUPKA (*in utmost despair*): Your Excellency! Hic-

GWENDOLYN (*furious*): Control yourself!

HUPKA: Your Excellency! Hic-

LADY P. (*softly*): Listen! The Astorian national greeting!

(Everybody passes the word.)

EVERYBODY: Your Excellency! Hic!

COUNT (*astonished*): Hic?

LORD R.: But the whole matter remains highly suspicious. Where is this Astoria?

COUNT (*steps up to him*): Lord R., you have always warmly recommended the revision of Astorian boundaries. Continue your noble efforts as Grand Nabob of the Astorian Fleece.

LORD R.: My last visit to Astoria convinced me that the integrity of your boundaries must be restored with all due speed!

SHAW: But tell me in the name of free critical thought within the European mind where exactly is this As . . . ?

COUNT (*interrupts*): Upon you, my dear maestro, I am bestowing, in recognition of your endeavors to spread Astorian ways of thinking and manners of thought throughout the world, the Astorian Order of the Beaver, Third Class, tax-exempt and deductible.

SHAW: My last visit to Astoria convinced me that Astoria is the most progressive country in the world.

LADY P.: But, dearest, where is your beautiful As . . . ?

COUNT (*interrupts*): To you, Lady P., I entrust, together with the Cross of the Order, Second Class, the patronage of our Astorian relief work for veterans and orphans. You have always been a good mother to our orphans.

LADY P.: Social welfare in Astoria, your beautiful country, is indeed exemplary!

ANASTASIA: Goood, but vherrre, vherrre . . .

COUNT: Grand Duchess! Upon you, as the most prominent victim of Bolshevism, I bestow the honorary citizenship of Astoria and an annual appenage of 30,000 pounds.

ANASTASIA: I know and luf your prrriimitive mystic countrrry! Oh, I luf the patient Astorrrian Mushik . . . Hah, good moter Astorrria!

HUPKA: (*has toasted each of these ceremonies and emptied his glass every time. He is utterly stoned. He turns the globe*): Girls and boys, I can't find this blasted Astoria.

EVERYBODY: But why not? (*All persons are pointing to the globe from the other end of the room.*) There it is!!!

HUPKA: Oh, I see . . .

(*Meterman from the power company enters. Gwendolyn bumps into him.*)

METERMAN: If the lady does not pay immediately, I'll have to turn off the electricity this very minute.

GWENDOLYN: Listen! We have a secret pact with Japan.

METERMAN: Why don't the Japs pay your light bill then?

GWENDOLYN (*rips Hupka's medal off his chest*): I herewith bestow upon you the Order of the Suspender, First Class.

METERMAN: Much obliged. And now I'll turn off the juice.

HUPKA (*rushing up to the Meterman*): One more minute! (*Rushes over to Lord R.*) Pardon me, milord, but could you, as a friend of our country, help us out with a trifling sum?

LORD R.: What amount are you thinking of, Ambassador?

HUPKA (*looks at the light bill*): Thirty-five even.
LORD R.: May I ask what for?
HUPKA: For—hmm—for investment in electrical energy.
LORD R.: I see! For military installations! In that case I am only surprised that D. could not help you out.
HUPKA: D. did not have anything on him. It's tough just a few days before the end of the month.
LORD R. (*has been thinking*): Not a bad idea. In the form of an investment I could—just to play a trick on Rockefeller—
HUPKA (*encouraging him*): Splendid! Let's play a trick on Rockefeller!
LORD R. (*shakes hands with Hupka*): It's a deal.
HUPKA (*holds out his free hand for the money*): Thanks.
LORD R.: You are welcome.
HUPKA: But, Your Lordship—
LORD R.: Yes?
HUPKA: Hi there! And what about the money?
LORD R. (*laughing*): You are a joker, Ambassador. No really, thirty-five-hahaha—I really don't have thirty-five million on me, hahaha!
HUPKA (*embarrassed*): Hahaha . . .
LORD R: Or were you thinking of Astorian currency?
HUPKA: Of course I was thinking of . . . (*wants to say whatchamacallit, realizes his chance of inventing the Astorian currency*) whatchama . . . of watchamas and . . .
LORD R.: And what is it worth, your currency?
HUPKA (*almost shouting*): One devalued whatchama equals 15 whatsits which is the same as 73 whoozis which again equals 98 whatchmawhoozis. (*He rushes to the meterman.*) I'll pay you in watchamas.
METERMAN: And I'll turn off the light.
HUPKA: Okay, go and turn it off then, you . . .
GWENDOLYN: Hupka, what are you saying?
HUPKA: Listen, we've already got a state system, we've got state medals, secret military alliances, a national greeting, and inflation. Naturally, there are still a few things missing, but things are nevertheless brightening up!
METERMAN: Without light.

GWENDOLYN (*to Hupka*): I understand. Not much can happen to us anymore. (*To the Meterman:*) Go ahead and turn your light off if you want. We'll say it was a short circuit. Just a second. There's one more thing we need at this moment! The most sacred heritage of our tradition! A national anthem! Hupka, think up a national anthem, but quick before the light goes out.

(*Hupka roars the anthem; everybody joins in. It is getting dark quickly.*)

Scene Four

(*In front of the gates of the Astorian Embassy. Paul and Pistoletti are asleep. Paul wakes up from the cold.*)

PAUL: Cold!
PISTOLETTI (*who is now waking up*): You can't ever be satisfied. Either frostbite or sunburn—man can't have both at the same time.
PAUL: If they only hadn't kicked us out of the joint . . .
PISTOLETTI: Did you by any chance actually believe that the innkeepers in London wouldn't kick out a bum?
PAUL: That's what I thought.
PISTOLETTI: And why did you think that?
PAUL: Because of the sportsmanlike character of the British nation.
PISTOLETTI: Then it serves you right. (*Lies down again.*)
PAUL (*after a pause*): Cold.
PISTOLETTI: Cold but sober. In a drunken state the human being is a brute. Aren't you at all happy about your human dignity?
PAUL (*shivering*): I am. But if I could sit somewhere in a human joint and have something to eat and drink . . .
PISTOLETTI (*raising himself; kindly*): The young generation has no logic. In such a case you would be stoned again, ergo a

beast again, ergo you wouldn't have no human dignity no more.

PAUL: But I'd be happy.

PISTOLETTI: Exactly. Either happy or a human being—man can't be both at the same time.

PAUL: I don't believe that!

PISTOLETTI: You'll have to believe it. Just take a look at the world.

PAUL: That's what I'm gonna do. And somewhere in this world—

PISTOLETTI: "Somewhere in this world!" That song I sang with the rest of them when I hit the road for the first time. Either young and stupid or old and smart. Man can't be both . . .

PAUL: You and your "either-or." And I'll say it anyhow: somewhere in this world . . . !

PISTOLETTI: And where is that somewhere, smarty?

PAUL (*despondent*): Where? (*A moonbeam falls upon the sign of the Astorian Embassy.*) In Astoria, for instance.

PISTOLETTI (*interested*): Astoria? Never heard of it.

PAUL: I haven't either. That's why.

PISTOLETTI: I see. You're nuts. Either nuts or hopeless—man cannot be both at the same time.

PAUL (*softly*): Shut up, Pistoletti. In Astoria the streets are heated in the winter so the homeless won't freeze. In every sidewalk beer-garden bunches of bananas grow, ripe ones, from the West Indies. In Astoria people don't get stoned 'cause they are unhappy but 'cause they're happy. 'Cause in Astoria everything's free. Even the money. And the girls wear summer dresses . . . (*The moonbeam leaves the embassy sign.*) But you ain't interested. All you want is sleep.

PISTOLETTI (*jumping up*): Who's asleep, you young whippersnapper? D'ya think anyone can sleep while you're talkin' like that? You want me to believe there is such a place? So much happiness in one spot?

PAUL (*firmly*): There's got to be a place like that. The bigger the misery's in other places, the bigger the happiness must be in Astoria. Automatically. Or nothing's gonna balance out in the world.

PISTOLETTI (*softly*): Why did I ever take you along, you nutty

Astoria, Chawwerusch Theater, Herxheim, 1991. Sabine Felix (Pisto), Ben Hergl (Paul).

of-a-gun. (*In sudden rage*:) Who says things have to balance out in this world?

PAUL: But they've gotta. Or what would we be livin' for?

PISTOLETTI: What for? I'll tell ya. Suppose I go to the grocery wholesaler round the corner and ask for a job unloadin' the trucks. Our chance is one in a hundred thousand. On the other hand, if we are dead our chance is zero. Do you now understand the difference between being dead and being alive?

PAUL: That difference is too small for me. (*Lies back in the shadow of the building. Pistoletti exits. Pause. Enter Hortensia and Rosa.*)

HORTENSIA: But Rosa, that was another gentleman you let pass without a word.

ROSA: That was no gentleman, Hortensia, that was a man.

HORTENSIA: He who scorns the penny deserveth not the pound. Pride cometh before a fall.

ROSA: You know, Hortensia, it is very kind of you to initiate me into the business and to let me work in your turf and all, but I'm afraid I don't have any talent.

HORTENSIA: You've got talent all right but you don't have any principles.

ROSA: Quite possible. And I am not thrifty enough.

HORTENSIA: Youth knows no virtue.

ROSA: That's probably it. I'm too indecent for a streetwalker. And because I'm so indecent, I'm always thinking of what I'd be thinkin' of if I were doing it, and it turns my stomach. And then I quickly think of somethin' else so that I don't have to think of—it.

HORTENSIA (*motherly*): And what else are you thinkin' of, child?

(*Moonbeam.*)

ROSA: I'm thinking of this country here, of Astoria.

HORTENSIA: You wanna go into business there?

ROSA: In Astoria nobody does business. In Astoria everything's done out of love. Or not at all. Even the most decent and most wealthy women there marry out of love. In Astoria women get babies not out of unhappiness but because they're happy. All people live in small houses in the country. Everybody has a little garden with glass ornaments and hammocks and violet-beds and deer and flamingos. And they've got a marriage law there that a man can marry a woman only if he invents a word of endearment for her that no one else has ever used.

HORTENSIA (*moved*): But there can't be a place like that. Impossible.

ROSA: But there's got to be. Or how else could I be thinking of it? We must get what we are thinking about from somewhere. Maybe we all heard about Astoria once and then somehow forgot it. But we've always had a feeling that we'll remember it again, some day. And that's why we went on living. Or what would we be living for, anyway—what else would we be living for?

(*Moonbeam disappears.*)

PAUL (*from the shadow*): For makin' the difference greater!

HORTENSIA: There you are, child, there is another customer. In your business dealings be correct and meet the buyer halfway but give him nothing on credit. Don't waste any time with formalities. Time is money, my child. (*Exits.*)

ROSA: Yes, Hortensia. (*Reluctantly she approaches Paul.*) Wanna come along?

PAUL (*smiling*): Just like that? Ever heard of sayin' hello to people?

ROSA (*shy*): Good evening.

PAUL (*laughs*): There you are. That's a good girl. You don't seem to have much experience, do ya? You don't seem to know life yet.

ROSA: Hortensia says she knows life. But I don't want to live that kind of a life.

PAUL: And you're not goin' to. Are you cold? Are you sleepy? Come on, sit here.

ROSA (*obeys*): So you wanna come with me after all.

PAUL: Of course! You'd be scared stiff to go on that long trip all by yourself.

ROSA: On what long trip? (*Moonbeam falls on the sign.*)

PAUL: That country is on the other side of the globe, on the antipodes, you see? The farther away, the more beautiful it is. Just imagine: The voyage was rough . . .
ROSA: The voyage was rough . . .
PAUL: But now we've finally landed in our new home country.

(Open scene change: Fantastic tropical landscape with palm trees and factory smokestacks. Bright noon. Paul and Rosa under a palm tree.)

ROSA: Look how big the sun is here. As big as a millwheel.
PAUL: That's what the antipodes are like. Just watch how fast you'll have a tan. (*A banana drops.*) Wanna banana? When the bananas are ripe, they fall off the tree by themselves.
ROSA: Really? Look, there comes your friend.

(Enter Pistoletti. He wears a gigantic straw hat and is loaded down with brightly-colored fruit.)

PAUL: Hi, Pisto.
PISTOLETTI: Damn it, it's hot. See how they loaded me up at the supermarket? (*Puts down his basket.*) As soon as the siesta is over, you get on it, hear? You young whippersnapper, on with your work!
ROSA: Work? Did I hear work? You've got work?
PAUL: Sure. In the supermarket.
PISTOLETTI (*laughs*): Hahaha! Supermarket? Hahaha—you nut, what are you doin' in a supermarket? I thought you worked at a lathe.
PAUL (*smiles*): Of course I work at a lathe. I was just pullin' your leg, Pisto. I've a job in the steel plant. In Pisto-Stroi.
PISTOLETTI (*with a gesture of modesty*): Well, really, that wasn't necessary.

(Ringing of bells.)

ROSA: Somebody is getting married.

(Enter Hortensia and Jacob as bride and groom.)

ROSA: My God! Hortensia and Jacob, her fiancé!
JACOB: My dear Rosa, I am through with bein' just a fiancé.
HORTENSIA: After thirty years. But now he's given up cards and smokin'—and drinkin' . . . and knifin' . . . and his second fiancée . . . and his third fiancée . . . and he's given up safe-crackin' and that's what he liked best of all.
JACOB: Oh yes. We change with changed circumstances. For you, my dear Rosa, it's high time to find your man, too.
ROSA: A customer, you mean?
JACOB: No, my child, a man, a husband.

(Hortensia and Jacob have paraded round the stage in a dignified manner and now they exit.)

PISTOLETTI: That's right. But don't show up late for work. Mr. Foreman! *(picks up the basket and exits.)*
PAUL: I'm a foreman now—now we can settle down and start livin'.
ROSA: Look how blue the sky is. That's the only real blue.
PAUL: Because the world is ours now, understand? The fields, the palm trees, the houses, the factories.
ROSA: And the sun. As big around as a millwheel! But that's . . . that's a happy endin'! *(Kiss.)* While you're up, dear, hand me a grapefruit from your buddy's basket, will ya?
PAUL: *(Looks up. Sees that the sun has disappeared and that everything is as it was before. Rosa, who has closed her eyes, is not aware of the change.)*
ROSA *(sleepily)*: Where's the grapefruit? What's the matter?
PAUL: Nothing's the matter. Just wait a little—sleep a little longer. You can dream a little longer.

(The sky has become gray.)

ROSA: I'm afraid that the sky's gray again.
PAUL: The sky isn't gray.

(Rosa goes on sleeping leaning on his shoulder. Paul sings the song "When the Sky Turns Gray":)

Far in the distance now the stars,
Our brothers, have died away.
And from a gray and leaden sky
Down weighs another day.
Mankind wakes up in wretchedness
And kills and prays and cheats.
The times are sick, their evil breath
Goes gasping through the streets.

Get up! You aren't at home, you bum,
Move on, it won't get lighter.
What you've been hoping for won't come.
The sky will not get brighter.
This is another poor folks' day
Of blood and tears and sorrow,
A day like a thousand days before,
Not our hopes' tomorrow.

It won't be the day that we have seen
In visions of brilliant sun,
Of blossoms bright in luscious green,
Of a world that we had won.
Pick up your pack, sneak out of sight.
The cops are around for sure.
Hide, oh hide the dream of night,
The sunlight dream of the poor.

PISTOLETTI *(from outside)*: Paul! Paul!

(Paul and Rosa have jumped up. Pistoletti comes rushing in waving a newspaper page.)

PISTOLETTI: There! Read!
PAUL *(reads haltingly)*: "During the international economic conference in London a sensational incident occurred. When the debate on the unemployment problem was opened . . ."

PISTOLETTI (*snatches the paper out of Paul's hand*): " . . . the Astorian Ambassador Hupka got up and made the following solemn statement . . ." (*He interrupts himself.*) Hupka? Hupka? I know that guy!
PAUL: Go on, will ya!
PISTOLETTI: " . . . solemn statement: 'Among the total population of Astoria there is, at this point in time, not a single unemployed person. (*Long pause. All three stare at the gate of the Embassy. Then Pistoletti pulls himself together and goes on reading:*) Not a single Astorian is sick, not one is starving. The infant mortality rate in Astoria is nil.'" (*In the meantime Hortensia has entered, dragging Jacob with her. They all listen. Long silence; they all stare at the gate. Then, as if under a compulsion, all three shout simultaneously:*)

ALL: Open up! Open! Open!

(*The door opens. Out comes Hupka, very elegantly dressed. He stops a second in surprise and indecision, and then tries to pass through the people in front of him. Pistoletti recognizes him.*)

PISTOLETTI: Hupka, buddy!
HUPKA (*coldly:*) I don't know you.
PISTOLETTI: So you've become a Mr. Hupka, have you? A Mr. Hupka!
HUPKA (*embarrassed*): What do you want?
ALL (*rushing up to Hupka*): An entry permit to Astoria!
HUPKA (*embarrassed, sneaks out through the wings.*)
PISTOLETTI (*sings the "Chanson of Honor":*)

> Want a place near by the fire?
> And some room for others, too?
> Noble Man must aim much higher,
> Creature comforts will not do!
> Higher spheres must fill your yearnings;
> Spirit sets off man from brute!
> Honor seek, not daily earnings,
> Honor, honor absolute.

Winter's merciless and cruel,
Sends its icy blast to kill.
Men of honor won't need fuel,
They're above all earthly chill.
Moral laws will keep them sweating,
Cheaper far than wood or coal.
Honor is their central heating,
Anti-freeze of lofty souls.

"Poor but honest" be your aim.
Honors always are to spare.
Honors will adorn your name,
Though you have no shirt to wear.
Scorn all things that are material:
Poverty is but a spleen.
Slums are phantoms, Honor's real:
Keep your Honor spotless clean!

Ready cash is hardly needed.
Big-scale gamblers play their game
Leaving payments quite unheeded,
Stake their honorable name.
From the big sweet Honor cake
Cut your slice like every rake.
Live on words of Honor till
The grave of Honor keeps you still.

Scene Five

(Behind the curtain a voice is repeatedly heard: "Next, please!" When the curtain rises, one sees the passport office at the Astorian Embassy. There are three windows, but only number one is open, with Hupka on duty behind it. There are posters on the walls: "Buy Astorian Oil Bonds!"—"Astorians, Pay Only Astorian Taxes!"—"Don't Visit Beautiful Astoria!" Hupka is completely worn out.)

HUPKA: Honorary citizen number 23,687, please! Don't push, please!

(In the window the applicant with the number tag 23,687 on his chest appears.)

APPLICANT: Your Honor, I'm deeply indebted to you. As you probably know from the newspapers, I was without nationality until yesterday. My home country expatriated me although, being a scientist, I gave it all I had. I shall be delighted to put myself at the service of science in my new home country, Astoria . . . Why are you laughing?
HUPKA: Why am I laughing? For 23,687 reasons, professor. But mainly I'm laughing out of sheer idiocy.
APPLICANT *(with forced smile)*: I see. Tired? Well, then let us settle the somewhat ridiculous formalities of the visa as quickly as possible . . . *(Hands him passport.)*
HUPKA: Yes, let's. Professor; unfortunately we are missing your police registration for 1934.
APPLICANT *(laughs)*: But the whole world knows where I lived in 1934. Every newspaper wrote about it, Your Honor.
HUPKA: A government official doesn't read newspapers. The only reading matter for a government official is the police registration forms. The next honorary citizen, please.
APPLICANT: But Your Honor, I . . .
HORTENSIA *(pushes forward. Says to Number 23,687)*: Go on, go on! How long are we goin' to have to listen to your drivel? I've been waitin' since five in the morning . . . *(23,-687, still protesting, is pushed aside.)*
HUPKA: The eggheads always give us the least trouble.
HORTENSIA: This time, Your Honor, I really have got everythin'. All the papers, the whole lot. Here's the inoculation certificate of my neighborhood grocer, Your Honor. Here's the marriage license of the witness at the wedding of my eldest niece. Here are 592 statements from all of my 592 fiancés testifyin' to my immaculate moral conduct.
HUPKA: You had a canary live in your household for three years without police registration?
HORTENSIA: How could I? Here, Your Honor, the police regis-

tration for the canary, and here, his death certificate.

HUPKA: But what if every canary who just took it into his head to twirp and trill all day without a permit . . .

HORTENSIA: Never without a permit! Here's the license of the Society for the Prevention of Cruelty to Animals and here the diploma of the fully licensed Twirp and Trill Society, Division Canaries . . .

HUPKA: Very well. One pound sterling tax advance and one pound oil bonds.

HORTENSIA: What? I thought the bonds were voluntary.

HUPKA: Wrong. They are spontaneously obligatory.

VOICES: Come on, come on! What's holdin' her up?

HORTENSIA (*holds on to the window ledge*): Here, Your Honor. My last savings, Your Honor!

HUPKA: All right. Can you speak Astorian?

HORTENSIA (*nonplused*): But where could I've learned . . .

HUPKA: The next honorary citizen, please.

(*Hortensia, protesting, is pushed away.*)

HUPKA Of course! (*To himself.*) The language! Ingenious idea of mine.

ROSA: If you please, Your Honor—for three weeks I've been comin' here every day, Your Honor, to get my visa, Your Honor.

HUPKA: Have you now, my child? And do you speak Astorian?

ROSA (*beaming*): Of course I can.

HUPKA: You caaaaaan?

ROSA: Perfecte! Studio applikado pane consulario. Tres semenas studio lingus astorica! Tante voluntes imigratione en Astoria. Soy pur piccolo girl. Sed enough pinke-pinke foer piccolo Toussaint-Langenscheidt, Astorian for Beginners.
(*Shows him the book.*)

HUPKA: Excellent! Well, my child, now I know only of one more clause that's tight enough to exclude all of you.

ROSA: I don't understand, Your Honor.

HUPKA: You'll understand in a minute. (*Speaking again in his official tone:*) Two hundred and fifty pounds immigration tax.

ROSA: Two hundred and fifty . . . ?

VOICES: Get on with it, go on. I've been waitin' long enough. You're not the only one.
HUPKA: The next honorary citizen—
ROSA: But where shall I get . . . (*Begins to cry.*)
HUPKA: Don't cry! (*Screams:*) Don't cry!! (*Slams the window shut, sinks down exhausted, covers his ears with his hands.*)
VOICES (*all at the same time, softly, but very urgently*): Your Honor! Your Honor!
VOICE: What about me?
VOICE: I am honorary citizen number 23,690.
VOICE: 23,692.
VOICE: 23,700.
VOICE: We have brought all the papers, Your Honor.
VOICE: All the papers! Your Honor!
VOICE (*demanding*): Right is right, Your Honor!
HUPKA (*rises*): Correct! Right is right! You must be shooed off, my friends. But at least in the proper official fashion. (*Takes a sign.*) "For details, go to window 2." (*Puts the sign over Window 1.*) And when you now come to Window 2 . . . (*Takes another sign.*) "For details go to Window 3." And at Window 3 you find out (*takes a sign*) "For details, go to Window 1." (*Has put all three signs over the windows.*) Now my friends. And since you are all pushing each other so hard and since you can only advance in one direction it will take you days before you land in front of Window 1 again. And then you'll have forgotten that you have been there before and you will turn to Window 2 and then to Window 3 and on and on like that *cum gratia ad infinitum.* With this merry-go-round, my friends, I have made an ingenious invention. At the moment I just don't know what to call it, this ingenious invention . . .

(*At this moment a hand rips the sign off Window 1. Paul appears.*)

PAUL: Dirty trick!
HUPKA: What did you say, young man!
PAUL: Damned dirty trick!
HUPKA: Thank you. You have said the word of the day.

PAUL: You miserable, cheap son-of-a-gun, you pencil pusher, you dirty son-of-a-bitch, you're tryin' to lead us around by the nose.

HUPKA: Thank you, again. High time that somebody tells me the truth to my face.

PAUL: Year after year we drag our feet through the world, covered with grime and lice—starving—and no place to call home.

HUPKA: Now you are calling back my dearest memories—one really ought to help you.

PAUL: I don't need your help. I want my right. I wanna be admitted to Astoria.

HUPKA: Say, how about givin' you a job as a lackey here at the Embassy? And your girlfriend, or whatever you have, could be a maid?

PAUL (*fascinated*): Lackey at a real palace?

HUPKA: With a gorgeous uniform, and—wait a minute—how about selecting for me thirty strong, regular young guys who would also like a fixed income? Fifteen pounds a month. And free clothing.

PAUL: But can the Embassy here use so many servants?

HUPKA: Since you have been paying your taxes so conscientiously and buying our bonds, the government has plunged into oil and extended its household considerably. Anything else you want?

PAUL: And where do we report to for the job and all that?

HUPKA: Servants' staircase. See Super-Lackey James. Anything else you want?

PAUL: And—is there any gold on the livery?

HUPKA: Nothing but. Anything else you want to say?

PAUL: No, Your Honor. Your most obedient servant, Your Honor.

HUPKA: Nothing else you want to say? Think carefully!

PAUL (*thinks carefully. Suddenly beaming, standing at attention*): Happy Easter, Your Honor! (*Exits.*)

HUPKA: Happy Easter. He can't think of anything else. Perfectly contented. And the great trip to Astoria? Forgotten. I knew that human beings could be bought, but that they could be bought that cheap! (*Sings "Song of Man Selling Himself"*:)

The raw material prices are a-booming,
The hopeful heralds of a bullish trend.
Dow Jones is stirring, Wall Street is a-blooming,
The Stock Exchange is sprouting dividends.
One stock alone cannot keep up the pace,
One kind of merchandise is losing in this race
And stays the cheapest thing in every land.
It is the reject product they call Man.

The price of Man in our modern age is
A couple of bucks apiece. Oh, Man is shrewd!
Free self-delivery and starvation wages
Make him the cheapest sucker to get screwed.
Man sells himself with all the proper wrappings,
With human dignity thrown in for trappings;
And if, dear buyer, you are low on cash,
Pay in installments for the human trash.

And if you're broke, don't think about their pay—
Just keep on buying, buy them by the herd.
Pay them with stale ideals of yesterday,
Man sells himself for any pretty word.
For of his kind there simply are too many,
He knows the market and stays cheap and meek.
He knows his value's minimal, if any.
The spirit is a bargain and the flesh is weak.

(The reply of the waiting applicants:)

Don't get too smart, you shining business light!
You overrate your creditors' good will.
A place to live and food's a human right.
If you deny it, we present the bill.
We've come at last to make you pay the price.
Man's sick and tired of being merchandise.

(*During the last stanza, noises of unrest have become audible behind the stage. The shouts of those waiting outside grow more and more impatient. People hammer so hard on the wall that it threatens to come down. At last the Butler appears.*)

BUTLER (*at the head of a group of lackeys, dressed exactly as he is, Paul and Pistoletti amongst them. Speaks very fast*): Don't worry, Your Honor. (*Blows whistle piercingly. Exits running at the head of the lackeys.*)
PAUL: Anybody who still wants anything? (*Exits.*)

(*Incessant blowing of police whistles while the choral song grows weaker and weaker.*)

HUPKA: Stop it! I don't want that either. You hear? Go back! I'm not to blame for this! Go back! (*Sinks down, powerless.*) This is chaos!

(*The whole bustle, which had lasted only a few seconds, stops quickly. The Butler reappears.*)

BUTLER: Chaos? If Your Honor permits me to make a remark: Not chaos—on the contrary.
HUPKA: On the contrary?
BUTLER: This is law and order. In this historic moment, Astoria, after a somewhat unusual initial phase of its history, has finally become what it so long pretended to be.
HUPKA: But what has it become, for God's sake?
BUTLER: A state, Your Honor. (*Exits.*)

Scene Six

(*On stage the head end of a long banqueting table the rest of which is meant to continue in the wings.*)

ANASTASIA (*whose notorious laughter was heard before the curtain rose*): Hahahahaha! Uncle Ambassadorrr is verrry funny today!

HUPKA (*with obviously forced hilarity, but all the louder*): By golly, that's me. Look at me, I'm the silver dragonfly; wheel in the champagne and the women!

GWENDOLYN (*to the guest sitting on her right who remains invisible*): Yes, milord, he used to be a simple corn farmer from Krawonian Astoria. Now the merry temperament of his ethnic tribe is coming through. And who of us can hold it against him? On a festive occasion like this one today, when our oil company is yielding dividends for the first time . . .

(General hush)

COUNT (*rises*): Ladies and Gentlemen! . . . as from a horn of plenty, or to speak metaphorically, as from a horn of plenty. (*Applause.*) Indeed. The Astorian horn of plenty has sounded louder than the vegetarian bassoon. Oil is the backbone of our national economy. With my accustomed thoroughness, I have examined the expert opinion of our consultants. Excellent, yes, excellent! Our oil is absolutely odorless. It is not inflammable and can be transported with absolute safety. Besides, it is the cheapest oil in the world.

(Applause.)

ANASTASIA (*softly to Hupka*): Is dat trrrue?

HUPKA: Why shouldn't it be true? If something doesn't exist, why shouldn't it be odorless and safe to transport? And the buyer pays as little for it as for the expert opinion of a consultant.

GWENDOLYN (*furious*): Hupka!

ANASTASIA: Chort poberi! Te dog speaks in rrrriddles! (*She hides a notebook.*)

COUNT: With its oil policy, the government of His Majesty Sedlatschek VIII, which we have the honor to represent, has achieved the status of a world power. If, up to now, Astoria's state insignia was a three-legged lion whose three legs symbolized the three points of the compass, from now on our coat of arms shall be enhanced by the addition of a horn of plenty from which lavish streams of gasoline flow over the three-legged lion. Furthermore . . .

GWENDOLYN: That's enough, darling.

COUNT (*raises his glass*): Gentlemen—The King!

EVERYBODY: Long live the King!

GWENDOLYN: Ladies and Gentlemen! Thanks to the far-sighted legislation of His Majesty's government, which we have the honor to represent, the Astorian people, through generous subscription to the government bonds, have given the state the financial means to exert a decisive influence on the Royal Oil Company. Every one of the 80,000 Astorians living in other countries has made his little contribution . . . Not to mention the citizens of the immense territory of the Astorian Kingdom who, without saying a word, have done their duty.

ANASTASIA (*to Hupka*): Vitout sayink a worrrd?

HUPKA: Not even a cemetery of deaf mutes could be quieter.

GWENDOLYN (*with furious looks at Hupka*): But our government shows its gratitude to the people. Everybody knows how hard the poor people must work in the oil fields of other countries, everybody knows how dirty that work is. In our operations you'll find nothing of the kind. Our oil is extracted in the most hygienic way imaginable. (*Applause.*)

ANASTASIA (*as above*): Iis dat trrrue?

HUPKA: I should say so! Is there anything more hygienic than speculations at the Stock Exchange?

GWENDOLYN: Cheers to the Royal Astorian Oil Company!

EVERYBODY: Cheers!

ANASTASIA (*with side glance at Hupka*): Expects me to solve puzzles, tis stinkink son of a sphinx! Must beguile hiiim vit converrrsation. (*To Hupka:*) Nice day, iis iit not?

(*At this moment Pistoletti enters and, together with James, serves. Hupka stares at him spellbound and does not answer. Instead of him:*)

GWENDOLYN: Very nice, indeed. It's pouring buckets.

COUNT: Excellent. And this magnificent virginal snow in all streets.

HUPKA (*suddenly breaking through his spell*): Be gone! Gone! Ghost. Abomination . . .

(*Pistoletti exits.*)

ANASTASIA: Vat iiis te matterrr, liiittle Astorrrian duf?
HUPKA: Was it him? Was it not him? Nonsense . . . it mustn't be him.
GWENDOLYN: Him who?
HUPKA: Who? The incarnation of my bad conscience. But that's nonsense. My bad conscience is in the hospital for the poor in St. Ulrich, and is betting with pink elephants for slivovitz.
GWENDOLYN (*to her neighbor on the right*): He is somewhat intoxicated, milord.
ANASTASIA: He iiis. Drrrunk like an Tungusian Isvoshtnik. Do you vant my soul, broterrr? Orrr my body gloink vite?

(*Pistoletti enters, and serves silently.*)

HUPKA (*is startled, and closes his eyes tight*): Both, both. Anything but to see that face again.
ANASTASIA: I sell you my verrry own daddy for two and a half kopeks.
HUPKA: Give me that daddy of yours!

(*Pistoletti glances at Hupka, then exits.*)

HUPKA (*hesitatingly opens his eyes*): Is he gone yet, that ghost of a lackey?
GWENDOLYN: Hupka! Stop it! Behave yourself, will you! You are not in a brothel but the opposite. (*To the person sitting on her right:*) But yesterday's weather, milord—that radiant blue . . .
COUNT: And, at the same time, that magnificent solar eclipse.
HUPKA: I know he'll come again. But why should I be blamed for that whole dirty business? This whole mess, the large scale swindle! When I got dragged into it, I had no idea it would turn out like this. (*Desperately he grabs the sleeve of the Count.*) That wasn't what I wanted. That was not it . . .

at all!

COUNT (*utterly unmoved*): There, one of those vandals smuggled a fish bone into my fish again. But I am the world-ash, I'm Yggdrasil.

HUPKA: Silly ass! It's easy for you. You're stupid.

GWENDOLYN: Hupka! Now be quiet and give a banquet speech, this minute!

COUNT (*after obvious nudges from Gwendolyn, knocks on his glass*): The Lord of Kravonia has the floor.

HUPKA: The floor . . .

(*Pistoletti enters.*)

HUPKA (*terrified, closes his eyes and starts screaming without opening them again*): Girls and boys! Good news! Yesterday our King, His Majesty Sedlatschek VIII of Astoria, celebrated his engagement to prince Ollapotrida Jonas Amandus, heiress apparent. So far this marriage has been blessed with twelve little boys of immaculate healthy breeding stock who are numbered, in sequence, with Arabic numbers. At the same time, my bad conscience which, from the realm of vermin-infested reality has infiltrated our presence, is standing behind me. He is about to empty a bowl of tartar sauce on my head. But without any right to do so. I am innocent. I said a magic word, girls and boys: the word "state." And all pandemonium broke loose. I called up magic powers and they got out of control. I'm like the sorcerer's apprentice: "Hence, hence you broom, To the corner of the room!" Be gone, be gone, everybody be gone! (*The speech was accompanied by catcalls expressing increasing annoyance. Finally a general scraping of chairs. Calls of "Shocking" and the like.*)

GWENDOLYN (*to the guest on her right*): But milord! He doesn't mean it that way. Why don't you stay . . . milord. (*She goes after the invisible milord and exits.*)

(*Pistoletti also exits.*)

COUNT: The company is leaving the room hurriedly, or are my

senses deceiving me?

HUPKA (*opens his eyes*): Now they're all deserting me, the cowardly dogs. They're afraid of him.

(*Anastasia mysteriously appears from behind a curtain. Hupka is startled.*)

ANASTASIA: Iiit iiis only I. I am vit you, uncle Hupka!

HUPKA: Thank God, another human being.

ANASTASIA: If you von't tell me state secrrrets prrrhaps you vill buy weapons frrrom me? Fine liiittle cannons, beautiful liiittle cannons. Uncle League of Nations need not know about it.

HUPKA: No, no. Let's not talk about little cannons.

ANASTASIA: Alrrright ten, let's talk about luf. Astorrrian luf . . . Hup . . . Hupka. Oh nos femina amadeaus mannlicher triumfadores. Nosostros sweetheart quasi Albatros non stopflight en amore.

HUPKA: Please! Don't make me lose my mind altogether.

ANASTASIA (*after a glance at her watch, suddenly in a completely changed tone*): What'ya think? I'm not losin' *my* mind with all these goings on?

HUPKA: Anastasia!! You can also speak normal?

ANASTASIA: From now till half past twelve my name is Annie, thank God. 'cause now I've my midnight break. What 'ya think? D'ya think 'cause I'm a spy I'm goin' to work overtime with no extra pay? My boss, the chief of espionage, would love that. (*She pulls out knitting things and starts knitting.*) He can go jump.

HUPKA: Go jump! Sweet sound that strikes my thirsting soul so long estranged from the dear speech of home. Miss Annie, you are the first human being in weeks who speaks to me like a human being. Praised be the Lord. (*Anastasia has stood up. Hupka is startled.*) Where are you goin'?

ANASTASIA: To the joint across the street for a bottle of pop. Let me tell ya—for eight hours a day I've gotta be around diplomats. At least in my break I wanna talk to some honest people; is that askin' too much? . . . Even if I'm only an employee of low rank. (*She exits.*)

(Hupka is alone. Pistoletti appears in the door.)

HUPKA: God Almighty! I wish the earth would swallow me up.

(Wants to disappear.)

PISTOLETTI: Has Your Lordship any other wish?
HUPKA: I—I don't even know you!
PISTOLETTI: Your Honor's most honorable power of memory apparently has been overstrained. *(Removes medals from Hupka's chest.)* With your permission, Your Honor?
HUPKA: Look, you don't know yourself what you want. Everything is in perfect order . . . in perfect order in our state. The Count is taken care of . . . I am taken care of . . . the oil is taken care of . . .
PISTOLETTI: Your Honor's memory is still too constrained. *(Removes the tie round Hupka's neck.)* Mr. Hupka has no objections, has he?
HUPKA: And the good lackeys are also taken care of . . .
PISTOLETTI: The gracious head of Your Honor is still not free enough. *(Takes off Hupka's top hat.)*
HUPKA: And as far as the others are concerned . . .
PISTOLETTI: Ah! The others! Now we are talkin', finally.
HUPKA: Look, Pisto!
PISTOLETTI: Well, whadda ya know! You even recognize me. We are makin' progress, sir!
HUPKA: Pisto? Why are you sirrin' me? How come you got out of the hospital? How did you get into this livery?
PISTOLETTI: I got into this livery 'cause that was the only way to get near you. I got out of the hospital 'cause a poor devil doesn't stand much of a chance in a game of chance.
HUPKA: I don't understand.
PISTOLETTI: Of course not. And that's why I'm sirrin' you.
HUPKA: Don't you have one good word for me?
PISTOLETTI: Sure I do. A very good one at that! Why don't you let us into Astoria?
HUPKA Why? *(Thinks desperately. Suddenly enlightened:)* Why don't I indeed! Why not? Why shouldn't I?

(Gwendolyn enters. Only Pistoletti sees her).

HUPKA *(enthusiastically)*: Now that we have money like dirt due to our oil . . . our ethereal oil . . . now we really could buy some land . . . a piece of forest . . . and settle all of you there and build factories for you and give you ploughs and land . . . give you land! *(He tries to embrace Pistoletti, but Pistoletti pushes him ungently away. Hupka sees Gwendolyn and tries to kiss her hand, enraptured with gratitude:)* You understand what I mean, don't you, Countess?

GWENDOLYN *(pushes him away)*: Oh, I understand very well what you mean. You are creating a public scandal! You have taken off your tie and are plotting with subversive elements. Your place is not with us but with the mob!

PISTOLETTI: In the name of the mob, I object vehemently!

HUPKA: But don't you understand what I mean, you two? Up to now Astoria hasn't had any land!

PISTOLETTI: No land—fantastic!

GWENDOLYN: And you want me to buy some, don't you? So that any fly-by-night geologist can *prove* that Astoria has no oil.

PISTOLETTI: No oil—even more fantastic!

HUPKA: Look here, Countess, now . . . remember the day when we met on the road and you said to me that you wanted to buy a country . . . Now that you are a stock exchange tycoon, you must show some understanding . . . !

GWENDOLYN *(laughs.)*

PISTOLETTI: A stock exchange tycoon and show understanding? That is the most fantastic idea of all. *(Gwendolyn laughs.)*

HUPKA *(helpless between the two)*: I . . . I don't understand the world anymore . . . Pisto, why don't I understand the world anymore?

PISTOLETTI: Because of your fancy collar. You don't object, do ya? *(Rips off Hupka's collar.)*

GWENDOLYN *(laughing)*: Really, my dear Hupka, I have to say no to your suggestion.

HUPKA: No? Then to hell with that Astoria of yours. And I am tellin' you right now that today I am goin' to pop the whole big Astorian bubble!

PISTOLETTI: Hupka! Buddy!
HUPKA: Pisto! Brother!

(Enter Butler.)

GWENDOLYN: James, arrest these people.
HUPKA *(exits through the window with Pistoletti)*: Astoria doesn't exist. The whole world shall hear it!
GWENDOLYN: James . . . James, you've always been my best lackey . . . Now you must help me!
BUTLER: At your service, Countess, but . . .
GWENDOLYN: But . . .
BUTLER: At your service, but now I want the power!

Scene Seven

(Coffeehouse. Journalist, Secretary.)

JOURNALIST: Write, Miss: Original report from our special correspondent in Astoria.
SECRETARY: And now what? Perhaps it wouldn't have been a bad idea if you had gone to Astoria at least for a couple of days.
JOURNALIST: Are you crazy? If a sixth continent emerged from the Pacific, no ten horses would drag me out of my coffeehouse.
SECRETARY: But what are we going to say?
JOURNALIST: We'll piece something together. Write: At this moment we are cutting our path with hatchet and machete through the impenetrable jungle of Slabovian Astoria . . .
SECRETARY: The air in this place . . .
JOURNALIST: Thanks for the tip. Write: The heavy air of the tropics fills our lungs with lead.
SECRETARY: Waiter! Bring me some café au lait, not too black.
JOURNALIST: Thanks. A black native of pygmy size appears in our path . . .
SECRETARY: Plenty of warm milk—but no skin on top!

JOURNALIST: Yuck! How cruel! His enemies had brutally scalped him.

SECRETARY: Water!

JOURNALIST: Since we are suffering from a tormenting lack of water, we cannot help the unfortunate creature. Tell me, do you know why Dr. Gerstinger has become so arrogant lately?

SECRETARY: You don't know? They've put him in charge of the official press agency of Astoria and he calls himself Chief Editor of the European edition of the Astorian National News.

JOURNALIST: Is that so? Is there such a thing?

SECRETARY: Since yesterday.

JOURNALIST: Splendid. Once there is an official news agency, *we* don't have to think up stories anymore! You can go home.

HUPKA (*enters*): You are the editor?

JOURNALIST: Who is that? Since when do we see strangers in this coffeehouse?

SECRETARY: Ambassador Hupka. He was fired yesterday. (*Exits.*)

HUPKA: I would like you to publish a very important news item, editor.

JOURNALIST: Very important? That's enough to make it dangerous. But I'll do it if you place a page-size ad in the Monday morning issue.

HUPKA: But I'm not talking about an ad; I'm talking about the fact that Astoria does not exist!

JOURNALIST: For such a fat lie you'll have to place three ads.

HUPKA: But it's true.

JOURNALIST: True? In that case it costs much more than that. I'm afraid you wouldn't be able to afford it. Perhaps we could agree on a lie of medium dimensions. I could offer to print that for two three-column ads.

HUPKA: But it is not a question of an ad in this case.

JOURNALIST: What do you mean, in this case? It's always a question of ads. (*Exits.*)

HUPKA (*calling after him*): But I am telling you, editor, Astoria does not exist.

LOUDSPEAKER (*rattles away*): Astorian power and Astorian ingenuity are taking possession of the whole world these days. At this year's World Exposition the pavilion of the Astorian Oil Company attracted special attention. (*Hupka listens with growing irritation.*) Waste-products of Astorian oil are being made into synthetic foodstuffs which are so inexpensive that for the near future the non-Astorian population of the world need not worry about nutrition problems.

HUPKA: But Astoria does not exist!

(*An apparition: a man with a charity contribution box*)

MAN: The number of Astorians living in foreign countries has exceeded the two-million mark. Contribute liberally! Help us to bridge the bitter time until we may find our fulfillment in entering our longed-for homeland.

HUPKA: Hey, buddy. Do you know where it is, this Astoria?

MAN: No.

HUPKA: And when they'll take you there?

MAN (*threateningly*): No!

HUPKA: Then why do you still believe in Astoria?

MAN: 'cause I've nothing else left.

HUPKA: But you'll never see it! Never!

MAN: Bastard! (*Tries to hit Hupka. The Man disappears.*)

LOUDSPEAKER: With the help of generous donations, the Kingdom of Astoria has succeeded in raising its armament to a level which . . .

HUPKA: Isn't there any power to stop that?

(*An officer appears.*)

OFFICER: There is indeed. And a superpower at that.

HUPKA: Your state considers Astoria its archenemy then?

OFFICER: For centuries . . .

HUPKA: . . . you have been preparing for war against a country that does not exist. There is no Astoria, therefore it has no territory.

OFFICER (*dismayed*): But where are we going to throw our bombs? Damn it, that puts us at a serious disadvantage. I shall immediately suggest to the Council of Ministers that at least our most endangered targets, the cathredals and museums be razed . . .

(The officer disappears. An old man appears.)

HUPKA: Who are you?
OLD MAN: I am Professor Ancient, the acknowledged authority on international law.
HUPKA: But is Astoria legal in terms of international law?
OLD MAN: Why not? To put it simply, in our definition, a state is identical with an army, a police force, a bureaucracy, etc. Astoria has all of those things.
HUPKA: Pardon me . . . but I've always believed that a state means fields and meadows, factories, houses, museums . . .
OLD MAN: That's what the layman thinks. The things you have enumerated belong to the concept of homeland. That's something completely different.
HUPKA: Then state and homeland have nothing to do with each other.
OLD MAN: As you see, my friend. *(The old man disappears.)*
LOUDSPEAKER: In response to numerous requests from our listeners, National Radio will start an Astorian language course for advanced students today. The course will be directed by Professor Aryano Racemaster who was awarded the state prize for literature for his Astorian peasant novel *The Sin against Astorian Blood*. As we reported earlier, Professor Racemaster recently addressed the Cultural Association in Vienna as a representative of the intellectual elite of his home country . . .
HUPKA *(in front of the loudspeaker which keeps talking, unperturbed)*: But . . . you don't have a homeland . . . You don't know what it means to have a homeland! What you are idolizing here is . . . *(Discouraged:)* They don't hear me. It's all for nothing.

(The loudspeaker falls silent. Anastasia enters.)

ANASTASIA: Of course, it's all for nothing. You're just wasting your breath. Witdraw into private life, like me.

HUPKA: Miss Annie! What are you doin' here?

ANASTASIA: Unattached lady not without means is looking for young musical retired gentlemen of principles who would like to enter into a soul relationship for the purpose of establishing a modest chicken farm. Under "Love in a Cottage."

HUPKA: But Astoria . . .

ANASTASIA: Forget Astoria! Believe me, Mr. Hupka, once this whole swindle is exposed, a bigger swindle will follow. A little house in the country . . . an orchard . . . a chicken yard . . . that is the only true Astoria. Nothing but white chickens. Wouldn't you like something like that?

HUPKA: Would I ever . . . Miss Annie.

ANASTASIA: Well, and what about me? Wouldn't you like me?

HUPKA: Would I ever . . . Miss Annie.

ANASTASIA: And have you bummed around the world enough?

HUPKA: Have I ever! See, that's why I'm so desperately looking for a piece of the world where I can say: this is home.

ANASTASIA: There you are! So why don't you want to raise white chickens under "Love in a Cottage"?

HUPKA: The white chickens aren't the point.

ANASTASIA: Oh! I like idealistic temperaments like you.

HUPKA: Actually . . .

ANASTASIA: Be sensible . . . Kilian.

HUPKA: Kilian? You said Kilian, Annie? . . . *(He is giving in:)* Oh, you . . . you white chick, you, my little chickadee . . .

(Paul enters.)

HUPKA *(sees Paul, suddenly)*: No, I don't want to.

ANASTASIA: What don't you want?

HUPKA: Be sensible. Look at this young man. He was one of those sensible people, and his sensibleness was . . .

PAUL: . . . a dirty trick.

HUPKA: This is the second time that you take the words out of my mouth, young man.

ANASTASIA: Who's that?

PAUL: This is . . . a servant whose servility is like a red-hot poker twisting in his heart . . . This is a bought soul with the thirty pieces of silver burning in his hip pocket like glowing coals . . . This is . . .

ANASTASIA: . . . a lackey who's off his rocker. Come, Kilian!

PAUL: Listen, Hupka, in half an hour they'll unveil a colossal monument to the State of Astoria in the garden of the Embassy. The speech'll be broadcast over all the stations in the world . . . are you listenin'?

ANASTASIA: So why don't you come?

PAUL: No, he's not comin'. Listen, Hupka, I am goin' to let you through the police cordon. You jump up on the speaker's platform, shove James aside and . . . and . . .

HUPKA (*in ecstasy*): . . . and hold the real unveilin' speech! Come to my heart, brother! With this liberating idea you atone for all your sins!

ANASTASIA: But gentlemen, think it through! It's already too late for all that.

(Pistoletti enters.)

PISTOLETTI: On the contrary, buddy, too early.

HUPKA (*scornfully*): Too late . . . too early . . . huh, if you're afraid, why don't you go raise white chickens with Miss Annie.

PAUL: Right! Hahahaha.

PISTOLETTI: With one rebellious lackey you wanna overthrow Astoria? Put your brains in order, buddy.

HUPKA: I'm not your buddy anymore.

PAUL: Chicken breeder.

HUPKA: You two are a pair. (*To Anastasia:*) His first name is Hypolit; in case you wanna know.

ANASTASIA: But I don't like the name.

HUPKA: You'll get used to it . . . Mrs. Too-late and Mr. Too-Early.

PISTOLETTI: You are a weather-cock, Hupka, and a fabulously stupid one at that. Mark my words.

HUPKA: We're just wasting our time. Every word's wasted on him. Come on, buddy!

PAUL: One prick of the pin and the bubble bursts.

HUPKA: Arm in arm with you I'm ready to face the slings and

arrows of outrageous fortune! (*Both exit.*)

PISTOLETTI: You'll come back with your head in a sling and the arrows in your butt.

ANASTASIA: Too bad. He would have made a first-rate chicken farmer.

PISTOLETTI: The white chickens aren't the point, Miss Annie. The point is that fate has to give this gentleman one punch in the nose after the other until he realizes that one doesn't ditch one's hobo buddies.

ANASTASIA: Punch in the nose? But he's such a handsome lad.

PISTOLETTI: There's no way out. Either a mug that's intact or a wholesome insight . . . Man can't have both at the same time.

(*Shouts offstage.*)

PISTOLETTI: You hear the shouting?

ANASTASIA: Sure. The dedication of the monument is about to begin.

Scene Eight

(*In front of the veiled monument. In the box for the dignitaries, Gwendolyn, Count, Butler.*)

COUNT: Folks! Before I begin my speech at this historic moment, I want to close it with the words: Glory is loyalty's horn of plenty!

(*Applause; Count steps aside.*)

GWENDOLYN: Dear, dear friends. Fellow sinners in this earthly valley of misery! As you know, I am not active in politics. I am only a simple businesswoman thinking of my accounts. My only concern was and is your material well-being. I am not the person to speak to you in this solemn hour. The only one called upon to speak now is our great stammerer, James.

I herewith ask our illustrious stammerer, this simple man of the people, to say a few words. Hic, James!

(Hic-calls and applause.)

JAMES: Men and Women of As . . . As . . . As . . .
CROWD: Ass . . . Ass . . . Ass . . .
JAMES *(motioning them to be quiet)*:   . . . torians. To . . . To . . . To . . .

Program of the production of *Astoria*,
Landestheater Magdeburg, GDR, 1985.

CROWD: Too . . . Too . . . Too . . .
JAMES (*motioning them to be quiet*): . . . day is a great day. I am also in the po . . . po . . . po . . .
CROWD (*after the tune of the national anthem*): Po . . . Po . . . Po . . .
JAMES (*motioning again*): . . . sition to explain to you why— Well . . . Today the last Astorian died, who was not yet a member of the voluntary association of lackeys and of would-be lackeys. A roof . . . roof . . . roof . . . roof . . .
CROWD: Ruff . . . ruff . . . (*Sounds like barking*).
JAMES: . . . tile killed him inadvertently. Peace to his ashes. From now on the Astorian population living abroad consists only of voluntary lackeys and would-be lackeys. I . . . I . . . I . . . (*straining*) . . . I'll . . . I'll . . .
CROWD: Heil! Heil!
JAMES: . . . I'll . . . I'll now share with you a confidential revelation which has been burdening my heart for some time. Astorians! For months the secret world powers, Bassoonism, Vandalism, and Vegetarianism have tried to spread the news that Astoria does not have any territorial existence. This infamous fabrication of lies is . . . is . . . is . . .
CROWD: Booooooooh!
JAMES: . . . is true. (*Thundering applause.*) Astoria has no land. What does Astoria possess? Astoria possesses the best bureaucracy, the best army in the world. What else does Astoria need? A still better bureaucracy and a still better army. And what else? Wheat fields? Ridiculous. Every modern person knows that bombers are more important than grain. Housing projects? The majority of our male population lives in the barracks of allied nations, the majority of our women in their canteens. That is together 30 percent of our population. Another 30 percent live in various prisons that have been kindly put at our disposal. (*Applause.*) The remaining 40 percent live scattered over the world on foreign soil. These noteworthy living conditions keep us from the greatest evil in this century: contentment! Our heads high, in eternal inner dynamics we tremble in excitement with accelerated pulse towards the future, be this future gloomy . . . or . . . or . . .

CROWD: Hurrah!

JAMES: . . . or gloomy. Who, then, dares say that the State of Astoria does not exist? I ask you: What deserves more to be called a state, the black Republic of Liberia which has an extensive territory but not a single tax collector, or Astoria, which has no territory but has instead the most elaborate state bureaucracy? Astoria, the most modern type of state, has raised its luminous stately head as the most consistent, most uncompromising perfection of the modern idea of a state. The state in and for and through itself. The state, freed of all side effects that in other lands pollute the very concept. The state, reduced to the state machinery. Astorians, let this epoch-making revelation be demonstrated to you through the unveiling of this triumphal monument. I have been silent long enough, have beaten about the bush too long, used too many pretty words. Let the veil drop! Men and women of As . . . As . . .

(Thundering applause. Hupka enters. He jumps up onto the speaker's platform.)

HUPKA: Folks! Fellow suckers! *(James tries to grab him.)*

GWENDOLYN *(smiling)*: Leave him alone, my dear James. It's not worth the trouble.

HUPKA: Believe me! Astoria does not exist. *(Silence. Hupka is confused.)* You don't understand. But it's so simple . . . What you have wanted, what you've been dreaming of when your stomachs were grumbling—that's a homeland, a country that is ours, understand? Our fields, our houses, our mountains . . . our piece of the world . . . yes, our homeland, that's what we want to love, that's what we want to protect. Say something! Why don't you say something? Why did you clap when this guy talked, this preserping utender . . . this pursstring surrender . . . this upursing suspender . . . this pretending usurper . . . or whatchamacallit?

(At this point the dignitaries begin to laugh. Their laughter echoes in the crowd and grows to a hilarious roar. Laughing, James takes Hupka by the collar and disposes of him with a

kick in the pants.)

COUNT *(laughing)*: James, who was this bassoonist clown?
JAMES: A bum.
GWENDOLYN: Do you know him, by any chance?
JAMES: A certain Hupka.
GWENDOLYN: Hupka? Never heard of him. *(Growing serious:)* But we are all sinners. Who would cast the first stone?!

(A moment of silence, then roaring laughter and triumphal music. Darkness.)

Scene Nine

(Country road as in Scene One. Hupka, Paul, and Pistoletti are bums again. All three singing.)

    No one would hold your ladder
    To pluck the stars out yond.
    Such are the times, such is the world,
    My brother vagabond.

HUPKA: Herewith our Astorian adventure seems to have reached its end. *Finita divina commedia.* And what did it all amount to? That instead of two, we are now three buddies without supper.
PAUL: That's something. The more the better
HUPKA: Very true. Left to himself, man either descends to the level of an ambassador, or he ascends to some kind of delirium tremens.
PISTOLETTI: Righto. You finally saw the light. Listen, I'm going to explicate the moral of the whole story. If only there was a place around here to sit down and rest a little . . .
POLICEMAN: *(enters).*
PAUL: Oh boy, here comes our chance for a . . . rrest.
HUPKA: Oh, an old friend of mine. A hearty good day to you!
POLICEMAN: Papers!

HUPKA: If I am permitted a remark, inspector, you're the same inspector who a year ago displayed such angelic kindness because your wife had delivered triplets. Why—if you pardon my asking—why are you so ill-disposed this year?
POLICEMAN: If you're so damned curious: because she got triplets again.
HUPKA: Measure for measure or, as the saying goes, *l'art pour l'art*.
POLICEMAN: Forged passports. Come with me.
HUPKA: But I beg your pardon, *au contraire*. Genuine Astorian passports.

Astoria, Scene Nine, Jura Soyfer-Theater, Vienna, 1991 from left to right: Klaus Uhlich, Christo Melingo, Franz Josef Koepp, Karl Dobravsky.

POLICEMAN (*sarcastically*): Sure. Made out by yourself. And you had the gall to sign them with your own "official" signature and to put a fake stamp on them to bamboozle the authorities.

HUPKA: No idea of intentional bamboozling. I myself was Ambassador at the time.

POLICEMAN: And you want me to believe that? Your Excellency is, as everybody knows, a former murderer with a price on his head. Come on now, everybody, you're all under arrest.

PISTOLETTI: You see, that's what ya get.

POLICEMAN: Quiet. Don't talk.

HUPKA: If we can't talk, maybe we could sing somethin'.

POLICEMAN: All right, sing somethin', to make the time go faster for me.

HUPKA: Ready?

PISTOLETTI and PAUL: Ready!

ALL THREE (*singing*):
>Are you going to bum it forever,
>Always in rags and alone?
>Is there between hell and heaven
>No piece of ground that's your own?
>Nowhere trees that blossom for you,
>No place where you belong?
>Listen, the wind in the poplars
>Is singing a new song.
>
>Look for a land that can be yours,
>Here, not in a far beyond.
>Stop searching for Astoria,
>My brother vagabond.
>And if your legs are weary,
>And your heart from hoping too long.
>Keep marching and keep singing.
>My brother vagabond.
>
>Begging for a coin in your hat
>You dragged yourself through the city.
>You won't get a homeland begging.
>They won't give it you out of pity.

So gather your friends together
And grab a shovel, a plow,
And wherever you just happen to be
Make it your homeland now:

Here is the land that will be yours,
Not in a far beyond.
Stop searching for Astoria,
My brother vagabond.
Time's worked for you all along,
For your future, there is no other.
So march with time and sing your song,
Vagabond, my brother.

(Curtain)

Vineta

CHARACTERS

Johnny, an old sailor
Anne, keeper of a harbor tavern
Kathryn, a prostitute
Town Watchman
Lady
Grumpy Senator
Merry Senator
Town Clerk
Beggar
Beggar Woman
Wife of Merry Senator
Lily, Daughter of Merry Senator
Soldier
Prisoner
Voice of Prison Guard
Citizens of Vineta

Scene One

(Inside a harbor tavern. Music and voices.)

JOHNNY *(drunk)*: Anne, hey, Anne! I say, Mother Anne! *(Anne enters.)*

ANNE: Come on now, Johnny, shut your trap!

JOHNNY: What did ya say? I'm supposed to hold my trap? In this 'establishment'? That's a new one!

ANNE: You've had enough.

JOHNNY: Enough? I'll tell ya when I've had enough, understand? I've . . . I've plowed four oceans, and I've gotten old doing it, if you wanna know.

ANNE: Kathryn, tell Johnny to shut up, will you.

JOHNNY *(enraged)*: What am I supposed to do? Shut up? Me, a paying guest? In this joint? What d'you think this is? A stinkin' old hole, that's what it is, a dump! If you wanna know. *(Kathryn enters.)*

KATHRYN *(gently)*: Sure, Johnny. You're right. And now cut it out, Johnny, you've had enough . . .

JOHNNY: Listen, Kathy, I could rock you on my knees, I could be your grandfather. When your unknown father, the rascal, wasn't even approximately born yet, I already made mulattoes in Hawaii, if you wanna know. Hey, another bottle, do you hear? Am I a payin' guest or not?

ANNE: You don't pay a damn cent, Johnny!

JOHNNY *(suddenly very depressed)*: I don't pay a damn cent is right. But it isn't very tactful to rub it in like this and tell an old man that he lives off your charity. Bah, that's not refined.

ANNE: Johnny, now . . .

JOHNNY: . . . hold your trap, hey, I know. That's what I hear all day in this whorehouse . . .

ANNE: Come here, Kathryn!

JOHNNY: Anne, what did I say? Half a bottle, I said. Remember the days when we were young! Our days of roses, Anne . . .

ANNE: I never shared any days of roses with you, not with you. And I don't want you to talk to me that way, you hear?

JOHNNY: I mean each of us separately. But at that time you still had a heart in you instead of nothing but blubber, didn't ya or did ya? For an old man.

ANNE: C'mon now, Kathryn. Mr. Ditje in box two wants to have a chat with you.

JOHNNY: Don't go away, girl. Don't leave an old man alone. I'll tell you a story from my life. (*Animated:*) Hey, boys! Everybody listen! (*He drinks.*) Johnny buys you all a drink. Johnny is goin' to tell ya a true story from his life. (*Noise continues unchanged. In the din a voice is heard:*)

VOICE: Like hell Johnny's goin' to pay! (*Laughter.*)

ANNE: And if you start bothering the guests, you'll be thrown out. Kathryn, quiet him down, will you, and then go and have your chat with Mr. Ditje.

JOHNNY (*extremely sad*): You see, Kathy? I'm supposed to be quieted down and Mr. Ditje just the opposite. You're supposed to chat—with someone else—'cause I'm an old man.

KATHRYN: You're not an old man, Johnny.

JOHNNY: You ain't foolin' me. Nobody gives a damn about me anymore. The boys don't even wanna hear my stories.

KATHRYN: Because you've told them a hundred times, Johnny.

JOHNNY: Nonsense, that isn't it! Nobody loves me anymore. And no one wants to hear my stories anymore. No one! Nobody!

KATHRYN: That's not true, Johnny. I wanna hear 'em.

JOHNNY: You do? You're a good girl, Kathy. But you know them all already, don't you? Or do you?

KATHRYN (*lying*): I sure don't. You've had so many adventures, Johnny.

JOHNNY: Haven't I? And Mr. Ditje?

KATHRYN: Mr. Ditje can chat with himself in box two.

JOHNNY: And the boys?

KATHRYN: Can go to hell.

JOHNNY: Hahaha! When those boys were still in their diapers, I was already huntin' polar bears in Calcutta. You wanna hear that one?

KATHRYN: Yes, Johnny.

JOHNNY: Or would you rather hear how I seduced the sea serpent?

KATHRYN: Yes, Johnny.

JOHNNY: Or how I drank the Flying Dutchman under the table?

KATHRYN: Yes, Johnny.

JOHNNY: No, I'd rather tell you how I lived on Vineta, in the drowned city. A whole long life I lived there. And there's a moral to the story, too. That we must be alive, girl! Alive! I mean, alive in our hearts! (*Kathryn yawns.*) Are you yawnin', sweetheart?

KATHRYN: Me?

JOHNNY: You know the story already?

KATHRYN: No, Johnny, I don't. Go right ahead, Johnny, tell me that one . . .

JOHNNY: Well, at that time I was still young, twenty-five perhaps, or twenty-six. In those days you'd have chatted with me, and all free and no charge, night after night. (*Kathryn fills his glass.*) Thanks, Kathy! Here's to you! In those days I wasn't a sailor but a diver. It was only later, after I'd been to Vineta, that I was through with divin'. Then I stayed away from the bottom of the sea. This is how it was: It was in July eighteen hundred and something, and our boat, a nutshell of three hundred tons, was anchored somewhere off the coast along the North Sea. I'd been in those parts, of course, years before. Anyway, a freighter had sunk, and we were supposed to salvage the wreck. All right. Who was the most dependable diver on board?

KATHRYN: Johnny!

JOHNNY: Right, Johnny. So Johnny's supposed to go down first and have a look around, two thousand feet below sea level. All right, I get ready. Diver's suit, lead shoes and the rest of the gear. And as I'm standin' at the railin' and I'm just gonna put on the diver's helmet, what do you think happens?

KATHRYN: A cabin boy comes runnin' . . .

JOHNNY: . . . and how! All out of breath, as if the devil had him by the neck. Johnny, he screams, don't go down, you won't come up again! Why shouldn't I, I says kind of surprised. And he: the bells! I've heard the bells ring. Well, the crew all started grinnin' of course, and the mate, who was a joker anyway, says: The cook's given you a good whack, that's why you can hear the bells ring, hahaha, but the boy says no, when the cook gives me one, it's more musical; these are church-bells, he says, and they're ringin' down in the sea. (*In the meantime Kathryn has left. The old sailor does not notice.*) And I says, your mother's fairy tales are still in your head, that's what it is, says I; what you're hearin' is nothin' but optical acoustics, that's all my boy, says I. And now reach me the helmet says I. The boy starts cryin'. Don't cry, says I, and I screw the gear right, and I go over the side, down the ladder and into the water. But as I'm sinkin' down and reach a thousand feet or so—what do I feel, Kathy? A pressure in my head, such a nasty pressure, I tell ya, and a headache just like I'm havin' now. Only now I have it from the racket in here—can't you tone it down a little, fellows!—oh well, we won't listen to them, will we, sweetie? A headache I have, and then a buzzin' in my ears—and then what do I hear? Bells! Honest to God, it's bells all right. Ding dong, ding dong. (*The tavern noises have subsided. Distant ringing of bells begins.*) I realize at once, of course, what the trouble is. Something's wrong with the air hose, understand? Well, I tug at the line, I give my signal: Pull me up, will you? Nothin' doin'. On the contrary! It's just like they were deaf and blind up there on deck, they let the line run out just as smooth as ever, and I go down and down and—damn the headache— and deeper and deeper I go. (*The bells become louder.*) Things go black before my eyes. (*The lights dim.*) I don't see nothin' no more, I don't hear nothin' no more, only those bells ringin', this damned ringin'. Do you hear it, Kathy—gettin' louder? I try to get some air, I don't get no air—there's a roar around me, a dull roar like breakers—and the bells keep dronin'—I feel like I'm about to die—like it's all over with me—all over—done and gone—and then I open my eyes and . . .

Scene Two

(Twilight. Medieval cathedral square. In the foreground, Johnny, lying on the ground. He is in the diving suit, without a helmet. The bells fade away. A Town Watchman in medieval soldier's tunic is standing in the middle of the square.)

JOHNNY *(looking around in amazement)*: Where am I? How did I ever get here?

WATCHMAN *(does not answer.)*

JOHNNY: Gee, have I been lucky. Looks like somebody saved me. But he sure didn't have any manners, whoever did it— to drag you half-dead out of the sea and then leave you lying in the street. What did you say? *(No answer.)* Or was it you who saved my life? Was it? *(He gets up.)* Damn it. Can hardly move my legs; feels like a weight's lying on them, like the air weighs a ton. Gee, am I weak! Say, you! Have I been lying here for a long time? Have I? Hmm. Excuse me, what time is it anyway? Hmm, I see, you think there's a clock here anyhow, so why ask—but that's a sundial, sir, don't you see? And since at this time, as you can see, no sun is shining . . . *(He looks at the sky.)* The sky sure looks strange today. Gray green, as if I was looking through water. Funny, isn't it? Hey! Hey, you! *(He points to the shadow of the style of the sundial which wavers strangely.)* That's why that clock keeps dancing about like crazy. Lost its direction. As if time stood still in this town of yours. Heehee. What did you say? I see, nothing. Hmm. I quite agree. But for me time is most important, man. If I've been gone for some time, the boys on board are going to worry about me. Hey, you! Do you understand? *(He looks at the silent Watchman, nonplused.)* Well, there are only two possibilities: either you're deaf and dumb or you're a monument. In the first case, you have my sympathy; in the second, I can't help remarking that you were unveiled in an extremely impractical spot because at a busier time of day you're going to be a most impractical obstruction to the traffic.

WATCHMAN: According to regulations. I regulate the traffic.

JOHNNY: Hurrah! He has God's gift of speech! Quick, my dear sir, before you fall asleep again: Where am I? What time is it? Which is the quickest way to the harbor? (*No answer.*) Oh dear! Is the conversation over again? You've spent all your energies in your detailed lecture, have you? In that case I guess I'll have to get going.

WATCHMAN: Keep going. Don't stop. Keep moving.

JOHNNY: But where shall I go? Where is the harbor of this blessed town? Which way shall I go—here? ... or ... ?

WATCHMAN: Keep going according to regulations.

JOHNNY: Sir, you must admit, for a drowned sailor communication with you is somewhat exhausting.

WATCHMAN: I regulate the traffic.

JOHNNY: I've heard that already. But what do you mean? What traffic?

WATCHMAN: The regulated traffic. According to regulations.

JOHNNY: Undoubtedly. What bothers me is that I don't see any traffic anywhere around here. (*No answer.*) Hey, I'm asking you: Is there any traffic here at all?

WATCHMAN: According to regulations, no.

JOHNNY: And?

WATCHMAN: I regulate same.

JOHNNY: I see. Well, in that case ... (*He is intimidated.*) And— tell me—maybe in this way I'll at least find out what time it is—tell me, since when have you been standing here? (*Cunningly:*) Since this morning?

WATCHMAN: Yes.

JOHNNY: Is it now noon or evening?

WATCHMAN: Yes, according to regulations.

JOHNNY: What?

WATCHMAN: Since evening.

JOHNNY: Since evening you've been standing here?

WATCHMAN: Yes, since noon. According to regulations.

JOHNNY (*he puts both hands to his head*): Now I have only one more request: Tell me that you've been standing here since the day after tomorrow and then I see clear.

WATCHMAN: Yes, according to regulations since the day after tomorrow.

JOHNNY: Thanks. Now I know you are cuckoo. But, let me go on . . .

WATCHMAN: Go on! Keep moving! Do not stop! (*Johnny is startled. He begins to feel uneasy and makes a wide circle around the Watchman and leaves. The bells begin ringing again.*)

Scene Three

(*Harbor. A Lady with luggage. Enter Johnny. The bells fade away in the distance.*)

JOHNNY: Well, here I am. A sailor will find a harbor blindfolded! (*To the Lady:*) Excuse me, madam, is this where the ships leave?

LADY: Yes, sir, this is where the boat leaves.

JOHNNY: Thank you. Do you happen to know where I could rent a dinghy? The thing is, I've been stranded in this town, so to speak, and it can't be too far out to my boat. Do you happen to know if the shipping offices are open yet? Seems to be rather early in the morning—I haven't met a single soul in the street, only a policeman in a funny outfit. And he was more dead than alive. Heeheehee. (*He is startled by the empty stare of the Lady.*) I'm sorry, just a little joke. I'm just a simple sailor, you know. Maybe the lady knows what time it is? People around here sure don't seem to talk very much. (*He clears his throat in embarrassment.*) Hmm. I see the lady is about to set out on a voyage herself.

LADY: Yes, sir. I am waiting for the ship. I want to travel to my husband. He and my little daughter are expecting me. She has blond hair and her name is Annelore.

JOHNNY: Isn't that nice? Pretty name. And where, if I may ask, do your husband and your daughter reside?

LADY (*quietly*): I don't know.

JOHNNY: I mean—well—what I mean is—where? In the sense of where?

LADY (*she looks at him without understanding him*): I have forgotten.

JOHNNY: But that's kind of embarrassing, you might say. (*Perplexed.*) I mean, if that's the case, where are you going to travel to?

LADY: Yes sir. I am waiting for the ship. I want to visit my husband. He and my little daughter are expecting me. She has blond hair and her name is Annelore.

JOHNNY: Well, well, you don't say. Pretty name. And when does the ship leave?

LADY: Yesterday.

JOHNNY: Oh, yesterday, is that so?

LADY: Certainly, sir.

JOHNNY (*crushed*): Then it was not the policeman—it's me! Please, madam, help me. Please tell me if the following sentence is crazy or not: If a ship leaves yesterday it doesn't leave today and it doesn't leave tomorrow, which means it doesn't leave at all.

LADY (*she smiles*): I am waiting for the ship, sir, I feel very lonely for my husband and my little daughter. I will be very happy when I can kiss them again. I cannot be without them.

JOHNNY: And the ship is leaving yesterday?

LADY (*very firmly*): Yesterday. She has blond hair and her name is Annelore.

JOHNNY (*utterly confused*): Pretty name . . . You don't mind, do you? I'm a little groggy. (*He lets himself drop on the bench next to the Lady.*)

(*The Merry Senator and the Grumpy Senator enter.*)

MERRY SENATOR: All right then, Senator, I'll give you the ten carloads of wheat for twenty-twenty. My last word. Take it or leave it. We are no babes in the woods. Hehehe. Hahaha.
GRUMPY SENATOR: Senator, you don't take our business seriously. You know that I'm only a shadow of my former self. If I give you twenty-twenty I'm giving you more than I can afford.
MERRY SENATOR: And the shipping costs, Senator?
GRUMPY SENATOR: I say twenty.
MERRY SENATOR: You are a nail in my coffin! Hahaha! All right, it's a deal. Hahaha!
JOHNNY: If these two fellows aren't two normal citizens, I abandon all hope. Good morning, gentlemen!
MERRY SENATOR: Good evening.
JOHNNY (*pleased*): Good evening, I mean.
GRUMPY SENATOR: Good afternoon.
JOHNNY: Excuse me, what time might it be right now?
MERRY SENATOR: Eight-thirty sir! Isn't that right, Senator?
GRUMPY SENATOR: Yes, it's exactly a quarter of four.
JOHNNY: What? Oh—thanks ever so much. Yes, and my congratulations on the transaction you've just concluded. Being a sailor, I know a little about that sort of thing myself. What kind of wheat is it that you are trading?
GRUMPY SENATOR: First class. First class. Twenty-twenty. Bad times!
JOHNNY: I mean where does the wheat grow? Here? In Canada? In Argentina?
GRUMPY SENATOR: Don't know.
JOHNNY: But—how come you don't know?
MERRY SENATOR: Just imagine, my dear friend, we don't remember that, hahaha!
JOHNNY: But—you've just bought that wheat, haven't you? And you even paid shipping costs . . . and . . .
ERRY SENATOR: . . . and? And? And I sell it again. You want it? First class. Twenty-twenty.
JOHNNY: But if the wheat doesn't exist?
MERRY SENATOR: Well, then it does not exist. Hahaha!
JOHNNY: And yet you make a living from it?

GRUMPY SENATOR (*angrily*): A living? We don't live, sir. Remember that. I will not stand such statements! This is no life! I am but a shadow of my former self!
JOHNNY: But in that case, why do you do any business at all? What do you make all that money for?
GRUMPY SENATOR: Don't know.
MERRY SENATOR: Don't remember. We forgot that a long time ago, my friend, hahaha!
JOHNNY: You forgot? This is the town of forgetting. But that is . . . And what kind of clothes are you wearing? Nowadays, people don't wear such clothes anymore. Please, do tell me which of all these ships is leaving first. Never mind where—I don't care anymore where it's going. I'm sure you've forgotten where it is going—no—and I'm not asking when it's going either—just tell me which ship it is. Which ship?
GRUMPY SENATOR: None of them.
JOHNNY: None of them?
GRUMPY SENATOR: Bad times. All shipping has died. A dead harbor.
JOHNNY: But all these ships?
MERRY SENATOR: So-called dead ships, my friend. Nothing but dead ships . . . hahaha!
JOHNNY: I must get out of here! Out of here! (*Exits*.)
MERRY SENATOR (*to Lady*): Good morning, madam!
LADY: Good evening, Senator!
MERRY SENATOR: The lady is waiting for the ship?
LADY: Yes, I'm waiting for the ship. I want to go to my husband and my little daughter. She has blond hair and her name is Annelore.
MERRY SENATOR: Give my respects to your husband, the Councillor, when you arrive. And give Annelore a hearty kiss from me! Hahaha!
GRUMPY SENATOR: When does the ship leave?
LADY: Yesterday, Senator.
GRUMPY SENATOR: Already? I am a convinced skeptic, but as far as our shipping traffic is concerned, all I can say is: hats off!

Vineta, Scene Three, Max Reinhardt Seminar, Vienna, 1990 Karin Resch (Lady), Paul Cornelius (Merry Senator), Gottfried Neuner (Jonny). Christian Schramm (Grumpy Senator).

Scene Four

(Town gate. A window in one of the gate towers. In the window the Town Clerk. Johnny comes running and bumps into the closed gate.)

CLERK: Your papers.

JOHNNY: What papers?
CLERK: All of them.
JOHNNY: I don't have any papers. I want to get out of here. Why does anyone need my papers?
CLERK: I don't know. It is only my duty to insist you hand over same.
JOHNNY: Well, I don't have any, I tell you. On the kind of trip I've taken one doesn't take papers.
CLERK: Then come the day after tomorrow.
JOHNNY: Damn it. I won't have any papers the day after tomorrow either.
CLERK: Then come the day before yesterday between five and two!
JOHNNY: How can I do that, for crying out loud?
CLERK: Then what do you really want?
JOHNNY: I want to get out!
CLERK: Where do you want to go? (*Emphatically:*) Consider your answer carefully. Everything is being recorded.
JOHNNY: To my boat, that's where I want to go.
CLERK: Where is your boat?
JOHNNY (*irritated*): Don't know.
CLERK: How did you come here?
JOHNNY (*pondering*): Don't know.
CLERK: Purpose of your stay?
JOHNNY (*at a loss*): Don't know.
CLERK: Do you know where you are?
JOHNNY: No.
CLERK: Why do you want to go back?
JOHNNY (*defiantly*): Because I've got to go on working!
CLERK: What for?
JOHNNY: In order to live!
CLERK: Why do you want to live?
JOHNNY (*taken aback*): Don't know.
CLERK: You don't know?
JOHNNY (*as if paralyzed*): I don't remember.
CLERK (*urgently*): Think again!
JOHNNY: I don't know—I think—I struggled—I—I—loved—hated . . .

CLERK: What did you struggle for? Whom and what did you love and hate respectively?
JOHNNY: I—I don't remember.
CLERK: Then why do you want to live?
JOHNNY: Why? Don't know. Don't remember.
CLERK: Good! That's enough to meet minimum requirements. Fill in the above answers on the questionnaire provided, and you will receive the document.
JOHNNY: What do I get?
CLERK: The citizenship papers of Vineta.

Scene Five

(In front of the cathedral. Johnny, a Beggar, a Beggar Woman.)

JOHNNY: And where do you live?
BEGGAR: Nowhere.
JOHNNY: And where do you sleep?
BEGGAR: Don't know.
JOHNNY: What poverty! But you love each other, don't you?
BEGGAR: Don't remember.
JOHNNY: You're damned forgetful around here. And where do you work?
BEGGAR: Nowhere.
JOHNNY: I haven't found any work either.
BEGGAR *(to Johnny)*: You're not from here.
JOHNNY: I am too. But only since—how long is it now, I wonder; well, it doesn't matter—only since a little while ago.
BEGGAR WOMAN: That's why you don't know that in Vineta nobody works. The rich don't need to and the poor can't. In short: The law of the land.
JOHNNY: If that's so, what the hell do you eat?
BEGGAR WOMAN: No one in Vineta eats. The rich have no appetite and the poor no soup.

JOHNNY: Dreadful. Well, let's hope . . .
BEGGAR: . . . that it will get better yesterday.
JOHNNY (*shaking the Beggar*): Tomorrow, man! Tomorrow, tomorrow!
BEGGAR (*obliging*): Yes, tomorrow, the day after tomorrow.
JOHNNY: Damn it all. I'm still a bad citizen of this place. I don't understand you folks. I don't understand how you can live without hope. Well, I'll try a different approach. What are you doing here?
BEGGAR WOMAN (*eagerly*): Oh, we are waiting until the mass in the cathedral is over. When the townspeople come out, their hearts are soft. Then they give us something.
BEGGAR: Sure, they give us something.
JOHNNY: At least some trace of hope. And when will the mass be over? (*Beggar and Beggar Woman look at each other without understanding.*) Well, didn't I speak clear enough? When?
BEGGAR WOMAN: Don't know.
BEGGAR: Don't remember.
JOHNNY (*furious*): Try to remember, for crying out loud, try to remember, will you!
BEGGAR WOMAN: I don't think it ever ends. I think the hearts of the townspeople are so hard that the mass will go on forever.
JOHNNY: And you are waiting . . .
BEGGAR WOMAN (*eagerly as above*): . . . yes, we are waiting until the mass in the cathedral is over. When the townspeople come out, their hearts are soft. Then they give us something.
BEGGAR: Sure, they give us something.
JOHNNY: Great, folks, just great! And you can live on that?
BEGGAR (*without any understanding*): Live? You want to live?
JOHNNY (*bitterly*): Yes, I do, you gentle imbeciles, I want to live! I don't know anymore why and what for and for whom because I've forgotten all that since I came here. But, damn it, I still want to live. I'm going to go into business, I'm going to work some deals, dirty ones maybe, I don't care. But I will be rich. I will move up in the world. And

then I will live. Even if time stands still in this place. Even if this damned twilight hangs above my head as long as I've been here, day and night, because there's no day and no night. I don't know who's put a spell on this town. But I'm going to live and work. Period. Good day, good night, good morning everybody! (*Exits.*)
BEGGAR WOMAN: He wants to live . . .
BEGGAR: And work . . .
BEGGAR WOMAN AND BEGGAR: In Vineta! (*They shake their heads.*)
(*Bells.*)

Scene Six

(*In the house of the Merry Senator. The Senator; his Wife; Lily, his daughter.*)

WIFE (*to Lily*): So you love him with all your soul, from the bottom of your heart, my child?
LILY: Yes, mother.
SENATOR (*not at all as jovial as he was when he talked with his business friend. Now a real tyrant; threatening*): In which case I hope, for the sake of your honor, that you have not the slightest idea what love is.
LILY: No, father. (*She speaks the truth.*)
WIFE: And after a long struggle, you have decided to take upon yourself marital duties, my poor child?
LILY: Yes, mother.
SENATOR: In which case, I do not doubt that you have no idea what these duties consist of?
LILY: No, father. (*She speaks the truth.*)
SENATOR: Good. And now to the real problem of your forthcoming marriage. The dowry will remain deposited in your name. It's true, of course, he's done me good service in the company for many years and he also piled up a little something on the side, but . . .

WIFE: . . . and naturally you have to look up to him as your husband in blind trust and devotion, my poor child . . .
SENATOR: . . . but you never know.
WIFE: You never know. Repeat!
LILY: You never know, mother.
SENATOR (*sharply*): What can't you ever know?
LILY: I don't know, father.
SENATOR: Good. You'd better not! (*With the coldness of a murderer:*) You are a lily, understand? And if you ever . . .
WIFE (*she notices that her husband has broken off suddenly and finds it advisable to whisper to her daughter*): Repeat!
LILY: I am a lily and if I ever . . .
SENATOR (*horse laugh*): Hahaha! (*He has heard guests arriving and suddenly changes over to being jovial:*) The dear guests!
WIFE: The dear, dear . . .
LILY: . . . dear, dear . . . (*All three exit.*)

(*Enter Johnny and the Town Clerk. Johnny is now about thirty-five; he is elegantly dressed in the fashion of Vineta.*)

JOHNNY: She is a lily. Do you believe that she loves me with all her soul and from the bottom of her heart?
CLERK: Have you ever seen anyone love anybody in Vineta?
JOHNNY: If she doesn't, she is going to hate me.
CLERK: Or hate anybody?
JOHNNY: She is an exception.
CLERK: No, she isn't. You are. When I made you a citizen, I sure made a mistake.
JOHNNY: You're right there, my friend. Because now that I am rich, I'm going to begin living.
CLERK: That's not exactly what I meant. In a town of de—oops!
JOHNNY: What's that?
CLERK: Nothing. A slip of the tongue. I only mean: No man is an island. No matter how hard he tries to be.
JOHNNY: You'll see. This town which now is submerged in mud I shall . . .
CLERK: In mud? So you don't know the story of Vineta?

JOHNNY: No, I don't. There aren't any books about that around here.
CLERK: On orders from the Senators, I had them pulped five hundred years ago.
JOHNNY: How long ago? Are you trying to be funny or something?
CLERK: You mean you really don't know? Most people up there know . . .
JOHNNY: . . . up on the second floor?
CLERK: On the ground floor up there, on land. But I'd be a fool to tell you . . .
JOHNNY: Speak, buddy, or I'll kill you!
CLERK: In the first place, you can't kill me since I am already . . . In the second place you'll try to kill me anyhow no matter what I say. Just wait till you find out tonight that you are going to be in bed with a girl five hundred and eighteen years old. Ergo, I might as well keep my mouth shut.
JOHNNY: Clerk, take pity on me!
CLERK: Pity? But it would amuse me . . . Tell me, didn't you hear in school about the legend of a town which, in the darkest Middle Ages, sank into the sea?
JOHNNY: Into the sea? God, I—I think I remember . . .
CLERK: Which only proves again that you are not a true citizen of Vineta.
JOHNNY: There was a tidal wave, I think—let me see, six hundred years ago it was—a huge tidal wave came over the town.
CLERK: Possibly . . . As far as this tidal wave is concerned, my memory really fails me; at any rate, it was a catastrophe—so terrible that one had to call it a deluge to make people up there understand. But I know more about what happened after that.
JOHNNY: And at the place where Vineta disappeared, one can sometimes hear bells ringing out of the sea—because Vineta goes on living . . .
CLERK: . . . "living" is not the right word. Vineta is dead and doesn't know it. Funny state to be in, isn't it? We can't live

and we cannot die. We do not age, we do not hate, we do not love, we do not fear. We do not fight for anything anymore, we have no hope. What should we hope for, since time has stopped, and yesterday and tomorrow are the same. But except for the Senators and the two of us, nobody knows the situation. And nobody must find out.

JOHNNY: Dead, and nobody knows it? So that's why! . . .

CLERK: That's why. Do you understand everything now?

JOHNNY (*beside himself*): Everything except for one thing, you . . . you fine-feathered friend! Why don't *you* tell people what you know. Why don't you?

CLERK: Me? . . . well . . . hmm, why don't I? In the first place, because it amuses me; in the second place, because it is to my advantage and, in the third place, because I am afraid . . .

JOHNNY: Afraid? Of what?

CLERK: Of the unthinkable that would happen if . . . just think . . . what we have here is a last remnant . . . only an illusion . . . a hopeless state of affairs . . . but if that too crumbles . . . disintegrates . . . whatever may come after . . . that very last nothing . . . I can hardly imagine . . . and yet, I'm afraid of it . . .

JOHNNY: In short, you think a lot, you know a lot, and act very little.

CLERK: Right, my friend! Even a dead intellectual remains what he was—an intellectual.

(*Noises and voices. The Merry Senator, his Wife, and Lily enter.*)

SENATOR: Oh, here he is, our runaway! The gentlemen are having a little stag party, no doubt? A farewell to bachelorhood, hahaha!

CLERK (*softly to Johnny*): I entreat you, don't ever mention to your father-in-law, now or at any time in the future, that he and his whole family are dead. He can't stand it. And you make yourself socially impossible.

WIFE (*whispers to Lily*): Go hide your blushes in his arms.

LILY: Yes, mother. (*She does as she is told.*) Johnny!
WIFE: My poor child.
SENATOR: Young friend! My son! This tender maiden flower . . .
JOHNNY (*between his teeth*): . . . of five hundred and eighteen years . . .
SENATOR: . . . eh, maiden flower . . . eh . . .
CLERK (*has passed around drinks, and now he raises his glass*): . . . we shall sprinkle appropriately. May she live and blossom and prosper!
EVERYBODY: May she live and prosper!
SENATOR: Here's to the good fortune and success of our now united firm. May it live and prosper!
EVERYBODY: Live and prosper!
WIFE: Our new son and partner—may he live and prosper!
JOHNNY (*to the Clerk*): He sure will live!
CLERK: No one can live alone, my friend.
SENATOR: What did the gentlemen say?
JOHNNY (*confused*): Oh nothing, dad. I only said that I'm always going to assist you in your business and . . . and . . . (*he finds himself compelled to finish his speech somehow*) . . . and if one day an inscrutable fate tears you from our side . . .
CLERK (*softly to Johnny*): Idiot!
SENATOR (*he turns pale. Bellows forth*): Be quiet, you young whippersnapper! Senator Hansen never dies! Do you hear? Never dies! And if this place rots and if the whole world gets wormy like an old pumpkin, Senator Hansen will never die! Because he doesn't want to! Doesn't want to! Doesn't want to! (*The last words are spoken in darkness.*)

Scene Seven

(*Johnny's garden with marine plants. Johnny is now forty-five; his wife looks the same as on the first day.*)

LILY: And have you heard the latest, darling? The Councillor's wife, such a sweet, nice lady, wants to join her husband and their daughter again after a longer period of separation. Annelore is the girl's name. Pretty name, isn't it? The Councillor's wife is already waiting for the boat which leaves last night at ten P.M. sharp. And the two beggars in front of the cathedral who were chased away by the town orderly yesterday were there again the day before yesterday. Impudent riff-raff, don't you think?

JOHNNY: Yes, it must have been a terrible catastrophe, that flood, that even the poor could forget that they are human beings . . .

LILY: And the very latest? The Councillor's wife, such a dear, nice lady, after a longer period of separation, wants to . . .

JOHNNY: Tell me, dearest, how old are you now?

LILY: Twenty-five, dearest.

JOHNNY: And three years ago you were? . . .

LILY: Twenty-eight, dearest.

JOHNNY: How come? Oh, I see. Well, it doesn't make any difference. I just wanted to tell you: According to the time system they use on land, I mean up there, it has been ten years now since I began trying to live with you. Have you noticed anything of my attempts?

LILY (*blushing*): But, darling—when you took me, I was a lily and . . .

JOHNNY: That's not what I mean. Try to understand! What I mean is that I have been trying to be *alive* with you.

LILY: But, darling, to be alive is so indecent, don't you know?

JOHNNY: Just tell me: Do you love me?

LILY: But of course, dearest.

JOHNNY: Do you know what love is?

LILY: Of course not, darling.

JOHNNY: You know that tomorrow I am going to the front. Aren't you sad that I must go off to war?

LILY: Sad? Of course not. On the contrary.

JOHNNY: I know I am a hero, but . . .

LILY: Vinetans are immortal.

JOHNNY: I am not. Don't you know what a woman who loves feels when her husband goes off to war?

LILY (*confused*): Darling . . . I think . . . once upon a time . . . a long time ago, I knew . . . but I have . . . I've forgotten.
JOHNNY: Forgotten . . .

Scene Eight

(Johnny and a Soldier in the trenches.)

SOLDIER: They won't forget us, pal. We are heroes.
JOHNNY: Sure, sure. Right now I'm interested in something else. Do you know where we're marching?
SOLDIER: No, I don't know, pal. But the bugle's going to blow attack very soon and . . .
JOHNNY: Undoubtedly. Just tell me one thing: Who's our enemy?
SOLDIER: Those over there.
JOHNNY: But who are they?
SOLDIER: Who? That . . . gee . . . damn it all to hell . . . that I have forgotten.
JOHNNY: Forgotten . . .

(Bugle.)

Scene Nine

(Town gate. Clerk behind the window. Johnny, older still.)

CLERK: Well, brother, long time no see. And to what circumstances do I owe this honor after so many years? As I see, you haven't died yet, I mean in that glorious war.
JOHNNY: Fortunately.
CLERK: Have you lived?
JOHNNY: God, no.

CLERK: In short, a good Vinetan.

JOHNNY: Save yourself the irony. What are you up to now?

CLERK: I have started to pursue philosophical studies in my spare time. I am considered the great thinker in academic circles.

JOHNNY: You don't say. Tell me, professor, what can you think about as long as you aren't allowed to think about the simplest thing . . . life itself? As long as it's more or less your very duty to forget what's most vital?

Vineta, Scene Eight. Landestheater Salzburg 1975.

CLERK: It's all very logical. I think about forgetting. A school of philosophers has gathered round me. We call ourselves the Circle of Oblivionists. Allow me to present you herewith with a copy of my standard work, *Forgetting as a Principle of Thinking for Nations of Advanced Civilization*.

JOHNNY (*reads*): "An integral, non-materialistic conceptualization, which, filled with the true essence of existence derived from a metapsychopathic perception of essentiality, aims at metaphysical phenomenology, teaches us . . . "—well, isn't that something. By the time you are in the second half of the sentence, you've forgotten the first.

CLERK: Excellent! That is exactly the purpose of my method. You've got it.

JOHNNY: Son-of-a-bitch.

CLERK: And you?

JOHNNY: Me? I started to live today. That's why I am here. I wanted you to know. I just gave a terrific speech in the Senate which is already the talk of the town.

CLERK: You mean the request for abolishing the housing shortage among the beggars?

JOHNNY: Request? Demand! And Action! I've just come from the ceremony of laying the foundation stone for the first beggars' housing project. I said: "Air, light, and life!" The audience was moved to tears. From this day on . . .

CLERK: You mean from yesterday on.

JOHNNY: How's that?

CLERK: Or from the day before yesterday on. How often have you, my friend, laid such foundation stones since you became senator?

JOHNNY (*utterly confused*): How often? Today was the first time, man!

CLERK: Oh yes, according to the Vinetan way of counting time. But a stroll through the country around the town demonstrates that said area is studded for miles with foundation stones laid by Senator John. One thousand and ninety-five, all told. According to the other system of time . . . the chronology of those who cannot forget . . . you've been

laying a foundation stone every day for the last three years. Each time you launched a new epoch, of course.
JOHNNY: Honest to God, that I have for . . .
CLERK: . . . for . . . for . . .
JOHNNY: Forgotten . . .
CLERK: Now, my poor friend, I told you on your wedding day: You will not be able to keep alive all by yourself in the middle of the deceased. Wasn't I right?
JOHNNY: I don't deny that anymore, but . . .
CLERK: But then you tried to wake up the dead. And the outcome of the miracle?
JOHNNY: Listen, clerk . . .
CLERK: The outcome? How far did you get . . . with your wife? With your pal at the front? With the homeless beggars?
JOHNNY: You have a sense of logic, clerk. Only death himself has that much logic. But let me tell you, in spite of all that, I will . . .
CLERK: Go right ahead, my boy, but do you realize that you haven't got much time left?
JOHNNY: How come?
CLERK: Right. Of all of those whom I keep a record of, you're the only exception.
JOHNNY: ???
CLERK (*moves his hand over Johnny's face*): Look at yourself! You're getting old.

Scene Ten

(*A prison. A Prisoner. Johnny, an old man by now.*)

JOHNNY: Speak openly to me. I am Senator John. I want to help you. Do you need help?
PRISONER: No, Mr. Senator.
JOHNNY: Are they treating you all right?
PRISONER: Yes, Mr. Senator.
JOHNNY: Don't you have any complaints?

PRISONER: No, Mr. Senator.

JOHNNY: You don't have to stand at attention for me. Sit down. (*Prisoner remains standing at attention; Johnny, irritated*:) Go ahead, sit down!

PRISONER (*startled*): Yes, Mr. Senator. (*He obeys.*)

JOHNNY: What crime did you commit?

PRISONER: Don't know, Mr. Senator.

JOHNNY: When will your sentence run out?

PRISONER: Yesterday, Mr. Senator.

JOHNNY (*looking around for a guard*): Guard, what has this man done? When will he be released?

VOICE OF GUARD (*off stage, like an echo*): Don't know. Yesterday.

JOHNNY (*to prisoner*): What's your name?

PRISONER: I've forgotten.

VOICE OF GUARD (*like an echo*): . . . forgotten.

JOHNNY: I'll tell you why I've come. Ever since I came to this town, I have been looking for life in vain. I haven't found it, not among the poor and not among the rich. I haven't got much time left. And it occurred to me: In the world where I was young, no one loved life as much as the prisoners. That's why you are my last hope. I give you your freedom. (*Prisoner is silent.*) Do you hear? You are free!

PRISONER: I hear, Mr. Senator.

JOHNNY: Repeat: I am free.

PRISONER: I am free.

VOICE OF GUARD (*like an echo*): . . . free.

JOHNNY: What are you going to do, now that you are free?

PRISONER: Don't know.

JOHNNY: Try to remember. Isn't there anybody waiting for you, somebody you want to hug and kiss when you come out?

PRISONER: No.

JOHNNY: But there must be an enemy waiting for you somewhere, somebody you want to get even with after all these years.

PRISONER: No, Mr. Senator.

JOHNNY: Man, listen to me! There is a world that is different. A world where night follows day, and where there is spring

and winter and spring again; storms blow, the sun shines. Grain is sown and harvested and sown again . . . without end. Human beings are born and grow like the grain. Because they have a restless heart, they must love and hate as long as they live, and they grow old and die. And new men are born to hate and to love, to grow old and to die . . . without end, and all this has no other meaning than itself. But it's a great meaning, it's called life. Do you understand?
PRISONER: No, Mr. Senator.
JOHNNY: I know, it's very hard for you, but a spark of longing for all that is still in you, isn't it? Or was once?
PRISONER: I don't know anymore.

(Voices)

VOICE OF THE GUARD: The Right Honorable and family are coming for an inspection!

(Enter the Merry Senator, his Wife, Lily, and the Clerk.)
LILY: And you know, mother, the councillor's wife, such a dear, nice lady, after a long separation wants to . . .
WIFE: But look, what a cute cell!
SENATOR: Hahaha! Whom do my eyes behold? Our dear runaway!
CLERK: The young senator is gathering material for the speech on prison reform he gave yesterday.
SENATOR: Conscientious as always, hahaha!
JOHNNY *(with difficulty)*: Listen to me . . .
LILY: And what a cute prisoner!
JOHNNY *(as above)*: Listen, citizens of Vineta . . .
SENATOR: Quiet! The naughty young Senator John is memorizing his speech! Hahahaha!
JOHNNY: I don't know why you perished and sank down so deep that even in the most miserable prisoner the last spark of life has died.
SENATOR: Oho?
LILY: But John, what's the matter with you today?

JOHNNY: I only know one thing. My last chance to call myself alive among you, even if it's only for one last breath and at the cost of utter unthinkable destruction . . .

SENATOR: Oho?

WIFE: John, you're crazy!

JOHNNY: . . . my last chance is to say the truth in public, the truth that I've helped you keep secret. Yes, I will tell everybody the truth and . . .

SENATOR: Young man!

CLERK (*sharply to Johnny*): Keep quiet!

JOHNNY (*rushing to the barred window*): . . . this one second I will live! (*Tears the barred window open.*) Everybody listen!

CLERK: Keep quiet!

JOHNNY: All of you whom this man has in his files here . . . listen! Vineta, your world, is . . . (*the clerk jumps at him, wants to close his mouth*) . . . dead! (*At this word, all other characters freeze in their positions. Johnny and the Clerk are wrestling silently. In their fight they knock against Lily. As if loosened by the impact, disconnected words drop out of her mouth. In the same way, dead words issue from the other dead Vinetans . . . A senseless, lifeless jumble of sounds accompanies Johnny's fight with the clerk; all "speak" simultaneously.*)

LILY: And you know, the councillor's wife, such a dear, nice lady, after a long separation . . . wants to . . . but, of course, darling . . .

WIFE: You are a lily, my child . . . remember that . . . You never know . . .

SENATOR: Take it? hahaha! Price: Twenty-twenty. Hahaha!

PRISONER: Yes, Mr. Senator. Yes, Mr. Senator. Yes, Mr. Senator!

JOHNNY (*to the Clerk*): Let go! You are death! I want to live! Live! Live! Let go! I need air! Air! Air! Air!

(*In this confusion, bells are beginning to resound.*)

Scene Eleven

(Tavern as in Scene One. Johnny alone.)

JOHNNY: Well, and when I opened my eyes, Kathy, there I was, lying on deck, and all around me the crew was roaring: "Hurrah, he's alive!" Half an hour they had tried to resuscitate me; half an hour I'd been hovering between life and death, half an hour or a whole lifetime, whichever way you want to look at it. And you know, sweetheart, then I knew, of course, that Vineta was just a case of acoustical optics. But I have been thinking a long time about what a man could learn from that story. Sure, I've often thought, in reality there is no town in the whole world that's like this Vineta. But if one day a tidal wave should come, some big war, some big barbaric outbreak, I wonder if the whole world might not turn into a Vineta. *(Kathryn has come in, unnoticed by Johnny.)* But that's only in my imagination—or what d' you think, Sweetie? 'cause if it isn't just in my imagination, then it's a pretty serious business, isn't it? In that case, all of us would have to put all our energies together, all of us and right now, and even then there might not be much time left, 'cause no one would know when it might come, that flood. Maybe it's already quite close by now, maybe right outside the door of this dirty old hole here. And that would be something to be scared of, don't you think?
KATHRYN: Sure, Johnny. You're right, Johnny. Such a cheapskate.
JOHNNY: Who's that now?
KATHRYN: Oh, that Mr. Ditje in box two. Such a mean old pennypincher. Disgusting, that's all I can say.

(Curtain)

Broadway Melody 1492

Adaptation of *Christoph Kolumbus*

by

Walter Hasenclever and Kurt Tucholsky

CHARACTERS

(in order of appearance)

Director of a cabaret theater
Portier of the Burgtheater, Vienna
Amerigo Vespucci, Professor of Geography
Christopher Columbus
Quintanilla, Minister of Finance
Santangel, Chancellor
Marquise de Moya, Lady in Waiting
Ferdinand, King of Spain
Voice of a servant
Isabella, Queen of Spain
Jose Vendrino, Finance Inspector
Recruiter
Listener
Supplier
Landlady
Minstrel
Egg Woman
Pepito Alibi, a criminal
Girl with flowers
Tax Collector
Sailor
Ship's Boy
Indian Chief
Medicine Man
Anacoana, an Indian girl
Minnehaha, an Indian woman
Indian Woman Tobacconist
Indian Post Office Clerk
Young Indian Woman
Old Indian Woman
Waiter

Prelude

(Tiny office of the portier at the Burgtheater in Vienna. The portier, and the director of an avant-garde cabaret theater.)

DIRECTOR *(timidly)*: Good morning. Excuse me, do I have the honor of speaking with the portier of the Burgtheater in person?

PORTIER: Indeed, you have the honor. And now go home. Your manuscript has been rejected.

DIRECTOR: Excuse me, but I didn't submit a manuscript.

PORTIER: Listen, you had the right idea. Because as you might know in this establishment I meet all the demand for new plays. For some time I wrote under the pseudonym Hans Sassmann, and recently I've been calling myself Josef Feiks. People like you can just forget it.

DIRECTOR: Of course, I am well aware of that fact, Mr. Portier.

PORTIER: Listen, who are you anyway?

DIRECTOR: I'm a theater director . . .

PORTIER: Oh, I see. In that case, have a seat!

DIRECTOR: Of an avant-garde theater.

PORTIER: In that case, get up. What do you want?

DIRECTOR: I would, most humbly, like to ask your artistic advice, Sir, if I may. We'd like to put on a historical play, and since the Burgtheater is exemplary in this genre . . .

PORTIER: Aha! Listen, very laudable, very laudable. What kind of material do you plan to use?

DIRECTOR: We are dealing with . . .

PORTIER: I'm not interested in any deals. I want to know what kind of material you have.

DIRECTOR: We're dealing with the discovery of America. The play begins . . .

PORTIER: Listen, are you hard of hearing or what? I want to know about the material. Look, at the Burgtheater we use gold brocade exclusively. There's nothing more effective than that. How many yards do you have in your costume stock?

DIRECTOR: We . . . uh . . . do you think cotton would do?

PORTIER: Cotton? Good Lord! Tell me, how much tradition do

you have anyway?

DIRECTOR: We've been putting on plays for four years.

PORTIER: Four years . . . Good Lord! And how high is your subsidy?

DIRECTOR: But, is that all that important?

PORTIER: Important? Good God! Listen, you don't seem to understand. Listen: For a historical play you need three things: 1) costume and property stock, 2) tradition, and 3) a subsidy. The stock creates the tradition, the tradition creates the deficit, the deficit creates the subsidy, the subsidy creates a bigger stock, the bigger stock creates more tradition, a new deficit, a new subsidy, and it goes on like that into metaphysics . . . Do you get it?

DIRECTOR: No, I don't.

PORTIER: See what I mean? Now let's go on: How often does Columbus sing the Prince Eugene March in the first act?

DIRECTOR: Excuse me, but how can Columbus be singing the Prince Eugene March?

PORTIER: What's the matter, can't he sing?

DIRECTOR: He can sing, but because of the historical truth . . .

PORTIER: What d'you mean? You're telling me the Prince Eugene March is not historical?

DIRECTOR: Well, yes, but . . .

PORTIER: See what I mean? Have you been to see Professor Gregor on the second floor yet to ask him about Renaissance buttons?

DIRECTOR: What do we need Renaissance buttons for?

PORTIER: What for, what for? For Columbus's fly, of course.

DIRECTOR: You see, actually we thought of taking a different approach, the other way round, so to speak. As far as the exact details are concerned, we want to be quite irreverent, but the essence of the thing, the underlying principles must be historically true. We want to disregard the facts in favor of the truth. We want to bring the past alive, make it relevant to today.

PORTIER: Aha! So that's what you want to do.

DIRECTOR: Yes.

PORTIER: Aha! Listen, I don't understand.

DIRECTOR: That's too bad. Perhaps we could, with your permission, show you the play?
PORTIER: Well O.k., I have no objections. But, wait a minute. How big is that stage of yours?
DIRECTOR: Our stage . . . well, I mean, forty-nine people . . .
PORTIER: That's nothing, a mere cubbyhole, if you ask me. You need at least a hundred supernumeraries.
DIRECTOR: I mean there are forty-nine seats in the auditorium.
PORTIER: In the audi . . . Jesus, Mary, and Joseph! Then how big is the stage?
DIRECTOR: About as big as your office here.
PORTIER: Hahahahaha! In that case you could put on the play right here. Hahahaha! At least you'll get some tradition, free of charge! Hahahaha!
DIRECTOR: Right here? Why not! With a little imagination? In the first act we are at the royal palace in Santa Fe. Then your easy chair would be a fancy seat fit for royalty and your desk a meeting table for the Council of Ministers. (*He begins to rearrange the furniture.*)
PORTIER: Very flattering, but . . .
DIRECTOR: We could hang a map up here. (*He rolls down a big world map, which from now on dominates the backdrop.*)
PORTIER: Hey, what are you doing?
DIRECTOR: I am making a model stage.
PORTIER: For heaven's sake, I was only joking. You don't really want to put on the play right here in my office, do you?!
DIRECTOR: I am accustomed to hardships.
PORTIER: But what about tradition?
DIRECTOR: Let Director Röbbeling keep it.
PORTIER: But for God's sake, can't I ring the bell, so that at least something is the way it should be?
DIRECTOR (*grandly*): Act one. A hall in the Royal Palace at Santa Fe!!!
PORTIER: Wait a second! (*He rings the bell frantically.*)

(*Darkness.*)

DIRECTOR:

>The world's a stage, or so they say.
>For us the world is just a cabaret.
>The play begins, but first, come on, Columbus,
>Let's look at who is causing all this rumpus.
>You are the hero, but don't put on the dog.
>In history's machinery you're just a cog.
>A halo will drive up the power bill;
>Heroes don't pay it, and our budget's nil.
>
>You are Columbus, captain of the sea.
>The debts you have will land you soon in prison.
>You are aflame with an illustrious vision
>That is the product of your storm-tossed day.
>You are inspired, but stop your ego's flight,
>You're not the only one who's seen the light.
>Who owns the visions that the age begot?
>The hero only dreams them. He owns them not!
>
>And so you must, a poor obnoxious pest,
>Go hat in hand from king to king,
>You see land in the west, land in the west!
>Your message has a most familiar ring.
>Too many are, like you, inspired,
>And your conviction sounds a little tired.
>You drag your mission like a curséd lot.
>A hero?—No, a hero you are not!
>
>Now for the umpteenth time you come again,
>The sorriest of pure fools in all the land,
>And hang around the royal court of Spain
>To scrounge three sailing ships from Ferdinand.
>You know yourself, inside you are so weak,
>And all your outward strength is rot.
>Your real destiny is about to speak,
>And you, Columbus, hero—hear it not.

Broadway Melody 1492, ABC in Regenbogen, Vienna 1937, program.

Act One

Scene One

(*Columbus, Vespucci, professor of geography*)

VESPUCCI: Here you are again, señor . . . what was the name again?

COLUMBUS: Christopher Columbus.

VESPUCCI: Right. Didn't I have the pleasure of seeing you a couple of years ago? What brings you here this year?

COLUMBUS: The same thing, professor. The most exalted highest grace, or whim, has granted me the opportunity to present my plans at this court once again, and I did not want to do that without having contacted you first.

VESPUCCI: One should bleed you with leeches, señor, because you suffer from an idée fixe. Surely you don't believe that the iron-clad laws of science have changed these last two years, do you?

COLUMBUS: I hoped that they would. More and more universities are accepting the theory that the earth is round.

VESPUCCI: Is that right? Well, remember this: as long as I teach at this university, the world is going to stay flat. Do you understand? Besides, you have no verifiable proof for your theory, and the Bible disproves it. (*He opens a Bible.*) It is written, Psalm 104, verse 2: "who has stretched out the heavens like a tent." You've got to have a flat surface for a tent that big, so the earth can't be round.

COLUMBUS: Now just a minute. Isaiah, chapter 65, verse 17: "For, behold, I create new heavens and a new earth, and the former shall not be remembered."

VESPUCCI: That proves nothing. We rely on facts. Revelations 20, verse 8: "And Satan will be loosed from his prison and will come out to deceive the nations which are at the four corners of the earth." How can a sphere have four corners? Now that's logic for you!

COLUMBUS: And if I prove by empirical evidence that I'm right?

VESPUCCI: By empirical evidence? Empirical evidence is totally unscientific.

COLUMBUS: I will sail west, straight west, I will . . .

VESPUCCI: You'll slip off the edge of the earth and break your neck.

COLUMBUS: I will land on the east coast of Asia. I will be the first to find the sea route to India, because the earth is a globe.

VESPUCCI: You will, eh? My dear senor, I just discovered—to top it all off—that your theory contains a contradictio in adjecto. Let's assume for a second, that the earth is a sphere; that means that you are sailing down on a sphere. But how, pray tell, will you ever get up again?

COLUMBUS: By following the motion of the globe.

VESPUCCI: Nonsense. I'm going to write a book about that very point.

COLUMBUS: And I, with the help of three sailing ships, will prove you wrong.

VESPUCCI: You won't be able to.

COLUMBUS: Why not?

VESPUCCI: Because I'm a voting member of the Royal Council for Cultural Affairs, and the Council won't approve even half a ship for you.

COLUMBUS: Is this what you call the competitive spirit of science?

VESPUCCI: Precisely, senor. You can bet your life on it. No one is ever going to find a continent in the west, or my name isn't Amerigo Vespucci.

Scene Two

(Santangel, Chancellor; Quintanilla, Minister of Finance; Columbus)

QUINTANILLA: I am not a magician. I am only human.

SANTANGEL: Excuse me, you are the Minister of Finance.

QUINTANILLA: It's a mystery to me how we're supposed to pay

our debts. We don't have any gold.

SANTANGEL: Tap the reserves of the Royal Bank.

QUINTANILLA: For one thing, that's against the law, for another, I'm on the Board of Directors, and for another there aren't any reserves left.

SANTANGEL: In this historic hour, in the year of our Lord 1492, when one of the greatest events of all times is about to happen . . .

QUINTANILLA: I know, I know . . . the stepped-up arms effort. Can't you wait till fall for the final victory?

SANTANGEL: Till fall? My dear Quintanilla, don't you know that the Queen has taken a vow not to change her undershirt until the land is swept clean of all infidels? It's January now . . . if she is to wait till September . . .

QUINTANILLA: Between you and me, Santangel, is it true, that story about the undershirt?

SANTANGEL: Shhh. She isn't the one wearing it.

QUINTANILLA: Who is?

(There is a knock at the door.)

SANTANGEL: We don't want to be disturbed. We are in conference.

VOICE: The gentleman says it's urgent.

SANTANGEL: So who is it?

VOICE: A sea captain.

SANTANGEL: What's the man's name?

VOICE: Christopher Columbus.

QUINTANILLA: I vaguely remember having heard that name before.

SANTANGEL: Oh dear, that obnoxious troublemaker from Portugal who wants to sail to India. Her Majesty the Queen has taken an interest in him.

QUINTANILLA: What do you know!

SANTANGEL: Tell señor Columbus to come in.

QUINTANILLA: But you were going to tell me the story about the shirt.

SANTANGEL: Listen. Do you know the Marquise de Moya? *(He*

whispers in his ear, both laugh. In the meantime Columbus has entered the room.)

QUINTANILLA: Impossible!

SANTANGEL: It's true! I swear. (*Laughter.*) . . . (*To Columbus:*) Just a moment.

QUINTANILLA: And her husband? What does he have to say about it?

SANTANGEL: He doesn't have a clue.

QUINTANILLA: Husbands never do. (*To Columbus:*) Yes?

COLUMBUS: I've been asked to present my plan to you.

SANTANGEL: Who are you, and what do you want?

COLUMBUS: I'm a sea captain from Genoa and have to go begging from court to court because the kings don't want to accept my empires. I've proven on the basis of geographical computation that the way west across the ocean must lead to . . .

SANTANGEL: Make it short please.

COLUMBUS: We obtain important goods from the Far East. But the land route is threatened by the Turks. People tried to sail along the coast of Africa to reach India. But it was all in vain. These thoughts were weighing heavily on my mind when God sent me the inspiration . . .

SANTANGEL: Just don't think of yourself as a misunderstood genius, señor . . . (*He has forgotten the name.*)

COLUMBUS: Columbus.

SANTANGEL: Nowadays we are inundated with so-called "discoverers" . . . and every one of them tells us a different story.

QUNITANILLA: What do you expect of your plan, señor . . . señor . . .

COLUMBUS: Columbus.

SANTANGEL: What do you expect to gain by it?

COLUMBUS: The opening up of a new world.

SANTANGEL: I wish I had your worries, señor! A new world?! We've got enough trouble with the old one. Don't you know that the Queen has taken a vow never to change her undershirt until our land has been liberated from the infidels? Do you have any idea how much of the soldiers' pay is used up

by the laundry bill every month?
COLUMBUS: But just think of the travels of famous men who reported fantastic treasures.
SANTANGEL: Fantasies don't make fiscal policy.
QUINTANILLA: I wouldn't say that.
SANTANGEL: And how do you plan to finance your voyage? Do you have any capital?
COLUMBUS: I have certainty.
SANTANGEL: That won't do.
COLUMBUS: Soon I will be richer than anybody.
SANTANGEL: Says who?
COLUMBUS: An inner voice.
SANTANGEL (*looking through a file*): Oh, is that so? And has this inner voice also told you that you haven't paid your taxes, señor . . . señor . . . Columbus? And that the Royal Bureau of the Inquisition has a file on you that could stretch from here to India?
COLUMBUS: God has inspired me, and God will protect me from my enemies.
QUINTANILLA: You're always talking about God. Are you Jewish?
COLUMBUS: My father is Count Colombo of Montserrat.
QUINTANILLA: That's too bad. (*To the Chancellor:*) That would have simplified matters. (*He makes a gesture of hanging*).
SANTANGEL: Señor Columbus, we want to conclude this amusing conversation. You have no money, you don't pay your taxes, a neighboring state is said to have a search warrant out for you; I'm warning you, señor Columbus. Since your last visit with us conditions have changed. A colder wind is blowing. Your theories almost border on heresy!
COLUMBUS: The world is round. I have to sail west, straight west.
SANTANGEL: We know that by now, señor. You are not the only one who says that, you know.
COLUMBUS: Doesn't that lead you to the conclusion that there is something to it?
SANTANGEL: I conclude only that our inquisition is still far too humane . . . unfortunately!

Scene Three

(*The King's private chamber. Fanfare as the curtain rises. The King; Columbus.*)

COLUMBUS: Your Majesty, I rushed to Santa Fe from Portugal to throw myself at your feet.
KING: From Portugal? From Portugal. I see. I've heard they have a new way to cook snails in celery there.
COLUMBUS: Your Majesty! A discovery of immeasurable importance for all of Christendom . . .
KING: Isn't it? Christendom will rejoice in knowing that I can eat snails again. As you know the doctor wouldn't let me eat them with pepper and vinegar.
COLUMBUS: In a thousand sleepless nights I have crossed the ocean . . .
KING: Is that a fact? You can't sleep either? Have you been having stomach trouble, too? I'm happy to hear that. Why don't you get up? So what can I do for you?
COLUMBUS: To my unspeakable dismay I've just heard from His Excellency the Chancellor that the resources of the Royal Bank are not sufficient to rid the country of the infidels even though the Queen has taken the vow . . .
KING: Come closer. Can you keep a secret? I'll tell you something, since both of us have stomach trouble, after all. Listen: My wife isn't wearing that shirt.
COLUMBUS: What difference does it make?
KING: What do you mean, what difference does it make? Do you know who is wearing it? Her Lady in Waiting, the Duchess of Moya. Do you know little Moya?
COLUMBUS: Your Majesty, the round shape . . .
KING: That's the one. I'll tell you a story about her. Do you know Vendrino? The little fat one, the Finance Inspector who used to be a wheat merchant? (*He whispers.*) She . . . with him . . . and he says . . . and then she . . . behind a curtain . . . in bed . . . and he to her . . . and she says: "With whom do I have the pleasure of . . . ?" (*He laughs.*) What do you think of that?

COLUMBUS: Your Majesty is very gracious to me. May I infer from that that I have Your Majesty's full confidence?

KING: Sure, sure, my friend, I only trust people with stomach trouble because I know them inside out. What can I do for you?

COLUMBUS: As your Majesty probably knows, there are already thousands of people in your kingdom who subscribe to the theory that the earth is round.

KING: I know. Don't worry about them. We'll catch 'em all in due time.

COLUMBUS: I myself, Your Majesty, believe, that the earth curves beyond our horizon.

KING: Is that so? Does the earth have permission to do that?

COLUMBUS: The earth doesn't bother about permission, Your Majesty.

KING: All right, all right! For your sake, I'll let it go this time. Let the earth curve, if it must. But I don't want anyone talking about it. It makes me dizzy.

COLUMBUS: I don't get dizzy, your Majesty. I'm going to submit the idea of my life to the Council for Cultural Affairs in one hour. I need three ships to give Your Majesty an empire on which the sun will never set. The Secretary of the Treasury does not seem kindly disposed towards me. I beseech Your Majesty to use your power as absolute monarch on my behalf.

KING: Look, my dear friend, don't be childish. What good is a world empire to me if Quintanilla cuts the antacids from my budget? What does Professor Vespucci think of your idea?

COLUMBUS: He opposes it, too.

KING: Are you insane? Don't you have any idea of the power structure in this country? Don't you know that Vespucci and my doctor are buddies? Do I have to eat gruel again for months just because of you?! Gruel, yuk!

COLUMBUS: Your Majesty . . .

KING: Shut your mouth! End of audience. I am bitterly disappointed in you, señor Columbus. It's not easy to wear a crown if you can't even depend on people with stomach trouble.

(*Fanfare, darkness.*)

Scene Four

(Duchess of Moya.)

MOYA *(sings the Chanson of the Duchess of Moya)*:

As you know, my name is Moya,
Lady in Waiting to the Queen.
I'm informed and I enjoy a
Furtive glance behind the scene.
And if two will kiss on Monday,
I already know on Sunday.
The spicy news I have today
Will simply take your breath away:
Our Queen took a vow on her honor
She'll keep the same shirt on her,
She won't put a new one on
Until victory is won.

You will see this very minute
The ingenious gimmick in it.
What a laundry bag of tricks!
Washing, too, serves politics!

It takes money to keep clean
The undershirt of our Queen.
And to wash it, wash it, wash it
Adds an item to the budget
And new taxes for the war.
The price of bread and salt will soar.
For defense funds you just sock it
To the poor and pick their pockets.
They'll just have to do with less.
Victory is near! God bless.

You have seen this very minute
The ingenious gimmick in it.
What a laundry bag of tricks:
Dirty washing's politics.

Scene Five

(In the private suite of the Queen. Santangel, Quintanilla, Vespucci, Columbus.)

SANTANGEL: It's a question of the Holy Scripture. Captain Columbus maintains that his inspiration comes from God. But in the Bible I can nowhere, and I mean nowhere, find any reference to a sea route to India. Therefore it does not exist. The whole thing is blasphemy. This case belongs in a very different tribunal.
QUINTANILLA: How do you know that your way is the right one.
COLUMBUS: I just do.
VESPUCCI: But we have proven to you that you cannot be right.
COLUMBUS: I'm certain of it anyway.
SANTANGEL: I think we can put an end to this discussion. Are there any questions?
QUINTANILLA: Thank you, we're no longer interested.
COLUMBUS: I have to sail westward!

(Fanfare.)

VOICE: Her Majesty the Queen.
QUEEN *(enters)*: Please, gentlemen, don't let me interrupt you. *(To Columbus:)* When did I see you last, Captain? It's been two years!
COLUMBUS: I throw myself at Your Majesty's feet.
QUEEN: Get up. Step more toward the light. Your hair has turned gray.
COLUMBUS: May I speak openly, Your Majesty?
QUEEN: Please do!
COLUMBUS: When Your Majesty in your grace permitted me to see you last time, I felt that it changed my destiny. For the first time, I looked into eyes that did not mock me. They were the eyes of my Queen. Years of suffering lie behind me. Does Your Majesty know how a person feels when he cannot eat or sleep, when he is pursued by one, and only one, thought?

QUEEN: Are you married?
COLUMBUS: I was married . . . when he finds no peace because everything revolves around that one point . . .
QUEEN: Is your wife still living?
COLUMBUS: She is deceased.
QUEEN: And where do you live now?
COLUMBUS: I just wander around the world aimlessly.
QUEEN: You lead a lonely life.
COLUMBUS: On sleepless nights I have crossed the ocean, westward, Your Majesty, westward. Through the endless expanse of the sea . . . following the path of the setting sun . . .
QUEEN: Don't you have anybody who is close to you?
COLUMBUS: I have my conviction.
QUEEN: What would you do if I granted your wishes?
COLUMBUS: I would carry Your Majesty's flag to the ends of the earth.
QUEEN: The flag . . . You were born in Genoa, Captain? They say Italians are very passionate.
COLUMBUS: I wish I could prove it to Your Majesty.
QUEEN: Are you that bold?
COLUMBUS: I'm prepared to die for my Queen at any time.
QUEEN: To die? Do you have to go to such extremes?
COLUMBUS: I'm determined to risk my life. My last cry will be: Long live the Queen!
QUEEN: Your last cry . . . what a shame. You're a man a woman might find attractive. (*To Santangel:*) You have the floor, Santangel.
SANTANGEL: After a thorough examination, the Council has come to the conclusion . . .
QUEEN: Do you consider the expedition at all feasible?
SANTANGEL: The expedition has no chance of success at all. I must add that certain statements of the Captain sound almost heretical.
QUEEN: I've just convinced myself that the captain is a devout Christian. What else?
SANTANGEL: Given the present condition of the kingdom there is no room for any experiments in our foreign policy. I strongly advise against it, Your Majesty.

QUEEN: And you, Treasurer?

QUINTANILLA: We would not survive any further demands on the treasury. I fully concur with the opinion of the honorable Chancellor.

QUEEN (*very quietly*): All right, gentlemen, in that case we'll do it. (*General astonishment.*) I'm aware of the difficulties, but I'm of the opinion that we have to take part in the conquest of the world. I want to incorporate India into my kindom before other countries beat us to it.

SANTANGEL: An expedition under the auspices of the state could be most advantageous.

QUINTANILLA: I fully concur with the opinion of the honorable Chancellor.

QUEEN: I thank the Council for its deliberations. Santangel, please be so good as to settle the details with the Captain.

SANTANGEL: Your Majesty, I see only one difficulty.

QUEEN: Don't we have any money left? (*Santangel and Quintanilla shrug their shoulders.*) Pawn my jewels then.

QUINTANILLA: Your majesty, they are pawned already.

QUEEN: Then pawn them again.

QUINTANILLA: We'll make that business deal with the English. They aren't very pleasant, but they do have money.

COLUMBUS (*kneels before the Queen*): Illustrious Queen, in undying gratitude I kiss . . . the hem of your dress.

VOICE: Your Majesty, the dressmaker.

QUEEN: I'm coming. (*To Columbus:*) I hope you won't disappoint my expectations. (*To Santangel:*) Send me the contract for my signature. (*Queen exits.*)

SANTANGEL: Have a seat, señor Columbus. I suggest we engage you in our navy with the rank and salary of a Sea Captain. You'll receive command of one ship . . .

COLUMBUS: Of three ships.

SANTANGEL: I beg your pardon?

COLUMBUS: I'll be needing three ships.

SANTANGEL: One thing at a time. For your personal equipment you will receive a subsidy; the Treasurer will determine the amount. You must submit an exact account of all the proceeds. Do you have any further wishes?

COLUMBUS: I demand the title of Viceroy and the office of Governor General of all the lands I discover; also a promotion to Sea Admiral and ten percent of all proceeds.
SANTANGEL: Tell me, my dear man, have you taken leave of your senses?
COLUMBUS: I'm not finished yet. I demand the ownership of one eighth of these lands and the income they generate. All the rights, titles, and honors are to be inherited by my descendants.
QUINTANILLA: That's the most extraordinary piece of insolence I've ever heard.
SANTANGEL: Are you serious?
COLUMBUS: Absolutely.
QUINTANILLA: Señor Columbus, I thought you were an idealist.
SANTANGEL: Do you think you can negotiate with us in that tone?
COLUMBUS: I'm not negotiating, I'm stating my conditions.
QUINTANILLA: You come to us as a beggar and then state conditions?
COLUMBUS: Too bad. (*He stands up.*)
SANTANGEL: Sit down. We can talk about the titles. You can become an Admiral for all I care. But you won't get any money.
COLUMBUS: If my conditions don't suit the gentlemen . . .
SANTANGEL: Señor Columbus, let's come to an agreement. Five percent and the Vice-Royalty.
COLUMBUS: Ten percent.
SANTANGEL: Seven-and-a-half percent, that's the absolute limit.
COLUMBUS: I'm sorry, good-bye.
SANTANGEL: Where are you going?
COLUMBUS: To the King of Portugal.
SANTANGEL: Nine-and-a-half percent . . . and the deal's on. But you'll have to forget about the property rights. We'd be the laughing stock . . .
COLUMBUS: I insist on all my conditions.
QUINTANILLA: Then go to . . . the King of Portugal.
VOICE: The Marquise of Moya.
SANTANGEL: Show her in. (*Moya enters.*) My dear Marquise!

MOYA: Her Majesty would like to know whether the contract has been drawn up.

SANTANGEL: It's a good thing you've come. You'll see for yourself how our modern day explorers behave.

MOYA (*eyes Columbus through her lorgnette*): Señor Columbus himself. Very interesting.

COLUMBUS: Will you be so kind, dear Marquise, as to convey to Her Majesty my most respectful farewell.

MOYA: Are you leaving so soon?

COLUMBUS: I'm returning to Portugal.

MOYA: One moment, gentlemen. (*She speaks quietly to Santangel and Quintanilla:*) Gentlemen, this simply won't do. The Queen insists on the contract.

SANTANGEL: But you can't talk with this man.

QUINTANILLA: Tell me, is it true that you are wearing the Queen's undershirt until Granada falls?

MOYA: Officially, the Queen is wearing the undershirt. Semi-officially, I am.

QUINTANILLA: And who's really wearing it?

MOYA: My chambermaid.

SANTANGEL: So what about the contract?

QUINTANILLA: The man is trying to rip us off.

MOYA: Then rip him off. I'm always for everybody making a profit. Why can't everybody rake some off? That's my policy.

SANTANGEL: Not bad, not bad . . . (*To Columbus:*) Señor Columbus, we'll accept your conditions. We might even want to participate in your venture. But we can only undertake this risk if a comptroller goes along.

COLUMBUS: I can't share my command with anybody.

SANTANGEL: Nobody is speaking of that. We just need a trustworthy person to examine revenues and expenses.

QUINTANILLA: But who would that be?

MOYA: Don't you have a very capable man in the Ministry of Finance by the name of Vendrino?

QUINTANILLA: Vendrino? Oh, really?

SANTANGEL (*softly to Moya*): Still?

MOYA: I thought we were talking business here.

SANTANGEL (*calling into the wings*): Tell Finance Inspector Ven-

drino to come up.
QUINTANILLA: I propose we establish a partnership. There's only one problem: Do you have any money?
COLUMBUS: No.
QUINTANILLA: Could you give us some security?
COLUMBUS: I offer my life as security.
QUINTANILLA: That's not a very stable collateral.
VOICE: Finance Inspector Vendrino.

(*Vendrino enters.*)

SANTANGEL: Inspector, we are dealing with . . .
VENDRINO: I know.
SANTANGEL: How do you know?
MOYA: Señor Vendrino has been informed of the facts.
SANTANGEL: So much the better. Would you be willing to accompany the expedition as Royal Comptroller of Accounts?
VENDRINO: What does the position pay?
QUINTANILLA (*quietly*): You'll be a partner.
VENDRINO: It's a deal.
SANTANGEL (*to Columbus*): Be so good as to put your conditions in writing. In the meantime we'll consult with each other. (*Columbus sits down at the table and writes. The following takes place behind his back.*)
QUINTANILLA: What do you think of a private trading company with head-quarters here in Santa Fe?
VENDRINO: That's not quite the way things are. We'll sell stock, let me finish, and establish a company with limited liability. He (*pointing at Columbus*) is personally liable . . . and we all share in the profits.
QUINTANILLA: But then we'd have to pay in cash.
VENDRINO: Here we would. But we'll transfer the whole thing to the Republic of Andorra and there we won't have to pay in cash. How's that?
MOYA: Isn't he clever?
VENDRINO: The transfer has the additional advantage that the partners don't have to be registered. All right then, how much?

SANTANGEL: Fifty thousand from me.
QUINTANILLA: Fifty thousand from me, too.
VESPUCCI: And from me, too.
VENDRINO: Thirty thousand from me. (*He notes down the amounts.*) And another thirty thousand from Marquise de Moya.
MOYA: Where am I going to get that kind of money?
VENDRINO: We're not paying here, we're just exchanging IOU's.
SANTANGEL: And if the thing's a flop?
VENDRINO: Then *he*'ll be in for it.
SANTANGEL (*aloud*): Captain . . . oh, sorry, Admiral . . . we've come to an agreement. The Comptroller of Accounts will take care of everything else. (*Columbus hands Santangel the contract, and Santangel keeps it.*)
VENDRINO: One more question. Who's going to take care of the supplies? I mean the equipment and the purchase of provisions? Let me finish . . . I'll take care of it. I have the know-how. I used to be the purchasing agent for the city. (*To Columbus:*) May I ask you to come to my office with me. You don't have to worry about a thing, señor Columbus . . . I'll do everything myself. (*He takes Columbus by the arm and leads him away.*)
MOYA: What if he really does discover something? Then he'll be getting way too much.
QUINTANILLA: How so?
MOYA: You've accepted his conditions.
SANTANGEL (*slowly tears up the contract and sings the "Chanson of Contracts":*)

> Friends, I do not want to prophesy,
> And I'll avoid all fibs, at least tonight,
> But, who knows, the earth might just comply
> And to please Columbus prove him right,
> And will be a sphere and not a plane.
> And who knows, when our century ends
> Out of mighty seas new continents
> Might grow like mushrooms after rain.

But we don't have to worry,
Columbus' territory
May stretch from pole to pole—
We'll be in control.
The game so bold that he began
We play along to fool him—
Break all the rules that fit his plan,
And our rule will rule him.
He speculates on earth and sky,
His vision has gone to his head
But one small thing escapes his eye:
His contract, his contract . . . is ripped to shreds.

Worthy friends, in, say, five hundred years
Explorations may be out of date,
Borders will criss-cross both hemispheres
And discoverers will come too late.
All the conquerers will kill each other
For a bigger sliver of the pie,
What today we get for nothing
Tomorrow only blood will buy.

True, those times are not yet here,
but Columbus is their pioneer,
All the gear to colonize:
Culture, progress, and deceit,
Profit, murder, enterprise
Are the cargo of his fleet.
In five hundred years the game
Of aggression is the same:
The smart guys speak of honesty
Of eternal peace ahead.
The dummies hear the words with glee.
Do what they're told, but they don't see:
The treaty, the treaty . . . is ripped to shreds.

Act Two

Scene One

(*A street, recruiter with drum. One person listening.*)

RECRUITER (*accompanies himself on the drum*): To all subjects of His Majesty! We, Ferdinand, King, by the Grace of God, of Aragon, Castile, the Two Sicilies etc.,etc., Count of Barcelona, Ribagorza etc., etc., make it known and proclaim:
LISTENER: And what?
RECRUITER: And proclaim:
LISTENER: I see.
RECRUITER: With undying concern for the destiny of our beloved people, we have decided to open up new lebensraum. A place in the sun will be created and an empire on which the sun never sets! To raise our status in the world . . .
LISTENER: I see.
RECRUITER: What do you mean, you see?
LISTENER: It's the price of bread again.
RECRUITER: Idiot. On the contrary. To raise our status in the world . . .
LISTENER: Didn't I tell you?
RECRUITER: Shut up! . . . we have equipped an expedition to prepare a sea route to India. We are looking for fearless men who are willing, under the leadership of Admiral Columbus, to carry the flag of His Majesty to the ends of the earth. We need lots of volunteers! Sign up now! (*He sighs and starts over again.*) To all subjects of His Majesty: We, Ferdinand, King by the Grace of God, of Aragon . . . Listen, you jerk, how long are you going to be loafing around here?
LISTENER: Huh?
RECRUITER: I've already drummed the announcement thirty-five times in this shitty little village. Don't you think I ever want to eat lunch??
LISTENER: To what?
RECRUITER (*roars*): To eat!
LISTENER: I knew it, the price of bread.

RECRUITER: Are you hard of hearing?
LISTENER: Unfortunately I am, señor drummer.
RECRUITER (*roars*): I want to eat!
LISTENER: Yelling doesn't do it for me. The louder you yell, the less I hear; it's real funny with me.
RECRUITER (*whispers*): . . . make it known and proclaim . . .
LISTENER: And what?
RECRUITER (*roars*): and proclaim . . .
LISTENER: Shhhh!
RECRUITER (*softly*): In undying attention . . . (*furious:*) Oh, to hell with it! Office closed!

(*Darkness.*)

Scene Two

(*Same stage as in scene one. Vendrino and a supplier walk up and down while conversing.*)

VENDRINO: Listen, señor, do you really think you can rip me off? Quite the opposite, let me assure you! The recruiting effort is going great guns, the recruiting office is jammed with volunteers, the masses are eager to conquer for a place in the sun, their enthusiasm knows neither limits nor . . . etc., etc. but the suppliers are still dragging their feet. What do you think you're doing? Let me finish. Where's the new offer for ship's biscuits?
SUPPLIER: But . . . the Admiral has accepted my first offer and . . .
VENDRINO: I know that.
SUPPLIER: . . . and you rejected it.
VENDRINO: That goes without saying. You don't think I'm paying the full price, do you? I've never done that in my life. Let me finish. I want to buy good and cheap. Good for the officers and cheap for the crew. Well? Do you get the message? How about a sample? Let's see. (*He chews the biscuit.*)

That's awful.

SUPPLIER: Those are the cheap ones.

VENDRINO: They are? (*He takes another bite*) Of course, much too good for the crew. What did you put in them?

SUPPLIER: Vanilla.

VENDRINO: Vanilla? You're certainly no merchant of the new age, you're medieval. Just plain antedeluvian. You know what you should have put in? Let me finish. Kitchen cleanser. That's good for the teeth.

SUPPLIER: But . . .

VENDRINO: You don't know a thing about modern principles of nutrition. Or don't you have any kitchen cleanser? Let me finish. I'll offer you one lot of first-class domestic kitchen cleanser at twenty-twenty, with five percent cash discount. Is it a deal?

SUPPLIER: But the Admiral . . .

VENDRINO: . . . made it easy for himself. There he goes with a hop, skip, and a jump, conquering colonies! But first I have to invent the economic policies to go along with them . . .

(*Darkness.*)

Scene Three

(*In Columbus's room*)

COLUMBUS (*alone, bent over papers, murmering*): twenty-three, twenty-seven and six is thirty-three, and seven is forty, carry the four (*A knock at the door.*) four and five is eight and three is eleven, carry the one . . .

LANDLADY (*enters hesitantly*): Hm, excuse me . . .

COLUMBUS: One and five is six and three is nine . . .

LANDLADY: Are you working on your calculations again, Admiral?

COLUMBUS: Yeah. It's really complicated, damn it. Maybe you could help me.

LANDLADY: I'd be glad to, Admiral. Let me see. What nerve. The tailor charged you ten ducats for that suit? My brother-in-law would have made it for half that. And the washerwoman charged two ducats? She should be burned at the stake! By the way, there's an error in your addition.

COLUMBUS: Arithmetic was never my forte.

LANDLADY: You let people cheat you right and left, Admiral. Your creditors are going to ruin you. Jesus, when I think what patient suckers we are, my husband and I. We've been waiting for our rent for three months. Wait, Antonio, I said, don't be so greedy. On the last day of the month, when the Admiral gets his first Admiral's salary . . . right?

COLUMBUS: (*says nothing.*)

LANDLADY: And today is the last day of the month!

COLUMBUS: My dear woman . . . I . . . you know . . . I'm only a civil servant . . .

LANDLADY: Are you telling me that you didn't get paid?

COLUMBUS: My dear woman, the state has tremendous financial obligations these days. The Queen has taken a vow . . .

LANDLADY: Jesus, you aren't going to tell me the story of that undershirt again, are you? Do you know what that dirty shirt has cost us, Admiral? Three percent sales surtax, six percent beer tax, six ducats mule fee! And now to top it all off, three months' food and lodging! Good God!

COLUMBUS: My dear woman, in seven days I'll be sailing west towards unknown seas.

LANDLADY: A wonderful consolation.

COLUMBUS: The earth is round.

LANDLADY: The sum you owe me is much rounder!

COLUMBUS: I shall be Viceroy of India.

LANDLADY (*scornfully*): And then you'll send me the money?

COLUMBUS: I certainly will.

LANDLADY: And you expect me to believe that? I've been in the rental business for twenty years. Really, Admiral.

COLUMBUS: O.K., so what am I supposed to do? (*With a helpless look at the bills*): I don't know where to turn.

LANDLADY: I have an idea.

COLUMBUS: I've already pawned everything.

LANDLADY: Who's talking about pawning? What a shame to pawn that beautiful watch.

COLUMBUS: What watch?

LANDLADY: Oh, I know a watch when I see one. I'm an educated woman. Whenever I dusted here, I couldn't take my eyes off it. And you know, señor Columbus, my sister-in-law's boy is getting confirmed today, And I'm his godmother . . . and I thought that would be a gift that nobody ever thought of . . . a watch, no boy has ever gotten that for his confirmation, and . . . señor Columbus, when you come back from India you could have another year free room and board . . . that's what I thought . . . I mean, just an idea, you know, señor Admiral.

COLUMBUS: You mean this thing here? (*He puts it in her hand.*)

LANDLADY: I sure do, your Excellency.

COLUMBUS: But, dear woman, I need that. Aside from the grace of Saint Christopher, this instrument is all I have to help me find my way across the seas.

LANDLADY: Maybe the grace will be enough, your Grace? Because, you know, a watch like that . . .

COLUMBUS: But this isn't a watch.

LANDLADY: It's not a watch?

COLUMBUS (*grandly*): This is my compass!

LANDLADY: A com . . . (*She throws the compass on the floor.*) Shame on you. Pack your bags and beat it! (*The landlady exits.*)

COLUMBUS (*falls on his knees and examines the compass terrified.*)

VENDRINO (*rushes in*): Morning, Admiral, old buddy. What are you doing? Practicing for sea sickness?

COLUMBUS (*rights himself*): It's a good thing you've come, Comptroller. I must reproach you severely.

VENDRINO: You reproach me? Now I've heard everything. I have to reproach you! Let me finish. Since I took the equipping of the expedition off your shoulders, the deliveries are finally being made on schedule. So far everything's fine and dandy.

COLUMBUS: Aren't you exaggerating?

VENDRINO: All right. Let's say fine, but not quite dandy yet.

The recruitment, however, which is still in your hands, isn't working at all. So far your recruiters have drummed fifteen drums to shreds and haven't drummed up one single sailor.

COLUMBUS: What more can I do than to remind the subjects of their duty, appeal to their honor and their . . .

VENDRINO: etc. etc. All right, the slogans are right, but the methods, the advertising technique, good God! Do you believe that nowadays, in the year 1492, people will swallow that garbage if it isn't served up properly? What you've been doing is downright medieval. You don't have the foggiest notion of modern propaganda techniques.

COLUMBUS: And you, señor Vendrino, don't have the foggiest notion of what a ship is. The boards you sent me for the repair of the Nina and Pinta are unacceptable.

VENDRINO: Why? You won't find cheaper ones anywhere in the whole country.

COLUMBUS: They're rotten! Worthless junk! The Santa Maria is more or less seaworthy. But the sailors on the other two ships will go to the bottom because of your cheap boards.

VENDRINO: Better to go to the bottom than not go at all. If we don't economize on the equipment, the whole Indian adventure will capsize. Let me finish. I simply don't understand your attitude. Whose idea was the whole thing anyway?

COLUMBUS: Mine.

VENDRINO: See what I mean? So why are you always interfering?

COLUMBUS: I'm . . . I'm speechless.

VENDRINO: Bravo. That's the way you should be. You're the man with the idea. I'm the man who makes it work. You've got the fame. I've got the headaches. Let's stick to this division of labor.

COLUMBUS: After half a life of hardship, I've finally succeeded in getting my idea accepted.

VENDRINO: That goes without saying. My respects. But believe me: you have no idea what it is you have finally succeeded in getting accepted, and that's a fact. You just don't. Why, you don't even have a clue to what possibilities your idea has. I can see that from the way you go about recruiting.

COLUMBUS: Now you just leave that to me. I will at least select my own sailors . . . if nothing else.
VENDRINO (*shrugging his shoulders*): All right then. Just keep on selecting. But be sure to find people to select from. It's been pretty slim pickings so far. Good-bye.
COLUMBUS: Hm . . . Señor Vendrino . . .
VENDRINO: What is it now?
COLUMBUS: Could you, I mean I'd be much obliged to you if you could lend me a modest sum till the fifteenth . . . my hotel bill . . .
VENDRINO: I'm awfully sorry, old boy. Your recruiting methods are not paying off; in fact they're costing us far too much time. And time is money. And I have no time. Good-bye.
COLUMBUS: Good-bye. (*Vendrino exits, the landlady's face appears*): Hey, Vendrino!
VENDRINO (*returns*): Now what is it?
COLUMBUS: Do you think you could organize the recruiting more effectively?
VENDRINO (*with a deep sigh takes out his wallet*): Boy, oh boy, I'm a sucker for you every time.

(*Darkness.*)

Scene Four

(*A Street. A minstrel sings, with the help of pictures, the "Song of the Dangers of the Sea"*)

Diego, poor sailor, poor sailor,
Your face is so yellow, say why?
I was in India, dad.
The pollution was pretty bad.
Pure sulphur rained from the sky.
Oh!

Diego, poor sailor, poor sailor,
What happened to your ear?
I was in India, uncle.
I got a nasty carbuncle
That left me but one ear to hear.
Oh!

Diego, poor sailor, poor sailor,
With no legs you look pretty sore.
I was in India, sis.
The snakes there, I still hear them hiss,
Took the legs I had before.
Oh!

Diego, poor sailor, poor sailor,
With no arms you are a sad sight.
I was in India, brother,
A serpent or something or other
Ate all my arms, left and right.
Oh!

Diego, poor sailor, poor sailor,
You're minus a head and a rump.
I was in India, my friend,
And lost my head and rear end
In the Himalaya swamp.
Oh!

Diego, poor sailor, poor sailor,
Why are your kisses so cold?
I was in India, darling,
The mermaids' tricks were disarming
And left me limp and old.
Oh!

Diego, poor sailor, poor sailor,
You're going to your grave to die!
The hardships I would have endured,

But my stomach cannot be cured.
The ship's biscuits killed me. Good-bye!
Oh!

Let us pray to God of the Earth and the Sea:
From the Indian fleet please deliver me!

VENDRINO (*enters*): Hey, old sport, what are you doing?
MINSTREL: Good sir, I'm bringing the common folk knowledge and news of the world at large.
VENDRINO: Stop that medieval gibberish! You're producing a tabloid.
How often do you appear?
MINSTREL: Daily at the market place, señor.
VENDRINO: Splendid! A daily for illiterates. Do you know, young man, that you are a superpower?
MINSTREL: Who me?
VENDRINO: You should produce a late evening edition. Well, some day. And just think, the King doesn't even know how valuable you could be for him. The main thing is, I know. What do you have on your pages today?
MINSTREL: I don't sing from pages. I sing as the bird sings.
VENDRINO: You mean, you're free to sing what you want?
MINSTREL: Most decidedly.
VENDRINO: We heard that one before. All journalists say that. All right then, shoot!
MINSTREL (*sings*): Rosita and Pedro were lovers, oh how that couple could love.
VENDRINO: The short story doesn't interest me. You can do whatever you want with the literature section.
MINSTREL (*sings*): It was on a Wednesday night, the moon was shining bright, They robbed the Danville train . . .
VENDRINO: Spare me the crime section.
MINSTREL: I wonder who's kissing her now . . .
VENDRINO: I don't care beans about the quiz section either . . .
MINSTREL: (*sings the first lines of the "Song of the Dangers of the Sea."*)
VENDRINO: Finally, the editorial on colonial politics. Let me

have a look at your illustrations. Listen, young man, this will never do. You don't have the foggiest notion about the duties of a responsible press towards the people, towards the state as well as . . . etc., etc.

MINSTREL: But dear señor . . .

VENDRINO: Shut up. If that's how the press works, it's no wonder we can't recruit a single volunteer. Pure scare propaganda.

MINSTREL: Señor, that's what the public likes to hear.

VENDRINO: Because the public has been educated wrong. You've got to take a completely different approach, young man. More heroism! More positive thinking!

MINSTREL: I'd go broke that way.

VENDRINO: Young man, you don't know who I am. I am Finance Inspector and Royal Comptroller of Accounts Vendrino.

MINSTREL: All right, so you'll take my license away. What can I do? If I sang songs praising the Indian expedition, I'd fold for sure.

VENDRINO: Boy, are you dense! Do you really live from your audience?

MINSTREL: What else am I supposed to live from?

VENDRINO: From ads, that goes without saying. All the suppliers are at my command. Without even trying, I can get you two ads a day for every folksong, ten to fifteen lines long. You pay me ten percent. That leaves you the other ninety since you have no printing costs. Of course, the condition is that you take a responsible, positive position on colonial politics. Then I'll have the press working for me at last . . . and you'll have a solid footing for your business.

MINSTREL: Hidden, o señor, is the meaning of your utterance.

VENDRINO (*sighs*): All right, then. Listen, I'll explain it to you one more time. Unfortunately you're not advanced enough for a late evening edition. This is the way you've got to do it: Hip hip hurrah, to India . . . understand?

MINSTREL: Yes, señor! (*He sings.*)

Hip hip hurrah to India,
To India's distant shore.
Through stormy seas we'll find the way

That no one found before.
We'll find gold and silver by the sack
And hot dark women on their back.
We'll conquer India far and wide,
'Cause God is on our side.

Hip hip hurrah to India,
We, the master race will come,
To teach them all our better way
In the name of Christendom.
We'll get gold and silver by the sack,
And hot dark women on their back.
We'll conquer India far and wide,
'Cause God is on our side.

Once India's ours, we'll no more roam
With hip und with hurray.
We'll be back at home, sweet home,
As if we'd never been away.
There'll be gold and silver by the sack,
And all the treasure we brought back
For our waiting, sweet, white bride,
'Cause God is on our side.

(*Blackout.*)

Scene Five

(*Egg stand, Columbus strolls by.*)

EGG WOMAN: Eggs, fresh eggs, good Sir. (*Columbus is about to go by.*) What's the matter? A regular customer like you isn't buying anything today?
COLUMBUS: Well, it's because . . . (*Quickly*): All right then, give me half a dozen hard-boiled.
EGG WOMAN: Half a dozen hard-boiled for his Excellency, the Admiral.

(*Columbus quickly takes an egg and eats it.*)

EGG WOMAN: That's better! Eggs are the best food for an active gentleman. I'm sure you have a lot of work with all the preparations for the trip.

COLUMBUS: You know, it's really strange. I, too, thought the last few days would be a rat race. The fact is, however, that I find myself just standing around, bored to tears. Maybe that's the way it always is on the eve of a historic feat.

EGG WOMAN: That's just the way it should be. You should never leave anything for the last minute. You'll need the last minute for the toothbrush you forgot to pack.

COLUMBUS (*at a loss*): It's not the toothbrush. The geographic calculations have been finished for a long time . . . and everything else has been taken care of by my assistants.

EGG WOMAN: That's exactly the way it should be. You, as Admiral, shouldn't have to worry about a thing. They should handle you like a raw egg. After all, you are a genius.

COLUMBUS: Do you really think so?

EGG WOMAN: Of course. You resemble my late husband just like one egg resembles another. And my late husband, he was a genius. He started with two chickens, and then by the time he passed away so peacefully, he could look back on four hundred eggs a day. You won't ever get that far. But you'll find the sea route to India, I'm sure. (*Columbus has eaten another egg.*) You do have a healthy appetite today, Admiral.

COLUMBUS: Healthy, I don't know about that . . .

EGG WOMAN: What do you think that sea route to India is like anyway?

COLUMBUS (*eagerly*): Look, it's really simple. (*He takes an egg and demonstrates the following.*) This is Europe.

EGG WOMAN: This is what?

COLUMBUS: Europe.

EGG WOMAN: I don't see nothin'.

COLUMBUS: This is Asia, another part of the earth.

EGG WOMAN: Nothin'! Not a speck! There are no specks of dirt on my eggs. My eggs are fresh and clean. And if you're gonna insult me, go and find yourself another egg lady.

COLUMBUS: But my dear woman. I'm using your egg as a scientific model.
EGG WOMAN (*suspiciously*): You are, huh? Of course that would be a great honor for me. If it's true.
COLUMBUS: Your eggs are a symbol of the greatest astronomical discovery of the century.
EGG WOMAN: You're kidding. Do you really mean that? My God, if only my chickens knew!
COLUMBUS: Apropos, my dear woman I . . . you know . . . such a nuisance, my wallet . . . I left it at home . . . and . . .
EGG WOMAN: That's quite all right, Admiral. You have credit with me, of course. I always did have a soft spot for a genius. But you should've told me right away that you don't have any money. You always act like you're a shrewd businessman who's always ripping other people off, but actually you don't have a clue about business.
COLUMBUS: I think you're right.
EGG WOMAN: Of course I am. Now my late husband, he was an all-round genius, and you are a little one-sided. Doesn't matter. But you should beware of businessmen or they'll cheat you.
COLUMBUS: You're no dummy.
EGG WOMAN: Well, smart enough for the egg business. You have to know what you want and then go for it, that's the main thing. O.k., the gentleman owes me a ducat fifty. What are you doing now?
COLUMBUS: I'm trying to make this egg stand up, but there are some problems you can't solve in this world.
EGG WOMAN: Says who? Let me try. (*She puts the egg down forcefully so that the end breaks in and the egg stands up.*) See? You've got to use force. There's the egg of Columbus!
COLUMBUS: And I thought I was the egg head.

(*Blackout.*)

Scene Six

(*Prison cell, Pepito, Vendrino.*)

PEPITO (*asleep*)
VENDRINO: Hey, old sport!
PEPITO (*wakes up*): Aha, a new one! (*introducing himself:*) Pepito Alibi, vulgo Pepo. Three years, public violence.
VENDRINO: Pleased to meet you. Finance Inspector Vendrino.
PEPITO: Hey, are you a fancy-looking customer. Are you in for bigamy or criminal bankruptcy?
VENDRINO: None of the above.
PEPITO: You're not in for a political offense, are you? 'Cause if you are, I've gotta protest violently. 'Cause, as a criminal who thinks positive, I refuse on principle to share a cell with a political offender.
VENDRINO: Young man, that's not even a possibility. On the contrary. Let me finish. Would you like to hit ship tomorrow morning?
PEPITO: Well shit, after all the things and people I've hit in my life, that'd be a change. Where do the honorable authorities plan to transport me in this boat of yours?
VENDRINO: To unknown shores.
PEPITO: If you mean a penal colony . . .
VENDRINO: You misunderstand me, my dear señor. You're going to be pardoned.
PEPITO: Don't feed me some fairy tale, señor. The day before yesterday, in a fit of temper, I beat up a guy on the cell block so badly that he had to be hospitalized. Yesterday I bit off a guard's ear. If you keep on yakkin' about a pardon you'll get a taste of my behavior that'll make it tough for your old lady to put you back together.
VENDRINO: Why, your behavior is exemplary.
PEPITO: My behavior is what? (*He raises his arm, ready to hit Vendrino, but suddenly changes his mind.*) Honestly, you slay me.
VENDRINO: Because you don't let me finish, my dear sir. Have you heard of the Indian expedition of Admiral Columbus?

PEPITO: I sure have. Last week a certain Diego was in my cell, a deserted volunteer. He told me that nothin' don't stink like the goulash in the barracks of the guys going to India. And then four recruiters came at noon. Big bruisers, real impressive . . . and then Diego volunteered again.

VENDRINO: You see my point. Now we're getting to the heart of the matter. Do *you* think they're ever going to find the sea route to India with wimps like that Diego? All the propaganda in the press is lost on guys like that; they fold before they ever leave the barracks. See what I mean? (*Pepito shrugs his shoulders.*) Of course you do, that goes without saying. We need five hundred men. So far we've got fifty, and forty of them don't have the slightest notion that they're going to be the heroic conquerers of new colonies.

PEPITO: What do they think they are in for?

VENDRINO: They think they're going to North Africa to grow cactuses.

PEPITO: What a bunch of birdbrains.

VENDRINO: You get my point. They're not the kind of crew members I need. What I need is you, Pepo, and four hundred like you who'll show the Indians what's what.

PEPITO: And all those going along get pardoned?

VENDRINO: That goes without saying.

PEPITO: You know, señor, I'm beginning to like you.

VENDRINO: Huh?

PEPITO: Yes, I am! You're a pretty respectable crook. And when I hear you making a proposal like that, I almost believe it's not the usual trick.

VENDRINO: How do you mean that?

PEPITO: Don't you get it? A pardon plus the life of a free sailor. Santa Claus offers us that every Christmas, and anybody stupid enough to fall for it ends up working his ass off as a galley slave.

VENDRINO: Señor Pepo, you know me well enough to know that I'm not talking about anything like that.

PEPITO: So what are we talking about? Anybody who comes and offers me a job gotta put his cards on the table or shut up. I'm nobody's sucker.

VENDRINO: All right, listen, my dear sir. Up to the end of the fifteenth century colonial politics was by and large restricted to the establishment of trade companies.
PEPITO: What a roundabout way to steal. Professional criminals don't have no respect for that.
VENDRINO: But now a new epoch is breaking out.
PEPITO: It's breaking out? I like it already.
VENDRINO: The task will be to civilize the newly discovered lands thoroughly.
PEPITO: Thoroughness is the foremost duty of a thief.
VENDRINO: It goes without saying that we come with peaceful intentions.
PEPITO: That's just what I do. It's only when somebody disturbs me in my work that I turn into a beast.
VENDRINO: We carry culture, civilization, and western ideals and values with us.
PEPITO: I've never worked with tools like that before. Sounds interesting.
VENDRINO: We are solely and purely interested in the beneficial exploitation of resources, the treasures that are just lying in the ground unused.
PEPITO: In the cellar or in the attic—it never made no difference to me where they were hidden.
VENDRINO: In other words, we'll occupy our place in the sun.
PEPITO: What?! You want to break in in broad daylight? What's the police going to say to that?
VENDRINO: The police are going to cordon off the street when we return in triumph.
PEPITO: Well, what d'ya know. And anyone who takes part in this job'll get an official pardon?
VENDRINO: Retroactively and in advance.
PEPITO: In advance? I get it. Hats off, señor. I'm in! And if I'm in on it, that means the underworld will have a hand in the new world empire.
VENDRINO: All right then, the four hundred boys . . .
PEPITO: . . . no problem! I'll be damned if I can't get a gang together for a deal like this.
MINSTREL (*enters*): Can I come in?

VENDRINO: Come right in. (*He introduces the two.*) Señor Pepito Alibi . . . Señor Perez, Chief of the Press.
PEPITO: Pleased ta meet ya. Three years, public violence.
VENDRINO: Have you heard his latest editorial yet?
PEPITO: I had the pleasure in today's morning edition. A pretty good con job. At last I get promoted from the crime section to the editorial page.
VENDRINO: This is a historic moment. You're going to tell me that three guys like the three of us can't conquer the world lickety split? Don't make me laugh . . .
ALL THREE: (*sing "The Ballad of the Three"*)
Watch out! We'll get you,
We gang of three will!
Our greed grabs the world by the throat
Like bloodhounds out for the kill!
First the man with the heavy blow—one!
Then the press and the radio—two!
Then the man who gets all the dough.
With force and lies and gold
The world is bought and sold.

Watch out, colored man.
White power's in!
If your skin ain't white as ours,
You must fight to save your skin.
First the man who breaks in, smash—one!
Then the liar of media trash—two!
And last the man who hauls in the cash.
With force and lies and gold
The world is bought and sold.

Europe, watch out!
We'll chain you, too!
We'll dress you in gold from head to toe,
Then beat you black and blue.
You'll serve that man with the iron fist—one!
The man who gives the truth his twist—two!
And the boss of the two, the capitalist.
With force and lies and gold
The world is bought and sold.

Scene Seven

(*Columbus, kneeling in front of a world map, says his prayer to Saint Christoph.*)

COLUMBUS:
   On mighty seas and distant sands,
   Saint Christoph, be my guide.
   My fate is always in thy hands,
   In you I will abide.
   Carry these ships and all they keep
   As once you carried God's own son
   Safely across the deep.

   Oh spare us meteors and plagues,
   Saint Christoph, hear me plead.
   And when my compass lets me down
   Only Thy grace can lead.
   Preserve the lie about my birth
   That everyone believed;
   The world is bad, my patron saint,
   And wants to be deceived.

   The world is bad, weak is my creed,
   Saint Christoph, forgive my hate.
   I'm only human in my greed
   So make me rich and great.
   Tell me how long my luck will last,
   My glory, my renown,
   And let me know my enemy
   So I can strike him down.

VENDRINO (*enters*): Admiral, Admiral, the ships are saddled! In two hours we can weigh the anchor, as they say so aptly, but that won't take long. I got a light one cheap.
COLUMBUS (*in a formal tone*): Thank you. (*He starts walking back and forth in long strides.*)
VENDRINO: Why are you rushing around like that?

COLUMBUS: That's how a sailor walks.
VENDRINO: That's good to know. (*He starts running next to Columbus with little steps.*) From prow to bow, from star to board . . . everything's shipshape. Even the crews are already complete. The prison management wasn't very cooperative but I was hard as nails and got them all out.
COLUMBUS: You hired criminals?
VENDRINO: You should see them. Perfect specimens, rough and ready.
COLUMBUS: And I'm supposed to conquer an empire with criminals?
VENDRINO: Who else would you suggest? Stamp collectors?
COLUMBUS: I refuse to set sail.
VENDRINO: Oh, come on!
LADY (*heavily veiled, enters*): Quiet, señor!
VENDRINO: Who's that now? Don't disturb the Admiral, he doesn't have any time.
LADY: Quiet, señor!
VENDRINO: What the hell do you want? For God's sake take off that curtain!
LADY: Please, more respect for my secrecy!
COLUMBUS: I definitely refuse . . .
LADY: Quiet, señor! Kneel down . . .
(*Columbus obeys.*)
LADY: I have traveled from Santa Fé to Palos to bring you a message from a lady who doesn't want to be named. The lady wants you to know that a stowaway has smuggled himself on board the Santa Maria to be victorious with your fleet . . . or to die. This stowaway is the heart of a queen!
COLUMBUS: Tell Her Majesty that I definitely refuse . . .
LADY: Quiet, señor. The lady wants you to know that at this very moment the eyes of the whole empire are upon you, that there is no turning back, only a going forward. You, Columbus, carry on your shoulders the future of mankind just as Saint Christopher once carried the divine child. You are a hero!
COLUMBUS: But . . .
LADY: Quiet, señor! The lady knows that you are dedicated to

your mission and that, in spite of all petty obstacles, you will be victorious. The lady sends you her tears, her blessing, and this medallion. (*She puts it around his neck.*)

COLUMBUS (*jumps up*): Comptroller, in two hours we lift anchor! We'll take the course to Africa and sail in the direction of the Canary Islands.

VENDRINO: Your command is my desire, Admiral!

COLUMBUS: We'll come to the twenty-eighth parallel and follow it straight west.

VENDRINO: You don't say.

COLUMBUS: Straight west!

VENDRINO (*pushes Columbus, who is in a trance, out the door. To the lady*): Beautiful mask. You'll get a percentage.

LADY: I should hope so, señor.

VENDRINO: What of all that did the Queen actually say?

LADY: She said, Bon Voyage.

VENDRINO: I'm impressed. With whom do I have the pleasure?

LADY: Do you remember Gibraltar?

VENDRINO: Gibraltar. Let me think. I did know a lady there . . . you're not Juanita, are you?

LADY: You guessed it!

VENDRINO (*kisses her hand*): That was that charming evening when we met secretly. Your husband was away . . . that is he wasn't really away at all, and he wasn't really your husband either. Why did you stop writing me?

LADY (*tears off her veil, it is the Marquise de Moya*): You rat!

VENDRINO (*very startled*): But darling . . . that was before your time.

MOYA: Before my time? How long have we known each other? Two years. And when were you in Gibraltar? Three months ago.

VENDRINO: Darling . . .

MOYA: Don't darling me! We're through! I'm sick and tired of your cheating on me over and over again! I never want to see you again.

VENDRINO: First give me kiss. (*They embrace.*) And with whom are you being faithful to me these days?

MOYA (*pulls at his ruff*): These men . . . how simple-minded they are.

VENDRINO: Do you love me?

MOYA: Of course. Otherwise I'd be much nicer to you. But I can't be alone all the time. Seize the day!

VENDRINO: Stop playing with my collar. Come here. Sit down. (*They sit down on a trunk.*) Beatrice, you can't imagine how busy I've been. I'm organizing the whole expedition.

MOYA: In Santa Fee they're wearing tiny hats now.

VENDRINO: Would you please stop looking at yourself in the mirror.

MOYA: How do you get along with the Admiral?

VENDRINO: He's a strange man. When you ask him something, he gives you such a weird look, as if he were totally occupied with something else. Aside from that, he does everything wrong. Nevertheless . . . there's something to him. That man could go places!

MOYA: He's not my type at all. I like fat men.

VENDRINO: He can thank his lucky stars that he has me. I made him what he is, after all. I think we made a good deal with him. You'll see lots of money!

MOYA: And who gave you guys the idea?

VENDRINO: I did. (*He pats her cheerfully on the behind.*)

MOYA: No, I did! Ouch, don't be so gross. I've told you over and over again: You don't have good manners, you don't have bad manners, you don't have any manners. You are much too loud. Even at court. That's no way to make a career.

VENDRINO: And how does one make a career?

MOYA: Like this. (*She kisses him.*) Are we going out to eat later? I love eating with you.

VENDRINO (*pulls a notebook out of his pocket*): I don't know if we'll have time before departure. When are you going back? I mean . . . one really ought to . . .

MOYA: What on earth are you thinking of??? I'm travelling in the entourage of the Archbishop.

VENDRINO: What a pity.

MOYA: Yes, Jose, it is a pity.

VENDRINO: A terrible pity.

Moya: Do you promise to write to me, fatty?
Vendrino: I'll write you every day, sweetie.
Moya: Tell me everything. Tell me what the Indian women are wearing. I'm dying to know. And if they don't wear anything, then write about that, too. And tell me if the men are well-built. And be careful not to catch cold during the crossing. You are the kind that catches a cold if there's a closet door open. Bundle up, do you hear? And don't do anything stupid with those Indian women. I want you back in perfect health! (*They kiss.*)

(*A girl appears, she is dressed in white, and holds a bunch of flowers in her hand.*)

Girl: Now let all your hearts sing,
Now let all your bells . . .
Vendrino (*surprised*): How do you mean that, my child?
Girl (*undaunted*): Today is our day of bliss,
That nobody will want to miss
Vendrino: Are you sure you haven't come to the wrong door?
Girl: want to miss . . . want to miss . . . day of bliss, that nobody . . .
Vendrino: . . . will want to miss. We've heard that.
Girl (*starts crying.*)
Moya: Why are you crying, my child?
Girl: I am . . . (*sniffle*) . . . a maid of . . . (*sniffle*) . . . honor . . .
Moya: That's no reason to cry. You won't be one for ever, give it time . . .
Minstrel (*comes running, breathless*): Where is she, where?
Vendrino: Are you looking for this girl, perhaps, Propaganda Chief?
Minstrel: What the hell are you doing here, you brat? (*He gives her a slap.*)
Girl (*bawling*): Now let all your hearts sing . . . let all . . . (*sniffle*) . . . bells . . .
Minstrel: But not here, silly goose. I told her to break through the police cordon suddenly the minute the Admiral arrives at

the harbor. What a moron. This gentleman is not an Admiral, can't you see that?

GIRL: I lost my way . . . (*sniffle*) . . .

VENDRINO (*to Moya*): As you see, the departure ceremonies have already begun. We won't have time to eat.

MOYA: What a pity, darling.

MINSTREL: Stop bawling this minute! Or no, go on, bawl away. That'll be an ear-catcher in a minor key. "Uplifting scenes of good-bye in the headquarters of the general staff. Populace storms offices with tears streaming down their faces."

PEPITO: (*in uniform, breathless*): Help! Help!

VENDRINO (*to Moya*): The leader of our volunteers. What's the matter, Señor Pepito?

PEPITO: They're on my tail.

MOYA: Who is?

PEPITO: Everybody, the whole town! Hear them yelling?

MINSTREL: Sure we hear them, Señor Pepito, they're giving you a big send-off.

PEPITO: You're kidding! Oh shit, and I thought they were shouting: Stop thief! Stop thief!

VENDRINO: It's high time you started gearing yourself up for your new position.

GIRL (*to Pepito*): Now let all your hearts sing, now let all your bells ring . . .

PEPITO: Huh?

GIRL: Today is our day of bliss, that nobody . . .

MINSTREL: Are you still here, you numbskull? That's not the Admiral either!

GIRL: . . . wants to miss . . . wants to miss . . . Today is our day of bliss . . . that nobody . . . (*sniffle*)

MOYA: Poor thing. (*She gives her a piece of candy.*)

MINSTREL (*writing in his reporter's notebook:*): "Lady of the High Aristocracy who wishes to remain anonymous takes starving child to supper."

PEPITO: O.K. Chief, we're ready. Let's get on with the job.

VENDRINO: Will you please make use of a more sailorlike terminology? In a minute or two you'll be face to face with your Admiral.

(*Enter Columbus, with him a tax collector.*)

COLUMBUS (*furious*): You're not going to issue me an exit permit?
TAX COLLECTOR: Regulations are regulations.
COLUMBUS: Just who are you anyway?
TAX COLLECTOR: Oh, I am nobody, just a tax collector.
COLUMBUS (*beside himself*): I will not stand for any more of this harrassment.
VENDRINO: Just a minute. What's going on here?
TAX COLLECTOR: Nothing's going on. The Admiral isn't going 'cause he hasn't paid his taxes.
MOYA: Good heavens, what shall we do?
PEPITO: That's easy, lady! (*He grabs the tax collector by the collar and raises his arm.*)
VENDRINO: Let go of him at once, you idiot. You're the pride of the nation. (*To the minstrel:*) Señor Editor, you'll keep mum about this incident!
MINSTREL: That goes without singing.
COLUMBUS: For crying out loud! What do I have to do to get permission to leave the country?
TAX COLLECTOR: Nothing. All I have to do is reclaim the three little boats you have out there in the harbor . . . and then, as far as the authorities are concerned, nothing will stand in the seaway of your seaway to India.
COLUMBUS: Finance Inspector Vendrino?
VENDRINO: The matter will be settled in no time. Hand me that rag!

(*The Tax Collector hands him the ordinance.*)

VENDRINO (*and the Maid of Honor speak to the Tax Collector at the same time*): Now listen carefully. According to the decree of April 24, 1488, the income tax quota, which does not derive from public utilities, is calculated with the capital gains tax in such a way that the sales tax plus the property tax minus the real estate tax is calculated with the uncommitted ten percent of the household tax. Assuming that the sum total would have been due on July 1st, the ordinance of November 18, 1474 takes effect whereby the tax-exempt portion of the income tax falls outside any claim of the IRS. Today is the third of August 1492, which means that the amount is not due until January 1st, 1493. Do you get it? Do you have anything more to say?

GIRL (*finally in gear*):

> Now let all your hearts sing,
> Now let all your bells ring.
> Today is our day of bliss
> Nobody will want to miss.
> For ye, the Admiral, we see.
> There's no braver man than ye.
> Now you're going far away.
> Come back soon, hip hip hurray.

TAX COLLECTOR (*overwhelmed*): Well, nothing. Regulations are regulations.
VENDRINO: But if you don't understand the regulation, señor?
TAX COLLECTOR: Well, in that case. (*He exits.*)
VENDRINO: Well, how did I handle that?
MOYA: Magnificently, fatty.
VENDRINO: You see, Admiral, anybody can go to India, but to get out of one's own country, that takes real talent.

Scene Eight

(*On board the Santa Maria.*)

PEPITO (*sings the Ship Song*):

> The waves of the ocean are blue, so blue,
> Santa Maria.
> You are our ship, we're proud of you,
> Santa Maria.

We sail every day from morn' till night,
But India never comes in sight.
Oh India, we'd be so glad to see ya.
Santa Maria, Santa Maria,
Lucky Santa Maria.

Proudly our flag blows in the breeze.
Santa Maria.
Our cook alone eats all the cheese.
Santa Maria.
Our cook alone drinks all the rum,
We're sailing dry through Christendom
Deep into geographia.
Santa Maria, Santa Maria,
Lucky Santa Maria.

One day when we no longer roam,
Santa Maria,
Happy again we'll be at home,
Santa Maria.
And if our Marie should get a ba-by,
We won't ask who the daddy may be,
'cause we all loved our Marie.
Santa Maria, Santa Maria,
Lucky Santa Maria.

Water is wet and earth is dry,
Santa Maria,
There was a smart guy who told us a lie,
Santa Maria:
Besides our world there's another one.
We've been all over and haven't seen one.
Who knows, maybe it's behind the sun.
Santa Maria, Santa Maria,
Lucky Santa Maria.

(*A ship's boy scrubs the railing. Pepito supervises the work. Enter a sailor.*)

PEPITO: Listen, boys, what's that funny noise I hear, that crunching sound?

SAILOR: Maybe we hit a sandbank.

PEPITO: I always knew you were an idiot, Rodrigo. But it takes more than one idiot to be as stupid as you are. How can we hit a sandbank in the middle of the ocean? Why are you here anyway, because you are a safe cracker or a sailor?

SAILOR: Ay, ay, señor . . . a safe-cracker. (*Sadly:*) I always dream of banks, I can't help it . . . and a sandbank is better than no bank . . . seventy days of sea and sky . . . as far as the eye can see there's not a thing to steal . . . one of these days, in my cabin fever, I'm gonna drill a hole in the side of the ship.

PEPITO: Shut up. There it was again, that crunching sound!!! Like sand . . . (*He gives the ship's boy a slap.*) . . . you low-down guttersnipe, eating stolen biscuits! Is that what I trained you for with such loving care? Every time you steal they catch you five minutes later, you amateur. What a loser!

SHIP'S BOY: Pardon me, señor. You said that once we have the colonies we can steal above board.

SAILOR: That's it, mate. That's the ideal that inspired us to go on this expedition. And now . . . where's the colony and where are we? I don't even know what a woman looks like any more; it's so bad I can't even dream of one.

BOY: Me neither, señor.

PEPITO: You snot-nosed twirp, you're not supposed to know anything about women.

BOY: But I did dream of one.

PEPITO: Shut up and keep swabbing!

(*Sailor and ship's boy resume work.*)

BOY (*sings softly*):

> Every day for fourteen hours
> We are scrubbing grime and grit.
> Instead of biscuits kitchen cleanser,
> Instead of India we get shit.

SAILOR (*sings along softly*): Santa Maria, ahoy!
BOY (*somewhat, louder*):

>Ham and beef are for the big cheese,
>Columbus dines just like a duke,
>We can chew on kitchen cleanser
>And get soup that makes you puke.

SAILOR: Santa Maria, ahoy!
PEPITO (*lost in thought, has sung the last stanza with the others, catches himself, furious*): Quiet, you scum! How long's it been since you were eye to eye with a shark? It's been a while since you died like heroes on the battlefield, eh? I'm going to toss you all overboard.
SAILOR: I wouldn't be so sure about that, mate, because out of cabin fever we could toss you first.
BOY: Ay, ay, señor.
PEPITO: What's that!? You plan to commit an act of insubordination?
SAILOR: We'd never do that. Just because I, a simple criminal, don't understand such highfalutin' words. But who knows, there are those ten guys in the crew that don't have police records, and some of them are from good families; they volunteered because they thought the ships were bound for North Africa, not the west. I could ask them what that is, "insubordination."
BOY: Should I run downstairs, señor?
PEPITO: Ya'd better not. What are you complaining about anyway, you slime-buckets?
SAILOR: Something's fishy around here. Rockets are falling from the sky. Grass is growing on the ocean. Remember when we saw fish flying? (*He crosses himself.*) But there ain't no such a thing. If a fish can fly, then it sure can't swim. No one at home will ever believe that.
BOY: And the cannibals, señor.
PEPITO: Where are there cannibals?
BOY: In India! Men with three heads and women as big as trees. And what about the food on board?

SAILOR: I wish we could at least get something to eat that doesn't make us glad to see a storm coming so we can throw it all up.
BOY: And why can't we sing, señor?
SAILOR: With all of that, at least we want to be allowed to sing.
PEPITO: Anyone who doesn't like it here can get out.
SAILOR: Right, and if you tell us to shut up, our cabin fever just might get out of hand, and you could be the one to end up eye to eye with a shark, mate, if you don't mind my saying so.
BOY: Yes, señor.
PEPITO: All right. 'cause I am a good guy: You can sing for all I care.
BOY: Much obliged. (*A tempo.*)

> Señor Vendrino did the shopping,
> This fine fellow did us in.
> Our rudder's out of cardboard,
> Our sails are paperthin.

SAILOR: Santa Maria . . .
BOY (*stops singing*): Shhh, the ol' fatso's coming!
PEPITO: Quick, sing something clean!
PEPITO, SAILOR, BOY (*sing*):

> When the sun is going down,
> Going down, going down,
> You'll see him no more.
> When your sweetheart's leaving town
> Leaving town, leaving town,
> She'll come back no more.
> Weeping willows
> And forgetmenots so blue,
> Love's a tear-stained pillow,
> That's why I think of you.

VENDRINO (*has entered and listens to the singing with approval*): Bravo, Mate! The morale of the crew is superduper! I see the soup is being served. Give me a taste, boys. On this ship there're no differences of rank. (*He tastes the water that has been used to scrub the deck.*) Oh, tasty! I wish we had soup that good in the officers' mess!

SAILOR: With your permission: you must have cabin fever, 'cause this ain't no soup.

VENDRINO: Did I say soup? Of course I meant to say: apple cider.

PEPITO (*to himself*): Birdbrain . . .

BOY: Señor, it ain't cider neither.

SAILOR: In as much as it is swab-water.

VENDRINO (*stiffens*): You dare to call your food swab-water? and you, Pepito, you tolerate that?

PEPITO: I tolerate that.

VENDRINO: But how can you?

PEPITO: Because it really is swab-water.

VENDRINO: Tie him to the mast!

SAILOR: Our cabin fever isn't that bad.

VENDRINO (*scared to death*): Holy Moses! Mutiny! Mutiny on board. Admiral! (*He rushes off.*)

BOY: That's his bad conscience.

SAILOR: Naturally, a severe case of cabin fever. But wait a minute . . . mutiny . . . not a bad idea.

PEPITO: Just what we needed. Now he's running through the ship screaming "mutiny." And the boys don't have to be told twice. What the hell . . . I'm with them.

SAILOR: With them or the others?

PEPITO: Where there are weak and strong, I'm always on the side of the latter.

BOY: Is this a brawl or what, mate?

PEPITO: You bet. Come on boys, we'll show 'em! Let's make mincemeat outa them! (*They rush off and collide with Columbus who now enters.*)

COLUMBUS: Stop! What do you want?

BOY: We wanna go home.

COLUMBUS: Back to jail?

SAILOR: Pardon me, sir, but big deal! At least we can break out of a jail. But here we can't break in or out.

PEPITO: And that rotten India doesn't even exist. That was just a gimmick of certain parties who wanted to get a certain rake-off from certain purchases.

BOY and SAILOR: Right on!

BOY: We wanna go home.

COLUMBUS: Sailors! Swarms of birds indicate the proximity of land. Yesterday there was a green twig adrift in the sea. In the face of such signs do you want to be robbed of your well-earned reward? Think of the riches that await you. Think of the prize of two hundred ducats for the first person to see land. Who's with me?

SAILOR: With your permission, Admiral, we'd go with you. But no one with an upset stomach has ever discovered India.

BOY: Please, señor, the soup is dishwater.

PEPITO: And why? For ten times seven days we have been languishing under the slavery of irresponsible profiteers. Ten times seven days . . .

COLUMBUS: Quiet. I didn't know about the soup. I was totally occupied with the inclination of constellations and with the ship's course.

SAILOR: That was an unfortunate case of cabin fever.

COLUMBUS: I demand an explanation.

SAILOR: The explanation is, if you please, that we can't eat constellations, unfortunately.

PEPITO: And why? Because a clique of greedy moneybags . . .

COLUMBUS: I don't want to talk to you anymore . . . Señor Vendrino.

VENDRINO (*enters*): Yes, that's right. I don't deny it, I never have denied it. The canned provisions are rotten . . . let me finish. Do you think you can discover India and have unspoilt food, too?

COLUMBUS: You deceived me.

PEPITO, SAILOR, BOY (*at the same time*): Damn you! (*Shouting.*)

VENDRINO: Let me finish! Why do you think you got these ships? Because they'll yield a profit. How will they yield a profit? With rusty cans. Would the ships be profitable with brand new cans? Not on your life. What follows from this? That one conquers colonies with rotten meats and vegetables . . . or not at all. (*Shouts of "Shame."*) Now let's see whether your country's faith in you was warranted . . .

COLUMBUS (*who has been listening to Vendrino during the general screaming with both fascination and effort*): I understand . . . Men, I appeal to your ideals.

BOY: Señor, there ain't no such thing.

COLUMBUS: Higher values are at stake, not just the well-being of the individual. Our people need lebensraum. Don't let your spirits sag! I'm willing to starve along with you.

SAILOR: An unheard-of case of cabin fever. We can't eat that either.

PEPITO: And why? (*He goes on speaking but cannot be heard in the boy's boos and the shouting in the wings.*)

VENDRINO (*shouting more loudly than the others*): Pin him to the mast!

PEPITO (*threateningly*): Whoooo?

VENDRINO (*pointing at Columbus*): Him!

PEPITO: Did he make the profit?

VENDRINO: No, but he thought up the idea, isn't that right, Admiral, old boy?

COLUMBUS: Right, I did.

SAILOR: With your permission, Admiral, your most disobedient servant! (*Sailor and boy tie Columbus up. The sailor takes his sword.*)

COLUMBUS: Vendrino, you're a traitor!

VENDRINO: Admiral, I'm a human being.

PEPITO: It was his idea, toss him overboard! (*Cheering off to the sides*)

SAILOR (*looking into the distance*): With pleasure, any time! Only right now it wouldn't make much sense!

PEPITO: How come, you . . .

SAILOR: 'Cause the purpose of the whole thing would be for him to drown. And if that's what we want, we'd have to move farther away from the land.

VENDRINO: What land?

SAILOR: Well—the land over there, on the horizon.

VENDRINO: Land?

BOY: Land?

PEPITO: Land?
COLUMBUS: Land!
THE WHOLE CREW (*the screaming is picked up behind the scenes.*) Laaaaand!!!
SAILOR: What's all the screaming about?
COLUMBUS: That is India . . .
VENDRINO: India!
PEPITO: India, you block-head!
SAILOR: Jesus, do I ever have cabin fever!
VENDRINO: Admiral, we are deeply moved; may we extend our most cordial congratulations . . .
PEPITO: Admiral, would you please forgive a habitual criminal a little tactlessness . . .
SAILOR: It's your fault, guttersnipe! 'Cause you always have to sing (*Gives the boy a slap.*)
COLUMBUS (*interrupts with a shake of the hand*): Men! The past is wiped out! A new world lies before us . . . All men on board! Hoist the flags, men, we'll sing the anthem!
EVERYBODY (*sings*):

Bravery and decency
And unity and honesty
You find in Spain alone.

Economy and purity
And unity and chastity
You find in Spain alone.

Now that is no small thing,
Long live the Spanish king.
Now that is no small thing,
Long live the kiiiiiing!

(*Darkness.*)

Act Three

Scene One

(Bay with palm-trees on the ocean, open hut, outside fireplace. The Chief and the Medicine Man are sitting outside, playing chess and smoking fat cigars.)

CHIEF: E2 to E4.

MEDICINE MAN: E2 to E4? That's what you're trying to do to me? You won't get away with that, not with me . . . D2 to D3.

Broadway Melody 1492, Act III, Scene One, New York, 1992. Donna Linderman (Chief), Wendy West (Medicine Man).

CHIEF: What's that supposed to be? A primitive, deceptive maneuver, that's what it is . . . In that case I'm going to . . . with my bishop . . . I'm going to . . . thwart your plans . . . I'm going to . . . thwart . . . I'm going to . . . No, that's wrong! Oh damn, damn. (*He ponders, sings:*) "Give me five minutes more, only five minutes more . . ."

MEDICINE MAN: Are we singing or are we playing?

CHIEF: "Give me five minutes more, only five minutes more . . ." F2 to D3. Haste makes waste. Or no, I'd better not . . .

MEDICINE MAN: Pièce touchée!

CHIEF: As you please! Just don't get excited. No matter what I do . . . you're a goner. (*He stares meaningfully at the board. The Medicine Man has jumped up and suddenly looks nervously at something in the distance.*) What's the matter? Get a move on, move!

MEDICINE MAN: Chief, I see something.

CHIEF (*without looking up*): What's there to see?

MEDICINE MAN: A warship.

CHIEF (*as above*): My good Medicine Man, you're nuts. There's no such thing as a warship anymore.

MEDICINE MAN: With cannons! Take a look, will you!

CHIEF (*as above*): Cannons have been done away with. You're just nervous.

MEDICINE MAN: Of course I'm nervous. Because you keep on singing that stupid song!

CHIEF: I'm not singing at all. Who's singing? Not me.

MEDICINE MAN: Check!

CHIEF: Check? Well I'll be . . . ! (*Thoughtfully*): "Give me five minutes more, only five minutes more." (*The Medicine Man jumps up.*) Why don't you stay put! I'll stop singing.

MEDICINE MAN: Look!

CHIEF: You're right . . . strangers.

MEDICINE MAN: White men!

CHIEF: Look at those funny feathered hats they're wearing!

MEDICINE MAN: They're all excited about something.

CHIEF: Do you think they're cannibals?

MEDICINE MAN: Shhh.

(*Columbus and Vendrino enter in dress uniform. Embarrassed silence. No one knows what to say.*)

VENDRINO: Bon appétit!
CHIEF: Nice day today.
COLUMBUS: Very nice day.
CHIEF: Did you have a pleasant crossing?
COLUMBUS: Yes, thank you.
CHIEF: With whom do I have the honor?
COLUMBUS: We come in the name of Their Majesties of Castile and Aragon. I am Christopher Columbus, Admiral in Chief of the Ocean and Viceroy of this country.
CHIEF: I'm the chief. And this gentleman is a brother-in-law of mine.
COLUMBUS: We come with peaceful intentions. We merely wish to take possession of this land.
MEDICINE MAN (*to Vendrino*): Pardon me, but are you cannibals?
VENDRINO: I'm the King's Comptroller of Accounts. We're going to establish order here . . . All this will have to go to make room for some regular houses. What's the meaning of these miserable huts anyway? Made of straw? What does the building inspector say about that? And you don't even have a proper harbor, do you!? Well, don't worry, we'll fix things up! But the first thing we've got to do is take possession of this country. That goes without saying.
CHIEF: Wouldn't you like to have a seat? (*Everybody sits down.*)
COLUMBUS: Their Majesties of Castile and Aragon send you their greetings. We have discovered you. I hope you will prove worthy of this honor.
CHIEF: Do you like it here?
VENDRINO: If you really want to see something, you should come visit us in Santa Fe! If you want to see some action!
CHIEF: Is it a big country you come from?
COLUMBUS: The biggest in the world.
CHIEF: Then why did you come here?
COLUMBUS: We need colonies.

CHIEF: What's that?
COLUMBUS: Colonies are countries which we civilize. We bring them the blessings of culture. We show them that their morals and manners are barbaric, and that they have to live the way we do.
CHIEF: And then what?
VENDRINO: Then they belong to us.
CHIEF (*smokes*): Very interesting.
MEDICINE MAN: Really, very interesting. (*The two blow thick clouds of smoke in front of them.*)
CHIEF: I'm afraid you'll be disappointed. There isn't much to conquer here.
COLUMBUS: What do you mean?
CHIEF: Because there's nothing here.
VENDRINO: May I see what you have in your ear?
MEDICINE MAN (*takes a ring out of his ear*): Here.
VENDRINO: Gold! Hallmarked? No. (*He hands the ring to Columbus.*) Do you have more of this stuff?
MEDICINE MAN: Of this worthless metal?
VENDRINO: Worthless? I beg your pardon . . . You people wear rings like this in your ears?
MEDICINE MAN: We put on a new one every day.
VENDRINO: Then, let's trade. You give us gold and we'll give you merchandise.
MEDICINE MAN: What are we supposed to do with that?
VENDRINO: Go into business!
MEDICINE MAN: But we don't need anything.
VENDRINO: Since when is merchandise there to be used? The main thing is production. A modern state has to sell its products to other nations.
CHIEF: So they sell to you?
VENDRINO: They would like to, but we don't allow it. We're the only ones allowed to sell.
CHIEF: And what if the others don't want to buy?
VENDRINO: Then we wage war against them.
CHIEF: Very interesting.
MEDICINE MAN: Really very interesting. (*Pause.*) But if everybody wages war and no one can buy anything, why don't

you open your borders and trade freely?
COLUMBUS: Because we are a nation!
MEDICINE MAN: And if another nation says the same thing?
VENDRINO: Then it's not a true nation. (*Pause.*)
COLUMBUS: You are a small country, and we are a large nation. Surrender and hand over your weapons!
CHIEF: We don't have any.
VENDRINO (*hits the chessboard with his fist*): Are you trying to make fun of us? We're the conquerors here!
CHIEF: You misunderstand. We really don't have any weapons. We have a few spears and arrows for hunting, and that's all.
COLUMBUS: You mean you don't have an army?
CHIEF: We did have an army once. We also had warships and weapons. We even had money. But that was a long time ago. Our forefathers, who were very wise, realized that all these things do is bring misery, and so they abolished them. We've had peace ever since.
VENDRINO: How can anybody exist on such a low level of culture? This has got to change). What we need here is *organization*. We'll establish a commercial colony. Under our authority. That goes without saying. We'll protect your legal rights.
PEPITO (*rushes in, excited*): Gold! Gold! All you have to do is pluck it from their ears. Gold! The cups, the pocket knives, the false teeth . . . everything's made of gold! You don't know what to grab first.
CHIEF: Is this what you call protection of legal rights?
VENDRINO: That's confiscation.
COLUMBUS (*to Pepito*): I forbid all looting! See to it that discipline is maintained.
PEPITO: But if even the chamber pots are made of gold . . .
COLUMBUS (*cuts him off*): Dismissed!
PEPITO: Very good, Señor! At your service, Admiral!
MEDICINE MAN: Why is that man making such weird motions? Is he sick?
VENDRINO: No, he's obeying orders.
MEDICINE MAN: Do your people always have to obey orders?
VENDRINO: Whenever a superior gives an order.

MEDICINE MAN: Who's considered a superior?
VENDRINO: Whoever has the higher salary.
CHIEF: Very interesting . . .
MEDICINE MAN: Really very interesting. (*Again they puff thick clouds of smoke.*)
COLUMBUS: What are those sticks in your mouths?
MEDICINE MAN: They're cigars.
CHIEF: Please, help yourself. (*He offers them cigars.*)
VENDRINO: Do these grow here? (*He bites into a cigar.*)
MEDICINE MAN: You don't eat them. You smoke them. (*He lights Vendrino's cigar with his own.*)
COLUMBUS: Odd custom.
VENDRINO: Doesn't taste bad! (*To Columbus*): Can you imagine the Queen putting something like this in her mouth? (*He swallows the wrong way and coughs.*)
MEDICINE MAN (*pats him on the back*): Don't blow on it, inhale!
VENDRINO: Thanks.
COLUMBUS: You sit around like this all day, smoking fat cigars and not doing anything?
CHIEF: What else should we do?
COLUMBUS: Work!
CHIEF: For whom?
VENDRINO: You'll find out soon enough!

(*The sound of muffled drumming is heard from afar. The Medicine Man goes and gets a drum out of the shrubbery and listens.*)

COLUMBUS: What's that?
MEDICINE MAN: Quiet! A news report!
COLUMBUS: From this village?
MEDICINE MAN: Oh no, it comes from very far away. (*He listens and then beats the drum rhythmically.*)
COLUMBUS: What are you doing?
MEDICINE MAN: I'm passing on the news.
VENDRINO: How much does a message like that cost?
CHIEF: Nothing. We all drum what we have to drum.
VENDRINO: Sheer anarchy!

MEDICINE MAN (*while drumming*): nine—ty—nine—ty—two—nine—ty—five . . .
VENDRINO: Are these stock reports?
MEDICINE MAN: No. They're game scores. We walk around and hit a little ball into holes with a club. The winner is the one who needs the fewest hits.
VENDRINO: Sounds pretty idiotic to me.
COLUMBUS: And that's what you're drumming through the whole country?
MEDICINE MAN: It's the only thing that really interests us.
VENDRINO: And for other matters you communicate by word of mouth only? Or how does it work?
MEDICINE MAN: We use knot-writing.
COLUMBUS: What's that?
MEDICINE MAN (*to Chief*): How do you explain that to an illiterate?
CHIEF (*shows them a knotted, colored string*): Look at this, for instance. It is a letter from my uncle on Condor Island: (*He unwinds the string.*) "Dear nephew. Unfortunately I cannot lend you anything because my last hunt was a flop." The rest is personal.
COLUMBUS: Then every knot is a character?
MEDICINE MAN: A character—what's that?
COLUMBUS (*to Vendrino*): How do you explain that to an illiterate?
VENDRINO (*looking at the knotted string*): I understand the thing in principle. That goes without saying. I just forgot my glasses.
COLUMBUS: Peculiar people, but not unlikable.
CHIEF (*rising*): We have a big favor to ask of you. I don't dare . . .
COLUMBUS: Please go ahead!
CHIEF: I'm afraid I might insult you.
COLUMBUS: Is there anything I can do for you?
CHIEF: We'd really like to finish our chess game. Perhaps we could continue our discussion tomorrow morning. Of course you'll be our guests for the night. (*To Columbus:*) May I offer you my humble hut? (*He points at the humble hut.*)

COLUMBUS: I can't accept.
CHIEF: But I insist! We realize what we owe to such a great chief. You'll share your bed tonight with the most beautiful dancer of our tribe.
COLUMBUS: Please don't go to any trouble.
CHIEF: Or have you brought your own women?
COLUMBUS: No, we haven't, but . . . I'm pretty tired from the journey.
CHIEF: Our dancers are very talented. It will be a lasting memory for us.
COLUMBUS: That's very kind of you. But perhaps one of my officers could take my place . . .
CHIEF: I'd be deeply insulted.
COLUMBUS: Heaven forbid!
CHIEF: Just go ahead and make yourselves at home here! Gentlemen, it's been a pleasure! (*Mutual bows. The natives take their chess board and leave.*)
COLUMBUS: What a mess . . . that dancer.
VENDRINO: You'll have to make a sacrifice.
COLUMBUS: But what will the Queen say?
VENDRINO: Admiral, greater sacrifices than this have been made for the fatherland.
COLUMBUS: Then you do it!
VENDRINO: After you, Admiral.
COLUMBUS: That's not what I came to India for. I am an explorer, not a lover.
VENDRINO: Sometimes the two are one and the same. Maybe the girl's very nice?
COLUMBUS: A colored girl? Impossible. I have Spanish blood in my veins.
VENDRINO: From Genoa . . .
COLUMBUS: What did you say?
VENDRINO: Nothing. The only thing I'm saying is that we mustn't insult these people.
COLUMBUS: What do you think, Vendrino? Isn't there a health hazard involved with a girl like that?
VENDRINO: Who for?
COLUMBUS: I'm not a coward, but this is going too far.

VENDRINO: But Admiral, we're pioneers!

COLUMBUS: Then, at least let me shave first.

VENDRINO: I'd like to make a few suggestions concerning the occupation. Out of consideration for administrative logistics, the first thing to do is to set up a military base. I'll set up a central agency for gold. Then one for colonial merchandise: lavender, myrrh, musk, camphor, and all that cinnamon. Yes, that's right . . . cinnamon, too. For purely financial and political reasons. One thing's clear, negotiations won't get us anywhere. This is how things really stand. An iron hand, that's what the situation calls for.

COLUMBUS: They're quiet, harmless people who aren't bothering anybody. I don't want any bloodshed.

VENDRINO: In that case, I must decline all responsibility.

COLUMBUS: I release you from that with pleasure. I have the confidence of the Court.

VENDRINO: You forget, Admiral, that you owe your success in no small measure to me. Without me you'd still be sitting at home. I obtained the money, I equipped the ships, I recruited the crews. I . . .

COLUMBUS: You took part in a mutiny.

VENDRINO: Who, me? When? Oh, right. Now wait a minute, you know me well enough to know that that was only a bit of Nordic cunning on my part. And what about you? What did you do?

COLUMBUS: I had the idea.

VENDRINO: Yes, Admiral, you had the idea. One man has the idea and another carries it out. Where would you be without me?

COLUMBUS: And where would you be without me?

VENDRINO: You've a much greater mission here. You have to represent Spain!

COLUMBUS: And who will bear the responsibility?

VENDRINO: There is no responsibility, there's only risk.

COLUMBUS: I know what violence is. I want peace.

VENDRINO: I know what peace is, I want to make money. (*He bows.*) Admiral . . . (*Exits.*)

(*Columbus, lost in thought, disappears into the hut. The stage is empty for a minute, then the Indian girl Anacoana sneaks on stage.*)

ANACOANA (*sings*):

From the cloud shapes in the evening sky
Our medicine man would prophesy:
New, white men will come to our shore
And change our lives for evermore.
Where now in storm the forest's roaring,
Rigid, stony masses will be soaring,
Houses just as high as mountains,
And a flood of light around them;
Deafening noises will surround them all
Louder than the mightiest waterfall.

When he told us what he'd seen,
I was no longer what I'd been;
I was seized as by a spell
And I could not tell
Was it fascination, was it fear?
The stone giants drew me near
In the forest's gloomy night,
And I dreamed of the dazzling lights.
There I wanted to be, and I wanted to flee,
And I danced in ecstasy:
One—two—three, one—two—three, one—two—three,
To the distant future's melody.

In some little birds' strange zig-zag motion
Our wise man saw big ships
Coming without sails across the ocean,
And where our humble huts now stand
Magic will transform the land.
In the towns that seem to have no end
Men will race on shiny wheels
Chasing time like antelope in fall,
Their moving pictures are running on the wall.

In the thundering cloud he read
A word that we had never heard.
And it drew me near
With temptation and with fear,
And Broadway was that word.
Yes, I want to be in a shining cart
Race along in seas of light,
My picture moving on the wall at night.
Then I'll dance as in a trance
One—two—three, one—two—three, one—two—three
To the distant Broadway Melody.

(*In the meantime Columbus has appeared and has watched her dancing.*)

ANACOANA: Did you like it?
COLUMBUS: I liked it very much.
ANACOANA: Do your people dance like that, too?
COLUMBUS: Not yet. But we soon will.
ANACOANA: May I come a little closer?
COLUMBUS: Please do.
ANACOANA: So you're the foreign chief? How old are you anyway?
COLUMBUS: I'd rather not talk about that.
ANACOANA: Our chief isn't all that young anymore either. You're wearing a nice dress.
COLUMBUS: This is not a dress. It's a uniform.

(*Anacoana bursts out laughing.*)

COLUMBUS: What's so funny?
ANACOANA: What kind of weird pipes are these?
COLUMBUS: It's a pair of pants.
ANACOANA: Do you always wear them?
COLUMBUS: The questions you ask! I'm not asking you for your secrets. Pants are pants.
ANACOANA: Take them off! (*Columbus is shocked.*) I must have said something wrong. Aren't you supposed to say that?

COLUMBUS: No, you mustn't say that.
ANACOANA: Why not?
COLUMBUS: Because . . . you don't say things like that.
ANACOANA: Oh! Now I understand. It's taboo.
COLUMBUS: What's "taboo"?
ANACOANA: Taboo is something that you mustn't touch or else you die.
COLUMBUS (*cannot help smiling*): Well, it's not that bad. There's no need to exaggerate. But there are things which you don't say because they're indecent.
ANACOANA: If they're indecent why do you wear them?
COLUMBUS: Tell me, are you always this inquisitive?
ANACOANA: I am not inquisitive. I just want to know exactly how things are.
COLUMBUS: What's your name?
ANACOANA: Anacoana. That means: Flower of the wild water.
COLUMBUS: Anacoana . . . I like the name.
ANACOANA: And what's your name?
COLUMBUS: Christopher.
ANACOANA: Christopher . . . Do you have many wives?
COLUMBUS: In our country a man has only one wife.
ANACOANA: Good heavens, the poor wives! Are your women beautiful?
COLUMBUS: Very beautiful.
ANACOANA: More beautiful than me?
COLUMBUS: They're not all as shapely as you are.
ANOCOANA: Do they wear pants, too?
COLUMBUS: Yes, but in a different way.
ANOCOANA: Oh, they wear them on top.
COLUMBUS: No!
ANACOANA: Where then?
COLUMBUS: Don't be so curious.
ANACOANA: But I want to learn. What do your women do when they love a man?
COLUMBUS: They marry him.
ANACOANA: What do they do?
COLUMBUS: They go to church and make a pact for life.
ANACOANA: Here they do something totally different. Are you

married?

COLUMBUS: No.

ANACOANA: Do you want to make a pact for life with me?

COLUMBUS: First of all, you can't rush something like that. Second of all, in my country, it's the men who ask that question, not the women.

ANACOANA: Ask me, Christopher!

COLUMBUS: Come here, child. I've got to have a serious talk with you. Sit down here. There. Now listen carefully. A barbaric custom of your tribe requires that I . . . that you . . . that I and you . . .

ANACOANA: Then you don't want to make a pact for life with me?

COLUMBUS (*smiles and strokes her hand*): No.

ANACOANA (*looks at his hand pensively, then suddenly*): Are you as white as this all over?

COLUMBUS: Yes, all over.

ANACOANA: Can I see? (*She opens his jacket at the neck and finds the Queen's madallion*): What's this?

COLUMBUS: A medallion.

ANACOANA: Did a medicine man give you that?

COLUMBUS: No, a queen.

ANACOANA: Do you love her?

COLUMBUS: You're not allowed to love a queen.

COLUMBUS: Does she love you?

COLUMBUS: When I think of her now . . . maybe she really did love me.

ANACOANA (*tears off the medallion with lightning speed*): I don't want any other woman to love you!

COLUMBUS: Give me that medallion right now! (*He grabs her by the arm and tries to tear the medallion away from her.*)

ANACOANA: Let go! (*She bites him.*)

COLUMBUS (*realizes that force will not work*): If you don't behave yourself, I'll send you away.

ANACOANA: But I won't go.

COLUMBUS: Then I'll call my men and have them take you away.

ANACOANA: Then I'll scream. In this country, if a woman wants

something, a man has to obey. The woman is always right.
COLUMBUS: Don't the men have any rights here?
ANACOANA: Oh yes. They're allowed to take care of us, to feed the children, and to say 'yes' to everything. Say 'yes'!
COLUMBUS: What do you really want?
ANACOANA: I want to have a romance.
COLUMBUS: Now, in the middle of the night?
ANACOANA: Come on, put your arms around me just once! (*She holds up the medallion.*) Then you'll get your totem back. Promise you'll do it?
COLUMBUS: Yes, but . . .
ANACOANA: I'll throw it into the woods! One, two . . .
COLUMBUS: I promise.
ANOCOANA (*gives him the medallion*): Now it's your turn.
COLUMBUS (*very embarrassed*): I can't embrace you just like that.
ANACOANA: If you don't, I'll call for help. (*He kisses her.*) At last!
COLUMBUS: What are you doing to me! I feel like a teenager.
ANACOANA (*sits on his knee*): But Christopher, you are so famous, and we women love famous men . . .
COLUMBUS: Am I really famous?
ANACOANA: Terribly famous, really, the whole village is talking about you.
COLUMBUS (*draws her passionately to himself*): Then come . . .
ANACOANA: Wait. Not yet. Tell me how you got here, but with all the details. I want to know everything. I'm so excited.
COLUMBUS: On August third of the year 1492 I weighed anchor in Palos and, in glorious sunlight, we sailed across the blue ocean . . .
ANACOANA (*interrupts him with a kiss.*)
COLUMBUS (*withdraws and goes on speaking unflustered*) . . . westward.

(*Anacoana slowly closes the curtain of the hut.*)

(*A longer pause. Pepito and Vendrino enter. The former holds a bunch of feathers like those the Indians wear.*)

VENDRINO: What's that in your hand?
PEPITO: Oh nothing, I just plucked an Indian! Hey, what's the old boy doing in there?
VENDRINO: He is representing Spain.
PEPITO: Well, what d'ya know! I never would've thought he was capable of that! Almost all of my boys are busy being representatives, too. The husbands around here close their eyes with a readiness that makes you wonder. Watch it, tomorrow they might come and collect their dividends.
VENDRINO: You don't have to worry about that. They write that off as part of our rights as guests.
PEPITO: Maybe. But it's not going to be easy to colonize these people. We're in it up to here.
VENDRINO: Oh, is there resistance?
PEPITO: Far from it. They are so accommodating, it's enough to make you tear your hair out. If I go and break into a grocery store back home and the owner gets the drop on me and threatens to blow me away . . . all right, that's part of my trade. But I would never have imagined in my wildest dreams that he would give me a hug and help me pack up the loot. It's mind-boggling.
VENDRINO: Don't you worry. This provoking non-resistance won't do them any good. We'll smash them.
PEPITO: In a case like this, I don't get a kick out of smashing anybody. Besides, the boss is against it.
VENDRINO (*contemptuously*): Him? Just leave him to me. Pepito, do you want to make a career for yourself . . . or do you want to go back to jail?
PEPITO: In court they call that a loaded question.
VENDRINO: So, if you want to make a career, remember: This is the last night this degenerate country will be allowed to indulge in its revolting laxity. Beginning tomorrow morning, no holds barred! In one year you won't recognize this place. Get what I mean? (*Both exit.*)

(*For a few seconds the stage is empty. Moonlight. Subdued music.*)

CHIEF (*enters and sings the Song of the Chief "Lands turn into maps"*):
Another island, and one more coastline,
One more mountain right to the top,
Another river, one more goldmine,
There is no limit, there is no stop.
Is there a corner still undisputed,
One apple tree in bloom, perhaps?
Where is the globe not yet polluted?
It is dissected and computed,
And land turns into maps.

Two more meadows and one more valley.
Like hungry locusts they cover the plane,
They climb the peaks and crawl through the gullies,
And carefully register inches of gain.
Is there one corner undisputed?
One apple tree in bloom, perhaps?
Where is the globe not yet polluted?
It is dissected and computed.
And land turns into maps.

And maps and charts become playing cards.
Every player wants more and more.
They're all in a hurry to win territory,
A world bridge tournament soon starts,
And the trumps, slam bang, will mark the score.
And south and north, and east and west,
They're all bluffing for a claim,
He plays best who cheats the rest,
And countries are cards in the game.

Scene Two

(Tobacco shop of an Indian Tobacconist. Rolls of knotted string hang on the wall.)

TOBACCONIST: Good morning, señora Minnehaha!
MINNEHAHA: Manitu be with you, señora Tobacconist!
TOBACCONIST: The morning paper for your husband? Here you are.
MINNEHAHA: No thanks. Don't bother. We're cancelling our subscription.
TOBACCONIST: Holy Pocahontas, but why?
MINNEHAHA: Who are you trying to fool? You know very well the junk the strings are knotting together these days. The morning string says the same as the evening string: nothing but strings of lies . . . ! The only section I'd kind of like to see is the installment of the fairy tale. I've just got to know what's going on. Would you mind letting me take a peek? *(She unrolls a roll of string on the wall.)*
TOBACCONIST: No dice. I'm not going to be your lending library, señora Minnehaha.
MINNEHAHA: Oh, come off it! Who do you think you are?
TOBACCONIST: I am the Royal Castilian Tobacconist, fully licensed by the colonial authorities.
MINNEHAHA: Yes, we know. And what were you a year ago, before the colonial administration established the tobacco monopoly? A piece of shit, that's what you were.
TOBACCONIST: I don't have to take that from you! What color is the skin of your last child? Tell me!
MINNEHAHA: Why dark brown, of course.
TOBACCONIST: Café au lait, very light!
MINNEHAHA: If I say it's dark brown, it's dark brown.
TOBACCONIST: We know, we know! Café au lait!

(The Medicine Man has entered and heard the last few sentences.)

MEDICINE MAN: Good morning, ladies. I hear you are discussing the coffee monopoly.

TOBACCONIST: No way! The hullabaloo is about the brat of that Minnehaha woman there.

MINNEHAHA: You just keep your mouth shut!

TOBACCONIST: A box of cigars, señor Medicine Man? Why don't you try the latest brand, Popocatapetl?

MEDICINE MAN: All right, but very soft ones! As I was saying . . . the coffee monopoly and the tobacco monopoly have both caused dissatisfaction among the people. That's quite understandable, psychologically speaking. Somewhere in our hearts we all cherish a longing for the good old days when we could still pick our own cigars and our own mocha out in the fields. But let bygones be bygones.

MINNEHAHA: Why?

TOBACCONIST: Don't act like such a dummy. How are tobacconists supposed to make a living?

MINNEHAHA: How did they do it before?

MEDICINE MAN: Pardon me for saying so, ladies, but the most important thing is that the Royal Castilian Colonial Company makes a living.

MINNEHAHA: And how did they do that before?

MEDICINE MAN: It didn't exist before it came here to establish itself.

MINNEHAHA: If that's the case then why, in Fitzliputzli's name, don't we kick them out?

(Enter the Chief.)

TOBACCONIST: Oh, the Chief!. My respects!

MINNEHAHA: My respects, Chief!

CHIEF: Good morning, good morning! Good to see you, doc. *(To the tobacconist:)* A package of tobacco, Queen Isabella, medium quality.

TOBACCONIST: But why not the top quality? My heart bleeds when I see that you roll your own, just to save money. Only a year ago you were smoking the finest cigars.

CHIEF: Yes, but that was a year ago . . . give me fifteen tax stickers.

MEDICINE MAN: Tax stickers again? They're going to be the death of you yet.

CHIEF: What am I supposed to do, Surgeon General? As long I'm still officiating as this ridiculous pseudochief, I have to hand all the petitions of my subjects on to the higher authorities. And since my subjects don't have any money, I have to pay for the tax stickers that go on every petition.

MEDICINE MAN: A fortune, in other words.

TOBACCONIST: You're much too generous, Chief.

MINNEHAHA: I think so, too. A little less generosity would have saved us a lot of trouble.

CHIEF: What do you mean?

MINNEHAHA (*can't restrain herself anymore*): I don't mean a thing. I'm not allowed to mean anything, since this riff-raff has been in the country.

CHIEF: Shhh.

MINNEHAHA: No shhh. I don't understand what these stupid tax stickers are for. I just don't understand it. And I don't understand why this cheap-looking money should be worth more than the pretty pebbles in the brook. I simply can't understand it!

MEDICINE MAN (*trying to change the subject*): If I follow you, you're discussing the money problem.

MINNEHAHA: What do you mean?

MEDICINE MAN: As long as we had it, we couldn't have cared less. Now that they've taken it away from us, we suddenly feel the need for it.

MINNEHAHA: But just tell me what for!

TOBACCONIST: For tax stickers.

MINNEHAHA: But what do we need tax stickers for, for crying out loud? Holy Manitu! It's going to drive me nuts. Why don't you throw the damned riff-raff out?!

CHIEF: My dear woman, I can't throw anybody out.

MINNEHAHA: Why not? We've got a hundred for every one of them.

MEDICINE MAN: The whites aren't human.

MINNEHAHA: Right! They're beasts.

MEDICINE MAN: You are wrong about that. Animals are much

less dangerous. The whites are . . . they are . . . you explain it, Chief.
CHIEF (*grandly*): They're gods.
MINNEHAHA: Gods?
TOBACCONIST: Gods! What have I been saying all along! It's because of their white skin, right, Doctor?
MEDICINE MAN: If it were only the skin, they'd just be freaks of nature. You tell them.
CHIEF: Just think of what the white man introduced to this country. The war dance, skalping, stakes for torture. And the hardest thing to accept is that they're training our young people to do these things, so that soon everybody will think that they are indigenous to our Indian culture. Can human beings really be that cruel?
MEDICINE MAN: Only gods are capable of things like that. I admit that they're pretty unlikable gods, greedy gods, gods equipped with an amazing thirst for blood, but . . . gods will be gods.
TOBACCONIST: I've said it all along. Now do you understand what tax stickers are?
MINNEHAHA: Offerings to the gods.
TOBACCONIST: Right. And what am I as a tobacconist? I'm the priestess in charge of the offerings.
MINNEHAHA: Oh, so that's what you are. Señora Tobacconist, if that's true, then let me tell you something: I don't want any part of that religion!

(*Darkness.*)

Scene Three

(*Headquarters of the Royal Castilian Colonial Company. Vendrino and Anacoana.*)

VENDRINO: Señorita Anacoana!
ANACOANA (*enters*): Señor Comptroller?

VENDRINO: Well . . . the situation is this. My private secretary is . . . has . . . let me finish. Unfortunately she can't come today. Would you do me . . . would you take a dictation for me?
ANACOANA (*coolly*): I'm at the service of all the gods in the company. Officially.
VENDRINO: Officially, of course. That goes without saying. You know me well enough, enough said . . . so without further ado: Dictation, please. Do you have enough string with you?
ANACOANA: Yes, I think so.
VENDRINO: You still haven't learned how to write on paper, have you?
ANACOANA: No, I haven't.
VENDRINO: Too bad. That borders on passive resistance. Well, what the hell. So let's go. I'll begin. Get knotting, señorita. (*He dictates*): To the Royal Castilian Ministry for Foreign Affairs, attention: His Excellency in person. Confidential . . . Do you have "Confidential?"
ANACOANA: Yes.
VENDRINO: Just to be sure, add an exclamation knot. Good . . . With reference to the latest communication from Your Excellency, comma knot, I humbly inform you that I intend to travel to Europe on the ship after next, comma knot, to submit my most detailed report to the most exalted office . . . Period.
ANACOANA: Period? What's that?
VENDRINO: Pardon me, I meant to say: loop.
ANACOANA: Most exalted office, loop.
VENDRINO: Good. This will be my last written report then . . . loop, loop, loop, and I regret to say, comma knot, that it is not any more encouraging than the last ones. Loop.
ANACOANA: Please slow down before I get all tied in knots.
VENDRINO: My secretary does sixty knots a minute. Let's go on. The crass inability of Admiral Columbus . . . do you have "crass"?
ANACOANA (*looks up suspiciously*): Yes.
VENDRINO: Then untie it. "Crass" is too crass. Let's say it this way: The regrettable inability of the esteemed Viceroy Co-

lumbus is becoming more and more apparent from day to day. His lax economic policy . . . say, do you understand what you're writing here?

ANACOANA (*lies*): Oh no, señor Comptroller. I'm just a dumb Indian.

VENDRINO: Good. I hate intelligent women. You're charming. Let's go on. His laxity in economic affairs falls miserably short of exploiting the possibilities of the colony . . . semi-knot. Is it any wonder that the dissatisfaction among the populace is growing by leaps and bounds, question knot . . . Instead of making short shrift of the complainers the esteemed Viceroy exercises a leniency which only increases the impudence of the redskins: Trouble is brewing everywhere; things are getting critical . . . loop, loop, loop . . . there is only one area in which the esteemed Viceroy doesn't stand for any nonsense . . . double loop, and that's where his personal cash box is concerned.

ANACOANA (*represses an exclamation of indignation.*)

VENDRINO: How's that?

ANACOANA: Oh, nothing, I'm just starting a new roll.

VENDRINO: Good girl. Your shorthand knotting is perfect. Your knottikens are calligraphically beyond reproach. On we go . . . But I entreat Your Excellency not to upset her Majesty the Queen . . . loop . . . None of the criminal manipulations in the Royal colony will escape my watchful eye. The "I" in "I entreat" you should write with a capital "I"!

ANACOANA: What's that, please?

VENDRINO: You don't have a capital I? What a stupid system!

ANACOANA: It's good for one thing though . . . (*She looks at the first part of the letter which Vendrino has playfully formed into a big loop*) . . . a business letter like this can be made into a noose.

VENDRINO: What do you mean? (*Sees what he has done.*) Oh, I see. (*He laughs.*) "Oh tender angel, unburdened by suspicion," as our Calderon says so beautifully. On we go! . . . Let me finish, Your Excellency . . . loop . . . And I certainly will not tolerate our precious racial stock being contaminated by mixed marriages with the natives . . . Just a sec.! (*Kisses her unashamedly.*)

ANACOANA: What do you think you're doing? (*She shoves him away.*) You want to commit a racial crime? It takes two, Señor Comptroller.

VENDRINO: No, it takes three, baby! There is no crime until a third party looks through the key hole! But since we're alone, sweetie . . . (*He embraces her*).

(*Columbus enters. Vendrino pushes Anacoana away.*)

COLUMBUS: Good afternoon, Comptroller.

VENDRINO: Let me finish. Señorita Anacoana's got to be fired this minute. She is spreading a tropical sensuality that has an unnerving effect on the Iberian master race.

ANACOANA: That's an infamous lie! He . . .

COLUMBUS: Señorita, you may go.

ANACOANA: But Christopher, you as a god should know . . .

COLUMBUS: In official matters, there is no Christopher . . .

VENDRINO: . . . only his Excellency, the Viceroy and Governor General.

ANACOANA: (*to Columbus*): Is that true?

COLUMBUS (*nods.*)

ANACOANA: Too bad. (*Exits.*)

COLUMBUS: Don't forget that the child has been spoiled by her pagan upbringing. She is *not* going to be dismissed.

VENDRINO: Your Excellency, really, I must say . . .

COLUMBUS (*emphatically*): The woman will not be dismissed.

VENDRINO: I submit to your granite will, Your Excellency!

COLUMBUS: Let's get to work now! What's the order of the day?

VENDRINO: Just a signature under a decree, the alcohol regulation. (*Hands him a document.*)

COLUMBUS (*reads*): You want to prohibit private beer-brewing under penalty of death?

VENDRINO: Your Excellency, the natives brew some kind of awful stuff out of plant juices and drink it until they're lost to the world. Nothing serves to promote public health as much as the death penalty.

COLUMBUS: Oh, all right. (*He signs.*) Then we'll cancel the rest of the brandy shipments from Europe.
VENDRINO: No. That would be a mistake, Your Excellency. The market here has a real thirst for brandy.
COLUMBUS: How do you square that with your prohibition of beer-brewing?
VENDRINO: Quite simply, Your Excellency. We want to eliminate the competition.
COLUMBUS: I thought we wanted to civilize these people.
VENDRINO: You can only civilize peaceable Indians. Indians are peaceable when they're drunk. Do you think they would tolerate the death penalty if they were sober? But, as I've already explained, the death penalty is an irrevocable prerequisite for fighting alcoholism. It follows that we need liquor in order to civilize them. Is that finally clear, Your Excellency?
COLUMBUS: Not quite. I must admit that continuing our research in the interior interests me much more than these boring administrative matters. Are the Blackfeet still obstructing our advances?
VENDRINO: And how!
COLUMBUS: In that case, forward march! I'll sign.
VENDRINO: What do you want to sign?
COLUMBUS: A declaration of war.
VENDRINO: What do we need a declaration of war for?
COLUMBUS: Don't try to make a fool out of me. To wage war, of course!
VENDRINO: I can't believe my ears, Your Excellency. Somebody must have kidnapped you out of the thirteenth century. Who in our day and age still operates with declarations of war?
COLUMBUS: Señor Comptroller, I will not tolerate any attempt on your part to tell me what to do and what not to do. I'm grateful to you for taking over certain boring administrative details, but that's where your rights come to an end. Do you understand? I'm in command in this colony, and I wish to be as powerful as I am just.
VENDRINO: Powerful *and* just? Excuse me, but you'll have to choose one or the other. You can't be both at the same time!

(*Darkness.*)

Scene Four

(An Indian post and telegraph office. Behind a large drum there is an office window. Signs: "Royal Post and Drumming Office," "Drumming messages accepted between 8 and 2 only." "For greetings to your loved ones use the reduced holiday rate," etc. A post office official sits at the large drum. In front of the window stands the Chief.)

OFFICIAL: No pushing or shoving.
CHIEF: I'm not shoving.
OFFICIAL: I didn't say you were. I'm just warning you. Everybody has to wait their turn. You're not the only one.
CHIEF: As a matter of fact, I am.
OFFICIAL: Now don't be obstinate. I have my orders.
CHIEF: How dare you talk to me like that? Don't you know that I'm your chief?
OFFICIAL: That's irrelevant. Chiefs come and go, the post office is eternal.
CHIEF *(sighing)*: And there's nothing anyone can do about it. That's western culture. If it isn't too much trouble, I'd like to send a drum-o-gram.
OFFICIAL: Where to?
CHIEF: To my uncle on Condor Island.
OFFICIAL: House number, street?
CHIEF *(smiles)*: That's not necessary. Everybody there knows my uncle.
OFFICIAL: Everybody, but not the post office.
CHIEF: Oh, come on. The drumming official knows him, too!
OFFICIAL: No, he doesn't. An official only knows his duty.
CHIEF: Well, I don't know my uncle's house number. A year ago he didn't even have one.
OFFICIAL: I'm sorry. Then you'll have to go home without sending your drum-o-gram. Or wait a minute; why doesn't he drum you his address?
CHIEF: But how can he? He doesn't know my address either. And this is urgent family business.
OFFICIAL: So why don't you just go there?

CHIEF: The trip takes three months.
OFFICIAL: What am I supposed to do about it? That's our new efficient postal system.
CHIEF: It's hard to be a redskin nowadays! (*Exits.*)

(*An Indian girl enters.*)

OFFICIAL: No shoving!
GIRL (*self-consciously*): Excuse me, please. Is this the place where you send drum messages?
OFFICIAL: Yes.
GIRL: To my fiance, 4 Chief Square, Troutville.
OFFICIAL: Here you are. (*He hands her a small drum.*) Are you familiar with the procedure?
GIRL: No, I'm afraid not.
OFFICIAL: All right then, listen: You drum the message on the form drum, and I repeat it on the transmitter drum. Patrons are requested to drum clearly and audibly so as to make the official's work as easy as possible.
GIRL: Could I have a different drum? This one has a hole in it.
OFFICIAL: Bring your own next time, if you don't mind. How many taps do you want to send?
GIRL: I don't know exactly.
OFFICIAL: You're a public nuisance, because now it's my duty to inform you as politely as I possibly can that messages of three taps or less go for a reduced rate. All right then, what do you want to tell him, your boyfriend?
GIRL: That I love him as the grass loves the dew, that he is my rising sun, that life without him would be like a rose without fragrance, that I await his return like the dry field awaits the young wind before the storm, the harbinger of blessing . . .
OFFICIAL: My dear girl, that'll cost you a fortune.
GIRL (*helplessly*): But what am I going to do?
OFFICIAL: You'll have to reduce your message to the bare essentials. A drum-o-gram is not a love poem. All right then, now what's the most urgent?

GIRL (*eagerly*): That he comes like the young wind before the storm!
OFFICIAL: Come on, haven't you told him that on other occasions?
GIRL (*hesitatingly*): Well, yes I have. But he must know that he is my morning sun.
OFFICIAL: I'd be willing to bet that's no news to the gentleman in question.
GIRL: That's true. But I've never told him that he is my morning dew.
OFFICIAL: All right. But do you have to tell him right this minute?
GIRL (*haltingly*): Well, not really.
OFFICIAL: All right. As far as I can see, the one concrete piece of information is that you await his return. Look, in your own interest, why don't you just drum: Await return, Maja. That'd go for the reduced rate.
GIRL: But it's not true!
OFFICIAL: What do you mean? Aren't you awaiting his return?
GIRL: Yes, but not like that. Besides, he's known for a long time that I'm waiting for him. I just wanted to . . .
OFFICIAL: He knows it already! Great! You can save yourself the whole drum-o-gram, since you yourself realize that you don't have anything to say to him. Why are you crying, my child?
GIRL (*sobbing*): Oh God, I don't have anything to say to my fiance! Nothing to say! Nothing . . . (*She exits. An old Indian woman enters.*)
OFFICIAL: No pushing or shoving!
OLD WOMAN: My son lives in the district of the Blackfeet, in the third house of the village of White Stag. There are no whites there yet. Give me the drum. I want to tell him how things are going with us here so that he will come and take his old mother back with him.
OFFICIAL: Here you are. (*He hands her the form drum. The old woman begins to drum. Pepito who has been sneaking up behind her listens. The old woman who has been drumming only haltingly now begins to drum in tense, agitated rhythms.*)

Versión del alemán:
Alfredo Bauer

Editado
por el Ateneo Argentino Alejandro von Humboldt

Broadway Melody 1492, Title page of the Spanish translation by Alfredo Bauer, performed at the Teatro General San Martín, Buenos Aires, 1992.

PEPITO (*grabs hold of her and rips the drum out of her hands*):
That's it, lady. For that last message you are under arrest!

(*Darkness.*)

Scene Five

(*In a tent. Columbus is alone and absorbed in his work. Now and then he whistles to himself. He is in a good mood.*)

PEPITO (*enters. He is wearing a showy uniform, but reports in the manner of a subordinate*): The Field Captain and Commander in Chief of the Royal Colonial troops wishes to speak to your Excellency.

COLUMBUS (*without looking up*): Please show him in.

PEPITO: Very well, sir. (*He salutes smartly and exits, reenters immediately, however, in the pose of a real Commander in Chief. He gives a lax salute.*)

COLUMBUS (*smiling*): Why did you announce yourself, Pepito?

PEPITO: I have to uphold the dignity of my position. I don't even go to bathroom without announcing myself, if you pardon my saying so. On the other hand, fame has not made me proud, so that I don't mind being my own underling. No duty is beneath me. I especially prefer to make my own arrests. Unfortunately you can't be everywhere at the same time. Christ, I sure wish that either I had a thousand hands or the whole colonial population had only one neck! (*He makes the appropriate gesture.*)

COLUMBUS: You're doing an awful lot of arresting lately.

PEPITO: You have to look at the psychology of it, Your Excellency. 'Arrest' is a verb that I knew before only in the passive voice—"to be arrested." That's why the active voice holds such a special fascination for me.

COLUMBUS: I wish you'd end the war against the Blackfeet faster. This penal expedition is dragging on and on.

PEPITO: That's not my fault, Your Excellency. We would've finished off that damned tribe a long time ago if something totally unexpected had not happened.

COLUMBUS: What was that?
PEPITO: They're fighting back! What unadulterated gall! All they have is bows and arrows, while on our side we have the just cause in the form of rifles.
COLUMBUS: Pepito, I'm glad to see you in such a good mood. I declare this day a holiday.
PEPITO: Because Vendrino's coming back from Europe?

(COLUMBUS *nods.*)

PEPITO: You sure do have funny ideas about holidays.
COLUMBUS: I had him take messages to Santangel and the Queen, important information, strict orders. He'll undoubtedly bring the confirmation of my offices and rights. And it's high time, by the way . . .
PEPITO (*ironically*): High time indeed!
COLUMBUS: . . . and I will finally rule as undisputed Viceroy to the benefit of the whole colony. There can be no doubt about my irreversible promotion.
PEPITO: You mean "demotion."
COLUMBUS: You've got to be joking.
PEPITO: Joking? I may be a man of violence, but I'm not inhuman. When I see how a poor sinner throws kisses to his approaching henchman, my calloused eyes can hardly fight back the tears.
COLUMBUS: Pepito, I forbid you to make stupid jokes. I'm the ruler here.
PEPITO: My devoutest apologies, Your Excellency. You are a baboon, a freshly pounded meat-head.
COLUMBUS: How dare you!
PEPITO: Just sit right back down again, Your Excellency, and listen to me! I just can't stand watching this anymore. It breaks me up! I'm blowing the whole intrigue! Maybe you can still rescue yourself.
COLUMBUS: Out with it, for heaven's sake!

(*Ship signals in the distance.*)

PEPITO (*with reference to the signals*): No, you're a goner. The ships from Europe are arriving. (*He salutes.*) Your Excellency,

I am paying you my last respects. You will be an unforgettable memory for me.

(*He exits.*)

COLUMBUS (*taken aback, looks after him, shrugs his shoulders, then calls*): Anacoana!
ANACOANA (*enters*): What are your wishes, my god and boss?
COLUMBUS: Forget the formalities, we're alone. Sit down . . . Listen, honey: Today is the start of my great career. I'll be rich . . . really rich. At last I will be a real Viceroy. A truly great ruler, invincible and powerful . . . perhaps even more powerful than King Ferdinand himself.
ANACOANA: Why not before now?
COLUMBUS: You can't understand that, of course. Vendrino is bringing me all of that from Europe.
ANACOANA: Vendrino?
COLUMBUS: Yes, he has been at the royal court.
ANACOANA: Why didn't you go yourself?
COLUMBUS: I didn't want to leave the country that I discovered. There's still so much here that interests me as an explorer.
ANACOANA: I see . . . (*She hesitates.*) And you let him go in spite of the letters he wrote about you?
COLUMBUS (*without having really heard her*): And you know, baby . . . now that I am the greatest man of the Empire . . . I have . . . I must . . . I have certain duties of representation . . . the etiquette, you understand . . . and the two of us . . . I personally am very fond of you . . . and I'll give you a nice farewell present . . . a royal farewell present . . . my honey bun . . . but . . . do you understand?
ANACOANA: I understand perfectly. You gods always talk so much. You want me to leave you, don't you? I've known it for some time already.

(*Columbus does not answer. Anacoana stares into space. Both are quiet. After a little while:*)

COLUMBUS (*suddenly remembers something which now seems more important to him than anything else*): What letters were you talking about just a minute ago?

ANACOANA: The ones Vendrino wrote to the Queen about you. You know the ones I mean.
COLUMBUS: I know absolutely nothing.
ANACOANA: Oh, of course you do.
COLUMBUS (*gets more and more agitated*): I don't know anything, I tell you. Why don't you say something, for heaven's sake!
ANACOANA (*apathetically*): All right, if you want me to repeat what you already know: Vendrino wrote that you're a thief.
COLUMBUS: You've got to be out of your mind!
ANACOANA (*unperturbed*): He wrote your Queen that you govern badly. That you are incompetent. That he has to watch over you carefully or else you would ruin everything. He often wrote things like that . . . and the last time was just before he left.
COLUMBUS (*petrified*): How do you know all this?
ANACOANA (*very quietly*): The last letter he dictated to me personally. You know that.
COLUMBUS: I don't know anything! (*Screaming:*) I don't know anything!
ANACOANA: Christopher, how can you joke around like this on the day we have to part? Of course you knew everything!
COLUMBUS (*softly*): So, that's what he did! That's what he did! (*He begins pacing back and forth rapidly in the room.*) And you! Why didn't you tell me?
ANACOANA: I don't understand. You must have known. You're a god. Gods know everything.
COLUMBUS: So that's what he did . . . That's what he did . . .
ANACOANA (*to herself*): We have a proverb: If somebody in the village commits adultery, the village dog hears about it after everybody else, but the husband hears about it after the dog. But you, you're a god. You know everything.
COLUMBUS (*screaming*): Will you cut it out! I'm not a god!
ANACOANA (*disconcerted*): You are . . . not a . . . god?
COLUMBUS (*as if in a fever*): The dirty traitor, he ran me down at court.
ANACOANA: Not a . . . god?
COLUMBUS: He tried to undermine my position . . . he won the Queen's confidence with deceit!
ANACOANA: Not a . . . god?

COLUMBUS: Maybe he's bringing orders against me . . . no, no, I bet they are just orders that restrict my powers . . . that reduce my percentage . . . that confounded percentage!
ANACOANA: Say that what you said was just a bad joke! Say that you really are a god! I beseech you!
COLUMBUS: I'm not a god. I'm not even of noble birth. It's all been a bunch of stupid lies. I am a sailor, a common, ordinary sailor. But a sailor is a good swimmer, and I won't drown. I will . . . I . . . I'll appeal to the Queen!
ANACOANA: He's not a god. Poor thing. Now I can see it for myself. (*She looks at him very sadly.*)
COLUMBUS: No, that's ridiculous! I'll turn to my crew! No . . . he's already bought them! I don't have a crew anymore. I must . . . I . . . I'll turn to the Indian tribes. They love me. They *must* love me!
ANACOANA: Poor Christopher! I thought you knew everything, and you don't even know . . .
COLUMBUS: What? What *else* is there that I don't know?
ANACOANA: What you yourself have done.
COLUMBUS: I brought culture to these tribes.
ANACOANA: Every day the tribes have been praying for your death the way they pray for good weather.
COLUMBUS: I know you're lying. (*He starts to leave.*)
ANACOANA: Where are you going?
COLUMBUS: I'm going to call the tribes together! (*He exits.*)

(*Fanfare. Vendrino and Moya appear, arm in arm. Pepito leads the way.*)

PEPITO: His Excellency the Viceroy Jose Vendrino of Veracruz and his illustrious consort!
VENDRINO: Where's Columbus?
ANACOANA: Go find him yourself!
MOYA (*to Vendrino*): Are you as conquerer going to stand for this sort of thing?
VENDRINO: That goes without saying, sugar. As you know, women and old men will be spared.
MOYA: Good, that's nice and generous, isn't it? A historical statement. (*She starts her babble.*) Wow, is it ever charming here! The men have such great bodies. But this hideous

carpeting has got to go. What low-class taste! Who was the vice-queen here?

ANACOANA: I was.

MOYA: A colored person? Shocking!

ANACOANA: If you don't like colored things, then why do you paint your face?

MOYA: I forbid you to talk like that, you half-naked thing!

ANACOANA: I'm half-naked because I have a beautiful body. Why don't you take your clothes off!

MOYA: Jose, are you going to put up with this?

VENDRINO: Of course not, baby, that goes without saying. But first, let's get this historical business over with. Where is he . . . this Admiral of ours who committed high treason?

(*Columbus' voice is heard off stage.*)

COLUMBUS: Indians, now they want to put me in chains. I brought you the blessings of civilization. I opened your land to culture. Indians! Now they want to drag me away from here like a criminal. Show them how you feel about this, folks!

(*Shouts of jubilation are heard off stage. Beating of drums. Rhythmic stamping of feet.*)

MOYA: Jose, what are those funny contortions those people are going through out there?

VENDRINO: That's a primitive dance of joy, sweetie pie. (*Through the muffled drumming suddenly marching steps and military orders can be heard.*)

COMMANDING VOICE: Company, halt! Admiral, in the name of Her Majesty the Queen, I order you to hand over your sword!

(*Drum roll.*)

VENDRINO: Etcetera, etcetera. Finished!

MOYA: And now at last show me the viceregal bed chamber, Jose!

(*They exit together.*)

ANACOANA: (*apathetic again, to Pepito*): And we thought that you were gods.
PEPITO: On the contrary, girl! We're devils . . . really vile . . . and poor devils. Don't you forget it! And don't make our job harder for us than it already is.
ANACOANA (*runs off.*)
PEPITO (*alone, sings "Pepito's Chanson"*):

And they believed that we were gods
Just because our skin is white,
Gods that would deliver them
From pain and plague and plight.
Instead of blessings, we brought terror,
By our actions they could tell:
Gods?! Good heavens, what an error.
We'd be glad to be just human
But that is hard as hell.

And what we are, no one can doubt
From this day on. Just look about,
Just look at all the ruling classes:
Devils all, poor wretched asses.

One day we lick the boss's boot,
The next we spit right in his face
If another shares with us his loot.
World history is one disgrace.
One day, when he still rules supreme,
His very loyal friend we seem,
Next day we dump him on the deck,
And wish that he would break his neck.
One could lose all self-esteem.

The world is turning in its spin
Proving one thing beyond all doubt:
One turn and the hero that today is in
Tomorrow's out, is out.

Scene Six

(*Prison cell in Santa Fé. Columbus, Chief. While Columbus walks back and forth taking long strides, the Chief sings.*)

CHIEF (*singing*):
Columbus thought his native land
Was long and wide and big and grand.
When more land he detected,
To his surprise it changed in size
In a way most unexpected:

It was not bigger, it was small!
When the embittered Admiral
Measured his space he found it
To be six steps from wall to wall
With iron bars around it.

COLUMBUS: That song again . . . Listen, Chief, I know that here in Europe you've gone out of your mind a little . . . probably because you're homesick. Still, I like to talk with you because you are the only human being whose company I have been granted . . . since yesterday, after having been alone for three months. But, please, don't always sing such unadulterated rubbish. A prison cell in Santa Fé is not my native land.

CHIEF: It is too. Your homeland is the space in which you can move around freely. Before you discovered my land across the sea it was my homeland. Now, that there isn't an inch of free ground there, I don't have a homeland anymore.

COLUMBUS: Where did you learn the art of fabricating aphorisms like that?

CHIEF: At the court of your King.

COLUMBUS: So that's why they brought you here yesterday.

CHIEF: My problem was the King's gruel. This is what happened: After the two of us were unloaded in the port of Palos and you were brought directly here, I was presented to the King. He found my red skin most decorative. And when I cooked potatoes for him, I won him over completely. From Vendrino . . .

COLUMBUS: Don't mention that name.

CHIEF: Excuse me. The King immediately ordered three tons of this exotic fruit from over there. I was graciously appointed court jester with license to cook.
COLUMBUS (*smiles*): A very good position.
CHIEF: Wasn't it though? Thus I learned how to compose fools' songs:

Not only that. I could afford
To criticize events at court.
The state police observed the peace.
And all the truths that I expressed
Were not warrants for arrest.

This privilege to use my mind
I shared with a dwarf of a boy
Who had two heads and one behind.
We and the King's horse enjoyed
Free expression without repression.

The dwarf was more careful than I was, even though he had two necks on his shoulders and could have risked one of them. But I took the liberty one day of making fun of the royal gruel. In doing that I touched the sublime at its most sensitive spot. I could have talked about anything but eating.

Potatoes raised me up to fame,
But gruel plunged my name to shame.
So allow me one suggestion:
What makes this world go round amounts
To a question of digestion.

COLUMBUS (*suddenly stops walking*): Do you have any news from over there?
CHIEF: It's probably not news to you anymore that my people are slowly but surely being ruined. Vendrino . . .
COLUMBUS: I don't want to hear a word about this man.
CHIEF: Pardon me.
COLUMBUS: What's he up to?
CHIEF: He's stealing as usual.
COLUMBUS: He's not going to be stealing much longer.

CHIEF: That depends. I'd guess about another five hundred years.

COLUMBUS: You talk like a raving lunatic, you poor bastard. I realize now the mistakes I made. But I'll set everything straight.

CHIEF: This noble resolution comes too soon.

CHIEF: Too soon?

CHIEF: Five hundred years too soon. I am convinced that you won't get another chance, fortunately. As Viceroy you're much more dangerous than Vendrino.

COLUMBUS: But Chief!

CHIEF: Vendrino doesn't make mistakes. Vendrino exploits us consistently. We know what to expect. You would exploit us inconsistently, and that would only muddy the water. But, as I said, there's no need to worry about you anymore. Your time is past.

COLUMBUS: In a one-hundred-page expose I have disclosed to the Queen all the intrigues against me, disproved all the slander . . .

CHIEF: That was three months ago.

COLUMBUS: That's all right. I'll stick it out in this hole. They wouldn't dare put me on trial. They want me to rot here. I know that. But Queen Isabella . . .

CHIEF: By the way, I read your hundred-page expose.

COLUMBUS: Where? How could you have?

CHIEF: As court jester I had access to all the rooms. Once I found myself in the wrong wing by mistake, in the room where the officers on duty spend the night. A pretty merry bunch. One of them was a young guy, a lieutenant Alvarez, nineteen years old at most. To pass the time between shifts, he used to make little paper boats and play "Sea route to India."

COLUMBUS: What are you driving at with all this nonsense?

CHIEF: I found your expose in the bedroom of this rather childish lieutenant.

COLUMBUS: You found it where?

CHIEF: Where? On his bedside table, I think it was.

COLUMBUS (*shocked*): How . . . how did it ever get there?

CHIEF: The boys get their paper from the waste baskets of the Foreign Office next door.

COLUMBUS: My God. It's all over. My voice doesn't get to the

Queen anymore. That's it for me. But no . . . you've got to be hallucinating or just plain crazy.

CHIEF: Why did you ever set your hopes on the Queen?

COLUMBUS: She loves me. Now that . . . (*Noise of keys jangling.*)

WOMAN'S VOICE (*outside*): Guard, leave me alone with him. Didn't you hear me, be gone.

(*A veiled Lady enters.*)

COLUMBUS: What can I do for you?

LADY: Quiet, señor. I'm here to convey greetings to you, illustrious greetings. The greetings of a proud and unhappy woman. Brace yourself.

COLUMBUS: Heavens! My star is rising.

LADY: Quiet, señor. When you came back across the ocean that you had discovered, came back in chains like a dangerous criminal, there was a stowaway on your ship: The stowaway was the heart of a Queen.

COLUMBUS (*overcome*): My Queen conveyed a similar message to me before.

LADY: She did? Not that I'm aware of.

COLUMBUS: It was before my departure.

LADY: You're mistaken. At that time the Queen could say no more than a trembling "Bon voyage." Because the Queen *loved* you then . . .

COLUMBUS: Then? And now?

LADY: Now the Queen . . . for the sake of old memories . . . is most kindly disposed toward you.

COLUMBUS: I don't understand.

LADY (*softly*): You don't understand this time either.

COLUMBUS: She believes in my innocence, doesn't she? Her heart spoke louder than all the slanderers, didn't it?

LADY: No, unfortunately not. She confesses that she was persuaded by those who discredited your honesty. But the expose that you then sent her convinced her and made her feel ashamed.

COLUMBUS: The expose?? Then Her Majesty did read it?

LADY: A despicable court lobby tried to remove it from her sight. But they didn't succeed. The Queen found it any-

how . . . one night. Brace yourself, Captain. Prepare yourself for a . . . (*She notices the Chief:*) Who is that?
COLUMBUS: Nobody. A redskin.
LADY: . . . for a reunion. (*She lifts the veil.*)
COLUMBUS: Your Majesty!
ISABELLA: (*moved*) Compose yourself. (*They are both deeply moved and do not speak.*)
CHIEF (*sings very softly*):

This proves again beyond all doubt
How wantonly fate jumps about;
It never takes the road ahead,
Sometimes it likes to dance by chance
Right through a lieutenant's bed.

ISABELLA: Who's that singing?
COLUMBUS: Nobody at all. A crazy Indian, Your Majesty. Tell me . . . ask me . . . no . . . go on with what you were saying. You found my expose . . . one night?
ISABELLA: Did I say "one night?"
COLUMBUS (*unsuspecting*): I believe so.
ISABELLA: Yes, it was one night. One of the most beautiful nights I've ever had . . .
COLUMBUS: I understand. It was the night of innocence triumphant.
ISABELLA: Well, if you say so . . .
COLUMBUS: Oh, Your Majesty!
ISABELLA: Compose yourself, old friend. I really feel so very sorry for you.
COLUMBUS: May I enjoy your favors once again?
ISABELLA: Of course; of course.
COLUMBUS: Will I be rehabilitated?
ISABELLA: Without a doubt.
COLUMBUS: And will I receive what I am entitled to?
ISABELLA: Your innocence of any wrongdoing will be announced publicly. You'll be set free and get back the title of Admiral of the Ocean . . .
COLUMBUS: Your Majesty . . .
ISABELLA: . . . retired, and with a fitting pension.
COLUMBUS (*shocked*): I . . . My ears must be deceiving me.

ISABELLA: You heard right. Now compose yourself, please. Your active life will come to an end with many honors.

COLUMBUS: But I want to begin it.

ISABELLA: You're very popular all over the country. People in the market places everywhere are telling each other the anecdote of the egg of Columbus.

COLUMBUS: Egg? What egg?

ISABELLA: The most obstinate of scientists no longer deny that you've discovered a new part of the world.

COLUMBUS: What egg? What new part of the world?

ISABELLA: You have discovered something much greater than a part. You've discovered a new continent: America.

COLUMBUS: What kind of weird name is that?

ISABELLA: Professor Amerigo Vespucci has written a book about the new continent. So they've chosen his name for it.

COLUMBUS: Another conspiracy. This Vespucci always was my enemy. I was in India. Period.

CHIEF: Your Majesty. I want to complain about this gentleman. It wasn't enough that he discovered us. He also misinformed us about who we were. Since his theory about India is wrong, we're not Indians, we are . . . how's that again . . . Americans.

ISABELLA: No. You remain Indians.

CHIEF: Pardon me, but do you really think it's fair that my people should be named after a misunderstanding?

ISABELLA: That's your name and that's that. It's too late for complaints.

CHIEF: Pardon me, but if anything, it's too soon. It'll take another five hundred years before we natives can call ourselves Americans.

COLUMBUS (*brooding*): What egg? For heaven's sake, what egg?

ISABELLA: Forget it, old friend. Time has left you behind.

COLUMBUS: So fast?

ISABELLA: Time goes much faster nowadays. Do you think that my colony still belongs to me? It already belongs to Vendrino and all the other Vendrinos in the world. They're the ones who are setting the tempo now.

COLUMBUS: You're mistaken, Your Majesty. I may die a pathetic senior citizen . . . my discovery may have been in error . . . it may now bear the name of an idiot . . . but mark

my words: from this country blessings will flow forth all over the world. It has riches far greater than any other country. The best of the Old World will settle there to harvest those riches. A new culture will come into being, a culture of freedom, of boldness, of justice.
ISABELLA: A Vendrino culture.
COLUMBUS: No. Vendrino will lose in the end. I believe in the future, Your Majesty.
ISABELLA: Strange dreamer. You remind me of yourself in your best times.
COLUMBUS: I believe in the future of America.
ISABELLA: You're a boy, a boy with gray hair . . .

(*They exchange glances. Silence. During the following scene change, the Chief sings softly.*)

CHIEF: Their heads are hot, their eyes burn clear,
   They argue whose land it will be,
   The land of the just, the land of the free
   Or the land of the profiteer.
   Their flaming hearts will soon be cold,
   Their argument is growing old
   And lasts five hundred years.

(*The music changes to jazz rhythms. Open scene change.*)

Scene Seven

(*The prison has changed into a restaurant at the top of a skyscraper on Broadway. The Chief is now a waiter, Columbus a grayhaired gentleman, Isabella a lady in an evening gown.*)

(*They all sing the jazz hit*):

   We tap, tap dance and never stop
   Our driving, driving beat.
   Our hearts are first-class steel;
   It melts when we think we feel,

When we get sentimental.
But the brain stays instrumental.
And we tap, tap dance, whatever may be,
To the beat of
The Broadway Melody.

We have gangsters and democrats,
Cave dwellers, bag ladies, film potentates,
Burn coffee to hold the profit rates,
We spill milk in gallons in the sand,
We, the United States,
God's own land.
We tap, tap dance and never stop
Our driving, driving beat.
Our souls are made of chrome,
We sing "My Old Kentucky Home"
When we get sentimental,
But the brain stays instrumental.
And tap, tap dance, whatever may be,
To the beat of
The Broadway Melody.

Our houses are higher than we can tell,
We've sent dirty niggers straight to hell.
In thirteen seconds we supplied
The oldest man with the youngest bride
That ever the good old sun espied.
We have gangsters and democrats,
Cave dwellers, bag ladies, film potentates,
We burn coffee to hold the profit rates,
And spill milk by the gallon in the sand,
We the United States,
God's own land.

We tap, tap dance and never stop
Our driving, driving beat.
Our God supports our greed,
Let Him care for those in need.
Our souls are made of chrome
And we sing "Home Sweet Home"
When we get sentimental.
But the brain stays instrumental.

    We tap, tap dance, whatever may be,
    To the beat, the beat
    Of the Broadway Melody.

COLUMBUS: Dear Isabella, come what may, I still believe in the future of America.
ISABELLA: Christopher. You're a boy, a boy with gray hair.
COLUMBUS: Let's ask the waiter to settle our argument. Waiter!
WAITER: What can I do for you?
COLUMBUS: You can give me some information.
WAITER: I'd be glad to.
COLUMBUS: Tell me, are you grateful or angry that we discovered you?
WAITER: Uh . . . sir . . . uh . . . I just serve here. Perhaps you would like to talk to the head waiter?
ISABELLA: Speak your mind. Don't be afraid.
WAITER: You're very gracious, M'am. Well, frankly speaking, we'd have preferred to discover ourselves.
ISABELLA: You see, Christopher, culture only brings misery.
COLUMBUS: But just think . . . technology, mechanized agriculture . . .
SECURITY GUARD (*rushing in*): Just a minute, what's goin' on here?
COLUMBUS: But consider this: Without the sacrifices that civilization demands, any progress . . .
SECURITY GUARD: I won't consider nothin'. I want to know what's goin' on here. What kind of scenario is this?
DIRECTOR (*enters*): This is a roof restaurant on Broadway.
SECURITY GUARD: Good God, what's Columbus doing on the roof?
DIRECTOR: It's a vision.
SECURITY GUARD: A . . . what?
COLUMBUS, ISABELLA, WAITER (*together*): A vision.
SECURITY GUARD: A vision?! In Radio City Music Hall? You've got a surprise coming, sir. By the way, I don't understand the play at all any more.
DIRECTOR: Don't you see, we want to discuss the question of whether . . .
SECURITY GUARD: Now don't be ornery. You've already taken advantage of my good nature. The manager might show up any minute . . . and then I'm up a creek. Now that's it. Enough! (*Everybody is talking at him at the same time.*) So

what's the deal, is the story of Columbus over yet, yes or no?
DIRECTOR: Yes, it's over.
SECURITY GUARD: O.K. then, get a move on. Close the curtain and be done with it. (*He goes to close the curtain.*)
DIRECTOR: Hold it! First we've got to sing the final song. That's part of our tradition.
SECURITY GUARD: Well, all right. If it's part of the tradition, I can't object.
DIRECTOR: O.K. Here we go:

(*Final song*):

> For two large continents and an ocean wide
> Just ten square yards of board was all we got.
> And from the cardboard props on either side
> The tradewinds swelled the topsails of our plot.
> We played a world in transition
> When history turns a page,
> Showed the truth behind tradition
> And behind our great new age.
>
> Yes, you discover your own present
> When you rub off the patina of the past.
> It's good and bad, but mostly it's unpleasant,
> And harder to control than we'd forecast.
> But until the final curtains fall
> Over all seas and lands,
> The future of us humans all
> Is held in human hands.
>
> Time goes forward, it never stops
> Its roaring beat.
> A captain's crazy notion
> Kept the world in motion.
> You saw his crooked heart,
> Saw him outplay his part.
> Time never stops, whatever may be,
> The beat
> Of the future's melody.

(*Curtain*)

Prelude

(Adaptation)

(*Lobby of Radio City Music Hall in New York. Glassed-in cubicle of the security guard; security guard; director of an off-off-cabaret theater.*)

DIRECTOR (*hesitantly*): Good morning. Excuse me, do I have the pleasure of speaking with the security guard of Radio City Music Hall himself?
SECURITY GUARD: Yes, you have the pleasure. And now, you can get lost. Your manuscript has been rejected.
DIRECTOR: Excuse me, but I haven't even submitted a manuscript.
SECURITY GUARD: Listen, you had the right idea. Because, as you probably know, in this establishment I meet all of the demand for new shows myself. People like you can just forget it.
DIRECTOR: I am well aware of that, sir.
SECURITY GUARD: Listen, who are you anyway?
DIRECTOR: I'm a director . . .
SECURITY GUARD: Oh, well. In that case, have a seat!
DIRECTOR: . . . of an off-off cabaret.
SECURITY GUARD: Well, in that case, get up. What do you want?
DIRECTOR: I should like, most respectfully, to ask your artistic advice, sir. We want to put on a historic play, a kind of revue, almost a musical, and since your theater sets the tone for this sort of thing . . .
SECURITY GUARD: I see! Listen, very laudable, very laudable. What kind of material do you plan to use?
DIRECTOR: We are dealing with . . .
SECURITY GUARD: I'm not interested in any deals, I want to know what kind of material you've got.
DIRECTOR: We are dealing with the Discovery of America. The play begins . . .
SECURITY GUARD: Listen, are you hard of hearing or something? I want to know about the material. Look, we like to use gold brocade in this establishment, or anything that's real shiny. There's nothing more effective than that! How many yards have you got in your costume stock?
DIRECTOR: Well . . . uh . . . do you think . . . gunny sacking

might do?

SECURITY GUARD: Gunny sacking? Jesus! How much glamor is there in that, for pity's sake?

DIRECTOR: We try to do without that.

SECURITY GUARD: Without it . . . Jesus! How many sponsors do you have?

DIRECTOR: Not many, I mean we don't have any. Are they absolutely necessary, I mean artistically?

SECURITY GUARD: Absolutely necessary? Jesus! Listen, you just don't understand. For a historical show you need four things: 1) costumes and property stock, 2) glamor, 3) patriotism, 4) sponsors. The stock creates the glamor, the glamor creates patriotism, patriotism creates the sponsors, the sponsors create more costumes, more costumes create more glamor, more glamor creats more patriotism, more patriotism creates more sponsors and it goes on and on like that, right into metaphysics . . . Do you get it?

DIRECTOR: No, I don't.

SECURITY GUARD: See what I mean? Now let's go on: How often does Columbus sing *Yankee Doodle* in the first act?

DIRECTOR: Excuse me, but how can Columbus sing *Yankee Doodle*?

SECURITY GUARD: What't the matter, can't he sing?

DIRECTOR: Of course he can. But what about historical truth?

SECURITY GUARD: What d'you mean? You're telling me *Yankee Doodle* is not historical?

DIRECTOR: Well yes, but . . .

SECURITY GUARD: See what I mean? Have you been up to Research on the second floor yet to ask about Renaissance zippers?

DIRECTOR: What do we need Renaissance zippers for?

SECURITY GUARD: What for, what for? For Columbus's fly, of course.

DIRECTOR: Well, actually we were thinking of taking a different approach, the other way around, so to speak. As far as the exact details are concerned, we are quite irreverent, but the essence of the thing, the underlying principles are what we want to be historically true. We want to disregard the facts in favor of the truth. We want to bring the past to life, make it relevant to today . . .

SECURITY GUARD: I see! So that's what you want to do.

DIRECTOR: Yes.
SECURITY GUARD: I see! Listen, I don't understand.
DIRECTOR: That's too bad. With your permission, perhaps we could show you the play?
SECURITY GUARD: Well o.k., I have no objections. but wait a minute. How big is that stage of yours?
DIRECTOR: Our stage . . . well, I mean forty-nine people . . .
SECURITY GUARD: That's nothing, a mere cubby hole, if you ask me. You'll need at least a hundred chorus girls.
DIRECTOR: I mean there are forty-nine seats in the auditorium.
SECURITY GUARD: In the audi . . . Good Lord and Father in Heaven! How big is the stage?!
DIRECTOR: About at big as your cubicle here.
SECURITY GUARD: Hahahaha! In that case you could put on the show right here, hahaha. At least you'll get some glamor free of charge! Hahaha!
DIRECTOR: Right here? Why not! With a little imagination? In the first act we're at the royal palace in Santa Fe. Then your easy chair could be a fancy sear fir for royalty and your desk a meeting table for the council of ministers. (*He begins to rearrange the furniture.*)
SECURITY GUARD: Very flattering, but . . .
DIRECTOR: We could hang a map up here. (*He rolls down a big world map which subsequently dominates the backdrop.*)
SECURITY GUARD: Hey, what are you doing?
DIRECTOR: I'm making a model stage.
SECURITY GUARD: For heaven's sake. I was only joking. You don't really want to put on the show right here in my office, do you?
DIRECTOR: I am accustomed to hardships.
SECURITY GUARD: And what about glamor?
DIRECTOR: You can keep that.
SECURITY GUARD: But for God's sake, can't I ring just the buzzer so that at least something is the way it's supposed to be?
DIRECTOR (*grandly*): Act One. A hall in the royal palace at Santa Fe!
SECURITY GUARD: Just a minute! (*He sounds the buzzer frantically.*)

(*Darkness.*)

THE NOVEL

Jura Soyfer, 1937

Thus Died a Party

(Fragment)

Prelude

Franz Josef Zehetner was used to his wife's reproaches for not exactly achieving a great deal in his life. In utter apathy he endured the violent scenes she made at almost regular intervals. In fact, he had learned to find something agreeable in these outbursts. When, an hour or two later, he joined the regulars in the back room of the pub for the evening glass of wine he would say with an amused sigh: "Gentlemen, another electric storm passed this afternoon. Looked like the thunder and lightning would never stop, oh boy!" It was reports like these that created the conspiratorial atmosphere real men and comrades need to feel. Most of the gentlemen present knew from their own experience what Zehetner was talking about.

Shortly before Christmas 1932, however, one of Zehetner's marital confrontations went beyond the customary and bearable: his wife used a crushing word (and having spent her youth in better circles, she must have been aware of its implications): "Proletarian!"

Franz Josef Zehetner bore, to be sure, the suspect title of master mechanic, but he nevertheless was someone who had to use his head and he was a government employee. Mark you: a government employee, even if one of low rank. He had an office in the roundhouse of one of the largest railroad stations in Vienna, and one of his purely intellectual, administrative functions was the setting up of shift schedules for mechanics, firemen, and engineers; in other words, he held a position of authority. Getting this far in his career had been hard enough. His father, a headmaster of an elementary school, had dreamed of the day when his son would attain the same honor if not a higher one. But when Franz Josef, in spite of cramming, was unable to advance beyond the third year of the *Gymnasium*, his father, in shame and fury, took the boy out of school and had him learn a trade. He regretted the move but, true to his principles, never took it back. He could not bear the disgrace of having a locksmith's apprentice for a son and died soon after. Franz Josef had no choice but to become a fireman and, in due course, an engineer. Throughout the years of his humiliation he had been sustained by an inner voice assuring him that he had been destined for better things and, as far as necessary compromises allowed, had kept his distance from certain elements among the work force. His exemplary conduct had gained him the goodwill of the roundhouse supervisor and eventually the position of master mechanic. His ego bolstered, he had dared to propose to the daughter of a higher official in the city administration. He claimed her as his own. The sins of his youth were redeemed. At this point, however, Zehetner's star seemed to have reached its apex. Apart from the fact that he now had a wife and four children, he was at the end of 1932 what he had been ten years before: master mechanic at wage level thirteen, and his highreaching promises which once had befogged the suspicious mind of the higher official in the city administration no longer found any credibility, not even in his marriage bed a few minutes before the light was put out. His wife's regrets came too late. The secret wound in Zehetner's soul had been brutally torn open and the pain was intense.

While still an engineer, he had been forced to put up with that appellation, though only when certain persons used it and certain compromises made it inescapable. But why was he now, as a civil servant, still, or rather again, within the reach of such name-calling? Why had he not advanced beyond wage level thirteen, that narrow margin of existence, made narrower and narrower by recent wage cuts? It never occurred to him that his modest mental abilities might have something to do with it. Nor did he ever feel any inclination to dive into the complexities of political economy. For Zehetner, to ask "Why?" was to ask "Who's to blame?"

"Who's to blame?" he asked himself as despair overwhelmed

him once more. He had known the culprits all along. They were always the same people. But one had to be careful.

In 1932 the Republic was fourteen years old. For all these years Zehetner had stored up hatred in himself and watched over it like a pedantic miser. Rarely had he dared to show it openly, never to vent it. The stationmaster, of course, could afford to declare that times had changed. But even the roundhouse supervisor was very unwise to repeat such assertions, Zehetner thought. And he himself, an employee so low on the wage scale, had no other choice but to shut up and swallow everything. Zehetner's caution, however, was no longer shared by the other gentlemen who were loyal to God and country. They certainly talked big in the main office; but Zehetner still hesitated to show his true feelings. In him alone fear was still as strong as hatred; they fought each other in his soul; they devoured, nourished each other. Dammed up for years, they tasted flat in his mouth like stale beer, and made him sick. He patiently endured his slow poisoning. After Sunday mass he thought of it as a punishment God had inflicted upon him. Disregarding the crease in his dark holiday pants, he knelt for a long time, the veterans' steel-helmet badge in his lapel, before the Virgin Mary, and quietly and repeatedly he uttered imprecations so bloodthirsty that not even at a veterans' table in the pub would anyone dare repeat them aloud. When he looked at his pallid, drawn face in the mirror he enjoyed some satisfaction at the thought of the revenge he would take one day: "So that's what you've made of me! Just wait! You've got a surprise coming, you scum!"

To be on the safe side, Zehetner had joined the most diverse associations and political parties. While in his lapel buttonhole he sported the red-white-red ribbon of the Christian patriots, there was in a secret compartment of his wallet a membership card that identified him as an Aryan, proud of his German blood. The plebeian manner of the latter party, which tastelessly enough called itself a "Workers' Party," went against Zehetner's grain as did everything Prussian. But the Brownshirts marched through the city so sure of themselves, as if Vienna were Berlin, and their shouts of "Germany, awake!" rang through the streets every day. And even if they had recently suffered a defeat at the polls in Germany, in the Vienna city election the number of their delegates had shot upward. In Germany, as in Austria, it was still quite possible that they would come to power. One had to give them credit, by the way, for being efficient organizers, and that was one of the reasons why in typically Prussian fashion they made high demands on one's convictions.

Not in Zehetner's wallet but carefully hidden at the bottom of the drawer where his wife kept her underwear, there was another membership card. He had not taken it out for many years—his last dues had been paid in August 1921—but there it was, like new, drenched with the sweet scent of lavender. There was no excuse for its existence. Whenever he thought of this membership card his self-esteem dropped. Sometimes, when he came home all fired-up from a political meeting at the pub, a smart parade or a rally—the pep speeches of the leaders still in his ears—he would go to the bureau and pull out the drawer with a jerk.

"What are you rummaging around in my things for?" his wife asked. He mumbled something about a spare collar stud and quickly shut the drawer. The membership card remained where it was—for all eventualities. Zehetner still feared it as much as he despised it.

Zehetner knew that he was considered a coward because he still did not dare act like his Heimwehr buddies, who left no doubt that they ruled the land or, like his distant colleagues at the German Transport Union, who behaved as if they were going to rule it tomorrow. Let them reproach him for being a coward! He saw deeper and knew: he who hated the enemy on the left without being afraid of him did not really hate him, was a fool and show-off who had forgotten the real issues, no matter how aggressive his rhetoric was. Zehetner had not forgotten anything. Whenever the boys at the pub turned their minds to the past they relied on his memory for the facts. "Say, Zehetner, who was the rat on the soldiers' council who made that stink in the boss's office in '18, or was it '19?"—"It was in 1919," Zehetner said, "in June. Lechner was his name—from Linz. He threatened the stationmaster at gun point. The issue was a troop transport of the People's Militia."

What was long past, swept away by fourteen years, was still alive in Zehetner's memory, depressing, almost as if it were happening now.

In trains packed to bursting the mutinying soldiers returned from the lost war. The roofs were black with troops; in shouting swarms they hung from the doors. Defying regulations, they slung their rifles muzzle down over their shoulders; they did not obey orders any longer, did not give a hoot for God and Kaiser, did not believe in the fatherland. Every day another rumor sprang up about one of those new fatherlands that were proclaimed in the streets of Prague, Budapest, Ljubljana and elsewhere, and then the soldiers of the former Imperial-Royal Army discovered all of a sudden that they were Czechs, Hungarians, Poles, Slovaks, Croats, Turks, or German Austrians . . . They put on their caps the insignia of the new nations or the red five-pointed star the prisoners of war had brought home from Siberia. The soldiers flooded Vienna. Every officer who still dared to show the Habsburg colors was chased through the streets. "Hey, Slowana!"—"Arise, you prisoners of starvation!"

When the flood subsided, a small state emerged. Its six and a half million inhabitants disbelievingly called it the Republic of German Austria. It was the Allies, not the Austrians, who prevented a union with Germany. The head of the government was a Social Democratic lawyer. Foreign policy was conducted by a Social Democratic Jew. It was then that Zehetner disgraced himself by obtaining that membership card, and he was only one of thousands who did the same thing with equal disgust because nobody knew what the next day would bring. It was true that in the government departments some good Christian gentlemen sat beside the Social Democrats. But in the communities all over the country, workers' and soldiers' councils were gaining ground. To be sure, in Hörlgasse in Vienna nineteen men who had shouted "All power to the councils" lay dead. But what was called army in those days consisted of gangs, which in every orderly state would have been liquidated long ago. On their caps these "soldiers" still sported the same red carnations with which they had come back from the war, they still sang the songs they had sung while mutinying. In overcrowded trains they left Vienna to protect the borders—borders which were so incredibly close to Vienna and so unclear to bewildered geography teachers that in the classroom they still stuck to the borders of the Austro-Hungarian Monarchy. And yet, on these borders of the tiny state that had just been born, these "bandits" kept watch and hesitatingly spoke of a "fatherland" again . . . for rather obvious reasons: next door in Hungary and Bavaria the dictatorships of the councils were collapsing and it looked as if order were to return to Central Europe.

The time came when Zehetner noticed to his amazement that in his own country, too, the situation had become stable. How and why, he hardly knew. No General von Epp had appeared on the scene, no Horthy, no Mussolini. Nevertheless, the soviets had vanished. The military began to look somewhat confidence-inspiring, and one could accept its protection without feeling quite so guilty and apprehensive. The army got rid of its red Minister of Defense (for the Cabinet had become purely bourgeois again) and finally shed its ominous name "People's Militia." The worst had been averted, but only the worst. Better not think back on those years of inflation! It was enough that Zehetner never could nor ever would understand how the unheard-of had happened: in those days, ordinary workers were unscrupulous enough to threaten a strike at any time, and for that very reason made more money than did college graduates!

The Social Democrats no longer held any positions in the Cabinet; in Parliament, however, they raised their voices all the louder. In the Vienna City Hall they ruled unchallenged. They were no longer masters of the whole country—and Zehetner had stopped paying his dues. But at the station he was careful to show them his respect. Even the stationmaster had to do that.

The new Chancellor went to Geneva and managed to secure a foreign loan to stabilize the country's economy. He was a Jesuit prelate. Always and everywhere he wore the tight, long black robe of the priest. Nobody would have been surprised to hear that this man had no body at all. In the minds of the people he was only a head, a completely bald ascetic head with a thin-lipped mouth, a thin aquiline nose, thin-rimmed glasses. He was not popular. He was not loved by anybody. Not even by the Tyrolese, whose piety was as deep as the misery on their mortgage-ridden mountain farms; not by the rich, self-important farmers of Lower Austria; not by the Styrians who, in spite of the infectious closeness of mines and metal works, had remained good Catholics; not by those small lease-holders in the Burgenland who would have profited by socialist land reform and yet supported the existing order; not even by the few thousand Christian Social workers, and certainly not by those in Zehetner's office who were proudly conscious of their German blood. None of these groups felt any affection for the Prelate-Chancellor, only self-consciousness and shy respect. He spoke to them with the voice of a Kalksburg Jesuit, a hollow voice which sounded as if it rose from the crypt where the Habsburgs' bones were rotting. His speeches, grudgingly and monotonously presented, contained references to Dante and quotations from Thomas Aquinas, and were not accompanied by any of the gestures popular speakers use. With barely concealed disdain for the Zehetners of the land he demanded sacrifices of them. As sole palliative he threw them one slogan: "Stabilization." For Zehetner it was enough. He did not resent having another slice cut from his wages. Order, surely, would return at last.

"Stabilization" proved a failure. Zehetner made the painful adjustment to the situation so well that in the end he convinced himself that "stabilization" was a success. What did he really care about all those people with small savings accounts who, after inflation had been tamed, found themselves reduced to the state of stabilized beggars? What did he care about unemployment, that chronic disease which had afflicted the ill-begotten state from birth? What was poverty in pious Tyrol to him? Zehetner never saved any money, he was not on the dole, was no peasant. He was a government employee. In his sky one bright little star twinkled: retirement. And now? Should he, for fear of losing his star, still bow and scrape to the Reds? Should firemen and such riffraff who sat on the shift-scheduling committee put their noses into his business for the rest of his life? And was he to pretend that he liked it because they just might run the depot one day? Would he have to accept his retirement benefits, the hard-earned support of his old age, from the hands of Jews and coal-shovelers? It was unbearable to grow old and ready for retirement in anticipation of such a nightmare. What did it matter if the financial stabilization was slow in coming? Zehetner was no materialist. But where was the stabilization of the soul which the Prelate-Chancellor had promised? It was true that His Eminence tried to curtail the rights of the loudmouths in Parliament and to push his foreign loan policy through by decree. But he failed. The Social Democrats had over a million votes and needed only three hundred thousand more for the absolute majority. And in the arsenals of their party militia—as was rumored again and again— the weapons piled up.

On July 15th, 1927 Zehetner thought: "This is it. We've had it. Done for." In the Burgenland a Heimwehr man had killed a member of the Socialist militia and been acquitted. Tens of thousands left the factories. From Floridsdorf, Meidling, Simmering, from everywhere they marched to the Inner City and flooded the Ringstrasse. From the windows of the Department of Justice crucifixes, portraits of Emperor Franz Josef and stacks of files were hurled down to the pavement. Policemen, disguising themselves as judges and clerks, escaped from the premises. While his wife was fighting over the last pound of lard at the grocery store to be ready for civil war and famine, Zehetner sat in the kitchen and kept a low profile so that the Revolution would not notice him. In the streets the first volleys cracked. When shortly afterwards he heard that only the police had fired, he repeated uncomprehendingly: "Only the police?"

"Why, sure. They chased the Reds through the streets like rabbits. They say ninety of them are done in."

Zehetner still did not understand what had happened. The Free Trade Unions called a twenty-four-hour strike in protest. He took part in the strike so as not to make an unfavorable impression in those stormy days. For twenty-four hours not one railroad car rolled over Austrian tracks. But when the twenty-four hours were over, Zehetner, pale and trembling, reported to the roundhouse supervisor. He did not strike, he said, only a sudden indisposition had kept him home. He spent hours in a state of unnerved anxiety, but the next morning it became clear to him that his instinct had not deceived him: all over Vienna, streetcar conductors and other employees of the City Transport System returned to work to do their duty. They looked disturbed. Many had their heads and arms bandaged. They had not dared to report sick.

Toward noon word got around that in Bruck an der Mur the dictatorship of the proletariat had been proclaimed but that after a few hours the proletariat had called it off again. That was all. Over the graves of ninety Reds the Prelate-Chancellor announced the order of the day: "No mercy!"

There were reasons for hope. Sunday after Sunday parish priests and high church dignitaries consecrated the pennons of new Heimwehr units. Zehetner carried his head higher, and on his hat he wore a cockfeather. On weekends busloads of Vienna Heimwehr toured the provinces where they marched four abreast through the streets of "infested" industrial towns. At first the shouts of *Heil!* and the crash-boom-bang of brass bands scarcely concealed their insecurity, but with every Sunday they became bolder as they paraded through workers' districts. The streets there were deserted as if the red plague had taken its toll. The local Heimwehr could openly vent their hatred of Vienna, that Babel of sin, where a schoolteacher was elected mayor and Jews were city councilmen. In the provinces the Heimwehr already talked of a "March on Vienna."

They were not quite ready for that, though. And yet, was the triumph of October 1928 not intoxicating enough? In immaculate formation tens of thousands of "cockfeathers" marched through Wiener Neustadt, the traditional bastion of the Reds. At the same time the Defense Corps, the Socialist militia, was marching through parallel streets, though kept in check by cordons of regular army soldiers, rolls of barbed wire, and machine guns. Obviously, the "Greens" (the Heimwehr) were the victorious invaders; the Reds were only the garrison holding a parade in home territory. The whole of Austria knew that. The whole of Austria was afraid the day would not go by without trouble. But it did. On the train ride home Zehetner and four dozen other Heimwehr men were packed in an open box car. As the train was leaving one of the stations between Wiener Neustadt and Vienna, suddenly a fellow in rags popped up at the foot of the railroad embankment. He opened his mouth wide to scream something incomprehensible, quickly aimed his rifle at them and fired. The shot went wide of its mark. Apart from Zehetner hardly anybody in the car noticed what had happened. The victors, elated by the free beer, sang their triumph out into the world. Zehetner, however, was not drunk. All day his throat had been dry with apprehension. When he recovered from the shock of the shot, the enemy was no longer in sight. The lump in Zehetner's throat softened and finally melted into a bittersweet sentimental sob. Like a bird at sunrise, he suddenly felt an instinctive urge to sing. Zehetner really yearned for a bacchantic air, full of feeling and charm, something like: "There will be wine and song, but we'll be dead and gone . . ." But his comrades bellowed forth military marches. And so, jubilantly chiming in, he alone tried to hold the upper voice to show off his high tenor in all its glory: "We are the Kaiser's soldiers of regiment number four . . ."

That day the Austrian workers had retreated another step before Zehetner. Almost every week thereafter brought him minor or major satisfactions. Thus one day he could announce in the roundhouse: "According to a decree of the central administration of the Federal Railroads, it is henceforth prohibited to decorate railroad engines with flags on the First of May." Prudent as he was, he added a congenial touch: "Unfortunately," he said, and after a pause: "There's nothing to be done about it, gentlemen. That's the way it is." Or, one morning after importantly unfolding the *Reichspost*, he had the pleasure of informing his wife at breakfast: "There you are. Now the English Labor Government has been overthrown too. 'Leh-bah'—that's how it's pronounced. They always had it in for the Heimwehr movement, MacDonald did, and especially that Henderson. Now they see how far it got them. It stinks to high heaven how they treat our fatherland in other countries; everybody thinks he can wipe his feet on it. But you just wait. Now that the German Chancellor is no longer a Red, you are really going to see something!"

When the shameless luxury tax levied by the red city government of Vienna unleashed the worldwide Depression, Zehetner invented a new pastime for his off-duty days. He postponed the customary family walk for two hours and set out all by himself, his hat cocked over one ear and between his teeth a carefully selected thin curved cigar which he balanced delicately so that it pointed straight forward.

With elastic steps he sallied forth into neighborhoods where no one knew him and strolled through measly, dusty little parks where the unemployed sat in the sun (there were so many of them that there was no room for mothers with small children). There he would start conversations and initiate discussions which seemed harmless enough but were sadistically spiteful in their most telling nuances: "As a government employee with tenure, I . . ."—"I know what it means to be poor, young man; I started from scratch."—"Who's to blame for it all? Ask Herr Breitner, the City Councillor. He isn't? Well, you heard him, didn't you . . . ?"—"Excuse my saying so, but for somebody who is really willing to work there is no such thing as an economic crisis."—"Seek and ye shall find."—"Idleness is the root of all evil."

As was to be expected, he barely escaped being beaten up even though he did not wear his Heimwehr badge on these occasions. This danger was not the least of the incitements that made him repeat his adventure; another was the chance to display his superiority by the elegant manner in which he averted blows. For he spoke not only in a provocative but also a stern, fatherly tone which intimidated many of the young unemployed, especially since Zehetner spoke a stilted, "refined" standard German. Dialect he only used in occasional jokes meant to quiet the tempers he had aroused. (Zehetner could be extremely jovial and charming.) The boys looked at him suspiciously, puzzled, surly, discouraged. Some would argue with him quite vehemently until one of them would reach his limit and approach him threateningly. Then the skinny little man whistled for his dog and left, smiling and shrugging his shoulders: "You're just brainwashed, young man. Too bad." He heard how behind him the peacemakers tried to quiet the hotheads: "Leave him alone. Everybody has the right to his opinion." Zehetner's eyes flashed; he whirled his cane like a drum major. No matter how the discussion had ended he was basically right. For he was indeed a government employee and did have tenure. Such excursions (he always made sure that there was a policeman around) he called "reconnaissance forays" or "needling Marxists."

At the station, Zehetner could tell when the workers had been to a meeting the previous night. He savored their disgruntled remarks and frustrated looks. "We are going through a slump right now," their leaders had told them. "Lower your sights. Strikes won't do any good." In the fall of '31 the Heimwehr in Styria tried a putsch. It was not government action that caused the venture to fizzle out after a few accidental fatalities. Nor had the Socialists done anything to squelch it. To them the attempted coup, as well as the subsequent acquittal of the culprits by a Graz jury, was, rather, a humorous affair. The 15th of July 1927 was sealed away in ninety tightly nailed coffins. But who could guarantee that they were nailed tightly enough? Who could say even at the end of 1932 that all the dams that had been piled up laboriously since then were strong enough to prevent another flood like the one of 1918? Zehetner mistrusted the pavement the Heimwehr marched on with their *Heils* and the crash-boom-bang of their bands; he mistrusted the quietness of the locked-up housefronts in the workers' districts. The fourteen years of the Republic had given him claustrophobia. They formed an epoch in themselves: the time "after the overthrow." In the preceding period, in "peacetime," life had been orderly, predictable, understandable. Everything that had happened "after the overthrow"—and was still happening—obeyed unknown, uncanny, chaotic forces.

Nothing was where it should be; nothing was stable. Of its state employees the government demanded due respect, but in Parliament it endured unheard-of insults and permitted itself to be accused of corruption, dependence on big money, demagogic double-dealing. One day it claimed unqualified support—which Zehetner gladly gave it; the next morning it was forced to resign, and for days the country was without leaders. In "peacetime," domestic and foreign policy had been based on inspiring guiding principles: "With paternal care for the well-being of our peoples . . ."—"In unending loyalty to our ancestral ruling family . . ."—"With an unfaltering elasticity in his gait our venerable aged monarch advanced a few steps down the palatial staircase to meet the young German Kaiser . . ." Now, "after the overthrow," no one talked about anything except moratoriums, budget problems, financial obligations to the League of Nations, interest on loans, loans to pay the interest on the loans, and on and on without end. And to top it all off: one was supposed to understand what it was all about! The country was run by shopkeepers who graciously allowed the people a voice in making decisions. Zehetner did not want a voice in making decisions. He wanted to be promoted to wage level fourteen. In "peacetime" he would have been there a long time ago. In "peacetime" the Imperial-Royal Railroads commanded a vast network which extended from Silesia to Northern Italy and from Salzburg to Przemysl. In those days amidst a conglomerate of subservient Slavic peoples it still meant something to be a German Austrian; and a person who worked with his head was respected. But even aside from such considerations, all that was needed in those days to move up to the wage level Zehetner had set his heart on was the assurance that one was not a materialist. But in these crazy times it did not help Zehetner to remind his superior of his idealism. The roundhouse supervisor knew well enough that Zehetner had always been willing to bear sacrifices and that he had pledged body and soul to God and country. And in spite of the proverbial hypertrophy of state-employed personnel, he had advanced his protegé two levels. More evidence of his personal goodwill, so the supervisor said, could not be defended before the others at the depot. Necessary compromises simply had to be adhered to. As the supervisor put it, Zehetner was not especially popular with the workers; even some of the Heimwehr men did not like him particularly. He should be patient. He should not forget that times had already changed significantly . . . all of which proved to Zehetner once more that times had not changed, were still the same lousy times "after the overthrow."

You could not buy a small goulash for less than forty groschen. Every time Zehetner remembered how little a small goulash had cost in "peacetime" he was shocked. Zehetner could not stop being shocked. Modern art raged unhindered, undermining the state and, what was almost worse, undermining him. The young generation, instead of learning discipline in the barracks, involved themselves in politics, spent their vacation in summer camps, boys and girls together, and the girls did not even get pregnant. The godless were allowed to throw mud at the clerics. A government employee who had received a *Gymnasium* education had to put up with being called "proletarian." Everybody could get away with anything. Anything was possible at any time.

Only one thing was not possible: to show one's hatred of those who were to blame for it all. One had to cooperate with them. They sat on personnel committees, were co-rulers of the depot. They were members of the executive committee in the head office of the Federal Railroads on Schwarzenbergplatz. They even held leading positions in the administrative council, those Jews and coal-shovelers. And the most confusing thing in all the confusion of these times "after the overthrow" was this: it was not only pressure that made cooperation with them necessary. One actually could not do without them. Were they not the dam to prevent the greater flood, the final chaos? Only the devil knew where they really stood, the devil or they themselves. Did they uphold the state or were they revolutionaries? Their newspapers wrote about their intentions in a language that was Greek to Zehetner. Their trade unions accepted wage cuts without batting an eye and at the same time spoke of a socialist planned economy. Their representatives in Parliament shut their eyes to hard-line government measures and at the same time threatened revolution. At times, Zehetner's confusion drove him to the verge of paranoia. When he passed the gigantic municipal housing complexes on the periphery of the city, which were named after Karl Marx, Friedrich Engels, Mateotti, or Lassalle, he did not see tenement buildings for the working population but civil war fortresses of the red militia. Municipal garbage trucks to Zehetner were tanks, kindergartens were arsenals, playgrounds drill grounds. They had made Vienna a camouflaged stronghold of world revolution. One could not see their faces; they wore masks, and masks under the masks. They were incomprehensible, elusive just like the times "after the overthrow." They were those times. They were to blame for everything. They were indispensable. They were to be feared as on the first day. And only he who could not do without them, only he who was afraid of them, could hate them profoundly enough.

  To hear that word from your own wife! Zehetner walked about with a deeply troubled look on his face. A proletarian. That's what he was, then. "So for you I am a proletarian, eh?" he said between his lips. Her attempts to smooth things over did not convince him. In self-torture he thought of his measly 195 schillings a month, of his unprovided-for children, of his trivial function in the office where, if the truth were known, he could be replaced by just about anybody. "A proletarian," he repeated, "so that's what they've made of me." For days no other thought entered his mind. He managed to do his job as usual merely because it could be done by any adding machine; only a machine would have worked more accurately because it did not have to worry about the payments on his office jacket or about the confused emotions the jacket covered.

Zehetner, raised as a Catholic in a very Catholic country and remaining a Catholic, had a great respect for emotions; the more confused they were the greater was his respect. He had learned to sense higher things behind them. A phrase, which one evening at the pub he had washed down with a pint of Vöslauer wine, suddenly surfaced: "Homesickness wells up within me," he said to himself, "homesickness for Austria, the true, Christian, German Austria . . . ." Uplifted by such yearnings, Zehetner absorbed the prophecies for 1933, which like similar prophecies at the end of previous years, were pronounced by the *Führer* on this side of the border and by the other *Führer* on the other side of the border. Zehetner, who had never really chosen between the two, was spared a dilemma for once; both said exactly the same thing: 1933 would bring powerful, final, epoch-making changes. Zehetner forgot that he had heard the same oracle a year ago. In quiet rapture he sat before the radio which called out to him the great message: "It is enough! Things cannot go on the way they are. Something has to be done!" Right! That was exactly what Zehetner felt himself. Fourteen years had made the cup full, and the big hand on the clockface of History finally approached the hour of decision. Yes, he, Franz Josef Zehetner, was a German, an Aryan, an Austrian, a Christian, he was the prisoner of Versailles and Saint-Germain, he was the victim of Marxist terror and was the oak at whose roots international Jewry gnawed. Even in him, most careful of the careful, something at last demanded a great breakthrough, only he was not quite sure whether this something was the call of the blood or the voice of the Lord. In any case, he, Zehetner, had been awakened! No one should reproach him any longer for being half-hearted.

It was in this tense state of mind that he received orders from the roundhouse supervisor to schedule the shifts for the intensified holiday train service, and along with the orders the hint, noncommittal of course, that he could, if he felt so inclined, use this opportunity to let some elements in the work force know that times had changed.

After office hours, Zehetner took the schedule of shift teams home and spent half the night over them. He was a specialist in petty chicanery. This time, however, he was not going to be satisfied with dilettantism; he was going to do a thorough piece of work, revenge work. Certain individuals would be amazed how tough Christmas and New Year's traffic could be for them. He was not going to restrict himself to harassing the substitutes, who in a case like this, were at his mercy anyhow. Oh no; others too would have their surprise. Overcome with joy, Zehetner felt in himself the uninhibited, daredevil readiness for violence which he had observed with envy in younger men who shared his convictions. In previous years, Zehetner's pen—scratching with hatred but calligraphically neat with fear—had placed certain names in the shift schedule exactly where collectively bargained contracts entitled them to be. Tonight he threw such considerations to the wind and treated them like any other names. For every twenty hours on the job he assigned them five hours of sleep. Zehetner held a merciless reckoning.

Only one name made him hesitate: Ferdinand Dworak. Was Dworak not the only man in the depot who was allowed to enter the boss's office without first wiping his shoes? (And the boss had such a fine ear for the dutiful scraping on the doormat!) Was Dworak not offered a cigar of politeness whenever, in his oil-stained overalls, he took a seat in the inner sanctum? Did the year 1918 not bear the same face as this Dworak? Had he not been the master of the depot then? Had he not saved the boss's life when, from the roof of a railroad car, he had shouted again and again to the unfettered mob: "Comrades, we must not lose our nerves now!" Was Dworak not the most dangerous enemy in the whole depot and at the same time the most respected person? Was he not as hateful as he was irreplaceable? Was he not, to put it briefly, the District Leader of the Free Trade Union?

Zehetner pondered a long time before he overcame his fear.

Then he rose, triumphant.

He undressed carefully, interrupting the process several times to indulge in a self-rolled cigarette. Still in socks, he sneaked up to the shift schedule once more to add a bold flourish, and finally, in shirt and underpants, he stalked back and forth in the room, rubbing his hands. He stopped to pat Schurli, the snoring Chihuahua. Tenderly he arranged the dog's little pillow. As Zehetner often emphasized, he loved this animal more than all the human beings in the world. ("A human like me, for instance, can defend himself when anybody does anything to him, whereas an animal, on the other hand, has not even the gift of speech.") When he walked the little, fidgety, nervously trotting creature, he liked best to take it near the Karl Marx tenement complex. He took a roguish delight in watching the dog lift its hind leg against the wall of the gigantic structure.

He said good night to the dog and crept into bed. His triumph did not let him sleep. He had to wake up his wife to tell her everything in detail. Would they be surprised, those gentlemen! And Dworak, too, would realize for once that big cheeses like him no longer had anything to say. Now the whole bunch of them would finally have to understand that their eight-hour day was dead and buried. Times had changed, that was all. He who cannot hear shall take the consequences. He, Zehetner, had shown no mercy! And what he had done was but a little foretaste of the greater, final, epoch-making changes that the coming year would bring!

His wife did not answer. ". . . practically, you see," he added, in an attempt to qualify what he had said, ". . . you see, practically it amounts to five hours."

Practically, they would not be able to sleep more than that. And they had no valid recourse to protest his decision. He had seen to that. He was no adding machine, was he? He knew his job inside out, did he not? They could not prove malicious intent. He would just shrug his shoulders. "Sorry, my dear friend."

He showed his wife how he would shrug his shoulders, and suddenly discovered that she must have gone to sleep some while ago. The quilt had slipped off her skinny body in places. In "peacetime" she had been pleasingly plump and full of charms.

Was this still a wife? Was this still an existence worth living? Zehetner's triumph evaporated quickly and left him shivering. Was he really satisfied? He was not. He had only imagined that he was. Was he awakened? Determined to march forward? God, how often during the past fourteen years had he been ready to march forward! Had he scored a victory? . . . In the nursery next door one of the tots began to cry. Zehetner gave a start. If only the old lady did not wake up and start whining too. A proletarian, so that's what I am to her . . . . Shivering, he sat in his unwarmed bed. And again he felt all alone in these dreary times "after the overthrow"—orphaned. Who would finally put an end to all this misery? The great awakener in Germany? He was but a Prussianized Austrian, which meant he was worse than a Prussian. The Heimwehr Prince? He knew how to use words all right, uplifting words one had not heard for a long time and wanted to hear, but he was young, very young, and irresponsible. The new Chancellor, Dollfuss? The other day, when he marched along the front row of their battalion, the fellows, even the Prince, could barely suppress a smile. This Chancellor was a barking dwarf, a cartoon come to life. Zehetner sighed and closed his eyes . . . . After a while his deceased father entered, grew into an enormous threatening form, looming above him. His eyes were flaming with rage, his bushy gray mutton-chops quivering. "Because you killed me!" he thundered from his height. "You good-for-nothing!"

Zehetner, tiny Zehetner, stood at attention. "Yes, Mr. Supervisor! Yes, Captain!"

"Bum," his father roared, "drop-out!"

As his father slowly raised his hand, a dark shadow moved along the horizon and across the sky. The hand hit Zehetner's face twice. He saw stars dancing. Tears welled up in his eyes; slowly they ran down his cheeks. Tears of relief. Soon his breathing was quiet and steady.

Ferdinand Dworak
Officer of the Railroad Union
District Commander of the Defense Corps

1

This run contained everything that Dworak had always and most bitterly hated: unreasonableness, unpredictability, disregard for order, arbitrary coercion.

Before an excessively polite Zehetner had informed him that "unfortunately" he would have to be on duty on New Year's Eve, he had carefully planned the evening. Dworak never wasted an hour. The plan had been: dinner at home with son and wife (he had finally given in to her entreaties), then an urgent (much needed) conference with the new treasurer of the local organization (which would probably have gone on and on), then a speech at the New Year's party of the Workers' Educational Association (so that the jolly crowd would not completely forget how serious the times were . . .), and finally a relaxed couple of hours at the restaurant "The Republic."

Nothing of all that was to be. There was no way of getting around it; he would have to spend this night, this mixed brew of snow, hail, and bitingly cold darkness at the engine, and Gellert the fireman was not the person to make a situation like this any more pleasant. Indeed Gellert made matters worse. And now, as the station signals—green, blue, and red—had just streaked by, he could already sense that it was going to be worse than it had to be. In the dance of flakes, Vienna faded into a foggy smudge of dim light, and somewhere in that haze was the restaurant "The Republic," the club room, the table for the regulars. And there Dworak's only really relaxing hour of the year ticked away without him.

Wholesome beer-haze hung over the group; the beer-bellied proprietor served the men himself. And as his fleshy violet arms swung the load of steins over the men, he showed off by rippling his biceps. Brimming with foam, the steins landed on the table. When everybody had been served, he moved up a chair and treated himself: "Your health, gentlemen!" They all knew him. In

1905 (he had been just a serving boy then), he had refused to serve some dragoons of the Eighth Regiment who were thirsty from their raids on suffrage demonstrators. That landed him in jail for a couple of days and cost him his job. Then every child in the district knew the story. Now that he was owner of "The Republic," not even the tattoo on his chest, a symbolic illustration of the event, made much of an impression. Only the older comrades appreciated his feat. "Here's to you, boss!" That's how the evening started.

By now they probably had moved beyond that point. Maybe the lottery in the large guest room was closed by now? Some of the guys used to come over for it from the club rooms. Last year little Kaliwoda from the Defense Corps unit "Friedrich Engels" had won first prize: a gigantic smoked ham, decorated with red paper carnations. He acted as if that were nothing special and distributed the carnations amongst the ladies. But then, across the measly small glass of wine and spritzer, he exchanged meaningful glances with his wife. They were both young pups; he had no job and had even been off welfare for some time. That hunk of meat would last them three weeks.

Or was the lottery over by now? Were the women already predicting the future from the coffee grounds, the men from the *Arbeiter Zeitung*? Had they reached the toasting stage yet? Then Spannmeier, chairman of Section Twelve, would raise his glass as he did every year to that scantily dressed lady in the curlicued golden frame on the wall below the large coat of arms of the "Friends of Nature", the Party's Alpine Club. In a flowing Greek gown, the Jacobin cap on her head, she strode with muscular, naked legs, unarmed and victorious over a heap of overturned thrones, discarded crowns, scepters, broken swords, powerless cannon. Behind her the sun was rising. She was Freedom.

Younger comrades made fun of the cheap reproduction, but no one took it down. In 1890, when it was not yet cracked and yellowed but shiny and new and a glory to behold, Victor Adler himself had, in her spirit, opened the Workers' Educational Association of the district, shortly after the very first May Day Parade.

Surely, as every year, people from neighborhood joints would drop in. From apartments, too, where they celebrated the New

Year privately, the host or his wife would drop in, pick up new supplies from the bar, clank their keys undecidedly, and finally decide to sit down for fifteen minutes. Young hoodlums would appear on their endless bar-hopping, already three sheets in the wind: notorious characters among them, neighborhood toughs or riffraff from the SA. Icy silence, emphasized by the waiters clearing their throats, soon drove them out into the night again. But last year a different kind of young set had appeared, closer to Dworak's heart. His son with a whole gang of boys and girls, all of them members of the Young Front. In ski clothes, their boards on their shoulders, they had come stomping along from the station. The elders gave them seats of honor in the club room. Their cheeks were still red from the sharp mountain wind. They had drunk hot tea—not a drop of alcohol, teetotalers all of them. Their talk: stem turns, ripped stems and smooth christies, schussing down icy sunk trails, gliding wax, climbing wax. And in the middle of it, Weigel, a student, had attacked little Ruth Eisner: "But listen, I am telling you, Marx says that the dictatorship of the proletariat is the dictatorship of the majority and that therefore . . . ."

And even if this year these young folks would not be there—still, any of the Party members in the district who lived within a reasonable distance, anybody who happened to be in the neighborhood, would pay his respects and drop in at "The Republic." Because that's where the the leading men of most of the sections would sit together. In bad times, this was the headquarters of that army; in good times, holidays, this was the festive meeting ground of that family which called itself the "Social Democratic Workers' Party."

Had they in the club room already reached the memories stage? Isonzo—prisoner-of-war camps in Siberia—the Party convention in the year seven—the big Schuhmeier rally on the Schmelz 1907—and everybody's memories mixed and fused with those of others until even the most reticent, like Dworak, dropped their reserve and indulged in uninhibited talk, doubly pleasurable for them. Then the talk subsided, they fell silent and sat quietly in the goodly beer haze, head and heart pleasantly cleared. Suddenly Spannmeier noticed that it was almost twelve, jumped to his feet, stammered something sublime through his mustache covered with foam, and then the moment had come, and all stood up: the men kissed their wives and everybody had so many wishes that no one could think of a single one, and Spannmeier raised his stein once more and all screamed with him: "Happy New Year!" and "Long live socialism!"

The starless cover of the sky curved over the last thin glimmer that was Vienna. Indifferent village lamps swam by. Back in the restaurant "The Republic" the celebration would pass without Dworak. It was a shame: a real nuisance.

And it was harder to put up with than Dworak had expected. He, the most level-headed officer of the district, simply could not get rid of certain tempting New Year's phantasies at the back of his thoughts while he felt the fast rocking of the engine pressing ahead. He refused to accept the fact that under the circumstances he was the man to bring this express to the border safe and sound. The routine duties were becoming amazingly difficult and bothersome. Whenever Gellert opened the furnace door the heat hit Dworak's lids like blows with a fist. The wind gushed in through the window, bit with icy cold at his neck while the sweat was pouring down his face. A thought now occurred to him that under normal circumstances would have appeared ridiculous: would he catch cold? Glowing heat, December cold, stench of soot . . . all that he had learned to accept the way any decent man would accept his craft. He had learned to perform the necessary actions with a minimum of physical action. He and his fireman knew how to communicate whenever necessary with a minimum of words. What had to be done was done automatically. He had worked out a system of strict efficiency as was indispensable to anyone who surrendered his strength, his sleep, and his health to a government operation that was so run down that it became an exploiter worse than Henry Ford. The point was to economize one's resources, which, at the same time, was good training for an official in the Party and the union. The unemployed young people did not have such training, and it showed. That was Dworak's opinion, and that was Dworak through and through.

But on this night run he obviously was not his true self. He read the pressure gauge, turned to the window to look down the line and suddenly did not know whether he had read eight-and-a-half or nine atmospheres. Then, wouldn't you know, the lever of the regulator stuck for a second. One time, when Dworak leaned out the window, the wind almost tore the cap off his head. The simplest thing demanded concentration.

For ten years Dworak had not been sick once. In the morning he looked in the mirror no longer than was necessary to see whether he had washed properly. "Damn it, what's the matter with me?" he snarled impatiently. And what made matters worse was Gellert. When Dworak, against his habit, started to curse, to curse Zehetner, it seemed at first as if Gellert would understand, understand how difficult it was for a man of Dworak's standing to take it all.

He is chairman of one of the most powerful railroaders' unions in the country. He is ex officio member of the executive board of the Federal Railway Administration, Vienna, and a high officer in the Republican Defense Corps of his district. In 1918 he was the second in command at the depot. The second in command? But what were those officially in control at the depot or anywhere else? Shadows. True, all that has changed. Since then a lot of things had happened. But nothing that should cause him to doubt that in the depot he is the person of authority. How does the top man negotiate with him? With the utmost courtesy. Like one superpower with another. Behind the Hofrat there is the power of the Executive General, behind Dworak, the engineer, the power of the work force, 92 percent of them members of the Free Unions. Who is more powerful? Each of them prefers to leave that question open until the economy has recovered. Each of them shoulders his responsibility to keep the depot operating smoothly. And yet, the engineer's responsibility weighs more heavily. At times, unexpectedly, an incisive government statement is heard over the radio, at some farmers' rally the little chancellor insinuates threats, the aristocratic playboy fires up his mercenaries for the destruction of Bolshevism. In response, the Party raises hell in Parliament, calls protest meetings. What would the people prefer? The dictatorship of a Prince Starhemberg or the dictatorship of the proletariat? The Hofrat and the engineer, each for himself, knows: neither nor. All that's nothing but dog-fights. The decisive battle had been postponed. Somehow one has to get along with the other, superpower with superpower. No change in the work schedule, no pay cut, ever passes without beeing cleared with the engineer. He knows the maze of schedules, master plans, wage scales, amendments and subsidiary regulations, disciplinary ordinances, bills for cutting the deficit of the Federal Railroads; he knows them all better than the Chairman of the Executive Board, and as well as the Board's own lawyers. Without any preparation he could become Minister of Transport, Minister of the Interior or of Defense. He would have been in Parliament a long time ago if, back in 1924, he had not preferred to stay with his men at the depot. Better not think of that now, during this night. Now, after all that has happened, in the fourteenth year of the Republic, he is being chased off to work by a measly, little pencil-pusher like an apprentice by his master mechanic. According to the letter of the law, he couldn't have objected even if times had been different; the intrigue is spun too finely. But when would this nonentity Zehetner ever have dared to think of hassling him? Up to now he had never even noticed this Zehetner. Or whenever he had heard the name, he had explained him historically, as he had been taught, that is to say, excused. "He is a petty bourgeois, so what do you expect? Let him have his convictions." Now Dworak has to take notice of what has happened. It is not more than a nasty flea bite, and yet he can't get over it.

Dworak started a barrage of curses against Zehetner. He didn't spit the curses; he drank them in, panting. He wanted to get really drunk on his rage. And at first Gellert seemed to understand what Dworak was up against, how hard it was for him, and that he kept cursing like that only to work himself up to the boiling point so that he would finally explode in a word that would somehow make him get over the infuriating mess. Gellert did not make one of his cynical comments. He helped him like a good friend. While Dworak stood leaning out, the fireman was feeding the fire again and flinging curses and chunks of coal into the furnace. "Such a coward, that bastard. When the time comes I'll be the one to stand him up against a wall! We'll get rid of him, you bet. I wouldn't play the big shot now if I were them. We'll lick people like that any time." That felt good. Dworak smiled over to the sleeping village whose lights swam by him in wide arches. He knew every field in this landscape. He had been driving through it for 25 years. He knew it by day and by night. The flakes came more sparingly. No need to worry that the line would be snowed over somewhere. He felt a lot better already.

And the night would have passed more amicably if Gellert's sympathy had lasted longer. Dworak, who had quieted down, turned half round in the cab while he kept an eye on the tracks and started talking about the New Year's party he had missed. He didn't talk very loud because the two had learned to cut out the noise of the engine. And he did not talk in an excessively irritated way either. Dworak was ready to put up with the bloody nuisance. After all, he lived for his work. But because he was used to routine, he had to have some substitute for what he had missed. All he wanted was to chat with his fireman for a quiet half-hour. About Spannmeier and Pawlik, about the gossip in the organization. About old memories shared in the district. In short, about all those small things which, together with weightier reasons in 1924 had motivated him to leave fame and advancement to others. He wanted just a bit of family coziness to bury for good all the unuttered worries, all the unfinished business, the accumulated self-reproaches of the year that had just passed. The one that just started would bring enough of its own. At times one needs such a half-hour more than anything, and Dowrak needed it now at the end of this year 1932, and he had been looking forward to it for a long time. But now Gellert left him in the lurch. Gellert, too, had been expected in "The Republic." He usually took part in those meetings in the club room. But again and again he annoyed them with his sneering remarks. Which doesn't mean that the regulars there didn't have a sense of humor or couldn't take criticism. Spannmeier's delight in scornful banter was feared. And last year Dworak's son Hans had made a malicious joke about the Party leadership and caused a lot of laughter and antagonism. When company commander Kaliwoda got tipsy (and for that he needed only three small glasses because he drank on an empty stomach) he would stare into his wine and mumble: "Jews, that's what they are . . . no matter what they say." All that was part of it. But Gellert's remarks were different. They only caused uneasiness.

They came from an alien province. Actually, they only invited him because Dworak had taken a liking to him.

Now Gellert let the furnace door come down with a bang. He rested his belly on the shovel handle and pushed his head up. The red reflection of the fire had slipped from his face like a mask. Gellert stared at Dworak, his face blackish, short and wide, tight-lipped and with upturned nose so that his large nostrils were visible. Under the beak of the cap that he had pushed up, a couple of wet strands of hair bulged out. In the soot-covered skin his light gray eyes looked almost white. Even before he spoke, Dworak knew what was coming: "Oh boy. Looks like you're really homesick for those old cronies of yours! Well, if you ask me . . ."

"I didn't ask ya!"—"So what? I can say what I want in a democratic republic, can't I? So, if you ask me . . ."

Dworak was furious and leaned out the window and didn't listen anymore. That's the way Gellert was. Whatever anyone did for him was done in vain. He had remained what he had been when he appeared six years ago, a foreign element. A decent worker should not expect any gratitude from a vagabond. One can't expect any gratitude from any human being.

"Ferdl—Dworak!" The fireman tapped him on the shoulder and held out to him two metal cups and a bottle of beer. He smiled awkwardly: "Pour, it's almost twelve." Suddenly he was embarrassed, his eyes didn't return the glance. His unusually broad shoulders turned limp. He was a head shorter than his lanky engineer. Dworak took the cup without saying a word. Gellert made a pathetic attempt to smooth things over. "OK, let's forget it. Prost! Skoal, as they say in Sweden! Long live the Party!"

That sounded embarrassed and yet, in Dworak's ears, it had a sarcastic undertone. He growled his Prosit and put the cup to his lips. Anyway, the beer was good. Where did that vagabond keep the bottle so that the pils was even cool. At this moment a panic fear shot through his body. Anxiety pressed his stomach together so that he almost vomited the beer. He had the certain feeling that he had just overlooked the stop signal at one of the log huts. He reached for the emergency brake, thrust his upper body out of the window. The signals glowed green. He had been mistaken; everything was as it should be. The terror trickled away. But an unrest remained, some indefinite foreboding . . . The perfectly healthy man did not succeed in getting a clear picture in his mind of what was going on inside him for the next hour. During the break at the next big junction, where, in an emergency, substitutes were available, for a minute he seriously thought of asking to be relieved. He was in a condition that, according to the regulations, made it a duty for any transport employee to declare himself unable to continue on the job. "Because of impairment of full mental and physical ability to work," the regulations said. Only he could not have said exactly what was the matter with him, and so he drove on. The fireman had not the slightest idea, or he would have immediately reported his colleague sick, if for no other reason than out of fear for his own neck, and those of the passengers.

It had stopped snowing. The sky had brightened. For stretches of half an hour at a time the whitish moon sailed along beside the locomotive. Visibility was good. Nevertheless, Dworak could not get rid of the worry that the line was blocked somewhere. Could one know how heavy the snowfall had been further on in the mountains and whether it wasn't still snowing there? The terror about the possibly overlooked signal came over him again and again, even if less violently, because he mistrusted himself. But the fact that he did mistrust himself was unsettling enough. Several times it was Gellert who had to regulate the speed. Whenever he did it himself, the gauges didn't seem to be reliable. In reality it was he who wasn't reliable, and he knew it. His routine responsibility for everything that might happen to the train had become almost unbearable. "What the devil is the matter with me?" he asked himself again and again without finding an answer. About three o'clock in the morning he couldn't stand being alone with his worries anymore, and he screamed: "That's how train wrecks happen. And then they blame us. The bastards, they don't think for a minute about the trains. Politics, that's all they've got in their heads, nothing else. They don't give a damn about a human being. Jesus Christ!"

"What's the matter?"

"Nothing," Dworak groaned. He had avoided the real issue, so there was nothing else to say.

Anyway, that ended the tension between the two of them. At least Dworak felt enough at ease to tell Gellert what he thought about the railroaders who wished them Happy New Year at almost every depot. That had already happened a dozen times and strained his frayed nerves. He would have liked nothing better than to curse every single one of these smiling men. Almost everybody who held some position in the Party was the subject of rumors, and Dworak, who on principle never thought that there was any truth to them, now suddenly believed all of them. Meanness and corruption stared at him from everywhere.

"Did you see Stationmaster Andreas with that oily grin of his? Nothing but fear, let me tell ya. They ought to check the finances in his local real good one of these days. And young Hagleitner? What d'ya want to bet that he's a Nazi? He says he's one of us just to spy."

"Come on, Hagleitner of all people? You don't believe that yourself . . . ."

"Of course Hagleitner! Still waters run deep. You can't trust any human being anymore, nobody, I'm telling ya. . . ."

But that, too, wasn't the issue, and didn't help. And again the fear of a catastrophe gripped him.

There was no catastrophe. Under the circumstances you could call it more of an accident that it had not happened than if it had. Shortly before five, in all good order, he handed over the engine at the roundhouse in the terminal depot. He had five hours to sleep; at eleven-thirty he had to take a slower passenger train back to Vienna. He was so exhausted that sleep was out of the question. And so he did not take the road down to the railroad hostel but the one to the town. Gellert came with him, and that was OK. The streets were covered with ankle-deep snow. No restaurant was open any more; the street lamps, turned low, hardly gave any light. This small provincial town, like so many others, was impoverished; it had to cut corners. In the sparse moonlight the little town lay dead. The two railroad men were familiar with the town, but now, with all the statues shrouded in snow, all the windows gone blind, and all the pubs closed, the town turned strange for them again. The temperature dropped sharply. And, inspite of their fleece-lined winter jackets, they began to freeze, but they walked on aimlessly through the narrow side streets. To light a cigarette, they stopped in front of an iron statue of a madonna who, with a snow cap on her head and a frozen smile, held a stark naked Christ child out into the cold. Dworak blew smoke in the virgin's face.

"A country of bigots."

They walked on.

"In 1904, when I joined the Party, I believed that in ten years, at the most, reason would rule mankind."

Gellert, fifteen years younger, did not understand the concept. "How do you mean that?"

"And after ten years the World War broke out."

For a while they stomped silently side by side. Without any transition, Dworak asked him: "Sepp, tell me honestly, are you a Communist?"

Gellert dug the toe of his boot into a pile of snow. "If Lenin were still alive, I'd be a Communist."

For a moment Dworak had nothing to say. Again he had not actually talked about the real issue. He just had wanted to get to the bottom of his own uneasiness, but had not succeeded.

As it always happens in a small town, they came back to the market place without noticing it. Each of them was busy with himself. Gellert's varied life had often given him this opportunity of thinking about himself. With Dworak it was different. For the first time in his life he was really thinking about himself, and facing so many new questions that he felt completely helpless. The cold went right through him, the wet seeped through his boots, his bones ached.

And then he made an unusual discovery. More precisely, he came across a very natural and not at all amazing fact that struck him as a discovery. He realized that he was almost fifty years old. Old? That didn't really make him old yet. Nonetheless: Fifty years!

2

In the following weeks, however, no railroad inspector had reason to file a complaint against Dworak for negligence. Nothing happened that would have impaired his reputation of impeccable dependability. The reason might have been that, during the month of January, Dworak only rarely was called to night duty. But apart from that, Gellert reported that at that time the engineer made his peace with the locomotives in a special manner. When he oiled and checked the important parts, he not only displayed the usual care but also a kind of affection. Longer than necessary he busied himself with pistons and valves. He also began to give the locomotives human names, a custom that went back to the relatively idyllic depots of remotest prewar times and which now could be found only in one or the other smaller engine shops.

It was above all in the Party organization of our district that people noticed a change in Dworak. It started in meetings when he, who had always been known as equanimity incarnate, displayed a behavior that was highly questionable in a chairman. In an abrasive manner and obviously according to arbitrary whim, he would cut off discussions or speakers, or would announce a time restriction for speaking altogether. At first people put up with that silently out of respect for Dworak's authority. The first to object was Weyer, a comrade who was made untouchable by his thirty-five-year-old membership card. He thought it sufficient to whisper a remark at the table where, next to Dworak, he presided over the meeting. At that—it was a trade union meeting—Dworak banged his fist on the table: "Leave me alone with your agenda. For thirty years you have had nothing in your head but your agenda!" That was pretty bad! That was downright incredible from the mouth of a man who, under Victor Adler's bust, used to throne righteously and imperturbably like the absolute agenda itself. What was even stranger was that, after this and repeated other outbursts, all of a sudden he would lose all interest in the meeting and, in the most heated discussion, with furrowed brow, seemed to be absorbed in his own thoughts. Several times he was late for the meeting. The first teasing reminder to be punctual caused an explosion: "For thirty years I have been sacrificing myself for you. Because of you

I refused a seat in Parliament. Because of you, I've wrecked my nerves." Etc.

It was at this very meeting of the district's executive committee that Dworak's peculiar behavior reached a climax. At his urging, the whole agenda was chased through at top speed because, under Miscellaneous, he was going to make some important organizational proposals. When that moment came, he rummaged among the pile of notes in front of him, and, shaking his head, he put aside one after the other, until finally, holding on to the last piece of paper, he launched into an extensive address. He spoke in the energetic, inspiring tone people were used to hearing from him on more impressive occasions. Big words like "Party discipline," "To be or not to be," "Freeedom and Progress . . . ," "Dead-end street . . ." were heard. But in the end all that led up to the incredibly simple demand that membership fees must be collected more industriously and handed in faster. There was nothing in the world that the district's executive board considered more obvious, more basic, or that it had discussed more frequently, than membership fees. The board members looked at each other taken aback. They couldn't even muster the energy for a formal response. Amid clearing of throats and scraping of chairs, the meeting dissolved while a few mumbled an embarrassed "Hear, hear."

On the other hand, Dworak was known to say only decisive things and to speak only on decisive matters. Besides, even then people in the Party had become used to ferreting out behind the words of leading comrades a hidden meaning which, for reasons of parliamentary negotiations, of foreign policy, domestic policy or other tactical considerations, could only be hinted at in public. The political atmosphere was one of excitement, especially because of rumors which came across the German border and the fascists' illegal weapons transport that the party press had exposed. When Dworak's speech, in even fuzzier form than the original, made the rounds among the Party officials, it found various interpreters. The most adventurous kept a low profile. With a knowing twinkle in their eyes, they would be satisfied with theories that were as bold as noncommittal. "It's only logical. The Entente expects Austria to apologize for our government that permitted the smuggling of Italian weapons to Hungary. Now, on the one hand, we must appease France, and, on the other, we must watch out that we don't fall in with Italy. And apart from all that, we need a government that doesn't stand for such a tone in diplomacy because Austria is naturally the last shit in all of Europe, but too much is too much. So there's only one way out: a coalition government." And with meaningful glances they would point to some sentence, even some word in the *Arbeiter Zeitung*—"There you are! Comrade Bauer will have to take a back seat for a while. You've got to read between the lines. If Renner isn't Federal Chancellor in February, I'll eat my hat. For anybody who has ears to hear, Comrade Dworak's statements said what there is to be said." At the same time, opposing suggestions were made. So there they sat as always, the blind clairvoyants at the tables in party meeting halls or restaurants, speculating about this, that, and everything. And they were going to sit like that for a while longer, underlining words in the *Arbeiter Zeitung* with their fingernails, the extinguished cigar end between lips curled with superiority, with cunning glances and short memories, contentious, and, in their way, happy.

And so this time, too, they didn't leave their chairs. But others with more or less hesitation directly approached this comrade Dworak who, hitherto cool and unapproachable, had undergone a change that couldn't be quite explained. It was amazing what wishes, doubts, hopes, plans, magnetically attracted by his odd behavior, rushed in upon him from all sides. Some members of Section Four asked him to support them in their fight against their section chairman who systematically loaded the committees with elements from outside the district and, to top it all, with intellectuals, while the manual workers had nothing to say. A group of petty Party officials demanded his help against female comrade Prischnigg who still sat on the district's executive board although she was a floozie with a record, and had bitterly insulted comrade Petschina. The religious members of the district implored him to protect them against the tyranny of the freethinkers. One by one, treasurers, members of the auditing commission, secretaries of various clubs brought their complaints to him—conscientious petty bureaucrats who, for some paper reason, had become zealots. Come to think of it, of all others, they were most justified in referring to Dworak's speech that evening.

But it was due to a total misunderstanding that a member of the Defense Corps' third company appeared in Dworak's apartment and, with a firm squeeze of the hand, said confidentially: "Good to know, comrade, that you as a comrade in a responsible position finally are going to do something in the matter. We of the third company fully agree with your point of view."

"Well, I am not sure I know . . ."

The man, blinking his eye knowingly: "Never mind, comrade Dworak, the third company won't breathe a word." And, as he was leaving: "Would be a shame if the SA could hoard dynamite by the hundredweight and we shouldn't have a pinch of explosives. No need to talk about it—we understand each other. Or we might really end up in that dead-end street, as you put it so aptly."

Old Fellhammer, too, came. His sparse hair bristled on his shiny pate. He spoke excitedly, his pale blue eyes turned dark with passion. Of all he said, the man he addressed grasped only two sentences: "You're absolutely right," and "The debacle started in 1907 when the late comrade Schuhmeier took that unfortunate walk to the Imperial Palace."

But Dworak patiently heard the old fellow out to the end like all the others. He knew the axe Fellhammer had been grinding for twenty years and had often laughed about it. For years he had known (and actually loved) all these groups and grouplets that besieged him all of a sudden. He considered them as parts of the life of the organization from its very beginning, the natural sediments of this life, composed of failed ambitions, failed bad and good will, political and unpolitical spleens, ideals, crazes, human weaknesses of all kinds. Now and then, mostly before the district's conventions, these passions got stirred up only to subside soon again. He was used to that. Any attempt to analyse this residue of discontent would have appeared absurd to him. Dworak did not have a high opinion of human beings in general. Compared to the high ideals of reason and justice that, his convictions told him, were set as their goals, they had always appeared to him as rather despicable creatures; to a high degree they needed the guardianship of responsible Party officials. Thus for two decades he had traced every nuance of this discontent back to the natural inadequacy of humanity. For Dworak the difference between the affair of honor Prischnigg vs. Petschina, that had been dragging on for five years, and, let's say, the left opposition that began unfolding a year and a half ago, and, in the fall of 1932 even came close to joining the Communists in an "antifa," was only a difference in the degree of their harmfulness, but not one in principle. Neither one had understood what that really was: the Party. And since there always had to be people who did not understand, either one was inevitable. But so far Dworak had known even here to differentiate sharply between the important and the trivial, and had exercised that sense of orientation which saves people in leading positions from getting stuck in the quagmire of a thousand marginalities. Now he seemed to have lost it. His face twisted with impatience, he seemed to suspect something hidden behind all that was presented to him, be it in a torrent of words or in a stammer. And so for more than a week he gave careful consideration to all who besieged him.

Then, in one of those sudden, irritated decisions that used to become his obsession in those days, he signed himself over to the bureaucrats, body and soul. Many of them had only become that way gradually. Some years back they had displayed a restlessness similar to that so noticeable in Dworak recently. Only they had not been holding any high office and had not caused any raised eyebrows. And then they had thrown themselves into petty busyness, had become deaf and blind to everything else.

He threw in his lot with them up to the end of January. They would meet for working sessions that would last half the night, and would get quietly intoxicated with industrious pedantry as with opium. They buried themselves behind file cards. When he was off work Dworak, a bulging briefcase under his arm, would stalk from bureau to bureau. Weyer, who needed him for urgent measures against opposition railroad workers, was finally forced to literally corner him. It was no use. Dworak didn't listen; he averted his eyes. "OK, OK, do what you want. One thing at a time. I've got to go now." And he mumbled something about "checking" something. Beyond the border in Germany shots shattered the quiet every night. Communists and SA were engaging in street battles that claimed many lives. Ancient Hindenburg spoke of the oath: "Loyalty is honor's marrow." The enigmatic Schleicher cabinet was the center of rumors: the scandal about subsidies for provinces in the east—the coup of the Reichswehr. In the restaurant "The Republic" the prophets had their heyday. In the sections slide lectures were canceled to make room for political presentations. The meetings proceeded boisterously and, what had rarely happened before, the discussion became the main point. Dworak ducked behind palisades of records and checked something.

"What the devil is he checking all the time?" Pawlik, the District Councillor, asked himself, plagued by a bad conscience. "Is he, by any chance, checking me out?" Although he had nothing to go on, he doubted no longer that Dworak had caught on to certain plans of his, plans that circled around the lucrative center of corruption of director Rupprich of Party-Moving-Picture Inc., circles so close that Pawlik could hardly wriggle out anymore. Did Dworak just pretend—thus Pawlik's bad conscience asked, illogically, as a bad conscience will—did Dworak only hypocritically act as if he were inactive and worn out by Party business only to suddenly expose Pawlik? Or did Dworak get ready to resign his position in the district because a higher career was beckoning? "For that," Pawlik said to himself disconsolately, "he doesn't have to trample on me and ruin me. With all the connections he has!" In any case, he warned Rupprich and prejudiced City Councillor Kollmer against Dworak. Thus, even in these high circles, a certain confusion took hold.

"What the hell is the matter with him?" Gellert, too, asked himself. When he had first noticed the change in Dworak, he had actually savored it. For what else had he wanted for years than to see this unshakable solidity finally shaken, and finally to penetrate the self-righteous, hermetic, impervious sphere of Dworak's thoughts. Whether he wanted this out of envy, downright hostility, or love, he never tried to figure out. But now he saw clearly enough that his success was no success at all. "Don't ask any questions, you better do your job!" And, "You don't understand things like that; you are just a bum."

And the most astounding discovery about his chairman was

in store for the fireman on the morning of January 31. They bumped into each other at a street corner. Beside Dworak trotted a certain Robert Blum, treasurer of section 12, a pathetic character, by the way, who had never achieved anything in his life but a correct account of a month's membership fees. Rumor had it that Dworak wanted to make him treasurer for the district, but how damned unimportant was all that on this 31st of January? Gellert, who since yesterday afternoon could not formulate a thought more precise than just this one: "It has happened after all—after all!" Gellert seized Dworak's hand: "What do you say to that?"

That Blum fellow opened his eyes wide behind his glasses. The fireman took no notice of him and repeated more urgently: "Say, Ferdl, what d'you say to Germany I want to know."

Dworak knitted his brow and withdrew his hand. "Leave me in peace with your constant grumbling about the toleration policy. Buy yourself the *Vorwärts*, then you'll know." Gellert opened his mouth wide. "So you don't know that yesterday . . ."

No, Dworak did not know anything. From the late afternoon on into the night he had been working with Blum and had not read the morning papers. Dworak, for twenty-five years chairman of the local section, member of the personnel committee, officer in the Republican Defense Corps, Member of the District's Executive Committee, had not read his *Arbeiter-Zeitung*, and went through his workers' district this January 31 not knowing that, the day before, Hitler had become Chancellor of Germany.

3

And there they were turning the corner already, the SA leading. Riding boots, brown shirts, shoulder straps, swastika armbands—everything tip-top. Drum rolls, blaring fanfares, thundering march steps. Students, salesmen, but among them again and again workers' faces. Unemployed? Sure, many unemployed, that was a consolation for Dworak and helped him to make light of them. But he also saw other workers, good people whom he had met in former years, no, even a few months ago, at union meetings. Then they had come less and less regularly, had become more and more reticent, grumpier, with eyes that reflected a bad conscience and defiance. Until they had stayed away altogether. Now he found them here again. It seemed to him as if their SA uniforms were a disguise. But they obviously did not feel like that. Behind them marched Hitler Youth and happily excited civilians. Curses followed them. A year ago people had laughed at them. They were not afraid. Now and then their hands went down to their belts threateningly. They moved, the flag raised high, their columns tightly closed, an invasion army through enemy territory. Their victory celebration was to take place on Karlsplatz.

Dworak left the fireman and the treasurer standing where they were, jumped into the next street car, and went home. On the second landing he had to stop a minute. He was short of breath. Short of breath? That was the latest. He leaned on the railing and looked at the neat name-tag on the door: Robert Blum, Civil Servant ret. Below, a paper label was affixed: Social Counselor. Office Hours: Tuesday and Friday 6 to 8. He realized that that kind of good fortune was not for him. The little party functionary could find his peace behind files and records. For him that avenue of escape was barred. He was up too high. He had too much responsibility. "Responsibility"—a devilish word. Formerly it had been a source of strength for him. He had hurled it with accuracy at excited meetings, and the know-it-alls, the smart alecks, the irresponsible had been silenced. Now this responsibilty weighed him down. If he had taken on such a great responsibilty, why not also the amenities that came with it? Why had he not left the depot that time in 1924? And what kept him from doing it now? He was ex officio member of the Vienna executive board. All he had to do was to have himself voted in as a regular member, and he would be released from his work at the depot, would receive a salary from the union, his railroad pension in addition and would have an office where he could bear his responsibilty which had become so great it could not be borne in any other way. One small step and this unnatural state would be behind him. Yes, that's what it was, an unnatural state. Because what was an officer of the general staff doing in the trenches?

The leader of Dworak's Party, Otto Bauer, for some reason

loved comparison with the military. As Dworak slowly climbed the steps up to his apartment, the words "Battle at the Marne" occurred to him. Didn't they say a sick officer of the general staff had all of a sudden found himself amidst the turmoil of battle? He had seen the confusing commotion of an army in operation from too close up: artillery stuck on the roadside, groaning wounded soldiers being carried past him, companies in dissolution, confused commanding officers, regiments marching to or away from the battle without knowing why. He had lost the perspective and ordered a general retreat . . . .

His wife and son already sat at supper in the kitchen that also served as living-room. She smiled, happy to see him, and put another plate on the table. Her features had become indistinct, her hair was gray, she looked years older than he was. He washed his hands. When he opened a wardrobe in the bedroom to get a fresh towel, he saw, tacked on the inside of the wardrobe door, a small picture of the Virgin Mary. He tore it off.

"Since when is that crap in my wardrobe?"

His wife was startled. Still and small, she sat behind the table. Her nose turned a waxy yellow and twitched. "But it's always been there, dad." "Don't lie to me! Why don't you come out with it right now and say that you have joined the bigots." She was silent and shyly ladled the soup into his bowl. It was quite possible that she did not lie, that the little picture had been there for years unnoticed by him. Quite possible that she went to church every Sunday without his knowing it. He had married her in 1909, mainly because a decent, class-conscious worker could not mess with all sorts of women forever, and he was sick of the brothels which railroad men frequented before they started the run back. After the marriage he had tried to bring the farmer's daughter who had been a hard-working, decent maid, into the movement. When he did not succeed, he paid less and less attention to her. Besides, the organization took every minute of his free time. In 1915 she bore him his son, nine months after his first leave from the front. He gave him the first name that was not the name of a Habsburg: Hans. He liked having him ride on his knees. When the boy was thirteen and a member of the Red Falcons, Dworak had given him a silver watch, so that the boy wouldn't feel bad about having lost out on the gift that other boys got at confirmation. And if Spannmeier called him a family tyrant, he probably did so only because Spannmeier himself was a henpecked husband.

Not a word was spoken at table. The political catastrophe that Dworak had just heard of was way beyond his wife's grasp, and his son's confused notions didn't interest him.

Hans pushed the half-full plate aside. "I don't want any more; every day that brew," he said and made a face. Dworak saw that his wife was hurt. And suddenly he felt sorry for her. She wouldn't have to feel bad about her soup now if he had taken advantage of his career chances. It was his fault. When they were young, she sometimes jokingly called him Mr. Representative and had built dream castles. But she never reproached him. She was a good wife and loved him. He had quite a bit to make up to her. He made a resolution to come home earlier from now on. Also, in the future, they should be together as man and wife more often. I'm still young enough for that for a long time to come, to give her that little bit of happiness, he said to himself. And disgruntled, he ordered: "Eat what's on your plate!"

Hans shrugged his shoulder. "But if I don't like it . . ." He reached for the bread and lard. The woman sighed. Dworak, who wanted to make peace gently stroked her head. "Don't feel bad, mother, the bum isn't worth it. He should be glad he gets anything at all as long as he doesn't bring home a groschen."

Hans had jumped up. "So it's my fault that I don't have a job, is it?"

Dworak quietly spooned his soup. "It sure isn't my fault. When I was your age I was independent and wouldn't have taken a single piece of bread from my late father without paying for it."

Only when he heard the door slam, did his anger give way to reflection. The boy had rushed out of the apartment. The woman was kneeling on the floor and timidly picked up the piece of bread the boy had spat there.

So not even to your own son could you say what you thought? No, he didn't understand anything anymore. For fifteen years—ever since he had come home from the war—he had seen the boy every day, had spoken with him, instructed him, raised him to be a reasonable, class-conscious human being, and now he had to ask himself whether he actually knew this eighteen-year-old any better than any other member of the Young Front. So what was it all for, all that care and love? And those SA brats—"Victory shall be ours . . ." If anybody had prophesied that to their fathers in the trenches . . . And now the fathers themselves were marching along with their sons. "No more wars!" had been the slogan then. Now Hitler was Chancellor! What good had it been, all that work? The rationalism that he had believed in above anything else, had it been a wrong kind of rationalism?

Was there no such thing as progress?

Dworak, his head between his hands, thought of his fireman. When Gellert had appeared at the depot, worn out and uprooted, how he had taken care of the boy! Had firmly planted him in the organization, had seen to it that he got some responsibilities, and thus had given him everything that, in his view, a person needed to find peace and the ground under his feet. It had been no good. What was it all for anyway? For what had he, Dworak, reached fifty years? Awkwardly, he stood again where he had been in that New Year's night: facing himself.

He took a letter out of his pocket. He had received it this morning from District Councillor Pawlik:

"Dear comrade Dworak!

Hope that you won't take it amiss from an old Party veteran when he is honest with you. Have the impression that lately you have been overburdened with responsibilities as, unfortunately, always happens to the best comrades in our Party who, without concern for their nerves, sacrifice themselves for the ideal; and for this reason you could use some recreation. By the way, that is also, independently of me, the opinion of City Councillor, comrade Kollmer, and therefore I'm giving you the friendly advice . . ."

Was this Pawlik then a scoundrel? That he was out for a career was not new to Dworak. He had known the man for thirty years. But now it seemed to him that he might have misjudged the man, that this flexible, perhaps a bit too aggressive but still usable Pawlik whom he had known might be just an empty dummy. How many such dummies—Dworak asked himself—were there in this world?

His wife tapped him timidly on the shoulder. Had anything

upset him at the depot? He looked so ill.

Dworak shrugged his shoulders. "It's nothing. Tomorrow I have an important conference with Representative Dreher," he lied only to say something, anything at all. And that's how the thought occurred to him that it wouldn't really hurt to see his old friend again.

However, the meeting was delayed for almost two weeks because first Dworak wanted to take care of the mountain of important matters that he had neglected. He did it with care and love. He even ordered matters that had fallen into disarray not because of his confusion in January but even before, that through no fault of his own had remained unattended, business he had planned to straighten out in his vacation. Areas that with the years had overlapped with those of others were sharply delineated again. Imminent conferences, meetings at Party Headquarters, rallies of the Defense Corps, and things like that which he used to keep track of in his head now were neatly marked on the calendar. And he did all that with a very precise sense of purpose.

"As if you were going on vacation tomorrow," Spannmeier said amazed.

"As if you were going to resign," Blum said jokingly.

"As if he had something else on his mind," Pawlik surmised suspiciously.

When towards the middle of February Dworak had the feeling that everything was shipshape and in exemplary order, he planned two hours for his visit with Dreher. Two hours on a Saturday afternoon, February 11. At the same time there was to be a big Party demonstration in response to the Nazi victory rally of last week. Dworak had decided not to take part in the demonstration. He was on day-duty these weeks and, for a long time, would not be free during Dreher's office hours. And to visit the Representative at home seemed to him inappropriate, for one thing because the purpose of his visit was official: to speed up the illegally delayed promotion of a brakeman to conductor. The case was urgent. And, of course, as the leader of the company of railroad workers in the demonstration, he had a substitute. At least that was Dworak's argument to himself.

Dreher's office was in the building of the Central Administration of the Austrian Federal Railway on Schwarzenbergplatz. (Since Dreher represented the union on the administrative council, he had an office there in a completely official capacity.) Dworak, only a minute from the building, hesitated to cross the Ring Boulevard. Both sides were already lined thick with supporters. The boulevard was thronged with marching masses; singing, slogans, flags filled the air. Dworak considered that it would take a long time before the column of his district would have marched on from the rallying point and turned onto the Ring. By that time he could be through with Dreher, and take over the command of the company of railway workers after all. He pushed himself through the people but at the edge of the pavement stopped again. Dworak had long ago become a Party official by instinct. Completely without reason some inhibition seemed to forbid him to leave while railroad men were marching. Undecided, he sighed and watched the passing columns.

February Eleventh 1933

On that eleventh of February we marched without music. To emphasize the fighting spirit of the demonstration, the Party had ordered us to leave the bands home. We had taken to the street as we had done for fifteen years, excited by the immediate cause but in the one, basic, unshakable knowledge that it was ours, this Ring Boulevard, lined by the pompous architectural ogres of the monarchy that had passed away. This ring round the district of the rich was familiar ground for our demonstrations. One belonged to the other. To the awful pseudo-Greek temple of the Parliament belonged seventy-two Social-Democratic Representatives; to the Gothic City Hall our two-thirds majority. And on the First of May and the Twelfth of November it was unthinkable that the Ringstrasse should not be flooded with people, athrob with our singing, aflame with our flags. Only once, in the year 1927, to our unspeakable terror, police volleys had shattered the air . . . Five years later their echo still rumbled threateningly through the country. But could that alter the fundamental fact that this city, this street was ours? And that's how we felt when we demonstrated on the eleventh of February. The danger whose deadly coldness was blowing in from Germany was an indistinct, unintelligible danger. After having ruled there for eleven days, it still had not exposed its face. We even hesitated to call it "fascism." At that time it bore only one name: all that was as yet unknown to us and was to be disclosed later on, was hidden behind that one name: "Hitler!"

Not only the music was missing at this rally; because of the humid weather, the varied colors of glorious May Day parades were absent: the blue shirts of the young, the white gym shirts of the athletes, the green blouses of the children, the bright gay dresses of the women. Only the banners on their light-colored bamboo shafts burned in their intense red in all that silent and roaring gray of sky, buildings, and masses of people.

Robert Blum, treasurer of Section Twelve, marched in the first row of his district. Already when the columns were forming, big-bellied Spannmeier had taken his arm and, with jovial phrases, pushed him to the front and got him to talk with District Councillor Pawlik. That didn't really mean all that much. When in a good mood, Spannmeier generously showed his favors indiscriminately. That Blum was to be pumped for information about Dworak was a second thought at the most. Blum felt flattered. Right in front of him moved the dignitaries of the district, and, towering above all of them, the powerful venerable figure of old chairman Kärndl, whose gigantic back blocked Blum's view. That didn't bother him. The broad, slightly bent shoulders, the fleshy nape of the neck and the silvery white hair, the pushed-back Homburg was view enough for him. On his left someone carried the district's banner. It was as old and venerable as Kärndl. Thirty-four years had darkened the heavy, wine-red material. "Knowledge is Power," the embroidery said in old-fashioned flourishes. For in the beginning was the Educational Association. It was unimportant that the venerable flag had the cut of Roman Catholic pilgrimage banners, that it was downright ugly with all its gold threads, that its wooden shaft decorated with a turner's artful knobs and grooves was uncomfortable to hold. What was important and precious emanated from it invisibly. Anyone who walked behind it, his head lowered, could read it on the cobblestones: Memories!

Although Blum marched in front only accidentally, he enjoyed a secret game with himself. With the restless checking glance of an organizer, he again and again turned round to look at rows of the organized who moved along with quick, or leisurely steps, or long strides. It was the old men and the women especially who, in these immense rows sixteen or twenty abreast, made any uniform marching step impossible. They, like Blum himself, had no sense for military precision. Out of this unrhythmical shuffling of feet rose a dull murmur of countless conversations. The women exchanged their worries about the children and the household. But almost all of them held on to their handkerchiefs and now and then waved to the supporters that thronged the side of the street. Again and again in the middle of their small talk they would shout "Friendship" or a shrill, furious "Down with Fascism!" Attempts by younger comrades to skip steps and initiate a marching rhythm were received with motherly scorn: "What are you doin', comrade Lechner, why are ya hoppin' like a billy goat," and then, a note softer, "Isn't he the one that danced with that girl, that Fritzi, from number 17 the other night at the WEA party?" and then, this time, very softly: "My ol' man is comfort-loving as any fat cat. Believe it or not, the other day when they drove out to the Vienna woods to bury the rifles for the Defense Corps, he wanted to play hooky. No beans, says I. Boy, did I get him out of bed in a hurry. You should've seen it!"

Blum's district was famous and respected in the working-class movement. Whenever they came in sight, uninterrupted cheers and applause welcomed them, an experience that for the little treasurer was as overwhelming as it was strangely new. For, in the twenty-nine years of his work for the party, he had not once been in a visible position. He knew that his appearance was not impressive, and that it was proper for him to remain in the background of life. Now that he was getting older, he accidentally savored the unexpected honor of marching at the head of a celebrated unit. While the younger comrades had come straight from work, he, the retired salesman, had had the leisure to don his Sunday best. The top coat wrapped around his body was black and, in the cloudy weather, not even the shabbiest spots along the edge of the velvet collar were noticeable. Black was the Homburg, black were the boots polished to a luster, and red was the little, twenty-nine-year-old silk handkerchief that fluttered in his hand. His cheeks were brutally clean-shaven. The neat steel-rimmed spectacles, though fogged up, sat firmly on his nose. The way Blum looked, he could well risk being seen alongside the highest functionaries of the district.

Somewhere singing welled up. The women stopped their talk. The old comrades, like Blum, dressed for the festive occasion because for them every march on the Ring, no matter for what reason, was a cheerful victory celebration for that First of May 1890 when they, between Royal & Imperial bayonets, had conquered the right to the street, the old comrades cleared their throats piously. Blum again looked at the back of the district chairman. Then the song had reached him. It was as ugly and powerful as the district banner. Blum had learned it long before the "International," and knew all stanzas by heart. So he intoned it, "The hymn to the noble bride, ordained to never leave man's side, ere human he would be. What now is his the world around resulted from this sacred bond. Work, hail! Work, hail to thee!"

Hans Dworak, eighteen years old, did not sing the "Hymn to Work" along with the others. For today he marched with the company "Friedrich Engels," and here song and chants were started only at the commandant's orders. That was the way Hans liked it. He marched with the Defense Corps for the first time. While his hobnailed boots (he had put hobnailed boots on because they looked more military) in the rattling beat of 120 march steps hit the pavement, at the back of his head there was a furtive echo of that other song about the soldiers marching through the town, and girls from the windows looking down, looking down . . . His uniform consisted of a blue, discarded city-transport jacket and a blue visored cap. But he felt the leather belt and shoulder strap, new and yellow, tight against his body; and the cap sat on his ear at a rakish angle, and a strand of hair hung down smartly. Now Hans didn't think of the difficulties with Paula, nor of how they treated him at home since he was out of work, nor of the day when his welfare would run out. There were other things to think about: first of all to present a defiant posture before all the people on the sidewalk. In secret anger he cast a sidelong look at some older workers in the company who didn't even think of putting out their chests and giving their eyes a stare of determination, but instead, tried to be as comfortable as possible in their negligently-belted jackets. Ready for the reserves, that's what they were, Hans thought, furious. Although many of them were just old enough to have been in the war, to him they seemed despicable old geezers. He completely forgot that they outdid him in a few things; they were excellent shots for instance, an art he hardly knew anything about yet. At that time he had a pretty inflated idea of himself in general. Carefully he checked again and again for places where the crowd on the sidewalk might fail to display the usual enthusiasm. Hadn't there been some talk about the Nazis trying to disturb the demonstration? Where were they hiding? Already he closed his hand round the belt, touched by the squeaking beauty of the new leather, eager to swing it on enemy heads. But there again, that transfixed smile was spreading over the faces of the onlookers, again hundreds of fists shot up with the shouts: "Hail the Defense Corps!" It was almost annoying. "Free . . . dom! Free . . . dom! Free . . . dom!" the marchers answered in the precise rhythm signaled by Kaliwoda's raised hand. But that was no sufficient satisfaction. And when Kaliwoda started dragging out, "Woooorking Claaaass!" and they roared their response "Awake!" and when he flung hoarsely in the air: "Hitleeeeer" and they, really stirred by hatred, followed with a stabbing "Go Croak!" and when this litany was repeated so often that finally the thousands around joined in the roar, and when it all turned into rhythm and song, Hans was in a trance. The singing, marching mass held him in its embrace. While he sang he was dreaming that the great moment had come, and they were marching into the last battle. Artillery thundered in the distance. In a side street machine guns were hacking. His heart contracted, not with fear but with passionate impatience. Hadn't Hermann raised his bugle yet for the signal? Hadn't the flags up front led the first rows in attack? The day of decision that had been promised for as long as he could think, exploded on the horizon, and Hans' wide-open eyes saw it as close as the next bend of the Ring.

To be sure, this was a very fantastic dream under an unfavorable February sky. To be sure, a very different future awaited them. To be sure, this dream, after a few moments would leave behind nothing but embarrassment. To be sure, with it Hans' self-confidence—this short-lived mixture of insecurity reversed and humiliations forcefully repressed—a self-confidence artificially incited by the rally's intoxication, would come to an end. In a few moments all would collapse in a heap of ashes. The uniform would not help nor the smart marching step. But for these few moments the words and rousing music of the "International" gave the poor dream courage.

Erich Weigel, twenty-four years old, sang along, and at the same time kept thinking all sorts of things. They all centered around the question: "Can the present phase of the dictatorship of the bourgeoisie in Germany, the Hitler-Hugenberg cabinet, still be called Bonapartism or already fascism?" Hastily he searched his memory for what Marx had said about Louis Bonaparte, and Trotsky about Kerenski. The thing was this: Right ahead of Weigel's Young Front unit a column of Communist Youth was marching. At yesterday's meeting of the district's youth leaders he had drawn emphatic attention to the historical importance of the fact that for the first time since the Austrian labor movement had come into existence, Socialists and Communists would demonstrate together. Still, it was pretty embarrassing to him that the Communists, boiling with energy and screaming, bristling with banners, had pushed themselves right in front of his Young Fronters. His apprehension had proven justified at once. Where the rear of the Communists and the head of his own column were touching, discussions had broken out. It was the fellows who carried the flags, harmless guys both of them, who were most vehemently besieged, and whenever they ran out of arguments, they turned to Weigel (not to their chairman Fink, whose position in the group was completely undermined by now). The truth was that Weigel had absolutely no objections to discussions with Communists, but they had to be civilized conversations between two of them, and not coarse polemics in public. Because Erich's by no means negative attitude towards Leninism (not towards the Communist Party, mind you, the difference must not be overlooked) was quite complex. Besides, it was combined with sharp critcism of the Social Democratic Party, and to express it publicly would have been unwise just before the election of the new chairman. If he followed the party line too closely, however, he ran the risk of ending up with arguments that were not his, and in consequences that he himself usually branded as criminal revisionism. (Apart from the fact that vis a vis the provocative clichés of the Communists, he unexpectedly discovered an irresponsible love for senile mayor Seitz or for fat Renner who had betrayed the working class. All these difficulties went through Weigel's head as he sang along mechanically. As long as both groups sang the same song, the truce lasted. Actually the Communists broke it prematurely by giving the end of the refrain their own twist. According to this version it was not just the International that would fight for human rights, but "Lenin's Third International" which was all the more noticeable and annoying because the extra words jarred the rhythm of the song. As soon as the last note had sounded, Fink raised his hand to give the signal for a freedom-chant. But the "Free—" remained suspended in the air. Not a single voice repeated it. And when he, walking backwards, repeated the attempt he failed again. The meaning of this was instantly clear to Fink's shock and to Weigel's joy. The silence was obviously demonstrative. The Young Fronters no longer tolerated a chairman appointed by Party Headquarters; they had decided amongst themselves to ignore him. Their silence was the final withdrawal of confidence. At the same time the silence told Erich Weigel that he did not have to wait for the general meeting in two days to consider himself the new chairman. The mission that had suddenly fallen into his lap, the doubts and little embarrassments that it might have meant for a person of a different nature did not bother him in the least. He had been a youth leader since his sixteenth year. He knew that from now on his words and movements, his habits, his happy and unhappy moods, his friendships with girls and boys no longer belonged to him. All these were going to be watched incessantly, had to withstand bitter criticism and, what was harder, serve as a norm and example to the souls who looked up to him. Already he felt how the glances of seventeen-year-olds followed him, importunate with unlimited devotion. That's how it had been during his four years with the Red Falcons and the three years at the Socialist Workers' Youth. The situation did not make him feel comfortable. Already the first decisions had to be made: The Communists had intoned the "Song of Soviet Airmen" and stopped briefly before the second stanza. The onlookers eyed them not unkindly but at the same time were noticeably uneasy at the passivity of their own young marchers. That's what you got when you marched directly behind the Communists. You could not spare your vocal chords; what the Communists lacked in numbers they wanted to make up with screaming. And there was not one person among the onlookers who at this moment more or less consciously did not compare the twelve times 100,000 Social Democratic votes with the few ten thousands of the Communists, and the 700,000 party members with those sectarians. One could feel the subdued displeasure of a rich family who had to welcome poor relations. And how embarrassing the situation might become when the shabby guests in the millionaire's house started a row, instead of gaping in admiration at the gobelins. Quick action was called for! Without hesitation and as a signal for all those who might still doubt that from now on the Young Front was the avant-garde of opposition in the district, Weigel loudly intoned the second stanza of the "Airmen's Song": "We thrust aloft our giant machines." The people on the sidewalks were hardly satisfied. The masses were not familiar with this song that came from another country. But since our boys sang it, many pricked up their ears, already more receptive to the strange lines that did not mention anything about Galileo, about noble brides or other symbols, but simply spoke of airplanes. And when the Young Front boys took revenge for "Lenin's Third International" by shouting at the top of their voices: "And every propeller sings whirring free—dom," the Communists' "Red Front" was drowned in the masses' echo. The Communist Youth did not throw in the towel. Without catching their breath, they started hammering their latest chant "Proletarians to the front! Cheers for the Red United Front." "Cheers!" the onlookers chimed in, finally carried along on the wave of the singing and chanting. But at this point, Weigel felt called upon to draw the line. He overtook the row of the Young Front's flag bearers, and tapped one of the Communists on the shoulder. The fellow turned round. Erich thought he had seen that face before. Possibly at the university or at one or the other political meeting. Had he not had a discussion with him one day in front of the Communist workers' bookstore?

The Vienna of intellectuals, the Socialists included, was a village consisting of libraries, meeting halls, and coffee houses, surrounded by the slopes of the Vienna Woods. And there were many faces that Weigel had seen throughout his young life without really knowing them. When the political opponent whom he was facing had been a boy, he had put his tent where the ground was still ripped up from the tents of Erich's Falcon group, had built his campfire on the ashes Erich's group had left behind. Later he had registered for the same courses because they professed to deal with economic development and then, disgusted, had cut them as Erich had done. If, at the university library, one of them could not get the *German Ideology* the reason was that the other one was reading it. Annoyed, he would rush to the library of the workers' organizations. But there dozens, insatiable like him, were already waiting for a copy to become available. They were the same people who, in the Cafe Schottentor over a cup of mocha, couldn't wait to snatch a *Manchester Guardian* or a *Weltbühne* out of each other's hands; the same people who on Sunday on the same meadows would play volleyball. Of course, not all of them knew each other. But once they had met, right away they called each other by first names. Without any trouble, the conversation continued a long chain of conversations that had never taken place. And that's the way it was to be later after times had changed brutally. "Haven't we met before? I mean, way back before we were outlawed?" But at this moment such thoughts hardly occurred to Erich. Marching along he thrust his pale, pointed face in front of the other guy and demanded: "Why don't you cut it out with your Red United Front?" The other countered the aggressive move with a provocative smile: "Why? Do you prefer the black one?"

There you had it. That's the way they were. Over a cup of coffee this same guy surely was willing to enter into a rational discussion, even about neo-Kantianism. Here in the street he thought he had to argue like a drunk cabbie. He probably thought that was the proletarian way to argue. "You know very well that your Red United Front means a united front over the heads of the leaders while we, my dear comrade, are for the united front, plain and simple."

"Also with Severing and Grzesinski?"

What was one to do with people like that? One couldn't simply say "no." One didn't want to lie "yes." Under the watchful eyes of his Young Front comrades, surrounded by roaring chants, he would have to explain the difference between the two brother parties. And that in sentences that were as complex as the whole relationship between the two camps. Erich evaded this necessity by shouting a short rejoinder: "Löbe has declared that if Hitler takes one step beyond the Weimar constitution, the SPD will march!"

"But is there still a Weimar constitution?"

"Of course not! But you can't really claim that what they've got over there now is fascism already." "What else?"

"You know as well as I do that things aren't as simple as you guys want them to be. If the coup of the 20th of July. . ."

No, the matter really wasn't simple. And as the discussion between Erich and the other student lost its focus, at several other places verbal skirmishes set in. It was a question of man against man or, in terms of numbers, one Communist against half a dozen boys from the Young Front.

The shots that were fired every night in the working class districts of German cities, these sporadic shots echoed in their hearts, alluring and at the same time frightening. The kinds of conversations they carried on these days, woven of hopes, pangs of conscience, assumptions, conversations that petered out into vagueness or ended abruptly, troubled their minds. Hitler had been governing Germany for almost two weeks now and in a way that wasn't all that different from the way Papen had ruled for a whole year. It already looked as if one could get used even to that as to so many other things. If the conversation turned to Germany, the old quagmire of problems that had been familiar for years appeared again. And it happened less and less frequently that one of these boys in the middle of a meeting, a discussion, a talk with his girlfriend suddenly turned around and saw the deadly shadow of the Sphinx falling on these days and suddenly felt terror gripping his innermost being: if you don't solve the riddle now, this very minute, then it's all over with all of us.

The imposing row of six banners had become quite irregular. Engaging in polemics the Young Fronters were in their element. The Communists liked nothing better. Louder and louder, the invectives shot back and forth.

"So you support the toleration politics, just like that?"

"You're nothing but a sect! The measly hundred you got together today—that's the whole C.Y.A."

"Of course, my dear comrades, we've got fascism in Austria already."

". . . the orders from Moscow . . ."

". . . why else did you de facto accept the Lausanne loan? And the twenty-eighth starvation amendment? And who strangled the Grünbach strike?"

"I am a Leninist myself! But you, you are Stalinists! If Lenin were alive today . . ."

"But why did you surrender the weapons of the working class to the bourgeoisie on July 15th?"

"Your stupid United Front politics . . ."

"The SP is tolerating just as much as . . ."

"But you call out a general strike every other day! But in Austria the workers are united, that's just it. And you are nothing but splinters. And that's exactly what . . ."

"I see, then tell me the difference between Zörgiebel and Hitler!"

In the most heated exchange, Erich Weigel suddenly caught Fink's sneering glance. Brought to his senses, he realized that they were hardly 600 feet from the Monument of the Republic, where they were to pass the grandstand, and that, at the moment, his marching column was a mess. He just had time to drive the Communists back to their group and to bring some order to his own unit. And there the Parliament Building came in sight already. They fell into a smart marching step. The flags, raised high, blew in the February mist and wind. Erich's eyes flickered behind the glasses. The unfinished discussion raged on in his mind. "They can say what they want," he thought, "they'll never get a demonstration together like that . . . not even in Germany. Such a magnificent show of power you won't find anywhere except here. 200,000 on the march—a demonstration of defiance and solidarity—and even if the *Arbeiter Zeitung* will describe it in the very same words—they are still true—they are no empty slogans . . ."

They were 60 feet from the Monument of the Republic. Erich gave the signal for a provocative chant of the left opposition:

"A republic's not enough,
Socialism is the stuff."

The Communists raised their fists to their shoulders and hammered their "Red Front!" Erich's unit raised their fists high above their heads and emphasized their military step. Their rigid eyes were beaming. The Communists unexpectedly unrolled a banner: "No more limitation to welfare benefits." But for the moment Erich did not notice this surprise attack. For the moment, he, with all his devotion, looked to the right. The Monument of the Republic bore, on blocks of smooth gray granite, the bronze heads of Hanusch, Reumann, and Victor Adler. Two men of the Republican Defense Corps stood guard by the flag of the Second International. It looked very much like the flag of the district. In front of it stood waving hulky Otto Bauer, slender old Seitz and, looking surprisingly like his father, only older, more weathered than the bronze head, eyes inflamed and shoulders bent from fifteen years of Social Democratic politics since the war: Fritz Adler, Secretary of the International, liberator of peoples. And, as always, Erich thought: "So he is the one who in 1919 shot President Stürgkh . . ." He was filled with unlimited love.

Käte Haider, twenty-seven years old, walked with a district not her own. She had stayed too long at the workers' children day-care. She would have preferred to stay there altogether and not to march at all since this time they had been told that it was not advisable to take the children along. But she had already arranged a date with her friend, Franz Seidel, and he was very particluar in things like that (too particular—and she knew that if she didn't wean him from this kind of sensitivity soon it would be too late; their relationship wasn't going to stay forever the way it was now, and before long he wouldn't be willing to change just for her sake). She had dawdled so long with the children because she worried about leaving them in the care of thirteen-year-old Rosl, and because Reiterer wouldn't and wouldn't come—although he had promised to sing with the children and take care of everything. And then it had gotten too late of course; she had no longer reached her district at the rallying point and not even caught up with it on the Ring. There simply was no sense in trying to squeeze herself through 200,000 bodies and ask where her district was. So Käte marched along anywhere and found out only later that she had marched with those from Floridsdorf.

She was surrounded by faces she didn't know. The worries about the day-care didn't leave her. She missed the group of little ones who, on May First and November Twelfth trotted behind her along the Ring. She missed the constant worry on those days: Aren't they getting too tired? Were they dressed warmly enough? And the difficult job of having to explain to the toddlers: "That's the Parliament. Do you know what that is, a parliament?"

Just as each of us demonstrating along the Ring had the thoughts and people around him that made up his everyday world, Käte needed her forty workers' children. Without them she felt superfluous, as if she had left her own active life and got lost in the crowd and had to wait until somebody remembered to take her back, or as if she had lost her way and ended up in a part of the city she had never seen before.

In situations like this, one is easily struck by things one might not even notice otherwise. Käte noticed a boy in his teens or early twenties, very pale, very run-down. Marching along, he kept his hands in his pockets; his cap was pulled down over his eyes. He didn't open his mouth. The glance that now and then he raised from the pavement and let roam around him was charged with hatred and contempt to a startling degree. What was he doing here?

Again, Käte heard the chant that dominated the demonstration: "Hitler, go and croak!" She asked herself: Why did we take this ugly word over from the Nazis? Don't we want to fight with spiritual weapons? Then three strange little old women caught her attention. Dressed in deep black, as if they were following some "beautiful" funeral procession which they undoubtedly were very fond of doing, they had a hard time limping along with the row, as they chatted with one another and fell silent again. And not one time did they in any way take notice of the human din around them. They did not utter one shout, did not wave a handkerchief. Not once did they look ahead or back on the gray avalanche of people that carried them along. In front of the Monument of the Republic they seemed apprehensive and whispered something into each other's ear. Then they went hobbling along round the bend of the Ring like old blind horses on a merry-go-round.

Käte thought again of the bright day-care center in the municipal housing block. And she remembered that she had become a Social Democrat because the city did so much for the children. That was ten years ago, and it had not been easy. Her father was a leader in the Christian Union, one of Kunschak's old guard, Roman Catholic to the bone and terribly bitter. And he had finally made home unbearable for her. She had suffered a lot. Until then the family had been her world. And then the unexpected happened: The Party gave her everything, replaced everything she had lost, even the family.

"Down with fascism!" the crowd roared.

Fascism? Käthe asked herself suddenly. What does that really mean? Does it mean that all this will come to an end? She tried to give this thought some concrete form. What would life be like?

She simply could not imagine it. The question proved unanswerable.

If all this came to an end, life itself would come to an end.

Josef Dreher

Social Democratic Member of Parliament

Representative Josef Dreher was not what one calls a spiritualized personality. Rather the contrary: a corporealized one. Dreher's body played an important role in his personal presence and public activity. To fanatical opponents this powerful paunch was the incarnation of bossdom. "Just look at the way he has stuffed his guts from your dearly saved-up membership dues," they taunted the railroad workers. They lied. Because already in peacetime, the master locksmith, a Viennese of the old generation, had cultivated eating and drinking, and since at that time he was only the unpaid secretary of his union, he had earned the means for it by the labor of his hands. Dreher's stomach knew nothing of orgies and senseless gluttony. Accordingly, it was not an inflated appendix, or repulsive pot-belly, but an almost natural extension of the body. The crimson red, which covered Dreher's impressive skull down to the neck and the nape, was nothing abnormal. His hair was thick: it was disheveled, a gray moss growing wild on head and upper lip and shadowing in dense bushels the baby-blue eyes. By the way, Dreher knew that even moderate excess at his age could threaten him with a stroke. For some time, he had been keeping to a gently prophylactic diet. He was a rational man who treasured life. He didn't have to fear for his health. In the trenches, the cheerful appearance of Sergeant Dreher had contributed to the fighting morale among the Deutschmeister-Regiment. When during the incessant artillery bombardment at the Isonzo this ruddy brother-in-arms came around a bend in the trenches the terror lifted ever so slightly, the terror which otherwise would have been unbearable beyond endurance and sanity. That he, this wide-assed target, had come through without a scratch, caused optimism, not envy.

What had helped him to achieve an evergrowing influence in the union? Undoubtedly his energetic common sense that was anything but common. But when he now, in all his innumerable responsibilities, found time to let the years of his youth pass through his head, his memory told him that his early rise had been spared an important obstacle: to be considered too young by his gray-bearded comrades. Actually, his girth made him look like thirty when he was only twenty.

He was below medium height, and his stomach made him look shorter, but more imposing. When a man like that is up on a platform, you can't help seeing and hearing him. At any rate, people trust him rather than one of those half-starved returnees from the Russian POW camps who, in confused words, told of soviets and civil war. That's how it had been in 1918. Already then, but now more than ever, his real specialty was a conference in a small circle with some good friends (be they Christian Social Representatives or red workers) whom he would kid around with and grab by the sleeve and drag off to a corner. Then the joviality of Dreher's physical presence radiated real power. The fanatics began to be ashamed of their rigidity; a feeling of physical inferiority stole over them in the face of this laughing mountain of flesh. Suddenly they were afraid of being taken for hysterical grumbling whiners. To find a common ground, to live and let live, to avoid ulcers, to find a modus vivendi—this goal in the name of the flesh drew the zealots within the range of reasonableness. When Dreher nimbly, in spite of his bodily mass, went striding through engine shops and train stations, the workers, poking fun at him lovingly, thought: "As long as we have hunks like that, nothin's gonna happen to us."

Dreher's appearance stood in stark contrast to Dworak's lean body, narrow head, and sharp nose. Before the year 1924, when Dreher, not yet raised to a higher position, was working with Dworak in the same depot, the Communist Depot Paper showed the two side by side, and that gave the caricature all the more bite. Then Dreher was elected to Parliament contrary to most predictions, because it had been the almost unanimous expectation that Dworak would be nominated and not he. Already then Dworak had been chairman of the local group and the real authority. Kidding around instead of explaining, the favorite voluntarily conceded the great career to the outsider. "Go ahead, fatty. You are a better talker."

And Erich Weigel, at that time a precocious high school student and a leader in the Falcons, had dropped the following aphorism at a small high-school gathering: "Comrades. Sancho Panza got the governor's island, and Don Quixote rides on."

When Don Quixote entered Sancho Panza's office, that affair of 1924 immediately stood between them. In none of the frequent meetings since had it been mentioned. Now, as if a silently agreed-upon deadline had come or a secret signal had been given, it slipped through the open door right in front of Dworak. Before the two men had exchanged hellos, they knew that somehow that was going to be one of the things they would talk about.

While the engine driver took a seat opposite the Representative, so that the massive desk remained between them, the conversation began with Dreher's usual jovial torrent of words:

"Nice of you to think of me again. How ya been? Dog-tired as usual, ol' buddy! Still playing the sucker for the ol'mob? Same ol' story—as soon as an official goes all out a little for the ideals of the Party, they shove the whole thing onto his shoulders. Just the same ol' belly-ache in our Party. So how's Hans doin'? Still no job? We'll have to give him a little push in the right direction. What's he again? Right, electrician. Tomorrow I've a meetin' with Supervising Engineer Swoboda in the Finance Commission—we'll see if there isn't a vacancy in Salzburg with the electrification project. By golly, wouldn't it be a laugh if an official of the railroad organization couldn't find a job for his own son. Things haven't gotten that bad by a long shot, thank God! So and how's Spannnmeier? What's he been up to? I must get out to the district again and look around. What a nuisance, this rat race here; can't get away from it. Nothing but bureaucrats in here. I'm tellin' ya, you've no idea what they are up to again, the gentlemen with their second bill for balancing the railroad budget. Never before were they so much set on chiseling on wages; I've never seen anything like it. They want everything at once. They think the wind's blowing their way. But don't you worry, you can tell the workers: their bark's worse than their bite. So, and how's the mandolin club progressing?"

Dreher still had not resigned his chairmanship of the workers' mandolin club in the district. Of course, for months he hadn't found any time for playing or for chairing. It was more the symbolism of the situation that he considered relevant: a Representative in Parliament, a member of the central committee and the administrative council of one of the largest operations in the country, and still chairman of this obscure circle of a total membership of twelve that somewhere "out there" met in the back room of some inn.

During this cordial flood, Dworak furtively eyed a German illustrated paper that happened to lie on the desk. The title photo showed the huge rally of the Iron Front in the Lustgarten. The caption read: "After Hitler it's our turn!" It seemd to him that the Representative wasn't in the best of moods. His joviality sounded a bit routine this afternoon, as if inside of this voluminous body a worn record was turning all by itself. Perhaps there was nothing to it. To anybody with the roar of the masses still in his ear, individual voices in a small room sometimes sound unreal. Maybe this was an instance of such an acoustic illusion. Right now, Dworak himself was by no means depressed. On the contrary, he had compared the demonstration whose roar came subdued through the window with the Nazi rally of February 1. And he had come away with this conviction: there hysterics—here quiet strength, there the drill—here the living life. At the same moment he had decided not to wait for his district but to go to Dreher immediately. And no sooner had this decision been made than it had a much greater effect than seemed commensurate with its insignificant weight. A wave of invigorating energy had lifted him up. It seemed to him as if a whole chapter had suddenly come to an end. A new page had been turned. Dworak, unskilled in reading his inner self, accepted the good mood without reservations. He bitterly needed it after those dismal weeks. And so he didn't question why Dreher was apparently out of sorts but described to him the case of brakeman Jakl who, in spite of having successfully passed all five conductor's exams, was still waiting for his promotion.

Dreher lifted the receiver. No problem, we'll have that taken care of in a jiffy. Over the phone came the nasal Austrian civil service twang of the Hofrat residing one floor up. Then Dreher's gray-haired paw threw the receiver back on the phone. The skin on his fingers was cracked and red as if all through the eight years in the halls of Parliament the biting wind of speed had blown around the former engineer. "His majesty had to search for the file. A disgrace that a case like that has to be dragged all the way up to the top office. Incompetent crew. But at the card table—there he knows what's what!" Dworak, in a congenial mood, did his friend the favor: "Really—you're playing cards with him?"

A childish smile spread under Dreher's gray mustache. His watery eyes sparkled. The merriment was gone in a second. Now there was no longer any denying that the flesh in his ruddy face had become rather flabby.

"And that deficit . . ." Dreher mumbled. "Because all they can think of in this place is damned politics. If for once we got ahold of operations—we'd show them what proper management can do . . ." He gave a snort. Nothing was said for a while. Such pauses in a conversation usually made Dworak uneasy. In most cases he began asking himself whether he wasn't keeping the extremely busy friend from more important matters, whether the silence wasn't a sign that the audience was over and the supplicant should leave. This feeling, the feeling of the poor relative (the reason, by the way, why he avoided Dreher's home and family) did not show itself this time. Both knew that everything they had talked about so far was only an introduction to the real topic of discussion. Originally Dworak had felt superior to Dreher but, in the course of time, the other's many high offices and honors had caused this feeling to wear off. Now it reappeared. Somehow he felt that this time pauses and delays worked for him. He waited.

Dreher knew exactly what for. He knew that Dworak had come to hear the proposal that had been made to him many times and that he regularly had dismissed with the argument: "They need me at the station." Perhaps this time Dworak only wanted to make sure that he still had that option. Perhaps he wanted to make use of it this time. Perhaps he didn't know himself yet that that was what he wanted. Undoubtedly this was what had him brought here today. Dreher was silent, breathing heavily. It had been he himself who had made that proposal. It had always been his fervent wish that Dworak would accept. Since that year 1924, his conscience had never quite been at peace. In spite of all he had done for the movement, now and then he felt that he had usurped that seat in Parliament. If Dworak accepted his advancement now, everything was all right again. Why hold on to his dilemma as long as higher up there was always room for so many more.

On the other hand, he must not forget that all of a sudden Dworak had come completely on his own. That in itself was nothing to be taken lightly. Did he suddenly aim higher, above Dreher's head? He certainly was capable—more than Dreher himself. One knew that. And at the very top where he was the railroad expert, there was room for only a few. He had enough enemies. And he had made enough mistakes—after all one was only human. So what was to be done now? Right now there wasn't anything that Dreher would have liked to push out of his mind more than this whole tangle of questions. Couldn't such worries wait for quieter times? Didn't he have enough to worry about as it was? Did he have to face again the danger rising out of his everyday life at a time when so much here in the office that had become a comfortable routine all of a sudden was becoming threatening, when so much that had become familiar all of a sudden was becoming uncanny?

But Dworak waited. Dreher knew that in dealing with this man, his genius for appeasement had always failed. It never rains but it pours, he thought and sighed. He got up. While he was walking up and down the room with his usual bouncy steps like a jolly rubber manikin he felt himself how phoney his jovial bass sounded today.

"Well, dear ol' Ferdl, we're getting old. All of us. That's just it. The day's comin' when I, here in my easy chair, am going to feel my fat, and you at your engine your bones. Ain't that right, ol' buddy?" And then on he went like an actor who hadn't learned his part very well. "Apropos, in the near future, the list of candidates for the personnel committee will be worked out. I really think you could let them elect you. It's ridiculous. You've done more work for a longer time than any regular member. You've deserved it, I should say. Or do you really want to work yourself to the bone at the station until you're ready to retire?"

Dworak had followed him with his eyes. As soon as the proposal had been made, he realized beyond any doubt that he had come to accept it. Now he didn't hesitate a second. Before he answered, he reeled off in his head all the rationalizations which had to come before the decision. Of course he deserved the well-paid position—wife and child—thirty years on the job—fifty years old—did he have to put up with the whims of a guy like Zehetner? Didn't the young members at the bottom scream that they, too, wanted their turn and wanted to move up? Hadn't he gathered so much experience that it was almost his duty to use it in a higher office?

He didn't even wait for the end, but simply said, "It's all right with me. You can nominate me."

Dreher's answer was even shorter: "Way to go, Ferdl!" and was accompanied by a side-glance that didn't conceal open suspicion. This side-glance was already assessing the versatility of his rival, his personal connections with the Party executive committee, his enemies, whom one might have to win over to one's own side. And when Dreher began to talk of the difficulties that for days had made life bitter, he did so out of calculation. "If you think, my friend,"—and that was the underlying sense of his saying this—"that it's nothing but a bed of roses up there . . ." The main purpose of his account was obvious in the following phrases: "And I says 'listen, Anton'—that's the Ministerialrat—"; "And then Secretary König says to me in private"; "At the Executive Director's, where I don't have to knock"; "And I naturally call a meeting of the executive committee of the Party just like that."

The state of affairs, disquietingly enough, was this: In the administrative commission, Chief Executive Seefehlner had described the budgetary situation of the railroads as desperate. If one didn't succeed in finding larger financial resources by the end of the month, one would be forced to effect "at this time not yet fixed postponements" in the paying of salaries and pensions. The representatives of the Free Unions had protested immediately. Following the proven strategy of avoiding larger sacrifices by making smaller ones, they had tried to raise the question of the workers in the repair shops. And Dreher had stated that one would be willing to discuss a possible payment in two installments if one received the guarantee that no more contracts would be awarded to private industry, which would protect the railroad workshops against further cuts in personnel. Seefehlner had remained uncompromising. He didn't seem to believe that the work force would no longer tolerate any further cuts, or he seemed to ignore it with unheard-of negligence.

Even more disquieting were the innumerable noncommittal, and yet so important talks behind closed doors and in private. The top management and people close to it started assuming a very strange, very unaccustomed tone. In the Chancellor's office, Dreher had been received by a close acquaintance in a strikingly cool fashion, or a semi-official source had made a strong statement like this: "In that case, nobody will be paid on March first." Of course that sort of thing was to be taken purely as a blackmail maneuver, and if this ridiculous threat wasn't withdrawn immediately, the Party would launch a campaign against it.

"But," Dreher concluded thoughtfully, "this doesn't smell good to me. I haven't smelled anything this bad in a long time—"

Dworak listened quietly to all that. He realized how serious the situation was. And yet he felt happy to be seeing it with new eyes. Last year, railroaders' wages had been gradually cut by twenty-five per cent, and at the same time, step by step, they had lost one right after the other. Whenever, after nerve-racking negotiations, Dworak finally was informed by the central committee—once again, one had to accept a so-called small sacrifice—he always associated it with the same picture that was becoming more and more depressing: He enters the depot, dozens of questions are thrown at him; he crosses the station hall, followed by hundreds of questioning looks. It's like running the gauntlet for hours. Finally a general meeting where he has to explain to his fellow workers that once again the management has to ask for their understanding, that this measure was a compromise achieved only after long hours of hard bargaining, that in the present crisis a strike was out of the question, that resistance would only make matters worse, etc. The opposition jumps to their feet screaming and hollering. Fathers of families awkwardly enumerate how much they have to spend on gas, light, and food. Nobody considers that Dworak makes the very same sacrifices. He tries to console everybody. Nobody tries to console him.

That's how it had been up to now. Now he would have different associations. He would sit at a desk and would check every figure in the proposals of the chief executive, would be tough in his negotiations with commissions, and would prepare a detailed analysis for the Central Committee. He thought: Now I shall have a better insight into the intricate situation. From a higher perspective. But for a fraction of a second his otherwise sober brain conjured up a crowded meeting hall, which was damned similar to parliament. Representative Dworak was giving a fiery speech against the exploitation of the railroad workers and finished off the catcalls of the right with his quick, sharp wit. Already at lunch he himself would read all about it in the papers (while the maid was setting the table and his boy came home from the college of engineering).

During the last weeks, the fear of aging that suddenly had begun troubling Dworak had restricted his consumption of cigarettes. Now he leaned back in the chair and, without hesitation, lit one. "Oh yes," he said, "now the gentlemen think they can get away with anything. By the way, what do you say to Hitler?"

The Representative served up some banalities: "That guy? He'll be down the drain in a year. If he doesn't lose blood already in the Reichstag election on March fifth. It all depends on the Center Party; they're the ones who can tip the scales." He reached for his pipe. "I've always said . . . ."

He stopped short. His hand too stopped in the middle of a movement. From some part of the gigantic head office the noise of a closing door could be heard faintly. For Dreher this noise seemed to be of the utmost importance. Listening, he stared into space for a second and hissed: "The department head." And already he was out the door which he forgot to close. He had hardly reached the corridor when he executed an outright grotesque movement. He raised his right hand somewhat above shoulder height and waved it a few times loosely from the wrist: the way one greets somewhat condescendingly and jovially an acquaintance from a distance. At the same time his whole upper body fell forward in the devoutest bow. And like a bowing waiter in any farce with a smooth wavy motion screws himself up into an erect position, and, on tiptoes, feet turned outward, silently rushes forward to the illustrious guest, Dreher shot away into invisibility. Dworak could not help laughing out loud. From the depth of the corridor the voice of the department head was to be heard, and again the visitor had the impression of hearing a gramophone record; this time it had a strong nasal twang, and the spring of the mechanism was almost run down so that with every sentence the unbearably drawn-out voice seemed to die in melancholy: "But don't you see—of course, but—that's just it—a precarious complication—" Apart from such obliging phrases nothing could be understood.

A few minutes later Dreher rushed in and fell into his easy chair. His fleshy features looked alarmingly troubled. His cheeks were two flabby pouches. Under his baby-blue eyes the wrinkled tearbags showed. In the redness of his skin irregular patches appeared yellow like wax. Like a blind man Dreher groped for his pipe, monotonous mumblings came through his lips: "Damned rat race—damned rat race—damned rat race—damn it . . ."

"Good heavens, what's the matter?" Dworak was amazed.

The fat man lit one match after the other, all of which went out before he could get them to the pipe.

"In three installments—they want to pay the March salaries and pensions in three installments—in three installments."

Dworak did not understand. "But that's not the end of the world. If one takes it as a kind of forced loan the management asks from the workers— without interest. The loss couldn't be more than a few schillings."

Dreher discarded that argument with a flick of his hand. "It isn't that, it isn't that, Ferdl. You don't get it. He told me—confidentially—if the union doesn't vote for it—then—then (now he spoke the broadest dialect) they'll do it anyhow. "What do you say now?" He thrust the fist that grabbed the pipe forward. From the fist the thumb shot up, stretched, a plump, curved number one of flesh and blood. "For the first time!"

Whenever some one else got agitated, Dworak always became all the more cool and collected. He began to speak in detail of everything that in this situation could have a quieting effect; first of all the information may not be authentic; secondly, the whole thing was no more than a plan and it wouldn't be the first time that the government of this measly excuse of a state lost its courage; number three: it was true that the threat implied a blatant violation of the bargaining contract which, as Dreher had said, had never been attempted with such directness, but perhaps for that very reason the measure was supposed to be taken as a preamble for a new contract to be presented to the union, a contract with certain extraordinary powers for the management; number four: in the past a compromise had always been found, even in more dangerous situations than this.

The big-bellied genius of compromise shook his head. Dworak stopped talking. The silence rose like masses of water . . .

Then the furniture began to be heard, softly creaking, crackling, ugly old pompous pieces transplanted from some ministry in the Monarchy, tarnished by time, heirlooms of many generations of civil servants. From the corners the first shadows of dusk came crawling. The portrait of Seitz, grade-school teacher and mayor of Vienna, had already drowned in darkness. But still through the window the noises of the demonstration could be heard, subdued like breakers on the seashore.

Without saying a word the two men in the room tried to assess the consequences of what they had learned. But only the immediate threat was clear. The government which for years had attacked the workers now started a first offensive against the Party machinery. Two partners had been playing cards: it had been an exciting game, but a game at the green table, following the same rules. And then all of a sudden one of the players got up and slapped the other in the face.

Dworak cleared his throat and said. "Listen, Pepi, you need not nominate me. I'm staying at the depot. The way things look right now, you'll need me there more than in the central committee. We'll have to quiet the comrades down, and I'm good at that like no one else."

He wanted to add something. Dreher wanted to answer, wanted hypocritically to try to persuade the other one to reconsider, wanted to feel satisfaction. Nothing came of any of it. While they were looking into each other's eyes both of them were gripped by an ice-cold panic. It was not caused by any rational argument but was one of those senseless fears that men sometimes experience at the first onset of aging.

At the time of such attacks, what one has built up in a life's work seems worthless and fragile. One sees oneself as worthless and fragile, surrounded by sickness and death. The friend is devious. On the very day you met he betrayed you. Behind your back he is laughing at you. The wife you love deceives you because you never satisfied her. The beloved cause is a fraud because you betrayed it. You have always deceived yourself because nothing that you could count as achievement can stand the test. And you have no more future. You will always fail. What you are holding is ripped out of your hand. What you have built will be blown away by a breeze. What you touch is dirt, dirt and fluff—that's what the world is. And you are worthless because you are old, an old man.

They both rose at the same time and, without looking at each other, as if they were afraid of seeing horrible wounds in the face of the other, they squeezed their bodies into their overcoats. Not until they were on the street did they feel any better. Slowly crossing Schwarzenbergplatz they consciously enjoyed the anticipation of the demonstration. From a little Falcon girl they bought red carnations and put them in their lapels. They exchanged surmises whether the rain wouldn't stop the demonstration after all. They came closer to the roar; it became deafening and they had to shout to each other. They stopped behind the onlookers on the sidewalk and for a while watched the red flags which passed in the gathering dusk, red sails on the river they couldn't see yet.

"Three hours already," Dreher said.

"A rally of 200,000," recited Dworak.

"A demonstration of defiance and solidarity," the Representative completed the phrase.

With experienced turns of the shoulders they started to work their way through the dammed-up bodies. They reached the first, happiest row of onlookers, and there they saw a singing unit of the Defense Corps marching by. Finally, they stood on the pavement; through the soles of their shoes they felt the gentle bumps of the cobblestones. Some district they didn't know marched by. Thousands shouted: "Freedom!"—"Freedom!" shouted Dreher and Dworak, and squeezed themselves into the marching row.

*

The next chapter deals with the strike of the railroad workers on March 1 (1933). Instead of putting all of the workers' demands on the agenda, the Free Union makes the payment in three installments the main issue, a strategy which takes the punch out of the strike because it is the only point to fight against. The strike is scheduled only as a protest strike of three hours. Nevertheless (at Dworak's depot) the participation is one hundred percent. Dworak who, naturally, represents the Union's strategy gets into an argument with Gellert who, in a confused and undisciplined way, represents the opposition's demands, which he misunderstands. Dworak's great authority prevails and at eleven o'clock he thinks the strike is a victory. But then he walks home with a railroad worker who had been very optimistic before the "victorious strike," but who now is discouraged and disconsolate. Dworak realizes that the strike, in fact, is lost. It has not brought the railroad workers any real gains because it had not been observed by all depots. Now the workers will be exposed to management's revenge rather defenselessly.

Gellert undergoes a serious inner conflict. People say that he had been bumming it all over the globe before he, with Dworak's help, found a home and peace in the Social Democratic Party. Now he feels that his faith in the Party is weakening. He feels as if home and the basis for his life are being torn away from him. He decides to go to his section of the Party and air his problems, and possibly find clarification. He is fighting for his faith in the Party.

Robert Blum

Treasurer of Section Twelve

It does not take long to tell the spare biography of Robert Blum, the treasurer of Section Twelve.

Blum's chairman, Spannmeier, liked to remind him repeatedly that his name was the same as that of the well-known revolutionary of 1848, and when the regulars sat round their table at the restaurant, he never tired of singing to them the well-known popular ballad: "... the Brandenburg Gate they open wide, and Robert Blum, his hands all tied, now marches forward with unfaltering stride ..." But that was pure scorn: nature had not meant our Blum to be a hero. It had given him a slight body, and eyes that were slightly crossed and of the grey-whitish color of the eyes of blind horses, and so nearsighted that already as a child he had to wear glasses. But he had plenty of brown hair on the top of his head, and his beard was full and did not grow sparse even in later years. He groomed them carefully, drew a precise part, sported a little sharply contoured mustache and an always well-combed little goatee. And within their modest limits his intellectual talents were well-developed. That is to say, he knew his arithmetic, even without pencil and paper. He was quick in grasping mental combinations, as long as they moved within the narrow confines of his everyday life, but he had absolutely no imagination. His handwriting would pass any calligraphy test. He insisted on cleanliness, punctuality, and order in every respect.

Even if his best faculties had long become outdated through typewriters and adding machines, he still was not an anachronistic individual case; in Vienna there were hundreds of thousands like him who had nothing more to offer than he had. Then why was he so much shyer than others? Why did the constant fear depress him that suddenly and unexpectedly some situation might arise that would push him into the foreground and force him to make a decision? Why did he, loved and even respected by all, move so timidly in the doings, events, business of our section? Because he thought of himself as a loser, an inveterate one, who also brings bad luck to others. Actually his self-confidence had suffered a rain of heavy blows.

By profession and inclination he was a commercial employee. His faculties for the job were adequate. But his appearance had worked against him. Not that he had not found jobs; on the contrary, he had no trouble finding one. But something in his appearance always landed him with businessmen who were on the verge of bankruptcy. Although he was most fastidious in taking care of his body and wardrobe, especially in his teens, he just did not look like someone you would have called "a great guy," but already at first glance he was recognized as second rate. There are commodities that serve their purpose well, dependable, solid commodities but they are marred by a small defect in the material, a tiny spot from a burn or a flaw in the weave. They are cheaper, and thrifty shoppers buy them. All his life, Blum had been just such a commodity. His ugliness made him shy in his youth, and he had gone from one job interview to the next. The thriving companies wanted two hours to think it over. ("If nothing better shows up, we'll take him. He isn't all that bad.") But the others looked at him favorably. He fitted in well with their old, shabby furniture: "I've got to watch my expenses," the businessman thought, "that's exactly the kind of employees I have to switch to.

Besides, if I ever owe him a month's salary, he won't say a word. He is the type that will starve for the company, if it ever comes to that."

Anybody who calculates like that, is already condemned to bankruptcy. And as part of the bankrupt estate, Blum was shoved from firm to firm. Wherever Blum entered, disintegration and bankruptcy entered with him. From his perspective it was all one overpowering, depressing disaster. But even if one considers his case perfectly rationally, even if one calls such a linkage of a person with a concatenation of events that was due, not to his will but to his nature, "demonic," just to give it a name, and even if one is willing to admit that the course of a person's life proves something, then the little existence of this man, who loved order, honesty, and life was demonically connected with disorder, deceit, and destruction. Finally his excellent references got him a job with a large shipping firm. There he worked his way up to the position of second bookkeeper. Then, in 1931 in the Depression, the company collapsed.

Discouraged, and by now too old to have any more decent chances, he withdrew into private life which he could manage due to his wife's tiny pension. He did not like to take this step. What began now was everything but a peaceful retirement. For his private life was cursed in a special way. When he was working there was at least some small prospect that with perseverance and some good luck he might defeat his destiny. At home, however, it knew no mercy. Shamelessly it used its superiority to deal completely unpredictable blows. Up to his thirtieth year, he had had women very rarely, and they had never been very desirable. Then he found one who was really pretty, solid, reasonable. He married her. She brought into the marriage a modest dowry, and a surprising wealth of passion. Then God (Blum would have said, if he hadn't been a freethinker) ordained her to become ill. What was wrong with her? Everything and nothing. The doctor threw up his hands. He couldn't even cure her insomnia. She went to bed, suffered, and complained about a hundred things; one morning she didn't want to get up, stayed in bed the next day, too, and lay there for years and never got up again. At the very beginning of this incomprehensible illness, Blum's sister-in-law settled in their apartment. She hated him, and he knew exactly why. She nursed his wife, and became an old spinster doing it. Invalid and nurse competed in torturing Blum. They succeeded best when the issue was the eternal money worries of Willi, the brother-in-law. He was an actor, a good-for-nothing who always needed money. Blum never found out whether the two women were actually fond of this Willi or not. At any rate, they turned the apartment into hell for him whenever one of Willi's begging letters arrived. And the apartment did not smell good. The bedroom window always had to stay closed because his wife couldn't have it any other way. And she hardly ever left her room. And the connecting door to the living room, where he held his office hours as a Social Councillor, always had to stay open. Or her griping would start. Sometimes the sister-in-law also made dangerous-sounding threats. Sometimes Willi's letters were of the kind one finds quoted in trial reports, trials about embezzlement, murder . . .

All that had already started in peacetime, had outlasted the world war, and had been going on now for twenty years. No end was in sight. It wasn't any great drama. It wasn't anything great at all, nothing serious. The whole district knew of it and had laughed about it since time immemorial. Some people found the whole story simply unappetizing.

Blum, however, did not stop loving precision, peace, and order. For twenty-nine years he was a member of the Social-Democratic Party.

2

On March 4th, shortly before seven o'clock in the evening, Blum left for a meeting with the section. With his briefcase, spectacles, graying goatee, and flabby stomach, he looked like a low-level civil servant. His advancing age, his worries, and his work in the Party had endowed his appearance with a modest dignity.

Blum was thinking: Thank God that we are over that. All this mess with the railroad strike and the hassles that followed, yesterday and the day before. Now he would be able to do his work in the Party in peace and quiet again. Good thing that Spannmeyer had scheduled the meeting for 7:30. The meeting of the council after that would surely last two hours. I will propose that the financial report be second on the agenda. Yes, that's what I will do. Even if the whole agenda has to be revamped. The new block treasurers that came from the Young Front are doing a lousy job. It's about time someone comes out and says so. I will not mince words—not I. All my life I haven't paid as much attention to politics as these whippersnappers who are still wet behind the ears. They can damn well leave politics to the comrades whose business it is. In their blocks more and more people are in arrears, and I'm the one who's responsible. That's just the way I'm going to put it. It is true—the editorial today was pretty cutting. These reprisals against the railroad workers—that's really something. And they speak of "ringleaders," as if we were still living under Taaffe and Badeni. The *Arbeiter Zeitung* sure let them have it for that. Four percent—out of two hundred schillings, that's eight. What are these people being punished for anyway, one would like to ask. It was really the management that broke the law. Got to have law and order. "Ringleaders"—How can anybody use a word like that nowadays? Well, thank God there's a session in Parliament today, and the whole matter will be straightened out. And at the council meeting tonight I will be able to get right to a couple of important questions. It must not be tolerated that comrades who have not paid their dues for a whole year are still carried along on the membership lists. Either—or. That's my principle. Where would we be without order? I'm the one who's responsible. Fortunately, in financial matters I possess sufficient authority . . .

And he began to prepare himself mentally for his uncompromising stance. Indeed, under normal circumstances, politics never assumed such importance in his thoughts as did now this question of the railroad strike—usually none at all. True, every morning he carefully read the *Arbeiter Zeitung*, but just as most good Catholics say their evening prayers: with a little patience, and a tiny little bit of devotion, the matter was always taken care of in due course. He was never engaged in nor was he dragged into discussions about budget cuts, fascism, party tactics, and things like that. Everybody knew that he was a completely unpolitical person. In public he only spoke when it came to his financial reports.

After he had crossed the courtyard of the municipal housing block and reached the hall to the meeting room, Chairman Spannmeier, trembling from head to toe, rushed towards him and pulled him aside.

"Listen, Blumekin," he stammered, "something awful just happened, something really awful."

Blum immediately got even more excited than Spannmeier. He had just come from an indescribably ugly scene at home. If one couldn't get peace and quiet even here, then where on earth could one? Fortunately here he had enough power to create order. Or at least to put in his two cents' worth. Only for heaven's sake, Spannmeier should not ask him to give a speech from the podium. Anything but that. A feeling of terror and courage made his blood run cold. He put his briefcase down on a chair and got ready. "Well?"

Spannmeier raised his fleshy arms helplessly. "Hadina is up to his old tricks again. He refuses to take over the ticket sale for the dance of the Education Association."

Immediately the treasurer's brain began to work. "Have you already told him that at the next council meeting he'll be elected third chairman?"

"A hundred times! He won't believe it. He says that we deliberately saw to it that in the last five years there was always something else that came up. He's not going to sacrifice himself for the ideal if he don't get no recognition. He wants us to elect him tonight, right after the section meeting."

"But that's ridiculous," Blum said indignantly. "With the kind of agenda we have tonight? Besides, he's always drunk anyway. Doesn't he himself realize that we can't elect a drunk as third chairman?"

The first chairman sighed. "Usually he gets the point. But today he just won't." Blum thoughtfully stroked his goatee. "Listen—there's only one way out." At that moment somebody stuck his head in the door "Comrade Spannmeier, the speaker is here."

"All right, tell me later," Spannmeier dismissed the matter.

They entered the lecture hall. The attendance was good: about a hundred and fifty people. A small section, like the twelfth, could be very pleased with that. When they had slide lectures, or light entertainment, up to three hundred and fifty would come, and they would have to move to the large hall. But that a topic that was no more exciting than tonight's attracted so many people surprised Blum. Then he understood: it was the tension of the times; people huddled around the Party eager to hear what it had to say . . .

Our section room was friendly, not overly large. Only a short while ago we had moved from the old gloomy quarters. The walls here were light brown, the doors painted white, the windows smaller than in the old building, but arranged more advantageously. Everything spic and span and brand new. In a word we were housed in a municipal apartment building that had just been finished. We had brought the furniture from the other place, including the speaker's podium that had served us so well. Years back Schuhmeier had spoken from it many times, Victor Adler occasionally. It goes without saying that the bust of Adler had not been forgotten either. It was now on a shelf in the left corner behind the podium. The Friends of Children, which shared the room with us, put up their gaily-colored bulletin boards, the teetotalers put up their slogans, and the "New World" Chess Club their tournament schedules. Right behind his chairman's seat, which is close to Adler's bust, Spannmeier had hung another copy of that allegorical painting of scantily clad Freedom, which was also hanging in the restaurant, "The Republic." ("Hey, I am a butcher," he joked. "I like plump women with an appetizing ham on them.") In fact, he was a retired male nurse, and not a butcher at all, even though he looked like one. Actually, retirees held the majority in the section's executive committee.

Approximately one half of the section comprised the petit bourgeois part of the district, and the other half, purely proletarian and immediately recognizable as such, had nestled in right next to the blocks where those "better people" lived. (In the entire district there were very few really wealthy people, or luxury shops, elegant private cars, and such. Only in the summer some rich people moved into a few dozen villas way out near the city limits.) For some reason, the members in our section with the most regular attendance were always people with their own small shops or businesses, clerks and sales personnel, and civil servants. On this evening Blum was amazed to see a solid block of about twenty railroaders, most of whom he had never seen before. Gellert was among them. They were in uniform, and had apparently come straight from the station. Blum shared the prevailing animosity towards Gellert. Now he thought: Well look at that! He's brought some colleagues with him. Doing something for the cause for a change. What d'ya know? . . .

Then he let his eyes wander over to another group that stood out. The young set, he thought without much good will, for reasons we already know. The young set crowded around the door, sat on window sills, tables, and some of them even on chairs. They liked being close to the door because, first of all, there were always those among them who, during the lectures, made an unobtrusive get-away, and second of all, they viewed themselves as a radical element, and thus wanted to be able to leave the room at any moment for an urgent meeting of their own, or even to show their opposition by staging an exodus.

Apart from that, no special groups formed. Those who were always crowding around the officials gabbing disbanded after a short while because most of the officials didn't stay in one place for long. Busily humming bees, they went swarming off after a brief stop. In short, this was simply life as usual for a small, active section that never "slept." Hardina was nowhere to be seen. Blum went to his chair in the last row. On the way he collected modest little signs of his popularity: the condescending greeting of a giant worker in the gasworks whose moustache was so magnificently twirled that one could almost think that all his life the master gas worker had been on his way to have his portrait taken for the jubilee column of *Das Kleine Blatt*; the "So good to see you," delivered in the man-of-the-world style of a smartly dressed salesman in a haberdashery; the respectful "Friendship" of a pale young unemployed fellow, a model among the block dues collectors that Blum used to hold up as an example for the young set; the playful punch from Nowarka, the streetcar worker and champion boxer in the sport club "Heros"; the motherly nod of an old woman whom he did not know by name, and who looked as if she always came to the section meeting right from church; now and then a handshake. And from the other end of the hall, Social Councillor Wolff was drawing mysterious squares in the air with her fingers. But that couldn't mean anything serious. She was only doing it to make herself seem important.

He sat down. At that very moment Spannmeier, towering weightily behind a carafe of water and a glass, shook the bell discreetly. Gradually the noise subsided; even the busiest ones had to take their seats. Now Blum was in a good mood. No doubt, his plan would lead to success. As a ploy, Spannmeier was to delegate the sale of tickets for the dance to him, Blum. Then Hadina would melt like wax, and the very next day . . . In a whisper, he outlined the plan to the man sitting next to him: Pollak, who was in charge of education. Pollak, an unemployed bank clerk and war invalid, looked up victoriously. "Without a doubt," he whispered back, "he'll accept, and be ever so grateful. That's the way to cut the Gordian knot. We'll force him to his knees."

Another ring of the bell. Complete silence.

"Comrades, tonight's section meeting is herewith opened and I cordially welcome our speaker, Comrade Steinbach. Comrades, it soon will be seventy years since the founder of socialism, Karl Marx, died. Tonight Comrade Steinbach will speak to us on the topic 'Karl Marx, his life and personality.' May I now ask Comrade Steinbach to begin with his lecture."

Blum straightened up. If it is permissible to take the liberty and compare him once more with a man in church: before the serious business of the meeting was to begin, Blum got ready to hear a mass, and hoped it would turn out elevating and inspirational.

Everything that was happening around him followed its proper order. He loved the room and the people in it. He even loved obstreperous Hadina and the hassles he caused. All the familiar business ran its course along the well-established track of agenda, proceedings, statutes. Here he had his duties, his responsibilities. More than that: he knew that he stood not alone, not in the forefront of existence, eye to eye with fate. He was not alone as a human being nor alone with his section. It was integrated with the organization of the district, the district was part of the city organization, the city part of the national organization. He was one of the seven hundred thousand, secure in their midst, not lost among them. He could rest assured: if I do my duty, all this will go on forever. He is turning the wheel of history—what pride there was in this knowledge! But he was not the only one turning it, heaven forbid. He was a cog in a gigantic mechanism of thousands of interlocking wheels and little wheels, in a powerful apparatus that functioned with unfailing precision. What security!

If someone had asked him, "What are you living for, Blum?" he would not have come up with an answer immediately. That's how completely his own little life had become part of this greater one, this world that seemed now so natural. What are you living for? You couldn't very well answer: I'm living for life.

The speaker (one of the less popular educational officers; his hair, starting at the back of his head and curling down below his collar, somehow gave him an "arty" look) began his lecture with a little dialectical aphorism: "Dear friends and comrades! Marx was not a scientist. Marx was not a revolutionary. Marx was a revolutionary scientist . . ."

Karl Marx or Karl Marx?

During the lecture, Spannmeier made a display of being attentive. While listening he inclined his head, now and then put his hand to his ear, and at some rhetorical phrases he shifted in his chair rhythmically, etc. He did all this without listening for a second. This is the unspoken privilege of chairmen. In their exterior behavior they must provide others with a good example. Nobody expects them to follow a lecture if they have other concerns. They're supposed to preside, not to listen.

Certain inflections of the speaker, as well as some sentence fragments he was catching, told his well-trained ear after an hour and a half that the lecture was nearing its end. When it was time to applaud, he was the first. In rising, he intoned the standard formulas: "I want to thank Comrade speaker for his excellent presentation. Does anybody wish to comment on the speaker's remarks—since there are no comments, I will close tonight's—"

At that moment he noticed that there was a comment after all. He acknowledged it without enthusiasm. Any chairman will be able to put himself in his position. Let's not forget that a protracted meeting still lay ahead for the council members. "Yes, Comrade? You wanted to say something?—"

A railroad worker stepped up to the lectern, a skinny man with dark features, clean shaven, his hair neatly parted and slicked down with hair tonic, a conductor obviously. Unknown to most, he immediately proved to be a poor speaker. He came from the station where ever since March first innumerable small intrigues, veiled and outright threats, mean-spirited Zehetner-chicaneries, vague hopes and anxieties had thrown everybody into a state of utter confusion. To sum up all these hellish details, to make it clear to the comrades that such trivialities in their entirety constitute a very serious, very dangerous battle for the union, to ask for help in this battle, all that was almost too much for the speaker in his awkwardness. And on top of this, he was talking about his own bread and butter. And he wasn't sure whether it was proper to speak about things like that so shortly after one had heard so many sublime words about Karl Marx, his life and personality. "Comrades. I would like to draw your attention to the question, I mean, what has caused our federal railroad workers such great upset these days, and also fears, comrades. As all comrades know, we have a strike behind us where we put ourselves in the front lines, so to speak, in the struggle for the right to form coalitions, for the entire Austrian proletariat. Now we must see, comrades, that a wave of punitive measures has started to break over us, such as lists circulating at the station, of who was striking, yes or no. Methods such as these are being used by the management, comrades, not to speak of forced retirements as reprisals—" He spoke with difficulty, often leaning on syllables while he groped for the next phrase, ending up in pitiful bathos. Only when he went on to speak about the parliamentary aspect of it did he seem to find his way a little better. So far as one can ascertain, he stated, the bourgeois parties will by no means vote in favor of retracting the punitive measures. In others words, the Parliament could not protect the railroad workers. So one would have to ask oneself what was to be done in a case like this . . .

Spannmeier let him go on for a few minutes more. Then he remarked politely: "Well, comrade, you understand, unfortunately I have to remind you that the topic of discussion is Karl Marx." Immediately the conductor became flustered. He stammered to the end of one last sentence, suddenly blushed from ear to ear and left the podium. To satisfy formal procedure, the chairman wanted to ask once more if there were any comments.

Before he could do so, Gellert was already standing beside him.

The heated scene that followed was later to become the topic of much controversy in the district. The railroad workers claimed outright that Spannmeier had prevented them from talking about their problems. In defending himself Spannmeier referred to his duties as chairman. Actually, he had acted correctly that evening. If a motion for changing the agenda had been accepted, he would not have given Gellert any trouble. Actually such a motion had been made by Weigel but was drowned out by the general pandemonium that Weigel's boys themselves contributed to so vociferously. Somebody even said that he had heard that one of the Socialist Youth had called out to Weigel: "To hell with the agenda!" Actually, the motion would have been defeated by a large majority, partly because the matter was considered strictly union business, partly because many were outraged by Gellert's behavior. In fact, he behaved with such an aggression, even despair that the railroad workers themselves were taken aback. Later the general opinion about the regrettable incident was that no single party could be blamed because in any other section the matter would have taken a similar turn even if perhaps in more polite forms.

The one person who had violated these forms was undoubtedly Gellert. Spannmeier had repeatedly attempted to interrupt him in the friendliest way imaginable. Gellert outscreamed his remarks as if he were in a meeting of political opponents. The speaker tried to mediate. He was not competent in union matters and willing to consider the topic "Karl Marx" closed. "If the comrades have to discuss other, more important matters . . ." Perhaps he felt a certain disappointment like any speaker who must realize that his lecture has found no echo. Was my presentation not interesting enough? Wasn't I in my best form tonight? Perhaps one could see his disappointment in his face. Who could reproach him for that or even blame him for what happened, even if it was this very remark that made Spannmeier lose his patience? "No, no, Comrade Steinbach," he exclaimed. "Things haven't gone that far yet, thank God!" Experienced chairman that he was, he felt that his honor was being assailed. He became determined; Gellert grew louder and more and more aggressive and, finally, flew off the handle: "What are ya sitting around here for anyway if the advance of fascism can't faze ya!"

Even before that, he had been interrupted by catcalls that had become more and more irritated. Now everybody felt insulted. They let him have it:

"You don't say!"

"Listen to him! Who does he think he is!"

"Shut up! Beat it!"

"Get lost, Commie!"

"Who's talking of Communists here?" Weigel flared up.

"Impudent slander!" the young set shouted.

For a few seconds the solemn voice of an old streetcar worker rose above the uproar. "Comrades, it is a disgrace, at this moment when over there in Germany the fate of the working class is being decided . . ."

Gellert banged his fist on the table. "That's the very moment when we must understand that the strike . . ."

"On with the agenda!"

And the chaos reached a new climax. (Only the railroad workers kept an embarrassed silence. Slowly a feeling began to take hold of them which only after gradually overcoming opposing emotions, barely a year later, was to determine their actions. Let no blame be attached to them!)

Unintentionally the speaker put an end to the row by suggesting that the topic "Railroad strike and reprisals" be put on the agenda for the next section meeting. By the way, that matter had already been smoothed over in Parliament this very afternoon. And while Pollak, the education officer, shouted that the section was no forum for such matters, and Gellert incensed everybody again by screaming that no Parliament could help once a strike was lost, suddenly a different person stood on the platform: a certain Mr. Rosen, LLD, a lawyer, Party member in our section, somewhat advanced in years. In the uproar a group had crowded around him listening to what he had to report. Then he was pushed and shoved and finally helped up to the platform.

"Quiet!" somebody shouted. "Dr. Rosen has something to tell us!

Through the gradually subsiding screaming old Rosen managed to put the following points across: Speaking of Parliament, he had been there this afternoon. A strange, rather serious incident had occurred there. Following a motion by the Social Democrats to vote on the retraction of the reprisals against the railroad workers, a "red" representative by mistake handed in two ballots with his name. Another Social Democrat, however, didn't hand in any. Although this did not effect the total count of votes, the Right created a row. "Things got almost as loud as here with us," Rosen added with a smile. "Renner demonstratively resigned as President of Parliament."

"Good for him!", one of the young set interjected.

"However," Rosen continued, "the Second President, the Christian Social Buresch, also resigned. And the Third President, the Pan-German Straffner, did the same. Thus the Parliament all of a sudden had no chairman, and since, apparently, no one had the authority to close the meeting and to call a new one, it disbanded in confusion and indecision."

After Rosen had finished, everybody instinctively turned to the speaker. I clearly remember the expression on Dr. Steinbach's face in the expectant murmur. He was pale and looked a little flattered. To say at least something, he advised us: "Well, comrades, undoubtedly this is the first case of its kind in the history of European and American parliamentarianism."

The Ides of March 1933

Although Dreher was a career man, up to this time he had never worried about "good" or "bad" luck. His own advance he considered an historic event and therefore a necessity that needed no justification. How else could the proletariat's increase in power manifest itself than by letting its best sons climb rung after rung up the nation's political structure? And in this country the climbing competition had less the character of a gamble than in France, for instance. Election by party, not by person, a two-party system, strict party discipline—all this meant that one had to gradually work one's way up. Only someone who had sat the sufficient length of time on office chairs, and had sat through the sufficient number of pants, had made it. Eccentrics and renegades had no chance, if only because the bourgeoisie in this country was so poor that it could hardly satisfy its own corrupt opportunists. The system of the lucky stars followed preset courses. Comets were rare. The fact that in 1924 Dreher, carried by a tremendous increase in votes (as Otto Bauer wrote at the time, only 300,000 votes were lacking to launch the classless society in Austria), got into Parliament at the age of forty, was considered a cause for wonder. But once you had "arrived," the prevailing circumstances provided such a sense of security that it simply never entered his mind that he could ever tumble down again. And since his rise, fast as it had been, had followed normal channels, even in his high position the healthy feeling never left him: I have served the proletariat selflessly long enough, and now I have every right to harvest the fruits of my labors. Undoubtedly, his sense of solidarity with his class was strong. At every stage that he had passed through, back to the lowest of them all, he had left behind him a group of friends, most of them without a grudge against him. He felt comfortable in any parliamentary committee; and he felt just as much at home whenever he visited the railroad station. Not for a second was he aware of any distance between him and the 700,000 party members. He considered himself a proletarian and was proud of it.

His ambition was satisfied for a long time to come. Higher goals would only come in sight when a coalition government became a possibility. Since the arrival of the Buresch cabinet with its intransigence, no one had talked about that apart from a few very vague discussions when the Dollfuss cabinet had formed. All this made it the more understandable that any problems of good fortune and bad luck hardly concerned him. Soberly he faced his sober destiny.

This needs stressing at this point because, during the weeks of March, a downright superstitious thought took hold of his mind. With that visit on February 11, Dworak had demoralized him, had infected him with some kind of a bad mood, had paralyzed him with some trivial worries, even disturbed his physical well-being. In short, it almost amounted to a belief in the 'evil eye.' Obviously none of this had any validity except the fact that the engineer, by evoking the circumstances of 1924 again, had touched, at an unfortunate moment, a sore spot in his life and his self-confidence. And true enough, during the day Dreher considered his suspicions pure nonsense. But at night he pursued them, when he could not fall asleep, the time when even the most responsible person will indulge in such irresponsible musings. In spite of his robust egoism, he was irresistibly drawn to such thoughts these days. For just in these days all sorts of things suddenly went wrong with him.

He knew it himself; all these phantoms that were so unlike him pointed to one thing: he had gotten out of shape. He was absolutely not in the ideal condition for facing the turmoil of political events that was breaking over him like a surprise offensive. Soon after the attack of depression that he had suffered (incidentally at the same time as Dworak), he felt physically out of sorts: he felt discomfort in his stomach after meals, violent belching, a light heartburn. Maybe he had always had that sort of thing without particularly noticing it. Now he went to a doctor right away. The doctor diagnosed an excess of acid in his stomach, nothing serious, usual with men who are very busy, probably due to insufficient chewing. He prescribed some powder. When Dreher, cautious and joking in a self-conscious way inquired about that awful change of mood, the doctor said it was nothing to worry about. Men in the change of life were often victims of such psychic phenomena. Of course the seriousness of the complaint partly depended on external circumstances. Writing the prescription for the stomach acid, he added smiling: "I'm not worried about you, Representative. If the political situation were as healthy as you are . . ." And he used this opportunity to feel out the influential man about the parliamentary crisis and about all that was in store for "this unfortunate Austria." The examination took place on March 8. The day before, the government had decreed pre-censorship, had banned all political rallies, and had empowered the district attorney to confiscate newspapers without a court order. This was a clear violation of the constitution.

"That's just it!" Dreher sighed, when, only slightly reassured, he left the doctor's office, "it's the external circumstances . . ." And again he asked himself why the devil, after so many years of health, he had to get sick at this of all times, why he now, instead of being allowed to take care of himself was burdened with a hundred important decisions. This coincidence of a phase of personal weakness and a political crisis—and a damned serious one at that—upset him so much that it developed into a separate sickness all by itself.

His car was waiting in the street. It was a car which was at the disposal of higher office holders who had no car of their own. For the last few days it was mostly used by Dreher. The situation had made him, the proven negotiator, one of the most important individuals in the Party. He knew it and knew that he was expected to perform. While he was driving to Party Headquarters, he tried to concentrate. Since March 5th he had been negotiating mostly with two influential Representatives of the Christian Socials. To be precise, due to personal connections, he had been to the home of one of them three times, and with the other one he had lunch every day in the same restaurant near the Parliament Building. Although Parliament had not convened since March 4th, both had remained loyal to their restaurant. Dreher had done so quite deliberately and on specific instructions. For Dollfuss and his Cabinet members had already begun to avoid contact as much as possible, and connections like Dreher's became precious. The first Representative had told Dreher that he considered the government's intention to keep Parliament from reconvening to be sheer nonsense. (Only he had put it in gentler terms, of course.) Also it seemed to him that the legal justification of the crisis was pretty far-fetched (and he added with a smile: "Very far-fetched!") If the three Presidents had all died in a train wreck—would that have been a reason to give up parliamentary government? (That was verbatim Otto Bauer's argument in the editorial of the *Arbeiter*

Zeitung. Dreher took it as a good sign.) And where was all this to lead? Was there anybody in Austria who was thinking of a dictatorship? He was convinced, he said, that the whole situation would straighten itself out in a couple of days.

He had said that, however, on the morning of March 5th; that was three days before yesterday's violation of the constitution. But only yesterday, that is on March 7th, the other and more important Representative, between his veal gulyash and Linzer-torte, had said something like this: "I personally am not informed with regard to the Federal Chancellor's intentions in this sensitive matter. But I don't believe that the Federal Chancellor himself—well—pursues a—I mean—a firmly defined goal, so to speak. As far as I am informed, it's primarily a question of extending the powers of the government, and a reform of procedures which should make a smooth execution of certain measures—what I mean is of primarily a budgetary nature. 'Cause, you know as well I do, in this respect our country's situation right now is no bed of roses, and in the coming session of Parliament we won't be able to take into account whether our laws will be popular or not."

For Dreher, the expression "the coming session of Parliament" struck a most welcome chord, and he replied that the Social Democrats would not find it hard to agree to said reforms. The Social Democrats by no means lacked a sense for the realities of the situation.

"That's what I keep telling myself," his lunch partner replied. "And undoubtedly the Chancellor will succeed in prevailing with this healthy attitude over the influence of certain circles—you know whom I mean. Unfortunately, this morning, for instance, I was prevented in no unclear terms from seeing the Chancellor . . ."

That was important! Dollfuss was under the intensified influence of the Heimwehr. Dreher had been one of the first to report this with certainty. Dollfuss was the Heimwehr's prisoner. The events of last night had confirmed it promptly and threateningly. Dreher had asked those two "democratic elements" to exert their influence, but as the violation of the constitution proved, his request had been in vain as had been the simultaneous maneuvers that other comrades had launched, either together with Dreher or by themselves. Today, shortly before he had been to the doctor, he had gone to that important restaurant. The Christian Social colleague had appeared on time. After all that had happened, Dreher had expected not to see him. Because his lunch partner belonged neither to the democratic group around Kunschak nor to the Kollmann circle, but to the younger Christian Socials like those around Schuschnigg, that is to say, those gentlemen who loved to call themselves the "generation of front line soldiers" and who displayed a certain skepticism toward the older democrats of their Party. It was important, perhaps decisive, to find out the attitude that this man took towards the violation of the constitution. Had he tried to prevent it? And if not, why not? Because he had not wanted to or had not been able to? Perhaps he also knew in what direction Dollfuss himself had drifted in the meantime?

The man gave the ridiculous answer: "The Federal Chancellor will say everything that one could desire in a radio address today." He didn't answer any other questions and shut up like a clam. It looked as though the violation of the constitution by his Party had sealed his lips. Was he afraid to talk?

Dreher took a more resolute approach. Early in the morning he had been asked to attend a session of the Party's Central Committee. He knew that the Party leadership considered the danger to be very high and had decided on incisive, hard hitting language. He told the Christian Social that, while he was talking, a proclamation was being printed preparing the people for a general strike and revolution. After that, he immediately changed to the jovial tone which after all was his very own specialty: was all of that really necessary? Did the government really want to bring things to a boil? Didn't one really have other common concerns in this "damned country that we all love?"

The answer was no "yes" and no "no," instead some eerily hollow cliché. This eloquent silence, the other's obvious fear suddenly made Dreher himself afraid. Indeed, only at this moment did he get scared of what had happened since the previous night. (Up to now a thousand hasty pieces of information, arrangements, meetings had left him no time for that). Now, all of a sudden, facing this hefty "connection" who, his mustache covered with beer foam, was finishing off lung and dumplings, now, in the quiet of the small club room, threateningly the specter of a world reared its head that at the time of the Pfrimer coup had caused roaring laughter as one pictured it in all detail: a world in which village pharmacists were transformed into all-powerful commanders of mercenaries, beerhall speeches into constitutions, factory owners into labor leaders, drug addicts, sadists, murderers, and arsonists into statesmen . . . Only now was he terrified by what was happening in Germany, only now he realized in a flash that soon no historical comparison, none of the usual political combinations sufficed any more to measure the scope of these events, and that very soon not even human imagination would be able to grasp them.

He realized what was threatening. His guts cramped up. And at this moment (he still couldn't forgive himself for it) he had stopped talking, had stopped chewing and, a half-chewed bite of meat in his mouth, tried to listen to his stomach. Something was going on down there, and the heartburn grew more vicious than ever before. The Christian Social had already reached the mocha stage. That was the stage when he usually became talkative. Dreher missed this opportunity. He did speak but not with the desirable intensity, not jovially enough. And it happened that he only half-registered answers that perhaps contained important hints. Because again and again his stomach demanded all his attention and, instead of thinking of more important matters, he decided in this perhaps decisive quarter of an hour to go to the doctor in the afternoon.

Now in the car Dreher reproached himself. He reproached himself instead of concentrating. The Party Executive Committee was in permanent session. He was expected. What could he report? Surely not what made him miserable in his work. He couldn't report what had happened early in the morning while he, before driving to Party Headquarters, was gulping down his breakfast (the hasty breakfast that had created all that stomach acid). He couldn't report the following: "Comrades of the Party Executive Committee. I have two sons: Ferdl and Eduard. Eduard is a fat student of medicine whom I like less than his brother, perhaps because, using my good name, he is pushing a little too hard up the ladder of higher Party offices. Ferdl is seventeen years old, about to graduate from high school, and I love him very much perhaps because he is so slim and looks somehow aristocratic so that I sometimes ask myself, 'where does he get it from?' And at breakfast this morning, as I slip him the paper with the news of the violation of the constitution, he suddenly lets out a 'Bravo.' My jaws drop with amazement and I ask him whether he's crazy. He turns red as a beet, starts stammering, and suddenly he jumps at me: 'Very good, they won't be able to insult statesmen from other countries any more. Now the Jews will have to think twice before spitting their venom at Hitler!' I demand an explanation. It's as if he were in a trance. He screams in my face: 'Yes, I am a Nazi! A man of the S.A.! And in few weeks the swastika flag will wave over Austria!'

I, Josef Dreher, admit that I don't like the Jews all that much myself. But that my own flesh and blood, in my own house . . ."

I can't tell them all that, can I, Dreher thought, consumed by fury and hurt. There are more important matters: I wasn't jovial enough with that papish lackey, that Jesuit. Nothing but hassles, goddamn hassles.

In this emotional turmoil he spat on the rug in the Austro-Daimler. When he rubbed the spittle into the fabric with his shoe, he noticed thin threads of blood. He forced himself to view the situation coolly and objectively like a stranger, like a doctor. He thought: stomach acid? That doesn't look like stomach acid to me. Funny—from the war I came home without a scratch; as a railroad engineer, I was in all sorts of shitty weather, and all I ever got was a cold now and then; as a Representative I get a vocational illness and that now of all times. Everything happens at the same time.

He saw that he was already driving along the Ring and had to reach Party Headquarters soon. Really now, that's enough of that nonsense, he decided and pulled himself together. He was determined to consider the new political situation and to weigh all possible consequences. But everything he could think of ended up in the one, actually quite unimportant question: what was it all for?

What for? From the first minute the whole situation had been as dangerous as it was silly. Now it was becoming a matter of life and death, and yet basically more and more ridiculous. A dictatorship? Who wanted a dictatorship? Dollfuss perhaps? Certainly not he. The coterie around him? Dreher was convinced: if you only had the opportunity to approach every single one of this coterie that had become so mysterious and could ask him point blank, not one of them would answer an outright yes. Except the Heimwehr leaders. And even among those there were some who had always been willing to listen. All right then: where was the dictator, the Hitler for Austria? Again: Dollfuss? Little Herr Dollfuss, a dictator? That idea was less ridiculous than it had seemed a short while ago but was still highly unlikely. Even within his own circles, the small man's authority was not any bigger than he was. Starhemberg, the playboy? A laughingstock even in these times when there was so little to laugh about. So let's go on: in spite of all that why would the bourgeoisie feel forced to want a dictatorship? The budget, the "unpopular" cuts? It was true, we had given them trouble with those, but not too much trouble. There had been times even when we had saved the government from being overthrown: we had tolerated the Lausanne loan, the bail-out of the Creditanstalt that had cost the people millions, the bail-out of the federal railroads; we had not resisted all that much when thousands were taken off welfare, and finally, on March 1 we had not gone beyond a demonstrative warning strike of two hours. "Gratitude from the House of Austria," Dreher growled furiously. But if need be, one could even be more accommodating. And the government knew that.

Or did they turn dictatorial because they were afraid of the Nazis? But who could help them against the Nazis better than the party of the 700,000, of the 41 percent? Or were they playing up to Hitler? Perhaps! But as far as Dreher knew, the drawn-out negotiations between the Nazis and the government had not become any more intensive. And was it really thinkable that Kollmann, Kunschak, the lower clergy, in short, the democratic counterforces in the Christian Social camp, would go along with that? Perhaps Mussolini was behind it all? But the government depended on France as much as it depended on him (if not more so because of the Lausanne loan). And Fritz Adler had learned from Leon Blum that Dollfuss had given Prime Minister Daladier firm assurances concerning Austrian democracy.

The end result: there really were no overpowering reasons for establishing a dictatorship. It didn't have much of a chance. Only a few people in the bourgeoisie wanted it. There was no dictator in sight. So what was the hassle all about? Dreher could mull things over and over as much as he wanted; he arrived at the same conclusion. For his party he still saw innumerable untapped possibilities to continue the cooperation with the bourgeoisie (for a long time this cooperation had seemed to him a well-founded necessity) because, he thought, Austria is not Germany. So once more: Why all these hassles? And yet, at Ballhausplatz, all sorts of forces were at play. No one pushed all the others, only the man right in front of him. Probably no one knew what he wanted, no one accepted the whole responsibility, no one followed a thought through to its final conclusion. Most likely countless cliques worked against each other as they always did. And the result was a blatant violation of the constitution. That was the situation: ridiculous and extremely dangerous.

So what was to be done?

When Dreher got out of the car in front of Party Headquarters, grumpy, nervous, his self-confidence shaken, "a sick man" (as he now called himself in secret), he answered himself in a loud voice: "Typically Austrian."

That was all he knew.

2

If a prosecuting attorney had asked Dreher shortly after these days: "What did you do during the week of March 8 to March 15," the Representative would have found it hard to render an exact account. In fact, not even on the evening of each of these days could he reconstruct precisely what had happened in the preceding hours. His general impression was: a breathtaking turmoil of the most varied meetings, all of them extremely important, centering around the question of life and death, and all of them proceeding in a somewhat cursory fashion, all of them ending in the same word: "If . . ."

Undoubtedly, we are making history now, Dreher thought again and again when he couldn't fall asleep. But in the whirl of the many questions that befuddled his brain, it didn't become clear, at least not yet, which of all the decisions would finally make "an historical impact." The year 1918 he had experienced from a different perspective. But now he asked himself: had it, maybe, been just like this? Perhaps that's just the way it is when one is making history?

In the offices of Party Headquarters and especially in the editorial offices of the *Arbeiter Zeitung* and *Das Kleines Blatt*, the daily routine proceeded under full steam. In the prevailing cocksure fighting spirit Dreher would snatch up phrases like: "Don't ya worry, we'll show them that Austria ain't Germany!" . . . "Well boys, this is it, the ball's rolling!" . . . "Time's up, no more fooling around!" . . . "They'll see that it's a different ball game altogether in Austria . . ."

When the *Arbeiter Zeitung* was confiscated several times, when white splotches interrupted its columns, when the immunity clause had to be appealed to in the provincial parliaments, the editors' fighting spirit only flared up more intensely. Above the name of the paper on the front page they printed the words "Under precensorship". Every day the same headlines announced: "Our defense." The smallest, shortest local news item was written with feverish élan.

Dreher despised scribblers. He rushed past the journalists as fast as possible. Most of his business was on the fourth floor where the Executive Committee met. Here, too, the militant atmosphere left nothing to be desired. Only the Lower Austrians, the rightest of the right in the party, played their part of defeatists. One of their leaders, who had gone to grade school with the Federal Chancellor and for that reason had become the personification of many hopes, prophesied: "Dollfuss, I am telling you, Dollfuss is not going to cave in. We've got to meet him more than half way, and that right now." He did not convince the committee. Otto Bauer's line "Talk tough!," "No compromise!" met with general agreement. The consensus was that Dollfuss would "cave in."

From the moment the parliamentary crisis erupted, Dreher

watched the leader of the Party with eagle eyes. His confidence in Otto Bauer was not unlimited. Only after Victor Adler's death had Otto Bauer, the leader of the opposition in 1916, risen to be the undisputed autocrat. The catastrophe of July 1927 had mightily shaken his authority. During the period of reconsolidation that authority had gradually reestablished itself. Now that Dreher realized that again a time of action and decisions had broken out, he first of all examined Bauer's face. (It was wide, had been clean-shaven for some years now, already covered with fine wrinkles which increased the liveliness of expression; nose and mouth finely chiseled; the smile mostly kind or cunning; the expression often concentrated, pondering: the type of face one would associate with a scholar or an older character actor in the manner of Emil Jannings). As a "sick man" Dreher viewed the general mood skeptically: his own was miserable. Whenever he looked at Bauer, he could not resist a wave of suspicion that suddenly rose within him. He remembered that in those July days Bauer had compensated inadequately for Julius Deutsch's nervous breakdown. He remembered that Bauer was Jewish; again he noticed his foreign accent. He thought: he sure could have gotten rid of that in all these years he's been living with us. Supposedly that's the German they speak in Prague. If you believe that, you believe anything. Can't he speak differently or doesn't he want to? Is he an Austrian labor leader or a scribbler snowed in from across the border? He got us in a mess before with his saber rattling. He always makes the government nervous with his radicalism. And when the time comes to face the consequences, he doesn't do anything, and hesitates and considers, that Mister Theory.

However—Dreher had to admit to himself—this time, Otto Bauer to all appearances was very calm and sure of his goal. Perhaps he put on his best face because all eyes were directed at him again. The morning the constitution was violated, Dreher was one of the first men Bauer pulled aside: "So, comrade Dreher, how's the spirit among the railroaders?" Dreher knew that Bauer respected him as a man of practical affairs. He even presumed that the theoretician felt somewhat inferior to men like himself. But that was only an assumption, and in spite of all his personal misgivings, every time Bauer displayed his confidence in him Dreher felt a little proud. He answered cautiously because in times like these you had to be on your guard or, before you knew it, you were to blame for everything. He concluded: "If it should get serious, the railroaders will be there," and immediately he posed the counter-question: "So how about the general strike now?" Bauer said "Well, the restriction of the press last night is by no means an adequate cause. Questions of press control don't excite the masses. Sitting at our desks, we must not overestimate such matters."

Dreher found this answer very reasonable. He inquired what, in Bauer's opinion, was to be done first.

"Look here, comrade Dreher," Bauer said, "we can make things very uncomfortable for the gentlemen in the provincial parliaments. We'll also have to take advantage of the main parliamentary committee. First of all, we have to try all legal means. If that fails, all our comrades know what we'll have to do."

We did make things uncomfortable for them in the provincial parliaments. In Lower Austria and Styria the majority voted against the government. The parliament of the Province of Vienna declared: "The government is not able to name one bill that it seriously proposed and that the National Assembly did not pass. The Independent Province of Vienna will not accept oppression! Austrian labor will not sit by and watch democracy's dance of death passively but will resist with life and limb any attempt to establish a dictatorship against the working people."

The last of the three Presidents of the Parliament, the Pan-German Representative Straffner, consulted with Renner and convened the Parliament for March 15. The government, ridiculously enough, replied that it would prevent such a move which meant bending the constitution. And how would it prevent it? The word was: "Not in a violent way." So how then?

The Party mobilized the masses. At a tumultuous meeting of the Vienna delegates, Bauer gave a speech which probably was one of the most powerful of his life. In a mass rally of the Party youth, their secretary Kanitz shouted: "You will defend freedom with your young lives!" In 482 sections, meetings (due to the new regulations they were camouflaged as meetings for invited members only) were held simultaneously all over Vienna. All the provinces were on the move. The executive committees of the Free Unions throughout the country in solemn and passionate terms empowered the National Union Council to call a general strike if necessary. It was on this occasion that Dreher spoke. As all speakers these days, he found rousing formulations for his indignation:

"As recent as March 7 we offered the government our honest cooperation. We recognized that unusual times demanded unusual measures, and we were ready to give the government the possibility for such measures. How did the government show its appreciation? What was the answer? A violation of the constitution. Comrades, we face the warning example of July 20 in Prussia. But in Austria we shall never see a day like that. *We* will not give in to force. *We* will not be intimidated by one lieutenant and three soldiers. *We* will not trust the oath of some Hindenburg until it is too late. Comrades, in the name of 40,000 railroad workers, I promise that on the day when somebody dares to touch Austrian democracy, on that day, on every railroad line of the country, not one wheel will turn!"

He hardly had time to wait for the applause to subside. City Councillor Danneberg was already waiting for him outside, and again he was on his way to countless negotiations, negotiations that took ten to twelve hours of Dreher's day. In the class war that had been unleashed, he belonged to the commando unit of those who had to keep badgering the few in the enemy camp who were at all accessible. The whole general staff knew that for the immediate future this section of the front was the most important one, and Danneberg coordinated the attacks. Danneberg, though Jewish, enjoyed Dreher's goodwill and respect. The union man liked that species. Danneberg was no abstract theoretician, no saber rattler. Working on the budget calculations for the City of Vienna, he performed miracles of diligence and devotion. A real magician with figures. And what a genius at the negotiating table! Compared with Danneberg, Dreher himself was just an understudy. He had always respected Danneberg; in these weeks he almost learned to venerate him. Because bargaining these days was damned tough, tougher than ever before, no doubt about that.

Dreher and Danneberg came to Vice-chancellor Winkler, the leader of the national-democratic "Farmers' Alliance" Party. Winkler always had kept confidential cross channels open with the Social Democrats. He shrugged his shoulders.

"Gentlemen, if you knew my present position in the Council of Ministers! Do you know that today again I was not asked to attend the meeting? Beware of Fey, gentlemen. He is a much more dangerous operator behind the scenes than we ever thought. I'm seriously considering my resignation."

They came to Resch, Minister of Social Affairs. The Austrian unemployed hated him almost as much as Hitler. But Resch was a good democrat. He had always kept up his contacts with the Free Unions. And he was quite personable and held humane views, his unspeakably brutal methods of throwing people off welfare notwithstanding. He smiled:

"I cannot help you any more, gentlemen. Just handed in my resignation. If you knew what's going on at Ballhausplatz now—thank you, I'm getting too old for that sort of thing."

"So will the government permit Parliament to convene?"

"Oh no, they won't do that, not a chance!"

That was the word three days before the date of the scheduled session. Every day the Council of Ministers decreed a set of new emergency measures, some of them vicious, anti-Marxist ones, some indifferent. They wanted the people to get used to being governed that way. Dollfuss was not always able to slip through the dense net of negotiators, but everytime he managed to escape again, and would not be tied down to specifics. It still was not exactly clear what he was up to. And that was three days—no, not days, by now people counted the hours—that was some seventy hours before March 15.

Because at Party Headquarters one began again to show an interest in the Chancellor's life and psyche, Dreher learned that Dollfuss had remained loyal to the barbershop he had gone to when he had still been a little secretary at the Chamber of Agriculture. Dreher had formerly lived in that part of town and been a regular customer of the same shop. On the morning of March 12 he entered the modest barber shop and had his stubble lathered. A few minutes later the Louis Bonaparte of the Austrian bourgeoisie took a seat next to him. Even Napoleon I had been taller, was Dreher's first thought. He granted his strained nerves a few minutes rest and savored the Chancellor's physical smallness. After all that had happened since Dreher had seen him in Parliament, he seemed even tinier; really, almost a dwarf. He watched him with a certain curiosity: the same disproportionately bulging forehead, the same puffy cheeks; in short, the embryo head everybody knew. And the screeching voice of the awkward speaker had probably not become any smoother. Why, after all, should the man have changed within one week? Inside, too, he must have remained the same. So what devil had gotten into this little squirt? With the help of quite a glob of hair tonic the barber flattened Dollfuss's part. All right, that was his new hairdo. Before he had let his somewhat unruly hair grow straight up to make him appear taller. Prince Starhemberg probably advised him that a brush like that was not the hairstyle for a dictator. Ridiculous, Dreher thought once more. Then he began the conversation: "My respects, Herr Chancellor."

"Good day," Dollfuss answered absentmindedly, shortly raising his eyes from the paper. Dreher mobilized the last reserves of his joviality: "It seems, Your Excellency, we are both regular customers of this hair stylist here. We know each other, don't we—from Parliament," he added as Dollfuss looked up once more.

"Oh yes. Tony, would you hand me the *Reichspost*, please, if it's already available."

"You know, your Excellency, the other day during that discussion . . ."

"Tony, the strong lotion, please."

Dreher blushed so much under the lather that his skin burned. He remembered that one day in the Parliament Building, shortly before the crisis, he had been talking in the corridor in a rather loud voice, saying that this man was the greatest bungler that ever handled the parliamentary machinery; with his majority of one vote he lived by the grace of the Social Democratic delegation. His place was not on the government bench but at best in a cattle commission. That statement was the absolute truth but this was not an opportune time to recall it. Yesterday in Germany, it occurred to Dreher, they were supposed to have tortured Representative Sollman to death. In a coal cellar. But the thought whisked by quickly. Dreher was no coward. Such rage overwhelmed him that the barber was startled and took the razor from his face. Oh that bastard, Dreher thought, that half-baked freak! He sure has learned how to cut honest people! That country bumpkin, that hick! That tool of the Jesuits! That people like me have to put up with that! Damned rat race, damned rat race.

He sat on pins and needles. When the barber had finished shaving him, he left the shop without returning the Chancellor's correct "Good bye." And he raced on to Streeruwitz, Chancellor ret., confidant of the bankers who through the Creditanstalt was connected with French capital and therefore a democrat. He told Dreher that he had been completely excluded from everything that was happening now . . . Then on with Danneberg to the Federal President. This high-school principal from Horn made some noncommittal statements in an unctuous tone as if he were sending the graduating class off into the life of hard realities. He looked obviously under the weather. Only yesterday he had spoken in more concrete terms . . . Then they met Renner who reported that he and Straffner had finally succeeded in having the first lengthy discussion with Buresch. The result: zero. The First and the Third Presidents of the Parliament had made their position clear: the parliamentary meeting on March 4 had been closed according to procedures, so Parliament was no longer in session, and it was therefore legally justified to reconvene on March 15. (Straffner's resignation of March 4 had not been validated so there could be no objections to having him call the meeting.) Buresch, the Second President, however, simply repeated the government position: the session had not been closed, so theoretically Parliament was still in session, and therefore no new meeting could be called, and therefore Parliament could de facto not reconvene. (Straffner's resignation, however, had been accepted, and he was therefore not legally entitled to call a new meeting. Only the Federal President could convene Parliament.) (That explained why the poor guy looked so obviously under the weather). In short, the situation had not become any less ridiculous, and with every hour, with every fruitless discussion like this one it became more threatening.

"That Buresch," Renner said, "is perhaps one of the sneakiest."

As if one hadn't known the man for twenty years! As if he had ever been any sneakier than any other Christian Social . . .

And on went the rat race to the next antechamber and to the one after that, with Danneberg, without Danneberg, with Renner, without Renner, with the Lower Austrians or all on his own, on and on, exhausting, deadly discouraging, for the good and the salvation of the Austrian Republic. Dreher already measured the time left in hours. He didn't think: the day after tomorrow, but: the day after tomorrow at three p.m. Because even on the last morning something could, something simply had to hold up the course of events.

And with all that he constantly had to deal with his physical discomforts. That white fizzy powder helped his heartburn only for a short time. He took it much more often that he was supposed to. He took his medicine box and spoon to every meeting, at the Federal President's or the Vice Chancellor's office he asked again and again for a glass of water to take the medication, and concerned questions he answered with: "I have stomach trouble, you know." At first he had to overcome anger and shame before he could say the unfamiliar phrase. Later he began to feel some strange enjoyment in saying it, a kind of vengeful satisfaction. He experienced real pain only when the rat race allowed him a minute to catch his breath. Then he anxiously "listened" to his insides. No doubt, there was that burning sensation. And again it was spreading. Wasn't there another kind of pain that he had not noticed before? (He had already begun to differentiate between the finest nuances of pain.) Was all of that just stomach acid? And as strange as it seemed to him later, in such minutes he could completely forget the feverish turmoil in the country around him, the agitated masses he had addressed only a short while ago, the third hour in the afternoon of March 15, the whole world. Or he thought of all that at the same time and then a wolfishly brutal egotism attacked him: "Everything at once," he protested bitterly, "twenty-five years of sacrifice and when I want to reap the fruits of my labor all that crashes down on me! It's like a conspiracy!"

That this stomach of his could still be a political issue was unbearable. In the *Red Flag* he read: "While the second bill for balancing the budget of the Federal Railroad conjures up the threatening specter of hunger before twenty thousand railroad workers and their colleagues who face disciplinary action against them, while six-hundred-thousand unemployed fearfully face March 15, the day of a new wave of welfare cuts, while the entire Austrian working class anticipate with baited breath that very day on which the last pitiful remnants of their political freedom are to be taken away from them, the union boss Dreher is carrying his well-stuffed belly from bargain to bargain, from compromise to compromise, from treason to treason. Proletarians, think about it!"

He did not laugh about things like this as he used to. He crumpled up the paper, threw it on the floor, and crushed it with his shoe.

On March 12 there was a mass rally at the Central Cemetery to honor those killed in March 1848. Since political rallies were forbidden, this gathering, registered with the police as unpolitical, amounted to a last assessment of strength in the face of destiny. The masses loved Otto Bauer's hard accent with its well-marked rhythm. This time, too, he spoke with infectious fervor. He called out to them: "This March nineteen-hundred and thirty-three . . . another fight for liberty!"

Then they all filed by the graves of honor decorated with red carnations. Dreher stood side by side with Otto Bauer. They acknowledged the ecstatic "Freedom!" of the Workers' Youth, the silent oaths of the Defense Corps company, the quiet self-confidence of the individual factory units. Dreher saw women and men weep in the increasing stillness. He was moved himself and had to swallow. He heard Bauer mumble something. "Few," he said softly, ". . . I wonder why there are so few." Dreher abruptly turned toward him. But Bauer's face matched his editorials: "Serious and confident." He greeted the crowd with raised fist.

Next day the mood in Party Headquarters plummeted. It became obvious that Dollfuss was not caving in. In his radio address the dwarf set forth his goals: expansion of the rights of the Federal President, introduction of a corporate state, reform of parliamentary procedures, and preservation of law and order. In a recent interview that he finally granted the negotiators, he had made approximately the same points. They had replied that they were not unwilling to talk about issues. After that Dollfuss had held out prospects for detailed discussions at the end of the month. But he had said he could not allow Parliament to convene; he was as determined as ever to prevent a session.

By force?

Under preservation of law and order.

"But the gentlemen must understand," Bauer shouted angrily, "that we have directed the fighting spirit of hundreds of thousands to insist on that session."

The gentlemen did not understand. In the downpour of emergency measures there was one that dealt with the regulation of the sale of fuel, actually a side issue, but important in as far as it legally belonged in the parliamentary main committee. Did they want to do away with the parliamentary main committee altogether? Another decree stipulated that permission for meetings for invited members of associations, so-called V 2 meetings, now had to be applied for eight days in advance.

"You see?" Cassandra Leuthner crowed. "Now you have it," the Lower Austrians seconded. But the tone of the Party Executive Committee remained belligerent. "Dollfuss is threatening!" the *Arbeiter Zeitung* exclaimed. "We will not negotiate under threats!"

On the fourteenth the situation was unchanged. By means of an emergency measure the government robbed the City of Vienna of four million schillings. A rumor: "Miklas interferes!" sprang up never to be heard of again.

In the hall of the secretariat of the Vienna Party, Dreher bumped into someone (he was so confused from all the hectic turmoil that he instantly forgot who it was). "Do you know," this someone jumped on him, "that the Defense Corps has no weapons?"

"Nonsense!" Dreher screamed back.

"No, no, it's quite possible. The word's getting around the whole Party. Do you know that Körner is supposed to have said he refuses to accept any responsibility for the Defense Corps?"

"Then we'll see to it that he won't lead the Defense Corp any more, if that's true, for God's sake."

"Very good. Who do you want to fire now, comrade? Twenty-four hours before Parliament meets?"

"Go hang yourself," Dreher snapped and raced down the steps. He was expected in the meeting of the Vienna shop stewards. As he stepped up on the platform he was greeted by demonstrative applause. They like me, he thought, and that helped. He flung the words at them: "Austria is not Germany!" The crowd roared. But during the speech this time he felt that at several passages his inner enthusiasm threatened to fail him. His routine effortlessly filled these blanks. The end of his speech was drowned in ovations.

Half the night up to two in the morning Dreher spent at Party Headquarters. All over the country the Defense Corps had been put on alert.

Through the Party machinery all sections would receive the signal for the masses to flood the streets. Destination: Ringstraße, Parliament Building. All important factories were in direct contact with a central command. At two o'clock in the morning news got out that Straffner, who had just fallen asleep, had been pulled out of bed by a letter from the Federal President: he should cancel the parliamentary session. Dreher swallowed his powder, drank a big cup of coffee, and raced to new negotiations. In the morning the flags were hoisted on the Parliament Building, the ceremony usual for days when it convened. No one prevented it. In front of the building people started milling around. They behaved in an orderly fashion and were not molested by the guards. Dreher's meeting lasted until twelve noon. Finally, Straffner's answer to the President was drawn up and sent: the 125th session of Parliament will take place today at three p.m. After electing the new president Parliament will adjourn. Straffner is in the right. He cannot and will not hand over his responsibility to anyone else. Or to be even more succinct: we are not going to budge.

It was a quarter after twelve. Dreher granted himself half an hour to relax. He wanted to go home, have lunch with his family. In the car excitement and sleepiness fought an exhausting, undecided battle in him. The districts around the city center glided by him. There life seemed to be going on as usual. In his district, a working class district, the picture changed radically: women were crowding into grocery stores; everywhere people were engaged in discussions; Defense Corps men in groups of three or four were on their way to rallying points. Greetings and jokes followed them. The district was getting ready for battle.

Dreher found only his wife at the lunch table. The sons had stayed away. The younger one without any explanation. We are not the only ones on alert today, Dreher thought as bitterness rose in him; so is the S.A., indeed, so is the S.A. My family life is in ruins, he thought. The nape of his neck was sore from the sweat-soaked collar. He pulled the damned thing off.

"Josef, please," his wife said, "how often have I asked you not to take the collar off at the table. That's so common."

He looked at her: her puffy forty-year-old face was overly made up. Last month she had started to play the piano. Four times a week a tutor came to give her English lessons. She took private classes in rhythmic gymnastics. Last month he had to hear how someone at Party Headquarters, some Jew to some other Jew, said behind Dreher's back: "Do you know Dreher's wife? And do you know *Le bourgeois gentilhomme* by Molière? Isn't she a Madame Jourdain right out of the book? Madame Jourdain, proletaire-bourgeoise!"

Dreher looked at the modern furniture, which he found uncomfortable. He looked at the maid who called him "Herr." He saw his wife's pearls. He looked her straight in the face. She was startled. The man in front of her was not her husband, not the one she had trained to keep his collar on at home and to kiss her hand in company. But the other one, the one she had married when she had been a slip of a sales girl in a ladies hat shop: the railroad engineer Josef Dreher.

The engineer forgot to chew carefully. A half-chewed bite of meat squeezed its way down his gullet. He washed it down with a mighty swallow of beer. Then he said ice cold: "You slut. Today civil war's breaking out."

*

The following chapter is to give you some idea of the figure of Hans Dworak who only now really takes an active part in the novel and is to be a main character.

To sum up the events [still to be dealt with] between this and the preceding chapter: Parliament has been broken up by the government, and, contrary to all expectation, the Social Democratic Party does not react. A spontaneous strike of the printers breaks out that could spark a general strike. The strike is squelched. Finally, on March 31 [1933] the Defense Corps is dissolved. The Party also accepts this defeat.

The following takes place during the night of March 31.

A Question of Nerves

That night over the Vienna Woods there was hardly any light from moon or stars. The muddy sky merged with the blackish-brown soggy earth. The wind blew in biting gusts. When it sprang up, it splashed its ice-cold spittle in their faces.

Through the lean, bare, restless trees, the Defense Corps men could see the road where the truck waited, its outline dim against the darkness.

"Deeper!" commanded Kaliwoda, and thrust his shovel fiercely into the ground. There were four others with him: Panetti, Franz Seidel, Erich Weigel, and Hans Dworak. They were burying the rifles of the Company "Friedrich Engels." They had left Fritz sitting on guard in the truck. The truck was loaded with empty milk-cans. The cases of rifles had been hidden under the cans.

They had already been digging for nearly half an hour, standing ankle-deep in mud and dead leaves. The soil was rocky here. Every time Kaliwoda pressed his spade down with his foot they could hear the wet mud squishing in his shoes. The soles and uppers were full of holes. It was when he was "in civvies"—in other words, when he was not wearing his old public transport uniform jacket with the embroidered cuffs—that you suddenly realized how desperately poor he was.

From time to time Panetti would look at Kaliwoda's soaking windbreaker and could curse himself. Why hadn't he brought his sweater with him? Then he could have suddenly complained that it was unbearably hot, working in this thing, and would Kali for God's sake take it. But he couldn't offer him his jacket, nor his overcoat. Panetti had on his snazzy (and only) overcoat, and under it his jacket and knickers—the splendid get-up which always bowled over the girls and which was reserved for spring, summer, and autumn Sundays, and Sundays only, mind you. He had spruced himself up like this out of sheer anger. For Kaliwoda had forbidden him to wear his Defense Corps uniform in the woods. First, one shouldn't wear a uniform in any case, and, second, to wear one on a dangerous job like this would be sheer madness. So, as a protest, Panetti had put on his Sunday best, so light colored and easily stained, and not yet entirely paid for. This was just as brave as wearing a uniform, and, worn on a milk-truck, looked just as conspicuous.

Thus, once upon a time, regiments of high-born cadets went into battle wearing kid gloves. (With the difference, however, that these were not the only kid gloves that the cadets possessed.) Panetti, now as muddy as the rest of them, and with no spare clothes at home, found fresh fuel for his anger. But a consoling thought was that his Mannlicher rifle was not being buried with the rest. It lay at home under the mattress. He slept on it every night. And how well greased and polished he kept it!

The initial tension had lessened during their wearisome digging. They talked together in low tones. Now they were talking about how the rifles had come into their possession. It was on a night in May of the previous year. Until then the cases of rifles had belonged to the Heimwehr. But then the district commander of the Defense Corps had told Kaliwoda that there were some rifles, belonging to the "Cock-Feathers" in such and such a place, and if they wanted them, all they had to do was to go and get them. Well, he didn't have to tell them twice . . .

"Bought with our tax money anyway," Franz Seidel reminded them. You could tell that he had never been unemployed. This kind of justification appeared quite unnecessary to Erich and the three boys who lined up at the Labor Exchange every week to get their card stamped.

"Boy!" said Panetti, "the informer who told us! I wouldn't want to be in his shoes. If they ever get him—! He's as good as dead. They'll lynch him."

"What are you talking about? They haven't got the guts to do a thing like that—not those Heimwehr suckers. You've got to pay them five schillings to march in their own demonstrations. Them, fanatics? Give me a break."

But Panetti, who liked to live in a world of drama, insisted irritably: "That's because you don't know them. They have their own special detachments for that kind of thing. They wouldn't lose a minute standing one of our spies up against the wall."

"They're only poor devils, though, really," said Erich.

Suddenly Hans Dworak broke into the talk. So far, he had been digging silently and with desperate energy. They all noted the curious tone of his voice.

"Only poor devils, are they? They're bastards! If I went tomorrow and sold myself to Starhemberg because I'm unemployed, I'd like to know whether you'd call me just a poor devil?"

There was something provocative about the way he said it.

"Hey, you wouldn't have to do that," said Panetti with good-natured gruffness. "Not you, the son of a party boss . . ."

Hans stopped digging at once and stood upright. In the darkness they could see his hands convulsively clutching the handle of his spade. He seemed to have turned dead white. He spoke shrilly, stammering almost tearfully.

"Oh, is that so? Who told you I haven't been to the Heimwehr, then—or to the Nazis? How about it, if I was a spy—and you didn't know it . . .? What about that?"

Hysterical, Erich thought. Suppose something has gone wrong again between him and his girl. Erich took this sort of conduct on Hans Dworak's part as a personal insult. Anyone would sympathize with Erich, who had helped so many young chaps to develop in the Falcons and in the Socialist Labor Youth movement, and then—just see how some of them turned out!

Erich had not seen or heard anything of Hans since New Year; none of them had. All he had known was that Hans was running around somewhere, in cheap dance-halls, playing pool in little shabby cafes, without really enjoying himself at all. Just the most miserable existence of an unemployed youngster. On New Year's Eve, up at the ski hut, he had sat all night hardly saying a word. During the discussions he never opened his mouth. He would just clutch at his Paula's hand under the table, or tell barroom jokes. And that a boy who turned out like that should come from Erich's group . . .

But while Erich felt personally hurt, the others were embarrassed.

"Looks like we better let him alone," Panetti murmured. "The stuff he's talking! Why did we ever take such a kid with us, anyway, that's what I want to know. You can see he's . . ."

"Shut up!" said Kaliwoda abruptly.

He had said that in a way that made them all look towards the road. They saw the lights of two bicycles gliding rapidly towards the truck. Then the lights stopped. The cyclists dismounted. They could see them in the light of the cycle lamps. Policemen.

They leaned their bikes against the truck, and unslung the rifles from their shoulders. Fritz jumped down from the driver's seat. One of the policemen switched on the truck's headlights. The other searched Fritz. Fritz was talking, gesticulating, showing them his identity papers. Then one of the policemen climbed up on to the truck and began to rummage among the cans. He was throwing them down on to the road, one after the other. Fritz stood there still, his hands in the air.

Hell! thought Erich. There was a cursed tickling in his throat. He was struggling to suppress it. He mustn't cough, and how he wanted to! He held his breath, bent his body forward, pressing his hand over his mouth, trying to "cough inside himself," and writhing dumbly as though seized by a cramp. The others saw what was wrong with him, and stood there rigidly, their hands clenched in anger at their helplessness, their faces twitching.

Then Hans Dworak gave a loud laugh. For a second they stood there, dumbfounded. Erich, of course, coughed then—it didn't make any difference. Panetti turned and grabbing Hans by his coat-collar raised his fist to strike. But Hans just went on laughing right in the big fellow's face, without making any attempt to defend himself. This so confused Panetti that he let go of him again. Hans went on laughing. Panetti lost his head then and made no attempt to stop Hans. Instead, he whirled round, hearing footsteps in the undergrowth, and expecting the policemen's sharp "Hands up!" any moment.

But it was his comrades' footsteps he had heard. The rest of them were running through the wood towards the road, while Fritz grinningly beckoned them on. The policemen were slowly zigzagging away on their bicycles.

It took the astonished Panetti six leaps to reach the truck. Fritz, jumping up and down with excitement, held up a card for him to see. It was a Heimwehr member's card.

"I pinched it, the day before yesterday. I just thought of it, at the last moment, while they were questioning me. 'Now, buddies,' I said to them—just think of me calling policemen 'buddies'!— 'Now, buddies,' I said, 'I'm not really carrying milk, as you can guess, but we've got a couple of cases we're burying over there— an order from our battalion.' And so they saluted me politely and took off like the wind."

Talk about luck!

But the even greater luck we had—luck that saved a life, as we told each other afterwards—was that Erich Weigel had known Hans Dworak for eight years, that perhaps after that fit of laughter he had really begun to understand what was going on inside Hans, so that he feared he might make more of a scene of some sort; or maybe it was because Erich was still smarting from that sense of personal injury and was sore at him. But, whatever the reason, the main point is that he turned round to look at Hans at the very moment when the kid was aiming a pistol at the disappearing policemen. It was also lucky that Erich didn't lose his head, but acted, and acted quickly.

It may be that Hans would never have pulled the trigger. It is very likely indeed that he would not have hit either of the policemen. For his hand was trembling terribly. It was a good thing that Erich didn't think of that or anything else but simply flung himself upon Hans. They fell to the ground and began to wrestle. The others had not yet grasped what was happening. They had not yet noticed the revolver, which Erich was trying to wrench away from Hans. The only one of the four who did anything was Fritz. He started the engine and revved it up. He did it instinctively; whenever there is some sort of a row on, the thing to do is to start an innocent noise to drown it out, so that the police will not notice.

The two boys were fighting on the ground, gasping for breath. Hans was not strongly built. But while Erich lay on top of him, trying to twist his right wrist round, Hans suddenly turned his right arm, still grasped by Erich, in an unexpected direction: outwards and backwards. He succeeded in doing that perhaps because Erich didn't know what he was up to. Hans' face was fearfully distorted. He was not gasping any more, he was sobbing now, his whole body moving convulsively. Only when he had already brought the point of the pistol up to his own temple did the others hear Erich suddenly yell:

"He's trying to shoot himself."

They dashed towards them. But the boys were lying a few yards from the road, among the trees. And the few seconds it took them to get there was the time when help was most needed.

Erich glimpsed that face, contorted with horror and desperation, which long ago had been the face of a youth he knew. He saw the quivering lips, heard the jerky whining. He saw the wide staring eyes upturned to the sky. He knew that now, in a fraction of a second, he must find the word which would save this life. If such a word existed at all—he must find it at once, there was no time to hunt about for it. He realized all this during the moment he was crying out: "He's trying to shoot himself!"

And after the wave of horror which swept over him in this scrap of time when all would be decided, there rushed through him a greater wave, of love for the slim quivering body and pain-crazed soul of his comrade. It was this swell of feeling which swept the right word into his consciousness. He pressed his head into the narrowing space between the revolver muzzle and Hans' temple and blurted out into his friend's ear:

"Hänschen—comrade—we need you. We're going to fight, I tell you. We're going to fight them!"

Slowly Hans' grip relaxed. The revolver sank down.

In the truck Hans hung on to Erich's hand. He tried to justify himself.

"You know, when I saw what a fool I'd been, the stupid way I've been acting and realized what I must seem to all of you—

well, nothing seemed to matter, you understand . . ."

He looked round shyly at the others.

"I suppose they'll kick me out of the Defense Corps now? When the District Commander hears about this . . .?"

Panetti smacked him heavily on the shoulder, shouting:

"He won't hear anything about it, you bloody big fool!"

"No?" Hans said, smiling. And then he collapsed, and lay full length among the clattering milk-cans.

They fussed over him like a bunch of sisters of mercy. Franz Seidel, shaking his head, said:

"Well, for Christ's sake. They're more grown-up in Käte's kindergarten."

"It's all right, Hans, it's all right now," Panetti kept on saying, stroking Hans's hair with his enormous paw. Kaliwoda was frowning thoughtfully and chewing on his lower lip.

*

On March 15, 1933, the Dollfuss government prevents Parliament from convening. On March 29 The Republican Defense Corps disbands. The workers are in uproar and want to defend themselves by force. The Social Democratic Party leadership considers the time inopportune. It hopes for negotiations which the government has promised. It takes the view that fascism faced with an unrelenting nonviolent defensive will exhaust itself, and so it limits its action to a demonstrative gesture: Karl Seitz, mayor of Red Vienna, dissolves the Heimwehr although the Heimwehr-leader, Emil Fey, can appeal that decision with the Minister of Security: The Minister of Security is Fey himself.

Ferdinand Dworak, chairman of the workers council at a large Vienna railroad station, leads a delegation to Otto Bauer, the leader of the Party's Left, to demand in the name of the railroad workers an armed insurgence. Bauer explains to them the position of the Party leadership. Now Dworak will have the difficult task of defending this position before the agitated crowd of workers.

A Revolution?

"Say hello to your fellow worker, comrades. And allow me one more comment. You've all been in the war. Do you remember the Battle at the Marne? The day when the unrelenting defensive of the French troops for the first time called a halt to the powerful German offensive? Well, comrades, we know what sacrifices are demanded of you today. But please don't forget that this day can become the Battle at the Marne for Austrian fascism. Listen, comrades, you are the trusted delegates of your fellow workers, officers in our great army. We in the general staff will do our duty. Do yours, each in his section of the trenches. We depend on you. Don't forget that officers have to follow one order above all others: discipline, comrades."

And then, as the three men were already passing through the door, he added in a softer voice: "I, too, have had to bow to Party discipline at times when I was of a different opinion."

They walked down the steps without speaking. All the clever words they had just heard went whirring through their heads. The last ones took hold in their hearts. They had been an appeal. Anybody who would not understand such words had no right to call himself an Austrian workers' delegate. But they knew that these were times when one had to understand what could only be hinted at. They understood! Never before had they been more proud of the long, hard training time that had schooled their ears and nerves. They understood. Without looking at each other, they were convinced that they all felt the same way. No, we will not leave you in the lurch, comrade Bauer. Not us. Your job's hard enough in this damned small country, it's hard enough for you in the International. Do what seems prudent to you. Who's going to follow you if it isn't us, comrade Bauer?

As soon as the streetcar turned into the main street and the noise of the demonstration could be heard with full force, Dworak decided to get off right there and then. "Go on to the station," he said to Weyr and Andritz. They could hardly hear him: the streetcar driver had started to sound the bell frantically. His nerves, too, were obviously raw after half an hour's run through the agitated district. Dworak got up, squeezed through the passengers who stared wide-eyed through the windows. To his satisfaction he felt that he was perfectly calm. He knew by heart what was happening here just as he still knew the Lord's Prayer by heart. The young conductor on the platform had pushed his cap to the back of his head, the strap of his bag was hanging loosely round his neck, both of which were against regulations. He let it dangle carelessly while he leaned out from the platform. Dworak remembered how in 1919 they had slung their rifles over their shoulders upside down. He pushed the man aside good-naturedly: "Not afraid of the supervisor? What about the joy riders?" The conductor looked at him absentmindedly. "They still haven't cut off the juice . . ." A roar rose from the street and drowned out his words.

"Down with the fascists!"
The streetcar bell rattled incessantly like an alarm signal. For a minute Dworak stayed on the running board of the moving streetcar and tried to estimate the number of heads. Three thousand—five thousand—but the arc lamps swayed in the wind too much, light and shadow alternated too rapidly over the crowd, it was too difficult to guess. Dworak only saw that people were marching right up to the houses on both sides of the street and neither in front nor in back was any end of the demonstration in sight. He was searching the crowd for green uniforms. There were a few, dispersed and wedged in by the multitude. "The best police of the world," Dworak said aloud, mockingly. Then he saw what he was looking for and jumped off.

Immediately he was surrounded by bodies that pushed him slowly but irresistibly to the right, down the street, in the direction of the outer boulevard. The voices, hoarse already, screamed the slogans until they cracked. Mixed in with the screaming one could hear the boos and shrill whistles of the young boys. Dworak knew such spontaneous demonstrations, he had studied them as carefully as doctors study epidemics. He remained calm. He began squeezing his way through to the police officer, and without losing sight of the entrance in which the officer was standing he threw quick side glances around to see faces he knew. Gattinger marched by him. In one breath and getting his words mixed up he screamed quickly: "Long live the Defense Corps. Down with the fascist government." The elegant stiff collar of the salesclerk in a men's store gaped wide open. Just as a chorus answered his call he brushed past Dworak, like a somnambulist, the eyes transfigured, directed straight ahead without seeing Dworak. Andraschek waved to him. Her fat face and the skin in her V-neck were flaming red. "Come on, comrade Dworak! To the Parliament, let's go! Those fascist brutes!" Kerner in the black oilcloth jacket of his working outfit was suddenly at his side. "What's new? You are coming from Headquarters? It looks like . . . ."

"Down with fascism!"

Kerner turned pale, his lower lip trembled, he grabbed Dworak by the lapel. "Dworak, what do ya think, it's worth it to day, isn't it—to risk the pension?" Then he had to let go of him. He was a slight man and the current that Dworak was crossing carried him along.

From the streetcar it had appeared to Dworak as if the police officer over there had been City Chief of Police Kusnitzki. But when he had forced his way through to the entrance door, he saw that it was somebody else, not such a V.I.P., somebody he didn't know. The slim man, squeezed into a tight-fitting dandyish uniform had an amazingly small, boy's head, and a typical aristocratic mug. He was white as a sheet, stood in a corner of the entrance way, crumpled up his kid gloves between his fingers and stared up the street. Three policemen standing around him and clutching their clubs in cramped fists, looked at his face, waited.

Dworak said: "Listen, you, I'm going to make a speech!"

The officer gave a start and turned to Dworak: "Huh . . . what do you want?" All the way down the officer's uniform jacket Dworak saw a slimy trace, spittle. If that guy didn't get inside that door in a hurry . . .

"I'm going to talk to the crowd, you hear?"

"Public—public meetings are illegal . . ."

Dworak felt anger rising in him. "Are you blind or something? Don't you see what's going on here?"

"I am informing you that in a few minutes the riot squad will . . ."

How Dworak knew it, this tense, arrogant grimace staring at him: How often he had seen them, these deathly pale, arrogant officers' mugs, in 1918 at the railroad depots in the provinces, in the threatening turmoil of dozens of soldiers streaming back from the front. Here he found it again, fifteen years later, the provocative conceit of superiority. Oh that was something Dworak hated with all his guts. He was a quiet man, a considerate man. But that had always been like a sickness with him, turning his innards upside down, a sudden anger, but ice cold. He gritted his teeth. Don't be foolish, Dworak, don't be foolish, not now.

In the street there were no more callers, no more choruses answering them, one big howl without pause, without end. No more known, no more unknown persons. Only faces rocking from side to side, mouths that opened and closed and seemed silent in the deafening roar. Heads that passed by, fists that shook. "In Berlin," Dworak thought coolly, "they would have made bastards like him into mincemeat long ago."

"You are under arrest," the officer said.

"I'm what?" One of the policemen grabbed his arm. "Am I a criminal? I'm a criminal for you, am I, a criminal? Hey, you scum!"

"Shut up, or else—! Come on!" Another policeman grabbed him, turned his arm behind his back. Red circles began to dance in front of Dworak's eyes. Everything he saw was red. He shook them off. They grabbed him again, one by the shirt collar so that he couldn't breathe. He opened his mouth, gasped for air, wanted to scream. Then everything happened much faster than he could think, just as fast as he could act. A fist hit the aristocratic snout right in the middle. Ridiculously fast, blood spurted out of the nose; one of the policemen let go of Dworak. A truncheon hit the back of his head, the scar from the war injury began to hurt like mad; the second policeman staggered to the door, dragged him along by the collar. He was close to suffocating. Then he felt free, saw truncheons swish through the air, then a fence slat; a brick crashed against the door beside him, a soft object came flying against his chest; he caught it. It was sticky; he held it up to the light, a policeman's cap.

Two words raced through his brain: July fifteenth.

Dworak turned right, grabbed the officer with both arms round the waist, opened the door with his elbow, dragged the man into the entrance, and put all his weight against the door handle.

But the rush on the door that he had expected did not happen. Only then did Dworak start thinking again. He looked the officer over from head to toe, sizing him up. The officer almost stood at attention in the dim light of the entrance. A red weal was swelling up right across his face that was now ashen gray. He looked at Dworak with fish eyes, sneered grimly, and began pulling on his kid gloves. "It's no good beating them up," Dworak thought, "you've gotta kill 'em." But the sickness passed. He said: "You had more good luck than brains."

The officer made a step towards him. "You are under arrest. Follow me."

"Cut out the jokes," Dworak growled, disgusted. He looked over the fool's shoulder to avoid looking at his face. "Listen, I'm going to go out there and give a speech. And don't get any ideas and interfere; now you can't anyhow, but I mean later when your reinforcement shows up. The situation . . ."

"Shut your mouth and follow me to the police station." Something banged against the door, somebody must have thrown a brick at it or kicked it. The screaming from the street echoed in the entrance.

"Listen, police commissioner, or whatever you are: why don't you start thinking for once in your life, for God's sake. We have already lost a couple of minutes. Your reinforcement hasn't come yet. They probably got busy on the way. But once they are here— you've got to distinguish between a demonstration and a demonstration, that's your job, for God's sake—when they come blood will flow. People are going to get killed, understand, killed!"

And because that incompetent guardian of law and order still did not understand what Dworak was after, and still stood there like a figure in a wax works, and because Dworak imagined how this bloke would fold up if Chief of Police Kusnitzki came through the doorway and greeted Dworak as he always did, and because he felt a kind of scornful pity for the fellow, he said slowly and persuasively: "Don't you understand? I want to quiet the people down, don't you see? I want to help you guys."

The officer's face changed instantly, it lit up: "Very good, very good, mate, I . . ."

"Who's your mate!?"

Dworak pushed him aside, rushed to the door, out into the street, into pandemonium. A green uniform jacket, one sleeve wound round the lamppost, hung down in tatters. Mate—mate. The crowd no longer moved forward, it was split up in insanely howling groups. A woman pushed herself forward next to Dworak. She screamed: "Beat them dead!" Dworak pressed forward, began to fight his way through with his elbows toward a huge truck on the other side of the street. Mate—mate. A man rolled in front of his feet, looked up at him with eyes full of the fear of death, jumped up and ran off hunched over. He wore no jacket, his shirt was torn, but the pants still betrayed what he was: a policeman. A young man raised his arm and without saying a word punched him smack in the face. Mate—who's your mate, scum?!

The driver of the truck guessed right away that Dworak wanted to speak and helped him up. Kneeling on the driver's wide shoulders Dworak reached for the edge of the high roof of the cab. He could still see how the driver looked up at him and said laughing: "Today we'll hear some bangs, right? You tell them good!" Then Dworak was standing up there.

"Comrades!" Fifteen years before, he had stood in front of them like that, at the provincial railroad stations, in front of the men with the red carnations on their military caps full of lice, and some of them even had Soviet stars, in front of the boys with the rifles slung upside down.

"Comrades!"

Some hundred people already crowded round the truck throwing back their heads and watching him with upturned faces. Hundreds of eyes—Dworak suddenly realized that he was dizzy. The scar on his head began to hurt violently. Quiet—he thought and was unsteady. It got black before his eyes—I must—officer—Battle at the Marne—maneuver (where the devil did that word come from all of a sudden?)—maneuver, but that lasted only seconds, and he was in control again.

"Comrades! The fascist government has dissolved the Defense Corps!"

He knew that would make them scream. They did scream, piercingly and for a long time. He knew that soon after for a few moments it would be quieter than before. It got quiet.

"In retaliation . . ." Now there were already a good thousand around the truck; only in a side street the beating was still going on.

". . . our comrade Seitz as Governor of the Province of Vienna dissolved the Vienna Heimwehr! Comrades . . ."

"Cheeeers for Seitz!" "Comrades, . . . equality before the law . . ."

"Braaaavo!"

It had worked. Dworak felt a bitter taste in his mouth as if he were going to vomit. Now he had to give his last: "The balance of the law is restored! Austrian Social Democracy is returning blow for blow! Now the word of the hour is: Join the Party Order Guard and . . ."

"Braaavo!"

". . . and now, comrades, back to Section Headquarters. Quietly back to Section Headquarters. Everybody quietly and disciplined back to Section Headquarters!"

First a few followed his orders, then a dozen, then whole groups. The movement began to take hold, prevailed, pulled those along who didn't want to follow it. After a few minutes Dworak saw large patches of bare asphalt, then he saw only a few standing around, undecided, saw men burying their hands in their pockets, saw women straightening out their dresses, a wildly gesticulating handful disappearing into a pub, four men strolling off laughing, saw the truck driver wave to him impatiently: let me go on; saw that he had won, and felt no triumph at all.

As he stooped to climb down, he heard whistles from the direction of Reiningergasse. They are coming to mop up, he thought bitterly; now they can come. As soon as he stood on the pavement, he started running to the telephone booth to call Party Headquarters and ask someone to intervene on behalf of those who had been arrested. The howling in Reiningergasse swelled up. Others ran beside him. Run, comrades, run so you won't bring home any bumps and bruises on your heads. He knew all that like the "Our Father."

But suddenly a call made him prick up his ears. "They're outlawed! Disarm!"

Who the devil did they want to disarm? The police? Now, as they were running away?

They did not run away. They ran into Reiningergasse. Reiningergasse filled with people, and the main street became alive again.

But down there where Mankgasse crossed Reiningergasse at the bottom end, stood a combat unit of Heimwehr behind a double cordon of police that had just arrived. He could see how the police commandant tried to persuade the Heimwehr to leave. He could see how the Heimwehr grinned and, through the police cordon, provoked the crowd. Then he couldn't see any more what was happening down there. Again the street was packed with a howling mass.

It's all over, Dworak thought tired. They were just waiting for the next spark, the heroes. And then—he took off his hat and wiped the nape of his neck as he did after work.

Beside him stood a skinny man he did not know. "In five minutes some people are going to get badly hurt," Dwoark said to him. The man threw up his fists. "They're outlawed! They don't have no right, no right, no right . . ."

Suddenly he fell silent and in a flash looked strange. His cheeks were sunken in and full of grey stubble, his mouth was thin, his face covered with wrinkles; he was an old man. But his features had relaxed, his eyes were beaming, the toothless mouth was slightly open. In the street you rarely see people that look so strange, so crazed: somehow Dworak thought he had seen the man somewhere, but where? The man stretched out his arm in front of him and said softly: "The Defense Corps."

Dworak turned around sharply. On the main street the company "Friedrich Engels," four abreast, came running towards them. At the head next to Kaliwoda District Councillor Pawlik was running, gesticulating wildly. Kaliwoda paid no attention to him, kept on running, his head thrust forward . . .

Dworak didn't think twice, rushed to them, reached them a hundred feet before Reiningergasse: "Company—halt!"

They were in full uniform, with chin straps tightened. In spite of everything that was happening here, discipline, drilled into them for years, was in their blood and bones. They halted.

Immediately the District Councillor harangued Kaliwoda: "Back! You're supposed to be in Alert Quarters!"

The skinny short commandant bared his teeth: "*You* don't give any orders around here!"

Pawlik's spongy face turned almost violet. He was not cut out for situations like this; when would he finally realize that? "Don't you see what's going on here?" he gasped.

"I sure do," Kaliwoda snapped back.

"That's why we're getting the shoot'n irons!" some shouted. "We won't watch our comrades being butchered!"

Down the street things were getting hot. "Let me handle this, Pawlik," Dworak said, "you have no idea about things like this, you don't get through to the men."

But fatty kept up his nonsense: "The weapons! You don't even know where the weapons are!"

"We don't, huh?" Kaliwoda grinned dangerously. The whole company grinned.

Pawlik lost his head, stamped the pavement. "No!"

They were through with him. Kaliwoda raised his hand. "Company—back!" Pawlik yelled. But they were already running ahead.

At that moment Dworak grabbed the small commandant by the front of his jacket, whirled him around. "As Batallion Commandant I take over from Company Commandant Kaliwoda!" They stopped. "Understand?"

Kaliwoda, surrounded by a hundred men who were willing to march straight to hell for him, looked at Dworak with the shy look of a boy who's afraid of being punished. "Dworak," he stammered, "we've been on alert since yesterday, waiting." He swallowed. "Don't send us back." The company was silent and waited.

"Comrades of the Defense Corps! We'll see each other tomorrow as units of the Party Order Guard. The hour demands that we prove that the Defense Corps is the most disciplined, most reliable vanguard of the working class! If in Reiningergasse peace and order are not restored in the next minutes there will be a blood bath! Therefore: to Reiningergasse on the double, force your way through, force the comrades apart, tell them to split up!"

Are they obeying? They were waiting. But Kaliwoda lowered his head and did not say anything to them.

Now Dworak had to give his last. "We won't surrender our comrades to the sabers of the police. Only the coolheadedness of the Defense Corps can prevent . . . Forward march, comrades! Company, on the double!"

They obeyed. Kaliwoda was leading. Dworak kept right behind him; he knew that one word from the little guy was all it took for them to run past Reiningergasse on to the rifles. Kaliwoda moved his legs in short, very regular jumps as if he still had a long way to run. But he kept silent.

"I refuse any responsibility!" the District Councillor screamed. He stood in the middle of the street, already far behind them, a fidgeting jumping jack. They had reached the corner. Kaliwoda turned abruptly like an automaton. They threw themselves into the turmoil.

It was hard work.

It was hard to cut through the enraged mass. Hard to make themselves heard in the storm. Hard to shove, to split up these roaring, whistling clusters that stuck together as if they were riveted. But Dworak had good nerves.

But: these were no ocean waves, no hurricane, no avalanche: these were human beings with faces that looked at him beaming, and then, when they realized what was going on, became helpless, annoyed, or terrified, even hostile. With mouths that cheered "Hurrah!" and then turned rigid, gaped or screamed "No!" But Dworak had learned to be hard, hard on himself, too. There was always a price to be paid.

But: they began singing. When almost all of them had realized what was happening, when many already obeyed and drifted toward the main street some one started to sing, very loud, very hoarse, and a bit out of tune as is usual with the one who starts.

And they were singing:
We are the builders of the world to be,
We are the sowers, the field, and the seed,
We are the reapers, the harvest are we,
We are the future, and we are the deed.
"Back to Section Headquarters!"

Flag, fly ahead
"Disband, comrades!"
So flaming red,
Fly ahead on the road we'll pass,
"Go back! Don't get provoked! Back to Section Headquarters!"
We are the future's fighting men
We are . . . .
Hoo-eeee——hoo-eee——hoo-eee——hoo-eee

"Thank God," thought Dworak. With lightning speed the short, vicious whistles of the riot squad rushed closer.

The crowd split apart, ran off in all directions. All side streets spewed forth green rows of policemen fanning out. Oh yes, now there were enough of them finally, now they became courageous again, "The world's best police." All of a sudden they dominated the street, now they were mopping up. And the Heimwehr helped them, hunted Defense Corps men, cursed together with the policemen when they caught one, when they grabbed him, ripped off his jacket: "Red bastard!", set the bayonet on his chest, they, the outlawed Heimwehr who, could anyone doubt it, were legal again.

But the hunted running, gasping, under a hail of blows, the hunted kept singing

. . . the future's fighting men,
We are Vienna's working class.

Not all of them were singing; The cowards weren't singing, those who were brave but whose faces said "wife and children," were silent. But

Flag, fly ahead
the young men
So flaming red
with fury and shame in their faces
Ahead on the road we'll pass!
they were singing.

And those of Kaliwoda's company
The Republic's defense,
were all singing. And only those fell silent
We are the revenge,
whom the mass of pursuers trampled down and who had their jackets ripped off them, the jackets

We are Vienna's working class!
on the back of which was written:
"Friedrich Engels"

"So there you are, comrade Dworak, high time you are coming, I've been waiting for you for ages in this quiet narrow street nice quiet narrow street peaceful isn't it really I must congratulate you your coolheadedness has prevented any bloodshed today I shall tell the Party leaders and if you want your name in the *Arbeiter-Zeitung* I see you're going home tired, aren't you, no wonder I'm going with you a stretch I never would have thought that of Kaliwoda that he'd behave so decent his men drove the people apart with such a determination some of them even used force you know you put a man in a uniform and right away he feels superior to the masses hahaha isn't that right you're hurt too you know that's why this dispersal today is so regrettable isn't it discontent is growing but man you look like a corpse well the wife will put you on your legs again hahah won't she—isn't' that right—isn't that right—"Thank God Ferdie that you're home they say the revolution broke out in the main street Hans is already home too man the way you look there's a gash in your head come into the kitchen let me wash it for you but where are you going Ferdie Jesus with the dirty clothes on the bed are you sick want me to get the doctor why don't you say a word, man, are you—"

"Revolution," Dworak murmured "Revolution? But why not? That's what it could have become, too, a revolution . . ."

He looked carefully at the picture above the bed. It was a picture that his wife had dragged over from the old apartment. She didn't want to get rid of it in spite of the fact that he had talked her out of religion years ago. It was one of those pictures that made the common people stupid. He studied the faces in the color print. He studied one face after another, how they stared after Christ rising to heaven. He was looking for something and he knew what it was only when he found it.

At the edge of the picture there was an old man painted with ice gray hair and skinny face. And that face, that face looked exactly like the face of the old man in the street. But so exactly as if they'd photographed him as he said: "The Defense Corps."

"So that's why," Dworak murmured and fell asleep.

*

Käte Haider, a young Socialist, nursery-school teacher by profession, but now unemployed, is a volunteer worker in charge of a day-care center for workers' children. By nature she is an exceptionally motherly woman and has wanted a child for a long time. Her boy friend, Franz Seidel, a loyal Social Democrat and member of the Defense Corps, well-paid worker in a garage, has no objections but wants first to save enough money to open his own workshop. So they both have a firm goal: a modest, solid happiness.

In the summer of 1933 (a time when fascism is slowly but persistently advancing and begins to force workers to join the Patriotic Front) Käte gets pregnant. She decides to tell Franz nothing for eight weeks, and for a long time has been playing with the idea, though without any firm intention, of having the child.

The Price of Resistance

Käte went to meet Franz at the garage after work. Walking along the street she was dreaming:

Franz is coming home, she has already heated the water for him. Beside the wash basin lies the glycerine soap so that he can get the grease off his hands. Franz slips off his shirt, stands by the wash bowl, face, ears, and neck, his whole upper body covered with lather. She asks him what's new at the garage, whether he's had any argument with the boss. He splashes and rubs with the brush and growls as he always does when he starts talking about von Russ, and he says, no, they had not had any arguments, that he and the boss never have any arguments because they both know that once they start arguing there's going to be a case of homicide; they both know that very well. He doesn't know why he hates the man so much, but he knows one thing: if there's a civil war and he and the boss meet somewhere, only one of them will get away alive. And she laughs because this has been the story for years, and she says he shouldn't ruin his life now that he has to think of the child. She leads him to the cradle, but first he has to take off his hobnailed boots because Peter is asleep. The child's name is Peter because he is a boy. Then they discuss what he's going to be one day, and she says he must not become a worker because that would be a waste considering how bright he is. And Franz laughs and asks how she knows since the professor doesn't have any teeth yet. But she tells him to be quiet and that she knows anyhow.

She bumped into an old man delivering packages.

"Oops, Fräulein. How dreamy can you get! Thinking of your fiancé?"

"Of my son!"

"I see, my congratulations! Well, can't be very old, that son."

"He hasn't been born yet."

In this way the old man was the first to know about it. Before Franz and before herself. Because only as she walked on did she make the final decision, now that it had been said aloud. Too long had she been playing with the idea "Peter." She became even fonder of the children at the day-care than she had ever been. I already love it, she thought, taken aback. She tried to erase it from her life. It didn't work. To have lied to Franz, to have waited so long until it was too late to simply scrape it out—all these pangs of conscience were silenced. She felt happy as never before in her life.

She walked with her long hiking strides so as not to miss Franz when they closed the garage. A song in her heart, she planned word for word how she would tell him: Franz, I have to tell you something important. I've been lying to you for eight weeks, Franz. I've thought it all out. I want the child. You have a job, and maybe I, too, will have a job soon. Prospects aren't rosy right now with the situation as it is in the city kindergarten, but times will get better one day. We'll make it. I'm already so happy just thinking about it. That's my firm decision. Besides, it's too late for scraping it out. We can get married if you want, or not.

What kind of a face will he make? He will look as if he were a baby himself. He won't say no. If she says: my firm decision, that's it. He's found that out. She gave a big laugh, threw her long legs out even farther, sang the song.

When she came to the garage it was past six thirty. She wondered why she didn't see him waiting for her. Russ is forcing overtime out of them again, she thought and entered the workshop. Immediately she sensed something was different but didn't know right away what. The paint of the cars that were parked here or were in for repairs sparkled in the dim light of the few bulbs. As always, backs in overalls bent over raised hoods, as always, legs in greasy work pants stuck out from under chassis. But—now she knew—it was quiet, completely quiet. No noise of a tool, no voice was to be heard. It was as if everybody had fallen asleep in the middle of work. But the face of the mechanic who was kneeling in front of a car and stared in front of him was not the face of a sleeping person; it was pale and taut in breathless suspense. She followed his glance and saw Franz. Franz stood in front of the glass door of the boss's office; facing him about four or five paces away stood Russ. Käte froze in her position and held her breath. She felt: if you move now, if anything moves now, there'll be a disaster. Franz's face, usually radiant with health, was distorted, his mouth pinched. He looked at Russ as if he wanted to cling to him with his eyes, as if everything depended on not letting him out of his sight for a second. His arms hung limp. Russ had his hands in his pockets. His right lid was half closed, and below it the steel-blue, unscrupulous, healthy eye threatened. The left lid was wide open, the glass eye below it had a greenish luster. He didn't dare either to take his eyes off Franz. Suddenly the fist in his right trouser pocket moved. The pocket stretched forward as if Russ were extending one or two fingers. A drop of sweat fell from Franz's forehead onto his cheek. Without moving his eyes from Russ, he reached aside to a fender where a heavy wrench was lying. Käte wanted to scream but couldn't; she felt a gag deep in her throat. She couldn't move. Suddenly the voice of old Schmidt trembled in the stillness: "Gentlemen," he said very politely, almost servilely, "please, gentlemen, don't, you'll end up in Stein penitentiary." Russ slowly took his hands out of his pocket. Finally her scream broke through the gag: "Franz!"

"All right," he said and finally took his eyes off Russ and

looked at her. Then he took some deep breaths. His body loosened up. "I have told you my position in no unclear terms. Joining the Patriotic Front is out of the question. The same is true for my fellow workers."

Russ was the elegant cavalier again: perfectly parted hair, upright stance, broad shoulders, tall, handsome in spite of the glass eye.

"The latter is certainly not true."

"And why not, Herr Russ?" (Why didn't he call him "von Russ" or "Captain"? Everybody did, the customers did too.

"Because your fellow workers joined this morning, to a man." (Like most Viennese aristocrats, he spoke with a kind of nonchalant whine through the nose. Franz couldn't stand it.) "I am surprised that your fellow workers haven't told you yet."

"Is that true, mate?" Franz asked. The mechanic next to Käte quickly began to exchange a spark plug. No one answered. Russ had again put on his furious grimace. Officers lose their cool if one doubts their word. Franz knew that very well. Why did he behave so imprudently?

"You, too, comrade Schmidt?" Schmidt mumbled something.

"In my garage there are no comrades, only workers, Austrians! Will you finally remember that!"

"I'll try, Herr Russ." Russ's right lid drooped again.

"And what do you say now?"

"I say that I am surprised how fast upright men give in to pressure."

Russ clenched his fist and gave his whine a fierce edge: "And?" Franz smiled mockingly and looked Russ up and down. Now Käte knew that it didn't make any difference what those two said to each other. Their facial expressions alone, the way they said things, were enough to make each other's blood boil. She didn't understand this mysterious hostility, but she tried to see behind it and, because her decision an hour ago made her love Franz more than ever, and in these minutes most of all, she, too, began to hate Russ as if everything that had to be hated in the whole world had become concentrated in his elegant body with its officer-like nonchalance.

"And what?" Franz said. "Political terror tactics don't scare me."

"That's exactly how far we were a few minutes ago." In his officer's gait, his shoulders threateningly hunched up a bit, toes slightly turned out, Russ took two steps towards Franz. "Exactly how far."

Käte thought: when men are very agitated their voices usually become ridiculous. At the same moment she realized what was threatening. No, she thought and tried to swallow her fear.

"In that case, Seidel, I am really surprised that in a place where such political pressure is being practiced, a gentleman like you could have worked for three years, two months, and ten days . . ."

"How's that? So that's what you are driving at!" Franz turned sharply to face the mechanics. "Comrades, did you hear that? I am shop steward and he threatens to fire me! That's against the law. Are you going to tolerate that, comrades?" No, Käte thought with all her strength.

Old Schmidt began to talk very fast: "Captain, that would be illegal. You know that yourself. You can fire a shop steward only after the case has been in arbitration court. To fire him just like that would be out of the question. And the other workers—would not—, the other workers would not—certainly not in this case—since, as we know, that would be illegal—." His speech had begun fast, but had become slower and slower while Schmidt had tried to see the faces of his fellow workers. When he started, he had stood up straight, his eyes ablaze, and he had looked real young. But then he had lost his vigor more and more, and slouched again. Can a man age so much in five minutes? His speech ended in the mutterings of an old man.

"No." Käte said and clenched her fists.

"This is a small business, Fräulein," the mechanic whispered, "a dozen employees all told, and the ones in the office are all Nazis, you must know."

Käte grabbed him by the shoulders. The time had come to fight. She screamed: "Has it come that far with you guys?"

The mechanic got red as a beet. "Damned times," he murmured, "damned shit." Hesistating for a moment, he glanced at the others. They had disappeared behind the cars just like soldiers seeking cover during a shelling. All of a sudden they were busily working as if they were being paid for piece work. Then he, too, lowered his head to the spark plug that had to be replaced.

"Comrades . . ." Franz began again.

When Russ let out his first scream, nobody could understand him. It sounded as if someone (someone completely unrecognizable and not Russ) had screamed "Help." But the second time it was clear what he was screaming: "Out."

That's quite impossible, Käte thought, completely impossible, no one screams "out" like that, that's how one cries for help, obviously he's crying for help. Nothing could be more obvious.

And then Russ pointed his finger straight at the illuminated sign: "EXIT."

The voice that a thousand years before had struck her as ridiculous howled for the third time: "Out!"

Suddenly Käthe saw the garage not as a whole but as different objects one after the other in a confused sequence, like a jigsaw puzzle that had fallen apart. She saw a glass door "Office," a sign "Exit," a driver's seat, a round trade mark "Steyr," a back in an overall, a green glass eye, a wrench. Then it all went round in a circle, faster and faster: wrench, tire, oil can, gas pump, Exit, Entry. Stop it, she thought, or I'll get dizzy. In the racing circle her eyes at last settled on a blond in a car coat. The lady smiled from the wall. Below her a sign said:

Learn to drive without a fuss.
Learn to drive with O. von Russ!

Quite impossible, Käte thought. Behind the lady on the wall a red convertible was parked and behind the convertible a green mountain rose. Leopoldsberg, Käte thought.

They had been walking through the streets for a while without saying a word before Käte dared ask him whether it was all over.

"The scoundrel," he shouted. "He knew the other workers would be witnesses against him, and he'd lose the case in court if he fired me without separation pay. You know what he did after you left? He ordered me into his office. He threw the money for the period of notice and two months wages on the table. 'There you are! I don't want to mess with you in the industrial court. You insulted me and I could send you off without a groschen but I can't stand the thought of possibly having to see you again in court. I give you the money. About turn! March!' He said that cold as a fish. And you can't even throw the bastard's lousy money in his face 'cause you need it too badly, and you can't even . . . you can't do a damned thing . . ."

"But you are the shop steward. You can sue him."

"A fascist like that doesn't give a damn about the shop steward bill. I can't deny that I spoke of political terror practices. Don't worry, he'd get out of it fine."

"But the other workers?"

"You've seen them yourself. I don't hold it against them. Russ would have fired all of them. That's what we get 'cause we swallowed that anti-strike bill without batting an eye. Oh boy, does that man hate me! But I swear I'll punch his nose yet now that I've got the money. And once the shooting starts and he gets in my sights . . ."

"Shouldn't you try to sue him anyhow, Franz?"

"Come off it, will you!" he shouted in irritation. "Nothing would come of it. You know that as well as I do. So why are you nagging me? The job? Forget it!"

Forget it, she thought. But that doesn't change things at all. Other people are out of work, too, and have children. One just must not be a coward. Everything else was nonsense. She was startled. What was nonsense? Who is talking about not having it? And who do I want to convince? Suddenly something collapsed in her soul, with silent crashing. Unexpected, incredible like the collapse of a building in an earthquake. But she averted her eyes and didn't listen for the crash. We'll be brave, she thought. We'll muddle through. After all, what does a little child need? But now he finally had to know.

She began: "Franzl, I've got to tell you something important."

"Go ahead."

But the little speech she had prepared didn't fit anymore. Everything had to be explained differently now. The thought: I want to have the child, had quite a strange feel to it now. She was searching for new words, but again and again she came back to the silly, inappropriate little speech till she finally gave in and began to reel it off without spirit: "Franz, I've been telling you fibs for eight weeks."

A long silence followed. She thought, we'll be brave. We'll fight it through, the three of us. After all, you can't be unemployed forever. Franz has two months' pay in advance, and he's saved some. That'll see us through for a while. And Peter will be little for a long time. What does a little child like that need? And then other times will come. Other women, too, have husbands who are out of work and have no job themselves and still have babies. But then, to her agony, she remembered how she had preached to these unemployed, suffering mothers, how she had reproached them. Had she, Käte, said all these things? Yes, she had. Was she, Käte, one of these unemployed mothers? Yes, she was. Which of the two was right? Nonsense! she thought. Then she remembered the children in the day-care center, the children whose mothers were unemployed like herself . . .

At that moment she noticed that Franz had taken her back to the garage.

"Wait for me right here, Käte."

"What do you want in there, Franz? For heaven's sake don't throw your life away!"

"Don't worry," he answered. He looked more dead than alive. "I'll tell Russ that I am prepared to join the Patriotic Front. Perhaps it'll still help if he sees me standing there in front of him and how I . . ." Somehow, she didn't understand how, he forced a smile, hesitated, gave her a questioning look, and disappeared.

Opposite the garage there was an electric clock showing seven-thirty. Käte looked up to the minute hand and folded her hands like a zealous old woman in church before the crucifix. For two minutes she was praying to the minute hand. Then a flood of shame engulfed her. And I let him go. I tolerated it that he went to sell himself, that he humiliates himself before Russ, before Russ! For Christ's sake, have I gone completely insane? For God's sake . . . what's . . . come . . . over me? She was fighting for breath. A streetcar came rumbling down the street. Throw yourself on the tracks, she ordered herself. The streetcar passed.

Oh, I'm a coward, a coward, a coward! She was crying.

"Come," Franz suddenly commanded behind her and pulled

her along.

Hope left her breathless. "Did he take you back?"

"He laughed in my face. Then he didn't say a word for a few minutes. He wanted to savor his triumph. And then he threw me out. I'm going for a drink."

She suffered waves of pain that swelled and abated in a regular rhythm like the tides, like labor pains. When they were ebbing she could think: she thought I hope the abortion won't hurt as much as this now. She thought: everything is going on as usual, the traffic, breathing, all of life. Impossible that everything goes on like that, there must be a mistake, that mistake has to be corrected. Now I understand why people commit suicide. She thought: And yet, no matter what! My firm decision!

She saw: Franz is coming home, and the warm water is ready for him, beside it there's the glycerin soap so that he can get the grease off his hands. Franz slips off his shirt, stands by the wash bowl, face, ears, neck, the whole upper body are covered with lather. She asks him what's new at the garage, and whether he's getting along with the new boss, and he smiles and says: sure, everything's hunky dory. She takes him to the cradle, but before that he has to take off his hobnailed boots because Peter's asleep.

But Franz's smile, the cradle, the child's sleep, all that lay behind a veil of torture, because Käte knew all the time: it was only a day dream, a poor, feverish day dream.

An Interrogation

He couldn't look to the right, that's where the seven were huddled together like a conspiracy of devils. On one plank bed three of them were squatting, on another two had their feet propped up against the wall, staring with completely empty faces at the ceiling; two were leaning against the wall, hands in pockets, just as they used to lean against the board fences in the crime districts before they took off on the disgusting adventures they were boasting about now. The greasy gambler with his bald head (they called him "ass with ears"); the young professional beggar with the snout of a greyhound who exploited the pity of his fellow men which only very base creatures can do; the con man who looked like a vulture and cheated poor people in the country; the blond fellow, the young one, who stole the paving stones from the Vienna Municipality; the other young chap, who had run off with the meal tickets for the city's restaurant chain; the drunk whom they had brought in only last night, and the super criminal, the giant with only one eye and gunshot scars in his cheek—all of them were equally repulsive to him and frightening, and the one-eye he feared more than any of the others. They boasted loudly of their misdeeds. At least for now they left him in peace. But he did not dare look at them from his corner or they would start in on him again.

He could not look to the left either. There was the wall and he knew that it was covered with obscene drawings and words, with swastikas, hammer and sickle, and, as he had seen to his chagrin, with three arrows. Unthinking, young Party members who'd been led astray had been here before him. Such were the times.

Behind him: the wall.

Above him, before him: the barred window, the barred peephole in the door. And he behind bars, behind bars for two weeks now—no, better not think about it, better not look around, rather—rather: better rest your hands upon your knees and study your palms. Then he could imagine them to be file cards. Then he could work through the dues collection for September. The gang of devils carried on their conversations at top volume, laughed coarsely, screamed words he didn't understand. But from home he was used to shutting out disturbances when he was doing his duty. He didn't have paper and pencil. But he was good at doing figures in his head. Only one thing upset everything: the awful thing had happened one week before the end of the month. If it had happened around the first, he would have had a chance to check the cash records. Then he would have been able to figure it all out in his head now, could have added it all up even if it wouldn't have been easy. But then, if they had brought him here on October first then today would be the fourteenth and not the seventh. Then he would have missed the section meeting, whereas now he still had a chance of making it. One thing was sure: today, tomorrow, the terrible error finally had to be cleared up. And the meeting had no doubt been postponed. No doubt: for twenty years there hadn't been one officials' meeting in the section without him. And now all of a sudden? . . . That would be a joke. Surely he would still make it now, but then he would have to appear with the dues records all balanced. How could he come to the meeting without the records all ready for approval? Spannmeier wouldn't believe it. How often had he said to Spannmeier: When it's getting close to the end of the month I get that funny feeling like rheumatism until I've seen all the cash records. I don't even need a calendar to know when it's time.

Tomorrow, the day after tomorrow, they'll have to let him go. In the detective superintendent's office they were informed about everything, and they knew when that section meeting was going to be. He had to get on with it. It couldn't be all that hard to figure out who had paid in September, who was still in arrears, who had paid up some of his late fees. The greedy, the poor, the hesitating, the dependable, the savers—hadn't they always been the same people for years and years? And most members paid regularly, that was the way it had worked in the district since he had taken charge. Of course, if things had been allowed to go on as they had for the past twenty years until he took over the finances from Orner— oh dear, that would have been a pretty mess. But Orner had been killed at the front, one shouldn't say anything bad about him. Off to work then! Only: yesterday the policemen had beaten him on the back of the head again, and slapped him around nose and ears. There was a roar in his head, that's why it was so hard to add up, that's why it was stinging like fire behind his eyebrows.

Block one: 1 Rossigasse. Weichsberger undoubtedly paid. All right, 50 groschen. Apartment 16, the Fenz family: the father 50 groschen; the wife 50 groschen, makes 1 schilling 50; the son, unemployed, makes 1 schilling 60, all right. 3 Rossigasse: Dr. Ungar surely contributed to the defense fund. But how much? In August it had been 2 schillings, in July five—wait a minute. Does Dr. Ungar live at number 3? Where does Dr. Ungar live? Ridiculous that I don't remember a thing like that—that's because they are screaming so much. "Hightailed it outa there." What does that really mean? And where does Dr. Ungar live? Nowhere. Nonsense. Everybody must live somewhere. Is there actually a person by the name of Dr. Ungar? Hasn't he died? Or been sentenced to death? That's because they laugh so much, the devils.

And there One-eye stood in front of him again.

"What's cookin', Blum, readin' palms again? Studyin' to be a gipsy, eh?"

Quickly he shoved the file cards together and put them in his coat pocket. They were no outsider's business.

"C'mon, move a bit closer, them guys can teach ya somethin'."

Repeatedly he had tried to put these criminal elements in their place. Ever since they'd been rough with him. So as not to provoke them, he sat down on the edge of the plankbed and kept quiet.

"At that moment two dicks turn up at the door, each of them a shooting-iron in his hand. 'Hands up!' You can imagine everybody in the joint raises his hands, and me a good two hundred tickets still in my inside jacket pocket; naturally I whisper to my brother: in the yard! One jump out the window and I'm in the yard, throw the crap in a corner, beat it, get home, you know, burn the three hundred I still had in the bedside table, and that was that. Everything would've been dandy if one of the lousy gang that had stuffed his gut at my expense for two weeks hadn't blown the whole thing, the bastard. I know exactly who it was. When I get out he'll be sorry. They can't prove a damn shit and I won't admit no fuckin' shit, remember that, you Mister political!" (Blum acted as if he had nothing to do with the whole matter, but the criminal could only mean him since he was the only "political prisoner" in the cell). "You gotta deny everythin'. Nothin' but deny! And when you're under the gallows with the rope round your neck, you've gotta scream: I'm innocent!"

He wanted to put his tie in order in a gesture of dignity and then remembered that they had taken it away from him when he came here. He got up and wanted to take some dignified steps—the suspenders were gone, his pants were slipping.

"Gentlemen," the drunk whined, "I can't remember nothin', not a thing, gentlemen! I'm supposed to have stabbed somebody, gentlemen of the jury, but I don't know nothin'."

All of this was sad and despicable.

And if that were not enough, the blond guy told them how he had stolen the paving stones. He had simply loaded them at one building site, carted them to another and sold them! In broad daylight. In full confidence the foreman had helped him load and unload and, without a question, had paid him. And he had done that fine business for months. How could a person like that not realize that he was harming Red Vienna?

He tried again to escape into his corner. But One-eye caught him by the collar, pulled him down on the plankbed and looked him up and down with a scrutinizing and pondering look. The others stopped talking. They always stopped talking when One-eye was speaking. He was very much respected by that honorable gang. But an honest man had to be afraid of him.

"Listen, Blum, listen to me. I'd have a dilly of a job for ya. In your party you sure got a lot of business-guys who're broke. O.K., now listen to me: you pick one of them and talk him into taking out insurance against theft. Then he goes on vacation on a Saturday night. That night I get in there, crack his cash box with nothin' in it. I just take twenty percent, the rest you can split between the two of ya."

One-eye didn't boast as much as the others. The corners of his mouth drooped as he talked, his voice sounded contemptuous, nostalgic. That was the way he philosophized about his craft.

"You don't have to worry about me, I won't squeal. I'm forty-five years old now, sixteen of them I've been in the slammer—I haven't squealed once. The dick department here has gotta lemme go pretty soon. What I'm in here for, that's just small potatoes; two, three months, that's all I can get. Actually I wouldn't have to crack the cash box, all I have to do is look at it for half an hour, and there ain't a system I can't get open. But it's because of the way it looks, see? You can depend on me, no one's ever gone to the dogs because of me, just ask any of the boys here."

The blond fellow nodded reverently. The giant began to blink seductively. His cheeks pockmarked by gunshot holes began to wrinkle up. With his one eye that he kept blinking (the blind eye remained closed) he looked like a real devil who wanted to tempt your soul. "You get to know some business people, make a pretty pile . . . , get a rake-off, hear?" Suddenly he broke out in gruesome laughter, and the others joined in.

"Herr Turer, I grant you the right to your own opinion, but I am a decent person in spite of the hardships in our time."

The beggar stopped laughing and pushed his fist under Blum's nose. "And what are we, huh? We ain't decent people, we ain't, huh?" One-eye told him to be quiet. "Criminals, that's what we are, all of us. Sure, we're criminals. That's life, God damn it. But you, Blum, you're a criminal just like us."

"I?" Oh why had he told them all about himself the very first night when he had still believed that they were human beings and not devils? Now they'd start torturing him again. "I want to draw your attention to the fact that for twenty-nine years, for twenty nine years I've worked for the good of the community."

Their laughter cut him to the bone.

"A criminal you are," roared One-eye. "You blew up the garage!"

"I did not!"

"You're a pimp! You pushed Frau Kainz into the City Councillor's bed!"

"No! I did not! You are lying!"

"I'm whaaaat?"

"I am innocent, I reject any responsibility for the consequences of the irresponsible . . . that is . . . measures . . ."

"Innocent like him here, huh?" One-eye pointed at the drunk who at once began whining: "I can't remember nothin', gentlemen, I'm supposed to have stabbed someone, but on my soul, I can't remember nothin' . . . ."

The devils were doubled-up with laughter. "I'll split my gut," the gambler screamed out of breath and kicked his legs up in the air. The con man giggled like an old woman and held his hand over his mouth so he would not lose his dentures. One-eye put his arms around the shoulders of the young fellows and roared with gaping mouth. His healthy eye bulged watery blue; from under the closed lid of the dead eye tears were running that got caught in the holes of the gunshot scars. "A criminal, that's what y'are!"

Only the drunk, lying on his stomach, whined softly to himself: "I can't remember nothin' . . ."

He, the honest person, with a troubled mind looked at the drunk as he lay on the ground, an older man already, his eyes bloodshot, his face gray, pasty, and deeply wrinkled, his jacket full of dust and grease stains which he, shaking his head and sighing again, tried in vain to wipe off.

"Criminal!" One-eye roared. How the eyebrows were stinging! No, no, for twenty-nine years he had worked for the common good, he was no criminal. He, the section treasurer, the oldest member in the district—what a joke. Blum . . . maybe he was, who knows. What nonsense. Maybe because they beat him on the back of his head.

"Sing along, Blum!" One-eye roared, grabbed him by the neck, began to conduct:

"When the father and his son
Jacking off are havin' fun . . ."

He didn't want to sing, it was an obscene song. But One-eye noticed that and forced everyone to start over again. And he squeezed Blum's neck every time he hesitated.

When mom and daughter have no date
And with a candle masturbate,
When the Emperor of France
Received the ladies without pants . . .

Blum blushed all over. His head was about to burst. What can I do, he thought as in a fever, while he sang along, and One-eye squeezed his neck together.

"Louder, Blum!"

Mouse, mouse, cutie mouse,
Come with me behind the house . . .

Then he had the idea that saved him. He tore himself loose, ran to the door and knocked quite softly: "Wanna go to the john again and don't have the guts to? Are ya afraid of the cop?" One-eye asked with a grin.

"Yes", Blum murmured and smiled submissively. Oh, he was smart, much smarter than this scum.

"All right then," One-eye decided and began pounding the door threateningly.

The policeman opened with a curse.

Holding up his pants, he rushed along through the guard rooms where the cops on duty were solving crossword puzzles. Then he closed the door of the toilet carefully behind him, let down his pants, and sat down smiling. The file cards were in his trembling hands again . . .

I'll start all over again, he thought. To work! Block one, 1 Rossigasse. Weichsberger surely paid. Good. That's 50 groschen.

It was very difficult. Nevertheless, (he hardly knew how) he got as far as block three. Gathering all his strength, he tried to commit the sum to memory. "47 schillings, 30 groschen," he kept saying to himself while he buttoned his fly and cleverly enough flushed the toilet so that the guards would believe that he really . . . oh yes, as section treasurer he had to know human nature . . . and again and again: "47 schillings, 30 groschen."

When he saw his sister-in-law sitting in the hall, he forgot the figure. At first he thought that it wasn't really his sister-in-law because in the past few days he had seen all sorts of people: his wife, Spannmeier, Dr. Ungar, Orner, and it turned out to have been nothing but his imagination because there was nothing there but air when he tried to shake hands with all these people. (Which was quite understandable if you just thought about it for a minute and the headache subsided. How could Mary, how could Spannmeier have gotten into jail? Only criminals get into jail like One-eye and maybe Robert Blum. But he, the treasurer, or Spannmeier, the chairman, or Dr. Ungar of all people, and Orner who had been killed in the war? What a joke!)

So he tried to walk right through his sister-in-law because naturally he thought that there was nothing there but air. But he bumped right into her, and the guards laughed.

"Hey, Blum, are you going to wrestle with your sister-in-law when she comes to visit you, are you funny!" One of them whispered in his ear: "Don't you dare talk about the interrogation yesterday!" But he didn't think of that at all. He was so glad she had come.

"Anna", he called, "how nice of you to come! How are things at home? How's Mary? When is the meeting in the section?"

He saw that she smiled, and he felt warm right to his heart.

At last, he thought, somebody will be kind and friendly with me in this place. At last someone has come who has known me for many years and knows that I couldn't blow up the garage. I've already started to hallucinate out of sheer desperation. When Spannmeier hears that, he'll laugh: Blum, Blumekin, I always thought you were a dull pencil pusher, and in jail you suddenly turn into a poet, think your hands are file cards and imagine all sorts of crazy things. Blum thought of the loud, good laughter of his chairman. His eyes filled with tears.

He was surprised that his sister-in-law didn't say anything to him, and suddenly it seemed to him as if her smile was like that smile of One-eye, vicious and scornful. Nonsense.

"How's Willi, Anna? How are you doing? Who is filling in for me as Social Councillor? When old Guenther comes, tell her from me her benefits won't be curtailed. Do you hear, Anna, that's very important; I prevented that. When is the officials' meeting? Have the police made enquiries about me yet? Did you tell them why I must be innocent! And Spannmeier . . ." The older policeman cut him short:

"You must not talk about the case. If you talk about the case once more, the visit will be terminated!" Blum was quiet and, smiling, took in his sister-in-law's presence.

"You criminal!" The sister-in-law said. "You dissolute character. I've only come to tell you that Mary has had a heart spasm today so bad that I thought that was it! And do you know why, you gangster? Because a man from the criminal police came this morning and told her that if he were in her place he'd divorce you, you, you . . ." She screamed: "The whole district is talking about you; I don't even dare go out in the street, not even across the way to the drugstore, to get the medicine for your sick wife; people are pointing their fingers at me!"

"But I'm innocent, Anna! For two weeks I've been trying to convince all competent agencies that the unfortunate situation . . ." "An infernally cunning criminal, that's what you are. I told Marie that on the day she married you! A life sentence you'll get, that's the minimum. Herr Spannmeier said that, and he's an educated person."

He moved his hand to brush away the horse fly that began

buzzing around his ear. "Oh no, I'm sure he didn't say that, you're mistaken, Anna. Do you perhaps know, my dear Anna," (he had to flatter her or he could not get her to do anything—she had not changed) "do you perhaps happen to know, Anna, what day the officials' meeting will be held?"

"What do I care about your meetings? As a matter of fact, I bet your good comrades have already taken your office away from you, and right they are because . . ."

"You're lying!" he howled. He wanted to grab her by the throat, but he had never even tried something like that, not even as a kid when he was playing with other boys. During the war he had been deferred. Awkwardly he stretched his hands towards her neck, stood on tiptoe (she was much taller than he). But she had already slapped his face.

With one hand the guard dragged him back to the cell. He didn't want to believe Blum that the woman had lied, unashamedly and maliciously. With the other hand he unlocked the door and pushed him into the cell.

He stumbled forward as far as the momentum carried him, stopped in the middle of the cell, closed his eyes and hunched his back. What he expected happened: the giant paw of One-eye dropped on his neck and shoved him toward the other six devils.

*

The police investigator always looked so stern and unrelenting. Everything about him was neat and immaculate. The moustache was like a brush and always cut to a precise length; the sideburns had sharp, shaved edges; his hair was smooth and shiny like patent leather; his eyes looked proud and severe. He was a decent person no doubt if one could judge by appearances. Comrade Pawlik had always raved about how understanding this police officer had been at trials. It is true, Pawlik had said once, that the officer held different political views, completely different ones, but one had to respect another person's views as long as the person concerned was otherwise decent and approachable.

When the investigator had him brought in for questioning, Blum always thought of what Pawlik had said, and he believed:

now at last everything must be cleared up. But the investigator had always disappointed him very much, if one were allowed to put it that way. Oh, the whole matter was a mistake, a terrible mistake which probably went much deeper than one knew. At least sometimes he had a frightening vague sense that all over the world misunderstandings had opened up like chasms. But it was too difficult to understand it all. Now the investigator even screamed at him again, and he had said nothing objectionable, nothing that could hurt the feelings of a person in public office.

"Leave me in peace," the investigator screamed, "with your incessant self-praise! I've heard it for the umpteenth time that you served the community. I'm sick and tired of listening to your drivel."

He answered without raising his head (because he knew how the face of the officer looked at moments like this). "I've always been an honest person!"

"I didn't ask you about that. What did you do on the evening of September 23?"

"I went for a walk."

"Where?"

"I don't remember any more."

"Were you in the vicinity of the Russ driving school?"

"Yes, I was."

"What were you doing there?"

"I walked up and down in front of the garage a few times."

"What were you thinking while you were doing that?"

He blushed. "I . . . well I thought—we should—I thought—take some action."

"What did you mean by that?"

"I don't know."

Now the investigator screamed again (why did he?): "That's as far as I got with you last week. How can you account for your behavior so stupidly. Franz Seidel, who's been falsely incriminated through your confused and untrue statements, has said that on the evening in question he had told you about his being fired by Russ. After that you thought of taking action. It is pretty obvious what you meant by that, for heaven's sake."

"Herr Inspector. You know comrade Pawlik, he . . ."

"In this office there are no comrades. And Herr Pawlik has nothing to do with the whole matter."

"But he always spoke of contacts with you which . . ."

"No contacts at all. In Austria we'll soon break off any contacts with your kind in a way that'll scare the wits out of you! Did you see the car with the explosive charges."

"I did."

"What did you do then?"

"I was thinking."

"Thinking again. You must be a great thinker. And what about?"

"About injustice. And who's to blame for it all. And . . ."

"And . . .?"

"And that—well that—out of protest so to speak and because there must be a limit, I mean a limit to this injustice—the driving school possibly ought to . . ."

". . . be blown up?"

He hid his face in his hands. "Yes."

"Well, finally." All of a sudden the officer's tone had changed drastically. He had leaned back, filled his pipe, sighed good-naturedly. Bashfully Blum tried to smile at the officer. The officer smiled back! Blum's heart jumped with joy. Finally. He had known it all along. Everything must be cleared up.

"Such a confession feels good, doesn't it?" the officer asked in a friendly way, took a new sheet of office paper, filled half a page with it.

"Sign here!"

Nice handwriting the officer had. You could tell the decent person. But at the end he read: "And I herewith declare that on September 23rd at twelve-thirty a.m. I with my own hands destroyed the Russ driving school by means of explosives."

No, of course he couldn't sign that. He handed the sheet back. "Well, Blum, what's the matter?"

"What is written here, you must pardon me, but that is not true. No." Getting scared he ducked. But the stern gentleman did not start screaming again.

"Now listen carefully, Blum," he said slowly. "I'll tell you a story with a big prize question at the end. When I'm through, you'll have a chance to guess the answer. On September 23 Robert Blum goes for a walk. He meets Franz Seidel and listens to his story about being fired from the Russ driving school. Robert Blum is outraged. He makes threatening remarks; we haven't seen the end of things yet, there must by a limit and other clichés we've heard a hundred times. Shortly after midnight, Robert Blum walks past the Russ garage. Blum sees a truck parked close by with explosives on it that are meant for a quarry. The driver and his helper are gone. Robert Blum sees that and thinks that actually one could blow up the garage. At twelve-thirty a.m. the garage is blown up. Robert Blum is found in the vicinity, unconscious. The big prize question: who blew up the garage?"

The officer had spoken quietly, even jokingly. But under the friendliness a powerful rage was trembling that would make your flesh creep because one sensed: any minute the investigator will rush out of the office, and you'll be left alone, and then policemen will come in . . . and the eyebrows were stinging so bad . . . . and what the gentleman had said was as logical and convincing as a problem in addition. Blum must have blown up the garage. Robert Blum. The investigator, too, believed that Blum had blown up the garage. The seven devils screamed: Blum blew up the garage. The sister-in-law, his wife, Spannmeier, the whole district said: Blum blew up the garage.

A terrible crime. A heinous deed. Dozens of people could have been killed. If one thought of that, one's head began to spin, one's temples pounded. Disgust filled stomach, chest, throat, mouth, nose. What a despicable wretch, this Blum! Everybody turned away from him revolted! Only he, the section treasurer, the decent person, should not renounce Blum, should not condemn this criminal element? But something held him back. He wanted to speak, clear up all misunderstandings that gaped on all sides, black and terrifying like chasms. But something was wrong. Something—he didn't know what. Oh it was a torture, like a nightmare. You want to run away, quickly, but you can't. Your feet are heavy as lead; you can't get them off the ground. And you must run, you must, or the abyss will swallow you up, the regrettable misunderstanding! Something's wrong in the agenda for the day, the whole meeting is taking a wrong course. But you don't know why, you don't know. No.

"No," he said and shook his head sadly. And now the investigator jumped on him again. (Why did he do that?) All his joviality was gone. You could no longer see the precise, orderly face, he was that furious.

"No? No again? What d' you mean, no? You want to deny again that you blew up the garage?!!"

He was supposed to have blown up the garage, *he*? That was a new accusation! His whole being rose in protest!

"But what are you thinking of, Herr Investigator?? *Me*? *I* am an honest person. For twenty-nine years I have worked for the common good."

"You scoundrel! Don't you try pulling my leg . . ."

"Since 1908 I have been a Social Democrat. I have done my part in building Red Vienna. Doesn't that count anymore?"

"No!"

"As a Social Councillor I have had a hand, so to speak, in the great social relief work of the Vienna Municipality. Doesn't that count anymore either?"

"No!"

"Excuse me for saying so, I have always been a loyal republican, a loyal pillar of our small country."

"I'm not interested in that!"

"You're not interested in that?" he repeated stunned.

"You blew up the garage!"

"Me? But that's absolutely impossible. For twenty-nine years I've . . ."

"Shut up!"

Oh, why did he always make the gentleman so angry? He knew: one should avoid all unnecessary friction with the police. Victor Adler and Schuhmeier had said that already. But he really was not to blame for the investigator's rage. He had not committed any rash action, had not shouted any provocative slogans, he had never listened to the inflammatory instigations of Communists and agitators. He had always been polite and modest. And yet the investigator had left the room in a rage, and he was sitting there alone, waiting. Oh he knew what was about to happen.

And here they were already. He already knew one of them,

the fat one with the red cheeks and the piercing, beady black eyes. He didn't know the other one yet, the one with the long horse's head and the morose look. But he knew what they wanted to do with him.

"What kind of a guy is this one?"

"Blum's his name. He's the one why there's always that row in cell four."

"*He's* the one!" the horse head snarled, and his morose eyes lit up.

But he was surprised that he was less and less afraid. Yesterday and the day before, when they had looked at him like that with knitted brow, gathering all the rage in themselves that one needs to beat a human being that hasn't done any harm to you and only stands there without saying a word, he'd almost gotten diarrhea for fear, fear not only of the pain. It had also been the apprehension that the policemen's wives and children could suddenly come in and see it all.

Now, too, his thoughts became confused, circled faster and faster like a merry-go-round gone out of control. But he was not afraid. He tried to get hold of the thoughts that were whizzing by, and there was one that flashed at him: perhaps they are going to beat Blum and not me! The thought had hardly appeared when it was gone again and others raced by. It was a merry-go-round after all. You only had to keep looking, the thought would come by again, any second, any second . . . . He was waiting for it full of suspense because he knew everything depended on that one thought. The regrettable misunderstandings would be cleared up, the meeting would go on to the next point on the agenda, the collection of dues, unsatisfactory in all blocks . . . in spite of the hard times and in spite of what certain gentlemen had set their hearts on, gentlemen who, like Taaffe and Badeni, against the explicit clauses of the Party statutes . . .

At this moment he felt the jolt, the burning of the first blow on his head. His ears were roaring, the pain in his nose was humiliating, it knocked all the courage out of him; it made tears come to his eyes.

"I refer to point one . . ." But now they hit him on the other side of his head. His nose became thick like an elephant's trunk.

"Tell us about the garage, huh?" the one with the red cheeks and the flaming eyes asked. "Huh?" His fist big as a house flew at his mouth. His mouth filled with blood that he swallowed timidly.

"You red gangster! You bastard!" And again the fist.

He sobbed. The blood went down the wrong way. He had to cough. Coughing he spat blood on the floor.

"Pig, you damned pig! Look what a mess you made!"

Obediently he lowered his head. It really was a big, unappetizing . . . .
The steam hammer hit his chin, flung his head backwards, threw his body against the wall. The tooth, the tooth was gone. He'd swallowed it! Would the health insurance replace it?

Again his eyes filled with tears. Softly and hoarsely Otto Bauer whispered in his ear: "Oh, comrades, we know, in 1848 Robert Blum, in the fight for freedom, he stood against the wall before the henchmen of Windischgrätz and Jellacic . . ." Sobbing he repeated: "Before the henchmen."

"Who's your henchmen, huh?" Again the fist threatened his face.

"Don't hit him in the face with your fist," the horse-head warned morosely, "they'll see it and then you're in trouble." Suddenly he had a wet rag in his hand and came closer.

"Come on, Blum, don't make our job harder than it has to be. Confess and that's the end of it. Did you blow it up, the garage?"

"Me? But for twenty-nine years, twenty-nine years I have worked for the good of the . . ."

Both of them let him have it. The rag smacked him around the ears, made wet burns on the temples, on the back of his neck. He screamed. The one with the red cheeks worked the back of his head over like mad. Every blow went right through his brain to the eyebrows. The eyebrows were stinging, a thousand fine needles. He screamed. The one with the red cheeks kicked him in the belly with his boot. He doubled up, fell down, couldn't scream any more. Before every blow he heard the enraged voice of the morose one.

"The dog! Messes up the police station; thinks we're his janitors, the bastard." A dull blow hit his ribs, cut through into the lungs. He groaned. "He gets cell four all worked up, the bastard. We can't have a little peace on duty." The rag burned his eyes. He groaned.

"If we hadn't caught him we'd have had a bomb in the police station by now." The steam-hammer smashed his nose. He groaned.

"Not with the fist in the face. The scum might give us trouble, that red dog." The rag wrapped itself around his head, snapped back, whipped the head around, ripped his skull open. He could scream again, He screamed.

They didn't speak anymore. Nothing but a hail of blows, a roar, thunder, lightning struck again and again. He had no body anymore: hands, feet, head, nothing but one big hole filled from his head to his waist with nothing but one boiling torture. And when he screamed he didn't scream with his mouth (where was his mouth?), when he screamed, it was his whole body that screamed. Then the red circles began—and Robert Blum, his hands—to dance—long hat pins stabbed into the craters of pain— all tied—that the crater screamed like an animal—now marches forward—and then suddenly a magnesium light flared up in his brain and illuminated the whole world, all the regrettable misunderstandings disappeared, everything had an unbearably blissful clarity, and Robert Blum, his hands all tied, now marches forward with unfaltering stride.

When they squeezed a sponge over his head, and the water ran down his face, and they called him names because he had made their job so difficult, he quietly asked to see the investigating officer.

"Are you going to confess now?" they asked.

"I will clear up all regrettable misunderstandings."

The officer did not look at him but began to thumb through some files. But that wasn't necessary. The gentleman didn't have to pretend, didn't have to be afraid that he would complain of the beating. Oh no, he only wanted to explain everything. In a lively and cheerful tone he began:

"The thing is this, Herr Investigator, this Robert Blum, it was he who blew up the garage. But you must not judge him too harshly. He did it because of the injustice. He allowed himself to be intimidated and provoked by rabble rousers."

"There you are," the officer sighed satisfied. "Why didn't you confess the act of terrorism before. We could have saved ourselves a lot of trouble."

Strange: the officer didn't understand him again, and he was such an educated person. One had to explain the misunderstanding a bit better.

"I didn't commit any act of terrorism. Not me. That's completely out of the question. For twenty-nine years I have worked for the common good, and I was, as they say, a firm supporter of our little country. I am supposed to have committed an act of terrorism? If that isn't a joke. Robert Blum did it. Just a short while ago you proved to me point for point that it can only have been Blum, didn't you? And the whole district says it, too, and my sister-in-law, and the seven devils."

The officer jumped up. Why did he scream again when the eyebrows were stinging so much. And what a funny, unintelligible question he asked me.

No, he had heard right. He asked the same question again.

He repeated every single word to himself: "Are"—he understood that—"you"—that, too, he understood—"not"—all right, that word he himself used a hundred times—"Robert Blum"—he knew him, too; that was the man who had blown up the garage, his hands all tied.

The question was very simple, but he had never heard it before, and that's why he did not understand it.

He shook his head sadly.

The officer, too, shook his head, called in the two policemen, began to whisper with them.

"Only with the rag," the one with the red cheeks assured him submissively.

Let them whisper as much as they want; he didn't care. He had cleared up everything. Nobody could ask more of him. One must not burden Party officials with too many responsibilities. He was tired and wanted to sleep. As always he had fulfilled his duty toward the community . . .

The officer gently woke him from his cat nap and held out

the minutes to him: "Sign."

A quarter of the page was filled with writing. A beautiful, orderly hand. The handwriting betrays the person, the head bookkeeper had always said when Blum had been learning bookkeeping. He was too tired to read what was written on the page.

"Sign!" the officer repeated impatiently.

Oh, he was so glad to sign. But the officer's finger pointed to the bottom edge of the page. And when Blum had started as bookkeeper, the head bookkeeper had always said: "When you sign a receipt or anything else, always make sure that you leave no room between the text and your signature. Remember that!"

Reverently, he pushed the finger aside and signed right under what the investigator had written.

And again the officer became so red in the face. And again he yelled at him unintelligible words: "You sly fox. You know all about minutes, do you! You want me to believe that show you're putting on for me? You faker! Don't worry, I'll get you where I want you!"

The investigator tore up the minutes. Why was he so furious? Why did his voice sound so disappointed when he ordered the one with the red cheeks and the horse head: "Take him away, that faker. You've got to watch out for that one! Put him in solitary confinement."

*

In the middle of the night, he woke up because he had heard noises as if the seven devils were scheming some nasty trick against him. Then he remembered that he had been taken to a different cell. Reassured he closed his eyes. But the bunk was made of hard wood. His whole body was stiff. Every bone, every inch of skin was hurting. No matter how he turned and changed his position, nothing but pain. It was impossible to fall asleep. He sat up. The lamp here was not as bright as the one in the cell he had shared with the others; it gave a dim yellow light. That did him good; his eyebrows were not stinging so much. He tried to finish the accounting of the September dues. But he was much too tired, much too beaten-up to even look for the file cards. So he supported his head with his hands and napped a bit. When he woke up again, he saw that he was no longer alone. Many gentlemen in checkered suits were sitting there smoking short stemmed pipes; beside them others, short gentlemen with black goatees, and again others, tall and blond, nordic types, and all of them very elegant, very intelligent-looking, very educated and calm and collected. They spoke English, French, Norwegian, Belgian. The countries of democracy, he thought joyfully. And then he saw in front of them, his hands all tied, Robert Blum. Robert Blum had very beautiful, large eyes, black, curly hair falling down to his shoulders. He was wearing a black velvet jacket and tight-fitting pants. The expression on his face was noble, but they had taken his tie away from him. Everybody was looking at Robert Blum; their faces were stern and reproachful. The countries of democracy are condemning Blum most severely, he thought. What was Blum to him? Let them condemn Blum. Tired he closed his eyes. But then he began to feel sorry for Blum. He thought: oh, comrades, we know, the Western democracies, the Scandinavian countries with their centuries-old democratic tradition, all those countries whose opinion is a matter of life and death for Austria . . .

Life or death. No, he had to defend Robert Blum, had to help him. He opened his eyes again. Now he saw among the foreigners some well-dressed gentlemen who spoke like fellow countrymen. Good, solid middle-class citizens, he thought. And then he jumped to his feet with decision. Robert Blum gave him a proud and grateful look. He placed himself behind Blum, opened his arms in a dramatic gesture, and began to speak:

"Respected gentlemen, dear members of the Party. I take the liberty of speaking here as a person whose heart has always beaten for the small Republic of Austria; who, with due modesty and circumspection, has always done his duty; who, his rifle at the ready, has kept the Republic free from all deceptive temptations of certain elements; who, with the weapons of the spirit, knew how to protect the hard-won rights of the proletariat and who, for twenty-nine years . . ."

It was the first time he had spoken in a meeting without having a financial report in front of him. In spite of that, he did not stutter, his voice sounded full and strong as always when he presented his report for audit. All eyes were directed toward him, admiringly. The longer he spoke, the larger the audience became. The investigator appeared, lowered his head attentively so that one could see his pate shining like patent leather. Blum's wife appeared, beautiful and radiant, put her hands over her breasts and pressed her thighs tightly together as she had done that night. The sister-in-law sat next to her and looked remorseful; at one time everybody in the room turned round and pointed their fingers like flashes of lightning at her. Then all the spokesmen of the section came and sat down in an orderly manner, block after block. Spannmeier carried a big wreath of flowers with the inscription: "To Our Hero!" Willi and the two policemen, the one with the horse head and the one with the red cheeks, wanted to come in, but the investigator turned red as a beet, and they disappeared.

He saw all that while he stood behind Robert Blum and spoke.

"You are judging the deed of a human being. But, respected members of the Imperial Court, even if Robert Blum's action was a rash action, you comrades will understand. Robert Blum did not leave any opportunity untried to show his willingness for negotiations. Robert Blum said to the government: 'The state is in danger? All right. Let's discuss measures which can alleviate the real needs of the people as well as lessen injustice. We are willing to cooperate positively within the framework . . .' Thus spoke Robert Blum, worthy members of the Party. He was filled with a sense of responsibility, an example of coolheadedness. He was a fighter for the people; for him freedom was worth more than pure gold. But what happened? Certain gentlemen wanted to satisfy their desires, and, oh comrades, we know those gentlemen, they are the same as in 1918 . . . Then the day came when Robert Blum's patience, strained to the breaking point, broke. His action may have been rash. But . . ."

At this point everybody shouted bravo. It was a rally of the 200,000. He only wished that those gentlemen who had certain desires were present.

". . . it is understandable. He regrets his action deeply. He knows that western democracies with their centuries of culture . . .

But I am pleading to you to understand his error. I am pleading for mercy and forgiveness because he was not responsible for his action. Members of the Court, I as a decent person promise you he won't ever, he will never do it again . . ."

"Shut up in there. You go to sleep or I'll fix ya up so you won't know your own name, you red dog."

Everything vanished. Timidly he looked for the devils. He'd forgotten he was alone. He tiptoed to his bunk and lay down. He gritted his teeth to suppress the pain.

When the officer started to interrogate him again next morning an excited policeman came in and reported that the man who had been brought in intoxicated during the night had awakened sober this morning and had told his cell mates that he had blown up a garage. The guard had accidentally heard it through the door.

"Bring him here!" The officer ordered and, pointing at Blum: "Take him away."

As they pushed the man by him in the corridor, his heart wanted to stop. It was Richard Kainz . . . Kainz was sober but very agitated. He screamed incessantly:

"You don't know a thing. I have nothing to do with the matter. I wasn't even near the Russ garage. I have an alibi."

That evening the one with the horse head came into his cell and morosely said nothing but: "Pack up, you can go home."

It was a wonderful, dry October evening. He could leave his coat open, the air was so mild. He gave a friendly smile to all the people in the street. His heart jumped with joy; he felt it all the way up in his neck around which he wore his tie again. He was just about to purse his lips to whistle a song when he heard a voice behind him: "Blum, Blum, Blumekin."

He wasn't Blum if that wasn't Spannmeier.

"Of course we all knew that you were innocent. Our treasurer Blum was supposed to have blown up a garage? Ha—ha—ha. Of course we postponed the meeting; Hadina objected naturally, that opportunist. He already thought he'd get your job. But everyone else said: Blum has got to get out any day, you bet your life. No meeting without Blum. Good heavens, are you a sight! They sure beat you up, the brutes."

"I can't remember", said Blum, "I can't remember a thing."

His eyes filled with tears of joy, his glasses fogged up. Spannmeier opened his arms wide. Robert Blum flung his arms round his neck.

The Corner

Erich lost the semi-final of the "New World" chess tournament after twelve moves. Then he tried to overlook Panetti's hand for a time. The latter's trumps rained down on the table like cannon balls. Erich lay down on a bench and pretended, for five minutes, to be asleep, so as to get to sleep in actual fact. But it was no good. He looked out into the street. He tried to pace the room for a while, then thought: what's the use? He watched the others. Fritz began to draw a plan of the city's sewer system on a sheet of paper. But his pencil described an arc at the second street corner, crossed the whole drawing out and broke with a faint, dry, cracking sound. Kaliwoda, the little Commandant, was pacing up and down. Suddenly he sat down at the big table, without knowing what he was doing. For a long time it seemed that Holzer had actually fallen asleep. But then he pushed his cap off his face and swung his legs from the bench to the floor. He groped for his cigarette case. His hand brushed his stubbly cheeks and he grimaced comically, rubbing his chin. Panetti's three companions at the cardtable played like sleep-walkers. Probably the only reason why Panetti himself did not throw the cards away was because it amused him to thump the table every five seconds with a shout of: "Bang! Crash!" Erich wondered whether a girl would give him any pleasure at this particular moment. He tried to sketch the figure of a naked woman in the smoke-laden atmosphere, but the figure melted away in the stinking haze of the Flirt cigarettes. The thirty men of the Defense Corps, who had now been on alert for five hours, had fallen practically silent by this time.

Then, suddenly, every head jerked round at one and the same instant. For some seconds the whole world shrank to a telephone. Thirty pairs of eyes stared at it. Steindl sat there, holding the receiver. He said: "Headquarters? Who's speaking?" Then there was nothing but silence and in the silence Steindl's face. Steindl's face listened. It said: "Thanks." Then there was nothing but Steindl's voice. It said in a low tone: "I repeat the message. If nothing happens during the next half hour the unit can be dismissed. Freedom!"

A few matches flared up. Someone said: "So they didn't find anything in the *Vorwärts* office?" Another answered: "Of course they didn't. You know perfectly well that there are no arms there." Sennhofer exclaimed: "Let's start the final. Fritz and Lederer!" Kaliwoda laughed. He said: "Steindl, you fathead, you forgot again to say, 'Any eavesdroppers can kiss my ass!'" He laughed again and added: "One of you might at least open a window. This room stinks like the plague with all you miserable scum having to smoke like you do." No one joined in Kaliwoda's laughter. He said no more. Paskus opened the window. Damp and cold air drifted into the room. A truck rattled by out in the street and made the lamp hanging from the ceiling rock to and fro. There was a little snow sticking to the window. It began to melt. A few drops rolled lazily, like tears, down the moist panes. The cigarette smoke slowly disappeared. Instead of it, some kind of disagreeable smell mounted to the room from the street.

"Where's that stench of soot coming from?" asked Warenberger. He lay down, tall and broad as he was, on the rickety bench.

Gstettner lifted his high forehead from the table-top and explained at some length that the stench didn't come from soot, but from melting snow.

Someone thumped the table, not Panetti's table, but the big one. It was Herrmann, who had crashed his fist down upon it for no apparent reason. "Almighty God in Heaven!" he shouted. But his moon face remained as expressionless as ever.

A dozen men were sitting and standing in a circle round Sennhofer. The latter was talking. "Yes. A little fat guy. You must know him. He's Chief Inspector. He wanted to know whether I was still the caretaker of the house. 'Of course I am,' I said. 'Why shouldn't I still be the caretaker?' Then he asked me whether the rifle-range was still being used. 'Certainly,' I said. 'So far as I know, shooting clubs are not yet forbidden.' Well, I had to take him downstairs. Of course, there was nothing more in his head but the idea of scaring me to death, as he had nothing better to do. You're sure to know him, a little fatso. Regular Nazi, the killer type. Well, as you can guess, he nosed round, of course, for a devil of a time. Then he actually started trying to trip me up. Wanted to know whether the range was any good. Well, that was too much for my patience, as you may imagine. 'No good at all,' I said and called my wife and daughter. 'Now watch, Inspector,' I said. My wife took aim. A bull's eye. The kiddie did the same. Another bull's eye. 'And I fought in the war,' I said to him. 'If you like you can have a look at my marksman's certificate.' He opened his eyes at that, I can tell you."

There were a dozen more sitting round the big table. Panetti was talking. "So if we had the Anna-Hof, at the end of Franz-Masarelli-Street, then, don't you see, we could command the whole of Tamas Square. Because there's a nice little domed roof up there, don't you see, and if we had a machine-gun up there . . ."

"We sit here talking," said Herrmann—his face was as flat as a pancake and equally expressionless—"We sit here talking about civil war, just like a lot of old widows plotting love-affairs."

"Shut the window," Kaliwoda said. Bobby limped to the window and closed it. The cylindrical stove crackled. Above it a bust of Victor Adler stood on a ledge against the wall and stared with its empty eyes over the thirty heads into a corner of the room, where there was nothing to see.

This was the eleventh time the men had been put on alert that January. Every movement and gesture, every hope had had its hour and was finally played out. Every word and phrase had been used up. They had now settled down into a little office on the top floor of a big building, and everything beyond it was foreign territory to them. This part of the city in which they had been born and had grown up, the splendid, noisy, teeming workers' district, was now silent, as if numbed in the January mud, for trucks full of soldiers were rumbling through the streets. The city, once known as "Red Vienna," had grown timid, almost hostile to them. It was a foreign city. They felt forgotten, abandoned, and very lonely.

The sound of many footsteps and the faint clink of metal

came to their ears from the staircase. They knew at once that it was the police.

In the breathless stillness of the room a harsh, forced laughter rang out suddenly. It was Kaliwoda's. "It's our turn for a little visit now, boys. Anyone who forgets himself will have to answer to me for it later. Understand?"

The door was thrust open and swung with a crash against the wall. Eight policemen, with leveled revolvers, stood on the threshold. "Hands up!" called the Inspector. It was the little fat fellow Sennhofer had been talking about. None of the thirty moved their hands. "Hands up!" repeated the fat guy. His voice was hoarse and lacked assurance. Gstettner stood up, his chair creaked. The uneasy faces of the policemen all turned in his direction.

Gstettner, the leather-worker, folded his arms across his chest. He looked as dignified as a high postal official. His fair, reddish whiskers gleamed softly in the light of the swinging lamp. Kaliwoda's laugh rang out again, unexpectedly. "Come in, Chief Inspector. Nobody here has anything illegal on them." There was anger in the eyes of the fat fellow as he let the hand holding the revolver fall irresolutely and advanced into the room. The other seven policemen followed him. They, too, had lowered their weapons. The Chief Inspector pointed to the corner of the room towards which the bust of Victor Adler was gazing. "Get over there, the lot of you!" he ordered. Bobby, who was standing in the middle of the room, immediately under the lamp, made three, hasty, limping steps in the required direction. Then he saw that he was the only one who had moved. He blushed to the roots of his hair and stopped.

"D'ya hear me?" the Inspector demanded in an expressionless tone, raising his revolver. Kaliwoda smiled, remained silent for a few seconds and then murmured: "Well, off you go then, comrades." Those who were seated or lying down stood up. Everyone moved sluggishly, as slowly and as near to the revolvers as they could, towards the corner. Erich saw the Inspector turn pale. Erich's heart was beating like a roll of drums. He perceived, without surprise, that he was ready, at that moment, to obey blindly whatever orders the white-faced little unemployed man with the harsh laugh, their Kaliwoda, might give. As soon as they were all penned in the corner, three of the men in green uniforms came forward and planted themselves so as to face the group. These three men were young, freshly shaved and shiny like racehorses with the health that comes from plenty of good food and hard exercise. Their eyes seemed vigilant, but when Erich gave one of them a steady glance the man lowered his eyes. Fritz, who was standing next to Erich, said in an unrecognizable voice:

"Well, I'll be . . ."

"Silen-n-ce!"

As if this warning had been an order addressed to themselves two of the policemen rushed to the windows, brandishing pickaxes, which Erich now observed for the first time. They started banging away at the wooden paneling. It splintered in all directions. Panetti, as though he were standing in an ordinary chance assembly in the street, pushed his way through the members of the Defense Corps and past the policemen.

"Are you going to pay for that damage?" he asked. With a movement of the shoulder he jerked himself free of a man in green who had seized his arm. Cries broke out of the closely packed group of thirty like a burst of machine-gun fire.

"Tell us what you want here!"

"What's the game, eh?"

"Who gave you permission to smash up a room like that?"

Another commented in a caustic mutter:

"Why don't you try the Heimwehr? You'll have better luck there!"

That was an imprudent thing to say, thought Erich, at the same moment realizing that it had been he who had said it. There was a shining red collar-tab within a few feet of his eyes. Suddenly he found that he could not tear his gaze away from it. The stuff's wide enough to catch hold of, he thought, and immediately afterwards, no, that's silly. He forced himself to look away and his glance fell upon the face of the young policeman. The latter's lower jaw was trembling. He was frightened. The pickaxes were hacking frantically at the paneled wall. Panetti and the Inspector were standing immediately under the lamp, within a few feet of one another. The fat guy barked: "Keep your mouth shut!" He tried to push Panetti back with his right hand. The revolver stuck in his left hand seemed a superfluous and inconvenient object. Panetti did not move. The two men in green uniforms at the window hacked away, blind and deaf to all else, the last remnants of the paneling, though the wall behind it had been well in view for a long time. The three young policemen's eyes leapt from one member of the Defense Corps to another, as if they were trying to guess which of them would make the first move to attack. The two by the door did not budge. All eight of them were afraid. "Come here, Panetti," ordered Kaliwoda.

"All right, I'll stand in the corner for a bit," murmured Panetti. He turned his back on the Inspector and joined the rest. It was clear from the Inspector's face that he understood the situation. He was thinking, "I have nothing to fear." And also, "I have lost my head." He threw Kaliwoda a glance full of open and irreconcilable hatred and gave an angry order to the two men at the window. "Stop that!" Then he spoke to the whole detachment.

"Frisk them!"

The fingers that felt Erich's clothes were trembling. He did as the others did. He raised his arms, held his tongue and smiled as scornfully as he could. No weapons were found on any of the thirty.

"Take the wardrobe now," said the Inspector. The wardrobe was not locked. But the police made no attempt to open the door. They demolished it with their pickaxes. Inside were a few overcoats and the file of the "Friends of the Children." The Inspector rapped on the walls. Kaliwoda laughed.

"Try the wall here," said the Inspector. The policemen got to work with their pickaxes on the wall behind the big table. The hanging lamp rocked, casting a livid light on the scene. Thick fragments of plaster fell to the floor.

"Almighty God in Heaven . . ." breathed Herrmann.

"Quiet, there," Kaliwoda enjoined him.

"Now by the stove," said the Inspector, swinging round on his heel. His voice was hoarse. The air was full of dust from the plaster. The walls behind the table and near the stove were laid bare to the brickwork, to a height of about six feet.

"Give me that thing," said the Inspector, putting his revolver back into its holster. He took a pickaxe from one of the policemen. With four blows he laid the big table in ruins. The telephone fell to the floor.

"Has he gone mad?" Warenberger shrieked.

"Quiet, there," Kaliwoda ordered him.

The Inspector turned to Kaliwoda. They could see that his eyes were bloodshot. He went to the bench and hacked it to pieces. Except for him, everyone in the room remained perfectly still. The policemen stood as though rooted to the floor, fidgeting with their pistols. The Inspector smashed a chair to pieces and turned again to Kaliwoda. Then he grunted something incomprehensible, stood on tip-toe and swung the pickaxe to the full extent of his arm as though he were going to strike someone dead. He aimed at the bust, but did not hit it. The blow struck the ledge upon which it stood. Victor Adler's head, with its empty eyes, bowed respectfully to the company, turned a somersault, fell against the stove and collapsed in a heap of fragments of plaster.

Kaliwoda laughed.

"Pack up!" said the Inspector, more to himself than to his men. The latter walked backwards to the door, like animal-tamers leaving a cage. The last of them, the one who shut the door, had a good-humored face with plump, pock-marked cheeks, mottled red and white from excitement. This face, before it disappeared, suddenly became distorted, grimaced and yelled at them: "We're coming back, you damned, dirty reds!" Then he slammed the door and it was all over. The clock on the wall above the hacked bricks and mortar near the stove struck the half hour shyly. What had seemed an eternity to them had lasted in all only ten minutes.

A torrent of words boiled up in Erich's breast. But shame prevented him from uttering them. Could a man hold his tongue all through that damnable business and then, the moment the police were out of the room, start yapping? All the others, too, stood silent in their corner for some seconds. It was not until Kaliwoda went to the telephone and knelt down beside it that their stupor broke. Erich found himself standing before the wrecked wall, gaping with ten others at the bricks, as though a miracle had happened. Then he discovered that he was pressing his forehead against the cold windowpane. Next, that he was standing beside Kaliwoda, who was talking into the telephone.

"I repeat the message. The unit is dismissed. Freedom!"

Then Erich found himself looking at the chess board, while Panetti commented on the situation. "That wasn't a proper search for weapons. That fellow cared far less about finding anything than about scaring the shit out of us."

Erich heard himself say:

"Perhaps they'd have made a decent job of it if they hadn't been scared out of their wits themselves."

Next, he was stumbling among the fragments of plaster.

Gstettner was kneeling near him and trying in vain to fit the smashed head of Victor Adler together again. He kept on saying: "We'll put him on our list, we'll get even with him, he won't get away with that." Erich heard himself say: "What a God damn shame that one should have to put up with such things, damnation.—Don't bother, Gstettner. You'll never be able to stick him together again."

The next thing that Erich saw was Herrmann standing under the lamp with his head thrown back, staring into the light. Herrmann was saying, almost without moving his lips, "I tell you I'm ashamed. I don't know how it is with you guys. But I'm ashamed."

Kaliwoda's voice shredded those of the rest into insignificance.

"Curtains, boys! Quit flitting about the room like chickens with their heads cut off, pack up and go to bed. And don't you worry about what's happened. They can all kiss our ass, as I said to the eavesdroppers on the phone. It won't be long now, we'll pay them back!"

But as Erich was taking down his overcoat, he heard Kaliwoda say quietly from behind him:

"You stay here, Weigel."

To sweep up the plaster, I suppose, thought Erich, as he sat down on the one sound bench. All the others left the room, till only he, the Commandant, and Hans remained. Kaliwoda told them to wait, and disappeared. The window had been opened. The lamp was hanging perfectly still at last. Their lungs inhaled fresh air. Recent events began almost visibly to retreat into the past. They already seemed so far away that it was possible to meditate on them. But what meditations could there be? And what else could one say but: "The same old story"? "The same old story!" said Hans, letting his arms go limp in resignation.

Erich watched him curiously. When was it that he, Hans' former leader in the Socialist Youth, had last had a proper talk with him? It had been a good six months ago, when they had been so badly defeated at the trade-union meeting. Had they still been allowed then to show their red flags or not? Had they still been allowed to speak against Italy? Had the edict against striking already been in force? God Almighty! How imperceptibly, with what devilish cunning one of their rights after the other had been taken away from them, had they been forced into a corner!

There were three, no, four dates to remember. The eleventh of March, the day of that great farmers' rally; the fifteenth of March, when Parliament was dissolved; the twenty-ninth of March, when the Defense Corps was disbanded—or was that on the first of April? In September the Heimwehr marched out to the Trotting Course, that was on the seventeenth, or was that the date when the *Arbeiter-Zeitung* was first censored? Between those three or four dates nothing seemed to have happened and yet everything had. A swamp had formed. And in that swamp the Party was slowly and helplessly sinking.

"Yes, that's right. But, Hans, I never see you nowadays. I thought for ages you'd cut loose, like Franz. But I trained you too well for you to do that, didn't I? What have you been up to, then, all this long time?"

"Nothing much," Hans said. His appearance had changed a good deal. His eyes were harder. His features were harder. His voice was harder.

"Been reading a lot?"

"Sure."

"What?" Erich asked, partly from former habit and partly for the sake of hearing a comrade's report as so often before in fervent, passionate, slightly stilted language.

"Well, Otto Bauer's *The Austrian Revolution*, Max Adler's *New Humanity* and Kautsky's *Materialist Interpretation of History*. But I only just looked through that last one. Then I read . . ."

Those were the days, thought Erich. Without listening to

Hans' reply he talked on, as he would have talked if Paula had been there, Paula, the stupidest of his group—his group? Where was it now, and where were those days?

"Did you lose a lot of time, having to be on alert tonight?"

"No."

"Got a girl just now?"

"Nothing special."

"Well, you know, it's the same with me. And I really don't want one. As a matter of fact, while we were sitting here and waiting again, as usual, sick and tired of everything, gestures, words, thoughts, and the rest of it, I was wondering what sort of action I could take in my life which could still interest me. I found only one thing I wanted to do: to level a rifle and pull the trigger."

"Same here," Hans said. "But there's not much sense in that."

"In what? In pulling the trigger?"

"No. In being sentimental."

Listen to him! thought Erich. He took a good look at Hans. The man's very glance had changed. His voice had changed. His whole being had hardened.

Kaliwoda returned to the room. He was carrying the very last things that Erich had expected to see. Three pickaxes, a trowel, and a bucket of lime.

Kaliwoda pointed to the corner where they had been standing while they were being searched for weapons. He said: "Cut open the wall, boys, and take out the boxes." Then he indicated the mutilated section of the wall near the stove. "We'll wall them up again over there. I'll show you how to do it. If that gang really comes back they'll look everywhere except there. Get the idea?"

"A—Arms?" stammered Erich.

Kaliwoda's harsh laugh rang out, the strange laugh he had had the whole evening.

"And—and what would you have done, Kali, if they'd looked in the right place?"

Kaliwoda closed his eyes. His tiny face suddenly looked very strange, as though it had been bruised and kneaded.

"Well, if you'd really like to know, I'd have gone for the fat guy's throat. And some of us would have had to take their medicine. And then we'd have done the whole eight of them in, dogs and brutes that they are."

Suddenly the little Commandant's body, as though seized by an unseen hand, shook from head to foot. He raised his clenched fists. His jaws parted.

"I'm hungry!" he yelled at the top of his voice. "D'you hear me, Weigel? I'm hungry, I tell you! And I can't stand it any longer!"

Then, without a tremor, suddenly and noiselessly, like a bundle of old clothes, he collapsed.

Erich turned helplessly to Hans. But the latter was already in the doorway.

"I'll get something from the restaurant. I've got the key to the door. Wait here."

"Eh—Hans . . ." Erich began. But Hans was already on the landing below. Erich had no clear recollection of what he did during the next few minutes. He only remembered, for a long time afterwards, the cold, sticky sweat on Kaliwoda's face. He must have stroked or rubbed his forehead. As he came back to the room from the landing with a glass of water—was water any use when a man fainted from hunger?—Kaliwoda was already sitting, with open eyes, against the wrecked wall.

"That's not necessary," he said in a hoarse voice. "My nerves are a bit ragged, that's all."

Erich knelt down beside him. Little Kaliwoda, pale as a corpse, with two thin, violet streaks where his lips should have been, and his jaw bones trembling, had already assumed the authoritative tone he used during instruction.

"But remember, Weigel, what I meant to do then had nothing to do with the state of my nerves. And what I now mean to do is the only thing possible in the mess we've got into. The Party chiefs have managed to get our cart stuck fast in the mud. Mark my words. The only thing that's going to help us now is action."

"Do you mean terrorism, Kali? I can't believe that from you! After all, you're a trained Socialist—I mean, a trained Marxist . . ."

Two red spots had appeared on the Commandant's high, pointed cheek-bones and were growing darker moment by moment.

"Everything you're trying to tell me, Weigel, would have some chance of convincing me if I hadn't been preaching it to my own fellows for the last year. I know the whole box of tricks by heart, do you get me? 'Bide your time!'—'Keep your weapons oiled!'—'Revolutionary patience'"!

He gave a dry cough and spat, irritated at having to interrupt himself. Little threads of blood showed in his spittle. "The only chance of success is by mass action, eh? Isolated acts of desperation only provoke aggravation of the terrorist methods of the police, eh? Well? Do I know the old chorus or don't I? I tell you I know it backwards! This very night I was grinding it out again, one pretty little bit after another, till the boys shouted that they had had enough of it. Because that's still supposed to be my job and I'm responsible, damn it! And already I've been saying to myself for weeks on end, 'Enough! Enough!'"

He coughed again, tried to go on speaking through the cough, gasped, coughed harder than ever and spat. Spat blood.

"No, Weigel. It's over now. Mark my words. Those Jewish leaders of ours at Headquarters have been ruining us long enough. We've got to start it now or else it'll be too late."

"First you'd better have something to eat," said a new voice behind Erich. He turned around. It was Hans, carrying a bowl of soup and a package.

Kaliwoda's face reddened all over. He stammered like a small boy, refused the food, then began to eat.

Hans lectured him gently as he ate. Erich's head whirled, in a storm of doubt, fear, and despair. He did not take in the sense of what Hans was saying. He only perceived, with stupefaction that grew greater and greater, somewhere beyond the storm that was raging in his head, that Kaliwoda was listening attentively to little Hans, the youngest of their circle. For this reason Erich murmured from time to time, when Hans stopped speaking. "I say, Kali! I say, Kali!"

As soon as Kaliwoda had finished eating, he laid his hand on Hans' arm and said:

"You're not going to convince me, Hans. But I'm pleased with you. Go on as you are, keep it up. If things do ever get as far as you say they will, if a real revolutionary party comes out of it all, you'll be a big noise one day—"he corrected himself without smiling—"You'll be a real leader."

"That's quite a secondary matter for the present," Hans answered, wrinkling his brows.

They stayed there for some time, crouching under the gently swinging, yellow lamp, among the pieces of plaster from which Gstettner had in vain tried to reconstruct Victor Adler's head. Then they took up their pickaxes and went to work on the wall.

EPILOG

Song of the Twentieth-Century Man

Human we were counted once perhaps,
Or one far-off day we may be so
When we've found an answer to these traps;
But, here and now, to call us human? No.

We're just a name that's written on a pass,
A dumb reflection in a looking-glass,
The echo of what once was finely said,
The rumor of a rumor that's long dead.

What was human long ago stamped out—
Why should we keep up the empty show?
In our faceless cities swirled about
Shall we still pretend we're human? No.

We are the dust that's blown from lamp to lamp,
The queue that waits for the official stamp,
The number in a bureaucratic file,
And our own shadows could not be more vile.

Something human struggles to be free,
One way only that can help us know:
All the time to ask if men we be,
All the time to give the answer: no!

A poor, half-finished sketch is all we are,
A glimpse of humans in their final state—
A tune suggested by the opening bar—
You call us wretches human beings?—Wait!

Translated by John Lehmann

"We are the dust that's blown from lamp to lamp, The queue that waits for the official stamp . . ."

From the program *It's up to us!* Soyfer Theater, Guest performance, London 1987.

Dachau Song

Over the entrance to Dachau Concentration Camp stood the words:
ARBEIT MACHT FREI Work makes free

> Pitiless the barbed wire dealing
> Death, that round our prison runs,
> And a sky that knows no feeling
> Sends us ice and burning suns;
> Lost to us the world of laughter,
> Lost our hopes, our loves, our all;
> Through the dawn our thousands muster,
> To their work in silence fall.

But the slogan of Dachau is burned on our brains
And unwielding as steel we shall be;
Are we men, brother? Then we'll be men when they're done,
Work on, we'll go through with the task we've begun,
For work, brother, work makes us free.

        Haunted by the gun mouths turning
        All our days and nights are spent;
        Toil is ours—the way we're learning
        Harder than we ever dreamt;
        Weeks and months we cease to reckon
        Pass, and some forget the years,
        And so many men are broken
        And their faces changed with fears.

But the slogan of Dachau is burnt on our brains . . .

        Heave the stone and drag the truck,
        Let no load's oppression show,
        In your days of youth and luck
        You thought lightly: now you know.
        Plunge your spade in earth and shovel
        Pity where heart cannot feel,
        Purged in your own sweat and trouble
        Be yourself like stone and steel.

For the slogan of Dachau is burnt on our brains . . .

        One day sirens will be shrieking
        One more roll-call, but the last.
        And the stations we'll be seeking—
        Outside, brother, prison past!
        Bright the eyes of Freedom burning,
        World to build with joy and zest
        And the work begun that morning,
        Yes, that work will be our best!

For the slogan of Dachau is burnt on our brains
And unyielding as steel we shall be;
Are we men, brother? Then we'll be men when they've done,
Work on, we'll go through with the work we've begun,
For work, brother, work makes us free.

                              Translated by John Lehmann

Afterword

"It's up to us!" Is it?—in a time when our lives are more and more determined by forces beyond our control, when what is still "up to us" is restricted to our personal lives that seem to matter less and less? Is the title of this book then another example of that irony that drapes desperation or indifference with an air of cool superiority? It is taken from one of Soyfer's works in which despair ends in a renewal of faith in human freedom. A passionate answer to that individualism that sanctifies social apathy, Soyfer's plea for personal responsibility and collective ethics permeates all of his work written in a time that year after year proved him wrong. He screamed it into the growing darkness. Soyfer's protest against any kind of determinism inspired all his writing up to the last poem that he wrote in a concentration camp. John Lehmann, Soyfer's English friend, said of him: "The story of this young writer stands for me as an epitome of all the dignity and tragedy of the time of fascist triumph and threatening war."

Jura Soyfer was born on 8 December 1912, the son of a Jewish industrialist in Kharkov, Ukraine. When the Bolshevik Revolution reached Kharkov, the family escaped via Georgia and Turkey. In 1921 they reached Austria, and in 1922 settled in Vienna. In the Soyfer household Russian and French had been spoken. At the age of nine, Jura learned German and soon spoke it like a native. His multilingual upbringing provided him, as it did Horváth, with a sensitivity to linguistic nuances which was heightened by attending Karl Kraus' lectures and reading his famous satiric magazine *Die Fackel*. Jura's friend Mitja Rapoport, also a son of a Russian emigré family, inspired him to read Marxist literature at the age of fifteen. All around him Soyfer saw Socialism in the making.

Young Soyfer's Vienna was the now legendary Red Vienna where the Social Democratic municipal government, defying the aftermath of the war, proved that the working masses could find welfare and civilized conditions of life without a Communist revolution. It was the Vienna of Julius Tandler's pioneering work in public health, of Otto Glöckel's school reform, of Hugo Breitner's ingenious finance policies that made it possible for hundred of thousands to live in decent housing. Every day on his way to school Soyfer passed the site where another of the municipal housing blocks was growing, symbolizing more visibly than anything else the new order.

And yet, early on, and in spite of its success, envied by the world, this visionary experiment was threatened. Austria of the interwar period was not a country of tolerance, of "social partnership between Capital and Labor" as we know it today; it was a country of heated conflict. After the war the suffering country, unaccustomed to the challenges of democracy, was split wide open into the violently oppositional camps: conservative, reactionary, and left-wing. The first showdown came in 1927 with the acquittal of right-wing extremists who, in a skirmish with Socialists, had killed two uninvolved bystanders: the incensed masses demonstrated, the Palace of Justice was set on fire, and police fired into the multitude. It was a decisive date in Austria's history, and, like all such dates of that period, decisive in young Soyfer's life. Peace was restored, but the fire smoldered, the battle was on, and Soyfer joined it, joined the Socialist Association of High-School Students, became one of their most active members and soon one of their "poets." Jura, who had started writing poems when he was fourteen, now found the audience that encouraged his talent. The *Schulkampf* (School-Struggle), the organization's journal, published the satirical pieces with which he took a still modest but impassioned part in the fight for a new pedagogic vision of creating schools for thinking instead of rote learning. Viktor Grünbaum, *spiritus rector* of the Social Democratic Party Cabaret invited Jura to join this collective of impertinent spirits that made fun of the Party leaders in the audience, but mostly supported election campaign rallies with agitprop sketches. Some of these Jura wrote in school to combat his boredom.

In 1931 he was relieved to graduate from high school and begin his studies of German and history at the University of Vienna. In the very same semester Josef Nadler, the pan-

German professor of German literature, began teaching there, an academic appointment symptomatic of the tendency in Austrian humanities. Soyfer's second subject, too, under the influence of Heinrich von Srbik, became a "deutsche Wissenschaft" (a German science). 1931 was a crucial year for Soyfer and for Austria. In September the Austrofascist Walter Pfrimer tried a coup to take over the country; his miserable failure made him a laughing stock. But Pfrimer's acquittal by a jury was no joke. The case prompted Soyfer's first poem in the *Arbeiter-Zeitung*. With its passionate exposure of the "conservative" government's hypocrisy and its defiant call for justice, it set the tone for many of Soyfer's poems that followed. For the next two years, the *Arbeiter-Zeitung* (Workers' Paper), the official organ of Austrian Social Democracy under its chief editor Oskar Pollak, with a readership of 100,000, regularly published Soyfer's satirical pieces. The name "Jura," with which he signed them, soon became a household word among the Austrian left. That most of them appeared in a satirical column entitled *Zwischenrufe links* (Catcalls from the Left) indicates Soyfer's position clearly enough. He belonged to the left opposition within the Party who criticized the schizophrenic attitude of the leadership who practiced defensive withdrawal in the face of the rise of fascism even as they preached revolution in their propaganda.

Soyfer and other young members like Ernst Fischer demanded that the propaganda of strength be followed by action. The battle lines of the Depression were clearly marked; Soyfer celebrated the imminent collapse of capitalism and attacked all the forces that prolonged its moribund system. He attacked the Austrofascists, the Nazis in Germany and in Austria, the trend towards authoritarianism that swept all of central Europe; he pleaded for unity of the working class, for international solidarity against the common enemy, capitalism. The passionate indignation of Soyfer's poems made them perhaps the most rebellious voice in the revolutionary chorus of Party propaganda. Hilde Spiel has called Soyfer's poems the most directly political in the Austria of the early 'thirties. They were battle cries on two fronts: against the aggressive attackers and the reluctant attacked. Their sharp satirical force castigating injustice, hypocrisy, corruption make them, very much like Heine's political poems, still readable today for those who are willing to ferret out the political intrigues, the skirmishes of the daily politics, the marionettes, long and rightly forgotten, who peopled the political stage of those two years. What made Soyfer's satires so effective in their time, the verbal games, puns, allusions that offered the reader the joy of recognition, makes their translation almost impossible and, for American readers today, pointless. There are, however, a few whose language and, unfortunately, themes transcend such limitations, and some of these are included in this volume. The first section shows variations of Soyfer's indignation about the "order," the capitalist order, that was held up as God-given. The misery addressed in these pieces was worldwide, and three poems show how much Soyfer shared the general European left-wingers' view of the United States. Soyfer's diagnosis of his own generation as victim of the Depression was valid, of course, not only for Austria. The escape mechanisms he exposed were, as we know, of special relevance in Austria and Germany. All these pieces of evidence in Soyfer's accusation show the fascination Socialism must have held for those who did not want to be ground up by "this order." That in another article of the time he also sensed the intoxicating, false security provided by Socialist rallies attests to Soyfer's realistic psychology. The few poems about Germany prove how clearly Soyfer saw what many in his time did not want to see: that Hitler's aim was war, and that concentration camps were established immediately after Hitler came to, or rather was given, power.

While Soyfer established his name as a satirical poet, he went on writing agitprop scenes for party rallies, simple but effective allegories of the class struggle that today are of historical value only. They appeared in *Die politische Bühne* (The Political Stage) which also published two of his theoretical pieces, one of which is included in this volume. It was selected not only to bring out the irony that slogans which once made the blood rise have long since become hollow phrases; his criticism of the insidious trash with which the entertainment industry showers public consciousness has lost nothing of its incisiveness.

Encouraged by his publications in the *Arbeiter-Zeitung*, one of the most respected papers of the day, Soyfer tried to gain independence from his family through a career in political journalism. The polarization between left and right that characterized political life in Austria was dramatically intensified in Germany and, in the summer of 1932, as a self-appointed reporter, Soyfer spent several weeks there, eager to observe developments. His poems, reportages, and letters of those two months are the record of an Austrian radical left-winger witnessing the agony of the Weimar Republic. Feeling secure in his un-Jewish appearance (Jura looked rather "Russian," his friends recall), he passed the night in the home of a German with whom he had participated in a Nazi torchlight parade. In Braunschweig he heard Hitler speak and was "amazed at the mindlessness and brutality of this magician of the masses." He arrived in Berlin a few days after von Papen had removed the Social Democratic Government of Prussia, and he was appalled by the passivity of the SPD. While in the reports he sent to the *Arbeiter Zeitung* in Vienna he followed the party line, in the letters to his girlfriend Marika Szecsi he gave vent to his true feelings:

"The S.P. did not fulfill your cherished hope and capitulated most shamefully, and missed a great opportunity since the State machinery and the workers' ideology were relatively advantageous for decisive action. The working class in Germany is revolutionized through and through, and tears come to one's eyes when one sees how these magnificent proletarians with all their fighting energy have to perish lining up at the unemployment office because Wels is Wels and Thälmann is Thälmann." [Wels was one of the leaders of the Social Democrats and Thälmann the leader of the KPD (The German Communist Party)].

Soyfer hoped for a revolution of a united left beyond the bickering of the party establishments. His hopes were rekindled by the Reichstag Election on July 31, but doubt, even disillusionment followed soon enough:

"As long we are talking about the Social Democrats, I firmly believe that the theory "I know that I know nothing" is the only correct attitude concerning German politics at this time. What I mean is that it would be naive to believe that even Hitler knows what he's doing, let alone what he is going to do. The "factors" of German politics, from the old idiot Hindenburg (if I say that aloud the next cop has me instantly arrested) to the confused degenerate von Papen and the poor pathological case Adolf Hitler, don't know what to do and would love to change places with me because I know at least where I'm going to be three weeks from now and they don't. They are the more or less manipulated exponents of the factions of the bourgeoisie—Papen of the upper, Hitler of the petty bourgeoisie—who now come to claim their right as creditors; these are the roles they play in this miserable flea pit which today calls itself the arena of historic events. The tragedy in all this is, however: who in all this fight will come out on top, whether Germany will be governed under brown or black-white-red colors, that is uncertain. Certain is that the German proletariat today is no longer a factor to be reckoned with. Certain is that some form of fascism, be it in D major or in C flat, is coming over this country like a crippling disease."

And yet Soyfer did not give up hope. His disposition during those weeks in Germany can be best described in his own words; on his way to Hamburg he leaves Berlin "in an incredibly depressing situation with an incredibly fervent fighting spirit."

In Soyfer's mind there was no doubt that Hitler's rule would eventually lead to war. He did not share the illusion so widespread among the left that Hitler would not last, and did not subscribe to the consoling slogan "Nach Hitler kommen wir!" ("After Hitler it's our turn!"). He warned all those who encouraged illusory patience:

> Keep your cool? And just stay calm?
> Easy does it? That's no joke!
> If you knew what truth you spoke:

> Soon the earth, hurt deep inside,
> Wounded, will open, yawning wide.
> Graves like one great corpse-filled chest . . .
> After hell has broken out,
> Raving above and all about.
> Earth will welcome souls to rest—
> You'll take your ease and feel the balm
> Of cemeteries . . . and stay calm.
> And those whom words can never teach
> The calm will shock, the stillness reach;
> If now no words of warning wake you,
> After the storm the calm will shake you!

Soyfer's letters of that summer are also a very personal account of a twenty-year-old introspective intellectual trying to find his bearings in his profession as a journalist and in himself, and there is always that self-irony that undercuts self-pity.

In some of his most acid attacks on Hitler's regime, Soyfer used montages following the example of the German *Arbeiter Illustrierte Zeitung* (Workers' Illustrated): he interpreted newspaper photos by adding satirical verses elaborating on the "message" of the picture, often ironizing the photographer's intention. The Austrian Social Democratic weekly *Der Kuckuck* (The Cuckoo) published these through most of 1933—a sign that Soyfer's talent was gaining recognition. Still, he could never satisfy his ambition: to be acknowledged not only as a satirist but as a political journalist in the Party's leading paper.

The parallels between Germany and Austria became more and more inescapable. Two months after Hitler's triumph, Austrofascism intensified its offensive against parliamentary democracy. In March 1933 Chancellor Engelbert Dollfuss (G.K. Chesterton considered him the defender of the true German spirit) eliminated Parliament and started on his authoritarian course. And Austrian Social Democracy, by hesitating to call a general strike, missed, as it turned out, its last chance to prevent a dictatorship. The workers began to lose faith in their leadership, mass unemployment undermined their resistance and, when in February 1934 the final showdown came, only part of the

Austrian workers rose in arms. The heroic attempt was drowned in blood. Nine Social Democratic leaders were executed, their Party was outlawed, its assets confiscated; many members were put in detention camps, many others lost their jobs.

Soyfer had taken the militancy of his own verse seriously. As a member of the Academic Legion, the students' unit of the Republican Defense Corps, he was ready to fight, but when he came to the rallying point nobody knew where the weapons were hidden. A few days later shell holes gaped in the Karl-Marx-Hof, the pride of Red Vienna, Soyfer's Vienna.

Deeply disappointed with his Party, he, like his closest friends and many other Social Democrats, joined the underground Communist party which, it seemed to them, offered the only effective resistance against Austrofascism as well as the Nazi danger from across the border. The destruction of the Socialist press by the Austrofascists had robbed Soyfer of any possibility of making a living as a journalist. He went back to school and played with the idea of getting a teacher's certificate, but under Austrofascism a left-wing Jew would not have had much of a chance to teach. Soyfer gave up his studies, but not his writing. In fact, the enforced public silence he took as an opportunity to develop his talent—without any immediate prospect of publication but also without any of the restrictions that a government censor or an editor of the party paper previously might have imposed on him.

The defeat of Socialism infuriated and saddened—and challenged him. How was he to treat it in literary terms? The left underground papers and propaganda handbills were full of threnodies for the dead of February. English and American writers expressed their sympathies. Stephen Spender in his poem "Vienna" condemned Dollfuss, eulogized Red Vienna and its martyrs. Stephen Vincent Benet wrote his "Ode to the Austrian Socialists." Soyfer was not interested in sublime emotions, no matter how justified they were, but in analysis, in tracing the case history of a political organism before its collapse, a theme with the scope of a novel. Soyfer made it a test of his gifts: "It may be that in half a year all my ambitions will crumble to a heap of dust," he wrote in August 1934.

It turned out to be a very productive and up-beat summer after all, a summer away from Vienna. A Socialist Zionist youth group had invited him to lecture at their summer camp in Yugoslavia. Practically all of Soyfer's friends were Jewish, but religion was of no concern to him; his friends remember that he considered himself an atheist. He, like so many Jews on the left, believed that Socialism's classless society would do away with anti-semitism and absorb the "Jewish problem." But, spirited himself, he was intrigued with the enthusiasm of the young Zionists, and his intellectual curiosity ruled out simple answers. "I'm learning Yiddish songs (marvelous) and discussing Zionism, one of the trickiest social imperialistic missions, which is not so easy to refute as you think," he writes to Marika. And: "I am in the best of moods. I wake up with lines from *Faust* in my head, wash ice-cold in the Sava River or more comfortably at the well, drink milk warm from the cow, and go to work." . . . on the novel, that is.

Back in Vienna he discussed the drafted chapters with his friends and did more research. Soyfer considered the novel his main literary work and struggled to perfect it. We don't know how close he came to finishing it; from the way he numbered the chapters we can assume that many more were completed than have been saved. So what does this fragment amount to?— to one of the most remarkable prose works written in Austria during the 1930s.

Soyfer's novel is not one of the many basically propagandistic novels of the 1930s written to persuade the reader of the author's left-wing point of view. Nor is it one of the proletarian novels by nonproletarians. It is one of those less common novels which, to use Orvill Prescott's definition, are "about characters involved in politics and so about politics themselves." As Prescott says, "a political novel must be judged on two separate counts, its merits as contribution to political thought and its merits as a work of fiction." Alfred Pfabigan has acknowledged Soyfer's insights from the point of view of political science. The novel's literary merits are equally remarkable.

Without any literary model to guide him, Soyfer combines characterization of individuals and diagnosis of political processes. The Prelude sketches the turbulent history of the young republic as witnessed by a petty bourgeois, an incarnation of the insecurity, frustration, timidity, aggression, and opportunism of a whole class of sociologically "displaced persons" who, uprooted by the collapse of the monarchy, is longing for a return to the "good old values" and "the strong man." In Franz Josef Zehetner, Soyfer gives flesh and blood to that dangerously manipulable mentality which years later T. W. Adorno was to diagnose as the "authoritarian personality." Within Austrian satire Soyfer's Zehetner belongs to that lineage of petty tyrants that runs from Nestroy's Peter Dickkopf and company to Merz-Qualtinger's Herr Karl; only Soyfer shows more clearly the political dimension of such an unsavory specimen and the sociological forces of which he is the despicable though pathetic product.

Against the foil of Zehetner's reactionary perspective on Austrian politics, Soyfer sets out to trace the gradual decline of the Social Democratic Party due not to corruption but weakness. By carefully selecting his characters from different levels in the party hierarchy, Soyfer analyzes the party structure itself. There is no central character except the party itself, and each of the individuals that make up its life is seen from multiple perspectives: his own, that of other party members, and that of the narrator. Personal fates are interwoven with that of the party. Psychosomatic disturbances of the characters unobtrusively reflect the sickness of the political organism. The aging of the upper eschelons, the accumulation of offices in a few individuals, the older generation's disregard for the younger, the tension between leadership and "base," the paralyzing bureaucratization at a time when dynamic action is called for . . . all the abstractions that a political scientist might enumerate in a post-mortem of the Social Democratic Party of Austria, are given flesh and blood. Soyfer shows the weakness of the structure as well as of the leadership—its illusory hope for negotiations, its half-heartedness, the fateful contradiction of its verbal radicalism and its continued retreat. Because he had been an insider, Soyfer's criticism is all the more convincing and incisive . . . and informed by a genuine empathy with all those who had gained in the party a meaning for their lives. It was more than a political party; it was a social organism, a community united by a humanistic vision. How much such a vision could blind those it saved Soyfer shows in the pathetic figure of the Section treasurer. Blum is a simple character but his function in the novel is complex: the irony of his name turns the party's heroic tradition into a travesty, and yet his suffering is true martyrdom. Soyfer's psychology is equally convincing whether he makes us feel the insecurity of men in their fifties or the impatient enthusiasm of those of his own generation, their militant romanticism, their camaraderie, the nervous tension of a frustrated group waiting for action.

Throughout the novel we feel the dramatic conflict between opposing forces: that between the Party and the fascists who take on an all the more ominous power for evading direct confrontation, and that between those in command of the party and the base. Again and again the base tries to assert its will to action, and again and again it is thwarted by the call to order, by the party leadership or by the clubs of the police—or by both as in the demonstration that could have sparked a revolution. Kaliwoda's "The only thing that's going to help us now is action" expresses the desperate hope that the future is "up to us!" in spite of everything. It was the desperate hope that made the Defense Corps open fire in February 1934 when it was too late.

Soyfer wrote the novel with the knowledge of hindsight, but his point of view was that of the left opposition long before the February tragedy. How justified his criticism of the Party leadership was Otto Bauer himself confirmed in his *Der Aufstand der österreichischen Arbeiter* (The Uprising of the Austrian Workers), written in exile in Czechoslovakia:

> Parliament was eliminated. The dictatorship established itself. The attempt to continue parliamentary government Dollfuss prevented by force. We could have answered with a general strike on that 15 March. Never before had the prospects of a successful fight been as favorable as then. The German counterrevolution [by the Nazis]

had enraged the masses in Austria. The workers waited for the signal to fight. At that time the railroad workers were not as demoralized as eleven months later. The government's military organization was far weaker than in February 1934. In March 1933 we might have been able to win. But we shrank from the fight. We still believed we could reach a peaceful solution through negotiations. We avoided the armed confrontation because we wanted to spare the country a bloody civil war. The civil war broke out nevertheless eleven months later but under circumstances far less favorable to us. It was a mistake: of all our mistakes the most tragic.

Soyfer's novel breaks off a few weeks before February 1934. But the description of the party's agony is so conclusive that we understand why it won't survive. "Although [Soyfer's work] remained a fragment," wrote Ulrich Weinzierl," compared to it, most other 'finished' literary treatments of February 1934 and its prehistory are nothing but paper." And Rolf Schneider has said: "If we had this novel in its completeness it would be the most significant novel in the German language. No other novel has taken the most important social organism as its theme: the political party." In spite of its fragmentary nature Soyfer's work remains a pioneering achievement in political literature that transcends the merely historical dimension. The death of the Social Democratic Party in 1934 is history; the disintegration of a mass party due to inner weaknesses is a phenomenon we witness today in more than one political camp.

The prospect of publication would have urged Soyfer to complete the novel. Of course it could not be published in Austria. Contacts in Czechoslovakia failed. Whether he had any hopes of publishing it in this country we will never know; the two letters from Simon & Schuster, which the police confiscated when they frisked Soyfer in 1937, are lost. The only part of the novel Soyfer ever saw in print was the chapter "The Corner," which John lehmann published in English translation in 1936. The police confiscated all that Soyfer had finished of the novel.

For a year and half after February 1934, Soyfer could be

creative only illegally: while, off and on, he worked for the Communist underground, he devoted most of his energies to the novel which, as Soyfer was to find out, was also considered a subversive activity. Then suddenly, in the fall of 1935, he had a chance to go "legal" again, so to speak. Bil Spira, whose cartoons had appeared on the same page of the *Arbeiter-Zeitung* as Soyfer's satirical poems and who now did graphic work for the *Wiener Tag*, got him a job with the same paper which, because it was part-owned by a Czech firm, could afford a slightly more liberal course, at least in its coverage of the cultural scene. Since Soyfer contributed only to the Sunday issue, the reviews, reports, sketches, and poems he wrote for the *Tag* during the next two years provided little more than pocket money. (He always could live and eat at home but preferred not to.) For the present volume I have selected pieces from the *Tag* in which Soyfer looks at the situation in Vienna critically, as critically as censorship, even of the *Tag*, allowed him to be. The two fictitious letters, imaginative sociological miniatures, juxtapose two Austrias: that of the petit bourgois on the move towards fascism, and that of a working class family facing unemployment and insecurity. The mother's letter combines kitsch-sentimentality and feeling in a way that reminds us of Horváth at his gentlest. The satire on the student and the university explains why Soyfer, after a second try at the same disciplines as those of his negative study partner (ironically he named him Feder—one of his own pseudonyms), gave up school shortly after he had written this farewell to academe. Foreign as this satire on university life may sound to American readers, *Be Prepared*?! will strike a familiar note at least for those who remember the insane ads for atomic-bomb shelters during the Cold War. The ads may be gone, but Soyfer's satire on our hi-tech primitivity has every chance of becoming a classic.

In their careful construction Soyfer's prose pieces prove his craft, in their themes and genres they demonstrate his versatility. He wrote theater and film revues, and commemorative pieces about writers who, he thought, had something to say to his own time: François Villon, Johann Gottlieb Fichte, Ludwig Börne, and Johann Nestroy whom he admired so much. Always concerned with social issues, he wrote an ironic reportage on a so-called success story and an imaginary case study of a pathetic failure so typical of "unpolitical" lower middle class people. Soyfer's criticism found ever-new expression. One day he was asked for a film script. In contrast to so many writers of his time who fed the lucrative dream machine, Soyfer, in his "All Thieves on Strike!", combined a montage of Hollywood clichés with a satire on capitalist society confirming Brecht's verdict "property is thievery." The project never advanced beyond the resumé stage, and the resumé was never published until 1980. Today it is as fresh, intriguing, hilarious, and worthy of production as it was when Soyfer wrote it.

If we compare these texts to any Soyfer wrote before 1934, we can hardly miss the difference caused by the political changes. The satires he could publish have lost their aggressive, passionate sting. The order, more than ever, "worked like hell"; the question "Must it always be this order?" had become all the more urgent in the two years since Austrofascism had established itself. But the answer, the confidence in the final victory of the proletariat, could no longer be given, and that not only because of the censor. The answers that Soyfer could give now, in the *Wiener Tag* that is, had to stay within the limits of his assignment: the cultural scene. Again and again he asked the question: Must it always be this "steppe of the arts in Vienna," as he once called it? The arts to Soyfer meant primarily the theater, the most social medium, and the film, in pre-TV times the most powerful tool of the "consciousness industry" (H. M. Enzensberger). Soyfer's verdict, "a future historian of the theater will have to discard this period with a few words of regret" has been confirmed by more than one "future historian." Unfortunately they also discard those fringes of the scene where Soyfer saw sparks of hope. He looked at all possibilities that might overcome the most infuriating disgrace of the art scene, the gulf between the arts and the concrete concerns of the people. No longer did he plead for that theater of agitation that he had demanded in his "Political Theater" in 1932 and that now, four years later, would be instantly boarded up by the police. But the indignation about what the masses were being fed as art and entertainment permeated his critiques and his demands for a truly democratic culture. For inspiration or even for the proper arguments, he had to look beyond the "steppe": he found them in an American or a Czech movie, a French play, or in a modest oasis right at home: an Adult Education Center.

In the fall of 1935 when he started writing for the *Wiener Tag*, Soyfer also found another outlet for his creativity. Again it was Jewish friends who helped and opened the door, this time to the basement of coffeehouses, where for some time exciting theater had been going on, and where Soyfer himself was to create plays that challenged the cultural machinery whose sterility he criticized in the *Wiener Tag*. Before discussing Soyfer's work for these theaters, their peculiarities should be understood because they shaped his plays.

During the Depression many theater people lost their jobs, and Hitler's ascent to power in 1933 drove many actors out of Germany who, however, were disappointed in their hopes of finding work with Austrian theaters. An entertainment industry interested in box office hits, a state theater policy which glorified an uncritical national ideology and higher values which mocked the harsh realities of everyday life, an officially unsanctioned, but unofficially tolerated, at times even encouraged, anti-Semitism—all this was bound to challenge the opposition of young writers and theater people who found an outlet for their activities only in a number of basement theaters that sprang up in quick succession and, in the four or five years before the Anschluß, created a subculture which became part of Austrian theater history. From their very origin it was obvious that the authors, designers, musicians, and audience of these theaters were mostly left-wing intellectuals, many of them Jewish, and it was only logical that sooner or later Soyfer would become part of this alert, talented, critical and very Viennese, very Austrian community.

Hans Weigel introduced Soyfer to Leo Askenasy (Leon Askin) who at the time was actor and director at the ABC in, or rather below, the Café Arkaden, just across the street from the back entrance to the University. And for the ABC, which more than any other of those "underground" theaters irritated the censor, Soyfer wrote his first play. What kind of play could it be under the circumstances? First of all, it had to follow the special form that had developed in these theaters which tried to go beyond the cabaret convention of individual numbers loosely strung together by a conferencier. Mundane considerations played their part. For the use of the basement, the cafe owner expected some return from the drinks the audience would consume. To ensure a smooth business transaction without disturbing the show, after a few opening numbers, there was an intermission for ordering drinks and, after fifty minutes or so, another one for paying before some more numbers closed the program. And those fifty minutes or so were the time span alotted to the dramatic skill of the playwright. Apart from such restrictions of time and those imposed by the censor, a police officer, who did not read the script but attended the dress rehearsal and often returned for the performances, there were the restrictions of a constant lack of money. "The Statue of Liberty for Five Schillings," a dialog between Soyfer and Bil Spira, conveys that limitation, but also the ambitions of all involved in the admirable adventures of the imagination to overcome obstacles that a suspicious, unimaginative, vengeful, ridiculous, and unpredictable system could come up with.

That programmatic dialog was occasioned by Soyfer's first play at the ABC: *The End of the World* (Weltuntergang), performed in the summer of 1936. Its apocalyptic title was more than justified: Hitler, who a year before had instituted general conscription in Germany, in March 1936 defied the treaties of Versailles and Locarno openly by marching into the demilitarized Rhineland. In May of the same year, Mussolini broke the last resistance of the Abyssinians. The Berlin-Rome axis, which was to form the foundation of fascist imperialist aggression, consolidated itself while England and France reacted with exercises in appeasement and ineffectual threats. Soyfer, like all liberal and antifascist writers throughout Europe, had to face Stephen Spender's question, "Who live under the shadow of a war. What can I do that matters?"—and his play was the answer to that question: all he could do from the stage was to shock his audience into facing the question themselves, to make them feel the shadow of imminent destruction and the need to overcome apathy. The political developments proved the urgency of Soyfer's plea with uncanny precision and irony: the play was last performed on 11 July 1936—the day on which Schuschnigg, who had become Austrian chancellor after Dollfuß had been killed by Nazis two years before, signed a "gentlemen's agreement" with Hitler which sealed the fate of the country; now the Anschluß was only a matter of time. Nor was it only the end of Austria that was approaching. A few days later, on 18 July 1936, the Spanish Civil War broke out; the dress rehearsal for World War II was under way. It was this ominous tendency that had started with Hitler's take-over in Germany, not just Austrofascist censorship that necessitated Soyfer's shift from his intense exhortation to class warfare to an equally passionate stand against Nazi aggression that could only lead to war between nations. It was a shift of policy in line with the strategy of the Popular Front, and, in a wider context, with that of the Austrian conservative liberal Ernst Karl Winter whose attempt to unite the Austrian right and left against the German danger was thwarted by a shortsighted Schuschnigg.

The End of the World is a cosmic farce in the spirit of Nestroy and Karl Kraus. The fantastic frame plot is modeled after the apocalyptic vision with which Kraus's *The Last Days of Mankind* (Die letzten Tage der Menschheit, 1922) ends. In Kraus's play, humankind, having degraded God's image, is sentenced to death. Mars has decided to free the vermin called "humans" "so that from now on into eternity the heavenly spheres won't have to complain about disruption of their harmony." Soyfer takes elements of this cosmic trial and gives them a comical twist in the style of nineteenth century Viennese magical farce. The main body of the play which more than any other of Soyfer's plays follows the cabaret style, consists of a number of loosely connected scenes, all variations on the central theme: mankind facing the final catastrophe. The one unifying element is the only sane figure in the play, the "concerned scientist," whose attempts to save the world only confirm his diagnosis: humankind, blinded by illusion and ignorance and manipulation is irretrievably staggering towards annihilation. The end of the world proves to be best boom for business yet. Destruction and business are synonymous. Business goes on as usual, language goes on as usual, life goes on as usual—on the level of everyday "realism." But the coming annihilation only brings out how surreal this everyday world is, and how absurd its logic. To this apocalyptic farce Soyfer adds a truly Austrian touch: the "End of the World Hit" that the street-singers perform for Professor Peep in Viennese dialect could have been written by Nestroy, or by Kraus, who called Austria "a testing ground for world destruction." Like his great teachers, Soyfer saw through his chic, happy-go-lucky, irresponsible fellow-Viennese. The song starts on a sad note but ends with a rakish flourish, a flirt with disaster: "So let's go dying just a little!/ It's risky, but it's chic!"

All-embracing as Soyfer's criticism is, it does permit nuances. In his vignettes of the poor and unfortunate facing destruction his satire is milder; their stubborn rejection of any warning is pathetically comic rather than despicable. In one episode satire even gives way to understanding: "People are too busy making both ends meet and never have time enough to even think about death." And "The Song of Cake-Mix Granny" shows how they are manipulated if they ever should find time to think. When Soyfer turns to the powerful his satire is acid. His indictment of the ruling classes in their stupidity and ruthlessness reaches its climax in the last scene, set in the USA. It is also a climax in Soyfer's satire of language, his exposure of empty words. Just before the expected annihilation, a flood of clichés breaks loose as if the catastrophe had already taken place in the language.

The play's ending, the comet's declaration of love, his by now famous, often quoted "Song of the Earth," is perfectly acceptable in the fantastic cosmic frame of the play. It is a declaration of defiance against a command of destruction, an assertion of life over death. But how can it be reconciled with the rest of the play which, scene after scene, confirms Kraus's verdict: the human race is beyond help and deserves being wiped out? Soyfer's dilemma lay in the fact that, realist that he was, he could not deny the pessimistic conclusions that the political situation since Hitler's ascent to power forced upon him. Just as impossible was it for him, the political activist, to subscribe to a defeatism that would only further the catastrophe. The song is not the credo of unconditional optimism as it often has been interpreted, but, juxtaposing life and death, poverty and unending wealth, it sets before us alternatives and ends in a passionate hope that the right choice be made . . . "It is up to us!"

Soyfer's next play, *Trip to Paradise* (Der Lechner Edi schaut ins Paradies) is again a parable demonstrating the need to drastically revise our thinking. The play once more proves Soyfer's claim that the cabaret theaters confronted their audience with the burning problems of the day. In the fall of 1936 when the unemployment rate in Austria was 24 percent, when half a million people in the small country were out of work, Soyfer wrote this moving, comic, grotesquely anachronistic dream play of Eddy, the "little fellow," who has been out of work and off welfare for years and wants to find out who is to blame for his misery. He finds out, but only after a long race on the wrong track (which makes the message a play). Soyfer's playful visual imagination takes Eddy's backwardness literally, entrusts him to a time machine which takes him back through the centuries to the creation of Man . . . a simple trick, maybe, but, at the very beginning of this journey through world history in reverse, the science fiction gag generates truly poetic images on stage. The lady who, walking backwards, reverses charity into the robbery it is, the beggar's transformation of the blind war veteran back into a proud recruit blinded by patriotic propaganda, the soldiers shouting "No more wars!" as they approach 1914—they all act out theatrical emblems not easily forgotten.

On a level deeper than the visual is the poetic magic in Eddy's relationship to the machine. Making the machine also an "unemployed" who is thinking of retraining for a new position, giving it not only a human name but also human needs, Soyfer removes the alienating barrier between Man and the technology he has created and reduces Eddy's initial machine-wrecking *ad absurdum*. Violence is overcome by magic. It is the witching hour after all, the time when machines talk and turn into good spirits. "A fairy tale, then?" Soyfer asked in his review of Voskovec and Werich's movie. "Yes, but one that is most welcome: a lively modern popular fairy tale full of humor and courage nourished by clear insights." *Trip to Paradise* is such a fairy tale. And the "clear insights," the other messages in the play, are not served with a heavy didactic hand but with the light touch of a playful cabaret comedy full of surprises. "Art should be a means of education," said Brecht, "its purpose, however, is pleasure." But humor and seriousness are never far apart in Soyfer, and the contrast of past and present, hilarious when Eddy, the simple guy, confronts the scientists with the consequences of their achievements, turns into bitter political satire in the trial scene, the "flash forward" from 1633 to 1933. The whole dilemma of the worker who, in the deadly grip of unemployment, chooses wrong over right, is summed up in Eddy's "I only said it because I've gotta get some kind of work again." The grotesque anachronism turns deadly serious when Eddy proves not only progress but also the creation of Man himself a mistake. And as if he, the half-starved wretch of the twentieth century, were not proof enough, he calls witnesses: allegories of the "image of God," disgraced by exploitation, greed, war. Eddy's "Ballad at the Gates of Paradise" turns into a dance of death, simple and powerful like a Masereel woodcut.

Convincing as Eddy's negation of Man is, it cannot be Soyfer's last word. Again he prevents an "end of the world," and from pathos he returns to the comedy of affirmation. But the "happy ending" is no foregone conclusion. The future of humankind is put into human hands. Soyfer's "It's all up to us" is a declaration of human self-determination, a rejection of technological or any other kind of determinism, as much as of a teleological concept of history. "Human beings are at the same time actors and authors of their own history." How much such views contradicted Austrofascist ideology was illustrated by the preacher at St. Stephen's cathedral who, to Soyfer's great delight, had based a sermon on the play he had gone to see—a unique acknowledgment of a Viennese cabaret theater! The sermon proved Soyfer's conclusion wrong, of course, and replaced it with "It's all up to Jesus!"

Trip to Paradise was Soyfer's only play that was not put on by the ABC but by Literatur am Naschmarkt with an auditorium twice as large as that of the other basement theaters (i.e. about a hundred seats instead of the usual legally permitted forty-nine!). The play ran for three months, longer than any other Soyfer play. But the very success of the play had its own irony. The declaration of human independence with which the play ends was also meant as a left activist's plea that the Eddys of the land should take charge of their fate, a Utopian hope, considering the political situation in 1936. Besides, in the enthusiastic audience there were no unemployed, hardly any workers. "I must confess," remembered one of them—a friend of Soyfer—many years later: "I didn't see any of his plays. In a working class family that had to pinch every groschen, it would have been reckless extravagance to go to a play."

Soyfer's "Ballad of the Bowl," written in 1933, had predicted the workers' plight under Austrofascism, but they were by no means as passive as the end of the poem suggests. The labor movement had been driven underground and could never be persuaded to support the new State, which covered its weakness with a theatrical facade, advertising the new Corporate State, a fortunately half-hearted imitation of the fascism north and south of its borders. It was designed as a *Parallelaktion* that would take the wind out of the Nazis' sails, but due to its in many ways parallel ideology, it prepared the way for them, weakening Austrian identity rather than strengthening it. Ever since 1918, Austrians had looked either back to the Reich of the Habsburgs or to the Reich next door. A true national identity had never developed. A conscious republican identity had existed only in Red Vienna, but up to 1933, the Social Democrats, too, had considered the Anschluß desirable. In the interwar years there were only a few who really "wanted this state"; for most it remained an abstraction. Soyfer's next play, *Astoria*, was his satire on this abstraction, on a state that does not exist at all.

Soyfer found the idea for the play in a newspaper story that had amused readers all over Europe. In London a group of bored diplomats had opened an embassy for the fictitious state

Astoria, had given receptions and handed out medals. Soyfer extended this practical joke into an ingenious satire on the state as an illusion and a brutal power structure to cover up the absence of a meaningful social organism. The very theme suggested that Soyfer, as in his other plays, followed the technique of the Viennese magical farce. Only in this, Soyfer's most complex play, a literal "first step" into the realm of the imaginary establishes the fantasy as the new reality, and, again, two levels of realism and fantasy are integrated in the plot that in hilarious, bitter, moving, and haunting scenes centers around the basic conflict between rich and poor in the years of the Depression and the triumph of fascism.

Soyfer's caricature of high society does not only criticize the English fops who fell for the Astorian hoax. It also satirizes the attitude of the rich to the State in general, the vanity which makes them easily susceptible to corruption, the personal motives behind decisions that affect the lives of millions, the nonsensical cocktail-party talk, and the noncommittal, supposedly witty verbiage of intellectuals. To an alert audience in 1937, Soyfer's satire was charged with political allusions. The senile Count is, of course, a satire on Hindenburg and a defunct aristocracy, and the British elite in the play includes well-known sympathizers with Nazi Germany and supporters of appeasement.

The Astorian swindle which, in the world of the rich, was a big joke turns into a criminal plot to take advantage of people in need, the homeless, the unemployed, the outcasts who dream of a life in dignity. By transforming the dismal London street into a fantastic landscape of palm trees and smoking factories, Soyfer creates a stage image for the poor people's idea of paradise: a country of full employment in an exotic tourist setting modeled after the posters in a travel bureau or a cheap Hollywood movie. This illusion only prepares the poor for the Utopia that Astoria promises: a country without poverty, without sickness—the irresistible bait for exploitation. But Soyfer does not present only a bitter satire on the abuse and the seductive danger of Utopian hopes, and an exposure of the kitschy, petty-bourgeois Utopian fantasies. Very much like Horváth, he also penetrates the kitsch through its twisted roots to its source:

genuine, basic human longings. And even beyond that: Rosa's dream of a world of happiness and gentleness, in its delicate lyrical transparency one of the most moving scenes in all of Soyfer's plays—and perhaps in all Utopian literature—is answered by Paul's realistic reasons for living: "for making the difference greater"—the difference between "being dead and alive"—between mere subsistence and a life worth living. In the interplay of Utopian thinking, in its ambivalence and political demands, this scene is Soyfer's most powerful statement of the dialectic between Utopia and reality that characterizes so much of his work.

More and more Soyfer equates the abuse of the poor people's dreams with political power strategies—and concrete allusions to the political repression of his time. The beaurocratic inhumanity at the Astorian visa office reflects the indignities which persons forced into exile had to undergo in the thirties; the applicants' uprising is squelched by force. *Astoria* becomes Soyfer's Marxist parable of a fascist dictatorship in the making: threatened by the masses, capitalism calls on its "lackey," fascism to restore law and order, and to save the system. The Butler's unveiling speech is Soyfer's satiric prophecy of Nazi-Germany at war.

Soyfer's social criticism discloses the effect of poverty on the masses; he satirizes their gullibility, their neglect of principles for the sake of a job, their submission to authority. When the leading character regrets his sell-out and exposes the pernicious system, he is jeered by the brain-washed mob—Soyfer's bitter comment on developments in Germany since 1933. And yet it is the poor, after all, the main characters of the play, the homeless on the fringe of society, who retain the vision of a true homeland that, in the Marxist sense, would replace the state. In Hupka's passionate plea, the Utopian dream again takes shape, not as a fantasy of petit-bourgeois idyllics but as a political blueprint for a future that grows more and more distant; the three subversives sing their hopeful song on their way to jail.

Astoria is the one play of Soyfer in which Brecht's influence is especially noticeable. The whore and her pimp could walk the stage in the *Threepenny Opera,* and Soyfer's "Song of Honor" and his "Song of Man Selling Himself" reflect the cynical aggressiveness and the rebellious spirit of Brecht's songs in the same work. But there are other songs in the play, the vagabonds' lyrics with their resigned bitterness that postpones hope and "hides the dream of our long night/ The sunlight dream of the poor." The songs in *Astoria* demonstrate how many registers Soyfer's lyric voice had gained since he wrote his political verse for the *Arbeiter-Zeitung.* The songs in this and the other plays justify ranking Soyfer as a poet of remarkable versatility.

More than any other of Soyfer's plays, *Astoria* is a comedy of language and the most tantalizing challenge for the translator. *Astoria* shows how much Soyfer owed to Kraus and Nestroy, how much he deserves his place in the Viennese tradition of verbal satire. With noticeable gusto, Soyfer plays all the comic tricks of punning, verbal buffoonery, the interplay of local idiom and flavor with formal flavorlessness. He exposes middle class hypocrisy in the righteousness of proverbs and, again and again, he pierces the bubbles of clichés.

The parallels between Astoria and Austria and especially Nazi-Germany were too obvious to escape the censor. The text had to be revised again and again and, in spite of an excellent cast, *Astoria* had the shortest run of all of Soyfer's plays. We have no evidence, but quite possibly it was closed by the censor. Since the agreement of July 1936, any criticism of Germany in the press, the theaters, the movies, and the radio was prohibited. All those who did not, like the Austrian Nazis, look forward to the German take-over with joyous anticipation were left to vague hopes, despair, or resignation. Soyfer, the antifascist activist, could only warn his fellow Viennese and try to break the paralyzing apathy. His dramatic parable *Vineta* put them in a nightmare world in order to wake them up.

In his review of a French surrealist play, Soyfer had asked whether there wasn't any alternative possible between the titillation of a sophisticated avant-garde elite and the cheap amusement of the masses. *Vineta* was Soyfer's answer to his own question, his most unconventional, most experimental play. He denies himself and his audience all humor, all dialect, all lyrics, anything that might create a familiar atmosphere. Instead he only sets in motion the mechanics of the absurd, in a language that is none, which disintegrates into fragments and meaningless repetitions. In the impossibility of communication, Soyfer demonstrated his awareness of the loss of language in a time of its inflationary manipulation.

Vineta is Soyfer's vision of the "great cold" that Horváth felt coming. In the city under the sea only a ghostly twilight prevails, the twilight of a world without time, without history, a world of total oblivion. The play is Soyfer's radical reversal of that principle that the Viennese so often quote, not without a self-congratulatory note: "Happy is he who forgets." And his protest is directed against the deadly consolation "that nothing can be changed anymore." He dramatizes his protest by showing how one individual desperately tries to stay alive in this city of the dead. The sailor Johnny almost succumbs to the Vinetans' pseudo-existence, but like the scientist in *The End of the World* and Hupka in *Astoria*, those voices crying in the wilderness, he, too, desperately tries to destroy the illusion that holds captive the people around him. And, like Peep and Hupka, he fails. In the *Prager Tagblatt* Heinz Politzer, who later as a Kafka scholar was to analyze modern anxieties, found prophetic words about Soyfer's play: "Through this Fritz Feder [Soyfer's pseudonym] time and fear themselves wrote this play. And yet that our time created such a convincing symbol of itself proves how strong, how valuable are the energies of its youth, and what an immeasurable loss it would mean if Vineta ever became a reality."

Politzer's comment reminds us that we must interpret the thirties and their literature not only with the knowledge of hindsight. What strikes us today as prophecy, gripping in its accuracy, was written as a warning, still sustained by the hope that the unimaginable would never happen. *Vineta* was no absurdist play after all. In the last scene Soyfer breaks the absurd spell and returns to reality with an impassioned plea to preserve it before it is too late.

There was not much time left for Soyfer. Just enough to write another play. He was inspired by a work of the two well-known German Jewish writers Walter Hasenclever and Kurt Tucholsky, a play that in Hitler's Germany was banned from the stage. The question of how Soyfer ever got hold of *Christopher Kolumbus*, the play that, after a short run in 1932, had never been printed and five years later was forgotten, has caused all sorts of speculations that might intrigue a detective of literature. The play that Hasenclever himself had described as "very funny, unpolitical, and yet not well-behaved" challenged Soyfer to write his adaptation *Broadway Melody 1492*, which turned out to be funnier, and definitely more political and aggressive. In contrast to Hasenclever/Tucholsky's rather conventional Boulevard comedy, Soyfer's version was certainly more "original" than the original.

Soyfer followed the main plot line of his source, and made his work easier still by taking over about a fourth of the text verbatim. As Hasenclever/Tucholsky had done, Soyfer presents the Indians not as the primitive noble savages, but as superior in their culture which, like that in Thomas More's *Utopia*, without army and commerce, has reached a higher level than that of the Europeans. But the rest of Soyfer's version is far more than an ordinary adaptation; over long stretches the source disappears and Soyfer's voice predominates. Still, the play is uneven. It is weakest where Soyfer expands the relationship Columbus—Isabella into melodrama; it is strongest in those parts that breathe the spirit of the critical Viennese *Volksstück* and confirm Edwin Zbonek's apercu "Soyfer was a Nestroy who had read his Marx"—in the many songs he adds, and in the short scenes that present history through the eyes of "simple" people.

In Soyfer's play the character of Columbus is more complex than in the source. The explorer's ambition outweighs his human decency; he becomes enslaved to commercial interests and delegates power to the ruthless. Accordingly Vendrino, the Royal comptroller, and Pepito, the criminal who commands the Colonial Forces, stand out as the most sharply drawn satirical figures. Vendrino's racist and other Nazi terms link Spanish colonialism with the Nazi threat in 1937. As in most of his works, Soyfer was concerned with the ominous development in Hitler Germany, and very likely it was this concern that ignited his interest in the play by Hasenclever and Tucholsky. The Spanish conquest of America became his historical metaphor for the threatening German conquest of Austria.

Soyfer's satire is amazingly many-faceted. The very first scene satirizes not only the way the Burgtheater travestied Austrian history in the spectacles about national heroes of the past. The principle he followed in his own anti-model play, i.e. "to neglect 'reality' for he sake of truth" ironizes the presentation of history in general. Finally a play with this title gave the lie to the Hollywood "Broadway Melodies" that during the twenties and thirties, year after year, dazzled American and European audiences with the glamour that glossed over the misery of the Depression. Soyfer's criticism of the United States does not lead him into ultimate pessimism. True to Soyfer's sense of history that rejected any teleological design, this play, like all his plays, has an open ending: "The future of us humans all/ Is held in human hands."

Even more than *Astoria*, this last play transcended all the limitations of a basement theater and demonstrated how ready Soyfer was to go beyond it. Soyfer never saw it on stage. Three days before the premier on 20 November 1937 he was arrested in the street. The prison was three blocks from the ABC where every night his *Broadway Melody* elicited rapturous applause from the audience.

The police had made a mistake. Soyfer was not the high functionary of the Communist propaganda machine they had hoped to catch. But they did not regret their error. The subversive material confiscated in Soyfer's room justified "detention while awaiting trial."

Conditions in jail were relatively tolerable. Every Thursday he saw his parents and his girlfriend Helli for a total of ten minutes. Although he was allowed to write only one letter a week, the amount of mail he could receive was not limited. His parents sent him money for cigarettes, he could write, he could read. We don't know whether he ever got all the books he asked Helli to send him (novels by Broch, Celine, Kafka, works by Freud); he got Schnitzler from the jail library, and he read "Goethe and newspapers."

In the long letters he wrote Helli he lost nothing of his humor, his wit, his insights into himself and others.

20 December 1937

Considered objectively, the whole thing is so comical and rules out any sentimentality. So I entreat you, darling: Don't give in to any of those weepy moods that I feel in the letters from my mother. I hope for instance that it wasn't you who had the stupid idea not to tell me that you lost your job. The idea that somebody out there thinks of me as a patient—mother actually wrote me once she would take care of me (!) once I am released—makes me nauseated.

A second perspective from which to consider my time in jail is to see it as a kind of punishment and trial period. As punishment, that is, for uncounted legally not punishable sins like wasting time, letting things slide, and all the others. When now, in the inactivity forced upon me, I realize ten times a day how much valuable time I fooled away; when in my meditation forced upon me, and in my actually quite salutary solitude I mull over the twenty-five years I have just put behind me, I gain all sorts of insights into myself. So far, being alone always did me a lot of good. The results are not only self-reproaches, but sometimes quite interesting ideas for work. But that this time my solitude came about the way it did, again is very comical. Which links pt. one and pt. two.

27 December 1937

At Christmas a commendable prison management sent a twig from a Christmas tree into each cell. Also gifts of packages of figs, apples, and chocolate. And that for prisoners who are only "detained awaiting trial." Just imagine all the goodies I'll get when I'll be a real convict as I've always wanted to be, ever since I was a child."

17 January 1938

    These Thursdays grow more and more brutal the longer our separation lasts. Don't think a minute that I don't feel the gloom and bitterness of it all as much as you do when I notice how those damned ten minutes go by without us having exchanged one real word. My mother always monopolizes the conversation. And who would hold it against her? She really loves me, you know. And Dad, used to her ways, keeps in the background with a hungry heart. And you and I have so much to say to each other that words fail us as soon we get a chance to open our mouths. But if I try and put a personal touch on our good-bye, with a glance for instance, I fail again. Last time I wanted to—as one says so thoughtlessly—"throw you a kiss," only you. What happened! The whole family threw kisses back. These visits are a real pain and afterwards I chew on my rage for hours over all the things that were left unsaid. So one by one we get to know the finer, special tortures of such a separation.

    And don't believe, my only one, that I have become estranged from you or you from me. That's a feeling that always comes over us when a great measure of love and need to be loved, through inner or outer circumstances, does not find satisfaction. I believe that great love, like anything great, always wants to go beyond itself, and considers itself small and inadequate—all the more so when iron bars are planted in front of it.

Following an amnesty for political prisoners, on 17 February 1938 Jura Soyfer was released into a world of uncertainty and ominous forebodings of worse things to come. Soyfer's letter of 21 February was more than a personal document; he wrote it to Marika and Mitja Rapoport who were already in the United States:

    For the first time in my life a turning point in the

political situation has hit me most miserably not only in ideological but also in very material terms. I have always hated to fight from a defensive position, and now I have to be afraid of being forced into one. Perhaps I will really have to face the question: What is a Jewish writer going to do, if . . . Isn't that terrible? On the other hand: Should I send my writing to the devil and just work? If my writing would let me send it. But it doesn't. So what else is there? Of course, there is also a decent way in spite of economic emigration, etc. I mean Heine's way. And that's the way one will have to go when it comes to that. But with how many self-reproaches that will never be silenced, whenever I think of Franz [an antifascist resistance fighter]. And then, in some forced menial job in Paris, with how many risks of losing the spirit instead of serving it.

An hour ago a friend came to see me, and I asked him what he is going to do in case, and he simply said: We have nothing to lose but . . . You are denied hearing such heart-warming things now. But you are also spared living through our old intellectuals' problems with an intensity we never experienced before. It's enough to make you sick. So much for the topic "ivory tower."

On 13 March 1938, one day after Hitler's troops marched into Austria, Soyfer tried to cross the Swiss border on skis and was arrested by Austrian border guards eager to demonstrate their loyalty to the new regime. On 15 June he writes Helli from the Innsbruck police jail:

> Ever since you wrote me of your imminent trip to England I have not stopped hoping that I would get free in time to celebate this good-bye together with you. We would have made these last weeks a good time, wouldn't we, and would have tried to catch as much as possible of the happiness that we had to miss and will miss. But now it does not look as if we were granted

these last weeks together; even if it were only a few days, I'd be grateful and happy. Yet even that is hardly sure. So it very probably means: Good-bye at a distance. Once more: For how long? I can give neither myself nor you any idea how long, darling. For in the three months that I have been in jail the world has changed rather drastically; only when I will have looked around in freedom will I have an idea of what's going to happen with me, with you, with both of us and with all of us. As long as I am in these four walls, only memories and dreams are at my disposal, and those you know as well as I do. You know Faust says: "Whatever it was, it was so lovely." Isn't he right?

A week after Soyfer wrote this letter, he was transferred to Dachau. During a long, hot day of slave labor in the gravel pit, he wrote the "Dachau-Song." Herbert Zipper, Soyfer's fellow prisoner, set it to music, and it was soon known throughout the camp. In September 1938 Soyfer was transferred to Buchenwald. When typhoid fever broke out, he was one of the team that carried the corpses. Soyfer died on 16 February 1939. His release had been approved a few days before. His parents and his sister were already in New York. His ashes are buried in the poor section of the Jewish Cemetery in Richmond on Staten Island.

Only Soyfer's poems and short prose were published during his lifetime. How did all his other writings survive? Otto Tausig, the editor of the first Soyfer edition after the war, wrote in his preface: "Before 1938, any antifascist had to pay for his convictions with months or years. Now they could cost him his life. In the storm that raged over Austria, who cared whether a few sheets of paper were swept away! And yet, hidden between a couple of shirts or the pages of books in the suitcases of persons who were driven into exile, a handwritten poem or a scene, a newspaper clipping or an almost complete play were saved. These persons hardly knew each other; they may never have met at all. They traveled in different directions. One went to Australia, another to America, England or France, to Cyprus or Manila." Helli Ultmann, Soyfer's girlfriend, in New York exile, had preserved the plays, parts of the novel, reviews, letters. John Lehmann had published two chapters of the novel in English translation. Towards the end of the war, Herbert Steiner and Tausig himself, both young Austrian Communist Jews, exiled in England, started preparing the first edition of Soyfer's plays, which appeared in Vienna in 1947.

The political and cultural situation in Austria after the war was not conducive to a lasting revival of Soyfer's work. He was remembered by a relatively small circle only. Soyfer material had been gathering in the Documentary Archive of Austrian Resistance ever since Herbert Steiner founded it in 1963, and the left press remembered Soyfer now and then, but for many years the inner strife of the thirties and the Nazi terror were conveniently forgotten. Performances of Soyfer's plays were few and far between. It was not until the seventies that the young generation forced the "return of the suppressed" and tried to penetrate the "Great Taboo" of the past, that the interest in Soyfer's work increased steadily. Today Austria has finally recognized Soyfer's achievement and importance. In 1980 a group of young actors formed a Jura Soyfer Theater. In 1988 a Soyfer Society was founded, whose board of trustees lists influential figures of political and cultural life. Government agencies support Soyfer research. A street has been named after him, and two of the houses in which he lived are marked by memorial plaques. Yet such acts of official respect do not, as so often, honor a writer who is forgotten by the public. Soyfer's work has become known to a growing circle of people. Through Helmut Qualtinger's reading of the novel over the radio, Austrians discovered Soyfer's achievement as prose writer.

Ever since 1975, the line of Soyfer productions has been unbroken. His plays have been performed in Austria, Germany, Switzerland, and occasionally in foreign countries—in small theaters, to be sure, experimental basements (as in Soyfer's times) and college studios, but also in a few larger houses, and always to enthusiastic audiences. Some of them have been translated into French, Spanish, Italian, Russian, and Czech. The collapse of the self-proclaimed "real socialism" has not devalued Soyfer's vision as anachronistic; the performances of his plays have increased in number since 1989. In the "Columbus and Anti-Columbus year 1992" his *Broadway Melody 1492* was produced not only in the old but also the "new" world, in New York and in Buenos Aires. And in 1993, almost fifty years after the end of the war, his Volksstück *Trip to Paradise* was finally staged at the Vienna Volkstheater, not in the big house but, perhaps more appropriately, in its outreach programs in working-class districts. The reception of his plays proves that their themes have retained their validity—the curse and blessings of technology; the apathy in view of possible global destruction; the ambivalence of Utopianism—its abuse and its indispensable impetus in political thinking. Nor are his themes only relevant in Europe, united or not. Like Peep in *The End of the World* scientists in this country warn in vain of the fatal reluctance to change; the homeless of *Astoria* walk the streets in all major cities of the USA; the abstractions of state machineries alienate citizens all over the world. And who, in the loneliness of his convictions, has not, like Johnny in *Vineta*, fought against a deaf, lifeless society around him. The division between rich and poor that Soyfer attacked during the Depression has not disappeared in the so-called developed nations, and has drastically separated the haves from the have-nots around the globe. Soyfer clearly diagnosed the dilemma of a betrayed young generation: frustration, unemployment as the cause of crime, the temptations of mass events, be they sports spectacles or political rallies. Soyfer's answers have not worked, but have ours? Soyfer, in miserably paid poems and prose sketches, in his plays on a makeshift, unsubsidized stage fathomed the contradictions of modern society. To point out the relevance of his themes today is not to relativize the evil and the horror of fascist rule that he attacked and that killed him. As a constant exhortation to strive for social justice and a truly human world, and to oppose all those irrationalisms that have reemerged in full force—national chauvinism, religious fanaticism, racist hatred—Soyfer's legacy is a living force in our time.

Editorial Note

After the first English edition of selections from Soyfer, *The Legacy of Jura Soyfer*, 1977, had been published, several important new texts by Soyfer were discovered which now can be presented in English translation for the first time: additional scenes in *The End of the World, Trip to Paradise,* and *Astoria,* the complete text of *Broadway Melody 1492,* and the novel, that is, the complete fragment of which only three chapters had been available in the 1977 edition.

Concerning the novel: In the manuscript the chapters are designated "Vorspiel" ("Prelude") Chapters 1, 3, 4, 5, 6, 19, 28, and "Waffensuche." For the present edition I have replaced the numbers with titles. All "Outlines" of unfinished work have been included in the translation to reflect Soyfer's total plan, as far as we know it.

Soyfer considered the novel his main work. The inclusion of this text (162 pp.) in this edition limited the selection from Soyfer's short prose (42 reportages, reviews, etc.); I selected those that are especially relevant to our time and reflect some of Soyfer's most basic concerns. The same principle guided my selection from his 110 satirical poems on politics of the early 1930s. All 27 lyrics in the plays are included in the present edition. Three poems and six prose pieces not included in this book were published in the first English Soyfer-edition (1977).

Since the Prelude to *Broadway Melody 1492* would not make much sense to an American reader, I have tried to transpose it into an American setting of the thirties. This adaptation is placed after the whole play.

Unfortunately space did not allow me to devote a special part of this volume to Soyfer's letters. To give the reader at least a limited opportunity to hear his private voice, I have incorporated some sections from them in the Afterword.

All translations in this volume are based on my German edition of 1984 (see bibliography). For problems of translating Soyfer and my approach to solving them see "Soyfer for Americans," in *Zeitschrift der Jura Soyfer Gesellschaft*, vol. 2

(1993), no. 4, pp. 3-5.

Any English edition of Soyfer's works must gratefully acknowledge the efforts of John Lehmann (1907-1989) to introduce Soyfer to English readers many years ago: In *New Writing*, which Lehmann edited, he published two sections of the novel: "The Corner" (under the pseudonym Georg Anders so as not to endanger Soyfer, transl. by James Cleugh, in no. 2, Autumn 1936, pp. 52-62) and "A Question of Nerves" (by Georg Anders, trans. by Charles Ashleigh, in: *New Writing*, New Series no. 3 Christmas 1939, pp. 260-265. Both of these translations were slightly revised for the present edition. Lehmann translated Soyfer's "Dachaulied" soon after Hugo Ebner, Soyfer's fellow prisoner, who was released from Buchenwald in May 1939, recited it to him in London. This translation circulated among Austrians who were exiled in England. Only the following publication can be documented: "Song of the Austrians in Dachau" in John Lehmann, *The Age of the Dragon*, Poems 1930-1951, London, 1951, p. 56 "Song of the Twentieth Century Man," Lehmann's translation of Soyfer's "Lied des einfachen Menschen" first appeared in John Lehmann, *Collected Poems 1930-1963*, London, 1963, p.90.

Acknowledgments

I want to thank Donald G. Daviau of Ariadne Press for including Jura Soyfer in his series of Austrian Literature in translation, and I want to thank Jorun Johns and Richard H. Lawson most cordially for their meticulous work and for helping this book over all the hurdles of the publication process. I am indebted to all persons who read all or parts of this translation and made valuable suggestions, especially Helli Andis, Beth Bjorklund, and Joan Birch. I am also indebted to the Computer Consulting Service at the University of Montana, who again and again saved me from despair when I was entangled in the "word-imperfect" of my own making.

My very special thanks go to my wife Lo. As she did many years ago when I prepared the first English edition of Soyfer she "never hesitated to make the jump from the England of Shakespeare to the Vienna of Soyfer"; she again improved the translation, and during the busy schedule of a full-time teaching load spent countless precious hours proofreading with me. Above all she was my "airy spirit" when I felt like lead. In fact, without her, this book would not have been ready for publication at the deadline—or ever ready at all.

I first read about Jura Soyfer thirty years ago in a book that I had borrowed from the British Council library in Vienna: John Lehmann's autobiography. It was my study of English literature at the University of Vienna that led me to Soyfer. Studying German at the same university, I never heard or saw his name. My first edition of selections from Soyfer's work was in English and preceded my edition of the German *Gesamtwerk* by three years. With the present volume the circle closes.

University of Montana Horst Jarka
Missoula
Spring 1996

Notes

Verse and Short Prose

Page
7 *wheat dumps in the sea*: in the 1930s huge quantities of wheat and other foodstuffs were deliberately destroyed to sustain a price level considered adequate by the producers.

8 *riot in the veterans' camp*: according to law American veterans of World War I were entitled to retroactive pay of $50 to $100. In the summer of 1932 thousands of veterans from all parts of the union assembled in Washington to speed up the payment. In conflicts between demonstrators and police on 28 July two veterans were killed. Then army units under the command of Dwight D. Eisenhower and Douglas MacArthur dispersed the "heroes of 1917" with tear-gas.

21 *Schleicher*: Kurt von Schleicher (1882-1934), German Chancellor December 1932 - January 1933.
Friedrich: Ernst Paul Friedrich (1894-1967), pacifist, anarchist, editor of *Die schwarze Fahne* (The Black Flag), in 1925 opened the anti-war museum in Berlin.

23 *Remarque*: publication of his book (1929) and showing of the film version (1930, 1931) caused violent protests by nationalistic circles in Germany and in Austria.

33 *Treitschke*: Heinrich von Treitschke (1834-1896), historian, decisively formed the interpretation of history of the nationalistic German middle class.
Chamberlain: Houston Stewart Chamberlain (1855-1927), philosopher, his *Grundlagen des 19. Jahrhunderts* (The Foundations of the 19th Century, 1899) was one of the ideological sources of the "Aryan"-cult of the Nazi era.

42 *Lessing*: Gotthold Ephraim Lessing (1729-1781), German dramatist and critic.
Schiller: Friedrich von Schiller (1759-1805), German dramatist.

45 *Hej Rup!*: Czech, "Heave ho!"

56 *Salacrou*: Armand Salacrou (1899-1989, French dramatist.
60 *Reinhardt*: Max Reinhardt (1873-1943), famous theater director.
61 *Nestroy*: Johann Nepomuk Nestroy (1801-1862), Austrian dramatist.
62 *Stranitzky*: Josef Anton Stranitzky (1676-1726), Austrian actor.
65 *Carl*: Karl Carl (Karl von Bernbrunn).

The Plays

The End of the World

87 *Führer*: In 1936 when the play was first performed this word would not have passed censorship. In the program it was replaced by "Lenker"—"captain," "helmsman," "director," etc.
89 *Jewish physics*: "One of the absurd stupidities of Nazi racism was the proclamation of a 'German mathematics,' 'German' or 'Aryan physics.' Even well-known scientists like Philipp Lenard and Johannes Staerk came down to that level, if only to strengthen their position in their feud with Einstein and other Jewish colleagues" (Karl Dietrich Bracher, *Die deutsche Diktatur*, 1972, p. 261f.)
91 *Lehar*: Franz Lehar (1870-1948), world-famous Austrian composer of operettas.
Slezak: Leo S. (1873-1946), famous tenor.
Kiepura: Jan Kiepura (1902-1966), singer, star in many film operettas.
Farkas: Karl Farkas (1893-1971), Viennese cabaret author and performer.
95 *Hermannskogel*: "mountain" (1,600 ft.) in the Vienna Woods.
107 *in Germany* such an explicit, negative reference to Germany would not have passed censorship (see note for p. 87.) The original version was: "Glei ums Eck"—"Right around the Corner."

108 *he*: Karl Kraus (1874-1936), greatest Austrian satirist.
the grumbler: a character in Kraus's satirical drama *The Last Days of Mankind* (Die letzten Tage der Menschheit).
He is silent: allusion to Kraus's response to Hitler's takeover on 30 January 1933: "Mir fällt zu Hitler nichts ein." ("I cannot think of anything to say about Hitler.")
his 800th silence: on 2 April 1936 Kraus gave his last, the 700th public lecture. He died on 12 June of that year. Soyfer had written this scene before that, and, considering his respect for Kraus in spite of the latter's support of Dollfuss, it is questionable whether this scene was performed after Kraus's death.

115 *the greatness of the moment* etc.: Jürgen Doll sees in Mr. Wood Soyfer's satire of the typical European intellectual of the political Right who like the Italian futurists and the German author Ernst Jünger glorified war and destruction.

Trip to Paradise

131 *another Italian*: Mussolini
stuttering bugs: reference is to the Austrian-made (!) automobile "Steyr 50" known for its performance on mountain roads.

137 *Isonzo*: river in Northern Italy, scene of several devastating battles in World War I.

140 *frogs' legs*: Galvani, Luigi (1737-1898) upon the accidental discovery of twitchings in the muscles of frogs' legs commenced research in dynamical electricity.
Popular Front: alliance of Communists, Social Democrats and Left Liberals in France (1934-1938).

154 *Cincinnati*: Soyfer's friend Mitja Rapoport was planning to do medical research, and eventually went there in 1937 with Marika Szecsi, Soyfer's former girlfriend.

158 *Vivat ille nunc renatus etc.*: approximate English equivalent of the Latin lines of the Humanists' hymn to the Renaissance:
First stanza: Long live the newborn Man, who ventures into life, the liberated Man.

Second stanza: Long live Man, hated and loved, not quite evil and not quite good, long live the liberated man! Third stanza: Long live the new state of things. Long live all who thought of all that's new, Long live the liberated Man!

Astoria

177 *Redl*: Alfred Redl (1864-1914), officer in the Austrian General Staff, found guilty of selling secrets to the Russians.

187 *Lord R.*: possibly Viscount Rothermere (1868-1940), British media magnate who in his papers (*The Daily Mail* and *The Evening News*) had praised the Nazi-regime and supported Oswald Mosley's British Union of Fascists. Soyfer's allusions to British sympathizers with Hitler were first pointed out by Jürgen Doll in his article "Astoria= Austria? Anmerkungen zum historischen Hintergrund und zur satirischen Zielrichtung in Jura Soyfers 'Astoria'" in *Jura Soyfer*, vol. 3, 1993, pp. 13-17.

206 *Tschort pabiri*! Russian: The devil take it!

216 *"The Sin against Astorian Blood"*: allusion to Arthur Dinter's notorious antisemitic *Die Sünde wider das Blut* (The Sin against the Blood, 1918).

Broadway Melody 1492

259 *Sassmann*: Hans Sassmann (1882-1960) Austrian literary critic and author, wrote several plays about famous figures in Austrian history (e.g. *Metternich, Maria Theresia und Friedrich der Große, Prinz Eugen*).
Feiks: Josef Feiks, Austrian author, wrote the drama *Ein Reiterlied* (A Horseman's Song), the radio play *The Wild Duke* (Der wilde Herzog), and others.

260 *Gregor*: Joseph Gregor (1888-1960), Austrian literary historian and scholar of theater research who in 1922 founded the Theater Collection of the Austrian National Library.

261 *Röbbeling*: Hermann Röbelling (1875-1949), director of the Burgtheater 1931-1938.

The Novel. Thus Died a Party

367 *steel-helmet badge*: badge of the *Heimwehr*
membership card: i.e. of the NSDAP (National Socialist German Workers Party).
defeat at the polls: at the election of the Provincial Parliaments in Lower Austria, Salzburg and Vienna on 24 April 1932 the NSDAP gained six times as many votes as they had done at the National Elections in 1930.

368 *another membership card*: i.e. of the SDAP (Social Democratic Workers Party).
Heimwehr: paramilitary organization of Austro-fascism.
German Transport Union: reference is to the *Deutsche Verkehrsgewerkschaft*; the great majority of Austrian railroad workers were members of the Social Democratic union.
People's Militia: the *Volkswehr*, a volunteer army with left orientation, established after the collapse of the monarchy in 1918.

369 *Social Democratic lawyer*: Karl Renner (1870-1950).
Social Democratic Jew: Otto Bauer (1881-1938), see noe for p. 401.
Hörlgasse: street in the Ninth District of Vienna where, during a Communist attempt at a coup on 15 June 1919, twenty persons were killed or fatally wounded (Gerhard Botz, *Gewalt in der Politik*, Munich, 1976, pp. 64ff.).

370 *General von Epp*: Franz Xaver Ritter von Epp (1868-1957), professional German army officer, commander of a *Freikorps* (right-wing volunteer army) which participated in the defeat of the shortlived Bavarian Soviet Republic in May 1919.
Horthy: Miklos Horthy von Nagybanya (1868-1957), Hungarian politician; after the defeat of Bela Kun's communist regime in 1920, Horthy became the Regent of the reestablished Hungarian monarchy (without a

monarch), gradually expanded his power to that of a monarch. During his rule Gulya Gombös of the radical Right formed a cabinet (1932-1936) with strong leanings toward fascist Italy and National Socialist Germany.
Mussolini: Benito Mussolini (1883-1945), Italian fascist dictator.
soviets: workers' and soldiers' councils
red Minister of Defense: Julius Deutsch (1884-1968), organized the *Volkswehr*.
the Cabinet...bourgeois again: in 1920 the coalition of Christian Socials and Social Democrats was followed by one of Christian Socials and Pan-Germans.
The new Chancellor: Ignaz Seipel (1876-1932), Catholic clergyman, leading Christian Social politician of the interwar period; Federal Chancellor 1922-1924 and 1926-1929; in 1922 secured the loan from the League of Nations; after the fire of the Palace of Justice in 1937, he incorporated the *Heimwehr* in to his reform of Austria according to authoritarian and corporative principles; Foreign Minister in the Vaugoin Cabinet (1930).

372 *their party militia*: the *Republikanische Schutzbund* (Republican Defense Corps), paramilitary organization of the Social Democratic Party, founded 1923, highest membership: 80,000.
Burgenland: province in the east of Austria.
ninety of them: in suppressing the mass demonstration, 86 civilians and 4 policemen were killed.

373 *reasons for hope*: the government's victory and the failure of the general strike in July 1927 accelerated the disastrous political development. "Actually, the weakening of democratic forces and the increase of fascist movements as well as the dictatorships of Dollfuss and Schuschnigg seem to be causally related to the 15 July 1927" (Botz, p. 142).
cockfeather: one of the *Heimwehr* insiginia.
schoolteacher: Karl Seitz (1869-1950).
at the same time: *Heimwehr* and Defense Corps leaders had agreed to hold their rallies in the Lower Austrian

industrial town Wiener Neustadt (7 October 1928) at a different hour and in a different part of town. In the morning, 18,500 *Heimwehr* men, of whom 16,000 had been brought in by rail, marched through the town. In the afternoon, 14,800 Defense Corps men and 21,000 workers in civilian clothes marched (Botz, p. 165).

374 *Reichspost*: semi-official organ of the Christian Socials.
English Labor Government: on 14 August 1931 the Labor Government (Prime Minister: James Ramsay MacDonald; Foreign Minister: Arthur Henderson) resigned. To combat the economic crisis and possible riots by workers, MacDonald formed a "national" coalition; in protest most Labor members of the government resigned.
the German Chancellor: after the Social Democratic Chancellor Hermann Müller (1876-1931) was ousted in March 1930, the Social Democratic Party of Germany no longer participated in the government for the remaining years of the Weimar Republic.
luxury tax: a progressive tax on entertainment, automobiles, liquor etc. introduced by the Social Democratic City government of Vienna

375 *Breitner*: Hugo Breitner (1873-1946), Social Democratic City Councillor of Vienna, introduced the luxury tax, see above.

376 *putsch*: on 13 and 14 September 1931 Walter Pfrimer (1882-1968), leader of the *Heimwehr* in the province of Styria, had attempted a putsch which, however, ended in a flop. The government exercised extreme leniency; Pfrimer and his men who had tried to overthrow the government went scot-free.
after the overthrow: after the collapse of the Habsburg Monarchy in 1918.

378 *Mateotti*: Giacomo Matteotti (1885-1924), Secretary General of the Socialist Party of Italy; exposed numerous acts of violence and corruption committed by the Mussolini government, murdered on 10 June 1924.
Lassalle: Ferdinand Lassalle (1825-1864), founded the first German workers party (1863).

379 *Führer on this side of the border*: Engelbert Dollfuss (1892-1934), Christian Social politician, Federal Chancellor 1932-1934, in March 1933 he eliminated Parliament to establish a dictatorship supported by the *Heimwehr*, outlawed the Defense Corps; reintroduced censorship and the death penalty, put out the socialist workers' uprising in February 1934, had nine leaders of the Defense Corps executed. Dollfuss was killed during an attempted putsch by the Nazis on July 27, 1934.
Führer on the other side of the border: Adolf Hitler (1889-1945).

381 *Karl Marx tenement complex*: Karl-Marx-Hof in the 19th District of Vienna, one of the most imposing housing projects of the Social Democratic City Government, erected 1927-1930, often considered a symbol of Red Vienna.

382 *Heimwehr Prince*: Fürst Rüdiger von Starhemberg (1899-1956), 1930-1936 National leader of the Autrofascist *Heimwehr*, 1934-1936 Vice-Chancellor.

383 *Workers' Educational Organization*: Arbeiterbildungsverein, founded in 1868 in Vienna.

384 *suffrage demonstrators*: the Russian revolution of 1905 and the Tsar's manifesto promising general suffrage inspired mass demonstrations by workers in Vienna and Prague. On 2 November 1905 about one hundred workers were wounded by police.
Adler: Victor Adler (1852-1918), in 1889 Adler united existing socialist groups to form the Austrian Social Democratic Party, whose undisputed leader he remained until his death.
first May-Day Parade: in 1890.
Socialist Youth Organization: Sozialistische Arbeiterjugend (SAJ).

385 *Schuhmeier*: Franz Schuhmeier (1864-1913), popular Social Democratic workers' leader, in 1913 assassinated by Paul Kunschka, brother of Leopold K., the influential Christian Social politician.
Schmelz: name of an open area in today's 15th District of

Vienna formerly used for military parades and drills.
387 *the little Chancellor*: Dollfuss measured only 5 feet.
aristocratic playboy: Rüdiger von Starhemberg
his mercenaries: the *Heimwehr*
395 *illegal weapons transport*: on 8 January 1933 the Social Democratic *Arbeiter-Zeitung* exposed the "Hirtenberg Weapons Scandal." Weapons had been shipped from Italy to the Austrian weapons factory in Hirtenberg supposedly to be repaired. In fact, some of them were handed over to the *Heimwehr*, while others were shipped on to Hungary. Such transactions violated the Peace Treaties of St. Germain and Trianon.
396 *coalition government*: see note on p. 370.
397 *that unfortunate walk*: Schuhmeier had attended the ceremony in the Imperial Palace where Emperor Franz Josef held the traditional annual speech to open Parliament. Schuhmeier had wanted to demonstrate that Social Democrats took the liberty of going to the Emperor as long as the Emperor did not deign to come to the Parliament Building. What had been meant as a gesture of strength was often criticized as one of servility.
398 *antifa*: antifascist united front.
399 *Hindenburg*: Paul von Beneckendorff und von H. (1847-1934), Head of Supreme Command of the German Army in World War I, 1925-1934 President of Germany, in 1933 H. appointed Hitler Chancellor.
Schleicher: Kurt von Schleicher (1882-1834), as German Chancellor from Dec. 1932 to Jan. 1933 he tried to prevent Hitler's rise to power. Murdered by Nazis during the "purge" in June 1934.
coup of the Reichswehr: according to rumors spread by the Nazis, Schleicher, who was also Minister of Defense, was preparing a military coup to gain power (*Reichswehr*: German Army).
scandal about subsidies: to bail out the debt-ridden junkers' estates 150 million Reichmarks were provided by the government; to raise the money new general taxes were levied and social services cut.

400 *Vorwärts*: official paper of the Social Democratic Party of Germany.
Arbeiter-Zeitung: official paper of the Social Democratic Party of Austria.

401 *Their victory celebration*: on 30 January 1933 Hitler had been appointed Chancellor of Germany.
Bauer: Otto Bauer (1881-1938), leading theoretician of Austro-Marxism, editor in chief of *Arbeiter-Zeitung* and *Der Kampf*, Foreign Minister 1918-1919, Member of Parliament 1920-1934.

402 *Red Falcons*: Social Democratic organization for girls and boys 10 to 14 years of age.

404 *Young Front*: Jungfront, youth organization founded by Manfred Ackermann with the purpose of activating the young people in the Social Democratic movement and, at the same time to prevent their radicalization under Communist influence.

406 *Twelfth of November*: on 12 November 1918 the Austrian Republic was proclaimed, national holiday during the First Republic (1918-1934).
the year 1927: see p. 372.

407 *in the beginning*: the Workers' Educational Association (Arbeiterbildungsverein), founded 1868, preceded the Austrian Social Democratic Party (consolidation of various groups in 1888).

408 *WEA*: Workers' Educational Association (Arbeiterbildungsverein).

409 *"The hymn to the noble bride,"* etc: from "Lied der Arbeit" ("Song of Work") (words: Josef Zapf; music: Josef Scheu), was first sung at the Arbeiterbildungsverein Gumpendorf on the first of May 1868, and became the Party song of Austrian Social Democracy.

411 *Hitler-Hugenberg cabinet*: in Hitler's first cabinet of January 1933 Alfred Hugenberg (1865-1951) of the German National People's Party was Minister of Economics.
Bonapartism: a dictatorship which, supported by the military and the police, tries to sustain the capitalist system by finding a modus vivendi with the workers and

other oppositional groups.
Trotsky: Lew Davidovich Trotsky (1879-1940), leader of the Bolshewik revolution 1917, opposed Stalin, murdered in exile.
Kerenski: Alexander F. Kerenski (1881-1970), Russian Social Democrat, emigrated after the Bolshevik revolution.

412 *Renner*: Karl Renner (1870-1950), Social Democratic politician, 1919-1920 first Chancellor of the First Republik, leader of the moderates in the Party, supported the *Anschluss*, first Chancellor of the Second Republic, 1945 to 1950 Federal President.
Young Fronters no longer tolerated: see note on p. 404.

413 *"Song of Soviet Airmen"*: the song "Rote Flieger" (words: Pawel German-Helmut Schinkel, music: Julius Chait).
noble brides etc.: allusion to the "Song of Work," see note on p. 409.
"And every propeller" from the "Song of Soviet Airmen," see above.
Communist Youth: KJV, Kommunistischer Jugendverband.
Red United Front: Rote Einheitsfront, Communist slogan in periods of tactical approachment to Social Democrats.

414 *after times had changed*: i.e., after the defeat of the uprising in February 1934.

415 *Severing*: Carl Severing (1875-1952), Social Democratic Minister of the Interior in Prussia.
Grzesinski: Albert Grzesinski (1879-1947), 1924-1926, 1930-1932 Chief of Police, removed by the Papen government, after 1933 leader of the German Social Democrats in exile.
Löbe: Paul Löbe (1875-1967), Social Democratic politician, 1920-1924, 1925-1932 President of the German *Reichstag*.
the 20th of July: on that day 1932 von Papen in a coup removed the Social Democratic Prime Minister of Prussia, Otto Braun, and Carl Severing (see above) from office.

416 *Lausanne loan*: on 19 August 1932 this loan was approved with 82 against 80 votes by the Social Democrats.
the twenty-eighth starvation amendment: (passed in the

summer of 1932) of the Unemployment Benefit Act.
Grünbach strike: in November 1932, 1,086 underpaid coalminers in Grünbach (Lower Austria) went on strike; the strike was called off although most of the demands were not met.
July 15th: of 1927, see p. 372.
Zörgiebel: Karl Zörgiebel, Chief of Police in Berlin (1926-1930) and in Dortmund (1931-1933).

417 *Hanusch*: Ferdinand Hanusch (1866-1923), Social Democrat, one of the pioneers of Austrian social policy.
Reumann: Jakob Reumann (1853-1925), 1919-1923 first Social Democratic Mayor of Vienna.
Victor Adler: see note on p. 384.
Fritz Adler: Friedrich A. (1879-1960), son of Victor A., in 1916 he killed the Austrian Prime Minister Count Stürgk to protest against conditions in the country and his Party's support of the war; sentenced to death, pardoned and released from prison in 1918. Secretary of the Social Democratic Party, fought Communist influence, 1923-1940 Secretary of the Socialist Workers' International.

419 *Kunschak*: Leopold Kunschak (1871-1953), leader of the left wing of the Christian Social Party, leader of the Christian Workers' movement.

422 *Iron Front*: Eiserne Front, founded in December 1931, coalition to fight Nazism in Germany, made up of the Social Democratic Party, the Free Unions, the *Reichsbanner* (Social Democratic paramilitary organization founded in 1924) and Social Democratic Sports Association.

428 *Center Party*: Deutsche Zentrumspartei, (Party of German Catholicism).

432 *defenselessly*: although it had only been a warning strike of two hours Dollfuss used it to demonstrate his hard line in dealing with the railroad workers most of whom were members of the Social Democratic Free Union. Army and police occupied the railroad stations, the leaders of the strike were arrested on the basis of a decree of 25. July 1925; many railroad workers had their wages cut or lost

their jobs. (Cf. Helmut Andics, *Fünfzig Jahre unseres Lebens, Österreichs Schicksal seit 1918*, Wien, 1968, pp. 214ff., and *Vom Justizpalast zum Heldenplatz. Studien und Dokumente*, Wien, 1975, pp. 343f.).
Blum: Robert Blum (1807-1848), Socialist delegate to the Frankfurt Parliament, came to Vienna during the Revolution in 1848, executed in Vienna on 9 November 1848.

436 *Taaffe*: Count Eduard Taaffe, 1879-1893 Prime Minister of Austria-Hungary, decreed laws against Socialist and other emergency measures.
Badeni: Count Kasimir Badeni, 1895-1898 Prime Minister of Austria-Hungary. Street deomonstarions finally led to his resignation.
Four percent: one of the punitive measures against the strikers.
broke the law: The management of the Federal Railroads had unilaterally broken a collective bargaining agreement. On March 4 the Social Democrats raised the issue in Parliament in terms of an "urgent inquiry."

438 *Friends of Children*: the Social Democratic educational organization Freie Schule-Kinderfreunde.

439 *Das kleine Blatt*: Social Democratic daily paper of a more popular make-up than the *Arbeiter-Zeitung*.

445 *Buresch*: error on Soyfer's part; the Second President of the National Assembly at the time was not the Christian Social Buresch but the Christian Social Rudolf Ramek.
the first case: the events in Parliament on 4 March 1933 described here initiated the Dollfuss authoritarian regime. Existing procedural avenues for overcoming the crisis were deliberately disregarded, and on 7 March the government declared itself untouched by the parliamentary crisis and started governing on the basis of the wartime emergency law of 1917, which had been carried over into the constitution of the First Republic.

446 *increase*: in the national elections in October 1923.

448 *violation*: in the emergency session of the Council of Ministers on 7 March, Schuschnigg, the then Minister of Justice, admitted that the planned press restriction

"amounted to a kind of pre-censorship, but that they must not create that impression in the public since the constitution prohibited any kind of censorship" (*Vom Justizpalast zum Heldenplatz*, p, 347).

450 *Kollmann*: Josef Kollmann (1868-1951), Christian Social politician who rejected the goverment's authoritarian course.
Schuschnigg: Kurt von Schuschnigg (1897-1977), Christian Social Minister of Justice 1932-1934, Minister of Education 1933-1936, Federal Chancellor 1934-1938, resigned under German pressure on 11 March 1938, 1938-1945 imprisoned.

451 *Pfrimer coup*: see not for p. 376.
drug addicts: Hermann Göring, one of the top Nazi leaders, was known to be a morphine addict.

453 *41 percent*: at the last national election of the First Republic (9 November 1930) the Social Democrats gained 41 percent of the votes and with 72 seats were the strongest party.
Blum: Leon Blum (1872-1950), together with Edgar Jaures founded the Socialist Party of France in 1902.
Daladier: Edouard Daladier (1884-1970), French Socialist; in 1933 D. was not Prime Minister but Minister of Defense.

455 *immunity clause*: a passage that had been censored could be "immunized" by being read by a representative in a provincial parliament and then be printed as part of that Representative's speech.

457 *Kanitz*: Felix Otto Kanitz (b. 1894, d. 1940 Buchenwald), Secretary of the Socialist Workers' Youth.

458 *July 20*: see note on p. 415.
Danneberg: Robert Danneberg (b. 1885, d. 1942 Auschwitz), Social Democratic expert for finances in the Vienna City Government.

459 *Resch*: Josef Resch, 1930-1933 and 1936-1938 Christian Social Minister for Social Administration.

460 *one vote*: the Dollfuss government was supported by 83 Representatives (Christian Socials: 66, Farmers' Coalition:

9, *Heimwehr*: 8), the opposition by 82 Representatives (Social Democrats: 72, Pan-Germans: 10).

461 *Streeruwitz*: Ernst Streer von Streeruwitz (1874-1952), Christian Social politician, Federal Chancellor May-September 1929.
Federal President: Wilhelm Miklas (1872-1956), Christian Social politician, 1928-1938 Federal President.
Buresch: see note on p. 445.

463 *Red Flag*: the daily paper of the Communist Party of Austria.

464 *downpour*: between 7 April 1933 and 30 April 1934 the Dollfuss government decreed 466 (!) emergency measures.
Leuthner: Karl Leuthner (1869-1944), Social Democratic Member of Parliament, represented the right wing of the Party.
Lower Austrians: the Social Democrats of the province of Lower Austria, led by Oskar Helmer and Friedrich Schneidmadl, favored a moderate course.
Körner: Theodor Körner (1873-1957), 1915-1918 Head of General Staff of the Isonzo Army (on the Italian Front), after his retirement from the army in 1924 he joined the Social Democratic Party and became military advisor to the Defense Corps. After disagreements (on strategy) with Alexander Eifler and Julius Deutsch, the commanders of the Defense Corps, Körner resigned as advisor in 1930. His refusal, alluded to in this passage, did not come about in March 1933 as the passage claims but in February 1934. Eifler had been arrested; the party leadership approached Körner, but after assessing the situation he concluded that it was hopeless. (Cf. Ilona Duczynska, *Der demokratische Bolschewik*, Munich 1975, p. 179f.) After the ill-fated uprising in February 1934, Körner was under arrest for a short time. In 1944 he was arrested by the Gestapo. 1945-1951 Mayor of Vienna, 1951-1957 Federal President.

467 *Parliament has been broken up*: On 15 March 1933 "the session of Parliament was scheduled for 3 p.m. But in order to forestall counter measures Dr. Straffner opened

it already at 2:30. The meeting hall was half-empty. Social Democrats and Pan-Germans were present, but not all of them because some plain-clothes-men had come just in time to close the doors before the noses of the latecomers. Inside Straffner was satisfied with opening the session and closing it after a few minutes. The idea was simply to demonstrate that the Parliament did still exist. When the police arrived in numbers the session was all over. But the whole maneuver had only demonstrated the helplessness of Parliament—a blow for the opposition, an encouragement for the government" (Andics, p. 217f.).

The strike was squelched: on 24 March the *Arbeiter-Zeitung* and *Das kleine Blatt* were subjected to pre-censorship. The printing staff of these two papers as well as that of all other papers struck, and on 25 March no papers appeared in Vienna. But due to lack of support by the Party leadership the strike was soon broken off. The fighting spirit of the printers, traditionally a politically very active and influential union, was considerably weakened. The result was that the printers did not participate in the strike in February 1934. (Cf. Pertinax [Otto Leichter], *Österreich 1934*, Zürich, 1935, p. 188).

five schillings: "The *Heimwehr* consisted for the most part of unemployed commanded by ex-officers and ex-corporals. To a certain extent, they were mercenaries willing to follow anybody who paid them more." (Quoted from Starhemberg's memoirs in Andics, p. 183.) In antifascist reports of the 1930s there are many references to the fact that *Heimwehr*-men were paid five schillings for marching in a demonstration (therefore their nickname "Fünfschillingmanderln" ("Five-schilling-boys"). See also Merz-Qualtinger, *Der Herr Karl*, Munich 1962, p. 14.)

473 *On March 29*: on 25 March the government decided to disband the Defense Corps; on 31 March it declared it illegal.

dissolved the Heimwehr: the *Heimwehr* appealed the Mayor's decree, and, within 24 hours, the appeal was granted (Botz, p. 213).

Fey: Emil Fey (1886-1938), leader of the Vienna *Heimwehr*, since October 1932 Secretary for Security.
crowd of workers: it could not be ascertained whether the events described in the chapter "A Revolution" were based on fact. The names of the streets are fictitious. Botz, who carefully documented all political confrontations during those years does not mention a demonstration comparable to the one described by Soyfer (Botz, pp. 210ff., 274ff.)

475 *the juice*: shutting off electric power was the signal for a general strike.
The best police of the world: publicity slogan of the Vienna police during the interwar period. (Cf. Franz A. Pichler, *Polizeihofrat P..* Wien, 1984, pp. 72 ff.)

485 *We are Vienna's working class*: the song quoted in "Wir sind das Bauvolk der kommenden Welt," words: Fritz Brügel, music: a popular Russian melody of the time.

486 *Patriotic Front*: Vaterländische Front, founded by Dollfuss to counteract political parties, and to create a general framework for propagandizing a corporate ideology and an authoritarian system. In 1934-1938 the *Patriotic Front* was the only legal political organization. In order to increase membership, pressure tactics were not uncommon. Attempts to win the workers' genuine support failed.

488 *Stein*: town on the Danube.
492 *anti-strike bill*: passed on 21 April 1933.
495 *restaurant chain*: WÖK = Wiener Öffentliche Küchen.
three arrows: emblem of the Social Democrats.
509 *Windischgrätz*: Fürst Windischgrätz and Freiherr von Jelacic commanded the Imperial troops to put down the revolution of 1848.
517 *Vorwärts*: name of the Party's publishing company.
524 *edict against striking*: see note on p. 492.
farmers' rally: probably the mass rally of 5 March 1933 in Villach in the Province of Caryntia, where Dollfuss gave an impassioned speech against parliamentarism.
trotting course: at the *Patriotic Front* rally on the Vienna

trotting course, Dollfuss announced his program of making Austria a "social, Christian, German state on corporate lines under strong authoritarian leadership."
first censored: see note on p. 492.
Adler: Max Adler (1873-1937), leading theoretician of Austromarxism. The work referred to here: *Neue Menschen. Gedanken über die sozialistische Erziehung*, Berlin, 1924.
Kautsky: Karl Kautsky (1854-1938), one of the most influential Socialist theoreticians during the Second International (1889-1914).

Bibliography

Works by Soyfer in German

Vom Paradies zum Weltuntergang. Dramen und Kleinkunst. Ed. Otto Tausig. Wien: Globus, 1949.
Von Paradies und Weltuntergang. Eine Auswahl. Ed. Werner Martin. Berlin (GDR): Volk und Welt, 1962.
Die Ordnung schuf der liebe Gott. Eine Auswahl. Ed. Werner Martin. Leipzig: Philipp Reclam, jun., 1979.
Jura Soyfer. Das Gesamtwerk. Ed. Horst Jarka. Wien: Europaverlag, 1980. (With bibliography).
Jura Soyfer. Das Gesamtwerk. Ed. Horst Jarka. Wien: Europaverlag, 1984. (Revised paperback edition of *Das Gesamtwerk*, 1980 in three volumes: *Lyrik, Szenen und Stücke, Prosa*).
Jura Soyfer. Sturmzeit. Briefe 1931-1939. Ed. Horst Jarka. Verlag für Gesellschaftskritik: Wien, 1991.
Jura Soyfer. Gesammelte Werke. Szenen und Stücke. Ed. Horst Jarka, Wien-Zürich: Europaverlag, 1993.

Works in English translation

The Legacy of Jura Soyfer, 1912-1939. Poems, Prose and Plays of an Austrian Antifascist. Ed. & trans. Horst Jarka. Montreal: Engendra, 1977.

Secondary Literature in English

Leon Askin. *Quietude and Quest.* Riverside: Ariadne Press, 1989, pp. 151-153.
Paul Cummins. *Dachau Song. The Twentieth-Century Odyssey of Herbert Zipper.* New York - Frankfurt am Main: Peter Lang, 1992. pp. 66-68, 78, 87-89, 91, 98, 99, 101, 103-105, 114, 255, 263, 266-269, 277.
Horst Jarka. "British Writers and the Austria of the Thirties."

Österreich und die angelsächsische Welt. Ed. Otto Hietsch. Wien: Braumüller, vol. two, 1968, pp. 439-481 (about Soyfer: pp. 475-477).

_____ "Jura Soyfer. A Jewish Writer under Austrofascism." *Shofar* (Purdue University) vol. 5, no. 3 (Spring 1987), pp. 18-27.

_____ "Jura Soyfer—A Writer of the Austrian Thirties Only?" *From Wilson to Waldheim*. Ed. Peter Pabisch. Riverside: Ariadne, 1989, pp. 125-155.

_____ "Life and Politics in the Literature of the Thirties." *Austria in the Thirties*. Ed. Kenneth Segar and John Warren. Riverside: Ariadne, 1991, pp. 155-177.

_____ "Jura Soyfer." *Major Figures of Austrian Literature: The Interwar Years*. Ed. Donald G. Daviau. Riverside: Ariadne, 1995, pp. 421-458.

Calvin N. Jones. "The Dialectics of Despair and Hope: The Modernist Volksstück by Jura Soyfer [*Der Lechner Edi schaut ins Paradies*], *Maske und Kothurn*, 1986, 32 (1-2), pp. 33-40.

John Lehmann. *The Whispering Gallery. Autobiography I*. London: Longmans, Green, 1955, pp. 294-302.

Alfred Pfabigan. "Jura Soyfer's *Death of a Party*." *The Austrian Socialist Experiment. Social Democracy and Austromarxism. 1918-1934*. Ed. Anson Rabinbach. Boulder, London: Westview, 1985, pp. 169-176.

Jura Soyfer and His Time. International Jura Soyfer Symposium 1992. Ed. Donald G. Daviau. Riverside: Ariadne Press, 1995.

George E. Wellworth. "Jura Soyfer. An Attempt at Rehabilitation." *American-German Review*, 55 (1969), no. 2, pp. 22-26.

Major Studies in German

Horst Jarka. *Jura Soyfer. Leben-Werk-Zeit*. Wien: Löcker, 1987.
Peter Langmann. *Sozialismus und Literatur. Jura Soyfer. Studien*

zu einem österreichischen Schriftsteller der Zwischenkriegszeit. Frankfurt am Main: Hain bei Athenäum, 1986.

Gerhard Scheit. *Theater und revolutionarer Humanismus. Eine Studie zu Jura Soyfer.* Wien: Verlag für Gesellschaftskritik, 1988.

Jura Soyfer, Europa, multikulturelle Existenz. Internationales Kolloquium Saarbrücken 1991. Ed. Herbert Arlt. St. Ingbert: Röhrig Verlag, 1993.

Jura Soyfer und Theater. Ed. Jura Soyfer Gesellschaft. Frankfurt am Main: Peter Lang, 1992.

Die Welt des Jura Soyfer. Zwischenwelt 2. Ed. Jura Soyfer Gesellschaft in Zusammenarbeit mit der Theodor Kramer Gesellschaft. Wien: Verlag für Gesellschaftskritik, 1991.

Index of Names

Adler, Friedrich 417, 453
Adler, Victor 384, 394, 417, 438, 456, 507, 519, 522, 523, 528
Adorno, T.W. 542
Andis, Helli (née Ultmann) 559, 562, 564
Angel, Ernst 45
Adler, Hans 106
Adler, Max 524
Ashleigh, Charles 567
Askin, Leon 82, 547
Badeni, Graf Kasimir 436, 508
Bauer, Alfred 340
Bauer, Otto 369, 396, 401, 417, 446, 448, 455, 456, 457, 463, 464, 473, 474, 509, 524, 543
Beaumarchais, Pierre-Augustin 59
Benet, Stephen Vincent 540
Brecht, Bertolt 546, 552, 555, 556
Broch, Hermann 559
Bismarck, Otto von 177
Blum, Léon 454
Blum, Robert 432, 509, 510, 513, 514
Börne, Ludwig 545
Breitner, Hugo 375, 534
Brüning, Heinrich 374
Buresch, Karl 445, 446, 461, 462
Carl, Karl 65, 66

Celine, Louis Ferdinand 559
Chamberlain, Houston Stewart 33
Chaplin, Charley 45
Chesterton, G. K. 539
Clair, René 46
Cleugh, James 566
Cornelius, Paul 239
Danneberg, Robert 458, 459, 461, 462
Deutsch, Julius 370, 456
Dobravsky 224
Dollfuss, Engelbert 379, 382, 446, 448, 449, 453, 454, 455, 459, 460, 463, 464, 473, 539, 549
Ebner, Hugo 567
Eden, Anthony 87
Engels, Friedrich 378, 384, 409, 467, 481, 485
Enzensberger, H. M. 546
Epp, Franz Xaver, Ritter von 370
Farkas, Karl 91
Feiks, Josef 259
Felix, Sabine 192
Ferdinand, Erzherzog 138
Fey, Emil 459, 473
Fichte, Johann Gottlieb 545
Fischer, Ernst 535
Franz, Josef I. 372
Franzmeier, Günter 142
Freud, Sigmund 559
Friedrich, Ernst 21
Friedrich, Erzherzog 24

Gerth, Hansjürgen 153
Glöckel, Otto 534
Goethe, Johann Wolfgang von 32, 42, 559
Gregor, Joseph 260
Grillprazer, Franz 64
Grünbaum, (Gruen), Viktor 34
Grzesinski, Albert 415
Hanusch, Ferdinand 417
Hardy, Oliver 46
Hasenclever, Walter 257, 558
Heine, Heinrich 536, 562
Henderson, Arthur 374
Hentzschel, Rüdfer 143
Hergl, Ben 192
Hindenburg, Paul von 339, 458, 538, 554
Hitler, Adolf 21, 26, 27, 30, 87, 88, 89, 90, 379, 382, 400, 401, 404, 407, 410, 411, 415, 416, 418, 422, 428, 452, 453, 459, 536, 537, 538, 539, 547, 548, 549, 551, 558, 562.
Horthy von Nagybanya, Miklos 370
Horváth, Ödön von 533, 545, 554, 557
Hufnagel, Wilhelm 128
Hugenberg, Alfred 411
Jannings, Emil 456
Jelacic Buzim, Josef von 509
Kafka, Franz 557, 559
Kanitz, Felix Otto 457
Kautsky, Karl 524
Kerenski, Aleksandr Feodorovich 411

Koepp, Josef 224
Kollmann, Josef 450, 453
Körner, Theodor, Edler von Siegringen 464
Kraus, Karl 62, 533, 549, 550, 556
Krupp, Friedrich von Bohlen und Halbach 30
Kunschak, Leopold 419, 450, 453
Lang, Fritz 43, 44
Lassalle, Ferdinand 378
Lehmann, John 529, 532, 533, 544, 564, 566, 567
Lenin, Wladimir, Iljitsch 393, 412, 416
Lessing, Gotthold Ephraim 42
Leuthner, Karl 464
Linderman, Donna 313
Lloyd, George 176, 177
Löbe, Paul 415
Louis, Bonaparte 411, 460
MacDonald, James Ramsey 374
Marx, Karl 378, 381, 385, 411, 440, 441, 442, 444
Masereel, Frans 552
Matteotti, Giacomo 378
May, Ricky 153
Melingo, Christo 24
Merz, Carl 542
Metternich, Clemens 64
Miklas, Wilhelm 461, 462, 463, 464, 465
More, Thomas 558
Mozart, Wolfgang Amadeus 58

Müller, Herrmann 374
Mussolini, Benito 21, 370, 453, 548
Nadler, Josef 534
Napoleon I. 460
Nestroy, Johann 61, 62, 63, 64, 65, 66, 542, 545, 549, 550, 556
Neuner, Gottfried 239
Nietzsche, Friedrich 33
Papen, Franz von 415, 537, 538
Pfabigan, Alfred 541
Pfrimer, Walter 451, 535
Pollak, Oskar 535
Pollitzer, Heinz 557
Prescott, Orvill 541
Preses, Peter 135
Qualtinger, Helmut 542, 564
Rainer, Fried 143
Rapoport, Samuel Mitja 533, 561
Redl, Colonel 177
Reinhardt, Max 60
Remarque, Erich Maria 23
Renner, Karl 369, 396, 412, 457, 461
Resch, Karin 239
Resch, Josef 459
Reumann, Jakob 417
Röbbeling, Hermann 261
Rohner, Dr. 56
Roosevelt, Franklin Delano 12, 179
Ruck, Christian 82, 88
Salacrou, Armand 56
Sassmann, Hans 259

Schiller, Friedrich von 42, 65
Schleicher, Kurt von 21, 24, 399
Schneider, Rolf 544
Schnitzler, Arthur 559
Schramm, Christian 239
Schuhmeier, Franz 385, 397, 597
Schuschnigg, Kurt von 450, 549
Seefehlner, Egon 426
Seipel, Ignaz 370, 371, 372, 373
Seitz, Karl 412, 417, 430, 473, 480
Severing, Carl 415
Shaw, G. B. 180, 181, 182, 185
Simon & Schuster 544
Slezak, Leo 91
Skofic, Margot 106
Slama, Tono 153
Sollmann, SPD. Abg. 461
Spender, Stephen 540, 548
Spiegel, Rudolf 18
Spiel, Hilde 535
Spira, Willi (Bil) 70, 71, 545, 548
Srbik, Heinrich von 535
Starhemberg, Rüdiger von 382, 387, 460, 469
Steiner, Herbert 564
Straffner, Sepp 445, 457, 461, 465
Stranitzky, Josef Anton 62
Streeruwitz, Ernst Streer von 461

Stürgkh, Karl Graf 436, 508
Szecsi-Rapoport, Marika;
   März Maria 537, 541, 561
Taaffe, Eduard Graf 436, 508
Tandler, Julius 534
Tausig, Otto 563, 564
Thälmann, Ernst 537
Treitschke, Heinrich von 33
Trotzki, Lew Dawidowitsch
   411
Tucholsky, Kurt 157, 558,
   559
Voskovec, Jiri 45, 46, 47,
   552
Uhlich, Klaus 224
Ultmann, Helli see: Andis
Villon, Francois 545

Walla, Marianne 135
Walter, Franz 106
Weinzierl, Ulrich 544
Weigel, Hans 547
Wels, Otto 537
Werich, Jan 45, 46, 47, 552
West, Wendy 313
Wilhelm II. 24, 176, 376
Wilson, Woodrow 177
Windischgrätz, Alfred Fürst
   zu 509
Winkler, Franz 459
Winter, Ernst Karl 549
Wolff-Plottegg 153
Zbonek, Edwin 558
Zipper, Herbert 563
Zörgiebel, Karl 416